MARTIN LUTHER
THE PRESERVATION
OF THE CHURCH

"Here, finally, for all interested in Luther's career, Brecht discloses an array of events, agreements, actions, and opinions involving Luther that most people know little or nothing about. . . . The single best description of Luther's later life available in English."

—Timothy J. Wenger*

"This third volume of Brecht's biogr⸌ ⸍ght into Luther's latter years, an era oft⸌ ⸍we see a man driven by his Christian ⸌ ⸍y his zeal for unity, qualities which were often⸌ ⸍ his era. . . . Clearly written and well translated, ⸌ ⸍ively easy reading. . . . The spirit and poignancy of the ⸌ ⸍tion and its challenge to all Christians are capsulated in these years. . . ."

—Jeffrey Gros, F.S.C., *Review for Religious*

MARTIN
LUTHER

THE PRESERVATION OF THE CHURCH   1532-1546

Martin Brecht

Translated by
JAMES L. SCHAAF

FORTRESS PRESS   **MINNEAPOLIS**

MARTIN LUTHER: THE PRESERVATION OF THE CHURCH, 1532–1546
First paperback edition 1999
First English-language edition published 1993 by Fortress Press.

This book is a translation of *Martin Luther: Dritter Band: Die Erhaltung der Kirche, 1532–1546* by Martin Brecht. Copyright © 1987 Calwer Verlag, Stuttgart, Germany.

Scripture quotations, unless otherwise indicated, are from the Revised Standard Version of the Bible, copyright © 1946, 1952, and 1971 by the Division of Christian Education of the National Council of Churches.

Library of Congress Cataloging-in-Publication Data
(Revised for vol. 3)
Brecht, Martin.
  Martin Luther.
  Translation of: Martin Luther.
  Included bibliographies and indexes.
  Contents: [1]. His road to Reformation, 1483–1521—
[2]. Shaping and defining the Reformation, 1521–1532—
[3]. The preservation of the church, 1532–1546.
  1. Luther, Martin, 1483–1546. 2. Reformers—Germany—Biography. I. Title.
BR325.B69313 1985   284.1'092   84-47911
ISBN 0-8006-0738-4 (v. 1)
ISBN 0-8006-2463-7 (v. 2)
ISBN 0-8006-2704-0 (v. 3 cloth)
ISBN 0-8006-2815-2 (v. 3 paper)

The paper used in this publication meets the minimum requirements of American National Standard for Information Services—Permanence of Paper for Printed Library Material, ANSI Z329.48–1984.

Manufactured in the U.S.A.   AF 1-2815
  03   02   01   00   99   1   2   3   4   5   6   7   8   9   10

Contents

CONTENTS

CONTENTS

CONTENTS

Translator's Preface

This volume completes the translation of the three-volume biography of Martin Luther written by Martin Brecht. The previous volumes, published by Fortress Press in 1985 and 1990 respectively, were entitled *Martin Luther: His Road to Reformation, 1483–1521* and *Martin Luther: Shaping and Defining the Reformation, 1521–1532*. It is a pleasure to have made this thorough and up-to-date work available to English-speaking readers.

The same general principles have been followed in this volume as in the preceding ones. Where translations of passages quoted from Luther's writings were included in *Luther's Works*, the fifty-five–volume American edition published by Concordia Publishing House and Fortress (Muhlenberg) Press, they have generally been used in preference to my own translation. References to this standard English translation have been added to the author's original notes. As in the first and second volumes, the word *Anfechtung* (pl. *Anfechtungen*), which may refer either to trials sent by God or to the temptations of Satan, has been consistently left untranslated.

Professor Brecht read through the translation and was extremely helpful in clarifying some expressions and correcting my errors. I appreciate his thorough scholarship and cherish his friendship. Working with him has been a joy and privilege.

I wish to thank my wife, Phyllis, for reading through the translation as a "nonspecialist," and making many helpful suggestions for improving its readability. The book has also benefitted from her careful proofreading. But, most of all, I thank her for her patience during this project, which has consumed a major portion of my time for more than ten years.

Columbus, Ohio
July 1992

JAMES L. SCHAAF

Foreword

In 1903 the fifth edition of the two-volume *Martin Luther: Sein Leben und Seine Schriften* by Julius Köstlin and Gustav Kawerau was published. To the present day it remains the single major scholarly comprehensive presentation of the subject and is justly valued because of the authors' solid knowledge of the material. In the course of the last decades, however, a comprehensive new Luther biography has understandably become desirable, one that takes into account new sources and changed viewpoints on Luther and the Reformation in general. Because they have not dealt with all the sources, and their interest has been more in the young Luther than the old Luther, recent presentations have treated the last two decades of his life more or less cursorily. Until now, therefore, the old standard work has only partially been replaced. Heinrich Boehmer's *Der junge Luther* was published in 1925 (ET: *Road to Reformation: Martin Luther to the Year 1521*, trans. John W. Doberstein and Theodore G. Tappert [Philadelphia: Fortress (Muhlenberg) Press, 1946]). Despite the long period that intervened, Heinrich Bornkamm's intention was to continue Boehmer's work. His book, *Martin Luther in der Mitte seines Lebens: Das Jahrzehnt zwischen dem Wormser und dem Augsburger Reichstag* (ET: *Luther in Mid-career, 1521–1530*, trans. E. Theodore Bachmann [Philadelphia: Fortress Press, 1983]), appeared posthumously in its uncompleted form in 1979. At the end of 1986 Reinhard Schwarz published his fascicle of *Die Kirche in ihrer Geschichte*, a cooperative work that deals with Luther. That condensed presentation competently demonstrates the current status of Luther research. Nevertheless, it, too, concentrates more on Luther's beginnings. The time after 1531 is treated relatively briefly. One of the intentions of the anthology edited by Helmar Junghans, *Leben und Werk Martin Luthers von 1526 bis 1546: Festgabe zu seinem 500. Geburtstag*, 2 vols. (Berlin: Evangelische Verlagsanstalt; Göttingen: Vandenhoeck & Ruprecht, 1983), was to fill the gaps in the biography of Luther. By working together, the several contributors were trying to accomplish what almost no author could do alone. In my opinion, however, the individual facets of such a joint work, as competent and qualified as their authors definitely were, cannot be a substitute for a full biography written from a unified point of view. As is always apparent, one cannot separate the necessary overview from a considered evaluation. At the same time, one must accept the fact that an individual author's field of view is necessarily limited.

FOREWORD

I was encouraged by the response that my presentation of Luther's road to the Reformation received, and therefore I undertook to expand it into a comprehensive new presentation of his life. The favorable evaluation that my second volume enjoyed has confirmed my intention. From the outset, it was clear that the magnitude of the subject, along with the immense number of sources and literature, meant that this task would impose extraordinary demands. Many times I was pushed to the limits of my own ability. After more than a decade of intensive labor and concentration, I present this work with a certain satisfaction, hoping that to some extent I have fulfilled one of the tasks of Reformation research. In light of the norm for interpreting texts that Luther himself humbly set forth in his very last written scrap of paper, a decade seems to be a relatively brief period of time in which to master this subject. I frankly acknowledge this, but the ability to continue to invest the necessary attention and concentration is limited by nature, and one's awareness of the limitations of one's own time and energy makes it imperative not to postpone the completion of this work. Moreover, Luther himself would have thought it improper for anyone to occupy himself too long with his life or work. Despite all my efforts at producing as exhaustive a discussion of all the significant aspects as possible, I do not claim that I have succeeded. People who have read very much in Luther know that they constantly find new insights that are rich and surprising, even in contexts that they know well.

The decision to begin this final volume with the accession of Elector John Frederick in 1532 has proved to be correct in the course of the study. The expectation that there were new discoveries to be made in the relatively little-used later volumes of the Weimar Edition did not prove false. Aside from insignificant trivialities, every text has been included in this presentation, although in different degree. New aspects and new interpretations appear in each chapter. Luther's part in the history of the Reformation in the 1530s and 1540s may thus be better seen. Until the end of his life he remained the leading figure on the side of the evangelicals, although the extent of his influence varied. Some developments obviously continued without him, and the Catholic opponents only paid partial attention to him. Not least were the great difficulties that confronted him in his own church apparent. It is well known that the personality of the old Luther displayed great tensions, both in deed and thought. His shortness and rudeness with his friends, although perhaps explainable, continually caused offense. In the many tasks that he had to perform, it was unavoidable that he also repeatedly made serious errors both in practice and in theory. To the end, however, his positive contributions and deep insights remained more significant. Abruptness and resignation were not able to stifle the tender tones and the fundamental trust in God that came from his belief in justification by faith, and, despite all the tensions, this was the consistent theme of his personality.

The subtitle of this volume indicates what was most important for the old Luther: the preservation of the church. For him, those who confessed the

Reformation gospel were identical with the true church. Because of this, the final phase of his life took on conservative outlines more strongly than ever before, but ones that were generally identical with what he had always wanted.

In this volume, too, it was important to organize the immense amount of material in a fashion that is easy to comprehend. Thus, chapters 1–3 and chapters 9–13, which treat Luther's private life, his congregation, Electoral Saxony and the other evangelical territories, and the controversy with his opponents, parallel each other to a certain extent. Chapters 4–6, on the Bible translation, the professor, and the Wittenberg controversies, give longitudinal treatments, and chapters 7–8, with their treatment of the problem of the council and the religious colloquies, provide the thematic point of contact with the major foci of the final portion of his life. Otherwise, I have followed the form and organization of the two earlier volumes. Most of the primary figures mentioned here were already introduced there. In addition to the index of persons and places in the present volume, a subject index of all three volumes is supplied.

Without the quiet assistance provided through the years by the Münster University library, which has been able to fill virtually all my requests, including some unusual ones, through interlibrary loan, this biography could not have been written. I wish to acknowledge my sincere thanks here. My work with the Calwer Verlag on this common task can be described only as productive and enjoyable. The effective and committed work done by my secretary, Frau Ingeborg Müller, my student assistants, Jens Voss and Ute Gause, and my assistant, Frau Bettina Wirsching, who, in addition to everything else, once again prepared the index, has contributed significantly to the successful completion of this final volume. The dialogue with them has been encouraging and helpful for me. I cannot adequately express the contribution that my beloved wife has made to the entire work with her support and partnership during all these years. My deep thanks extend beyond all the people who have helped me. Despite all the tiring work, I ultimately regard it as a gift that I have been able to pursue my calling as a church historian with this work.

Münster/Westphalia   MARTIN BRECHT
January 1987

SUPPLEMENTARY FOREWORD
TO THE ENGLISH EDITION

I greet the speedy completion of the English translation of the three-volume biography of Luther with admiration, respect, and gratitude. This is primarily and almost exclusively due to the perseverance of James L. Schaaf. Except for myself, no one but he knows exactly how complex this task was. Once again I must boast of our good teamwork. The translator has become more and more attuned to my text, so that very little additional revision has been required.

FOREWORD

Part of the work of revising was again done by my assistant, Frau Ute Gause-Leineweber; for this I express my gratitude. Moreover, thanks is due for the financial support of the translation provided by Inter Nationes, without which the project would hardly have been realized. The translator's diligence in working through the annotations should also be acknowledged. Some tiny errors that had escaped my attention were first discovered by him. In general, our common effort on this translation has made this for me one of the best experiences of my scholarly work in recent years. Now I can only hope that the completed translation will be as well accepted by the English-speaking public as the German edition has been here.

MARTIN BRECHT

January 1991

Sources of Illustrations

Dust jacket: Martin Luther, woodcut by Lucas Cranach the Younger, 1546

Plate I: Elector John Frederick of Saxony, photograph courtesy of the Toledo Museum of Art, Toledo, Ohio

Plate II: Croy Tapestry, Ernst-Moritz-Arndt-Universität, Greifswald, photograph by Günther Stelzer, courtesty of Christel Stelzer

Plate III: Cast of Luther's hands, Staatliche Lutherhalle, Wittenberg, photograph courtesy of Wilfried Kirsch

Plate IV: Andreas Osiander the Elder, photograph courtesy of the Biblioteca Apostolica Vaticana, Rome

Plate V: Elector John Frederick and Luther beneath the cross, Lucas Cranach the Younger

Plate VI: Inscription by Luther in a Wittenberg Bible, 1541

Plate VII: Martin Luther at the age of fifty, photograph courtesy of the Germanisches National Museum, Nuremberg

Plate VIII: Woodcut of "Cardinals Cleansing the Church with Foxtails," Cranach's workshop, 1538, photograph courtesy of Wilfried Kirsch, Wittenberg

Plate IX: Luther in the Classroom, drawing by J. Reifenstein, 1545, Staatliche Lutherhalle, Wittenberg, photograph courtesy of Wilfried Kirsch

Plate X: Katherine Luther, née von Bora, Staatliche Lutherhalle, Wittenberg, photograph courtesy of Wilfried Kirsch

Plate XI: Luther room, photograph courtesy of the Institut für Denkmalpflege, Arbeitsstelle Halle

Plate XII: Katherine doorway to the Luther house, photograph by Hermann Michels, Essen

Plate XIII: Luther as preacher, predella of the Wittenberg city church altar, photograph by Kühn

Plate XIV: Interior of Torgau castle church, photograph courtesy of the Institut für Denkmalpflege, Dresden

Plate XV: Jewish sow, sandstone relief on the Wittenberg city church, photograph courtesy of Burkhard Bartel, Simmozheim

Plate XVI: House in which Martin Luther died, photograph courtesy of Wilfried Kirsch, Wittenberg

MARTIN LUTHER
THE PRESERVATION
OF THE CHURCH

I

Peaceful Beginnings under Elector John Frederick— But with Most of the Old Problems (1532–36)

1. ELECTOR JOHN FREDERICK

From the beginning, the fate of Luther and of the Reformation was dependent on his current sovereign. Frederick the Wise had protected him. Elector John had made possible the new organization of the church after 1525. After John's death in August 1532, his son John Frederick (born 1503), who later was known as "the Magnanimous," succeeded him (Plate I).[1] Raised by supporters of Luther, John Frederick regarded Luther and his advice highly, and already during his father's lifetime had become an energetic supporter of the concerns of the Reformation. There was thus no fundamental reason to fear for the continuity of the Reformation politics of Electoral Saxony. Nevertheless, the change in government occasioned some uncertainty about how things would go in Electoral Saxony. John Frederick was twenty years younger than Luther and, because of his age alone, was more energetic than his father had been. It was uncertain whether he would pay as much attention to the reformer as Elector John had. And it also remained to be seen how he would deal with the concerns of the university and the situation of the Electoral Saxon church, which was still as difficult as ever, and what shape his evangelical politics in the empire would take. Nevertheless, the Religious Peace of Nuremberg had just gone into effect, and this averted the immediate threat to the evangelical estates. The beginning of John Frederick's reign thus coincided with a relatively calm, undramatic phase of the Reformation period. Initially, Luther's life also followed a smooth course.

In discussions around the table at that time, Luther openly stated his concerns that had grown out of his previous experiences with his new sovereign. Wisdom had died with Frederick the Wise, and piety with his brother John. He considered John Frederick arbitrary and little inclined to listen to the scholars. In contrast, one had to reckon with the initial experiences of an increase in the influence of the nobility, something that was problematic for

1

the church. Luther recognized that the new sovereign did not want for wisdom and courage, of course, but he still saw him lacking in the piety of his father, and he also doubted whether his reign would be successful. They would have to pray that God would help the elector. Luther later judged resignedly that the new rulers would act rashly when they learned that they could not immediately achieve everything they desired.[2] One of the officials who was immediately dismissed was the chamberlain, John Rietesel, the godfather of Luther's son Martin. Luther comforted him in his distress and assured him that he was in solidarity with him, without directly criticizing the elector.[3]

Despite John Frederick's new style of governing, Luther's fears generally proved baseless. The ruler took his responsibilities for governing seriously. He exceeded others in his support of the evangelical church.[4] The good contact between Wittenberg and the court continued, and there was no sign that the elector did not have a high regard for Luther. During the elector's not infrequent visits to Wittenberg, Luther had to preach in the castle church.[5]

John Frederick had great respect for Luther and identified completely with the evangelical cause. In important matters he sought Luther's advice and frequently summoned him to the court in Torgau for this purpose. Nevertheless, he always kept his own counsel. Occasionally he also attempted to enlist Luther's support for the objectives of Electoral Saxon politics. Luther, however, was far too independent to listen uncritically to his sovereign. Occasional differences of opinion could not be avoided in this relationship, so that one or the other had to refrain from forcing his view, but the two partners were able to deal with this without creating more difficult conflicts. This firm relationship between the two was one of the foundations underlying Luther's work in the last period of his life. It is not by chance, therefore, that in all the chapters of the biography of the older Luther we meet John Frederick and his active and influential interest in the concerns of the church, theology, the university, and, not least, Luther's own welfare.[6]

When the wedding of Duke Philip I of Pomerania and John Frederick's sister, Maria, took place in Torgau in 1536, Luther was to marry the couple according to the *Order of Marriage*. He preached seriously about the estate of matrimony and its dignity. Later he frequently criticized the immoderate drinking at this celebration. Those who took part were also aware that this union between the ruling houses of Saxony and Pomerania was significant for the Reformation. The famous Croy tapestry of 1554, which depicts the members of both families listening to Luther's sermon on the crucified Christ, was a later documentation of this connection (Plate II).[7]

Chancellor Gregory Brück, a veteran expert who was praised by Luther as the "Atlas" of Electoral Saxony, was retained by John Frederick and provided continuity in politics and administration.[8] John Frederick frequently used him as his intermediary with Luther and asked him about Luther's current opinions. Luther also appears to have had a good relationship with the vice-chancellor, Christian Beyer (died 1535), and his successor, Francis Burchart, both of whom were also members of the Wittenberg faculty.[9] In contrast, the professional, secular high-handedness of other officials gave reason for complaints. The reason Luther in 1533 called Marshal Hans von Dolzig a knave who was "destroying the land" is unknown. In 1535 he gave unqualified praise to the elector, but he complained in general about the distrust his "commanders" had for the Wittenberg theologians.[10] Luther considered it a problem that, contrary to earlier practice, they were spending money like water at the court. Although John Frederick was a robust man, Luther increasingly had justified concerns about his fondness for drink, behavior that was setting the tone for the court. He was particularly concerned because the elector was offering a target for his vigilant Catholic opponents.[11]

Elector John had granted most of Luther's numerous appeals on behalf of third parties. In contrast, John Frederick, as a precaution, immediately informed Luther that he would not be able to read all of them. Luther fully understood this. It was also an imposition on him to be enlisted as an intercessor, and he himself would have liked to reduce the burden. He was sure that the elector would know which appeals were important to him. He reluctantly passed on to the vice-chancellor a matter concerning his relatives in Eisenach, something that could not be settled there and that he could not resolve himself.[12] Nevertheless, after some initial hesitation, there was no appreciable change in Luther's petitioning. In October 1532 he was already forcefully appealing for a reduction of an excessively severe verdict, probably in a marriage case, for this was especially inappropriate at the beginning of John Frederick's reign.[13] He appealed to the elector to give two gulden to an aged man who was not being helped by the officials or others who were responsible.[14] Luther characterized his advocacy on behalf of Martin Sangner, who had been expelled from Schneeberg for making unjustified demands, as "reluctant." The elector clearly informed Luther that he knew only one side of the matter and that his decision stood.[15] Before Luther would take up the cause of a mad Wittenberg woman who had been imprisoned, Vice-chancellor Burchart should investigate the possibilities for her improvement. In this case, Luther did not think it made sense to incarcerate her, and felt one should especially be concerned about her daughter's marriage chances. The chains of human misery should be broken by mercy.[16]

With his commentary on Psalm 101, "a mirror for how David should rule (*Regentenspiegel*)," which was written in 1534 and published at the beginning of 1535, Luther, in a way that behooved him, intended to orient the young sovereign to his task.[17] This was not said in so many words, of course, but its context in the situation in Electoral Saxony is easy to recognize, although Luther frequently asserted that he had had no experience at court. This work, which has been somewhat forgotten, is one of his most basic and wisest statements on the subject of politics, which, in contrast to the Catholic clergy and the Anabaptists, takes a positive stand on secular office. For Luther, good political order is not simple to achieve, as both alleged and genuine experts claim, but it is a gift of God and a gracious endowment. Likewise, political results ultimately depend on whether God grants success. This was saying nothing against political sagacity; instead, it was a sober acknowledgement of its limits. Political principles and the law could not usually be applied directly but had to be realized through compromising with the realities of the situation and reconciling them. Political charismatics like Frederick the Wise or his counselor Fabian von Feilitzsch—"miracle men"—had the necessary wisdom for this; the smart theoreticians did not. The business of politics could be learned only in part, of course, but the wisdom of the miracle men did offer an orientation.

The ideal politician governs his land with God's Word, something, of course, that can be done only in felicitous, exceptional cases. It is impossible to keep a ruler's surroundings free from the enemies of God—examples from the Old Testament and the relations among the old believers prove this; even here God's support is needed. In some cases a prince must deal with dangerous counselors around him and yet not make common cause with them. The older Luther believed that to govern rightly meant to proclaim the Word of God and guard against seductive sects. This, too, could only be partially achieved. The abolition of papal compulsion brought with it a general relaxation of restraints. In the long run, this could be combatted only by carefully instructing the young people.

Despite the prince's obligation to provide for the external welfare of the church, Luther, as before, did not want to mix spiritual and temporal government. "Constantly I must pound in and squeeze in and drive in and wedge in this difference between the two kingdoms. . . ."[18] This did not mean that the two kingdoms were unrelated to one another, of course. In the name of divine authority, preachers had to proclaim God's commandments to political rulers, too. On the other hand, neither the spiritual nor the temporal side should attempt to change the rights of the other area. Yet a political and social order at peace was something like a model of the kingdom of heaven. Luther was certain that the current imperial (Roman) law was profane. To him, it was the quintessence of the political wisdom of the ancient world, and the present had nothing better to offer, although "the government and jurists may well be in need of a Luther."[19] Nevertheless, such a political Reformation might easily turn into a Müntzerian revolt. "Miracle men" were needed once again to apply the law properly. In a different way than in the psalm, the problems of defamation, envy, and arrogance in politics and society were discussed. In no way were wisdom and virtue the exclusive property of the upper classes. Luther could thus imagine an elected monarchy unrestricted by social barriers. Undoubtedly with a view toward the court of Electoral Saxony, he then spoke about the special devil of the Germans, "a good wineskin [who] would bear the name Guzzle, because he is so thirsty and parched that he cannot be cooled even by all this great guzzling of wine and beer. And such an eternal thirst, I am afraid, will remain as Germany's plague until the Last Day."[20] On the other hand, he praised dependable loyalty as a special virtue of the Germans. In no way did Luther keep silent about David's serious mistakes or failings, but the decisive factor was that he had a gracious God.

The commentary on this psalm intended to be critical of the existing situation. If it pleased only a few people, this would show that it was good. No direct response from the court is known, but Luther's theological friends praised his political wisdom.[21] In fact, it is remarkable in the way it combines sober insight into the relativity of political circumstances with the thoroughgoing consciousness of dependence upon God and the commitment to his will. Here the perspective from which the old Luther evaluated the world is apparent.

2. ELECTORAL SAXONY AND ITS CHURCH

At the end of Elector John's reign, only a few years after the first visitation that began in 1528, it was already apparent that the situation in the parishes of Electoral Saxony called for renewed changes. Pastors were being treated shabbily and were financially not well supported. Conversely, there were also complaints about their life style and their teaching. The committee of the *Landtag* that dealt with rural affairs recommended that a new visitation be undertaken.[1] When he was first invited to dine with the new elector on 21 August 1532, Luther, at Jonas's request, immediately presented John Frederick with the urgent matter of a new visitation, which was in fact initiated that same year, along with additional expropriations of church property.[2] Jonas was again named as one of the visitors.

In his first sermon before the elector, Luther also mentioned the low esteem the peasants, burghers, nobles, and public officials had for pastors and how they neglected them.[3] At that time he referred frequently in his Table Talk to these burning problems. It seemed to him that it was more important to see that pastors be supported by the congregations than to prevent vice. He also complained regularly about the arrogant attitude of the nobility toward the pastors.[4] A sermon delivered in Kemberg in October 1534 was permeated with his disappointment about the ingratitude displayed for the gospel.[5] Luther sought to explain this by stating that manifestations of evil were also to be understood as a result of the gospel. Even with his drastic warnings, Luther was unable to touch people's consciences, and over time this must have been tiring. Society had become immune to stinginess.[6] The insufficient remuneration corresponded to the minimal authority of the pastors, whose criticisms of the morality in all classes of society therefore had little effect.[7] In his preface to Caspar Aquila's *Sermon on Almsgiving*, Luther interpreted ingratitude as a

5

sign of the last days, for the loss of God's Word would inevitably lead to being abandoned by God and to judgment. He had to content himself by turning to the tiny group that received the Word with love and thanks.[8]

Except for substituting for Bugenhagen in 1534–35, Luther did not participate directly in the second visitation, but he was still frequently concerned with difficult matters. For example, Elizabeth von Reinsberg, a former nun, had been dismissed as the headmistress of the girls' school in Altenburg, and now she had to be supported in some other way from the church property.[9] Occasionally Luther tried to correct a problematic decision the visitors had made about church property.[10] In Dabrun the parsonage had been burned, and the pastor had lost everything. He needed funds promised by the elector, or else he would be forced to leave the parish.[11] Conversely, Luther also had to convince the elector to pay the allowances that the visitors had recommended for the clergy in Grimma, especially for the pastor who had heavy medical expenses for his wife.[12] Support had to be assured for the pension of a poor village pastor in allowing him to inherit a small glebe.[13] The income due Pastor Michael Cramer was being withheld, another example of the ingratitude of the peasants and nobles toward the gospel in the last days.[14] For unknown reasons, Hans Metzsch, the Wittenberg high bailiff (*Landvogt*), had expelled John Schlaginhaufen from the Zahna parish. When Luther tried to intervene for Schlaginhaufen, his good offices were rudely rejected. He was so infuriated by this that he threatened to leave Electoral Saxony himself; if this was the way the officials and their followers acted, the territory would lose its preachers and pastors. Other arbitrary dismissals of pastors by their nobles occurred. Luther let Spalatin be the sole advocate at court for the exiled pastor Wolfgang Götze, lest he arouse suspicion of a concerted action.[15] In 1535 the four pastors of the Baruth estate complained to Luther and Jonas, the visitors who were responsible for them, because the Von Schlieben family, which possessed the right of patronage, was withholding part of their compensation and not contributing to the urgent repairs that the parsonages required. The pastor in Crossen was encountering difficulties from his peasants concerning the construction of his quarters.[16] In one case, about which nothing further is known, Luther and Melanchthon advised the visitors not to start an argument with the steward (*Hofmeister*) Hans von Minkwitz. They had to show consideration for this important man at the court.[17]

The visitation still had to deal occasionally with cloisters of nuns. In 1534 the nuns who were continuing to reside in the Nimbschen monastery wanted to leave. Because of his experience, Luther could encourage this only if their support were assured. He thought it would be best for the old nuns to remain in the cloister. The dissolution of the cloister also presented the question of how to make further use of Johannes Petzensteiner, Luther's onetime traveling companion on his trip to Worms, who at this time was the preacher there, although not a very capable one. Luther had no advice. In Wittenberg there

6

were already twenty needy people who could not be supported. Burdens like this were being passed on to him, although it should have been the task of the other visitors with their greater resources to relieve the Wittenbergers.[18] In contrast to the Nimbschen nuns, the ones at the Plötzky cloister wanted to continue their communal life even after adopting the Reformation. Luther, however, feared that this might lead to a relapse into the papacy, and the elector did not authorize the new election of an abbess that they desired.[19]

Luther usually became involved with the problems of assigning pastors in connection with the visitation, but sometimes on other occasions as well, e.g., when pastors with no positions had to be housed. The deacon Valentine Paceus in Leisnig was allegedly not capable of performing the duties of his office because of illness, and therefore he and his large family had to be supported by alms from the elector. Luther also appears to have supported him personally, but later he had to acknowledge that Paceus, who never stayed long in any one place, did not deserve it.[20] Luther then filled the Leisnig diaconate with one of the residents of his house, Antony Lauterbach, who was preferred over another applicant. When Lauterbach soon became involved in a dispute with Wolfgang Fuss, the local pastor, Luther and Jonas energetically supported Lauterbach. Direct intervention in Leisnig, however, would have been possible only if Luther had received orders from the elector. Under the existing circumstances, Lauterbach did not have an easy time, and several times he had to be admonished to be patient. Luther recalled him in 1536. Lauterbach next became a deacon in Wittenberg. He occasionally asked Luther for advice, e.g., about pastoral care in the not infrequent cases of women who died in childbirth or in the case of stillbirths. Luther advised Lauterbach's wife not to let a certain person treat a sick child by using a biblical formula as a magic charm.[21] In order to avoid even the possibility of creating a controversy, Luther rejected the establishment of a preaching position at the Altenburg castle that would be independent of the pastor.[22]

When Luther was asked to give his approval to the appointment of Simon Haferitz in Kamenz in 1532, he emphasized: "I do not intend to be a new pope, appoint all pastors, fill all pulpits, etc.; but I grant that I am obligated to give my counsel and help to those who need it." He felt that the reason for the shortage of suitable pastors was the poor treatment they received, coupled with the lack of encouragement of schooling for new candidates. Nevertheless, it proved difficult to advocate Haferitz, because he once had been a supporter of Müntzer.[23] The congregation in Torgau was demanding the removal of their pastor and the chaplains, because they did not preach loudly enough to be understood. In light of the other qualifications of the clergy there, Luther was of the opinion that the visitors should reject this demand.[24]

How to handle pastors who had to be punished was a special problem. As long as criminal acts were not involved, Luther believed that the visitors, not the civil courts, should deal with them. In view of the tension between the pastors, on one side, and the peasants, burghers, and nobility, on the other, that led to criticism of the pastors' morality, secular courts were not the proper forum.[25] Luther wanted to have the superintendents, Myconius and Menius, deal with the troublesome case of a pastor's marriage, and he himself would step in only if the case were presented to the "centaurs," i.e., the electoral counselors who came from the nobility. However, he had to accept it when the judges decided the case, and not in the way he thought they should.[26]

By no means, however, did Luther protect pastors in every case. He demanded remorse from the Weida pastor, Johann Gülden, who had been arrested for rape but still had the temerity to demand a new position. Melanchthon asked that Gülden be pardoned, but the elector had him executed.[27] According to the initial information Luther received, the accusations against Johann Weybringer, the pastor of Hildburghausen who had been deposed for adultery, were based on evil gossip; therefore, the elector should have the matter investigated. He conceded: "It is true that perhaps we preachers are not pious; but because everyone is our enemy, Paul teaches—perhaps from experience—that one should not accept everyone's complaint against the preachers." The clergy's unfavorable position in society should not be made worse. Nevertheless, if clergy committed crimes they deserved severe punishment. In time, Luther became more unsure which side should be believed in this matter. He accused Weybringer of at least bringing suspicion upon himself, and a cleric had to guard against this.[28]

The clergy who deserved to be punished were exceptions. In this context, however, as in the matter of providing financial support for pastors, it became surprisingly clear that in no way had the new status of pastors achieved or regained its former position within society. After the experiences of the second visitation, for the time being the only dependable supporter of ecclesiastical authority—something essential in a church of the people (*Volkskirche*)—was the sovereign. Without him, the pastors and their preaching could not hold their own in the larger society.[29] In Electoral Saxony there were thus not only political arguments for a government of the church by the sovereign, but also significant ecclesiastical ones.

Luther had theological difficulties of a special sort with Michael Stifel, a pastor who was actually very close to him.[30] From 1525 to 1528 the former Augustinian monk from Esslingen had been preacher to the noble Jörger family of Tolleth in Upper Austria. When Stifel was driven from there as a result of anti-Reformation politics, Luther obtained the Lochau parish for him. Stifel married the widow of his predecessor, Franz Günther, and Luther performed the ceremony.[31] Stifel not only wrote one of the earliest hymns about Luther, but he also had exceptional mathematical gifts. His *Arithmetica Integra* (1544), *Deutsche Arithmetica* (1545), *Rechenbuch* (1546), and additional publications proved him to be a noted teacher of mathematics.

Stifel's mathematical interests also led him to manipulate words in such a way that apocalyptic dates could be ascertained by applying various cabalistic processes to the letters of the alphabet contained in certain Bible passages. In 1532 Stifel published his insights in *Rechenbüchlein vom Endchrist: Apocalypsis in Apocalypsim* (Booklet for calculating Christ's return: An apocalypse within an apocalypse). In the fall of 1532, Luther made a clear statement about the nearness of the end of the world: Affairs could not continue to get any worse; a change was needed. Nevertheless, Luther refused to write a preface to Stifel's booklet. In 1533 Luther had already condemned Stifel's calculations as fanaticism. In the meantime Stifel had set eight o'clock in the morning of 19 October 1533 as the time of Christ's return and had already given away his household goods. Luther sought to convince Stifel of the arbitrariness of his calculations but had little success: "In all my life no enemy has spoken so ill of me as he." Stifel reviled him for being a "Pilate and Herod."[32] In a letter on 24 June, Luther sought to pacify Stifel by classifying the problem as an indifferent one. One had to reckon that Christ might return at any hour. Stifel's passionate insistence on a specific time, however, gave rise to suspicions that the devil had bewitched him.[33] The matter could not be settled in complete privacy, of course, for it was feared that his prediction might lead to a riot. Stifel was therefore summoned at the command of the elector to Wittenberg for a theological inquiry at the end of August, and then several times subsequently. He stubbornly maintained his position, and consequently at the end of September he was forbidden to preach on this theme. Luther himself, accompanied by Melanchthon, preached in Lochau from 1 to 3 October, but without mentioning the imminent second coming of Christ.[34]

According to the account of Peter Weller,[35] a resident of Luther's house who had gone to Lochau to investigate, the people began streaming from great distances to Lochau days before the expected event. Stifel admonished them to repent and heard their confession. Early in the morning on 19 October, the predicted day, he conducted a communion service in the church, during which he preached once again on his prophecy, concluding with a tearful threefold, "He will come." At nine o'clock in the morning, when nothing had yet happened, the people went home. Stifel was brought by officers of the elector to Wittenberg, not least to protect him from the disappointed crowds. The elector removed him as pastor in Lochau for causing great offense in the German empire. The derisive song, "Stifel Must Die," was even recorded in the students' songbook (*Kommersbuch*). Luther himself seems to have viewed the affair with equanimity; Stifel had "fallen prey to a tiny temptation, but it will not hurt him. . . ."[36] His confidence in Stifel was not shaken, and thus the episode did not become a great theological affair, particularly because Stifel displayed good sense. The elector, however, refused to reassign him immediately, which Luther advocated. Instead, Stifel was to live for a time in Luther's house, with a drastically reduced income, and learn from him. At the beginning of 1535 he became the pastor in Holzdorf.[37] After Luther's death he began his apocalyptic speculations again and also became involved in other theological conflicts.

9

Luther continued to be confronted with questions about marriage laws, primarily from Electoral Saxony, but occasionally also from other territories. For example, a nobleman, Nickel Sack, had a relationship with the daughter of a peasant, whom he then also married secretly. The dispute concerned whether the daughter born before the marriage was equal to the other children, and, in addition, whether the children could inherit their father's title. Luther thought the answer to the second question was doubtful, and therefore he was reluctant to take up Sack's cause with the elector. But then the elector decided the issue in Sack's favor.[38] Luther used the case of a frivolous engagement in Torgau as an occasion to urge people to choose their partners carefully.[39] The Wittenberg theologians, on the basis of Lev. 18:18, held that it was impermissible for a man to marry his deceased wife's sister.[40] A Wittenberg student who came from Breslau had secretly become engaged to a girl. Because his parents had not given their permission, such an engagement was invalid, and it appears that the student appealed retroactively to this. Luther considered it impermissible to use "evangelical freedom" in this way for the sake of love, and he therefore attempted to secure the father's permission for the marriage.[41] When the father of another student would not permit his son to marry, Luther interceded on his behalf.[42] Luther did not seek to decide marriage matters that were the responsibility of Spalatin or Jonas, although he did not withhold his counsel. He did not want to be a marriage judge, because this brought him into conflict with the jurists who were still oriented toward canon law, as well as with the peasants who were lovelessly insisting on evangelical freedom. He tended to leave marriage matters to the jurists and to limit himself to giving advice to people's consciences. With an eye toward the jurists, he resignedly stated his opinion: "The world wants a pope."[43] The Reformation also pushed the limits with regard to marriage law. The conflict that can already be seen developing here later broke out openly.

Luther occasionally had to deal with matters that were foreign to him. He cautioned the Torgau *Schösser* (an electoral official) about failing to deal impartially with a legal matter, and reminded him that he, too, had a judge over him.[44] He did his utmost to see that the former *Schösser*, Kunz Pfeilschmidt, who owed the electoral treasury a sum of money, might repay the amount in installments. In this case, Luther was touched by the especially difficult situation: "Raising seven children without a mother would wear down an otherwise well man."[45] For a similar reason he supported a man who was unable to obtain property that was legally his: "The jurists carry things too far, and they have no regard for the pitiable condition of the poor people who have to seek their rights."[46]

In August 1535 Luther commended to Menius in Eisenach a woman who had stayed in Wittenberg for several months and there had given birth to a child. Luther had been a sponsor at the baptism, and he had compassion on the woman, although it is not impossible that in this case, too, he had been deceived as he often had been by "alleged nuns and elegant whores." Only later did he learn that she was the sister of Hartmut von Kronberg, who had followed her to Wittenberg. She had a remarkable fate. After her first husband died, Lorche von Kronberg became the second wife of an already married Jew, who was also in Wittenberg with her, but who shortly thereafter was murdered by relatives of the Von Kronbergs. Even after Luther learned of this, he continued to plead for the woman.[47]

In 1534 Luther came into contact with Hans Kohlhase, a merchant from Köln on the Spree and his exciting case, which became the inspiration for Kleist's novella, *Michael Kohlhaas*. While Kohlhase was on the way to the Leipzig fair, his horse was illegally taken from him by a Saxon nobleman. When he was unable to obtain justice from the electors of Brandenburg and Saxony, he started a feud with the Saxon nobility in March 1534. His armed action was supported by many classes of the populace. Until the real culprit was discovered, he was blamed for several acts of arson in Wittenberg in April 1534. The fair on 20 April was canceled. At the end of the year, Kohlhase also turned to Luther. As he once had done with the peasants, Luther clearly warned him not to seek his own revenge. If Kohlhase could not obtain justice, he would humbly have to leave the matter to God. There was no excuse for the new injustice he was committing with his feud.[48] At that time a solution was reached through arbitration, but it was one that Elector John Frederick did not accept, whereupon Kohlhase continued his feud for years. Luther repeatedly took note of these events. In November 1538 Kohlhase plundered the village of Marzahna near Wittenberg. Luther was critical of John Frederick's inability to preserve the public peace. The father of the country dared not disappoint his subjects who were trusting in him. For a time, Luther suspected that the elector of Brandenburg was making common cause with Kohlhase, until Kohlhase also turned against his own sovereign.[49] Rumors about alleged attacks by Kohlhase spread. He himself was even allegedly seen in Wittenberg, and this led to defensive measures about which Luther commented sarcastically.[50] The report that George Reich, a Wittenberg citizen who had been taken prisoner by Kohlhase, had been able to escape filled Luther with satisfaction. He was certain that this lawbreaker would come to no good end. When Kohlhase was captured by the elector of Brandenburg in 1540, Luther felt sorry for him, because he had brought this blood guilt upon himself.[51] For Luther, Kohlhase was not an isolated case, because the Saxon nobles also engaged in legal abuses.[52]

3. WITTENBERG

The Wittenberg congregation, too, in Luther's opinion, had a dual appearance. In appearance, it was a "manure sack," a miserable stable, not even a poorhouse, but the presence of the divine gifts of Word and sacrament turned it into a priceless royal palace. In view of this, he left no doubt when telling the old believers: "Here we have and are the Christian church."[1] How these gifts were used, of course, was often perverted: "The law attracts those who are good, and the gospel attracts those who are bad."[2] Here, too, dealing with evangelical freedom was problematic. Satiety and weariness with the Word of God were always a problem. The common people thought it most sensible to dispense with the preaching of the gospel and simply to read a chapter from the Bible, pray, and add moralistic exhortations.[3] Sometimes Luther was overcome with exhaustion: "I've preached here for twenty-four years. I've walked to church so often that it wouldn't be at all surprising if I had not only worn out my shoes on the pavement but even my feet. I've done my part. I discipline myself." Nothing was so exhausting as his cares, however, especially at night.[4]

To what extent Luther was involved in the new edition of the Wittenberg church order, which was prepared in connection with the second visitation in 1533, cannot be determined. No extensive changes were made in it. As before, his chief activity in the Wittenberg congregation continued to be fulfilling his preaching responsibility. Probably for reasons of health, after the end of March 1532 he preached in the city church on only one Sunday morning for the remainder of that year. This did not mean that he ceased his preaching, however, but rather that he was delivering sermons to small groups in his house. He expressly denied that this was in any way a protest against the way people were scorning the Word of God.[5] After August 1532 Luther preached sequentially on Sunday afternoons in the city church or in the castle church on 1 Corinthians 15.[6] This series continued until April 1533. In it he gave one of his most thorough expositions of the resurrection. In contrast to the general anxiety over death and the widespread orientation toward this world, he held up the realism of his faith in Christ. Of the seventy-six known sermons of the year 1533, only twenty-three were delivered in the city church, a few in the castle church in the presence of the elector, several in other places, but most of them in his home.[7] Beginning in September 1533, Luther preached sequentially on Sunday afternoons for a year on John 14–16.[8] In 1534 he was able to participate more fully in the Sunday morning preaching in the city church, but on thirty Sundays he chose to preach at home.[9] At the beginning of the year, when he preached six sermons on baptism directed primarily against the Anabaptists, Luther realized a plan he had entertained for a long time. From November 1534 until August 1535 Bugenhagen was away introducing the Reformation in Pomerania, and Luther again had to substitute as pastor for him. This time, however, he did not assume his weekday preaching duties. Beginning in July 1535, and also in the following year, Luther preached chiefly on Sunday afternoons on the epistle pericopes. No sermons in his home have been preserved from these two years.[10]

When, from the end of 1533 until 1535, the melancholy Jerome Weller, who was plagued by a lack of self-confidence, had to preach on the Gospel of

Matthew, Luther helped him by providing sermon sketches that dealt with the chief point of the texts. They were later published against his wishes. When the elector was in Wittenberg, Luther himself participated in these sermon series. Twenty-two outlines for Sunday sermons were produced in 1534 and 1535 for the same reason.[11]

Luther was occasionally asked by the residents of his house about the art of preaching. In accordance with the introduction to the First Commandment, what was to be done was "to preach hell fire to the proud, paradise to the pious, afflict the evil, and comfort the pious." Luther never referred back to his previous sermons, but gave the text a new form in the given situations. He therefore also considered it problematic for anyone to use his postils directly. In any case, one should preach simply, not for the scholars. "In the pulpit one should bare one's breast and give the people milk to drink, for every day a new church is growing up, and it needs the rudiments." Often even the best outline proved to be unworkable; in contrast, a sermon could also "come together" with meager preparation. The gift for preaching was varied, of course. Luther's style of preaching could not simply be imitated. After him, Cordatus and Rörer were the most highly respected preachers. Luther also knew that a sermon that a preacher himself did not regard highly was capable of accomplishing things that were not apparent.[12]

Luther himself thought Bugenhagen's instructive sermons were theologically stimulating, to be sure, but they were notorious for their excessive length, which tried the spirit, and, to Luther's dismay, they were little appreciated. He also considered Bugenhagen's or Deacon Fröschel's sharp, hortatory sermons, which were very general, as problematic.[13] When the deacon Johannes Mantel suffered a stroke in 1535 and was incapacitated, the other clergy assumed his duties, and Luther asked the elector to continue supporting him.[14]

Occasionally, Luther was asked to serve as a counselor (*Seelsorger*). Along with Bugenhagen, he comforted a mercenary who spoke to him following a sermon because he thought the devil wanted to grab him.[15] While substituting for Bugenhagen, Luther had to stand beside an arsonist, Valentine Teuchel, who was condemned to death at the stake for setting fire to twenty-six houses in the settlement outside the Fisher Gate and three houses near the castle. Luther reproached him again for the seriousness of his crime. It was no cause to despair, however, for God himself had comforted delinquents through the servants of his Word. He should willingly accept the bodily punishment, which ultimately was meaningless, in order to save his soul.[16]

The son of the Wittenberg jurist and burgomaster, Benedict Pauli, was fatally injured while bird hunting. Luther understood the grief of the father, but in faith he should accept this misfortune as coming from God's gracious hand. Many pious people in the Bible had also experienced such sorrow. The loss of his only son and his terrible death could not separate the father from a gracious God. The accident was not to be interpreted as a sign of God's anger and punishment.[17] The wife of Hans Breu was, with her husband, driven out of Leipzig because of their faith. Later, in 1536, the husband drowned. She fell seriously ill because of this. Luther interpreted her suffering as a father's loving chastening, and said she would not lack the power to bear it. It seems that this proved salutary for the woman.[18] In his final illness, Master John Bernhardi felt that his faith was being tried by the devil. In no way was this something out of the ordinary for Luther, but Bernhardi had to hold fast to faith in Christ. He should take comfort that he was not one of the Zwinglians, Anabaptists, Turks, or Jews. His strength lay in his relationship to Christ, and therefore all the weaknesses that the devil was exploiting were of no consequence. In this way one could chase away the devil, and he would have to depart. The gracious God also pardoned his own for their momentary blasphemous doubts.[19]

Peter Beskendorf, the barber and surgeon, is well known as one of the first Wittenberg citizens with whom Luther had a closer relationship.[20] He was a quartermaster (*Viertelmeister*), and at various times he occupied most of the honorary positions in the city, although complaints were sometimes raised about him. The image of his personality that we draw from the sources is many faceted. He must have been interested in religious matters, for it was an inquiry from him that motivated Luther at the beginning of 1535 to write *A Simple Way to Pray: For a Good Friend*, which was frequently reprinted.[21] In it, Luther described how "I do personally when I pray." When his tasks and thoughts distracted him and caused him to become cool or joyless in praying, it was then time to withdraw into his room for prayer. Above all, prayer in the mornings and evenings should frame the day, and one had to set aside a certain time for this, even though in themselves all activities of a believer could be considered prayer. Aside from the "evening blessing" in the catechism, a brief evening prayer from Luther in response to a question has been preserved: "My dear God, now I lie down and turn your affairs back to you; you may do better with them. If you can do no better than I, you will ruin them entirely. When I awake, I will gladly try again."[22] As he had already suggested in the *Personal Prayer Book*,[23] prayer should be practiced as meditation on sections of the Lord's Prayer, the Decalogue, and the Apostles' Creed. Situations and problems that were not in accord with God's will should be laid before him, in order that he might turn them into good. Luther favored free prayers from the heart, not ones that were bound to fixed formulations. In praying, one had to concentrate just as much as did a barber when he worked with his razor. This did not mean that a conversation with the Holy Spirit might not follow its own paths. Combined with the meditation on the Commandments and the Apostles' Creed should be an acknowledgement of God's will, thanksgiving, confession of sin, and petitions, including intercessions for others. Thereby the world became involved in the prayers of an individual. Nowhere is the connection between order and freedom in Luther's practice of prayer so clearly seen as in his advice for Master Peter.

Plate I
Elector John Frederick of Saxony and his Reformation co-workers
Painting by Lucas Cranach the Elder, ca. 1532/39

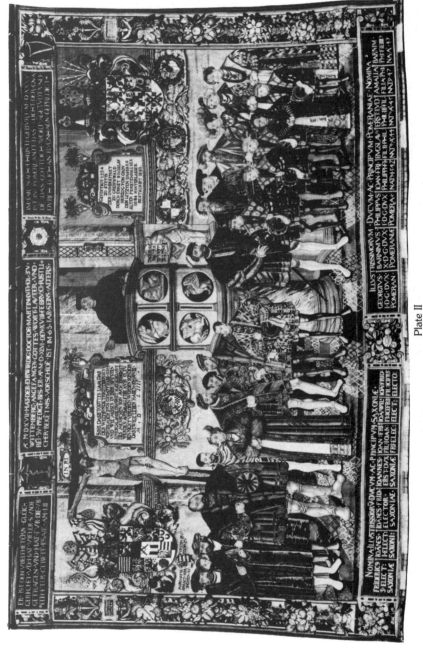

Plate II

Luther the preacher points to the crucified Christ, while in his audience are members of the ruling houses of electoral Saxony on the left, and of the duchy of Pomerania on the right

The so-called Croy tapestry by Peter Heyman, 1554

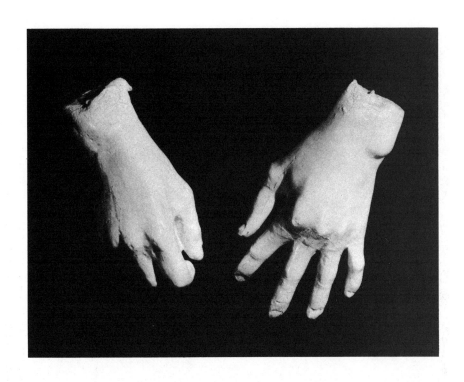

Plate III
Mold of Luther's hands, made after his death
It shows the deformity of his joints caused by kidney stones

LVSTRA·NOVEM·CVM·DIMIDIO·VIXISSE·FEREBAR
ANDREAS·TALIS·QVANDO·OSIANDER·ERAM

1544

Plate IV
Andreas Osiander the Elder
Oil painting by Georg Pencz, 1544

Plate V
Elector John Frederick and Luther beneath the cross
Title woodcut by Lucas Cranach the Younger for the Wittenberg New Testament that
appeared after Luther's death, 1546

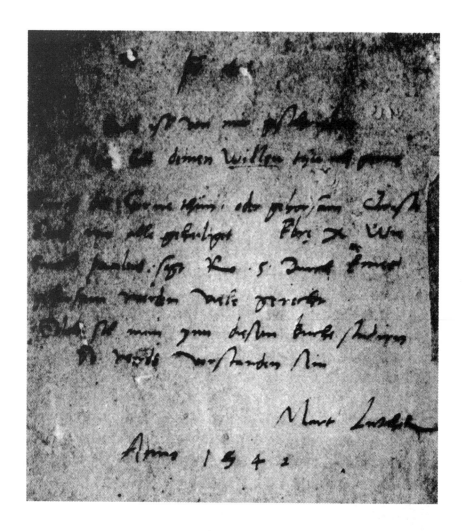

Plate VI
Inscription by Luther in a Wittenberg Bible, 1541
Psalm 41 [41]: In the roll of the book it is written of me; I delight to do thy will, O my God.
And by that will we have been sanctified through the offering of the body of Jesus Christ.
Hebrews 10.
As St. Paul says in Romans 5: So by one man's obedience many will be made righteous.
Those who study this book will understand.
Martin Luther
1542

Plate VII
Martin Luther at the age of fifty
Painting by Lucas Cranach the Elder, 1533

Ratschlag von der

Kirchen/eins ausschus etlicher

Cardinel / Bapst Paulo des namens dem
dritten/auff seinen befelh geschrieben
vnd vberantwortet.

Mit einer vorrede D. Mart. Luth.

Sophisma Chrysippi.
Si mentiris, etiam quod uerum dicis, mentiris.

Plate VIII
Cardinals cleansing the church with foxtails
Title woodcut for *Counsel of a Committee of Several Cardinals,* produced by Cranach's
workshop according to Luther's instructions, 1538

Plate IX

Luther in the classroom, showing the signs of illness

Drawing by Johann Reifenstein, a resident in Luther's house, 1545

The inscription referring to Luther's death comes from Melanchthon

Plate X
Katherine (Katy) Luther, née von Bora
Painting by Cranach's workshop

Plate XI
Luther room in the Luther house

Plate XII
Katherine doorway to the Luther house, 1540

Plate XIII

Luther as preacher points the congregation to the crucified Christ

Painting by Lucas Cranach the Elder on the predella of the Wittenberg city church altar, 1547

Plate XIV
Interior of the Torgau castle church, dedicated by Luther in 1544

Plate XV

"Jewish Sow"

Sandstone relief on the choir of the Wittenberg city church, early fourteenth century

Plate XVI
House of Johann Albrecht, the city clerk in Eisleben, in which Luther lived and died

Plate XVII
Funerary monument of Katherine (Katy) Luther, née von Bora,
in the Torgau city church

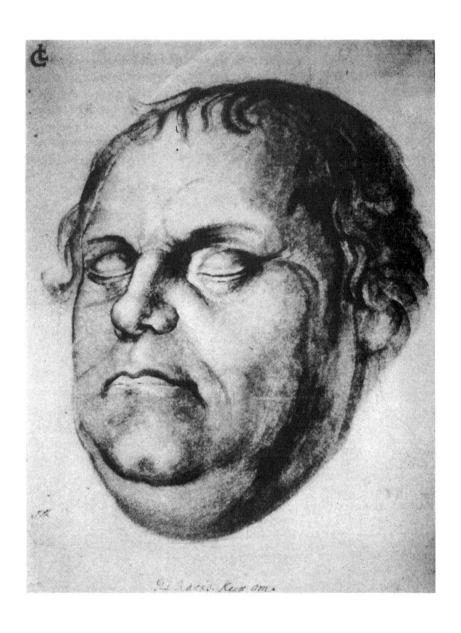

Plate XVIII
The dead Luther
Colored drawing by Lukas Fortennagel (Furtenagel), 1546

Plate XIX
Luther's grave marker in the Wittenberg castle church

Plate XX
Luther's bronze funerary monument
Because of the Smalcald War, the original by Heinrich Ziegler is in the
city church in Jena; a copy is in the Wittenberg castle church

Luther also remained close to Beskendorf when Peter became involved in a frightful crime. In 1533 the barber Dietrich Freyenhagen had married Beskendorf's daughter Anne. Luther was a sponsor for the first child born to the couple. Very soon arguments erupted between Beskendorf and his son-in-law. On 27 March 1535, Beskendorf stabbed Freyenhagen at the dinner table. In the ensuing trial, his advocate, Francis Burchart—supported by pleas from Luther and Melanchthon—was successful in having the deed regarded as manslaughter instead of homicide, and Beskendorf was punished leniently, with banishment instead of execution. A mitigating argument seems to have been that he had been seduced by the devil. Earlier, Beskendorf himself had boasted confidently that he was going to write a book of his own against the devil. After his banishment he lived with his daughter in Dessau. In 1536 he raised an objection to her remarrying, but in Luther's opinion it should be given no credence.[24] In connection with the pastoral counseling of the criminal, and possibly at Luther's initiative, a book of testimonials (*Stammbuch*) in support of Beskendorf was produced, in which a number of current or former Wittenberg theologians signed their names and wrote references to his deed. Luther's own contribution, partly in verse, was an urgent warning against the devil, the "murderer" (John 8:44), who could be overcome only by Christ.[25]

We catch glimpses of specific situations and problems in the Wittenberg congregation primarily from the exhortations at the end of the sermons as well as from the Table Talk. As before, Luther complained about the congregation's unwillingness to give, which he considered ingratitude for the gospel.[26] The rise in the prices of foodstuffs threatened to starve out the university, thereby endangering the education of theologians.[27] He considered greed in general a spiritual problem, for it was certainly incompatible with the gospel. "Wittenberg scratches, scrapes, and grabs everything for itself," and yet feels safe in doing so. Punishment could not long be delayed.[28] In the growing university city, profiteering in the housing market was rampant. Luther mentioned one case of a thirteenfold increase in price. He wanted to take action against the speculators by excluding them from the Lord's Supper.[29]

It was urged that an appropriate period of mourning intervene between the death of one's spouse and one's remarriage, but for social reasons this could not always be observed. In such cases the marriage festivities should at least be limited.[30]

Luther was aware that there were unmarried couples in the community involved in sexual relationships, e.g., meeting in the woods. He blamed this on the devil, who was invading the church in this area, too. Young people should either be prevented from doing this or they should get married. Luther considered adultery even worse than this sort of offense, which was committed by unmarried people, and he threatened to name the adulterers publicly from the pulpit. Along with the preachers, the government had to take action against immorality. The evangelical city of Wittenberg should not come into disrepute because of this. For the same reason he frequently urged that the prohibition against frequenting taverns during the preaching services should be enforced.[31] Luther was not opposed to modest dancing or to students and sons of the citizens associating in the inns, but he warned against certain disreputable public houses.[32]

Frequently the preacher also had to warn against sorcery. Witches were unable to do anything that God did not allow, but nevertheless they belonged at the stake.[33]

The exercise of church discipline in Wittenberg prescribed that the clergy should warn offenders, e.g., those who lived immoral lives or who stayed away from the Lord's Supper, that the elector would punish them or banish them from his territory. If this warning did not help, the pastors were to instruct and admonish them for a month. If they still remained obstinate, they were expelled from the congregation. No one was to be absolved who did not promise to amend his life. Absolution was not, however, to become a spiritual means of applying pressure.[34] Church discipline thus lay in the hands of the pastors, who, however, employed it only in flagrant cases. In contrast to southwestern Germany, for example, it appears that there were no struggles with the civil community concerning jurisdiction.

In July 1535 the plague struck Wittenberg once again. As he had done previously, Luther minimized the danger and rejected the elector's counsel to move somewhere else, especially because Hans Metzsch, the high bailiff who loved life and took very good care of his health, remained in the city. The danger was exaggerated by the students, to whom an interruption of their studies was not unwelcome, and by their anxious mothers. One had to be careful that this did not become a mass psychosis.[35] Luther gave some suggestions in his sermons. He had no use for special clothing for those infected. The supply of foodstuffs for those who were ill had to be assured. On the other hand, those who were infected had to stay away from those who were healthy. Husbands should not leave their wives. Unchristian despondency was inappropriate, but not everyone was able to conquer his fear with the confidence of faith. The congregation was invited to participate at the services of the Lord's Supper, which now were also being held on Wednesdays and Fridays. This should make it unnecessary to hold special celebrations of the Lord's Supper for the sick in their homes, because the clergy could not keep up with them. Luther especially rejected private communions when they were requested by those who previously had absented themselves from the communal worship service.[36] Among his instructions about health was also the warning against bathing in the Elbe, because this frequently led to accidents. Luther believed that the devil dwelt in the water, and that a person could less easily resist him there than on dry land.[37]

Luther made only a few statements about other conditions in the city. As before, he had little use for the building of the new wall, for he did not understand the significance of this fortification in an age of cannons. For him, the regular flooding of the Elbe showed how vulnerable the city was. Here only trust in God could help in the battle with the devil.[38] An application from the widow of the wealthy goldsmith Christian Düring, probably for the privilege of operating a tavern, was endorsed by Luther and Jonas.[39] The two were also expected as guests at a marriage arranged by one of the most noted booksellers, Moritz Goltz.[40] On his part, Luther had social obligations concerning the city and the university, which, under some circumstances, he tried to avoid because of the considerable expenses involved. This was why he arranged to have Caspar Cruciger's wedding, which ordinarily would have been held in Luther's home, celebrated in the Eilenburg castle. When Jerome Weller wanted to get married in Wittenberg, Luther advised him not to, for the same reason. If need be, a limited number of guests could be entertained in the Luther house, but this would be impossible, because Weller was a doctor of the university, and especially because of Luther's position in the city. Luther naturally did not want to act "dishonorably": "Our market [Wittenberg] is a mess, and if a crowd is to be invited, the university with bag and baggage, and others as well, which as far as I am concerned certainly cannot be left out, it will not be limited to nine or even twelve tables."[41] Nevertheless, Weller apparently did celebrate the large wedding in Wittenberg.

Luther believed that Burgomaster Tilo Dene was one of the magistrates who was able to guide a community rightly by using good words or severe punishment.[42] There are no signs of tensions between Luther and the Wittenberg magistracy. The city provided him building materials without charge. He was not billed for the wine that he occasionally requisitioned from the city's wine cellar.[43] As a whole, the preacher's relationship to the city at this time appears to have been rather normal, objective, and devoid of fundamental conflicts, but also without significant successes. Luther had to tolerate some problems. Possibly his relationships with the congregation had become somewhat more distant because his preaching activity had been reduced.

4. HOME, FAMILY, AND PERSONAL HEALTH

In 1536, Elector John Frederick renewed his father's assignment four years earlier of the Augustinian monastery to Luther and his family.[1] Luther's salary of two hundred gulden a year was to be paid from the tithe on beverages (*Getränkezehnten*). Beginning in 1535, he received an additional one hundred gulden from the revenues of the All Saints Foundation. Luther and Melanchthon were thus the most highly paid professors at the university. The increase in compensation was, at least in part, merely an accommodation to the increased cost of living. In addition to the salary, there were considerable payments in kind: one hundred bushels of wheat, 106 bushels of malt for two brews of beer, one hundred cords of wood, and two cartloads of hay. It is noteworthy that the Wittenberg bailiff was admonished not to short or reduce any of the quantities. Moreover, Luther occasionally received allowances of wine, grape juice, game, pike, chickens, and apples, in part as a type of official reimbursement for his expenses in entertaining. The two kegs of cider that the elector sent Luther in the fall of 1536 along with a personal letter were simply to be "drunk and enjoyed on our account" by Luther and his family.[2]

Despite the considerable income, money was usually in short supply in Luther's house, and it was spent only too quickly. Luther does appear at least at times to have held back his gifts to the poor out of concern for his family's support, especially because he believed that there were no truly needy people in Wittenberg, just loafers. Wherever there was real need, he considered himself obligated to help. Not infrequently, however, Luther was deceived into performing acts of charity and lending money.[3] It was not only Katy who became angry when a pastor—their friend Conrad Cordatus—wanted to sell Luther grain at an inflated price, as the peasants did.[4] At the end of 1534 Luther was not in a position to purchase the house adjacent to the Augustinian monastery, which at that time was owned by the former Augustinian prior, Eberhard Brisger. He did not even have half of the 440 gulden needed. He considered himself poor but was not greatly concerned about it.[5] In 1534, out of concern for his needy brothers and sisters, he was not expecting to receive the 250 gulden due him in accordance with his father's estate until years later.[6] A few months later, because of obligations for his own large household, he was unable to support Bernard the Jew. This was a difficult societal situation. Although Bernard and his wife were in good health, they depended on continuing assistance, and Luther, despite his desire to help, was unable to support this Jewish Christian.[7]

Already in 1532 Luther thought it was amazing that he had been able to survive financially, because it cost five hundred gulden a year just to maintain the household, substantially more than he earned. In reviewing the year 1535–36 he wrote an *Amazing Accounting between Doctor Martin and Katy*.[8] Just the larger expenditures—specifically, for example, twenty gulden for linen and thirty gulden for Katy's hog raising—without counting the regular payments for foodstuffs, totaled 389 gulden. In it we learn that at that time Luther purchased for ninety gulden an additional garden and a plot (*Hufe*) of land in what was called the *Kabelhufen* outside the Elster Gate.[9] Forty gulden was a loan to the cabinetmaker Gregory Blankensteyn for purchasing a house. Luther also had had to borrow half of this amount for a short term from the bookseller Moritz Goltz. Blankensteyn was to repay twenty gulden to the common chest, thus discharging one of Luther's debts, and he was to work out the rest.[10]

In the *Amazing Accounting*, Luther presented a catalog of goods, services, and circumstances that occasioned expenses. He offers such a revealing glimpse of his household and economic situation that it is worthwhile to repeat it here in full. His first list dealt primarily with foodstuffs: grain, barley, hops, oats, hay, wheat, flour, wine, beer, peas, hemp, flax, groats, small barley, rice, millet, sugar, spices, saffron, fruit, cabbage, carrots, turnips, onions, poppies, parsley, caraway seeds, oxen, swine, geese, chickens, ducks, birds, doves, eggs, butter, salt, wood, coal, straw, dried and fresh fish, meat from the butcher shop, bread, rolls, nails, hooks, iron wares, tallow, twine, wax, oil. A second category dealt with services, personal obligations, and building materials: the butcher for in-house slaughtering, the shoemaker, tailor, furrier, cooper, blacksmith, locksmith, barber, bathkeeper, glazier, knife maker, rope maker, strap maker, belt maker, harness maker, clothier, garment maker, shearer, brewer, potter, miller, joiner, linen weaver, girdle maker, bag maker, apothecary, physician, preceptor for the children, mason, carpenters, day laborers, bricks, lime, roof tiles, construction lumber, lath, boards, beggars, thieves, expenses for weddings, sponsorships at baptisms, gifts, hospitality, bookkeepers, bookbinders, gifts at fairs (e.g., those that Elizabeth Cruciger and Katy once exchanged),[11] Christmas gifts, servants, maids, maidens, boys, shepherds, swine castrators. Finally, he enumerated household effects and equipment: linen, beds, feathers, pewter ware, bowls, plates, candleholders, bowls, kettles, pans, shovels, spades, trays, wheelbarrows, forks, scoops, barrels, tubs, pails, brewing equipment, animal harnesses, wagons, silk, velvet.

On the basis of what was obviously his precarious financial situation, Luther drew the conclusion that only by trusting in God could one venture to manage a household. In fact, the money needed to supplement his salary came from Katy's own gardening and cattle raising, as well as from the income from the students who lived in the house. Luther left the responsibility for this area largely in the hands of his wife, and frankly admitted: "If I had to take care of building, brewing, and cooking, I'd soon die."[12]

Some information about the way Katy ran the household has been preserved: She drove the wagon, cultivated the fields, fed the animals, did the shopping, and brewed beer. Luther urged her not to become absorbed in these tasks. Once he promised her fifty gulden if she would read through the Bible within several months.[13] Under orders from Katy, his "chief cook," Luther had to order all sorts of delicious birds and poultry, along with rabbits and other delicacies, that were needed for a large doctoral banquet. The large quantity of beer that was also necessary had already been brewed by Katy.[14] She was not always successful in brewing beer. Occasionally what came out was thin *Kofent*, "monastery beer." Luther sometimes confessed that bread grain was needed in order to brew thin beer.[15] In August 1534 beer was in short supply in Wittenberg. Katy, however, had laid in a supply, so Luther's thirst did not have to go unquenched in that thirsty time.[16] The housewife was thrilled when a big barrel of large salted fish arrived from Speratus in Königsberg.[17] The garden on Zahnischer Weg that they had purchased in 1531 contained a fishpond, and from it pike, gudgeon, trout, ruff, and carp enriched their table. Although Katy regarded the fish as a welcome supplement to their menu, Luther used them as an occasion for expounding on the wonder of creation and its gifts, and on how one should use such gifts in thankfulness.[18] God had richly given the peasants his gifts of creation, but then he withdrew from them because they dishonored his Word. God himself wanted to be recognized in his bountiful gifts.[19] Conversely, drinking adulterated wine and eating rancid bread at a wedding moved Luther to state something that is still applicable today: "Now they are accustoming us to brimstone and pitch, so that we'll be better able to get along in hell."[20]

Luther did not approve of the trapping of birds done by his servant Wolfgang Seberger. He wrote a fictitious *Complaint of the Birds . . . against Siberger*.[21] In it the thrushes, blackbirds, finches, linnets, goldfinches, and other respectable birds complained that they were being persecuted, while the sparrows, swallows, magpies, jackdaws, ravens, mice, and rats were doing much more damage. Appealing to Seberger's laziness, they requested that grain be put out for them in the evenings and that the servant not go to the fowling floor until after eight o'clock in the morning. These birds were an example of God's solicitude, and that was something on which humans also could depend. Seberger, Luther's longtime famulus, had a modest income of his own from an ecclesiastical foundation at the castle chapel in Colditz, so he was only partially a financial burden for Luther. In 1535 Luther planned to buy him a small house so that Seberger would have something after Luther's death.[22]

Luther's family was still quite young. In 1532 most of the father's attention was centered on the then one-year-old Martin, and Luther was conscious of the strong attachment of a father's love. He noted how the child made his own will felt. His comment on putting the child to bed sounds like a lullaby: "Go now and be godly. No money will I leave you, but a rich God I will leave you. Only be godly."[23] In November 1532 Katy was again in the advanced stages of pregnancy. Luther regarded this as a divine blessing of marriage, but he was seriously concerned for his wife, for she had a fever and was troubled with insomnia.[24] Their son Paul was born on 28 January 1533 and baptized the next day in the castle church. The sponsors, who were to aid the child in being reborn in Christ so that he might possibly become "a new enemy of the pope or of the Turk," were Duke John Ernest, the hereditary marshal Hans von Löser, Jonas, Melanchthon, and Margaret, the wife of the court physician Caspar Lindemann. The name was selected out of reverence for the apostle Paul, to whom Luther was indebted for "many a good passage and argument."[25] The small child made Luther realize how Adam must have loved his first son, Cain, although despite this love Cain turned into someone who murdered his brother. Just as a mother's love is far stronger than the "refuse and vernix on an infant, however, so is God's love stronger than human stains," and thus sins do not separate the believing sinner from Christ.[26] For Luther, having children was not a self-evident result of his relationship with Katy but rather also had to do with believing in God the creator.[27] Their last child, a daughter, Margaret, was born on 17 December 1534. Her sponsors were Prince Joachim of Anhalt, for whom Hausmann served as proxy, and Anna Göritz, the wife of a jurist driven out of Leipzig.[28]

Luther cherished Katy as a charming wife, but even while she slept at his side, the devil troubled him with his *Anfechtungen*. Nevertheless, the devil with his evil thoughts was unable to interrupt Luther's enjoyment of Katy. This had nothing to do with sexual difficulties, but rather with the trials of faith. In such situations there was nothing to do but rely on God's Word.[29]

Luther was convinced of man's superiority over woman. If Katy were ever to talk back to him, he would give her a slap in the mouth, but there is no record of whether it ever came to that. There once was another source that complained about Katy's quarreling and squabbling. She could have her way with the family, but not with her husband. Luther was happy to leave the running of the entire household up to her, but she could not manage Luther himself. Where rule by women led could be seen in the example of Eve.[30] Despite the screams of sick children, and despite the peculiar nature of women, Luther stood by his positive evaluation of marriage, and he was well aware that he was thereby diverging from the church fathers. Before the last day, thanks be to God, marriage, government, and the ministry of the Word were now being restored as divine ordinances.[31]

Members of Luther's household included the students who lived there. Lodging here was in such demand that not all applicants could be accommodated. "Lord Katy" participated in the selection process.[32] Until 1534, Veit Dietrich supervised the students as a "vicarius," but then departed with his students because of disagreements with Katy. Nevertheless, he later stated how deeply grateful he was for the glimpses into the exemplary piety of life in Luther's house. When Dietrich married in 1536, Luther reminded him, undoubtedly referring to events in Luther's house, that a man must also yield to his wife, but without letting her dominate him. At the same time, in light of Dietrich's new position as preacher at the St. Sebald church in Nuremberg, Luther warned against self-conceit and self-love, which had already done such damage in the Reformation churches. Dietrich's successor as "vicarius" until 1541 was the nobleman Martin Weyer, who came from Farther Pomerania and later became the bishop of Kammin. Luther thought as highly of him as he did of Dietrich.[33] Ignaz Perknowsky, a member of the congregation of Bohemian Brethren who lived with Luther along with Burgrave Borziwog von Dohna, whom Perknowsky served as steward, frequently was a stimulating partner in the discussions at table.[34]

After the meals, Luther frequently commented on individual psalms. Among them was Psalm 23, the commentary that Rörer published in 1536.[35] A composer who cannot definitely be identified sent Luther a composition and a shipment of Borsdorf apples. Luther reported: "We sing at table here as best we can." That "sows" happened, i.e., mistakes, was not the fault of the composer, but of "our skill, which is still very modest." It was the same way with good political ordinances, which were being practiced in such an unsatisfactory way that an entire marketplace could be supplied with sausages from these "sows" (mistakes).[36] The dog Tölpel in Luther's household should not be forgotten. Luther marveled at the bodily gifts God had given his creature, a beautiful and intelligent animal.[37]

Celebrations took place not only on official occasions. On Luther's forty-ninth birthday, Jonas, Melanchthon, Bugenhagen, and Cruciger were invited to enjoy a boar sent by one of the princes of Anhalt. The twenty-third anniversary of Luther's doctorate was also celebrated with a festive meal. Luther commented at it: "Christ grant that this year I may enter heaven."[38] It was presumably at a social gathering that Luther's admiration for the jurist Francis Burchart's skill in playing chess originated.[39] Occasionally Luther let it be known that he had no aversion to alcoholic beverages. This was the special vice of the Germans. Once when his nephew George Kaufmann came into the room while drunk, Luther sharply admonished him not to ruin his health.[40]

In the last months of 1532 Luther appears to have recovered his health. His only complaint was one in September about a headache and diarrhea.[41] From December 1532 until the first weeks of the new year, he was particularly overburdened by literary deadlines, but he was also vexed by numerous other affairs, "so that I cannot disappoint my beggars and tormentors, the printers at the Leipzig fair." Among other things, he was to write prefaces for several books and had therefore let his correspondence pile up.[42] On 9 February 1533 he had a severe dizzy spell in the castle church, and he thought his end had come. He exhorted the clergy present to continue after his death to make their chief concern the preaching of the gospel, which gave them their identity as servants of the Word.[43] A few days later another dizzy spell happened. By evening he had already recovered, and for the clergy visiting him he was able to depict the struggle with death as an entirely normal thing. Ultimately, what counted was Christ's Word: "Because I live, you will live also" (John 14:19). This was not simply self-evident even for Luther. His comment reveals this: "Reason says, 'This is a big lie.' "[44] For Luther there was a connection between his illnesses and the *Anfechtungen* sent by the devil at that time during his sleepless nights; they were caused by things that were not just physical.[45] In March, Luther still thought it possible that he might die. Whenever he tried to concentrate, he became dizzy or had a roaring in his ears, and as a result he was hardly able to work. In May he was "still half sick," and he was occasionally unable to write his own letters. Hans Honold, an Augsburg patrician, sent him medication and a prescription for this complaint.[46] The severe pains in his toes in the fall of 1533 were symptoms of the kidney stones that afflicted Luther severely in the following period (Plate III).[47] The abscess on his lower leg that persisted led him to realize that the human body is a "disgraceful bag of lye" from which all kinds of "rivers" flow. Bodily excretions could not be stopped, and therefore he said that the "ass" was the best example against the regulations of men.[48]

At the beginning of 1534, Luther described himself as busy with many things, sick, and tormented. In March he was more or less healthy, but he was accomplishing little and felt useless. In his sermon on 10 May he spoke publicly about feeling weak. In September he was troubled by a cold and cough.[49] Nevertheless, in general Luther's health was better in 1534 than in the previous year. An interruption of his preaching for several weeks in February and March 1535 again seems to indicate a cold. In April he categorized his condition as changeable. Four months later he felt that he was weak from age. Shortly thereafter, he was severely plagued by diarrhea: "In the last two days I have had fifteen bowel movements."[50] At the end of October 1535, and also after the middle of January 1536, he again had a cold, so that he was unable either to preach or to travel.[51] At the princely wedding in Torgau on 27 February Luther was able to officiate at the marriage, but because of an attack of vertigo he had to let Bugenhagen conduct the worship service on the following day. Shortly thereafter, unbearable sciatic pains confined him to bed for two weeks.[52] Before Easter (16 April) he was again so sick because of the kidney stones, which became acute for the first time, that he wanted to die, and afterward he continued in a weakened condition. At the beginning of June he passed stones with a great deal of pain.[53] On 19 December Luther suffered a severe heart attack, and the worst was feared, especially because a winter storm and a halo presaged grave incidents.[54] There were lengthy intervals between the severe attacks of illness, but Luther had to live with his maladies and accept, however grudgingly, a diminution of his strength. He accepted the possible nearness of death, and sometimes even longed for it.

II

Luther's Role in the Reformation's Progress in Other German Territories, the Agreement on the Lord's Supper, and the Relationships with France and England (1532–36)

As expected, the Reformation in Germany continued to expand after the Religious Peace of Nuremberg of 1532. Luther was frequently involved in this process in various ways. He often assisted in introducing the Reformation into additional territories. Territories and cities that had already become evangelical continued to require his counsel and support. He warned against Anabaptism, which was clearly revealing at that time that it was a danger for church and society. Within the Smalcald League the cities in southern Germany were now drawing nearer to Luther theologically. Even France and England were seeking contacts with Wittenberg. More strongly than before, political interests were affecting these external relationships. Not infrequently, both within and without Electoral Saxony, the joint counsel of the Wittenberg theologians was requested or given, and frequently Melanchthon was assigned the task of formulating their mutual decision.

1. THE REFORMATION IN
THE PRINCIPALITY OF ANHALT

Aside from Electoral Saxony, there was scarcely any other Reformation territory in which Luther was more involved than the one in the principality of Anhalt, which lay to the northwest of Wittenberg.[1] As in the two Saxonies, the government there had similarly been divided between two lines of the princely house. Prince Wolfgang (b. 1492) resided in Köthen. Through his mother, Elector John's sister, he had close connections with the ruling house of Electoral Saxony. He had already joined in signing the Augsburg Confession in 1530. In the Dessau portion of the territory his cousin, Prince John (b. 1504), ruled. John's brothers were Prince George (b. 1507), the cathedral dean in

Magdeburg, and Prince Joachim (b. 1509). Until her death in 1530, their mother, Margaret, the cousin of Duke George of Saxony, had kept the Dessau portion of the land from turning to the Reformation. Subsequently, on the basis of their personal studies and contacts, George and Joachim drew closer to Luther. They also influenced their brother John in this regard. George Helt (b. 1485), the sometime tutor of George and Joachim, was studying in Wittenberg at this time, and he became an important contact between the princes and Luther.

In September 1532, through Luther's efforts, Nicholas Hausmann became the first evangelical court preacher in Dessau.[2] He maintained the close contact with Wittenberg that he had already enjoyed while in Zwickau. Certainly not unintentionally, Luther, Melanchthon, and Cruciger were invited to a great hunt in Wörlitz organized by Princes John and Joachim, one in which the electoral prince, Joachim of Brandenburg, also participated. On this occasion, on 24 November, Luther preached one of his basic sermons, *Sermon on the Sum of the Christian Life*. He began by explaining what service to God (*Gottesdienst*) is. All human efforts might be regarded as service to God, but in a special sense to serve God is to preach and listen to God's Word, and it is to this that God has attached his highest promise. Luther was concerned about emphasizing the importance of the evangelical worship service in order to counteract the widespread disdain for it. Real preaching dealt with both law and gospel, and the essence of the law was identified as the all-encompassing commandment of love that ruled out any kind of selfish motive. Before God, a person had to confess freely that he had not lived up to what God demanded. He was dependent upon Christ's forgiving grace, which he could receive only by faith. The law brought him before God's judgment seat (*Richtstuhl*), while the gospel brought him to Christ's mercy seat (*Gnadenstuhl*). Therefore, under no circumstances should the two be merged. Any trust in one's own accomplishment would adulterate faith. On its part, the experience of faith made possible the selfless love of one's neighbor. In this context Luther could clarify why everything depended upon the purity of this doctrine, but in so doing he did not fail to criticize the legalism of the old believers. In conclusion, he justified the necessity of his polemics very specifically vis-à-vis Electoral Prince Joachim of Brandenburg, who was indignant over them. When Luther later saw the printed version of this sermon, which Cruciger sent to him, he himself was impressed by it. The discussions in Wörlitz had concentrated primarily on theological subjects. Luther regarded the princes of Anhalt as exemplary because they were so well informed and exhibited such pious zeal.[3]

As before, however, Duke George of Saxony attempted to keep Princes John and George in the old faith. At Hausmann's urging, Luther thus attempted to convince Prince John that Christ's authority was superior to that of the councils. He praised Prince George as the only one among the spiritual princes to take a stand in favor of Christ's Word. On the basis of his own experiences,

Luther tried to assist Gregory Rosseken, a Franciscan who was Prince George's father confessor, in withdrawing from his monastic piety. He encouraged Prince Joachim to continue the reformatory work that had been started. The argumentation in all these letters from Luther is based on the doctrine of justification and faith in Christ. Organizational questions are not mentioned.[4] In October 1533, Duke George of Saxony, Archbishop Albrecht, and probably also his brother, Elector Joachim I of Brandenburg, came to Dessau. It was expected that they would exert pressure on Prince John because of his religious stance. Luther cautioned him not to get involved in a greater argument. Likewise, Hausmann should bravely defy the "Goliaths."[5] When Hausmann somewhat later had to preach to the princes of Brandenburg on what was then the delicate problem of baptism, he sought Luther's counsel.[6]

In March 1534 Hausmann sent Luther the Anhalt order of worship for his evaluation. In numerous places it differed from the Wittenberg practice, and Luther appears to have suggested extensive changes. He was concerned that the differing ceremonies not give the old believers a reason to criticize it. It was important, however, in the meantime not to print the order until it had been proved in practice. Luther did not regard the publication of numerous evangelical church orders, something that had started with the printing of his German mass in 1526, as a fortunate development. In fact, this first Anhalt order of worship was not printed.[7] The first evangelical celebration of the Lord's Supper in Dessau took place on Maundy Thursday 1534. Luther congratulated the three princely brothers for the courage they displayed, despite the pressure from their Catholic neighbors. Acting in a Christian way was always a risk undertaken in weakness, but one that Christ was able to bring to glorious completion.[8]

When Prince Joachim was afflicted with "depression and melancholy" in the summer of 1534, the Wittenbergers also tried intensively to help him. Luther encouraged him to be happy and enjoy the pleasures of life. He pointed to himself as an example: After his earlier "grieving and grumping . . . I now seek pleasure and take it wherever I can." On the basis of the evangelical awareness that had been attained, one could be happy in good conscience and gratefully enjoy God's gifts.[9] Because of Joachim's illness, Luther went to Dessau for several days at the beginning of June. In one of his sermons there he impressively expounded on the three ways of ruling mentioned in Psalm 45: ministry, government, and family. The admonition to hope patiently in God, who with his Word is near to man, applied to Luther's princely client.[10] When Joachim's condition initially improved, Luther regarded it as an answer to his intercessory prayers. The Wittenbergers did everything they could to sustain his condition. When he suffered a relapse, Luther had to comfort the prince by saying that this, too, was God's gracious gift, as difficult as this was to see.[11] From mid-July until the beginning of August, except for a brief interruption, Luther had to be in Dessau constantly, until Master Francis Burchart relieved him in caring for the patient. Luther did not feel completely well in Dessau. The local beer did not agree with him, and he longed for his wife.[12] Joachim's depressions persisted. In one place we learn that he regarded Luther's visits and words as helpful. At Christmas 1535 Luther pointed out to him that Christ had taken away our sins and our bad conscience, and that his power was strong in those who were weak.[13] This was probably one of the final arguments yet remaining in this difficult counseling situation.

Luther's contribution to the Reformation in Anhalt thus consisted less in organizational proposals and activities than in instructing the sovereign and providing pastoral care for him. In this predominately spiritual endeavor with people in responsible positions we see a distinctive feature of his reformatory activity in general. This was completely appropriate for the evangelical cause, and should not be casually belittled.

2. RELATIONSHIPS WITH OTHER TERRITORIES AND THEIR REFORMATION

There were varied experiences with the spread of the Reformation into additional territories. Through the princes of Anhalt, Luther had frequently come into contact with Joachim, the electoral prince of Brandenburg. After Joachim began his reign in 1535 there were reasons to hope that he might introduce the Reformation into the Mark Brandenburg. These expectations were not immediately realized. In fact, in 1536 Luther even believed that the elector had fallen away from the gospel.[1] Joachim II, a member of the house of Hohenzollern, steered a course between the confessions and always maintained a certain distance from Luther.

In Mecklenburg, Duke Henry had been advocating the introduction of the Reformation since 1533, while his brother Albrecht, the son-in-law of Joachim I of Brandenburg, opposed it. Albrecht initially did not look unfavorably on an attempt by Luther at mediation, but then he decided against it. One reason for this decision may have been the publication in Wittenberg of a book by Ägidius Faber, the Lutheran preacher in Schwerin, which was critical of the practice of venerating the relic of the holy blood in the Schwerin cathedral. Luther had provided a preface for this book that likewise mercilessly pilloried the papists' "atrocious idolatry."[2] Nevertheless, at the beginning of 1534, for political reasons, Albrecht did agree to permit evangelical preaching.

In 1534, after a fifteen-year exile, Duke Ulrich of Württemberg, with the support of Philip of Hesse, was able to reconquer his land from the Hapsburgs. Although this presented the possibility of winning for the Reformation an important territory in southwestern Germany that might be a political support for the evangelical imperial free cities there, Luther and the other Wittenberg theologians rejected the undertaking because it endangered the peace of the empire. Only subsequently did Luther recognize that God was active in the matter.[3]

As before, Luther was approached by cities and territories that had already become evangelical with questions about personnel matters, clergy recommendations, and concerns about ecclesiastical controversies. Hamburg wanted its superintendent, John Aepinus, to get his doctor of theology degree in Wittenberg.[4] Nicholas Glossenius was sent to be the superintendent in Tallinn after he had previously obtained a licentiate degree in Wittenberg.[5] In 1536 Elector John Frederick asked the Wittenberg theologians to find a preacher for Naumburg, an episcopal see of no little significance. Because no suitable candidate was available at the time, Jonas had to help for several months in Naumburg.[6]

In Erfurt both evangelical and Catholic worship services continued, a situation that caused constant friction. In 1533 the influential party of the old believers in the city council not only sought to curtail the incomes of the evangelical preachers, but also denied that they had been properly called. The conditions were so unfavorable that the preachers were thinking of leaving Erfurt. The Wittenberg theologians, however, had no doubts about the legitimacy of the Erfurt preachers' position. They had been elected by their congregations. In this critical case in Erfurt, the Wittenbergers decided in favor of election by the congregation over call by the council. Besides, the council had not previously forbidden the preachers from exercising their duties. Moreover, the Wittenbergers trusted that the Saxon elector, as Erfurt's protector, would support their cause. The difficulties in Erfurt also continued in the time following. Not much more could be done from Electoral Saxony except to encourage the preachers to stand fast in their hard-pressed situation.[7]

In 1536 a decision was made by the imperial supreme court to restore the possessions and rights of the Catholic clergy in Minden, a city in Westphalia that had become evangelical in 1530. The city therefore sent its superintendent Gerhard Ömiken to Electoral Saxony. In this case, however, Luther could do nothing more than send the petitioner on to the elector with his own recommendation.[8]

In 1532 the city of Bremen had forced the introduction of evangelical worship in the archiepiscopal cathedral. When the archbishop subsequently complained to the Diet of Regensburg, the city refused to restore the former situation and requested comments from its allies in the Smalcald League. The Wittenberg theologians took a strictly legal stance, saying that the city had no authority over the cathedral and thus its attack was improper. Because restoring the old cultus in the cathedral could lead to an uprising in the city, however, the cathedral chapter itself would have to bear that risk. For political reasons, Elector John Frederick did not unqualifiedly adopt the Wittenbergers' opinion. Until a council met, nothing should be changed in the existing situation in Bremen. If the opposing side were to use force, Bremen was assured of support from its ally.[9] In September 1533 Luther declared his approval of the Bremen church order, which had been sent to him. He also had no objection to the traditional practices of criminal law, only advising leniency in trifling situations. An admonition that preachers should be properly compensated was of course necessary in Bremen, too.[10]

As in the case of Bremen, the Wittenbergers held that the attempt of the city of Herford to usurp the rights of the abbess there was impermissible. On her part, however, the abbess should be understanding when the church's income that she controlled was appropriated for the support of the clergy, but the Wittenbergers rejected using ecclesiastical revenues for secular purposes, such as building the city wall.[11] The city, supported by its evangelical pastor, also continued to seek the abolition of the brotherhouse. Although the residents of the house accepted the evangelical doctrine, the continuation of the monastic manner of life and the special rights of the brothers were regarded as an alien element. Moreover, in 1534 it was expected that they would take over the city school. Once again, Luther and Melanchthon supported this. The life style that the brothers had freely chosen was not unevangelical. The city had no right to expropriate the brotherhouse for its own purposes. When the final phase of the conflict occurred in about 1540, Luther was no longer involved. Ultimately the brotherhouse was able to survive, but in the course of time it adapted itself more strongly to its evangelical environment and its expectations.[12]

In some territories in Westphalia the Reformation had indeed been introduced, but many traditional ceremonies had been retained. Luther received a number of inquiries about them from a county that we cannot precisely identify. He had nothing against continuing to bless wax or baptismal water for the time being, for example, but he rejected everything connected with the celebration of the sacrifice of the mass.[13]

In 1533 the clergy in Hesse asked Luther and Melanchthon about a more intensive application of church discipline. Luther praised their zeal, but he felt the time had not yet come for regulations of this sort. On one side, there was the danger of legalism, while, on the other, experience suggested that it would touch off major disturbances. They should be satisfied with applying the so-called lesser ban, i.e., excluding the unworthy from receiving the Lord's Supper and from serving as baptismal sponsors. But the church should make no use of the "greater ban," with its exclusion from society and from political life, especially because it could not be employed without the cooperation of the government. Such intervention by political power in the matter of church discipline was especially undesirable, because of the separation of the two kingdoms.[14] Not even the right to exclude people from the Lord's Supper, which Luther claimed belonged to pastors, would be granted everywhere by the government. He perceptively saw that any further introduction of strict church discipline in order to create a holy community was unrealizable.

Likewise in 1533, a new conflict occurred in Nuremberg between Andreas Osiander (Plate IV) and the other clergy. As in Electoral Saxony, so-called public confession, along with private confession, had been practiced in Nuremberg since 1524. This was a general confession of sins said by the congregation in a communion service, following which the minister pronounced the absolution. At Osiander's insistence, the church order of 1533 no longer made any provision for public confession. This caused troubles. The simpler general confession was much more popular than the private confession that Osiander demanded. The Nuremberg council therefore asked Luther and Melanchthon for an opinion. Their reply had a scope that grew out of the subject. They had no objection to the general confession, for, after all, the sermon itself was a declaration of the forgiveness of sins; however, an individual hearer had to receive the absolution in faith. This could be done more directly in private absolution, and therefore private confession should also be retained along with the general confession. The Nuremberg council instructed the clergy to act accordingly. Although Osiander initially raised no objections, clergy in Nuremberg feared—not without cause—that the conflict was not yet at an end.[15] Osiander's colleagues collected his objectionable statements and sent them to Wittenberg. Luther reacted differently than they expected. In insistent letters to Wenceslaus Link, to Osiander, and to the Nuremberg clergy in general he encouraged reconciliation. He, too, believed that Osiander was once again stubbornly thinking in his own way, and that his colleagues had the truth on their side, but a controversy because of this was senseless. Luther was hoping that Osiander might let himself be corrected in love. In this case, the peace of the church was of greater concern than the subject of the controversy. After Osiander acknowledged the position of the other clergy, they should let the matter drop. This great appeal for unity culminated in a direct address by Christ to the Nuremberg clergy. Luther hoped that with Christ's help peace could indeed be restored, but he was also aware that the antagonists were fallible men. It was precisely because of this that he admonished them to forgive one another.[16]

Luther's letters were unsuccessful; the controversy in Nuremberg continued, and the council therefore requested a new opinion from the Wittenberg theologians. This time the reply addressed Osiander's objections more directly. The Wittenbergers agreed with Osiander that absolution had to be received as a personal experience. Yet the general absolution or the proclamation of the gospel dare not be dismissed on that account. They likewise found Osiander correct in his criticism that thereby the general absolution might also be addressed to people who neither believed nor were penitent. It should be pronounced only presuming that these conditions existed. Osiander himself should not be forced to practice public confession, but he, on his part, should no longer attack it. The Wittenbergers were thus again indicating a rational resolution to the conflict. In a very approving personal letter, Luther sought to win Osiander's support for this proposal of mutual toleration of the differing viewpoints. The Nuremberg council rewarded the efforts of the Wittenbergers with one hundred taler.[17]

After a pause, Osiander began the conflict anew in 1535. Luther saw the machinations of the devil behind this. He attempted to comfort Link with the comment that even in Electoral Saxony they had to swallow hard because of the arrogance of the nobility and the peasants. Luther said that Link should enter the conflict only if Osiander first attacked him publicly.[18] Osiander again dealt with this topic in a sermon in August 1536. He was certainly correct that it was more appropriate to exercise church discipline in connection with private confession than with a general one. During a visit in Nuremberg, Melanchthon attempted to mediate. At his encouragement, the council presented the matter once again to the theology faculty in Wittenberg. The Wittenberg faculty, however, was content with reiterating its earlier view.[19]

Luther's advice was occasionally sought in cases of alleged demon possession. Special attention was attracted by a girl in Frankfurt an der Oder who constantly conjured up coins and then swallowed them. In each case Luther recommended that the congregation join in intercession, and that they investigate carefully to see if some sort of sleight of hand were being practiced, for this seemed to him to be a concoction of the devil. The devil was a living reality. But Christ, whom the devil (!) had crucified, had triumphed over him.[20]

Part of Luther's correspondence beyond the limited area of Electoral Saxony was pastoral in nature. Usually he already knew the addressee from somewhere else. He comforted Lorenz Zoch, the chancellor of Magdeburg, when his wife died. It was the lot of a Christian, in communion with Christ, to bear grief patiently. Luther frequently had to write such letters of condolence.[21] To Jonas von Stockhausen, the city governor in Nordhausen, who harbored thoughts of suicide, Luther wrote: "Bind your ears firmly to our mouth, and let our word enter your heart; thus will God comfort and strengthen you through our word." Despite all its weariness, a life given by God must not be cast aside. One must systematically turn away from the dark suggestions of the devil. He also charged Stockhausen's wife under no circumstances to leave her husband alone.[22] Luther reminded the ailing Mansfeld counselor John Rühel: "*Domini sumus,*" i.e., living or dead we belong to Christ and therefore we are masters of all adversities.[23] His words of encouragement to the Mansfeld chancellor Caspar Müller sound similar, yet different: God's good will must be accepted; "He is a good trader and a gracious merchant, who sells us life for death, righteousness for sin, and who asks as interest one illness or two, just for a moment. . . ." The patient therefore had reason for thanksgiving, despite all else.[24] With the ailing reformer of Lüneburg, Urbanus Rhegius, Luther used the memorable formula: We must bear Christ and at the same time be borne by him.[25]

It was not without reason that Luther addressed Dorothea Jörger, the Austrian noblewoman whom Michael Stifel had served, as "my good friend in Christ." Not only was she constantly sending gifts to Luther and his family, but in 1532 she also established an endowment of five hundred gulden, the interest on which was to benefit Wittenberg students. This may have been one of the first endowments of this sort in an evangelical territory. Here Luther experienced the willingness to give that he found so lacking in Wittenberg and Electoral Saxony. A large portion of Luther's further correspondence with Dorothea Jörger deals with the establishment and administration of this endowment. In 1534 he wrote her: "I myself did not know, and would also not have believed, that in this tiny city and poor school there were so many pious, capable lads, who have lived throughout the year on bread and water, and suffered from the frost and cold, so that they might study the Holy Scriptures and God's Word; for them your charity is a great refreshment and delight." In 1535 he distributed the money chiefly to poor refugees from the faith from other territories who were studying in Wittenberg.[26]

At the request of Dorothea Jörger, Luther sent her a draft for her will. It dealt only incidentally with the disposition of her maternal inheritance. The main portion was a thankful, evangelical confession of faith that was given as a legacy to her children, who moreover were admonished to live in harmony.[27] Here was the initial sign of a new evangelical custom. Lazarus Spengler, too, the Nuremberg city clerk who had courageously supported Luther since 1519 and who died in 1534, included in his will an extensive and unmistakably Lutheran confession of faith. In 1535 it was published in Wittenberg with a preface by Luther. For him, this was a testimony to a Christian faith, life, and death—a "legend of a saint" in the best sense, one that was able to strengthen weak, tried, and persecuted Christians. Moreover, Spengler's confession refuted the strident criticism of their opponents that there were no longer any pious people among the scholars.[28]

The problems that came to Luther from the other evangelical churches of Germany were extremely varied, and thus he had to deal with them in correspondingly different ways. Nevertheless, a certain common thread can be seen in his reactions: He was not concerned merely about political success or the spread of the church's influence. He realized that he was bound by the law, even when it stood in opposition to evangelical interests. Moreover, the solutions to problems had to be theologically correct. Within these prescribed limits, Luther advocated what could practically be achieved and what made for peace in the church. Not least, the central statements of the faith had to serve as a comfort for his fellow believers.

3. DEFENSE AGAINST
THE MÜNSTER ANABAPTISTS

Although Luther intervened in the Reformation taking place in individual territories only when he was called upon, and his participation thus did not follow any schedule, he made use of every available opportunity to oppose the spread of Anabaptism. At the end of 1532 he warned the council of Münster in Westphalia and Bernhard Rothmann, the local preacher, not to fall prey to Zwinglianism and Anabaptism. This warning was not without foundation: At that time Rothmann had already drawn close to Zwinglian positions. Luther's comment that Zwingli, Müntzer, and some of the Anabaptists had come to no good end was to be only too true for Münster as well.[1] At the beginning of 1534 Dutch Anabaptists came to Münster and soon thereafter took over the government of the city, which touched off an empire-wide action against the city. Luther apparently paid little attention to the events there at first. In July he replied to a question from Myconius, who had been shaken by Rothmann's argument that Christ had not assumed true humanity from Mary: The true humanity of Christ was not to be doubted. Later in the year Luther, at the request of the elector, sent an emissary to Soest to obtain more precise information about the situation in Münster.[2] In mid-November he knew that John of Leiden had been crowned king in Münster and that eight of his messengers had been executed in Soest.[3]

In addition to military action against the Münster Anabaptists, a theological conflict with them was already underway in 1534. Amsdorf published theses attacking Rothmann's doctrine of baptism.[4] On the Catholic side, John Cochlaeus several times published refutations of Anabaptist articles, in them pointedly blaming Luther for the abominations in Münster.[5] At the beginning of 1535, a *Refutation of the Confession of the New Valentinians and Donatists at Münster* was published in Wittenberg by Urbanus Rhegius, the Lüneburg reformer. It was directed against the *Confession of Faith and Life of the Church of Christ at Münster*, which Rothmann had published in the spring of 1534, and it identified his statements as ancient heresies. Its preface was written by Luther.[6] In it he took issue with two accusations. In Münster people had said that he was a "false prophet," even worse than the pope. Conversely, the papists regarded him as partially responsible for the insurrection in Münster and the heresies there.[7] Luther took this with self-confident equanimity: Without him, the "fanatics" would never have been able to criticize the pope, and, conversely, the papists would not have been able to withstand them. He did not deny that the fanatics had come from him. It had always been that way. Judas had been one of the disciples. All heretics had arisen in the church itself and they drew their false teaching from the Bible. Therefore, the accusations of the old believers were illogical.

Probably immediately afterward, Luther wrote another preface to the *New Newspaper about the Anabaptists at Münster*, previously printed separately, which reported on the accession of "King" John of Leiden and the sending, capture, trial, and execution of the Anabaptist apostles.[8] Luther regarded the events in Münster as a warning to repent. The introduction of polygamy and the establishment of the Anabaptist kingdom did not much trouble him. This affected the secular government, of course, but it was so manifestly unchristian that it would be no danger to the church. Only an incompetent beginner of a devil was at work in Münster. Nevertheless, the examples of Müntzer and Mohammed showed that even such crude deviltries attracted adherents. The best defense against them had to be the preaching of God's Word and not simply the use of military measures. Accordingly, Luther concentrated on refuting the false teachings of Rothmann's *Confession of Faith and Life*, which he apparently knew in the original and not only through Rhegius's rejoinder.[9] Exegetically, the view that Christ had merely passed through the Virgin Mary and had not been born of her as a true man was clearly untenable. Baptism was a divine work, not merely a human action. Not even human abuses of baptism altered this. According to Rothmann's earlier teaching, which had already been superseded in 1535 with the introduction of polygamy, only a union of believing partners was a valid marriage. From this, Luther drew the conclusion that all the residents of Münster were whore's children and consequently that existing relationships were also illegitimate. In sum, for him the Münster kingdom was so unambiguously seditious that it was unnecessary to deal with it anymore. Luther and the political authorities from all parts of the empire shared the view that the situation in Münster had to be attacked primarily because it was seditious.[10] This helped to make Luther's attitude against the Anabaptists even more harsh.

In sermons in October 1535 and in May of the following year, Luther occasionally reminisced about the example of Münster, one that showed how easily a false preacher could lead many people astray within a short period of time.[11] In 1537 he was still cautioning the nobleman Dietrich von Plesse, who resided near Göttingen, about Petrus Wertheim, the former Münster preacher who for a time had sympathized with Rothmann.[12] The plight of Minden was a symptom for him of how Münster's defeat had given fresh impetus to attacks on the Reformation.[13] In 1536 in Wittenberg there appeared a book written by Henricus Dorpius and with a preface by Bugenhagen entitled *Truthful History of How the Gospel Began at Münster and Subsequently Was Destroyed by the Anabaptists*. Until the eighteenth century it was the most important source of information about the Anabaptist kingdom in Münster.[14]

The events in Münster could only confirm Luther in his rejection of Anabaptism. In January and February 1534 he carried out a long-standing intention and dealt extensively with baptism in six sermons, in them of course taking issue with the Anabaptists and with the old believers as well. He informed Hausmann in Dessau of the main points in them, because Hausmann likewise had to preach on baptism in the presence of Albrecht of Mainz.

In the doctrine of baptism there was essential agreement between Luther and the old believers, although they taught it "more coldly" than he. Baptism was commanded by God, not a human invention. It was God's new covenant with all people for eternal salvation. Human abuses could not take away its character as a divine work. Repeating it would be an insult to God's work. Baptism must be received in faith, or else it is of no avail. Throughout one's life it is to be adorned with the fruits of faith, which of course are something different than meritorious works. With this basic concept of baptism as a divine work there was no need at all to discuss the problem of infant baptism.[15] In 1535 the baptismal sermons appeared in print without Luther's instigation. In his preface he said he wanted them to be regarded as a defense of the living Christ. Next to the devil, he regarded as enemies of baptism the Catholic "Arch-Anabaptists," who with their works baptized anew, and the "Epicureans"—meaning the Münster Anabaptists—who with their practice failed to recognize it as a divine work.[16]

Regensburg was an important stopping point for Anabaptists on journeys to their communities in Moravia. In the summer of 1534 Luther wanted the council there not to tolerate any settlement of Anabaptists. In previous years they had infiltrated cities, "and I was more confident of them than I am of your city." As the surest defense against them he thus recommended the pure preaching of the gospel according to the Augsburg Confession.[17]

In October 1534 Anabaptists appeared in the city of Zerbst in Anhalt. Their articles were sent to Luther. For him, their unbidden infiltration into the community was reprehensible, even deserving of death. He labeled the articles as seditious, "approving even the damned Müntzer."[18] In 1535 Luther apparently also approved of taking sharp action against three Thuringian Anabaptists.[19] At the beginning of the following year he complained about the continual appearance of false prophets, something that made him long for death.[20]

In Hesse they had been content with expelling those discovered to be Anabaptists from the territory. Some, however, returned secretly and continued their agitation. In 1536 Landgrave Philip thus asked a number of evangelical estates and the Wittenberg theologians how one should deal with such recidivists. The Wittenbergers replied with an opinion entitled *That Secular Government Is Obligated to Restrain Anabaptists with Bodily Punishment*.[21] The responsibility for punishing Anabaptists belonged to the government, not in any way to the preachers. Before they were punished, however, they were to be instructed. In any case, sedition had to be punished. The Anabaptists' rejection of authority, oaths, and private property and their view of marriage were considered sedition, along with the chiliasm propagated in Münster. The landgrave's reservations about the government punishing anyone for a matter of faith were answered with the comment that this was punishment not for holding a personal opinion, but for propagating it. Nevertheless, the Anabaptists' theological teachings, e.g., those on infant baptism, original sin, and Christology that were held in Münster, were also to be punished because they were blasphemy, and this the government was obligated to punish. Government, of course, had an obligation to investigate such crimes thoroughly. Therefore it needed instruction from the preachers. Establishing a separate ministry in the church and breaking fellowship likewise deserved to be punished. The death penalty was fundamentally permissible as a sentence not only for political crimes, but also for religious offenses because of their significance. Imprisonment should suffice for those who had only been led astray. One should proceed with all severity against rebels, especially when they propagated sedition as in Münster. The harsh opinion was unmistakably in Melanchthon's handwriting, but it also bore Luther's signature. He distanced himself from it somewhat, however, by adding the limiting sentence: "This is the general rule, yet may our gracious Lord grant grace along with punishment in accordance with the circumstances of the situation." To be sure, Luther did not rule out imposing the death penalty on Anabaptists in 1531, but in view of the recent experiences with them, he did agree with prescribing execution for crimes committed by Anabaptists, despite his qualifying statement. The Wittenberg theologians raised no objection to Electoral Saxony's action against the Anabaptists, which was harsh in comparison with that of other evangelical territories.[22] This de facto recourse to enforcing the laws against heretics was in keeping with measures that Luther later proposed against the Jews.

In practice, nevertheless, Luther made a nuanced judgment, as he had done earlier. In February 1536, Matthes Lotther, a painter of cards from Freiberg in Ducal Saxony, made unguarded statements about evangelical worship, and, among other things, claimed that laypersons could also administer the sacrament. Thereupon, Luther cautioned his fellow citizens about him. This had grave consequences for Lotther. He feared for his life and fled. Luther interceded for him with Duke Henry of Saxony, who was responsible for the government of Freiberg. Luther thought an appropriate punishment would be not exile from the land, but imprisonment for a time, combined with the requirement that he forever refrain from repeating his earlier statements. In the course of the hearing, when Lotther denied that he had said anything against the sacrament or that he had instigated conventicles, Luther immediately demanded a thorough investigation. Ultimately Luther became convinced of his innocence. At Luther's request, Elector John Frederick also interceded with Duke Henry on behalf of the accused. The charge that Lotther had broken his bond and left Freiberg, something that Luther thought understandable in view of the death penalty he had to fear, was sustained. He threatened, if necessary, to make the matter public. The duke was formally in the right, and thus he also stood by his position. When Luther learned this, he was beside himself, especially because he "was a little drunk." Chancellor Brück did all he could to dissuade him from attacking Duke Henry any further. Luther could not be induced to apologize for his threat.[23]

Only occasionally during the following years did the Anabaptists become a concern for Luther. In 1537, as he had done previously, he interpreted Jesus' blessing the children (Matt. 19:13-15) as an argument in favor of infant baptism. At the beginning of 1538 Luther dealt with baptism once more in the usual series of sermons. Again he explained it as God's sacramental action that preceded all human actions, and from this also came the justification of infant baptism. The train of thought is quite similar in the catechismal hymn on baptism from 1541, "To Jordan When Our Lord Had Gone."[24]

In January 1538 Luther expressly warned his congregation against sectarians who were infiltrating the church. They should be directed to him, the authorized preacher. He also mentioned that Anabaptist agitation was a crime punishable by death. At that time there was a marked influx of Anabaptists into Thuringia from Hesse. Two emissaries were executed and one imprisoned at the Wartburg, which aroused great attention. The superintendent in Eisenach, Justus Menius, justified this harsh action in his book *How Every Christian Should Conduct Himself Fittingly against Diverse Doctrines,* for which Luther wrote a preface. Punishment of the Anabaptists was not mentioned in it, but Luther did take issue with the offense caused by the appearance of sectarians in the church. He understood this as an *Anfechtung* that taught one to pay just that much more heed to God's Word.[25]

In the fall of 1538 Landgrave Philip summoned Bucer to Hesse in order to dispute with the Anabaptists. This developed into a plan to use the Anabaptists' former associates to convert them and win them back for the church. Persuasion instead of punishment would thus be attempted. Bucer was to solicit Luther's opinion of this new procedure against the Anabaptists. Luther did not advocate the death penalty, to be sure, but he decidedly advised that Anabaptists, the "devil's seed," should be expelled from the territory. Even if their actions occasionally seemed impressive, it was to be feared that ultimately a disaster like the one in Münster would result from their activity. Luther would not accept the argument that expelling them would merely contribute to the spread of Anabaptism. One had to chase a wolf away, even if he then caused harm somewhere else.[26] In 1539 three Anabaptists in Eisenach were induced to recant through the clergy's attempts at converting them and through torture. At the elector's request, the Wittenberg theologians had to express an opinion about their punishment. In this case they unambiguously rejected the death penalty, for this would only cause other Anabaptists to become more stubborn. Their recantation should be repeated publicly. The only punishment they recommended was imprisonment for two months. The former Anabaptists had to remain faithful to the evangelical church in the future, and the government should keep an eye on them. In Wittenberg, too, the theologians favored treating converted Anabaptists relatively leniently. Otherwise, however, Luther remained firm: Seditious Anabaptists should be executed, and the others should be expelled from the land.[27] In order to counteract Anabaptism in Mühlhausen, Justus Menius in 1544 wrote a third treatise on this subject, *On the Spirit of the Anabaptists*, for which Luther again wrote a preface. From Menius's denunciation of Anabaptism as the equivalent of Müntzer's enthusiasm, Luther understood it as something that led not only to heresy, but also to criminal offenses. At its conclusion he lamented once again the *Anfechtung* that the Anabaptists were causing the church.[28] Although two decades had gone by, Luther was thus still identifying the Anabaptists and sacramentarians with his onetime archenemy.

4. THE AGREEMENT BETWEEN THE SOUTHERN GERMANS AND LUTHER ON THE LORD'S SUPPER IN THE WITTENBERG CONCORD

The most significant development in the evangelical camp during these years was the consummation of an agreement on the Lord's Supper between the southern German cities and Luther. The initiative did not come from Luther, but originated after 1530 from the Strasbourg reformer, Martin Bucer. Following promising beginnings, the project came to a standstill after the summer of 1531, a state of affairs that was exacerbated by Luther's continued public rejection of Zwingli and his followers. His lectures on the Psalms between 1532 and 1535 are full of sarcastic comments on this subject.[1]

Irritations and Perspectives

Incidents were frequently occurring, of course, that must have irritated Luther. At the end of 1532, John Cellarius, the Lutheran preacher in Frankfurt, was dismissed. Thereupon Luther published an open letter to the people of Frankfurt at the beginning of 1533, clearly stating that the preachers there were teaching differently than he was. He did admit that some other places agreed with him, while others only pretended to do so, although they did not accept Christ's objective presence in the Lord's Supper, but only a presence for believers. For Luther this was a devilish trick that did not tender the sacrament to people. What a person was receiving in the sacrament had to be stated clearly. For this reason people ought to avoid Zwinglian pastors. Preachers who did not clearly say what was happening in the Lord's Supper should be expelled. Luther believed it intolerable to have two views of the Lord's Supper within one church. Moreover, he was disturbed that private confession was rejected in Frankfurt. As an appendix he purposely reprinted the open letter of 1524 to the city of Mühlhausen in which he cautioned against the seditious Müntzer.[2]

In view of this "vicious book," Bucer could do nothing but complain about the machinations of the devil that were continually causing schism in the church, where unity should really exist. In Constance, Ambrose Blaurer thought it best to ignore Luther's book and not stir up a hornet's nest. It seemed to him that Luther was too sensitive on the question of the Lord's Supper and so rigid that none of the books of the southern Germans could calm him. They, of course, were not going to be unsettled by Luther. Blaurer simply scorned Luther's accusations and "bloody pen." The effect of Luther's polemics was also limited elsewhere.[3] In a letter to the Frankfurters on 22 February 1533 Bucer attempted to smooth things over by mentioning how greatly they were indebted to Luther, God's agent. The injustice that had been caused by rumormongering simply had to be endured. Bucer then made suggestions to the Frankfurters for their response to Luther, which, above all, should contain biblical formulations. They should mention that while they thought it possible but problematic to speak about oral manducation, they did not want to question the presence of Christ in the Lord's Supper. It was not the substantive body of Christ that was given in the Lord's Supper, but the true body, and therefore it was not "mere" bread that was present. Capito advised the Frankfurters to overcome the antagonist Luther with moderation. The printed *Apology* of the Frankfurt preachers generally followed the line suggested by Bucer.[4]

As before, Bucer also attempted in the summer of 1533 to prevent the Swiss from breaking completely with Luther despite the latter's regrettable unfriendliness. Bucer was able to do this out of respect for Luther's proclamation of the gospel and because he believed it possible to interpret Luther's doctrine of the Lord's Supper in a sense that was also acceptable to the Swiss. Bucer was no more interested in giving up his relationship with the Swiss than the one he had with Luther. To be sure, he had to endure the bitter complaints from Leo Jud in Zurich about Luther's pope-like arbitrariness and his ranting against the Swiss: Luther was disrupting the southern German and Swiss churches with his accusations of heresy. There they were in no way disposed simply to adopt Luther's views or even to tolerate them. Not everything "that Luther poops is a rose."[5]

Proof that, under certain circumstances, Luther could also be charitable in passing judgment on questions of doctrine is seen in his attitude toward the Bohemian Brethren, who since 1531 had renewed the contact with Wittenberg that had been broken in 1524.[6] For this purpose they had prepared an *Account of the Faith*. The problem that had initially appeared in a German translation with Zwinglian overtones, published in Zurich in 1532, was remedied at the beginning of 1535 in a revised version, for which Luther wrote the preface.[7] On the basis of his conversations, he was convinced that the Bohemian Brethren agreed with him on the doctrine of the Lord's Supper, although they used different terminology. One had to be patient, "until finally we are able to praise Christ identically and unanimously with one and the same word and mouth." He did not refrain from mentioning that he was convinced that in Wittenberg they were speaking "more clearly and surely" about justification. From this preface Ambrose Blaurer drew new hope for an agreement in the sacramentarian controversy.[8] In 1535 the Brethren were planning to obtain legal recognition in Bohemia on the basis of their own confession. In preparing the confession, two of the Brethren made a trip to Germany and Switzerland. After they spent four weeks in Wittenberg, Luther and Melanchthon again confirmed that they were agreed on the doctrine of the sacrament. Variations in ceremonies and customs did not outweigh this agreement.[9] The next year the Brethren sent their completed confession to the Wittenbergers, who, after carefully examining it, declared that they were generally in agreement with it. One of their few reservations concerned retaining priestly celibacy.[10] The confession was to be printed in Wittenberg with a preface by Luther, but because no printer was willing to assume the financial risk of printing it, Luther regretfully sent it back to the Brethren at the end of 1537.[11] The Brethren themselves then paid the printing costs, and the confession was finally published in 1538. In his preface, Luther, following St. Paul's example, gave an account of how since his papistic days he had gradually altered his original rejection of the Bohemians until he could now state that they too belonged to "one flock under one shepherd."[12] Under Luther's strong influence, the Bohemians had drawn closer to his views on the decisive points in a remarkable way. Otherwise, there never would have been an agreement.

Not only in Frankfurt did the sacramentarian controversy break out again. In Kempten the Lutheran clerics Johann Seeger and Johann Rottach were dismissed from office because they would not commit themselves to a mediating view of the Lord's Supper. In July 1533, therefore, they sought Luther's advice, but his reply is not known.[13] The Lutherans in Augsburg urgently requested Luther to sanction special celebrations of the sacrament in private homes, but Luther refused because of his aversion to secret worship services. When the Augsburg preachers, appealing to Luther's approval of the *Account of the Faith,* boasted that he agreed with them, Luther demanded in August 1533 that the Augsburg council take steps to prohibit this. Despite the ambivalent formulations, he condemned the doctrine of these preachers as Zwinglian and denied that they agreed with his position. Luther threatened the council, saying that he would make this known in a public writing. The preachers, who were summoned by the council to answer, emphasized their unity with Luther and stated that their only difference concerned whether unbelievers ate. They believed they agreed with Luther in substance, if not in words. Luther replied bluntly and harshly to the Augsburg council on 29 October, announcing that he was going to make a public declaration against the "slippery word" of the preachers. At that time Wolfgang Musculus of Augsburg advised Bucer against reaching an agreement with Luther at the expense of the truth.[14] Luther's preface to the new, 1534 Wittenberg edition of *On the Wrath and the Good-*

ness of God by Caspar Huberinus, an Augsburg Lutheran, contained a polemic against sects and fanatics. In his book *The Private Mass and the Consecration of Priests* at the end of 1533 Luther had already struck a few blows against the "sacramentarians." Ambrose Blaurer wrote indignantly to Bucer on 23 February 1534 about this and about Luther's writings against the Augsburgers: "What sort of emetic can we use to cure this leader?" Understandably enough, in view of the comments about humility in Luther's preface to Brenz's commentary on Amos, Blaurer also wished that Luther would exercise some self-criticism in his attacks on the heralds and agents of the same faith. Luther's rage made Blaurer shudder. Bucer reacted more calmly. He knew Luther's righteous and unrighteous anger, and, moreover, the Augsburgers had provoked Luther.[15]

New Impulses for a Concord

In contrast to Luther, Melanchthon had already written appreciatively to Bucer in March 1533 concerning his efforts on behalf of an accord, although they had not accomplished much. One would just have to endure the fateful outcome (!) of the conflict, which had its roots in Luther's disposition. Melanchthon and Bucer should try to reduce the controversy and not add fuel to it. On 1 September Melanchthon even expressed the hope that he might work together with Bucer for a unification of the church. On 10 October Melanchthon mentioned the proposal of a discussion with Bucer to this end, something that was raised again on 15 March 1534.[16] At the beginning of March 1534 Bucer's *Account from the Holy Scriptures* was published, in which he distanced himself from the Anabaptists in Münster and from Schwenckfeld precisely in his statements about the presence of Christ's body and blood in the Lord's Supper, which showed that he had come closer to the Lutheran position and which Bucer called a basis for new consultations about reaching a concord.[17]

Then, for several reasons, achieving a comprehensive concord seemed especially urgent in August 1534. The progress of the Reformation in France appeared to depend on it; Bucer as well as Melanchthon shared this opinion. Moreover, the Peace of Kaaden, which Elector John Frederick had negotiated with King Ferdinand, had indeed permitted the introduction of the Reformation into Württemberg, which had been reconquered by Duke Ulrich, but it had expressly excluded the "sacramentarians." This made the legal situation within the empire more difficult for the imperial free cities that were inclined toward Zwinglianism. In Württemberg itself an agreement had been reached between the Lutheran Erhard Schnepf and Ambrose Blaurer on the basis of the Lutheran proposal of unity, which had not been accepted in Marburg in 1529.[18] This seemed to almost all the southern Germans, including Bucer and even Melanchthon, to go too far, because it acknowledged the true and substantial presence of Christ in the Lord's Supper.

When Melanchthon broached the subject of a general project aimed at reaching a concord with Luther in August, Luther indicated he was not unwilling. Melanchthon was already thinking about a synod that would be called by the princes. Melanchthon had found a ready ear in Philip of Hesse for his request that he do something to achieve an agreement. Philip therefore wrote Luther on 25 September and asked him to support a concord, now that the theological prerequisites for one seemed to exist and the provisions of the Peace of Kaaden made one politically necessary for the southern Germans. As a preliminary step, the landgrave was planning a meeting between Bucer and Melanchthon in Kassel after Christmas of 1534. Luther also declared on 17 October that he was prepared, for political reasons, to do whatever was compatible with his conscience. Nevertheless, a solid solution had to be found. He was afraid, however, that only a few of the southern Germans would follow Bucer.[19]

In the fall of 1534 Bucer, who was then in Augsburg, sought to present his views on the Lord's Supper contained in his *Account from the Holy Scriptures*, which Luther and Andreas Osiander had approved, to the Swiss and southern Germans. Bucer's optimism about the chances of reaching an agreement was not generally shared, however, and his efforts were again premature. To be sure, in mid-December, immediately before he left for Kassel to meet with Melanchthon, Bucer did agree at a meeting in Constance with representatives from the imperial free cities on the "true and essential presentation and distribution of Christ's true body and true blood" in the Lord's Supper, "on which everything depends in this matter against Dr. Luther," but the Zurichers boycotted the meeting because they did not share this opinion. They merely sent a confession in which, although formulated in a cordial fashion, they stated their disagreement with Luther.[20] The divergence between the southern Germans and the Swiss was becoming clearer.

The Wittenberg theologians, too, were preparing for the meeting in Kassel. Melanchthon called Luther's attention to a series of quotations from the church fathers that were difficult to reconcile with his view of the Lord's Supper. This did not prevent Luther from assiduously interpreting these passages in his own way. Melanchthon did not want to bear sole responsibility for the discussions with Bucer. Luther, too, did not want to decide everything himself and wished that Justus Jonas might also be involved. Because Jonas was ill, the instructions for Melanchthon were finally prepared by Luther alone. He thought that no accord could be achieved, and therefore he did not consider Melanchthon's trip promising. The matter was so great that nothing could be accomplished by only two or three people, even acknowledged authorities. Luther saw that he was in no position to alter his position, "even if the whole world comes to an end."

In his Table Talk Luther formulated his position on the presence of Christ's body and blood in the Lord's Supper unmistakably bluntly. Accordingly, he stated in Melanchthon's instructions: There should be no claim that previously they had misunderstood one another, because this would do nothing but create new confusion. He declared it impossible for conscience's sake for either side to declare that it countenanced the other's opinion. The gospel and the tradition of the church were claimed in support of the Lutheran view of the presence of Christ's body and blood. Not even Augustine's doctrine of symbol was regarded as a contradiction. It was impossible to substitute love for truth. These demands had to be met. In addition, Luther once again declared his interest in resolving the dispute, and for this he was willing to give his own life. He foresaw specific possibilities of a different sort for each party. If those on the opposing side were trapped in another opinion by their conscience, this would have to be tolerated. If the partners were sincere, God would set them free. Luther himself declared that he was also a prisoner of conscience, and if the partners could not adopt this view they would have to tolerate him. In the hope of future unity, Luther spoke in favor of mutual toleration for the time being, but he left no doubt that for him there would be no fellowship in faith until an agreement was reached. This did not need to be an obstacle to a political alliance among the partners. For Luther, "This is my body" meant that the body of Christ was truly eaten with or in the bread, and its reception could not be separated from the bread. Anything else would be contrary to his conscience. "Remorse is a grievous worm in the heart," he therefore informed Philip of Hesse. Melanchthon was thereby committed to Luther's view, with which he did not entirely agree, and thus he later referred to himself at the meeting in Kassel as an "ambassador in a foreign affair" (*nuntius alienae sententiae*).[21] Although this distancing of himself from instructions, which he himself requested and then also accepted, seems remarkable, to a certain extent it was characteristic of Melanchthon. He did not dare to contradict Luther, but he also could not follow him unreservedly. He evaded the responsibility of choosing the way to be followed and left it up to Luther.

The discussions between Bucer and Melanchthon took place in Kassel on 27 and 28 December. The unity they were seeking had to agree with Luther's demand for the presence of Christ's body and blood on one hand, and on the other it could not give any support to the misunderstanding of the old believers. They settled on a formula, one for which Bucer had already secured agreement of the Augsburg clergy and had specifically determined was consonant with the Augsburg Confession of 1530 and the Apology: With the bread the body of Christ is essentially and truly received. Melanchthon and Bucer should each work with their own sides to ensure that they were satisfied with this formula. After the meeting in Constance, Bucer was already assuming that the southern Germans would accept it, especially because the Augsburgers, who previously had been regarded as outspoken opponents of the real presence, agreed with this formula.[22] Vis-à-vis Luther's instructions, Bucer insisted that each side had previously misunderstood the other. The Swiss and southern Germans had ascribed to Luther a natural union between the elements and the body and blood of Christ, where only a "sacramental" one existed. Luther, in contrast, had assumed that his opponents accepted only a symbolic understanding of the Lord's Supper. Bucer left for further discussion the question of whether to refer specifically to this "theory of misunderstanding." The formula of agreement was not a compromise. Rather, on the basis of accepting a special sacramental connection, it was possible for the southern Germans to declare that they were supporters of Luther. Nevertheless, it was impossible for them in conscience to speak about a physical connection between the bread and the body of Christ, or about its being food for the belly, or about the sacrament automatically effecting salvation, and in this they wanted Luther to respect them. According to Bucer, there was agreement with Luther. If Luther could not accept the Kassel formulation, he would be asked to be patient in hopes that his partners might be able to convince him. Bucer thus believed that with his formula he had confirmed an essential and decisive similarity between Luther's understanding of the Lord's Supper and that of the southern Germans and Swiss, one that permitted the southern Germans to call themselves followers of Luther.[23]

Agreement depended on whether the results of Kassel would be accepted. Philip of Hesse expressed the hope to Luther that a lasting unity had been achieved, which, for political reasons, was very important for the Reformation, especially because no lasting peace with the papists was to be expected. Elector John Frederick would accept the formula of unity only if he could do so without offending God and his conscience. At the end of January, Luther, in his opinion on the formula, which referred specifically to the Augsburg Confession and the Apology and stated that the body of Christ was given and eaten, could find no fault with it, "if their heart is really in it." He was thus not yet completely free of mistrust. Therefore he was also opposed to a quick adoption of a concord. Previously some on the opposite side had been enemies of the Lutherans. If action were taken too quickly, it might touch off strife in the Lutheran camp. Through friendly, mutual association it would be evident whether the partners meant it "purely and rightly." The concord should not lead to a troublesome discord. Positive experiences with the opposing side would make it possible for the Lutherans to overcome their suspicion and resentment. Only when the troubled waters had calmed did Luther think it would be possible to conclude a concord, but further discussions were still necessary for this. Moreover, Luther wanted to await opinions from the Lutheran theologians—Urbanus Rhegius, Osiander, and Brenz, who was skeptical on this matter—and from the southern German cities. On 3 February 1535 Melanchthon nevertheless could inform Bucer that Luther had a more charitable and affectionate opinion of Bucer and his colleagues than before.[24] Doubts about the possibility of a concord were also expressed in southern Germany, primarily concerning one that included the Swiss. In addition, a reprinting of

Luther's major polemic work from 1528, *Confession concerning Christ's Supper,* caused embarrassment. Opposition toward a concord was becoming stronger in Constance. Luther spoke positively to Schnepf about Ambrose Blaurer's apology, in which he had defended concluding the Württemberg Concord, but he was irritated by Blaurer's nervous protestations that he had never thought any differently about the Lord's Supper.[25]

A genuine breakthrough in the negotiations on behalf of the concord was effected by the ostentatious change in Augsburg's position toward Luther in the summer of 1535. After it had previously been ascertained through mediators that Luther was expecting Augsburg to appoint a preacher congenial to the Wittenberg view as a sign of the city's change of heart—they were thinking of Urbanus Rhegius or Johann Forster, a native Augsburger who was then living in Wittenberg—Gereon Sailer, the city physician, and Caspar Huberinus were officially dispatched to Wittenberg. The Augsburg clergy announced their zeal for peace and for the concord, and they declared their displeasure over the sacramentarian controversy. They sent a confession of faith on the Lord's Supper that agreed with Bucer's formulations, and stated their intention to call Rhegius back to Augsburg. They expressly asserted that they desired to improve their bad reputation. Luther responded with genuine delight—he is even said to have shed tears of joy—at the hope for a genuine concord following this discord. The wound—as he regarded the controversy over the Lord's Supper—was now virtually healed and suspicion had been removed. Until then he had not believed that the opposing side seriously intended to draw closer. Now he could die in peace and leave a peaceful church behind him. At the same time, as confirmation of this unity, he sent Forster—because Rhegius was unavailable—to be the preacher in Augsburg, although he still was concerned about whether the Augsburg clergy would accept him. Luther was already thinking about a meeting with his former opponents. He gave up his earlier skeptical reticence about the attempt to reach an agreement and assumed an active role. As before, however, there were still those on both sides who opposed unity. Amsdorf and Brenz were among them, and on the other side were Constance and particularly Zurich.[26]

In southern Germany and Switzerland they took immediate advantage of the agreement between Augsburg and Luther, which presaged a comprehensive accord. The years of effort by Strasbourg and its preachers at overcoming the dissention appeared to have achieved their goal. Immediately after returning from Wittenberg, Sailer was sent off on a trip through the imperial free cities of southern Germany. No major resistance was expected from them. The Strasbourgers expressed their optimism to Luther concerning the Swiss as well. Capito was to see that the Concord was accepted in Basel and Zurich, despite the old resentment that still persisted. After meticulous preparations, Bucer negotiated, among others, with John Brenz, who was in Stuttgart at the time. All the difficult points of the Concord were discussed, including the Lutherans' demand for a retraction from the southern Germans and the problem of feeding the ungodly. Already on this occasion they dealt with the alternative formulation of feeding the unworthy. Thereby the major topics of the later discussions on the Concord were already introduced. Bucer was able to persuade Brenz to put aside his reservations.[27]

Sailer's mission at bringing the Concord to the cities was not simple. He regarded his modest success as the work of God. From Augsburg he could report to Luther that the sects had stopped their work and dissention had ceased. The Augsburg clergy and council reemphasized their will to reach an accord, but they also had to ask Luther not to believe anyone who might possibly denounce it. Forster did feel that his situation in Augsburg was somewhat uncomfortable, but he did not impute any ill will to his new associates. Esslingen declared its acceptance of the proposed accord at the end of August, and Ulm did the same at the beginning of September, referring to their previously declared readiness to accept the Augsburg Confession and the Apology. The clergy in Ulm were aware that Luther had expressly questioned Sailer about them, which was probably connected with their earlier aloofness toward the Lutheran doctrine of the Lord's Supper. They therefore asked him to extend to them the same fellowship as the Augsburgers enjoyed. On 28 September Luther was able to inform Elector John Frederick that the cities were more favorable toward the Concord than expected. Whether the Concord should finally be adopted at a special convention or whether a formula written by Luther might simply be accepted was still unresolved.[28]

In a series of similar letters to the cities and clergy of Strasbourg, Ulm, Esslingen, and Augsburg on 5 October, Luther proposed that the Concord be adopted at a meeting of the theologians at a location in Saxony on a date yet to be determined, and that Pomerania and Prussia should also send representatives. The group of participants should not become too large. The tenuousness of the new relationships is seen in the fact that Luther again had to suppress his suspicion that the Augsburgers were not at one with him. Conversely, Gerbel in Strasbourg wanted Luther to expunge the attacks on the "sacramentarians" from a new edition of his well-liked and widely distributed postil, which Luther then promised to do in order not to hinder the Concord. Nevertheless, the critical statements about the "sacramentarians" in Luther's large commentary on Galatians, which had become known in the summer of 1535, were still an offense.[29] Luther's improved relationship with the southern German cities became apparent in October when the city and clergy of Frankfurt asked Luther for advice in a legal matter involving the city that was pending before the imperial supreme court. Luther initially was reluctant to offer counsel because he knew nothing about the internal situation of the Frankfurt church, but by the end of November he was ready to send a clergyman to Frankfurt.[30]

At first it was unclear whether the authorities were also to participate in the conference of the theologians that was to adopt the Concord. Luther did not want to make the meeting depend on their approval, but he felt it was prudent

47

to instruct them. On 27 November he suggested to the Strasbourg clergy that the date be set after Easter 1536. On 25 January 1536 he informed Elector John Frederick of the necessity of a meeting with the southern Germans, at which, however, the continually agitating "nervous geniuses," who could ruin the undertaking, should not be allowed. The elector should appoint the site for the meeting; he suggested Eisenach and declared that he himself was prepared to cover the expenses.[31]

Bucer felt that before the conference with Luther there should be a special meeting of the southern Germans, especially involving the Swiss. The difficulties in including them in the Concord were becoming increasingly obvious. Moreover, the Constance theologians were trying to subvert the Concord. On 1 February 1536 the Swiss theologians, along with Bucer and Capito, gathered in Basel. The Swiss agreed on a confession—later known as the First Helvetic Confession—which stated that the Lord's Supper is a symbol that offers what Christ himself promises. In contrast to papistic teachings, all human merit was to be excluded from the celebration of the mass. Likewise, a natural union between the bread and the body of Christ was rejected. Bucer was hoping that Luther would also accept this formulation, which did not go as far as the one made in Kassel. The Swiss confession went too far even for Thomas Blaurer in Constance. He did not wish to join in Bucer's esteem for Luther, through which the Lord's Supper had been obscured, and preferred instead to remain with Zwingli and Oecolampadius.[32]

In a letter to Bucer on 25 March, Luther had suggested 14 May as a date for the meeting in Eisenach. Bucer was to inform the southern Germans and the Swiss, and also Brenz and Schnepf. On 1 May the Swiss declined to participate because of the lengthy journey and the lack of time, but they declared that they were interested in the Concord. The true reason for their refusal was the fear that one individual, i.e., Luther, would be too dominant in Eisenach. Even before this, Melanchthon had expressed his concern to Philip of Hesse that because of some individuals there would be more disunity than improvement created in Eisenach. A possible schism in Christendom seemed to him a high price to pay for a formulation of the Lord's Supper that was as correct as possible. Melanchthon therefore favored canceling the meeting. In the middle of May—because of Luther's illness the conference was postponed until 21 May, and ultimately moved to Wittenberg—Luther also informed the elector that, because of the now unambiguous dissenting stance of the Swiss, he had little hope for the Concord, whereupon John Frederick once more pledged Luther to the Augsburg Confession and the Apology.[33]

The Negotiations in Wittenberg and the Establishment of the Concord

On the Lutheran side at the Wittenberg negotiations[34] were Luther himself, Melanchthon, Justus Jonas, Caspar Cruciger, John Bugenhagen, along with

Justus Menius from Eisenach, and Frederick Myconius from Gotha. The participants from Pomerania and Prussia did not attend. The southern Germans were represented by Bucer and Capito from Strasbourg, Martin Frecht from Ulm, Jacob Otter from Esslingen, Bonifacius Wolfhart and Wolfgang Musculus from Augsburg, Gervasius Schuler from Memmingen, Johannes Bernhardi from Frankfurt, Martin Germanus from Fürfeld in Kraichgau, and Johannes Zwick from Constance, who, however, was not at the opening because of illness. The two representatives from Reutlingen, Matthew Alber and Johannes Schradin, belonged more to the Lutherans than to the southern Germans. It proved impossible—possibly intentionally—for the strict Lutherans Osiander, Brenz, and Schnepf to attend, although their participation had been envisioned.

Shortly before the meeting the prospects for the negotiations took a turn for the worse in the wake of the deliberate reprinting of Zwingli's *Fidei christianae expositio* (Exposition of the Christian faith) of 1531, along with letters by Zwingli and Oecolampadius, prefaced also with one of Bucer's letters. This was an extreme irritation to the Wittenbergers, because they no longer knew how they stood with their allies. Not until they received the favorable reports from Myconius and Menius, which covered the last portion of their trip with the southern Germans, did some hope revive. On the morning of 22 May Capito and Bucer met initially with Luther in order to set the agenda. At that time they delivered the confession of the Swiss and expressed their hope for unity with Luther. At midday the participants met in Luther's house. Before this meeting there may have been a scene that was suggestive for the still tense atmosphere; Musculus sneered at Luther's papal attitude, whereupon Schradin sharply took him to task: "No one asked you to come here."[35]

Bucer first gave an extensive summary of his efforts. Then Luther, in an unexpectedly blunt and virtually intimidating manner, described how the situation appeared to him: They were hailing their unity with him, but were continuing to teach the same old thing and claiming that the dispute was just a matter of words. Luther referred to the Swiss editions of Zwingli's works and demanded that his opponents expressly repudiate them. The proposed agreement would have to be an authentic and stable one, but Luther doubted that there was a common ground. He would prefer to leave things as they were rather than conclude a hypocritical agreement. Posterity—or at least God—would be aware of such duplicity. With one blow the years of efforts of the southern Germans at improving the atmosphere of their relationship with Luther and the small steps taken toward rapprochement appeared in question. Obviously, Bucer must have been deeply disturbed over this abrupt beginning. Initially all he could do was protest that his intentions were sincere and that he was innocent with regard to the Zwingli editions. Luther thereupon clearly formulated his requirements. The opinion that was contrary to Christ had to be repudiated. His opponents had to declare that in the future they desired to teach in conformity to Luther. He did admit that he had written too

49

harshly against Zwingli and Oecolampadius, but he could do nothing other than condemn Zwingli's formulations. Thereupon he very precisely traced Bucer's process of rapprochement and demanded, as a final admission that would dispel the doubt and suspicion he was having such difficulty in shedding, that Bucer make this statement: The bread is the body of Christ by the power of Christ's institution, regardless of the worthiness or unworthiness of the minister dispensing it or of the recipient. With this, the discussions on the problem of what the ungodly ate was broached. At this point the first round of discussions had to be interrupted because of Luther's weakness. Not until noon on the following day could more conversations take place. The southern Germans were irritated, even shocked, at this turbulent opening, which did not let bygone matters rest.[36] If they had foreseen this, they would not have come. Intentionally or unintentionally, Luther had put them on the defensive.

In his reply on the afternoon of 23 May, Bucer stated in a roundabout way, but more clearly than he had before, that previously he had not understood and taught all things correctly until he recognized his error, and he declared that he was prepared to make retractions. Nevertheless, he also stressed that he had difficulties with Luther's all-encompassing statements. Bucer essentially gave in to Luther's position. As problematic as before, however, was the assertion that the ungodly ate. Bucer had always wanted to teach a real eating in the sacrament, something he thought could not be conceded to the ungodly, unlike the papistic doctrine of the sacrament. When asked, the other southern Germans declared that they agreed with Bucer and asked that no one suspect them. Their governments would acknowledge the real presence of Christ in the Lord's Supper and recognize the Augsburg Confession and Apology, and therefore they asked that a Concord be concluded. Thereupon Luther conferred separately with the Wittenbergers. They felt that the statements of their opponents were sufficient, but they wanted reassurance in regard to the question of whether the ungodly ate. Bugenhagen proposed substituting the biblical expression "unworthy" for "ungodly," a suggestion discussed earlier. Luther could hardly have any objection to this scriptural term. This term made it possible for the other side to distinguish between ungodly pagans and believers who were misusing the Lord's Supper. As Bucer later reported, the southern Germans would have preferred to avoid the problem, but, once the negotiating position of the southern Germans had been worsened so much by the Zwingli editions, the Concord would never have been achieved without conceding that the unworthy ate.[37] After this concession by the southern Germans—a similar one on Luther's part, after the whole course of events, was not forthcoming—peace and concord would be established. Capito and Bucer wept. A prayer of thanksgiving was offered. All shook hands. A modification of the doctrine of the Lord's Supper in the southern German churches was to take place cautiously.

On the following day they discussed baptism, the power of the keys, and questions about schools. Luther wanted to assure himself of unity in these questions as well. The work ceased on Ascension Day. The task of drafting the Wittenberg Concord was assigned to Melanchthon, and it was discussed on the afternoon of 26 May. They decided not to give final approval to the Concord, but first to submit it to the governments and churches. On 27 May the confession of the Swiss was discussed. Luther had not anticipated their interest in participating in the Concord. Some items in their confession appeared obscure to him, but he felt they should discuss with the Swiss the possibility of their joining the Wittenberg Concord. In addition, they deliberated that day about the government's power over ecclesiastical affairs, a question that was especially acute in those cities where cathedral chapters were situated. As he had previously done in the case of the city of Bremen, Luther considered it impermissible for the city authorities to interfere with the cathedral chapters, which were independent according to imperial law.

After the difficult beginning, the atmosphere of the conference relaxed. Luther's sermons on Ascension Day and the following Sunday contained no sarcastic remarks. The guests from southern Germany were amazed at the difference between the Lutheran mass and their own plain worship service. In addition to the discussions, there was time for banquets in the homes of Lucas Cranach and of Luther, who once also engaged singers and pipers for entertainment there.[38]

The Concord[39] was signed on 29 May 1536 by all the participants except Johannes Zwick of Constance, who had no authorization to do so. It was in the form of a protocol that reiterated the opinion of the southern Germans: In the sacrament there were two things, an earthly and a heavenly. With the bread and wine the body and blood of Christ were truly and substantially present and were tendered and received. There was no transubstantiation or local inclusion of Christ's body and blood. The bread was identified with the body of Christ by virtue of the sacramental union, and the body was present with the tendering of the bread, although not outside the eating. The unworthy receive Christ's body and blood, but because they receive it without true repentance and faith and thus abuse its intent, it works judgment upon them. Thus the gift of the Lord's Supper, independent of the worthiness or unworthiness of the recipient, was unequivocally formulated. Contrary to some scholars' interpretation, there was no hint here that Luther allowed the opposing side any latitude of interpretation or even acknowledged such a possibility.[40] His partners in the negotiations had to accept his viewpoint. The most significant outcome of the Wittenberg negotiations was that the sacramentarian controversy, at least as far as it involved the evangelicals in Germany, was decided almost entirely in Luther's favor.

Efforts at Getting the Concord Accepted

The Concord was not finally adopted in Wittenberg; it first had to be submitted to the authorities and the other preachers. The next steps were to inform the governments and theologians who had not participated in the Wittenberg meeting, and to secure their approval. Luther was concerned about this. In the following days, he remained—along with Bucer who continued his active support of the Concord—the key person to whom the southern Germans and Swiss related. He had to request assistance from the Electoral Saxon chancellory in order to deal with the flood of correspondence. He immediately wrote Strasbourg and Augsburg, among others, and also Amsdorf, informing them "that we are agreed on the matter, as far as one can humanly determine." He expressed his hope for a unity that existed not only in words, but also in heartfelt trust ("all suspicion eradicated"). He warned the Lutheran Margrave George of Brandenburg-Ansbach against any polemics that might frighten the opposite side, who expressly protested their sincerity. The southern Germans were not held responsible for the Zwingli editions. Nevertheless, Amsdorf expressed his rejection and there was also opposition in Franconia, so that Melanchthon felt that his earlier fears about undertaking such a Concord were confirmed. Luther himself emphasized to Forster in Augsburg how frankly they had acted because of the consequences of any Concord reached through dissembling. Osiander, who was informed very quickly and clearly by the people from Reutlingen, expressed a favorable opinion.[41]

In Frankfurt on their journey home the representatives from southern Germany had agreed on a common report concerning the Wittenberg meeting. Bucer sought to commit his side to the Concord and offered, if necessary, to give more information. In Strasbourg he emphasized the demarcation from the papal interpretation contained in the Concord, and he offered his explanation of the "unworthy" as those believing Christians who received the sacrament unworthily. He also emphasized that as a result of the course of the negotiations they could not refuse to accept the articles of the Concord. Before the end of June there was an announcement from the pulpit in Strasbourg that corresponded with the agreement.[42]

From Frankfurt Capito had already thanked Luther almost devoutly for the ease (!) with which the discussions had proceeded and for the hospitality shown the secondary participants from southern Germany. His earlier oppressive anxieties had been replaced by an optimistic attitude and a new high estimation of Luther. He stated that a salutary relief had already come over him and that he had no doubts about the permanence of the union. He particularly wished that Luther would praise the Swiss for their enthusiasm for the Concord and let them know that he was not displeased with their confession but rather favored a simpler formulation along the lines of the Concord. Capito expressly apologized once more for Johannes Zwick's missing signature. He promised Katy a golden ring. In July Capito reported on his activities on behalf of the Concord, especially in Basel. To be sure, once again he had to mention threats to the peace, for example, Forster's dispute with Michael Keller, the former Zwinglian in Augsburg. Such incidents among the southern Germans, which made the harmony appear doubtful, should be brought up frankly by Luther.[43]

On 23 July the Augsburg clergy informed Luther that they had signed the Concord, which they had thoroughly examined, so that Luther's suspicions of them should be allayed. They called it a work of heaven. Nevertheless, Luther once again had to be warned about those who wanted to sow discord. Luther could do nothing in his delighted reply but encourage the clergy to continue in this vein and inform the people accordingly. Some doubts about their loyalty were awakened in him by Musculus's attacks on the Augsburg cathedral chapter, which were not in harmony with the Wittenberg agreements.[44] On 22 July Bucer could report to Luther that Frankfurt, Worms, Landau, Weissenburg, Esslingen, Augsburg, Memmingen, and Kempten, along with Strasbourg itself, had accepted the Concord. Ulm was delaying. Johannes Zwick was working to secure its acceptance by the Swiss. He hoped to be able to send the signatures to Wittenberg before the Frankfurt fall fair. Bucer himself was working on the promised retractions of his commentary on the gospels.[45] On 13 September Reutlingen reported its acceptance of the Concord.[46] The southern Germans who had been present in Wittenberg had worked intensively on behalf of the Concord, but in so doing they constantly met considerable resistance. Thus Frecht in Ulm wrote on 19 July: "Everyone is afraid, where there is nothing to fear, that we have conceded much too much to the monk [!] Luther, but they judge the great man hastily and think that we, who are defending Luther in this matter of the Concord, are completely Lutheran." Among those who successfully incited animosity against Luther was also Caspar von Schwenckfeld.[47]

The chief problem in the following period was winning the Swiss for the Concord. Joachim Vadianus of Saint Gall believed that he would be able to prepare them for it if he placed the emphasis somewhat differently. Capito and Bucer worked intensively and successfully to win the Basel clergy, who were themselves promoting the Concord in Zurich and Bern. As before, the Constance clergy remained aloof. They wanted to withdraw their signature, pretending not to be affected because of their previous acceptance of the Augsburg Confession. At the same time, they naively claimed that in so doing they were not intending to cause offense.[48] Luther stated the difficulties in a letter on 23 October, but he was still full of hope because of the faithful efforts of the southern Germans: The church travels a difficult way, but it attains the goal.[49] On 30 October the Ulm council, albeit somewhat reservedly, declared its agreement with the Concord because it conformed to the Augsburg Confession and the Apology, but at the same time it prevented its preachers from making a declaration of agreement that was too unreserved and appreciative. Here Schwenckfeld's agitation against the Concord could be seen. Ulm also reported Biberach's acceptance to Luther. In his reply Luther charged the preachers and citizens of Ulm to abide by the Concord.[50]

On 24 September and 14 November the Swiss deliberated on the Concord in Bucer's presence. The result was reported in a letter from the Swiss that was not written until 12 January 1537. Bern had demanded changes in the

Concord. Zurich would have no part of them and presented its own *Declaratio.* Constance strengthened the resolve of the Swiss by labeling the Wittenberg articles as not clear enough to be a Concord. The Swiss would not abandon their own confession they had presented in Wittenberg and wanted to maintain their freedom, but they did express the hope that unity could be established.[51] On 28 November and 9 December Vadianus and Oswald Myconius from Basel had already attempted to explain the attitude of the Swiss to Luther. Vadianus admitted that in Switzerland there were also radical "sacramentarians" who thought in purely symbolic terms. Here they had initially gone too far in the campaign against the papists. Nevertheless, he attempted to demonstrate that the Swiss view accorded with Luther's. Myconius encouraged Luther not immediately to doubt the Concord nor to repudiate the Swiss, who in principle were very willing to reach an agreement. Luther should deal fraternally with them and indicate anything that was desired that might possibly be a matter of different methods of formulation. They had to bear one another in love.[52]

At the end of 1536 the Concord was finally rejected in Constance. Ambrose Blaurer, Bucer's one-time faithful supporter in regard to the understanding on the Lord's Supper, withdrew after the bad experiences that he had had to suffer in 1534 because of the Württemberg Concord. It seemed unacceptable to him to acknowledge that the unworthy ate; it conceded more to the Lutherans than was compatible with his conscience. Not even Bucer's importunate letters could shake his reservations. Equally negative and hostile were Thomas Blaurer and Conrad Zwick in Constance. An unsuccessful attempt was made through Melanchthon to relieve Constance of the obligation to sign. Following this, a similarly fruitless attempt was made to convince the southern German cities to renew discussions with Luther. In November the Strasbourg clergy insisted on the acceptance of the Concord and made it clear that Luther otherwise would not be convinced that unity existed. The Strasbourgers were only able to persuade Constance, after many revisions, to send a letter to Luther that undoubtedly minimized the problems by declaring that the Wittenberg negotiations were unnecessary. They appealed to the Tetrapolitan Confession of 1530, against which Luther had never raised objections, denying entirely that there was a divergence. In part this attitude can be explained as fear on the part of Constance, a former episcopal see, of any rapprochement with the papal church. Although they then declined to send the letter, the dangerous isolation of Constance from the rest of the southern Germans was unmistakable.[53]

On 26 December 1536, in a letter to the imperial free city of Isny, Luther brusquely denied the repeated assertion that he had made concessions to the southern Germans in the Wittenberg articles and had gone over to the opinion of the Zwinglians. He was as sure as before that Zwingli had taught wrongly, and therefore there was no question of his making any concession. Nevertheless, he hoped that at least some of those among his southern German colleagues took the Concord seriously.[54] Luther continued to be convinced of Capito's and Bucer's sincere efforts, although in Augsburg a "Satan" like Keller had caused difficulties. He regarded the ring that Capito had sent Katy Luther as a symbol of the unity between Wittenberg and Strasbourg. He continued to have great hopes for the Concord, and he was sure that Christ would complete the matter.[55]

Luther reacted insightfully to the rejection of the Swiss on 17 February 1537 in a letter to Jacob Meyer, the Basel burgomaster who was favorably disposed toward the Concord. He was not surprised that there was still suspicion on both sides, for this was a serious matter. Luther emphasized the necessity of patiently striving for unity. "Resting birds"—meaning the old suspicion of the Lutherans—should not deter the Swiss. The existing circumstances had to be accepted for the time being. The letter was carefully composed. When Bucer and Wolfhart met in Gotha on 1 March 1537 after the meeting of the Smalcald League with the ailing Luther on the subject of the Concord, Luther once again expressed his view in an almost testamentary fashion: As a sincere man, hypocrisy was impossible for him in this matter, and his partners should also deal with it without dissembling. Luther was prepared to be patient. He again rejected the assertion that the matter had not been rightly understood. His opponents should either be silent or confess their error, as Amsdorf and Osiander continued to demand. If necessary, this might not happen for some time. In his letter to Jacob Meyer he had been concerned not to offend. In case of his own death, they should refer to this letter. Bucer, in his report on 1 April about the meeting of the Smalcald League, informed the Swiss once again about Luther's view of the Lord's Supper. Luther had never been concerned about *how* Christ was present and received, but rather about the presence and the reception themselves. In case no agreement could be reached on this point, it would be better to dispense with the Concord. It was intolerable to him that the Swiss had imputed a massive "fleshly opinion" to Luther. In Bucer's opinion, they should therefore let bygones be bygones, or old wounds would be reopened. Luther considered it problematic that the Swiss were constantly making spiritualizing qualifications in their statements about the presence of Christ, and this made him doubt their sincerity. Like Luther, the princes in Schmalkalden favored encouraging the Concord, or at least they opposed stirring up the old controversy. Ambrose Blaurer alone played an unfortunately ambiguous role in Schmalkalden with his statements about the Lord's Supper that corresponded to Constance's position; Luther did not know how to deal with them.[56]

Luther did not reply directly to the Swiss position until 1 December 1537. At that time Bern appeared to have abandoned its reluctance, and therefore Luther's letter was intended to promote peace. Again he showed that he understood that the scar of discord would not heal quickly. The opponents of the Concord should be silenced. Luther protested the sincerity of his intentions. It was left to Bucer to overcome differences. Luther hoped that the murky water would clear up, but harbored no illusions about the actual differences that existed. He informed Bucer in an accompanying letter that the Swiss confession pleased him even less than the Tetrapolitan Confession. The Bern clergy were happy with the letter; they recognized that they had incorrectly understood the Concord as a relapse into papalism. In a letter to Luther's co-worker Jocodus Neuheller on 2 February 1538, the Bern cleric Peter Kunz praised Luther's marvelous simplicity and integrity and polemicized against his opponent Caspar Megander, "Zwingli's ape." As requested, the Bern council forbade controversy over the Concord. Simon Sulzer, the Bernese who visited Luther in the spring of 1538, found Luther very disposed toward the Concord. Bucer considered the letter in January 1538 a timely gift. Leo Jud and Theodore Bibliander in Zurich did not cease their opposition, however. The difficulty of Bucer's task of mediation is seen in an almost simultaneous letter from him to Luther in which, among other things, he explained why he occasionally argued in Switzerland with Zwingli and Oecolampadius. It must also have awakened Luther's mistrust that in the meantime Karlstadt had taught in Basel, although, according to Bucer, without great influence. Bucer may accurately have characterized those who were agitating against the Concord: They did not want to have fought in vain and to have lost face. The dead weight of the Zurich Reformation, above all, was becoming apparent.[57]

In March 1538 Henry Bullinger sent Luther his Latin treatise *On the Authority of the Holy Scriptures* from Zurich and mentioned that he was interested in mutual contacts, although he did not mention the Concord. Luther replied on 14 May, admitting that he had not yet read Bullinger's book, although at that time he was already expressing himself very critically on Bullinger's estimates of the Anabaptists on one side and of the Lutherans on the other: "He is wrong. . . ." Luther let Bullinger know that he had almost died because of Zwingli's and Oecolampadius's deaths. This was no contradiction of those statements in which Luther had referred to the deaths of each man as punishment, because it was precisely this concept that had frightened Luther so deeply. Luther frankly declared that both sides thought different things were true. Moreover, he criticized the new editions of Zwingli's writings prepared by Bullinger. Each side still fancied that the other was in error, and yet Luther still wished to see unity before his death. On 6 May he had informed Duke Albrecht of Prussia: "Things are on the right track with the Swiss." He believed that he had Strasbourg, Augsburg, Basel, and Bern, along with the other cities, on his side, and he was hoping for a good outcome of the efforts on behalf of the Concord in order to vex Rome.[58]

It was not easy for the Swiss to answer Luther's letter of 1 December 1537. The Zurich clergy prepared a draft in February 1538, which stated that they were not united on how Christ was present and that Luther had not altered his previous conception. Here not even a retraction by the Swiss would be of any help. They should therefore let the differences continue to stand and yet be one in Christian love. Bucer and Capito, on whose shoulders Luther had laid the task of restoring unity with the Swiss, pointed out the contradictory nature of the Zurich draft. They knew that among the Swiss Zwingli's views were still being held. Therefore they demanded a clear reply about whether they thought Luther's opinion was Christian or not. They should either clearly confess their unity or else continue the discussion on any existing differences, rather than break off the negotiations. The letter from the Swiss on 4 May was written as if Luther had accepted the earlier Swiss confession and Zurich's declaration. Once again the viewpoints and misunderstandings were clarified. The existing differences in formulation should not disturb the relationships and the allegedly existing Concord should remain in force. Thus, contrary to Strasbourg's demand, they refused to deal with the problems that did exist.[59]

Luther replied on 27 June in almost the same way as in his previous letter. The actual task of mediation he entrusted anew to the Strasbourgers, and he also informed them who in Switzerland he still considered suspect. Capito praised Luther for this balanced and thoughtful letter, which was also well received in Basel. Among other things, he mentioned the advantage of the Concord, that the Swiss preferred to read Luther's books, and that those who sympathized with him were being strengthened by them. On 1 September Bullinger continued the correspondence with Luther. He praised Luther's sincerity also in his statements about Zwingli, but he could not understand why Luther did not see that unity was already established. Bullinger also defended the new edition of Zwingli's writings, and he claimed that he did not understand what was offensive to Luther in Zwingli, for Zwingli had certainly also affirmed the presence of Christ in the Lord's Supper. He asked Luther to state exactly his objections to the Swiss. Bullinger was concerned that suspicion and discord come to an end and that people practice love toward one another. On 28 September the Zurich clergy proposed to Basel that they let the project of seeking the Concord rest. In contrast to Luther, they saw no chance for any further rapprochement and believed that enough had been done in this respect. The Bern clergy agreed with this on 23 October.[60] Thus it was the Swiss and not Luther who put an end to the almost two years of efforts to persuade them to join the Wittenberg Concord. The enormous and long-term consequences this would have for their mutual relationship and thus for the history of the Reformation could not be foreseen by those involved at the time.

In August 1538 the durability of the Concord was endangered anew in Augsburg. The city council complained to Luther about Forster's accusations that the Augsburg clergy were deviating from Wittenberg and the Concord. At that time Forster, who had a difficult personality and was continually causing friction in Augsburg, was virtually conducting an inquisition against his colleague Keller, the former Zwinglian, to force him to adopt a Lutheran position. Luther was unwilling to judge the controversy with Forster, but he announced his dissatisfaction with the way the clergy were talking about the Concord in Augsburg. He warned them not to keep fanning the fire. That Keller had once been a Zwinglian was not forgotten and it could also be proved from his own writings. Otherwise, in this case, too, Luther left the task of mediating to the Strasbourgers. What had most annoyed Luther in the Augsburgers' letter was that they acted as if they had always agreed with him. The following statement by Luther attracts attention: "Therefore I never liked this fictitious Concord." This made it sound as if the period of the Concord was coming to an end. In fact, Luther was afraid that the relationship would worsen. For the time being he left it to Bucer to spoon up the spilled soup. Forster, unable to remain in Augsburg, assumed a professorship in Tübingen, where he became involved in new tensions with Ambrose Blaurer.[61]

That the Concord would come into existence and be sustained was never self-evident, and it was frequently endangered. One reason for this was that it was not an elastic compromise in which each side made concessions; rather, Luther remained absolutely firm in the matter and did not yield a hair's breadth, no matter how desirable the Concord may have been for ecclesiastical, political, or human points of view. In part the firmness had a positive result: The southern Germans could be won for the Lutheran view. Nevertheless, this also demanded a price: The Reformation in Switzerland ultimately went its own way. These were the historically significant positive and negative results of the attempt at concluding the Concord.

Human factors played a prominent role with Luther alongside the theological arguments, of course, and therefore in the course of these events we obtain significant insights into the range of his personality. The mistrust he had long harbored, which he never completely abandoned, was once again revealed by how strongly he was affected by the antagonism of Zwingli and the Swiss and by how deeply he felt their opposition. He therefore insisted on the retraction of his opponents, who on their part were not prepared to disavow Zwingli. The great achievement of Bucer and his friends consisted not least in being able, selflessly and with clear insight into conditions that could not be changed, primarily those of Luther's personal and theological standpoint, to set aside suspicion and create a relationship of trust that was the indispensable prerequisite for the Concord. They undertook these tasks—sometimes thankless ones, as are all efforts at mediation—with integrity, if also occasionally with too much optimism. They learned that the positions were in part so opposed to one another that they could not be reconciled. Wherever and as long as trust existed, it was possible for Luther also to change and act charitably and patiently. It would therefore be incorrect to consider him doctrinaire or stubborn in his relationship with the southern Germans and the Swiss. The basis for trust was ultimately not destroyed by him, but primarily by Zurich's breaking off the efforts at adopting the Wittenberg Concord. The contrast between the two sides immediately appeared more clearly than ever before, and it remained so.

5. FRANCE AND ENGLAND

With the exception of the Reformation in Denmark, which will be discussed later, Luther had only occasional relationships with the non-German countries. The appearance of an Ethiopian cleric in Wittenberg in 1534 was a unique event. It was difficult to communicate with him, because he spoke only a little Italian. Nevertheless, Luther believed he was able to determine that they agreed on the doctrine of the Trinity. The differences in worship ceremonies were not regarded as divisive of the church, and their eucharistic liturgies appeared especially compatible. Luther and Melanchthon provided letters of recommendation for the visitor.[1] This was one of their few contacts with the eastern church.

Since 1535 both Francis I of France and Henry VIII of England, for obvious political reasons, had been concerned about the Wittenbergers. In France, in 1534, the so-called affair of the placards, the appearance of sharply anti-Catholic pamphlets, had led to severe persecution of the evangelicals. This severely strained the relationship between Francis I and the members of the Smalcald League. It was feared that the adherents of the league would turn more strongly toward the Hapsburgs, i.e., to the real enemies of France. Among the measures taken to prevent this was an invitation to Melanchthon from the king, delivered on 8 August 1535 by Barnabé de Voré, one of the advocates of the unity project, for him to come to Paris in order to participate in negotiations aimed at solving the ecclesiastical dispute. Voré also delivered a letter to the German Protestants from the cardinal of Paris, Jean du Bellay, who together with his brother Guillaume, one of the trusted advisors of Francis I, had worked to arrange Melanchthon's invitation.[2] It was no accident that Melanchthon was invited instead of Luther. He was considered a man of compromise, and in the preceding year he had already sent an opinion to France that, in accord with the tendencies he had displayed at the Diet of Augsburg in 1530, minimized the existing differences with the old believers.[3]

Despite certain reservations, Melanchthon was ready to travel to France. To do so, however, he needed the elector's permission. In mid-August he discussed this in Torgau. Because of concern for Melanchthon's safety, but primarily out of consideration for the emperor and King Ferdinand, the elector forbade the trip.[4] A renewed request from Melanchthon was supported by Luther, for the journey might allow the possibility of lessening the persecution of evangelicals in France; Melanchthon should not decline the invitation, because it was possible that God was working through it. Luther gave no thought to any possible political implications of the trip. The elector continued to withhold his permission. The journey was not in the political interests of an

Electoral Saxony that endorsed loyalty to the emperor. In addition, once the contents of Melanchthon's opinion became known in Germany, it was feared that he was prepared to make too many concessions.[5] Melanchthon was bitter about the abrupt denial of his trip, especially because his fundamentally irenic intentions were also involved. He even considered leaving Electoral Saxony. Luther initially shared his position, but then he became more and more suspicious of the French envoys, to the point that he even doubted their identity.[6]

This episode had a sequel. Duke John III of Jülich and Cleves gave one of the summaries of Melanchthon's irenic opinion to the city of Soest in order to demonstrate that it was not necessary to enact a new ordinance. The preacher in Soest, Brictius thom Norde, thereupon sent the articles to Luther and asked what comments he had about them. Luther immediately published the *Articles That Have Now Recently Been Forged and Maliciously Extolled against Us Lutherans,* adding some critical comments and appending a letter to the Soest clergy.[7] He did not deny that offers of a compromise had been made by his side during the Diet of Augsburg, but he did not mention that the articles first originated with Melanchthon, a fact of which he was aware; instead, he presented them as a forgery on the part of the Catholics, although each article had not been altered in the same way. Nevertheless, the summary claimed that the Wittenbergers were prepared to recognize the pope without mentioning the precondition of allowing freedom for the gospel. Luther now declared that any agreement between themselves and the pope was utterly impossible. He thereby rejected Melanchthon's plans to achieve an understanding, as the Electoral Saxon court had already done. No tensions in Wittenberg were apparent because of this, but differences did exist.

In September 1536 Luther received a letter from Amadeus Roberti from Amiens that endeavored to enlist Luther in favor of Francis I's politics and against the emperor. Luther did send it to the elector, but it does not appear that he replied to it.[8]

For understandable reasons, France's dealings with Melanchthon and its attempt to reach an understanding with the Lutherans caused Henry VIII of England to approach the Lutherans again. An alliance between France and the Smalcald League would have isolated England politically. Henry VIII therefore sought to join the Smalcald League. In addition, he was still concerned about getting the Lutherans to approve his divorce.[9] In March 1535 Melanchthon had already dedicated the second edition of his *Loci Communes* to the English king, something that was occasionally regarded with indignation on the evangelical side.[10] Not only did he emphasize in it his agreement with the church fathers and his rejection of the Anabaptists, but he also stated that a discussion by learned men on disputed theological questions was desirable.

First, Robert Barnes, who had been influenced theologically by studying in Wittenberg and who had just been named Henry's court chaplain, was sent to Wittenberg for theological discussions at the end of July; he was followed a little later by Edward Foxe, the bishop of Hereford, and Archdeacon Nicholas Heath. Barnes delivered an invitation to Melanchthon to participate in theological conversations in England, which would also keep him from going to France.[11] The Wittenberg theologians—except for Melanchthon who was still with the university in Jena because of the plague—arranged an audience for Barnes with the elector and advocated allowing Melanchthon to make the trip, which could be compensation for rejecting the invitation to France. In Luther's opinion, Henry VIII's political and theological approach to the Smalcald League was in the evangelical interest and well suited to thwart the pope's plans for a council. The continuing differences concerning Henry's divorce should be left to the theologians: "The princes have nothing to do with that."

The elector agreed that the Wittenberg theologians might undertake discussions with the English envoys, but no definite agreements should be made without consulting him.[12] At that time Barnes had his history of the popes up to Alexander III (d. 1181) printed in Wittenberg. He dedicated it to Henry VIII, who had freed England from these personifications of the Antichrist. Luther wrote a preface for it in which he expressed his satisfaction that the a priori identification of the pope with the Antichrist from the Bible was now confirmed a posteriori by history.[13]

Because the arrival of Foxe and Heath was delayed until the end of November 1535, Luther feared that they had fallen victim to papal persecution.[14] In December at the meeting of the alliance in Schmalkalden the English envoys then presented Henry VIII's wish to join the Smalcald League and stated his willingness to engage in theological discussions, which was received favorably by the allies.[15] The theological discussions between the English emissaries and the theologians in Wittenberg did not begin until the latter half of January 1536, after Melanchthon had been summoned from Jena. Out of consideration for the emperor, the elector warned Luther against making too extensive concessions in the matter of the divorce. Luther was able to reassure the elector: He would stand by his previous verdict, that Henry's first marriage to the wife of his deceased brother, once it had been consummated, was valid, despite the Old Testament's prohibition. He would not let political opportunism prevail upon him to change it. Thus, oddly enough, the Wittenberg theologians considered themselves the only advocates for the recently deceased Queen Catherine and her daughter Mary.[16]

The negotiations with the English proved to be difficult and tense. This was not only because of the divorce question, for in it the envoys were willing to make concessions to the Wittenbergers. Rather, Luther felt that their method of negotiating, primarily Foxe's, was sophistical and unproductive, so that after a few days he had already had enough. In his opinion, the strife was not worth the substantial expenditures the elector was making for the envoys.[17] Nevertheless, the discussions went on for weeks more, although Luther deferred in them to Melanchthon.

The disputation *Against the Private Mass* took place on 29 January 1536, probably in connection with the negotiations with the English delegation, which also took part in the event. In the theses that Luther prepared he again rejected the private mass as human error, godlessness, and idol worship, while the English maintained the possibility of retaining it, which Luther then did not exclude entirely, e.g., in the context of a court worship service.[18] Not until the end of March did the discussions reach a definite stopping point. Regarding Henry VIII's divorce, they were agreed that according to Lev. 18:16 a marriage to a brother's wife as such was prohibited, but the Wittenbergers expressed no opinion on whether Henry's marriage, now that it had been consummated, had to be dissolved.

The common statement, the so-called Wittenberg Articles, was formulated by Melanchthon on the basis of the Augsburg Confession, the Apology, and his *Loci Communes.* As he had done in the articles written for France in 1534, Melanchthon similarly met the conservative English halfway. Nevertheless, the English envoys did not feel authorized to approve the articles without Henry VIII's assent. They particularly had reservations about the giving of both kinds in the Lord's Supper, the marriage of priests, monastic vows, and the veneration of the saints. Thus the final theological agreement with the English would have to be left to a later mission of the Smalcald League to England. Luther was agreeable to using the wide-ranging articles as a basis for a political alliance. He informed the elector, however, that there was no room for Henry VIII to negotiate any further changes: "For the sake of our churches, which have just barely been brought to rest and tranquility, we absolutely cannot again create discord and error." Upon the elector's repeated inquiry, he declared that they could not grant the king what they had refused the emperor and the pope. Whether one could conclude an alliance without a common confession was a "secular thing," about which the elector would have to decide. Luther still had his earlier reservations against the Swiss.[19] Henry VIII did not adopt the Wittenberg Articles. The Smalcald League was in no hurry to conclude an alliance with England. The king was also reluctant, because external political relationships seemed to be developing in a way more favorable to him. Moreover, he had to take into account the strong opposition of the old believers in England. The Wittenberg Articles thus only indirectly influenced the development of theological doctrine in England.

Not until May 1538 did the Smalcald League send a mission to England, but even then it was to engage only in preliminary talks and not to conclude an alliance. In it were Vice-chancellor Francis Burchart from Electoral Saxony and the Gotha superintendent, Frederick Myconius, from the ranks of the theologians. Luther took this opportunity to write a letter to Bishop Foxe, who, however, had died shortly before. Since the departure of the English delegation two years earlier Luther had received little direct information about the development of the Reformation in England, and he was now hoping for good news from the Saxon emissaries.[20] This delegation accomplished no tangible results either. When the Smalcald League achieved peace with the emperor in the Frankfurt Standstill in 1539, Henry VIII broke off the negotiations with them and again set the English church on a clearly Catholicizing course. Luther felt that his original opinion of Henry in 1522 had been confirmed and was happy that he had not become a member of the Smalcald League.[21] In contrast, Landgrave Philip and Bucer wanted to send a new delegation in order to prevent a disruption of the association. In addition, they felt that Melanchthon should write an admonition to Henry VIII. The Wittenberg theologians thought nothing would come of new efforts to win the English king. They thought he was stubborn and acting contrary to his conscience with his new religious politics. They clearly saw that Henry's ecclesiastical decisions were made only for political reasons and that he interpreted the truth however he pleased. In a case like this there was no sense in instructing him theologically; at most they could consider sending another admonition, which was then written by Melanchthon.[22]

At the end of July 1540 Thomas Cromwell was executed for his pro-evangelical politics and Robert Barnes for his dispute with Bishop Gardiner on the doctrine of justification—not, as Luther later thought, for his opposition to Henry's new marriage with Anne of Cleves—thus becoming victims of the Catholic reaction. Luther published the confession of faith that Barnes had written before his death, one that was clearly permeated by the spirit of Wittenberg, and himself wrote a preface for it.[23] For him, Barnes, who had been a guest in his home, was now a holy martyr. Luther once again made it clear that in Henry VIII's contacts with the Wittenbergers, initiated by Barnes, he had been interested only in having his marriage recognized and not in the evangelical faith. Luther understood that Barnes had always been hoping to be able to win the king for the gospel, although Barnes ultimately became a victim of Henry's despotism. The Wittenbergers had long since recognized this problem. Even a devil like Henry VIII and his persecutions had to serve to save Christians.

The overtures of the French and English kings to the Reformation were politically motivated. Both monarchs wanted to use Melanchthon, above all, to reach a religious compromise if circumstances permitted. It was impossible for Luther not to become involved; moreover, in the matter of Henry VIII's divorce it also concerned his judgment. In their involvements in European politics the Wittenberg theologians—primarily Luther among them—did keep the possibilities of a spread of the Reformation continually in view, but ultimately they relentlessly argued theologically and not politically. In this way they remained true to their cause. It was not their fault that their sincere efforts bore no results in either case.

In most cases Luther reacted to the developments of the Reformation rather than taking the initiative himself. Only with the Reformation in Anhalt and with the Anabaptists did he take an active role, encouraging it in the former instance and opposing them in the latter. This did not mean, however, that he thereby renounced his own creation. On the contrary, political concerns scarcely played a role for him. Instead, his concern was to emphasize his theological standpoint. Through this his influence on the Reformation in the cities was determined. With the Wittenberg Concord he was able for the time being to establish and preserve the Lutheran profile of the Reformation in Germany. The limits beyond which he was unprepared to go became evident in the unsuccessful negotiations with England. Within the German Reformation this firmness had a consolidating effect.

III

Renewed Strife with
Old Opponents

1. DUKE GEORGE AND THE
REPRESSION OF THE REFORMATION
IN DUCAL SAXONY (1532–39)

The Reformation also continued to spread in territories that were governed by
Catholic rulers. In them the usual practice of communion, giving only bread
and not the cup, could become a matter of conscience for the evangelicals. In
August 1532 Luther unmistakably informed the councilman and mine owner
Martin Lodinger in Gastein, Austria, that he dare not take part in this sort of
sacramental practice. Either he had to refrain from communing or he would
have no choice but to emigrate.[1] Lodinger was not the only one confronted by
this problem.

Comfort and Protest in the Face of Persecution

Despite considerable pressure from the government, the number of adherents to the Reformation in Ducal Saxony also grew. Residents of Leipzig
went to listen to sermons and receive the Lord's Supper in the nearby villages
of Electoral Saxony. On orders from Duke George they were placed under
surveillance and interrogated by the Leipzig council. Fourteen citizens who
were unwilling to return to the old faith were expelled in September 1532. An
additional nasty trick was to refuse them a certificate of dismissal with its
testimonial of good conduct, which was important in order for them to resettle
in another location. Luther comforted the exiles in this situation with a letter.
He presumed that the reason for this increased persecution was Duke George's
anger over the recently concluded Religious Peace of Nuremberg. This was
incorrect; the measures had already been initiated during Lent. The circumstances convinced Luther: "There will be no peace until the Lord himself
comes and topples the enemy of peace." He was convinced that God was the
God of those who were oppressed and suffering, not of the proud. He thought
that the duke's heart was hopelessly hardened.[2] When the Leipzig preacher
Johann Koss suffered a stroke in the pulpit on 29 December 1532 while attacking Luther and shortly thereafter died, Luther viewed it as a manifest sign of
God's judgment.[3]

Several groups of citizens, for the same reasons as in Leipzig, were expelled from Oschatz. Among them was the wife of Franz König. Because her husband was unaffected, the question arose of whether he was obligated to share her fate. Luther also wrote a letter of consolation to these exiles, whose resettlement in Electoral Saxony was not made easy either. Like the fleeing David, they should be certain that their exile was "a great thing" to God and to his angels, and that all their tears were "in God's sack."[4] Luther did more than write, however; for example, several times he interceded on behalf of the Dame family from Oschatz, advocating that they be granted monastery property for a farm.[5]

In the spring of 1533 new repressive measures were initiated against the evangelicals still in Leipzig. Dr. Augustine Specht, who died in March, had refused to receive communion under only one kind before his death and was therefore buried in unconsecrated ground, although "almost the whole city" attended. In order to prevent demonstrations like this, the duke forbade anyone to participate in such funerals in the future. Moreover, those participants at Specht's funeral who could be identified were interrogated by the council, which inquired whether they had fasted, gone to confession, and communed according to the old practice during Lent. One of the first to be expelled was the merchant Peter Gengenbach. In all, at least eighty people were affected by this massive order of expulsion. Surveillance of the citizens was carried out by giving lead tokens to those who went to confession and communion, so that they could prove they had performed their religious duties. In this situation some of the evangelicals asked Luther if, under certain circumstances, communion under only one kind might be permissible. Luther had to reject this. At the same time he condemned Duke George's supervision of consciences as forcefully as possible. The sovereign was not entitled to do this; rather, he was committing a grave sin by doing so. There was nothing else for those involved to do but openly to reject the immoral demands of the "murderer and robber" and suffer the consequences. Luther made the drastic recommendation, incongruous in expression: "One must smite the devil in the face with the cross"; in this case no sort of concessions could be made.[6]

As might have been expected, not all the evangelicals in Leipzig stood firm. A physician, Dr. George Curio, received communion under only one kind, although his wife could not be induced to do so and was therefore to be expelled. Curio subsequently suffered pangs of conscience because of his relapse. At the request of his friends, Luther sought to help him: If Curio would stand up and by his action risk being banished, then he too would already have been forgiven by Christ. Curio did then leave Leipzig, and at the end of the year Luther commended him to Nuremberg.[7]

Copies of Luther's letter of consolation to the Leipzigers also came into the hands of the council there, which sent them on to Duke George. George complained to Elector John Frederick about Luther's seditious writing, which contained blasphemies and also violated the 1531 treaties between the two Saxon states that had resolved the quarrels existing at that time. John Frederick discussed his reply with the Wittenberg theologians, and accordingly it was negative. Luther was not to be forbidden to write a letter of consolation for persecuted Christians. Moreover, in Ducal Saxony malicious publications had been published against him. Finally, the elector appealed to George's conscience, admonishing him in his old age to be reconciled to God and no longer to persecute the evangelical truth. John Frederick would pray that God "might make a Saul into a Paul" out of George. In his reply, George insisted that Luther had incited his subjects to revolt and thereby had also violated the Religious Peace of Nuremberg. He prayed that the elector might return to obedience toward church and emperor, from which this "runaway, perjuring monk" had enticed him. As might have been expected, John Frederick on his part now rejected George's polemic "pastoral care." In his opinion, Luther's letter of consolation could not be regarded as fomenting insurrection. He left no doubt that he would tolerate nothing of this sort. He therefore challenged Luther himself to reply.[8] This apparent concession to George's complaint could not help but exacerbate the conflict. In fact, the elector stood completely on Luther's side.

Luther already had a hint of what his reaction would be in the incident of an inquiry sent independently of Duke George by Wolf Wiedemann, the Leipzig burgomaster who was an old believer, asking whether Luther acknowledged the letter of consolation circulating in Leipzig: Luther treated the messenger delivering the communication from Leipzig so inhospitably that he would gladly have forgone his tip if he would not have had to deliver the letter. In his terse reply Luther first wanted to know who induced Wiedemann to make this inquiry. He suspected that the person behind it was Pastor Arnoldi in Cölln (Meissen) or the one he had earlier titled the "traitor of Dresden," both pseudonyms for none other than Duke George himself. "Then you'll get an answer, good measure, pressed down, shaken together, running over" (cf. Luke 6:38).[9]

Because of his ill health, Luther's *Vindication against Duke George's Charge of Rebellion* did not appear until July 1533.[10] He protested the charge of insurrection and assured Duke George that he did not want to infringe upon him as a secular prince. No such charge could be substantiated on the basis of his letter to the Leipzig evangelicals. If George had been characterized in the letter as an apostle of the devil, this was a spiritual verdict that referred to the forcible measures that the duke had employed against the spiritual realm, over which he as a secular ruler had no authority. Likewise, the statement that the evangelicals should "smite the devil in the face with the cross" could not be interpreted as encouraging the use of arms. This sooner applied to the oath to assist in condemning and persecuting the Lutheran doctrine, which the duke allegedly demanded of his subjects, for thereby the religious peace was threatened. Thus it was not difficult for Luther to refute George's accusation. If he were still labeled an agitator, he shared the same fate as Christ and the gospel.

Luther did not let things rest with this refutation. Self-confidently he pointed out once again that "since the time of the apostles, no doctor or scribe, no theologian nor jurist has so gloriously and clearly defended, instructed, and comforted the secular authorities as, by the special grace of God, have I; this I know for a certainty." Luther's writings and his action in the Peasants' War showed how ludicrous and slanderous George's accusation was. The duke, although he knew better, was attacking Luther and should be punished for lying. The real rebels were the clergy of the old faith, who despised the secular estate, and the laity, who had accorded the clergy a privileged status. The real rebellion was not the deserved critique of a prince, for it accorded with God's Word, but rather this agitation of the laity, which Duke George in his blindness was still covering up.

To his *Vindication* Luther appended a new letter of consolation to the Leipzig exiles. In his opinion, they did not need it, for with their innocent suffering they had already proved that they belonged to Christ. The letter of consolation likewise became a plea for freedom of conscience, about which Luther had already appealed to the duke in 1522: The guilty ones were not the evangelicals, but rather it was Duke George, by interrogating people's consciences about participating in the Catholic worship services, who had attacked God "in his office and judgment." "Such power has no angel, no man, neither pope nor bishop." Even less is a secular sovereign entitled to employ such measures. Here Duke George was acting as a tyrant and rebel against God. He should be delivered over to God's punishment. In his hardness of heart he was already condemned to hell, but the innocent victims of the persecution, with their good consciences, had both "paradise and the kingdom of God." One could only grieve over Leipzig and Ducal Saxony, because there it was not only Luther's doctrine, but also Christ and the gospel that were deliberately being denied.

Luther knew, of course, that Duke George would regard it as an affront to be labeled an enemy of Christ, but here he appealed against the prince to his own higher authority as a doctor of the Holy Scriptures. He could not spare George. The strength of the evangelical movement in Leipzig, which by then numbered about eighty families, should give the duke cause for serious reflection. The arguments for communion in only one kind, which were advanced by the Leipzig commission that had interrogated the evangelicals, were extremely weak. Through his political activity Duke George made himself equally guilty of all the bloodshed that had happened in the Catholic church, while it was the evangelicals who were advocating keeping the peace. In conclusion Luther made it clear to the persecuted ones: The cross is part of following Christ. The losses they had suffered would ultimately be worthwhile. The raging of God's enemies could not last forever.

Duke George's obligatory complaint to Elector John Frederick about Luther was not long in coming. Surprisingly, it was directed not against the general tone of the book, but rather concentrated on the oath allegedly required of the evangelicals, something unknown to the Saxon authorities. The elector, therefore, should distance himself from Luther, a "mendacious, perjuring, and apostate monk." John Frederick did not address the problem of the oath at all, and it is unclear what information Luther was relying on. John Frederick categorically defended Luther against the accusation of rebellion, referring to him as the one "whom God has selected as a special man to preach his holy Word clearly, purely, and faithfully," and also stating that "the elector of Saxony intends to hold this belief all the way to his grave." The sovereign was thus completely behind Luther.

Because of this, Duke George could only attack Luther in print. Yet the printing of a book written by him—once again under the name of Pastor Franz Arnoldi—was discontinued. Instead, it was principally John Cochlaeus who took up the attack on behalf of the duke with his *Duke George of Saxony's Honorable and Thorough Apology against Martin Luther's Seditious and Mendacious Letter and Vindication*. Cochlaeus amply demonstrated his polemic ability and was undoubtedly convinced of the weight of his arguments. Luther was "more vile than an enraged boar" and "a changeling born of a bathmaid," against whom George had to be protected. Cochlaeus was particularly concerned about presenting Luther as an insurgent and as a perjuring monk. He published another book: *Answer to Luther's Letter of Consolation to Some People in Leipzig and Basic Instruction about What They Did: And about Both Kinds in the Sacrament: With a Preface about the Great Damage to the German Land Caused by Luther's Writings*. In it he enumerated the enormous costs that had arisen because of Luther's writings, the negotiations at the diet concerning him, and the preparation of armaments. He defended the refusal to administer both kinds with the traditional Catholic arguments.[11]

In response, still before the fall fair in Leipzig, Luther, after a pre-publication copy of the *Apology* had come into his possession—once more with the help of the Wittenberg burgomaster—published *The Small Reply to Duke George's Latest Book*.[12] Because discussions between the two Saxon houses had been initiated once again, Luther contented himself with a provisional response to the "snot-nose" (*Rotzlöffel*) Cochlaeus. He had not invented the alleged oath demanded of the evangelicals in Leipzig, but even if the facts had been otherwise, that would not make Luther's book a lie.

Luther dealt with the secondary accusation that he was a perjuring monk and an apostate. He used this as the occasion for taking issue with monasticism once again, and in so doing mentioned many personal reminiscences. In this matter the duke was not his judge; rather, Luther would have to be refuted from the Holy Scriptures. The real apostates were those who by their many works were denying redemption through Christ alone. By leaving the monastery, therefore, Luther had accomplished a necessary correction and was a "blessed perjurer." The opposing side could not deny that monastic vows had been seen as surpassing baptism. The monks therefore were the real "Anabaptists." In contrast to his opponents, Luther was qualified on the basis of years of study, teaching, writing, and suffering. Monasticism was a human competitor with Christ's redemptive work and consequently a repudiation of Christ. Monks and nuns were unable to attain certainty of salvation. Bernard of Clairvaux, one of the most pious monks, ultimately did not trust in Christ but in his monastic piety. He saw the advantage of government and marriage as secular estates in the fact that people fulfilling these respective tasks did not intend to attain salvation. The chief outrage of monasticism was that it denied the grace of God. Anyone turning away from monasticism to the truth could ironically be said to have twice committed perjury. Next Luther dealt with the theological theory of "evangelical counsels" that went beyond the commandments of God: Poverty and obedience were in fact observed only with conditions; chastity was equated with celibacy. This allegedly evangelical life of the monks deserved nothing better than to be abolished, although he did not entirely exclude the possibility of a genuinely Christian monastic life. Duke George might scold Luther in any way he wished, as long as he did not label him a faithful, pious monk. The slanderous designation of "perjuring and apostate monk" had thus provided the opportunity for Luther once again to give an impressive justification of his reason for leaving the monastery. Luther did not discuss any of the other charges in the *Apology;* by his own admission he had not even read it completely, for he was long since fed up with the simplemindedness of the "snot-nose" (Cochlaeus). The only other thing he did was to take issue with the defamation of the deceased Elector John. Naturally, Cochlaeus responded to this *Small Reply* by publishing his *Small Response,* but it contained nothing new.

This final literary exchange between Luther and Duke George appears to have remained an internal Saxon affair. There were no reprintings elsewhere. In November 1533 the dispute between the Saxon princes was settled by a court of arbitration. No longer were the theologians to mention the affairs of the princes or their names in their writings. Defamatory books and letters were prohibited altogether. Luther was apparently satisfied with this resolution of the matter.[13] He had not begun this dispute, but only defended himself and his cause when he could not escape the controversy.

Duke George's Defeat in the Fight against the Reformation

The confessional friction between the two Saxonies continued despite the arbiter's decision, and therefore the advice of the Wittenberger theologians was again solicited. In 1534 Duke George wanted to attach to parishes of his duchy those villages of the counts of Einsiedel that belonged to his territory but were incorporated into Electoral Saxon parishes. The duke was entitled to do so on the basis of earlier agreements, and even the Wittenbergers recognized the legality of this. The most they could do was advise that they be attached only to such parishes that would not prevent people from going to listen to sermons and receive the sacrament in the territory of Electoral Saxony. Otherwise, the counts would have to make clear to their subjects that in this case they could not protect them, although believers nevertheless should not fall away from the gospel.[14]

At the end of 1534 Duke John of Saxony, the son of Duke George, complained to Elector John Frederick that Luther had attacked his father and Archbishop Albrecht of Mainz in his sermon on All Saints' Day. Because this would have been a violation of the agreements made the previous year between the Saxon princes, Luther was instructed to substantiate thoroughly any of his statements with facts and biblical references, so that a new conflict would not arise. Luther advised the elector not to go too far in accommodating Duke George, but he did write the requested letter. He wished that the elector did not have to bother with the matter. He would prefer to refrain from giving a more precise report. It would be better not to reopen the old wounds. Duke George could certainly make no regulations about what people in Electoral Saxony might say. Luther would not acknowledge him and Albrecht of Mainz as his schoolmasters, but, if necessary, he was prepared to answer before the elector. He admitted to Chancellor Brück that he no longer knew whether he had also criticized Duke George in addition to Albrecht of Mainz. His polemics against George, properly speaking, had ceased since the agreement the previous year. Evidently George also had no interest in pursuing the matter further. The elector then merely admonished Luther, for the sake of peace and compliance with the agreement, to spare the duke as much as possible. In contrast, he did not need to impose any limitations upon George's theologians.[15]

When 130 people were expelled from Mittweida by Duke George in 1535 because they wanted to commune under both kinds, Luther declined to send them a letter of consolation because of the agreement and recommended that Lauterbach, the Leisnig deacon, comfort them verbally.[16] In the same year Duke George also expelled some nobles who had received the Lord's Supper under both kinds. Thereupon Elector John Frederick employed the same measures against some Catholic nobles in his territory. The duke did not comply with an agreed-upon date for mediation in February 1536. For Luther this was new evidence of Duke George's vindictiveness, for which God would punish him. It filled him with satisfaction that in his hardness of heart the duke, unlike the elector, was unable to pray. When in 1536 Landgrave Philip did succeed in effecting a compromise whereby the expulsions of the nobles were rescinded while they on their part had to obey their respective church constitutions, Luther also rejoiced, although he continued to doubt that Duke George would cease his hatred and wrangling.[17]

In the first half of 1535 Luther used the withholding of both kinds in the sacrament as the theme of one of the practice disputations that were resumed at that time. It was directed against the decrees of the Council of Constance on this subject and against its defenders. The theses were not only printed in Latin, but Luther also published an expanded version in German.[18] Undoubtedly he wanted in this indirect way to take a fundamental stand on these acute arguments in Saxony. The decision of the Council of Constance was presented as an arbitrary repudiation of Christ's own command. The subtle arguments supporting it were exposed as untenable, and the council, along with the pope and the anti-Christian opponents of the true church, were unmasked.

After 1536, defending the old faith in the duchy became increasingly difficult. George's brother, Henry, who governed the districts of Freiberg and Wolkenstein, drew close to the Reformation under the influence of his wife, Katharine von Mecklenburg. In 1531 he himself had already asked the elector to summon Luther to Torgau in order to listen to him preach. Once in 1534 he was in Wittenberg and held a friendly conversation with Luther.[19] Among the evangelicals in Freiberg in 1535 was Jerome Weller's sister, who asked Luther's permission to celebrate the Lord's Supper with bread and wine in her home, a request that Luther rejected here—as he did in other situations—because of objections in principle.[20] Duke George's increasing oppression of his brother Henry led to the latter's entrance into the Smalcald League in 1536. Henry's temporary displeasure, which was caused by Luther's advocacy on behalf of the alleged Freiberg Anabaptist Matthes Lotther, did not change this rapprochement. In 1536 Henry's wife asked the elector for an evangelical preacher, who out of consideration for the situation in the duchy was to be unmarried and ordained. Luther obtained Jacob Schenk, still single at the time, who then created the first Reformation order for the Freiberg area.[21] When Schenk had to leave Freiberg in 1538 because of difficulties with the preacher Paul Lindenau, Nicholas Hausmann was to become the superintendent in his native city. Luther composed the formal letter for him to present the bishop of Meissen announcing his assumption of the position, which made no secret of his rejection of the papal errors, but also stated his basic acceptance of the bishop's office. Immediately after his initial sermon Hausmann unexpectedly suffered a stroke. At first the news of his friend's sudden death was kept from the ailing Luther, but Luther knew the deceased was in God's hands.[22]

At the beginning of 1537 Duke John, George's son and heir presumptive, was seriously ill. Luther prayed for him in the worship service on 14 January, that he might realize his errors and have a blessed end. At the time he did not know that John had died three days earlier. The young duke had promised his father to continue his anti-Lutheran politics. Luther saw his death as a judgment of God that forestalled the actions of the tyrants.[23]

George now tried, with the cooperation of the estates, to ensure that his last son, the mentally handicapped Duke Frederick, would succeed him so that Henry, his evangelical brother, would not come to power. At the end of January 1539 Frederick did in fact marry. Luther was convinced that George's plans would not come to fruition. When Frederick died only four weeks later, Luther could not help but feel vindicated in his view that the curse of God was upon Duke George.[24]

After Duke John's death, some of George's counselors, unlike him, sought to reach a solution to the religious question, something that was absolutely essential. Already in 1534 there had been a religious colloquy in Leipzig between the electorate of Mainz and Electoral Saxony, at which on one side were Michael Vehe, dean in Halle, and—representing Duke George and the bishop of Meissen—Julius Pflug, and on the other Melanchthon and Brück. An agreement was thwarted principally by the question of the mass. This first Leipzig colloquy did not signify any concession on Duke George's part. He would have agreed only with a conclusion that was acceptable to the old church.[25] Apparently Luther hardly took notice of the second Leipzig colloquy in January 1539, at which Brück and Melanchthon again attended from Electoral Saxony, Chancellor Feige and Bucer from Hesse, and the counselors George von Carlowitz and Ludwig Fachs—accompanied by George Witzel as theologian—from Ducal Saxony. An agreement based on the doctrine of the ancient church seemed too vague to Luther from the beginning, and no settlement was reached. In his opinion it was the evangelical church that came closest to the apostolic ideal.[26] Luther even saw George's attempts to reform the churches and monasteries in the summer of 1538 solely as an illegitimate attack on the property of the church.[27]

Duke George died on 17 April 1539. Understandably, the death of one of his most persistent opponents occupied Luther and his associates many times in the following period. In his first reaction Luther associated the death of George and of his sons with his inexorable anti-Reformation attitude. In this case, however, it was not joy in someone else's misfortune that motivated him, although for him, in view of the fate of the Reformation, George's death was an answer to prayer. Luther would have preferred it if the duke had not died and had repented, as Luther had earlier advised. George's accursed death was an admonition to repent. Mixed with Luther's bewilderment was also his amazement that he had survived his bitterest enemy. He believed it was impossible to pray for the deceased duke. One might pray for Abel, but not simultaneously for the accursed Cain.[28] Luther also found it worthy of thought that, as could already be seen, it was now to be the fate of Duke Henry—whom his brother had treated badly, had excluded from any influence over the government, and moreover had tormented because of Henry's inclination toward the Reformation—to take over everything.[29] Henry began at this time to introduce the Reformation into Ducal Saxony. The animosity between Duke George and Luther had lasted for two decades, chiefly over religion. At the end the duke, unable to stem the evangelical movement set in motion by the rebellious monk, was the loser.

2. THE PRIVATE MASS AND THE CONSECRATION OF PRIESTS

There is no known direct occasion that induced Luther to write *The Private Mass and the Consecration of Priests*[1] in 1533, and probably there was none. In form it belongs to the controversies with Catholic doctrine, such as those Luther pursued in 1530 with *Disavowal of Purgatory* and *The Keys*.[2] The three drafts that have been preserved show that Luther had been occupied with the project for a long time but that he was prevented from completing it by illness. Originally he had wanted to concentrate on the consecration of priests, but then he placed the problem of private masses in the foreground.[3] In December 1533 he reported to Hausmann that with this attack he wanted to test the wisdom and power of the papists to see whether they were able to reply with adequate conviction to the devil's possible objections to private masses; if not, they would demonstrate that they were the abomination of the Antichrist. He assumed from the outset that there would be a negative outcome of his experiment of seeking papal wisdom, "that arrogant judge over God and man."[4] In the preface to the later Latin translation, which was made by Jonas, Luther did acknowledge that with the book he had wanted more to strengthen his own supporters than to attack the opposing side. At the same time he was happy that they felt they had encountered the truth in it, just as they had earlier in the Augsburg Confession.[5]

Luther began with an interesting retrospect. He had originally been declared a heretic because of his attack on indulgences, but at the Diet of Augsburg the papists themselves wanted nothing more to do with indulgences. Possibly the consecration of priests might become as obsolete as indulgences and purgatory. Luther's explanation took the form of confessing that he had been tempted by the devil, and he expected the Catholic clergy to absolve him.[6] Such temptations were not unknown to him, but in this work the ostensible confession was merely a literary device. It is nevertheless interesting, in observing Luther as an author, that he made use of such an artifice.

The devil's temptation was the question of whether the private masses that Luther had celebrated fifteen years before, in which he worshiped only the bread and wine, were not actually idolatry. Appeals to Luther's status as an ordained priest and to his appointment by the church were easy for the devil to demolish. The priests had nothing but a historic faith in Christ; in reality they trusted in the saints. In contrast to Christ's institution, private masses were not celebrations of the community. Also, in them the death of Christ was not proclaimed as he had commanded, but instead they had been turned into a sacrifice and a work, not something to strengthen the congregation in faith. The "mass priests" thus acted in opposition to Christ's intention. In private masses faith was lacking on the part of both priest and congregation, and they were not being performed in accordance with Christ's institution. The defect in the person administering the sacrament alone called the mass into question. The theory that the priest was acting in accordance with the intention of the church did not apply here because the church's action was not in accord with God's Word. Such objections could not be brushed aside by simply calling the devil a liar. The only help was to confess one's sins and flee to Christ with confidence: "Apart from myself [i.e., outside my own existence] and in Christ I am not a sinner, for he has blotted out my sin with his holy blood; I do not doubt that. [As proof] of this I have baptism and absolution and the sacrament as sure seals and letters." In this way Luther himself had overcome the devil's *Anfechtungen* and obtained absolution.

Both private masses and the consecration of priests were given up, but then began the real controversy on this issue with the papists.[7] Luther left unresolved whether Christ's body and blood were present at all in private masses. If they were not, the masses would be a fraud. Appealing to the church's practice and to the fathers of the church was of no value; the church, too, could be led astray. Even if Christ's body and blood were present in them, private masses had defrauded the congregation and become a scheme for making money. The mass priests were doing something criminal, and they would call God's wrath upon themselves. The fact that there were also parish masses in addition to private masses did not change the abuse. The laity should therefore stay away from private masses. Luther raised even greater doubts about the presence of Christ's body and blood in private masses. The words of institution were spoken inaudibly, and therefore there could be no control over whether they were even said at all. Luther could refer to quite a few spiritual shenanigans being carried on in Rome, and by Müntzer as well. Even if the words of institution were spoken aloud, there would still be no certainty that the priest spoke them in faith, especially because the whole institution of sacrificial masses in the church was wrong. The church had been perverted when it abandoned the norm of God's Word and set up its self-made articles of faith.

Because priests were consecrated in order to perform the sacrifice of the mass, the question arose whether theirs was a legitimate calling to an ecclesiastical office that authorized them to administer the Lord's Supper rightly. It was in this context that the fundamental problems of ordination and the understanding of the church came into view. Although the Antichrist had established himself in the papal church, it continued for Luther to be the church, for it had baptism, the gospel, absolution, congregational masses, prayer, and a series of other genuine signs of the church, which, however, were not being practiced by the priests saying private masses. Thus true and false practices existed side by side within the church. The secret masses and sacrificial masses had overwhelmed and perverted the Lord's Supper in the church. Baptism had become insignificant because of competition from satisfactions and good works. The consecration of priests had given the clergy a special status higher than the common Christian life initiated in baptism, and thereby devalued baptism. Consecrating a priest, however, was nothing but bestowing a commission to fill the office of a pastor or preacher. The spiritual estate, allegedly superior to that of being a Christian, was a carnival mask, a fiction. Luther did not abandon his earlier view of the priesthood of all believers. It was likewise easy to show that in many respects the church had allowed the preaching of the gospel to become corrupt. The call to the office of the ministry had been corrupted and it was restricted to the ability to perform the mass. Its real function, viz., to preach and to strengthen faith, which was the issue, had been invalidated.

Although Luther had been prepared in 1530 to permit the old hierarchy to exercise certain supervisory functions in the church,[8] he now announced: "We shall see to it that we get pastors and preachers on the basis of baptism and God's Word without their chrism, ordained and confirmed by our election and call." The evangelical church was entitled to perform such an ordination because it possessed God's Word: "Where God's Word is pure and certain, there everything else must be: God's kingdom, Christ's kingdom, the Holy Spirit, baptism, the sacrament [of the Lord's Supper], the office of the ministry, the office of preaching, faith, love, the cross, life and salvation, and everything the church should have." Bishops were not necessary for ordination. Here, too, Luther held the view that each pastor was the bishop of his congregation and if necessary, as happened in Wittenberg, he could also ordain for other congregations, i.e., convey the ministerial office. He characteristically had a different understanding of ordination, not as a consecration of a priest, which allegedly bestowed the ability to change bread and wine into Christ's body and blood. In Luther's opinion, it was the gospel itself that did this; a minister only mediated it as he did the gospel in preaching. In baptism, too, it was really Christ who was the baptizer, and the pastor functioned only as his agent. The authority officiating in the church was not the minister, but Christ and his Word. In this respect, the church was independent of its ministers and their blunders, in a sense, but despite them it still remained the church.

In this context Luther masterfully described what the evangelical celebration of the Lord's Supper was for him:

> For, God be praised, in our churches we can show a Christian a true Christian mass according to the ordinance and institution of Christ, as well as according to the true intention of Christ and the church. There our pastor, bishop, or minister in the pastoral office, rightly and honorably and publicly called, having been previously consecrated, anointed, and born in baptism as a priest of Christ, without regard to the private chrism, goes before the altar. Publicly and plainly

he sings what Christ has ordained and instituted in the Lord's Supper. He takes the bread and wine, gives thanks, distributes and gives them to the rest of us who are there and want to receive them, on the strength of the words of Christ: "This is my body, this is my blood. Do this," etc. Particularly we who want to receive the sacrament kneel beside, behind, and around him, man, woman, young, old, master, servant, wife, maid, parents, and children, even as God brings us together there, all of us true, holy priests, sanctified by Christ's blood, anointed by the Holy Spirit, and consecrated in baptism. On the basis of this our inborn, hereditary priestly honor and attire we are present, have, as Revelation 4 pictures it, our golden crowns on our heads, harps and golden censers in our hands, and we let our pastor say what Christ has ordained, not for himself as though it were for his person, but he is the mouth for all of us and we all speak the words with him from the heart and in faith, directed to the Lamb of God who is present for us and among us, and who according to his ordinance nourishes us with his body and blood. This is our mass, and it is the true mass which is not lacking among us.[9]

The pastor appears solely as the representative of the congregation, which is fed by Christ. In the congregation there are no spiritual or social distinctions. There is no room for a special role of the priest or arbitrary and selfish ecclesiastical machinations. Luther can do nothing but give thanks that, after all the former abuses, he can now experience the proper way of celebrating the mass.

With his presentation of the right and wrong forms of ecclesiastical practice, Luther's work had unexpectedly become longer than he planned. He therefore interrupted his exposition and gave a much briefer treatment than planned of the seven ranks within the priesthood and of ordination. He expressly warned the "fanatics" not to misunderstand his radical questioning of the private mass as if he were doubting the presence of Christ's body and blood in the Lord's Supper altogether. The constant interplay between the true and the perverted church within the papal church alone precluded this.[10] Luther's book became more than a polemic. With its understanding of ordination it established a basis for the evangelical procedure that was soon being practiced in Wittenberg. It also indicated clearly and unmistakably that Luther was intending to deal even more thoroughly with the topic of the church in connection with the Catholic plans for a council.[11]

As might have been expected, *The Private Mass and the Consecration of Priests* with its pointed formulations was subjected to criticism from various sides. Naturally, Cochlaeus and Arnoldi in Ducal Saxony rejected it and wrote rebuttals, but Luther paid little attention to them. Some of his statements were also taken out of context and used to justify the worship services of the old believers. Luther's dismissal of private masses as invalid was also unacceptable to some conservatives in his own camp, e.g., Prince John of Anhalt in Dessau. Despite all his assurances, Luther with his doubts about whether Christ's body and blood were present in the private masses appeared to be dangerously close to Zwingli's views.[12] Luther was therefore induced by

George of Anhalt in March 1534 to write *A Letter of Dr. Martin Luther concerning His Book on the Private Mass, to a Good Friend,*[13] employing the form of a letter to a fictitious recipient. Once again he declared that, despite all the abuses, Christ's body and blood were present in the masses of Catholic congregations; he himself had earlier experienced this to his comfort. This was not true of private masses; they had essentially departed from Christ's institution in many ways. Therefore a distinction had to be drawn between the sacrament and the private mass. The church was not allowed arbitrarily to change the ordinance of Christ. Where it did so, it could lose its identity as the church and become heretical. The papal church's interest in private masses was a purely financial one. Moreover, it would not accept the reformation of this mendicant monk. Luther might boast that he had done more reforming of indulgences, pilgrimages, bulls, and covetousness than had five councils, but reform of the mass, which was one of the commercial pillars of the church—the other was celibacy—was too much to take. Luther, however, expressly compared himself to Samson who had toppled the two pillars of the house of the Philistines—and thereby he may again have elicited sympathy for his side.

3. ERASMUS AND WITZEL

In 1525 Luther carried on one of his most intense theological disputes with Erasmus of Rotterdam.[1] It is less well known that later he was unable to put aside the controversy with the great humanist, and that it led to another direct confrontation in 1534. Although he otherwise scarcely took notice of the writings of his opponents, Luther was acquainted with surprisingly many of Erasmus's writings. As numerous scattered comments in the Table Talk show, he appears to have dealt with this author strikingly often. There is no indication that he read any other writer with similar frequency, a sign of the intellectual significance the scholar from Rotterdam had for his time. In the new edition of the Greek New Testament published by Erasmus in 1527, which Luther used in his later years, he made many marginal notes, usually critical ones, primarily on the *Annotationes*.[2] They continued to be the old objections he had raised against Erasmus: Erasmus was interested only in the moral teachings of the biblical stories. Luther supposed that Erasmus did not believe in God and that for this reason he was treating these topics so ambiguously and with such ridicule. Because he wrote so well, no one ventured to contradict him, but for Luther the frivolity he encountered in the *Colloquies,* for example, was unbearable.[3] The features of Erasmus's face, which Luther probably knew from the woodcut by Hans Holbein, revealed his craftiness, as did his style of writing. Erasmus's use of language in his famed *Praise of Folly* and his satire on Pope Julius was clever, to be sure, but it was extremely frosty. He never let himself be pinned down. It particularly bothered Luther that in his theology Erasmus did not know how to deal with Christ's incarnation. He made Christ into a jurist. In this context Luther announced in May 1532 that he was

78

beginning a new controversy: "God has given me strength for one more year. My intention is to pay back Erasmus and other enemies." Luther inculcated animosity toward Erasmus among his friends, for he believed that Erasmus was an enemy of religion. This was evident in Erasmus's dialogue concerning pilgrimages in which, because of only one abuse, religion in general was ridiculed. Luther later characterized Erasmus as his hated "Hydra." A single page from Terence was better reading than all Erasmus's *Colloquies,* which Luther wanted to forbid his sons to read.[4]

From the end of 1532 on, Luther once again was intently occupied with Erasmus. Erasmus thought he understood everything. That was a delusion. Because he could not grasp the "foolish" way God worked, he was not wise at all, but utterly stupid. Like the skeptic Epicurus, Erasmus was judging God from a worldly point of view. His ridicule of papal ceremonies was too weak because it was not founded on the doctrine of justification. He ultimately acknowledged the Catholic rites, e.g., in his dialogue *Puerpera* (the boy-bearer), and thus revealed himself as a papist, but at the same time he did it with such skepticism that it seemed God was not in a position to guide the world's confused course.[5] Luther did not agree with Erasmus's translation of John 1:1, "In the beginning was the sermon," instead of "the Word." Erasmus's poems inspired Luther to write his own Latin couplet: "Whoever hates not Satan, loves your songs, Erasmus. . . ." Possibly he may have been thinking of Erasmus's poem about Jesus, which Luther found ambiguous and derisive. Therefore, after serious deliberation, he had decided to slay Erasmus "with the pen," the way he once had done Müntzer. Luther railed against Erasmus and all of God's opponents with the petition of the Lord's Prayer, "Hallowed be thy name." Erasmus knew nothing of the mystery that "Another bears our sin." In his writings nothing could be found about faith in Christ or victory over sin, and this was in line with his critique of the evangelicals. Because this "villain" thought faith in Christ was one of the less important things that could be ignored, he was damned "by the power of Luther's authority."[6]

On 1 April 1533 Luther used the idleness imposed on him by illness to read Erasmus's prefaces to the New Testament books. Naturally, he was disturbed once again: The Epistle to the Romans was called difficult instead of salutary. Nothing more was said about its contemporary significance than about that of 1 John. There was no difference between Christ and Solon, the Greek lawgiver. Although Erasmus was hard to grasp, the evangelical church should condemn him and his writings, although many wise people would be offended. It would be better to lose them than to deny the Savior.[7] On the festival of the Annunciation (25 March) Luther had been angered that Erasmus had cast doubt upon the joy of Christ's incarnation with his explanations.[8] The cautious and ambiguous formulations in Erasmus's recently published *Enchridion,* which failed to give clear guidance, proved to Luther that Erasmus was not a genuine teacher of the church and prompted Luther to refute him.[9]

79

The proposed "condemnation" of Erasmus was not immediately produced. Early in 1534 those around Luther believed that he should first turn his attack against George Witzel. In 1531 Witzel had left his parish in Niemegk in Electoral Saxony because he was suspected of being a follower of John Campanus, the anti-Trinitarian. Witzel, however, was actually not a spiritualist. The difference between him and the Wittenbergers was that he wanted a conservative reform of the Catholic church in the spirit of the ancient church. In 1532 he had attacked the Lutheran doctrine of justification in his Latin work, *Defense of Good Works against the New Evangelists*. The humanist Crotus Rubeanus, once Luther's supporter in Erfurt but who then had become disenchanted with him and was now a canon in Halle in the service of Albrecht of Mainz, wrote the book's preface. Early in 1533 a book by the Hersfeld pastor, Balthasar Raida, against Witzel's "blasphemous and lying booklet" appeared, in which Raida strongly supported Luther. Luther himself wrote a preface for it. It labeled Witzel's critique an obvious lie, which was motivated—like that of "Doctor Toad [Crotus]"—by his desire to lick the boots of the papal party. Exaggeratedly, he reported that he had recently suffered a bellyache. But, after relieving himself of "such worms and toads" he felt better. "Whatever doesn't want to stay should just fly away." The process of purification vis-à-vis the conservative humanists was inevitable. These opponents ought to be prohibited from agitating because they were endangering the religious peace.[10]

Luther, and particularly Jonas, prevented Witzel from getting an appointment in 1532 to teach Hebrew at the University of Erfurt. In 1533 he was called to be the pastor of St. Andrew church in Eisleben by Count Hoyer of Mansfeld, who, in contrast to his brothers, remained a Catholic. In the city, however, which was almost entirely evangelical, he was in a difficult position. Luther advised the schoolmaster John Agricola and the preacher Caspar Güttel to leave Witzel alone.[11] The fact that Witzel was married put him in an especially delicate situation. Cochlaeus therefore advised him in a letter in 1534 to keep his marriage as secret as possible. Unfortunately, the wind blew the letter out the window. It landed in the neighboring garden of Agricola, and he immediately sent it to the Wittenbergers who saw that it was published with glosses.[12] Luther himself took no notice of the many works with their criticism of the Lutheran church and their defense of the Catholic church that Witzel wrote in the succeeding years, or he did so only incidentally. He did not consider him really dangerous and therefore ignored him in silence. Luther did not take seriously Witzel's attempt to bring about a reunification of the church at the second Leipzig colloquy in 1539. Later, too, he did not let himself be provoked by Witzel.[13]

Nicholas von Amsdorf had already dissuaded Luther from writing against Witzel in January 1534. Witzel had learned everything from Erasmus, against whom he himself later took issue. Amsdorf wished, however, that Luther would attack Erasmus and his ignorance and malice, who out of sheer avarice and toadying to the cardinals, bishops, and Catholic princes, was maligning Luther's doctrine as heresy.[14] Amsdorf was apparently referring to the Latin work published in the fall of 1533, *On Restoring the Unity of the Church,* which had made overcoming of the schism a primary Catholic concern.[15] This, for their contemporaries, was what Witzel and Erasmus had in common. In March Luther responded to the request with a lengthy letter to Amsdorf, which was immediately printed.[16] Luther first expressed his surprise that Amsdorf had totally rejected Erasmus. He himself had regarded Erasmus simply as theologically imprudent in the controversy about free will. But now he acknowledged that Amsdorf was right: Malice and ignorance were keeping Erasmus from acknowledging the substantial dogmatic commonality in the evangelical church and the papal church. He had shown this in *The Private Mass and the Consecration of Priests,* but Erasmus was not interested in doing so.

Luther exemplified this with Erasmus's *Enchridion,* which had likewise appeared in 1533.[17] It lacked clear, simple statements of faith; instead, the youth were confused by unnecessarily difficult questions. This complicated organization of the *Enchridion,* however, may have been more the fault of the intellectual humanist's pedagogical ineptness than of his theological intent. At this time it was apparent how much Luther's reading of Erasmus's writings the previous year had heightened his suspicions. He mentioned Erasmus's disparaging of Romans and his alleged belittling of the author of 1 John in his *Paraphrases,* which, however, Luther had misunderstood. Luther considered the *Methodus,*[18] which introduced the famous Greek New Testament, so complicated that it was unable to engender anything but loathing and hate for a religion presented in such a complex way. The *Epistle on Evangelical Philosophy,* which likewise was a part of his introduction to the New Testament, presented Christ as a more perfect man, but not as a savior.[19] In about 1522 this had originally aroused Luther's suspicion that Erasmus was a skeptic like Epicurus and a denier of Christ.

Luther distrusted Erasmus's oblique, slippery form of speaking, which was neither rhetorically nor theologically permissible, because it shook religion altogether. He considered it imperative to interpret Erasmus critically instead of complimentarily; otherwise, nothing could be considered a heresy and nothing would be certain. Luther accepted the accusation, which the Catholic side had raised, that Erasmus sympathized with the Arian denial of Christ's divinity and of the Trinity, because some of his statements indicated this. He had no intention of continuing to suffer "the tyranny of Erasmus's ambiguity." For example, he mentioned Erasmus's use of the risqué expression, "God's coitus with the Virgin," as a way of interpreting Mary's conception.[20] Luther thus assumed the freedom to condemn the tyranny of these ambiguities in a twofold manner, first by interpreting them against their author, and then by denouncing their use in his deficient, likewise ambiguous commentary. Erasmus should be regarded as the evil enemy sowing tares among the wheat.

Luther let it be known that he did not regard this open letter as a true rebuttal directed against Erasmus—which it was in a basic sense—but rather as an explanation of why he no longer wanted to dispute with him. It would only keep him from doing more important work. He had already learned while writing *The Bondage of the Will* how difficult it was to carry on a disputation with Erasmus, who was so hard to pin down. At that time Luther himself was depicted by his opponent as damned, full of envy, arrogance, and bitterness, even possessed by the devil. After these initial statements, which sounded as if he were resigned, Luther proceeded to draw the conclusion: It may have been difficult earlier to canonize a deceased monk, but with their hate toward him they could easily become saints themselves even during their own lifetime, and, moreover, it would prove to be a lucrative business. In this Luther himself was suffering the same fate of apostles, saints, bishops, and of John Huss. This was not all, for he continued sarcastically: Luther thought it advisable to refrain from replying to Erasmus and to do nothing but bear witness against him, so that Erasmus might be relieved of his old fear of being considered a Lutheran. "For, as Christ lives, they are doing him [Erasmus] a great injustice, and I must protect him from his enemies, who accuse him of being a Lutheran, for in no way—I am a reliable and true witness—is he a Lutheran, but just Erasmus." Otherwise, he wanted Erasmus kept out of the evangelical schools. Erasmus's speech was not edifying. He should be delivered over to the papists, who deserved such an apostle. Unequaled self-confidence echoed in his concluding words: "Our Lord Jesus Christ, in whose power I know and am certain that he often has freed me from death, in whom I have begun all this in faith, and in whom I have done things that amaze even my enemies, will preserve us and keep us free until the end. . . ."

In form alone this was one of Luther's greatest letters—it did not lack polished elegance—and it is also one of the sharpest ever written against Erasmus. When we look closely we see that Luther refrained from totally condemning him as he had originally planned. He concentrated on attacking Erasmus's rhetoric and his use of language, which was truly Erasmus's own medium, and by so doing he deftly emphasized the difference between subtleties—elegant but dissociated from dogmatics—and public, clear statements of faith. In this respect Erasmus was plainly exposed. Surprisingly, there was little wider response. The letter was not reprinted, perhaps an indication that the scholars' interest in this controversy had waned.

Melanchthon was concerned that the controversy was being reopened because of the passion of old age, and he did not conceal this from Luther. Luther secretly hoped that Erasmus would take a stand and that the result would be a clear separation between him—and his supporters like Crotus and Witzel—and the church.[21] Some scholars in Wittenberg were irritated with Amsdorf for inciting Luther to write his letter. Amsdorf defended himself before the end of March 1534 with a book of his own, but Luther did not want it printed in Wittenberg in deference to friend (!) and foe. In this context, nevertheless, he declared that he had assuredly not yet expended all his ammunition against Erasmus.[22]

Before the end of April 1534 Erasmus published his *Vindication against Luther's Rash Letter.*[23] He did not believe he had given Luther any new reason to write it, and he deliberately limited himself to presenting a defense against the "demonic" charges made by Luther, who was motivated by hate and a lust for power. He was at a loss to understand the criticism of his way of speaking, for in his opinion there was never any doubt about his intention of supporting the church. He had never been under suspicion by the church, but it had been proved that Luther himself was. It was self-evident that Luther would take issue with his rules of grammar, and consequently that he would maliciously interpret his way of speaking in images. In some places he could show that Luther had quoted him in a way that was contrary to his meaning. In conclusion, Erasmus presented himself as justified, and Luther as a pathological complainer who had gotten almost everything from Huss and Wycliffe. His polemic language was obviously not Christian. Instead of this, Erasmus recommended that Luther take issue with those polemic treatises that were uncomfortable for him—probably thinking of Cochlaeus and Witzel—which he considered unworthy of a reply.

Unlike Luther's letter, Erasmus's book enjoyed a certain response, primarily by the Catholic side, and it was reprinted several times. At the end of June 1534 it was also known in Wittenberg; it was initially kept from Luther himself by his friends for fear that it would rekindle his wrath. He had also not decided whether he should reply.[24] Erasmus's 1533 book on unity was answered the following year by the Hessian pastor Antonius Corvinus, and Schirlentz, the Wittenberg printer, asked Luther to write a preface for it in order to improve sales.[25] Luther accommodated himself to the measured style of Corvinus's argument. He was convinced that the Lutherans would never lack interest in unity for the sake of love, and he referred to their efforts on behalf of peace. He never considered that the opposing side was expecting him to pursue the controversy in a different style. For neither side could there be an agreement on the doctrine of the faith that took the form of a compromise. Unlike Erasmus, Luther could not accept the church as the arbiter of questions of truth; that would be a capitulation to the pope. The church needed the certain Word of the Bible as its firm anchor. This exclusive norm was not accepted by the opposing side, nor by Erasmus. Consequently, no real agreement was possible. After Corvinus became aware of the *Vindication,* he conceded to Luther that no "conversion" on Erasmus's part was to be expected.[26]

Luther never wrote a new work against Erasmus. The *Vindication* had given him no reason to do so. Any discussion between these two great intellectuals of their time was hopeless. They were using different languages and they intended thereby to say different things; thus they were talking past one another. Erasmus died in 1536. Although he died with a prayer on his lips, Luther assumed that his opponent had come to an evil end because in the Protestant city of Basel he had refused the ministrations of a cleric.[27] In later years when the conversation around Luther's table occasionally turned to Erasmus, he usually repeated his earlier negative opinions. Only occasionally did he also have a favorable word, e.g., about the *Adages*, Erasmus's great collection of proverbs, which Luther also enjoyed using. He considered the famous edition of the Greek New Testament and its notes outdated. It should be suppressed, especially because the sacramentarians, e.g., Zwingli, had been led astray by it.[28]

Luther certainly had read the edition of the *Apophthegmata*, a collection of classical sentences published in 1543, and in it he made marginal notes, which generally ridiculed Erasmus's pagan moralism. In his lectures he mentioned that even the vilest work of a Christian peasant or of a Christian handmaid would be regarded more highly by God than all the valiant deeds of the ancient heroes.[29] Luther had no use for the humanists' synthesis of antiquity and Christianity; nevertheless, it was able to survive in the intellectual world of Protestantism and became a competitor of Luther's heritage. Seen from this perspective, Luther was unable to discern the spirits in this controversy.

4. THE INJUSTICE OF ARCHBISHOP ALBRECHT OF MAINZ

As with Duke George of Saxony, Luther also continued to have nothing good to say about Archbishop Albrecht of Mainz, who was then residing in Halle.[1] At the end of 1533, Albrecht, together with his brother, Elector Joachim I of Brandenburg, had enjoined a strict anti-Reformation policy on the dukes of Brunswick and on Duke George. At Pentecost 1534, as previously in Leipzig, he similarly expelled seventeen evangelical council members from Halle because they had refused to commune at Easter by receiving only bread without the cup. Luther asked Elector John Frederick to intercede for the exiles. His previous experience made him think that a forceful writing might possibly make an impression on the "hopeless coward" in Halle. Luther himself only occasionally polemicized in sermons against this "creature of the pope," but since 1534 he had been planning a new literary attack on him.[2]

The Schönitz Affair

In contrast to his conflict with Duke George, Luther's dispute with the archbishop in the following period had less to do with religious matters than with the legal case of Hans Schönitz, a great merchant in Halle. For years Albrecht had entrusted him with complicated financial dealings involving high expenditures and expenses, and Schönitz had exploited this to his own advantage. He probably also profited illegally from doing do. Because of his increasing debt, Albrecht resorted again and again to levying taxes on his estates, but he failed to keep his promise to use these funds to discharge his old obligations. In 1534 the estates refused to approve new taxes unless Albrecht rendered an accounting, which would have been a great embarrassment for him. As far as can be determined, Albrecht blamed his complicated financial dealings on Schönitz, his chamberlain. He had him arrested and forced a confession from him on the rack, which, however, the accused later retracted. Schönitz's family instituted charges against Albrecht before the imperial supreme court, but in the summer of 1535 Hans Schönitz was condemned to death on the gallows, and the sentence was carried out at once.[3]

This was not the end of the matter. Anthony Schönitz, the offender's brother, fled from Halle and sought a legal clarification. His appeals for lodging and legal support were commended by Luther several times to Elector John Frederick, with success.[4] Luther also came to deal with the Schönitz affair in another way. Ludwig Rabe, the chamberlain's clerk (*Kammerschreiber*) in Halle, had criticized the archbishop's practices of collecting taxes. He escaped imminent arrest by fleeing to Wittenberg, where he lodged in Luther's house. Apparently afraid of Luther's criticism, Albrecht of Mainz dispatched a threatening letter in order to intimidate Rabe and keep him from saying too much about Schönitz's case. Luther took this as the occasion to write a letter attacking the cardinal on this issue. He stated that he could not be prohibited from forming an opinion about the Schönitz affair, nor could he be prevented from expressing it. The "hellish cardinal" could not hang everyone in Germany who thought ill of him because of this. Luther spoke uninhibitedly about judicial murder and recalled that he had brought discredit upon Albrecht many times since the indulgence controversy. The new wave of public criticism that was engulfing the cardinal could not be stemmed. The threatening letter to Rabe only revealed Albrecht's evil conscience. Luther did not expect Albrecht to listen to reason. His letter was a sort of prophetic announcement of judgment: The "real hangman" would come for Albrecht.[5] On the basis of his earlier experiences with the archbishop, Luther's attitude toward this high representative of the papal church was dominated by deep distrust from the outset, and to this extent confessional considerations also played a role in the conflict.

In the troublesome dispute with Schönitz's family, Albrecht of Mainz attempted to enlist Prince George of Anhalt, who as cathedral dean in Magdeburg was in a certain sense obligated to him, as a mediator. Luther could only warn George not to get involved with the untrustworthy cardinal. In February 1536 he sent to Albrecht himself another letter with a pamphlet (*Zeitung*) about the judicial murder of Schönitz, in order to make it clear to him that the affair could not be covered up with an amicable settlement. Thereby he once again assumed the role of a prophet of judgment who was speaking to his counterpart's conscience. The accusations now became specific: Schönitz had been arrested at the Moritzburg in Halle, although it was not the archbishop who had legal jurisdiction there, but the elector of Saxony. Albrecht claimed authority in this case because Schönitz was his official. The accused had not been permitted to make a defense. The execution had been carried out while the case was still pending before the imperial supreme court. Schönitz was being blamed for Albrecht's dishonest financial policies. Therefore, Luther said with unmistakable clarity: "Because your electoral highness shits upon the emperor and his supreme court, takes the law from the city of Halle and the sword from Saxony, and moreover thinks that reason and the whole world are soiled toilet paper . . . and treats everything so pope-like, Roman-like, and cardinal-like, our Lord God will make sure through our prayer, if he pleases, that your electoral highness himself will have to pay for this crap." If Schönitz, who was acting as Albrecht's agent, was a thief, then the cardinal should be hanged ten times on a far higher gallows. Luther therefore announced that he was going to write a book against the cardinal, for which the cardinal was not prepared, and this time Luther would not spare him personally the way he had in 1527 at the murder of George Winkler, the preacher at the Halle foundation. Luther closed his letter by ironically presenting his respects to the blood-red cardinal's hat. Melanchthon was offended by the form of the letter and thought it politically inopportune. In contrast, however, the reaction of Albrecht himself was both surprising and characteristic. Not only did he bestow gifts on the letter carrier and offer Luther himself the role of media-tor—which he rejected—but he sought to effect a reconciliation with the Schönitz family.[6]

Luther had little success with his repeated pleas to George of Anhalt to stay out of the Schönitz affair because the cardinal was interested only in stalling. George did not believe that his mediation was serving to delay things. Ulti-mately Luther agreed that, along with Prince George, Jonas should become involved as a reliable advocate for the Schönitz family's interests. The result-ing proposal for a settlement, however, once again confirmed for Luther how rotten Albrecht's case was. Jonas appears to have shared Luther's viewpoint. The supposition that Albrecht was interested only in delaying matters proved to be correct. The discussions dragged on through all of 1537 so that in December Jonas, with Luther's agreement, threatened to withdraw from his mediatorial activity, but he then did not follow through.[7]

Luther's announcement that he intended to attack Albrecht of Mainz in print roused the other princes of the house of Hohenzollern, at Albrecht's request, to action. At the end of September 1536, Elector Joachim II of Bran-denburg had a discussion with Luther at the court in Torgau. Together with his cousin, Margrave George of Brandenburg-Ansbach, he also had a subsequent meeting with Luther on 1 November in Wittenberg, where the chancellor of Duke Albrecht of Prussia was staying at the time and for the same reason. In December, Luther had to report to Chancellor Brück. It would have made more sense, Luther thought, for the Hohenzollern princes to talk to Albrecht of Mainz. If he vilified the cardinal for being a rascal, he had no intention of bringing reproach on the house of Hohenzollern; Albrecht had already done that. It was the task of a prophet to call even the mighty to account. If Luther thereby committed an injustice against the cardinal, he was subject to the law of the elector of Saxony. Luther also probably promised Brück to refrain from issuing his book against the archbishop if Albrecht would cease persecuting the evangelicals in Halle. At the beginning of 1537, Albrecht of Prussia urgently asked Luther to admonish the archbishop privately once more, and he promised that he and other nobles would support him.[8]

In February 1538 a conference in Zerbst, which was attended by ten princes of Saxony, Hohenzollern, and Brunswick, along with Landgrave Philip, discussed the Schönitz affair and attempted to reach a settlement respecting the interests that Mainz and Electoral Saxony had in Halle. Albrecht of Mainz was the only one who did not attend, and his chancellor resorted to the crassest legal machinations, appealing to the decision to place the case against Schönitz before the imperial supreme court, which had been ignored when he was executed. Luther's announcement that he would expose this fraud was understandable. He could not help but feel his opinion was vindicated: If any criminal were deserving of death here, it was Albrecht of Mainz. Luther was adamantly opposed to Elector John Frederick relinquishing Saxony's legal jurisdiction in Halle to Albrecht, even though it might be of little value. In a sermon, probably in May, he denied altogether that Albrecht possessed the title of bishop. Because of Albrecht's limited rights of sovereignty in Halle, Luther occasionally referred to him as the "hangman and city clerk in Halle." Several times during the course of 1538 Luther revived his old intention of publicly attacking the archbishop's crimes.[9]

The Scandal over Simon Lemnius's Epigrams

Luther's aversion to Albrecht of Mainz was heightened once more by an event in Wittenberg. Since 1534, Simon Lemnius (ca. 1514–50), from Graubünden, had been studying there at Melanchthon's encouragement. Because of his interest in ancient languages, a career as a humanistic scholar seemed to lie before him. He was highly regarded among the circle of younger Wittenberg humanists for his translation of Homer and his gift for writing elegant Latin verse. His frivolous life style was not entirely suited to Wittenberg, but it was not particularly conspicuous.[10]

At Pentecost 1538 a small collection of Lemnius's epigrams, which had been printed by Nickel Schirlentz without the usual approval of the university, was offered for sale outside the Wittenberg church. Allegedly it was Luther who immediately noticed that some of the poems struck too close to leading Wittenberg personages. For example, they mentioned the drunkenness of the city captain, Hans Metzsch, cast doubt on the marital fidelity of the wife of the printer Hans Lufft, and questioned the looks of a girl who never went to the public bath. After closer scrutiny, some readers claimed to find insults directed against Chancellor Brück, even against the elector. All of this was so disguised, however, that, except perhaps for the ostentatious moral laxity, it might have been completely overlooked. (Later, even Lessing supported Lemnius's poetic freedom.) When those who were mentioned complained to Melanchthon, the university rector, Lemnius was placed under house arrest on the same day, his volume of poetry confiscated at the printer's, and the printer himself immediately locked up. Breaking his bond, Lemnius fled the next day when the city gates were opened to let the cattle out. The rector's attempt to cite the fugitive before him was naturally in vain.[11]

On the following Sunday, Luther, in his capacity as Pastor Bugenhagen's substitute, read from the pulpit an admonition, which then was also printed and posted on the church doors.[12] Members of the congregation should burn the "slanderous poetizing." In this way conspicuous action should be taken against evil gossip. The admonition shows that Luther was opposed to the epigrams for other reasons. Lemnius had dedicated them to Albrecht of Mainz, who was regarded as a patron of the humanists, and in several poems he had flattered the archbishop and those around him. For example, he had praised his love of peace and even his zeal for the old religion, which distinguished Albrecht from the evangelical princes. Lemnius was not alone in cultivating such contacts. His friend, George Sabinus, Melanchthon's son-in-law, had occasionally done so, and even Melanchthon himself had dedicated his commentary on Romans in 1532 to Albrecht. Luther considered such public toadying to the archbishop intolerable, especially from Wittenberg, "because this same shit-bishop is a false, deceptive man and yet he likes to call us Lutheran knaves." If the duplicitous poets did not stop this, Luther would take action against them. Once again a showdown with Albrecht loomed. This was the real nub of the scandal that Lemnius had initiated; it dealt with Reformation politics. The vehemence of Luther's statement attracted attention as far away as the evangelicals in southern Germany and Switzerland. Chancellor Brück and then the elector as well took offense at the allusions to themselves, somewhat differently than had Luther. A thorough investigation was therefore ordered, which was primarily intended to ascertain who was responsible for the printing. It was discovered that Sabinus and other friends had conspired with Lemnius. Harsh measures were imposed on the printer Schirlentz. Only through Luther's intervention was he able to escape banishment, and initially he was prohibited from pursuing his trade. Finally in September Luther was able to arrange for him to resume his printing.[13]

As the rector, Melanchthon had an awkward part to play in handling the matter. He was the first to see the epigrams, but he did not recognize their explosiveness. Even in the final condemnation of Lemnius, which he formulated, he merely decried abusing poetry by using it to spread evil rumors. He was held responsible for Lemnius's escape. It was believed, to a large extent unjustly, that he had known about the poems in advance. In July he thought that he would be driven out of Wittenberg. Only then did he write an apology to the elector in which he defended his innocence, but he was uncertain whether this would still the storm. For a while he himself considered leaving Wittenberg, but then he thought it better, because of his obligations, quietly to await the outcome.[14]

In September 1538 Lemnius published an enlarged edition of his epigrams that was full of malicious references to the Wittenbergers, including Jonas and Luther, who, as he declared, was raging like a tyrant. Some of his indecent poems also mentioned Luther's alleged unchaste marriage. In contrast, Melanchthon was conspicuously spared. Luther responded with a poem about the filthy "shit-poet," whom Albrecht of Mainz patronized, and it was not difficult for him to write it because he was suffering from diarrhea at the time. Melanchthon, too, was now in favor of taking immediate action against Lemnius.[15] In 1539 Lemnius crowned his rage against Luther by writing a drama, *Monachopornomachia*, the "monks-whores-war." This time his verses, in the opinion of some Latinists, were good, but the plot was weak. In it the wives of Luther, Jonas, and Spalatin spoke in an explicitly obscene way about their married lives and illicit affairs. Lemnius, incidentally, also cultivated this obscene genre in later love poems after he returned to his homeland. The play stood in the tradition of the ancient poet Martial and it picked up the earlier polemics against Luther's marriage, although it far surpassed them and was one of the most disgusting concoctions of the age. It failed to have much of an effect, however, because it lacked any reference to reality. Cochlaeus was the only one with whom it found favor, and later he worked on a similar level, which thus distorted the Catholic image of Luther for a long period of time. Luther himself reacted to the libelous work with "Christian" imperturbability. Years later he declared with fervor that it was absolutely impermissible to talk obscenely about women the way such a "horsefly" (*Arschhummel*) like Lemnius did. Anyone who loved reading such things could not have a gracious God.[16]

A Letter Carrier for the High Judge

Luther's impassioned attack on Albrecht of Mainz, and his repeated announcement in the work against Lemnius that he was going to write against Albrecht, brought forth the house of Hohenzollern once again. Joachim II of Brandenburg complained to Elector John Frederick, who also conceded that "it would be better if Doctor Martinus had refrained from such writings and were to refrain from them in the future." But, like his predecessor, the elector would not impose any conditions upon Luther in this regard, "for his doctrine, God be praised, is becoming purer and more powerful in the church from day to day."[17] Duke Albrecht of Prussia approached Luther directly concerning his work against Lemnius. He acknowledged that there were abuses among the clergy, but he admonished Luther to be patient. Luther's acerbity was offending many. He should also have consideration for the house of Brandenburg. In his reply Luther said only that illustrious houses also produced spoiled children. Also, the other Hohenzollerns were unable to agree with the politics of the archbishop, for they had demonstrated as much at the meeting of the princes in Zerbst. Duke Albrecht did not dispute this, but once again in October 1538 he attempted to dissuade Luther from attacking his cousin.[18] A last attempt in this direction was undertaken by Prince Wolfgang of Anhalt on 22 December when he sent Augustine Schurf, the physician, and Jonas to Luther. They spoke to him in the church about this, but accomplished nothing. Luther himself wrote to the prince that it was the fault of the cardinal himself, blinded and hardened in heart, that Luther needed to attack him, but he was certain that his book would have no effect on the one to whom he was writing. Later he looked back and said with some justification: "I had difficulties about the book because they wanted to stop it."[19]

Luther had been involved with this book against Albrecht of Mainz for almost two years. He had given considerable thought to it and had spent some effort in preparing an outline. Before starting to write, around mid-December, he had some initial anxiety, but then his pen moved rapidly.[20] The work, in fact, came all at once. Because of Luther's previous attacks, people were generally expecting a vehement vilification, but now Luther was writing not on the spur of the moment but on the basis of careful reflection. Thus with this indictment, *Against the Bishop of Magdeburg, Cardinal Albrecht*,[21] one of the most significant of Luther's statements on questions of justice came into being, one which went far beyond the specific circumstances of its origin and which has unfairly been almost forgotten. It was completed at the beginning of 1539. In it Luther referred frequently to an account—printed in Wittenberg the previous year, perhaps with Luther's support—by Anthony Schönitz of his brother's case and to a "rebuttal" by Albrecht's Magdeburg counselors, which he belittled as a plagiarizing "copycat sermon" (*Gänsepredigt*) because in it the accusations in Schönitz's account were refuted point by point. Moreover, the "rebuttal" intended to prove that Hans Schönitz had cheated and deceived his master. The material it contained, however, was of some weight.

First Luther explained why he had refused Albrecht's request that he serve as a mediator. He wanted to support Hans Schönitz, who had been unjustly put to death; this he had long since decided. Vis-à-vis the wily cardinal, this was a dangerous venture. Luther seemed like a sheep before the wolf. In so doing he would rely not on legal skills, but solely on the Holy Scriptures. In response to the interventions of Duke Albrecht of Prussia, he stated once again that he did not want to attack the house of Hohenzollern, but with many examples he demonstrated that even from good houses come spoiled children. That was true of human nature in general: "No human body is so beautiful and healthy that no snot, scabs, pus, and other filth comes from it." Noble lineage may not serve as a cover for injustice, and no one should say that this was only a single episode. "For princes are not appointed by God in order to plague widows, orphans, and poor, suffering people, but to protect, rescue, and help them, and so are jurists and counselors."

Luther expanded this into a fundamental principle: The nobles rejected any criticism of themselves as "shameful preaching and shameful books." Nevertheless, one could not refrain from criticizing the "shameful nobility." "A praiseworthy noble is one who fears God, honors his Word, is faithful and obedient to his prince and lord, chastely and honorably rules his house, and protects and supports his poor people wherever he can. A shameful noble is one who despises God's Word, practices villainy, is proud and arrogant, oppresses and mistreats poor people, and is unfaithful and disobedient to his prince and lord. And there are certainly more shameful nobles than praiseworthy nobles." Here we catch a glimpse of Luther's opinion of a leading class of society. The nobility are like women: The honorable ones deserve all respect, "for they are our mother, sister, wife, daughters, aunts. We have all lain under their hearts and have been nourished by blood from their hearts before our birth and have sucked their breasts after our birth and have been nurtured from the cradle with great effort and care." This should not prevent us, however, from criticizing whores, adulteresses, and witches. When criticism is necessary one cannot be concerned about status or family.

In this preface considerable objections were already included. Skillfully and impressively Luther continued the book by describing his own role. He abandoned the attitude of a prophet of judgment he had adopted earlier. He did not understand himself to be a judge at all, "but because, miserable as I am, I am a servant of the high and just judge and for thirty years I have sat in his chancellery not far from the door and I have also been a messenger and letter carrier, so that I have learned in a seemly way what sort of verdict is usually issued in that chancellery. . . ." Thereby he once again created a literary device that was appropriate for him. The interpreter of the Scripture found the verdict on Schönitz and the cardinal in the Bible, specifically in Job 31:13-15, where it said that the right of a servant was to be respected. Legally, servant and master are equal. Luther operated on the basis of this legal principle: "The thing speaks for itself." This meant that Albrecht was a party to the Schönitz case and could not be a judge. As he previously had done in the case of the peasants and with Hans Kohlhase,[22] Luther confronted the archbishop and elector with the same legal principle, which confirmed the unity of his political thought. Anthony Schönitz, too, had applied this argument in his account. This culminated in a frightful attack on the legal process. Albrecht was *richter nullus*, a non-judge. Schönitz and his family had declared they were willing to accept a legal ruling on the affair, and finally the imperial supreme court had assumed jurisdiction over the matter. Albrecht anticipated its action by executing Schönitz and confiscating his property, and thus he was a "murderer, bloodhound, tyrant, robber, and thief." This was not Luther's verdict—he was merely the messenger—but God's verdict. And God demanded restitution.

Then the entire case was reviewed. Albrecht's defenders appealed to written proof that Schönitz had embezzled. Nevertheless, this did not justify taking justice into one's own hands. The accused should have received a hearing. From his own experience Luther acknowledged how much legal cases occasionally had impressed him when he had information from only one side. "But when the other side came out, everything was false." Cases in which Luther unjustifiably advocated one side on the basis of partisan information are still apparent today. Luther may have too quickly passed over the actual substance of the allegations against Schönitz. Additional accusations were flimsy. He had allegedly demanded gifts from Albrecht, and this was construed as theft. Schönitz could no longer answer, but in this case the facts spoke against the cardinal. In addition, the great expenditures were blamed on Schönitz. If that was criminal, matters were even worse with the cardinal, who loved to build, and also with the pope in Rome.

Schönitz's confession had been obtained on the rack and he later had repudiated it. Luther therefore introduced a fundamental discussion of the problem of using torture as a means of ascertaining truth. He gave examples to show that it was an extremely uncertain means, which often led to false statements and, at best, it could be nothing more than a stopgap measure. "Wherever one can have the law in the light of day, one should refrain from such dark injustice." Only with hardened criminals was torture appropriate, for otherwise, according to Luther, the freedom of the law could not be preserved. By employing torture in exercising his office, a judge brought guilt upon himself, of course, but he did so in order to prevent greater injustice. This was anything but carte blanche for the use of torture. The cardinal, especially, was not entitled to do so.

Albrecht's aversion to the light also made him suspect in the matter at hand. Luther wanted to show this by delivering a "copycat sermon" of his own, i.e., one that refuted the "rebuttal" of Albrecht's jurists item by item. The extant documents raise the suspicion that the cardinal himself had put Schönitz up to his intrigues. With the money, which was gone, Albrecht had financed his own living expenses. He himself should therefore hang. The swift execution of Schönitz, without allowing him time to bid farewell to his family members, was inhuman and unjust. A priest, especially, should not act this way; instead, Albrecht should have stood by his servant. The archbishop's various tricks were mercilessly exposed. Luther declared that he was not exaggerating, for the matter itself was so bad. Here his criticism was also directed toward the "silver and gold jurists," who with their "rebuttal" had let themselves be bought in order to justify Albrecht's evil cause. According to the verdict of God, the "high judge," Albrecht had broken nearly all of the Ten Commandments.

The purpose of Luther's work was, first, to take a stand on behalf of someone who was unjustly persecuted, and, second, to call the cardinal to repent, although there was little expectation of that. If Albrecht did not want to be damned, he would have to acknowledge his guilt and make restitution. It was the task of the jurists to see that their lord obeyed the law, not, as often happened in the service of princes, to accept good pay simply to be obsequious. In general, the jurists, e.g., Luther's Wittenberg colleague Jerome Schurf, would have done better to accept Schönitz's case instead of abandoning him to Albrecht. Schurf had even approved of using torture against Hans Schönitz.[23] Luther saw here a widespread new danger: Officials did not prosecute the misdeeds of highly placed people, jurists did not uphold the law, and theologians were reluctant to criticize. The collapse of law and order could result from this. Luther himself would not go along with it. He protested again that he had not assumed the role of a judge. He was only interpreting the Word of his Lord. To it he would answer; for it he also requested the protection of his sovereign. In conclusion, he once more emphasized the spiritual perspective. Luther had not attacked the cardinal because he was a sinner—Luther was one too—but because he was defending his sin by appealing to God and thereby involving God in his injustice. Albrecht no longer acknowledged his sins, quite the contrary, and therefore a gracious God could no longer forgive them. This was blasphemy, and pope and cardinal were both guilty of it. Against them, Luther prayed: "Help, O God, dear Lord and Savior, that we stay pious sinners and not become sainted blasphemers."

As turbulent as the history leading up to the appearance of this accusation had been, the expected storm of protest did not occur after its publication. Luther so obviously had the law on his side that it must have been difficult to refute him, although he was unable to substantiate all of his accusations. At the very least, the allegation that the cardinal was guilty of judicial murder may have been justified. There was agreement: "Praise God that there are still people who can tell the truth!" Nevertheless, Elector John Frederick, responding to the intervention of the elector of Brandenburg, prohibited Luther from publishing any further reports of this sort against highly placed personages without first submitting them to the court.[24] Naturally, Luther accomplished nothing with Albrecht of Mainz. During his lifetime the Schönitz affair was not resolved. Nevertheless, Luther covered himself with glory with his theologically committed support for the law. For this he truly should deserve a place in legal history.

IV

Completing the Translation
of the Bible

1. TRANSLATING THE PROPHETS
AND THE APOCRYPHA

The German translation of the Bible progressed without interruption until 1524, first the New Testament and then the Old Testament as far as the Song of Solomon. The next installment, the translation of the Prophets, was not ready until 1532. Hence our account must once again return to an earlier date. In 1525 Luther blamed the regrettable delay in completing the publication of a complete German Bible partially on the thieving reprinters who published pirated editions, for in such a lengthy printing process there was a danger that portions that were already completed would be stolen from the Wittenberg printers and be published elsewhere, and this would mean that the Wittenbergers would suffer a considerable loss in sales of the costly edition. In fact, such an unauthorized advance printing of the Wittenberg Latin Bible did happen in 1529.[1] The many other demands upon Luther and his illnesses were the real reason for the delay. Nevertheless, he never lost sight of the ultimate goal.

The German commentaries on Jonah and Habakkuk in 1526, along with the one on Zechariah in 1528, each contained a translation. At the beginning of 1527, Luther turned directly to the translation project, "which this barbarous and animalistic nation has taken from me," undoubtedly meaning primarily the Peasants' War and its consequences.[2] In May he learned with some disappointment that Ludwig Hätzer, an Anabaptist with a humanistic education, and Hans Denck had already published a translation of the prophets in Worms. Luther fully acknowledged their achievement, although he felt the translation was somewhat confusing. Nevertheless, he was still determined to complete his own. Later, he was more reserved about this work by the "fanatics," and he criticized them for using the assistance of rabbis.[3] In his own translating, Luther made use of the "Worms Prophets" in an independent and critical way. Some things he adopted, but often he intentionally went his own way. Occasionally he used this work to correct his own, but the accusation—which George Witzel had already raised in 1536—that he borrowed from it without acknowledgement has proved to be without merit.

95

When the university was moved to Jena in September 1527 because of the plague, the translation of the Prophets had to be interrupted because Luther was dependent on his co-workers. He asked his friends to intercede that this devil-sent hinderance to the spread of God's Word might come to an end.[4] In May 1528 he referred to the difficult work of translating the prophet Jeremiah as "giving birth"; in June Luther and Melanchthon were already working on revising it. The sweat-producing task of teaching the Hebrew writers to speak German was compared to the story of the nightingale that was supposed to teach her song to the cuckoo.[5] Because it was obvious that completing the translation of the Prophets would take much more time, the German version of Isaiah was initially published separately in the fall of 1528.

A new interruption occurred because of Melanchthon's journey to the Diet of Speyer in the spring of 1529. When Luther was unable to preach and lecture in April and May because of a cold, he used the time to translate the apocryphal Wisdom of Solomon. He did not think much of Leo Jud's translation of it, which had just appeared in Zurich, but he believed that his own surpassed not only the version in the Vulgate, but even the Greek original itself. His subtitle, based on Wis. 6:10—"To the Tyrants"—and his preface reveal that Luther had selected this book in view of contemporary circumstances so that he might employ it against the oppression of the Protestants by the Catholic authorities.[6]

Again because of a current situation, this time the acute danger from the Turks, Luther turned in the winter of 1529–30 not to Jeremiah but to the Book of Daniel, for the Turks seemed to be the final, antigodly kingdom prophesied in Dan. 7:24-26 and, moreover, Daniel, chapters 8 and 11, had foretold the anti-Christian papacy. It was unusual that Luther dedicated the separate printing to Crown Prince John Frederick, who later thanked Luther by presenting him with a ring with the Luther Rose, probably specially made in Nuremberg. Because all the prophecies seemed to have been fulfilled, Luther anticipated that the world would end even before the Bible translation was completed. It was especially rewarding for kings and princes to read Daniel's political prophecy. They should learn from it that pious princes could depend on God, and that evil ones would be destroyed. That authority and sovereignty were gifts of God was something about which pagans knew nothing. The crown prince, otherwise a lover of the Holy Scriptures, should love Daniel as did the mighty ones in Daniel's time. The extraordinarily long preface provided a historical introduction focused on the present, which was based on intensive study of the sources and culminated by pointing to Christ's kingdom. A unique map of the world was included in the translation in order to help in understanding it.[7] Likewise precipitated by the danger from the Turks was the separate translation at the Coburg in 1530 of Ezekiel 38–39, which dealt with the attack and ultimate defeat of Gog, who was identified with the Turks. For Luther this was both a call to repentance and a call for courageous resistance to the Turks.[8]

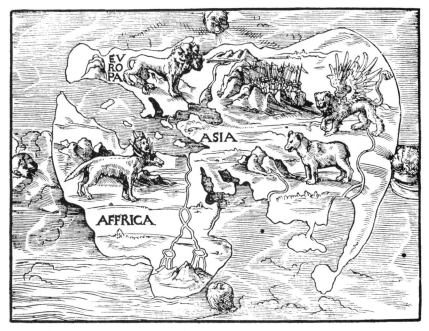

Map of the world according to the vision in Daniel 7, depicting animals and the
Turkish army
Der Prophet Daniel Deudsch, Hans Lufft, Wittenberg, 1530

Luther wanted to use the time at the Coburg not least to complete the
translation of the Prophets. On 8 May 1530 he was completing Jeremiah,
which he had already begun in Wittenberg. He was energetically applying
himself to the task, hoping to complete all the Prophets by Pentecost (5 June).
His poor health, however, prevented him from doing so. By 20 June he had
not even begun Ezekiel. Because of his illness, and also his weariness in
dealing with the obstinate text, he had not completed the translation at the
beginning of August, but Hosea was finished. Soon, only Haggai and Malachi
remained to be done. Working with the minor prophets was more of a comfort
to Luther than a task. After completing them, he turned again to Ezekiel, still
in August. The necessary work of revising them with his Wittenberg colleagues probably was not completed until the fall of 1531.[9] During his stay
with the ailing Elector John at the end of February 1532, Luther worked on
the general preface to all the Prophets. His health was so bad at the time that
he did not know whether he would be able to complete it. If necessary,
Melanchthon should jump in and use his "skill and eloquence." The preface
commended the Prophets as witnesses of Christ. Their solemn enjoinders of
the First Commandment had a contemporary significance, because the subtle
idolatry of the Jews' arbitrary worship was continuing in the present church.[10]

The prefaces to the individual prophetic books made frequent references to this. Self-confidently, Luther regarded his *Die Propheten alle deudsch* as the best of all translations, one which made it easier to understand the text than all the previous commentaries had.[11]

Now all that was unfinished was the Apocrypha. Creating a suitable translation of Ecclesiasticus also proved to be difficult, and although Luther complained about the work in the fall of 1532, he was ultimately satisfied with the result. The previous translations had been truly unusable, "but we have reassembled it like a letter that has been torn up, trampled underfoot, and scattered, and we have washed all the muck away. . . ."[12] Luther appears to have left the translation of the other books of the Apocrypha to Melanchthon and Jonas. He had grown weary of this work, and the Apocrypha did not have the same significance as the other books of the Bible. They were not even numbered in the table of contents in the 1523 Old Testament. In 1534, they were given the well-known title: "Apocrypha: These Books Are Not Held Equal to the Scriptures, but Are Useful and Good to Read." However, he continued to participate in the process of revision, and the prefaces were also written by him. Occasional references in the Table Talk, e.g., to the books of Judith and Tobias, which were belittled as "poetry," show that he continued his interest in the translation. He made no secret of his dislike of 2 Maccabees and also of the Book of Esther, "for they Judaize too much and have a lot of pagan crudeness." He would have preferred to "throw out" 2 Maccabees from the Bible.[13]

In March 1534 Luther was still thoroughly involved with the Bible translation, and in September, twelve years after the New Testament, the complete Bible was published.[14] It contained 117 woodcuts, almost all of them new and most made by someone identified by the monogram MS, who was associated with Cranach's workshop. Later information from the assistant proofreader of the Lufft print shop, Christoph Walther, indicates that the specifications for the illustrations came in part from Luther himself. According to his instructions, nothing that "did not serve the text" was to "deface" it. Incorrect illustrations were changed. One can usually accurately determine which Bible passages and what interpretation of them lie behind the illustrations.[15]

Luther's own contribution, obviously, was also the previously mentioned prefaces and the glosses (marginal notes). Aside from the translation itself, they made Luther's German Bible one of the most effective of his works, something that has still been scarcely recognized. Here too, all material centers around the doctrine of justification. One can trace the interesting process of Luther's theology in the changes and continual development of the glosses. In them we become acquainted with the experiences he was having at the time. Wherever appropriate, he clearly stated his rejection of the papal church. Likewise, he made political and social instructions for subjects and for rulers clear, and discussed the right relationship between men, women, and children. Criticisms of the "big shots" and rich people are loud, although ownership of

Gottes wort
bleibt ewig.

Biblia / das ist / die
gantze Heilige Sch=
rifft Deudsch.

Mart. Luth.

Wittemberg.

Begnadet mit Kür=
furstlicher zu Sachsen
freiheit.

Gedruckt durch Hans Lufft.

M. D. XXXIIII.

Title page of the first complete Wittenberg Bible, 1534

property is not radically rejected. Luther's criticism of moral laxity in general is also recorded here.

The Luther Bible, with its prefaces and glosses, is an essential document for determining Luther's theological and historical position. It reflects specific situations, with their options and condemnations, together with the whole range of world, church, politics, and society. To a considerable extent, Luther's own church was molded by it, and thereby the Luther Bible became one of the fundamental pillars of the Lutheran church in Germany. In its substructure there were some things that were conditioned by the time, and some that were also theologically one-sided. With this Bible, nevertheless, the church was essentially built on its own solid foundation. Its verdict on conditions in the world around the church, including politics and society, is one that is neither approving on the one side nor condemnatory on the other, but one that must rather be characterized as open, sober, and critical. Neither the authority of the state nor the existence of social classes was accepted uncritically. The Luther Bible was also an impartial and independent judge of existing conditions, as the Holy Scriptures had to be, and as their interpreter wanted to be in commenting on them. As it was put, not inappropriately, in a Latin gloss from 1545 on the value of wisdom and understanding (Prov. 16:16), which can hardly have come from Luther himself, "As it is done in the works of Dr. Martin Luther."[16]

The printer of the complete Bible was Hans Lufft, who acted as the agent of the consortium of Wittenberg printers, Moritz Goltz, Bartholomew Vogel, and Christoph Schramm. They had purchased the publishing house from Christian Düring, the indebted goldsmith, who since 1524 had published the portions of the Bible, first together with Lucas Cranach and then by himself. Luther once hinted that they had been very energetic in promoting their own interests in it.[17] For a long time the printing of the Bible was one of the most profitable businesses in Wittenberg. The 1534 Bible cost two gulden and eight groschen for an unbound copy, five times as much as the New Testament of 1522.[18] In 1543 the three booksellers were the richest men in Wittenberg.

As had previously been done with the portions of the Bible translation and the Postils, Elector John Frederick granted a privilege for the complete Bible, which was renewed again and again, to protect the Wittenberg publishers from reprints within the sphere of Electoral Saxony's influence.[19] Ever since 1524 the Agnus Dei and the Luther Rose emblems had been used to protect the copies of the Bible from unauthorized reprinting. In 1532 Luther himself besought the council of Magdeburg through Amsdorf, evidently successfully, to have the printer Michael Lotther cease reprinting the Prophets.[20] After Ducal Saxony adopted the Reformation in 1539, the Wittenberg publishers enlisted Luther's aid in obtaining protection for their imprints for two or three years from the Leipzig printer Nicholas Wolrab, who previously had been active as a printer for the Catholics. Luther was also opposed to having this

Dis zeichen sey zeuge / das solche bucher durch
meine hand gangen sind/deñ des falschē druckes
rnd bucher verderbens/vleyssigen sich ytzt viel

Gedruckt zu wittemberg.

Luther's seal for his Bible translation in the second part
of the Old Testament, Wittenberg, 1524

former underling of his opponents compete with the Wittenbergers at the important Leipzig book fair, and he therefore appealed to the elector. His effort, however, was only partially successful.[21] After 1541 the complete Bible contained a warning from Luther against any printers who for shameless profit reprinted it at the expense of the Wittenberg printers. Thereby greed, the root of all evil, was threatening the German translation of the Bible, which by God's grace had been produced in Wittenberg. For Luther himself this was not a financial matter: "For I have received it for nothing, and have given it for nothing, and also desire nothing for it. Christ my Lord has paid me for it many hundred thousandfold." Nor did he allow for the many years of hard work: "No one should know what we have had to suffer for this, what we have done and what we have spent, for this is his gift and he has accomplished this through us, his unworthy, miserable, poor tool." In contrast, he was offended at the frequent poor reprints that distorted the contents: "They ruin it, willy-nilly. It's all for money." The Wittenberg printers, however, were aware of their responsibility to produce an unadulterated version of the Bible.[22]

During Luther's lifetime a total of ninety-one printings of the Bible or portions of it were published in Wittenberg, including twenty-one editions of the New Testament and eleven complete Bibles. In addition, there were 253 partial or complete editions that were printed elsewhere, and these contributed considerably to the circulation of the Luther Bible. This does not include the Low German versions or the translations done by Luther's Catholic opponents like Emser, Eck, and Dietenberger, which were based on his. It is said that before Luther's death there were 430 complete or partial editions with a total of about a half million copies.[23] Thus approximately ten percent of Luther imprints were Bibles. In 1530 Luther was already regarding the pure (*clara*) German Bible, along with his commentaries on the Bible and his restoration of the doctrine of justification, as his most important achievement.[24]

2. REVISIONS

The work of translating the Bible never ended, although time and time again Luther thought that he had put his hand to it for the last time. Alongside the translation work as such, there was the preparation of new editions of portions that had already been printed. Several times this involved an extensive revision of the translation.

In the original preface to the Psalter of 1524 Luther explained that he had translated the phrase "mercy and truth" with "goodness and faithfulness," because this better expressed God's personal relationship with man. He then added a general afterword to the Psalter of 1525 that emphasized two thoughts: The commands of God are fulfilled by faithful believing, and the cross of persecution belongs to a believer's existence. In 1528 the old preface had to be removed, because Luther did not consistently follow his earlier freer translation. It was replaced with a general praise of the Psalter as the best collection of examples and legends of the saints, which gave a comprehensive illustration of their attitude toward God. It was superior to the usual stories of the saints because it preserved not the works of the saints, but their much more important prayerful sayings, which provided a glimpse into their hearts and into their praise and thanksgiving, as well as into their needful laments. The Psalter therefore offered something like a new grammar that taught the pious to acknowledge their sins and formed them into a community, to which the new translation gave them access.[1]

Luther was concerned not only with making the best possible German translation of the Bible, but also with improving the Latin text, with Melanchthon's assistance. In 1529 a partial edition of the Vulgate was published in Wittenberg. It contained the Old Testament (from Genesis through 2 Kings) and the New Testament, and also a Latin version of the Psalter. More than a mere correction, the text was frequently closer to the Hebrew original. The work was designed only for study purposes. In the worship services the customary Vulgate text was still to be used. In the preface to the new edition of the Latin Psalter of 1537, Luther emphasized that he was expressly limiting himself to improving the Vulgate. He thought a Latin translation of his own was even more problematic than the translation into his German mother tongue.[2]

In 1529–30 Luther and Melanchthon completed a thorough revision of the New Testament. In a prefatory remark Luther protested against arbitrary emendations of his text by the reprinters: "This Testament is to be Luther's German Testament. . . ." In a new preface to 1 Corinthians he warned against the fanatics. In a newly added preface to the Revelation of John he now gave an interpretation of its visions, which, like the Book of Daniel, which he was also revising, he applied to the course of the church's history. The Apocalypse thereby became a contemporary solace and a warning in the face of threats from the pope and the Turks. Reason could not clearly discern the church, which was beset by laxity, sects, and conflict. One simply had to believe that it was in communion with Christ, and there should be no doubt of this as long as it held fast to the pure gospel.[3] In 1533 the Acts of the Apostles received its own preface.[4] Contrary to tradition, Luther did not want to have it understood as a book of examples of pious living and good works, but rather as instruction in the righteousness of faith and thereby virtually as a commentary on the Pauline epistles. The Jews had once persecuted the Christians because they were no longer observing the law, and so it was understandable that the Gentiles were repeating this in the present against those who followed the message of the gospel; "this is ten times more annoying."

At the beginning of 1531, a new edition of the Psalter was necessary once again. Luther decided to undertake a thorough revision, "so that David might sound purely German," although he acknowledged that this would give his critics new fuel, because the Psalter was "closer to the German and farther removed from the Hebrew." Luther had regularly been making notes about a better understanding of the Psalter in his personal German and Latin copies. Melanchthon, Cruciger, and Aurogallus, the Hebraist, joined in the task of revising it, which took several weeks. Their protocols, which have been preserved, offer us a unique glimpse into the translation process.[5] The leading person in the effort, as would be expected, was Luther himself. He frequently gave spontaneous expression to his intimate relationship to the Psalms. Psalm 17 was "a fine little psalm and my little prayer." Psalm 28 was "pure gospel"; Psalm 33, "a fine, beautiful psalm." Psalm 49 could be characterized as an "obscurus psalmus"; Psalm 141, as a "very intricate psalm." Of Psalm 50, in contrast, he said: "This one is not difficult, but it is powerful." Psalm 51:17 "is a fine, precious verse, that our Lord God takes such pleasure in one who causes him so much trouble. It is a powerful psalm and it has great life in it. . . ." On Psalm 55: "Now here again is a wholly difficult psalm." Psalm 58 "has many good phrases." In translating, Luther constantly experimented with different possibilities of expression and breadth of experiences that the German language offered, not least its proverbs, occasionally intentionally even at the cost of faithfulness to the Hebrew source. He wanted thereby to capture the text's emotional content and its specific situation. Self-evidently, his own experience could also be seen. Of Psalm 72 he recalled, appropriately: "I have studied this psalm more intensely than any other." Psalm 107:14 had proved its worth in pastoral care. Luther knew that understanding a text exegetically and rendering it in German were by no means the same. With Ps. 6:6 he referred to the symptoms of the English sweat, the epidemic of 1529. Of Psalm 23 he said respectfully, "These people were really good at speaking"; of Ps. 50:10, "It is fine poetry, this thing." The translation process was not limited to philology, however. The Psalms spoke about specific situations of the present, including politics, church politics, society, and science. Luther illustrated the actions of the enemies of God by comparing them with those who opposed the Reformation and in this way he frequently found the proper expression. John Eck, John Faber, Archbishop Albrecht of Mainz, Duke George of Saxony, the emperor, the Turks, Müntzer, Zwingli, Erasmus, Karlstadt, and many others were mentioned. The representatives of the evangelical side like the elector of Saxony, Philip of Hesse, or Melanchthon appeared more infrequently. There are many reminders of the Diet of Augsburg. Occasionally the social actions of the peasants and the common people, the jurists and public officials, the court, the counselors, and the princes are mentioned critically. Good or bad personal reminiscences, or those of acquaintances, are associated with certain passages. Along with these contemporary references, they also kept an eye on the literary horizon; Terence, Vergil, and Homer were particularly mentioned.

Transposing a biblical text into one's own situation and understanding it on the basis of one's own situation and time is a complex phenomenon, and it must be evaluated in a discriminating way. The old historic text thereby becomes alive and contemporary, and in this way the translation achieves an incomparable force, but there is a danger that the original situation may be ignored or subjectively reinterpreted. Here the historical biblical documents are read as generally applicable testimonies to the limitations of human existence. Luther's generalization is one of the greatest achievements in the history of translation. It is based on the assumption that the Holy Scriptures shed light on the situation of all humankind, indeed, that they are the revelation of man's salvation. This expectation leads one to focus on listening to them and asking ever newer questions about the correct sense of the text.

In connection with the new edition of the Psalter, Luther worked on *Summaries of the Psalms*, which provided a terse, explanatory précis of each Psalm. These were to appear separately from the Psalter, so that text and interpretation could be kept cleanly apart. However, the execution of the project was delayed. Luther worked on it during the summer of 1532 and finally completed it in November. Melanchthon thought the *Summaries* were the best commentaries on the Psalms ever. Justus Menius called them a gift of God. Luther used the preface, *Defense of the Translation*, i.e., the new version of the Psalms, which he thought was the final one, to give an explanation.[6] In some places he had deliberately departed from the literal sense, as the rabbis and grammarians presented it, in order to achieve an understandable and unmistakably German way of speaking. In so doing he frequently hit upon the right expression, but occasionally the translation became virtually a free rendering, which altered the imagery of the original text in a questionable manner. He also hit upon brilliant solutions in this way. Originally he translated Ps. 63:6 literally: "Let my soul become full as with lard and grease, so that my mouth may render praise with joyful lips." Because that was incomprehensible in German, Luther rendered it according to the sense: "It would be my heart's joy and delight if I were to praise you with a joyful mouth." He expressly stated that he favored a translation according to the sense instead of a literal one, but even this principle he used with freedom. He would have preferred to translate Ps. 68:19 as, "You have set the prisoners free." He correctly noted, however, that this would be too weak and he kept the somewhat more difficult, but Christologically significant wording, "You have ascended the heights and imprisoned the prison." On the whole, Luther was confident in his method, although he thought improvements were possible and reckoned that as a fallible man he might have made mistakes. Nevertheless, he would not suffer petty criticism.

Because the process of group revision had proved itself with the Psalter, the same procedure was adopted in 1534 for an edition of the complete Bible. Not much is known about it, however. In January they were already hard at work. In August, Luther was still working on the text of the Book of Job.[7] When a new edition again became necessary in the summer of 1539, it was an opportunity for Luther to make another complete revision, which, with interruptions, took more than two years. Luther had to check the New Testament in the summer of 1541, and he complained about the pressure of time caused by its scheduled publication in the fall. This time it was primarily Bugenhagen, Jonas, Cruciger, Melanchthon, Aurogallus, and occasionally additional experts who worked together, with Rörer serving as proofreader. The members of the committee prepared themselves for the sessions with the original text, and they utilized the Jewish and Christian traditions of translation and interpretation. The results were recorded in the protocol and in Luther's personal copy. Once again, Luther's personal and intimate association with the text can be seen, and, just as before, he preserved awe in the face of specific statements and situations.[8] For the translation of corrupted or obscure passages he depended as much as possible on the philological experts, without, however, always following them.[9] This time, in distinction to the Jewish commentators, he understood the vision in Ezekiel 1 in a Christological sense. He interpreted it in this way in a new preface to the prophet and had the illustration altered accordingly. In addition, he offered assistance in understanding the description of the Temple in Ezekiel 40ff.[10] Luther considerably expanded the 1530 preface to Daniel, which was already lengthy because of the contemporary applications in it. He included an explanation of the "seventy weeks of years" (Dan. 9:24-27) and of the twelfth chapter with its treatment of the Antichrist,

105

Der Prophet Hesekiel.

Vision of the throne and wheels in Ezekiel 1
Woodcut by Lucas Cranach the Younger in the Wittenberg Bible, 1541

so that it became a comprehensive reckoning with the outrages of the papacy, which mirrored the final intensification of the conflict with Rome.[11]

At first Luther thought the Bible of 1541 would be the final version. He did not anticipate another revision and also thought that his health was not up to it. The edition, of which fifteen hundred copies were printed, was handsomely decorated and printed in a special format that provided an area 28 by 16.6 centimeters for the printed text. At first, the intention was to produce a few copies on parchment for the elector and the princes of Anhalt at a price of sixty gulden. At the end of 1541 the twenty-four Wittenberg bookbinders worked at capacity for months on the task of binding them. Because of this, Luther did not receive the first of his own three bound copies until June 1542. When the printing occasionally did not measure up to this high standard, Luther thought that, as with all businesses in the world, one would have to accept it graciously.[12]

Luther continued to improve the translation. The tenth Wittenberg edition of the complete Bible of 1545 was the final one that appeared during his lifetime. Like the two editions of 1543, it contained only a few corrections that came from Luther himself. One more partial revision of Romans and the two Epistles to the Corinthians had been done in 1544, and Rörer inserted them in the posthumous edition of the New Testament (Plate V) and of the complete Bible in 1546, which caused him to be accused falsely of forging the Luther text.[13] Thus, in fact, Luther was engaged almost to the end of his life in overseeing the translation work.

3. ARGUING WITH THE CRITICS

An undertaking that aroused such public interest as did the translation of the Bible naturally did not lack critics. Hans von Dolzig's objections to Luther's disposition to shorten things can be disposed of relatively easily. It simply sounded better: "I won't let it go," instead of, "I will not let go of it."[1] Duke George of Saxony could not let the matter rest with confiscating the translation of the New Testament in 1522. The following year Jerome Emser justified this in his great polemic attack: *The Reason and Cause of Why Luther's Translation of the New Testament Has Been Justly Forbidden to the Common Man: With a Clear Description of How, Where, and in What Passages Luther Has Perverted the Text and Unfaithfully Rendered It, or with False Glosses and Prefaces Has Led People Away from the Ancient Christian Way to His Own Advantage and Delusion.* Emser, in examining the entire translation, claimed that he had found about fourteen hundred errors. He conceded that Luther had translated "somewhat more gracefully and sweet-soundingly" than his predecessors, but it was precisely this that made his work dangerous.[2] The prefaces and glosses, in which Luther had stated his theological interpretation of the text, naturally aroused Emser's opposition; moreover, he rightly criticized a few errors. In general, he demanded a literal translation instead of one that followed the sense, and one that more closely conformed to the Vulgate instead of the original text. The substance of this critique could scarcely apply to Luther. Calling Mary "lovely," instead of "full of grace," at the beginning of the Magnificat (Luke 1:28) was something Luther had already defended in 1524 and 1525.[3]

Emser was not satisfied with just criticizing. At the encouragement of Duke George, in 1527 he offered his own version in competition with Luther's translation. In the main, it was a corrected version of Luther's text, and Emser acknowledged as much, although somewhat disguising it. Its format was even modeled after the Wittenberg original, going so far as using the same woodcuts as illustrations. In a preface, Duke George went to great lengths to justify his prohibition of Luther's translation: It destroyed the ancient worship, piety, and tradition of the church. Now, with Emser's purified version, the Catholics also had a German translation available.[4] It accomplished its purpose. There are a total of thirty-eight editions of Emser's New Testament known. With few changes, its text was adopted by the Catholic Bible editions of the Dominican Johannes Dietenberger (after 1534) and of John Eck (after 1537). Dietenberger, in addition, depended on Luther's translation of the Old Testament. Therefore, until the eighteenth century Catholics, too, were reading the German Bible in the linguistic form that Luther had given to it. Luther thought that Duke George had brought great shame upon himself with his preface, but he refrained from responding.[5] In 1529 he sought to prevent Emser's Testament from being reprinted in Rostock. He was not concerned about the text, "which the rascal maliciously stole from me, for it is virtually the same as my text," but about Emser's annotations, which he considered pernicious.[6]

In September 1530, while staying at the Coburg, Luther was provoked into one more conflict with Emser's Testament because he had received inquiries, perhaps from Nuremberg, among other things, about his translation of Rom. 3:28, "We hold that a man is justified without the works of the law, by faith *alone*." He replied with a work on the task of translating that has become famous, *On Translating: An Open Letter*, which is at the same time a personal document about his work of translating and therefore must be quoted more extensively than usual.[7] Luther was well aware of what he had accomplished with his translation. He thought his opponents were incapable of turning a single chapter of the Bible into German. They themselves had learned how to speak and write German from him, and this filled him with satisfaction. He had nothing against better translations if anyone could produce them, but he thought the papist asses were incompetent to judge his work: "It is my Testament and my translation, and it shall continue to be mine." Nevertheless, a translation, once published, was fair game for the critics. What the papists were capable of doing had been shown by Emser, "the Dresden scribbler," who had largely stolen Luther's text. Duke George had prohibited Luther's New Testament and then subsequently endorsed it in Emser's version. Luther would not even discuss the translation with the incompetent papists. To them, he simply decreed: "Dr. Martin Luther will have it so." Imitating Paul's boasting (2 Cor. 11:22-23), he stated: "I can expound psalms and prophets; they cannot. I can translate; they cannot. . . ." In addition, Luther himself knew the traditional philosophy of Aristotle better than his opponents. One should therefore simply say to the Catholics who criticized the translation of Rom. 3:28: " 'Luther will have it so, and says that he is a doctor above all the doctors of the whole papacy.' It shall stay at that." His old opponents like John Faber, the bishop of Vienna, and "Dr. Snotty-Nose" (Cochlaeus) were not suitable discussion partners.

Vis-à-vis his own supporters, however, Luther was prepared to give an account of his principles of translating. He first referred to the result of his efforts:

> Now that it is translated and finished, everybody can read and criticize it. One now runs his eyes over three or four pages and does not stumble once—without realizing what boulders and clods had once lain there where he now goes along as over a smoothly-planed board. We had to sweat and toil there before we got those boulders and clods out of the way, so that one could go along so nicely. The plowing goes well when the field is cleared. But rooting out the woods and stumps, and getting the field ready—this is a job nobody wants.

Regarding the "by faith *alone*," which did not appear in the original Greek text of Rom. 3:28, Luther believed that it was necessary, for "it belongs there if the translation is to be clear and vigorous," and he could refer to the common manner of speech: "Rather we must inquire about this of the mother in the home, the children on the street, the common man in the marketplace. We must be guided by their language, the way they speak, and do our translating accordingly. That way they will understand it and recognize that we are speaking German to them." Luther referred to solutions that he thought were especially good: The literal, "Out of the abundance of the heart the mouth speaks" (Matt. 12:34), had become the proverb, "What fills the heart overflows the mouth." As before, he also thought it better in Luke 1:28 to address Mary as "gracious," instead of the Latin "full of grace." He would not tolerate any attack on the purity of his motives in undertaking the difficult task of translating. He had not made any profit in doing it:

> Rather I have done it as a service to the dear Christians and to the honor of One who sitteth above, who blesses me so much every hour of my life that if I had translated a thousand times as much or as diligently, I should not for a single hour have deserved to live or to have a sound eye. All that I am and have is of his grace and mercy, indeed, of his precious blood and bitter sweat. Therefore, God willing, all of it shall also serve to his honor, joyfully and sincerely.

The verdict of pious Christians was what mattered, not that of his opponents. He declared, accurately, that he had not simply translated freely. Where it seemed appropriate, he followed the wording of the original. Not everyone was able to translate at all: "It requires a right, devout, honest, sincere, God-fearing, Christian, trained, informed, and experienced heart." The "alone" was therefore theologically necessary in Rom. 3:28 because here it concerned a primary principle of Christian doctrine, namely, justification by faith alone. Luther was aware of his opponents' criticism that he was thereby making good works superfluous. In this passage Paul was not only rejecting good works, but the law itself as a way of salvation. Of course, no one should take this as an endorsement of evil works, but one had to hold fast to this: Christ's death and resurrection alone free us from sin, and faith accepts this. The "alone" was therefore demanded not only by the language, but also by the very nature of the subject: "Therefore it will stay in my New Testament." There was virtually no other aspect of his activity about which Luther gave so much personal information as he did here regarding the business of translating. Thus it is apparent how directly it related to the heart of his faith.

Luther's continuing involvement in translating the Bible meant that he frequently commented on the task. He emphasized that one could never translate in opposition to grammar. At the same time, he always sought to give a theological force to the words of the text, relating them either to grace or to the law, to wrath or to forgiveness, occasionally to the three "estates" of the state, the home (or economics), and the church, and referring them to the main topics contained in that book of the Bible.[8] Although Luther did not react to the criticisms of his translation by Witzel and Eck, he frequently took issue with the objections of Sebastian Münster, the Basel Hebraist who was thoroughly acquainted with the rabbinic interpretation, and who had incorporated it in his *Biblia Hebraica* in 1534. Münster's philology bound him too closely to the Jews; he possessed no sense for figures of speech or for the faith. In Jon. 2:5 Luther had justifiably heightened the prophet's lament, and Münster had criticized him. Luther defended himself: "Yes, dear Münster, you have never experienced these *Anfechtungen*. But I sat with Jonah in the whale where everything seemed to be despair." Münster had no understanding of the meaning of the whole Bible, which occasionally gave Luther the freedom also to discard the rabbinic philology that lacked a theological perspective.[9] Luther also knew what he had accomplished in the area of scholarly philology. Referring to the new edition of 1541, he declared: "The Bible—I do not praise it, but the work praises itself—is so good and precious that it is better than all translations Greek and Latin, and you find more in it than in all the commentaries." Again he praised its readability, but he declared his concern that people might already be growing tired of it because the number of reprintings had declined at the time. His concern that people would alter his translation after his death, or that every schoolmaster and sexton would make one of his own and thus displace his, continued to prove groundless for a long time.[10]

4. PRAISING AND RECOMMENDING THE BIBLE

Beginning about 1541, it became increasingly common for people to give Luther copies of the Bible and, occasionally, other books, and to request that he inscribe them. The owners were mostly theologians and nobles, and some-times burghers from the upper class. Luther usually wrote a Bible verse with a brief explanation, and signed his name. Almost three hundred such inscrip-tions are known, and they were soon collected and published (Plate VI). They are extremely personal documents of Luther's pious attitude toward the Bible and the Word, which have, undeservedly, been nearly forgotten.[1]

On Josh. 1:8, "This book of the law shall not depart out of your mouth," he wrote, "This is a glorious promise for someone who likes to read and study the Bible, and also does so diligently: Namely, he shall be joyful and can depart in wisdom."

Luther frequently used the first and last verses of Psalm 1 to encourage someone to keep living in the Word. This conviction that one can exist merely by holding fast to the Word in faith is also found elsewhere. God's presence in the valley of the shadow (Ps. 23:4) was understood as mediated through the words of Scripture. "Dwelling in the house of the Lord" (Ps. 27:4) was believ-ing in the Word. The Psalms repeatedly call us to obey the First Command-ment, i.e., to be firm in hope and confident in prayer. Psalm 37:30-31 was explained in this way: "Note, God's Word must be in your heart and taken seriously, purely without any additions, and thus your way will be certain and secure. But human teachings are a slippery path. . . ." His explanations of Old Testament passages frequently emphasized that Christ was to be found in the promise and law in the Scriptures. The soul was wed to Christ by hearing (on Ps. 45:11-12). The Word of the Scriptures is *the* means of healing in every need (on Ps. 107:20). Psalm 118:14 was interpreted Christologically: "No one but Christ can be our strength, for by ourselves we would be powerless and crucified with all sorts of suffering. But when he is our psalm, hymn, and song, then comes the victory and salvation for eternal life. Amen." For Luther, all of Psalm 119 was an appeal to live out of the Word as the only way of life that would endure. On Ps. 145:5 he noted: "Flesh and blood, born in sin, keep us from seeing in this life what sort of splendid work and miracle God has done in us. Therefore we must preach, speak, listen, so that we may believe through the Word and begin to realize this, until we come to that place where with the blessed angels we shall see what now we preach and hear; yet we will never have our fill of it, but live eternally from it. . . ."

On Prov. 8:17 and Prov. 8:36 he said: It is the same Word as in creation "that speaks with us humans in the Holy Scriptures and through the mouth of every saint. And it gives nothing but life to all who seek it and gladly hear it. For it longs to be found, and longs to be with men in order to counsel them and help them. . . ." The prerequisite for understanding the Scriptures is trust and faith, for they deal with things that are yet to come and are unseen. "Therefore you must believe and hope, for surely if you believe and hope not only will eternal life come, but also temporal help in your present need, which seems to last a long time, because it's hard to endure" (on Prov. 30:5). Another inscription on the same passage said: "It is a danger above all dangers for one to be bold and insert one's own interpretation into God's Word. Again, it is a blessing above all blessings to be in awe and humbly to read and hear God's Word. . . ."

Isaiah 40:8, "The Word of our God will stand forever," was interpreted in this way: "That is, it remains fast, it is certain, it does not yield, it does not waver, it does not decline, it does not err, it does not let itself be diminished. Now wherever this Word comes into someone's heart with true faith it also makes the heart firm, certain, and secure, so that it becomes unyielding, upright, and hard against all *Anfechtung*, the devil, death, and whatever may come, that it confidently and proudly may despise and disdain anything that wishes to doubt, waver, grow angry, or become enraged, for it knows that God's Word cannot lie to it." He specifically applied Isa. 55:11, "My Word shall not return to me empty," to the biblical Word: "This is indeed a comforting saying. Wherever we can believe that God speaks to us and that it is God's Word that we read and hear in the Bible, we will find and feel that there it is not read and heard in vain without bearing fruit. But our accursed unbelief and our suffering flesh keep us from seeing and believing that it is God who speaks with us in the Scriptures, or that they are God's Word; instead, we think that it is Isaiah, Paul, or some other ordinary man who speaks, not he who created heaven and earth. Therefore it is not God's Word and does not produce his fruit, until we recognize it as God's Word in us." He commented on the important passage in Hab. 2:4, "The righteous shall live by his faith," in this way: "It is a magnificent saying, that faith shall be life. Why? Because it hangs on the Word through which everything was created, lives, and continues, which is Jesus Christ, John 1 [1 and 14]."

For Luther, condensing things somewhat, it was the Word that satisfied one's hunger and thirst for righteousness (Matt. 5:6). Receiving the apostles in Matt. 10:40 was reinterpreted as being willing to read and hear the Word, through which Father, Son, and Spirit were received as guests. His interpretation of Luke 11:28 emphasized the necessity of keeping the Word, as well as hearing it. On John 3:16, "For God so loved the world . . . ," he commented, "the Bible must really be a precious, invaluable book for anyone who can believe this, especially the New Testament, for no other book shows us such unspeakable love. . . ." It was similar in John 5:39, a passage often cited by Luther: "No book teaches us about eternal life, i.e., about Christ, the Son of God, except the Holy Scripture. All other books teach mortal matters, even the very best ones." This was coupled with 1 Tim. 3:16, on which he commented: "If we could believe that God himself speaks with us in the Scriptures, we would zealously read them and consider them our blessed workplace." Luther interpreted John 8:31-32, "The truth will make you free," in a manner that was very characteristic of him: "It is the freedom of Christ's disciples so to keep his Word that they are free and secure from the devil, from sin, from death, from hell and all evil. It means being free and confident and certain of everlasting blessedness here, and also having a glad conscience in the life to come. It means to be a nobleman, high born, a rich and great man." One of his comments on John 8:51 is vivid: "A person would be called a good apothecary, if he could give such medicine that not only would it conquer death, but that death would never appear again. And it is a miracle that a person must die, and yet not see death when he has God's Word in his heart and believes in it. This sort of strong medicine is God's Word, when held in faith, for it turns death into eternal life. Oh, if someone could believe this, how blessed would he be in this life as well!" The communion between Christians and Christ (John 15:7) was created by their relationship to his Word, and from it came the Christians' superiority to the world. Occasionally, although not very frequently, Luther also applied Rom. 1:16-17 to the Word of God as a whole—i.e., not just to the gospel—as the power of God and to the righteousness of faith that came from it.

The inscriptions in these books give an indication of how the old Luther related his faith to the Word of the Bible. The way he frequently identifies the Word with Christ is characteristic, as is taking ethical or legal injunctions and subordinating or reinterpreting them in favor of faith, or in favor of prayer as a personal relationship to God. Luther's confident faith lived in this relationship, mediated not least by the Word of the Bible. It was the source from which he drew his certainty and hope, his specific direction, and his criticism of events in the world. Here, too, the expectation that the Bible would speak directly to each person dominated. This made his piety vital and specific. For Luther, the Bible was a Word that spoke, not merely letters.

V

The Professor

1. THE UNIVERSITY:
ITS ORGANIZATION AND CONSTITUTION

Immediately upon entering office, Elector John Frederick, in accordance with his father's will, issued regulations concerning the financing of professorships at the Wittenberg university and thus guaranteed the institution's continued existence. Moreover, new ordinances were necessary for each of the faculties, primarily ones reflecting the changes that had been introduced by the Reformation. In 1533 Melanchthon wrote new statutes for the theology faculty. The norm for teaching was to be the Augsburg Confession of 1530, "the true and reliable conviction of the catholic church of God." The professors of the faculty were to devote themselves primarily to expounding the Old and New Testaments. Disputations and graduations, which had been discontinued for years, were to be reintroduced. The office of dean was to be filled by the professors in turn. If circumstances made it necessary, however, the oldest professor could occupy the position for a longer time. In fact, that is what happened. In 1535 Luther assumed the office of dean from Jonas, who had held it for many years, and he then kept it for the rest of his life.[1] This was a statement of who the head of the Wittenberg theologians was. It appears that there were no longer any legal or political reservations about Luther's serving as dean.

In 1536, after thorough preparations, the elector granted the university a new *Fundation*, which primarily provided a secure financial basis for it and assured that it could continue to offer regular instruction. The elector explained that there was a special obligation to maintain the institution because the proper understanding of the divine Word had emerged anew through Luther's teaching and the ancient languages had been promoted through Melanchthon's efforts. The chief purpose of the university, above the tasks of all the other disciplines, was to spread the gospel and the Word of God. Luther, Jonas, and Cruciger filled the three theological professorships, and, in addition, Pastor Bugenhagen held a teaching appointment. In addition to teaching, the professors were obliged to advise the elector on ecclesiastical matters and questions of marriage law, and this could occasionally cause difficulties in maintaining their teaching activity. Luther received the highest salary, three hundred gulden, and his colleagues, along with Melanchthon, received two hundred gulden; thus they remained the most highly paid members of the

Caspar Cruciger
Woodcut by Lucas Cranach the Elder

faculty. Luther and Melanchthon were given freedom in determining how much they would teach. In the arts faculty, instruction in the ancient languages, which was assigned primarily to the theologians, was in the highest position. As before, the revenue from the All Saints' Foundation was designated as the primary source of income for the university; the remainder came from subsidies from church lands.[2] In 1538 the elector audited his *Fundation*. Luther praised his zeal for the university, for it was "the foundation of the true religion." The elector appears to have understood this, and therefore one could only wish him a long life.[3]

Luther participated in the administration and politics of the university only to a limited extent, i.e., primarily in matters that were of personal interest. Only in exceptional cases was he consulted in the censoring of theological books, which was the responsibility of the theologians. He did not get involved in general university politics. In 1541 he recommended that the university appoint a music instructor. Future pastors and teachers needed a musical education for liturgical singing alone, and certain deficiencies had been evident.[4] Luther tried to arrange a permanent position at the university for the physician George Curio, for he could not make a living with his practice alone. Luther, for example, had never paid Curio a honorarium for his services. In 1543, when Curio was found guilty of assault and also suspected of adultery, he was threatened with the loss of his professorship. Luther thought the action of the university against Curio was too severe, and therefore interceded for him several times with the elector, but made no excuse for his actions. He, too, thought Curio was a black sheep, but for the sake of the university's reputation he should be let off lightly. Out of consideration for Luther and his health, the elector let the matter rest.[5]

After Aurogallus, the Hebraist, died in 1543, the former secretary of the Wittenberg castle library, Lucas Edenberger, applied directly to the elector for the position. Luther supported his application. Luther thought Edenberger was beyond reproach as a theologian, while many of the Hebraists were "more rabbinic than Christian." Theological qualifications should thus be more important than philological ones: "Anyone who does not seek Christ when he looks in the Bible or in the Hebrew language, sees nothing at all and talks the way a blind man talks about color." The elector subsequently requested that the university make a regular recommendation about the appointment. The professorship was then divided between Edenberger and a young man from the territory of Venice, Matthias Flacius Illyricus (1520–75), who later became a controversial Lutheran theologian. However, this could not be a permanent solution. Chancellor Brück ultimately saw to it that Flacius, who was well qualified, was given the full position.[6] The first new appointment to the theology faculty since the reorganization of the university was in 1544, when Jonas left to become superintendent in Halle. In accordance with the university's recommendation, and after discussion with Luther and Melanchthon, his position was filled by George Major (1502–74), the former preacher at the castle church who had been educated in Wittenberg. Nevertheless, because Jonas continued to receive a portion of the revenues of his professorship, Major wanted to retain his position at the castle church as compensation; moreover, he requested that his additional income from a benefice in Altenburg should now go to his sons who were still students. Luther supported this request, although it was not modest, because Major was so esteemed a preacher at the castle church. For good reason, however, the elector rejected such an accumulation of university positions in the hands of one person.[7]

We must briefly discuss Luther's attitude toward astronomy, for significant changes were occurring in that field. Since 1536, along with Erasmus Reinhold (1511–53), George Joachim Rheticus (1514–76) taught mathematics and astronomy in Wittenberg. It was already known at that time that Nicholas Copernicus, a cathedral canon in Frauenburg, Prussia, was teaching a heliocentric or heliostatic view of the world, although his significant writings had not yet been published. In 1539 Rheticus visited Copernicus and encouraged him to publish his revolutionary book, *De revolutionibus orbium coelestium*, which then appeared in Nuremberg in 1543 with a complimentary preface by Andreas Osiander. At Luther's table, in the summer of 1539, they had already discussed Copernicus's view that the earth revolved around the sun. Luther considered this one of those tiny scholarly discoveries that wanted to introduce something new at any price and thus upset traditional opinions. He considered this view incompatible with the biblical view of the world, which was that the sun moved. Melanchthon and Reinhold, for different reasons, also rejected Copernicus's new discovery, while Cruciger supported it. Nevertheless, no significant arguments arose in Wittenberg because of this. It was many more decades before the Copernican worldview became established at Protestant universities.[8]

Luther had had reservations about the jurists for years, and these finally led to serious conflicts. This was primarily a result of the tensions between the new theology and the traditional canon law, as well as of the differences in practice that came from them. Moreover, Luther strongly took issue with the discrepancy between imperfect human jurisprudence and divine justification, between transitory earthly law and the law of God. Because the jurists did not want to subordinate themselves to theology, a mutual distrust had developed. Luther therefore would not permit any of his children to study law. In his opinion, the jurists needed a Luther just as much as the theologians did. He commented on the forthcoming granting of a law degree: "Tomorrow there will be a new viper created against the theologians." The reputed greediness of lawyers naturally did not improve their reputation with Luther.[9] His displeasure was understandably aroused when they also defended the nobles' claims to church lands, and on this subject he considered their judgment worthless.[10] An episode from 1540 shows how sensitive Luther was about jurists. An Augsburg patrician, Hans Honold, had bequeathed a valuable cup to Luther. The executor demanded a receipt before he would deliver the bequest. Luther reacted very indignantly and vulgarly to this legal formality, for, to him, it seemed to impugn his honesty. After he received the bequest, he then had to apologize and concede that things had been done in an orderly way.[11]

One of the points that offended the jurists was digamy, the remarriage of a widowed cleric, which was forbidden by canon law. Luther considered this entirely permissible and far better than the previous moral derelictions among the clergy. The jurist Jerome Schurf, who originally had been one of Luther's supporters but was fundamentally conservative, unequivocally rejected it, as he did the new practice of ordination and conditions in the evangelical church in general. He refused to receive communion from deacons who were not episcopally ordained or who had married for a second time.[12] In his sermons in February and March 1539 Luther publicly warned the jurists against continuing to support the injunctions of canon law against digamy. "We will not and cannot permit you to split my [!] church." On this question the jurists had to submit. Luther appealed to the young people not to become such jurists who blasphemed God by appealing to church law.[13] It does not appear that Luther's challenge to the jurists had any consequences.

Another controversial point was secret marriages, i.e., engagements entered into without parental consent, which canon law recognized, but which Luther, appealing to the commandment to obey one's parents, strictly rejected. In the lectures on Genesis in 1540 he gave a lengthy and polemic explanation of his viewpoint against the canonists in connection with his exposition of Isaac's courting his bride (Genesis 24).[14] Luther's ire was particularly kindled at the beginning of 1544 by the case of Caspar Beyer, a student who lived in his house. Beyer had become engaged to a girl on condition of his father's approval, but then he promised himself to another. The relatives of the first fiancée sought to obtain the approval of Beyer's father for the union, and he did consent, although the father was not accurately informed about the facts of the situation. After this occurred, he also endorsed the second engagement. The case was complicated. The Wittenberg consistory, which functioned as a marriage tribunal and in which the jurists of the university also participated, declared that the first engagement was valid.

Luther believed that once again the jurists had made a decision according to Catholic matrimonial law, an opinion that was possibly not totally correct. He therefore attacked them vehemently from the pulpit on 6 January. A week later he withdrew some of his criticism: He had not wanted to condemn the jurists as a whole, but he warned against a jurisprudence that took a stand against theology and led consciences astray. As the preacher responsible for the Wittenberg congregation, he explained in a subsequent Sunday sermon why secret engagements should not be allowed. Confronted with the wrath of the jurists, he picked up the topic again on 3 February and protested that he had not wanted to offend the legal scholars, but that certain abuses nevertheless had to be abolished. He had previously informed the elector of the controversy and asked him to affirm the non-recognition of secret engagements, thus overruling the decision of the consistory in Beyer's case.[15]

Immediately following the first sermon, the law faculty itself appealed to the elector, particularly because they feared that Luther would attack them in print. The elector instructed Bugenhagen, Brück, and Melanchthon to mediate. He also announced that he would not tolerate any Catholic interpretations among the jurists. If Luther's criticism were to prove correct, he also should be allowed to publish it. Luther stated his point of view before the group of mediators in general and also in regard to this specific case. In March the conflict was still not totally resolved. This caused a great deal of trouble for Melanchthon, who was concerned about the faculties that had to work together. He thought that the blame should be placed upon Luther, who with advancing age was becoming more and more irascible.[16]

Regarding this specific case, Luther was still unwilling to make any concession in June. If necessary, he would pronounce the verdict himself. As far as legal formalities were concerned, what he had to say would have been only personal advice in the confessional, but in fact Luther was assuming the authority of a judge in a problematic way. He based this on his authority: "Of course I do not consider myself a private person, and I insist that God will impose my sentence on many people, rather than the one of our consistory." At that time, however, it was already evident that Beyer's appeal would be successful. Beyond this individual case, Luther's protest resulted in a requirement that the theologians and jurists were to agree in principle about secret engagements, as well as about prohibited degrees of relationship, which were likewise controversial. Luther was skeptical that anything could be achieved. It was his experience that the jurists did not accept the Reformation ordinance of marriage, and that they delayed the cases. In accordance with the instructions, however, he invited them to meet with him, although he was not prepared at this time to get involved in a debate or a compromise, and he simply informed the jurists that, as a preacher, he was bound by the Fourth Commandment, and, moreover, that parental approval of engagements was necessary. At that time he also emphasized in a sermon that the way the Bible formulated the law was a given for the jurists as well as for himself, and that it was binding on both of them. To Luther's surprise, the jurists declared that they agreed with him. In January 1545 Beyer's appeal was also granted, so that, with his father's permission, he could marry the girl whom he had actually chosen. Thereby Luther ultimately triumphed against the jurists. Because of gaps in what has been preserved, it is difficult to determine whether the jurists simply decided the complicated individual case differently than Luther, or whether they first had to reach the fundamental agreement that Luther demanded. The fact that the jurists' protests about Luther's provocation were apparently kept within bounds speaks in favor of Luther's action, although his demeanor seems harsh and excessive. He would have chosen to leave Wittenberg rather than consent to the validity of canonical marriage law in his church.[17] Therefore this controversy between the faculties of the Wittenberg university had to be endured.

Efforts on behalf of scholarships for students required many letters from Luther and his colleagues. Otherwise, many students who came from large families or were orphans could hardly have been able to study. Initially, the scholarship program in Electoral Saxony was not organized; each individual case required a special application, and then usually the revenues from an ecclesiastical benefice that was no longer filled would be designated for the purpose. In his requests to the elector, Luther continually stressed the necessity of encouraging new students in view of the shortage of personnel in the church. He also mentioned that educated theologians were indispensable, although in principle all Christians should be theologians. He was concerned, first of all, about developing theologians. When a student wanted to transfer from theology to jurisprudence, he reacted cautiously: "For I do not want, and it is also not my concern, to help a *theologus* who diverts theologians' stipends to the jurists." Occasionally Luther applied directly to the court officials instead of to the elector, or he dealt with the city councils himself.[18]

Even when a scholarship was granted, it could be difficult to get the money. Luther frequently had to try to obtain payment of the income of a benefice at the Wartburg, which the elector had assigned to Jerome Weller, for the Eisenach administration caused difficulties. The elector himself therefore had to become involved. There were new difficulties when this benefice was taken over by the administrators of the church lands and Eisenach again did not pay. After Weller, the Wartburg stipend was then received by George Scharff and subsequently by George Schnell, a resident of Luther's house. Because it was not paid in full, Luther again had to threaten to bring a complaint before the elector. Each year he practically had to extort the money from the administration, which naturally was irksome. For Luther, the case was a perfect example of the unfriendliness of administrative officials, but he was determined to proceed "with the most pious insolence against the devil's insolence," and he therefore turned once again to the elector.[19]

The elector himself had already become convinced in 1538 that the assignment of stipends needed a comprehensive regulation, one that would give special preference to students of theology. Chancellor Brück discussed this with Luther in 1541, and the result was a decision to exercise better supervision of the way scholarship recipients pursued their studies. The list of recipients of stipends, which Luther himself drew up, included thirteen students of theology, one of medicine, and eight who probably were in the faculty of liberal arts. This was a small number in view of the needs of Electoral

Saxony, but by 1544 had increased so that there were seventy students being aided, most of whom came from the larger cities. Despite Luther's intercession, a small city like Kemberg near Wittenberg went away empty-handed.[20] In Electoral Saxony no generous solutions to the problem of financing students were initiated as in Hesse and Württemberg, where institutions for scholarship holders were established.

The efforts on behalf of scholarships were not limited to Electoral Saxony. For George Schnell, who was mentioned above, Luther had already applied in 1533 to the magistracy in his hometown, Rothenburg ob der Tauber. Here he argued on the basis of the lack of new personnel for the church, the responsibility to educate people, the gifts of the student, and not least the advancement of the kingdom of God and the glory of Christ. At Luther's request, Duke Albrecht of Prussia financed a two-year period of study in Italy for Peter Weller. In another case the duke continued the stipend of a student who had become ill. Luther asked Margrave George of Brandenburg-Ansbach to extend a scholarship grant from four to seven years so that the prince would later have a suitable preacher; in contrast, it would be a sin if the student would have to discontinue his studies because of poverty. Luther later sought to have the same stipend granted to another student. In doing so, he made it clear to the margrave that such stipends are "alms given by princes and lords for the benefit of all Christendom." He sent other requests to Duke Henry of Mecklenburg, the council of Görlitz, Prince George of Anhalt, and King Christian III of Denmark. How important Luther considered such letters is revealed in one sent to Nuremberg, which he forced himself to write after a severe illness—while "dying," so to speak.[21] Occasionally he also interceded for nontheologians. The members of the Cotta family in Eisenach should make it possible for a relative to continue his studies in law in France. When it became apparent that the health of a student from Breslau would not permit him to become a preacher, Luther successfully encouraged the council to allow him to switch to medicine. Later he supported the student's transfer to the university in Leipzig.[22] Luther advised the Austrian nobleman Christoph Jörger that it was better to pay his son's student expenses in advance, because "prevention [Vorsorge] is better than cure [Nachsorge]."[23]

Duke Albrecht of Prussia or Franz von Waldeck, the bishop of Münster and Osnabrück who was sympathetic to the evangelicals, provided letters of recommendation to Luther for students from the nobility. On his part, Luther promised a concerned father that he would take care of his son and provide him guidance and help. Once he cautiously advised that two Mansfeld students who were entrusted to his care should have their allowance cut.[24] Special counsel was needed by Martin Weyer, one of the students living in Luther's house, who was summoned home by his father, an old believer: The son should not give any offense to his father, but fully participate in all the traditional pious exercises while at home, yet at the same time he should tell his father about justification and the preaching of Jesus. In this way it might be possible for the son to become the spiritual father of his physical father.[25] Among the obligations of a professor was also that of informing a father that his son had died during a fever epidemic. Luther was able to sympathize with the father's pain: "I, too, am a father and have seen some of my children die, and I have seen other suffering greater than death, and I know that such things hurt." His comfort was in stressing that with God the children were not lost.[26]

Luther sometimes exercised his responsibility for the students' morality from the pulpit. In 1535 he was not against their visiting the taverns, enjoying themselves, and singing, but they should not squander their money there. This was particularly true of the wicked saloons, which deserved to be nailed shut more than did the houses of people who were sick with the plague at that time. If the students did not comply, their parents would be notified so that they would not lose their morals in Wittenberg.[27] In February 1539 a masquerade and nocturnal riot took place, during which a student challenged a citizen. Luther strictly admonished the students that they were in the city in order to study and that they had to keep the peace. The burgomaster should use the watchmen to make sure that this happened.[28] A student who had expressed doubts about the Christian faith, and had also made notes to this effect, was interrogated about this and sharply reprimanded. He was considered a shameful example of the depravity of the time.[29] In the 1542 shrovetide there again were considerable excesses on the part of citizens and students. Because Luther's health did not permit him to issue a warning from the pulpit, he had one printed. As a "poor, old preacher," he urgently asked "Brother Student" to conduct himself quietly and respectably and devote himself to studying, or else he would be in peril of God's punishment. He believed he personally did not deserve such insubordination.[30] Although Luther could express himself very clearly this way, especially when public order was disturbed by the students, he did so only on relatively few occasions. Naturally, disciplinary problems were constantly arising at the university, but they appeared to have been limited.

Elector John Frederick had both of his sons study in Wittenberg. In order to display the progress in their studies, in 1543, at the age of thirteen and fourteen, before the university and in the presence of their father and invited princely guests, they recited some elegant Latin verses, which presumably were brilliant achievements of their preceptor. Of course, the elaborate poems later had to be printed, and Luther had to provide the preface.[31] He knew how to make something out of even this task. In addition to the obligatory praise for the boys, he mentioned the fact that here a new sort of education for princes was being practiced. He related this to an appeal to pray for the young princes, in whom the devil had a special interest, that they might be especially preserved from false counselors, unfaithful friends, treacherous servants, and greedy nobles. A good prince, one who seeks, multiplies, and preserves the glory of God as well as the good of his state, is one of God's special blessings. Thus the preface was his own pastoral contribution to the education of the youthful evangelical princes.

2. THE ORDINATIONS

On 12 May 1535 Elector John Frederick instructed the superintendents of the districts of the church that applicants for ministerial positions should first be sent to Wittenberg to "our scholars of the Holy Scriptures, who have the command to ordain them and also to bestow the power and authority of their office of priest and deacon." This measure was based on the fact that there was now a lack of episcopally ordained clergy; the elector was therefore instituting a new regulation. The calling to a church office was not to be left to the individual congregations or the superintendents alone, but it was to be preceded by an act of ordination by the Wittenberg theologians, which would replace the episcopal consecration of a priest. It did not state precisely which body in Wittenberg was to be responsible for doing this. Originally it was probably the theology faculty that was envisioned, but soon the clergy of the Wittenberg church took on a prominent role, because ordination was really an ecclesiastical act and not an academic one. When Vergerio, the papal nuncio, visited Wittenberg in November 1535 and inquired about the practice of ordination, Luther told him that Bugenhagen was the one who performed this episcopal function because the Catholic bishops refused to ordain. Bugenhagen, Luther, and the Wittenberg deacons later served as ordinators, but the theology faculty and Melanchthon remained involved in the process of ordination through examining the candidates. The task was therefore performed by the Wittenberg church in connection with the university theologians.[1] The plan to ordain people in Wittenberg with the laying on of hands was not entirely new. Luther had spoken about it in theory in 1523 and had installed the unordained George Rörer into his office as deacon in the Wittenberg city church in this way in 1525. But it had not become a regular practice. The expression "to ordain" was used in the following period very generally when someone was sent into the ministry, although this did not also preclude an installation within a worship service.[2]

The elector obviously did not act on his own in centralizing ordination in Wittenberg; he had agreed with Luther about it on 8 May during his stay in Wittenberg. On the following day, Luther was already announcing in his sermon: "We are planning on ordaining in a public ceremony." Because the bishops refused to ordain evangelical clergy unless they repudiated their doctrine, it would have to be done in Wittenberg, where they understood themselves to be the true church, and in so doing they were acting in the name of Christ. This action thus did not depend on a special power of bishops to ordain.[3]

124

One of the first ordinations took place on 20 October 1535, and Luther explained its significance in his sermon: The one who officiates in the worship service is Christ; the clergy are merely his instruments, "spoons [*Löffel*], hands," although this did not mean that they could not also be inadequate. He expressly emphasized that ordination was not to be understood as consecrating a priest, but as bestowing an office. The congregation participating in the ordination was exhorted to pray for qualified pastors. The intent of the elector's regulation was to prevent the appointment of unexamined clergy, who might then teach falsely. Therefore the examination before it was part of the ordination, which, contrary to what had previously been intended, was now no longer left to the individual congregation. Bad experiences with unqualified applicants, and even false teachers and Anabaptists, led to a centralization of the territorial church in place of the autonomous supervision of teaching by the congregations. Bugenhagen, however, raised objections to this. He favored an ordination performed by the pastors of the local church. Luther would not exclude that possibility in the future, when the practice of ordination had been firmly established, but the procedure that was initially introduced in Electoral Saxony remained in effect. The measures were in accord with the existing circumstances, in which, however, congregations gave up a portion of their autonomy, although they still retained the right to elect and call pastors.[4]

Luther himself formulated the ordination liturgy.[5] It began with a prayer for ministers of the church and their perseverance in sound doctrine. The office of the ministry was necessary for the church, and it was created and preserved by God himself. While the clergy present laid their hands on the candidate, prayer was offered that he might receive the Holy Spirit, so that as an evangelist he might build the kingdom of God and withstand its opponents, as well as "the detestable abomination of the pope and Mohammed." The worship service was normally conducted in the German language. There was, however, also a Latin formulary if the ordinand was a foreigner who did not understand German. Except for the prayers, the congregation was not actively involved in the ordination; it was a matter for the clergy. This indicated a heightened sense that the office of the ministry stood over against the congregation.

The Wittenberg ordination book that was started in 1537 listed the impressive sum of 738 names by the time of Luther's death.[6] This documents the great role Wittenberg played in providing the evangelical churches with clergy. By no means did all the candidates come from Electoral Saxony; they came from all parts of Germany and beyond. Conversely, clergy were not ordained exclusively for service in the church of Electoral Saxony. Other territories and cities as far away as Transylvania availed themselves of this service of Wittenberg, which contributed greatly to the theological uniformity of the evangelical clergy. The prerequisite for ordination was that a call to an ecclesiastical position had been issued. Occasionally, the authorization for an ordination was issued by the elector.[7] Not all the candidates were Wittenberg students, and some had not studied at all. At that time, an academic education had not yet been introduced everywhere as a prerequisite for ecclesiastical office. Normally, Bugenhagen, who was the pastor, performed the ordination. Until 1540 Luther frequently substituted for him, and, later, the deacon Sebastian Fröschel did. The ordinand was given a certificate that attested, on the basis of testimonials, or, in the case of Wittenberg students, on personal knowledge, to the good moral character of the candidate, as well as to his orthodoxy that accorded with the true church—evidenced in his examination—and to his abhorrence of false teaching. In an ordination examination, for example, Luther would ask whether justifying faith could be described as a work. The certificate further mentioned the candidate's promise to fulfill his office properly and to advocate true doctrine. It concluded with confirmation in a public ordination that, in accordance with the authority of God's Word, the office of preaching the gospel and administering the sacraments had been committed to him, and that God's assistance had been sought for him in prayer.[8] Reminders of the earlier practice of consecrating priests were thus avoided. Functioning on behalf of more than one location, which was what Wittenberg was doing, was substantiated by the example of the ancient church, without thereby claiming anything like an episcopal dignity for itself.

3. GRADUATIONS AND DISPUTATIONS

At the end of April 1533 the head of the parish treasury in Hamburg applied to the Wittenberg theologians on behalf of John Aepinus, who had been chosen as Hamburg superintendent, asking that he be granted a Doctor of Theology degree, which was appropriate for a position of this rank.[1] Doctoral degrees in theology had not been given in Wittenberg since 1525 because the legal basis—the papal privilege—that allowed the university to grant this title, which was highly regarded in the church, had been called into question. The request from Hamburg may have served to make the Wittenberg theologians aware that this problem needed a solution. When the elector came to Wittenberg in mid-June to discuss the council that had been announced, the theologians pointed out that there were only a few theologians with doctorates and that they wanted to grant degrees to Cruciger, Bugenhagen, and Aepinus. Not only did the elector declare his approval, but he also ordered that it be done speedily. The formal ceremony was to take place within the next few days. The elector would pay the expenses and be present himself. The theses for the doctoral disputations, which dealt with justifying grace, the church, and human traditions, were prepared by Melanchthon. The fact that the elector was present, with Dukes Francis and Ernest of Brunswick, Duke Magnus of Mecklenburg, and other members of the nobility, including the chief Wittenberg public officials and the former preceptor of the Antonians in Lichtenburg,

Wolfgang Reissenbusch, who was chancellor of the university, intentionally gave the event a solemn character, for which Jonas, speaking on behalf of the university and the theology faculty, expressly thanked them. Jonas likewise presided at the actual graduation ceremony in the castle church. Luther had composed the order for the graduation program. It stated that the graduation was taking place on the basis of apostolic and imperial authority, both of which were derived from God. This was ultimately a divine calling, one which pledged the doctor to withstand the enemies of God in a responsible, active way. As would have been expected, all mention of papal authority was omitted; indeed, the papacy was undoubtedly one of the enemies of God that was to be resisted. The indirect secular authority was recognized. The doctoral banquet that followed was laid on "royally" by the elector at eighteen or twenty tables in the castle. During 1533 Cruciger was made a member of the theology faculty. Bugenhagen, who held a special position as the Wittenberg pastor, did not receive this honor until 1535.[2]

In 1538, when the University of Tübingen, which had become evangelical, could no longer confer doctoral degrees because its Catholic chancellor had left Württemberg, Luther responded to an inquiry by advising it to follow Wittenberg's example and to exercise and defend its leadership position and privileges as the true church. In Tübingen, however, there was no attempt to operate on the basis of this newly defined legal foundation.[3]

The request from Hamburg about Aepinus's degree already clearly showed the need that had led to the resumption of granting theological doctorates. The doctor's degree from Wittenberg would serve as evidence of the theological qualifications of those clergy who held leading positions in territories or cities and who also were responsible for teaching and overseeing other teachers. The theology faculty considered itself authorized to grant doctorates because it held the pure, evangelical doctrine—presented in the Augsburg Confession in 1530—that conformed to the ancient councils of the church. Like ordinations, graduations were ceremonial acts to which members of the university were invited. The doctors received a certificate from the theology faculty, usually formulated by Melanchthon, that testified to their studies, particularly of Holy Scriptures, their morals, and the result of their examination.[4] Some of the new Wittenberg doctors became leading evangelical theologians of the next generation.

Beginning in 1535, graduation ceremonies for doctors of theology again occurred with some regularity in Wittenberg. These were preceded by disputations, for some of which Luther prepared the theses that the graduate had to defend. The subsequent replies to the rebuttals presented were frequently given by Luther himself.[5] Moreover, Melanchthon's statutes for the theology faculty had already provided for the resumption of the quarterly practice disputations at which the professors took turns in presenting the theses. The elector's *Fundation* of 1536 made the rotating disputations obligatory for all faculties. In the long term, however, it proved difficult to reintroduce and maintain the old practice.[6]

At that time there was a resurgence of interest in Luther's earlier theses. Melanchthon published them in a collected edition in 1534, quite accurately referring to their significance for theology and the history of the Reformation, as well as mentioning their enduring contemporaneousness. In a preface of his own, Luther declared himself in agreement with this documentation of his struggle and his efforts on behalf of the true church. Those who came after him should use the soundness of his arguments as a model, for nothing less than eternal life or eternal death was at stake. He called the disputations "evangelical fragments," worthy of being collected because they contained the chief articles of the gospel; without an understanding of them and without dealing with them the church could not survive. In 1538 the collection was republished, enlarged by the addition of series of theses written since 1534. In a new preface Luther emphasized the insufficiency and incompleteness of his earlier statements. This gave him an opportunity to look back at the development that had led him out of the papal church. This was not an occasion for arrogance for him. Nevertheless, one could praise the God who had led Luther—not without struggle and *Anfechtungen*—from weakness into strength, from ignorance into knowledge, from timidity into boldness: "In short: We are nothing, Christ alone is everything. If he turns aside his countenance we are lost and Satan triumphs, even if we ourselves were saints, Peter and Paul." Personal experience was continuing to teach Luther humility.[7]

It was not until after 1535 that theological disputations again became a regular institution in Wittenberg. Luther presided at a total of fourteen circular disputations and thirteen graduation disputations, limiting himself after 1540 to the graduation disputations, of which, in three cases, the theses were prepared not by him but by Melanchthon.[8] Ever since his days as a student, Luther had been accustomed to presenting a concise development of a theological topic in a series of theses. It was precisely through such a literary form that he had initiated the Reformation. Preliminary drafts of his books and lectures that have been preserved frequently resemble theses. To this extent, theses as a literary form are a significant element in Luther's writing, one that reflects not least his critical and polemic character. Luther obviously also devoted great care both to the form and content of his later theses, and they are thus prominent and important documents of his theology. Here once again his solid schooling in dialectics and in drawing precise conclusions came discernibly to the fore in the service of theology. He wished to pass on this technique, as well as its contents.[9] The disputations themselves clearly do not measure up to the level of the theses. Frequently the applications are sketchy, not infrequently formalistic, sophistical, far-fetched, and repetitious. Nevertheless, at times they provided Luther with further opportunities to clarify important points. Unfortunately, the transcripts of the disputations have been preserved only in a second-hand, reworked version.

The significance of the theses also depends on the subject chosen for them. Until 1538 Luther concentrated primarily on the doctrine of justification, with the theses against the antinomians also intended as a clarification of a conflict that had broken out in Wittenberg. In later years Christology and the doctrine of the Trinity were treated in the same way. In addition to these topics, Luther repeatedly addressed contemporary problems, such as the right of resisting authority or questions relating to the general council and the church. He was never content to deal merely with his theological preferences.

Each disputation that addressed specific challenges will be considered in its own context. The particular character of the disputations and the theses prepared for them shall now be demonstrated on basic theological themes.

Doctorates were to be bestowed on Jerome Weller, a one-time resident of Luther's house, and on Nicholas Medler on 11 and 14 September 1535. Weeks in advance Luther was preparing meticulously for the event in every respect. He was delighted about it. The elector was asked to provide venison and wine. Prince George of Anhalt also made a contribution. Jonas was to seek additional fowl and game for the "splendid" doctoral banquet planned in Luther's house. Colleagues from the university, which had moved to Jena because of the plague, were expected, as was Bugenhagen, who was then on a journey.[10] For the disputation there were two series of theses on Rom. 3:28: "For we hold that a man is justified by faith apart from works of law."[11] Luther later returned to this theme in two more disputations. The first series of theses clarified the understanding of faith. Faith was a gift of the Holy Spirit, not a mere historical faith acquired by humans. It laid hold on Christ who died for our sins and was raised for our righteousness. The essential mark of this faith was confidence that this had taken place *for me*. It constitutes the relationship of love between a believer and Christ. It is this faith, not the law, that justifies. From it, good works necessarily and spontaneously proceed, but they are not the cause of justification. This had implications for the understanding of biblical admonitions. They could be fulfilled only by those already justified by Christ, and they must always be seen in this way. All statements of the Bible are to be interpreted in reference to Christ. If this is impossible, they lose their inner authority. Moreover, one can make the audacious claim: "When we have Christ we will easily create new laws and judge everything correctly, even more, we will make new Decalogues," clearer than the old one. Nevertheless, because of the weakness of the spirit and the continuing burdens of the flesh, Luther advocated holding fast to the apostolic teachings. Justification was understood no less in terms of rebirth and new creation. Self-justification by works, in contrast, would mean that one was blasphemously usurping God's creating activity.

In addition to ensuring a proper understanding of faith, it was necessary to do the same for the law. It was not just the Jewish ceremonial law that had been abrogated by Christ, but the universal moral law that applied to all humankind, along with its power to lead someone into condemnation and despair. Luther's opponents could produce no evidence that one was justified by works of the law; when confronted with the law, even the saints realized that they were sinners. On the contrary, the law is fulfilled by Christ and by him we are saved. The teaching of works was the devil's attempt to distract men from their salvation and thus to cause them to lose it.

Jonas presided at the graduation. Luther made a suggestion for his speech in praise of theology, with which the disputation concluded: Theology was necessary after all other arts in this life had been employed either brilliantly or poorly, when what was at stake was dying and one's departure from this earthly sphere. "Then one must run to, seek for, and call out for that pitiful, wretched, and despised manger in Bethlehem." Crowns, the most exalted titles, riches, skill, or intellect will then no longer be of help.[12]

At the conclusion of the actual graduation ceremony Weller, one of the two new doctors, likewise had to deliver an address in praise of theology, which was also written by Luther. Here, once more, he took issue with the practice of disparaging theology and again emphasized that it was competent in dealing with the kingdom of God. Theology was God's servant, friend, and companion, but it enjoyed little respect on earth. He did not fail to mention that the calling of a theologian had its dangers, its *Anfechtungen,* cares, and concerns, but, seen correctly, non-theologians are prisoners of their inadequate reason and its laws. In contrast, theologians possess certainty and truth through the Word of God, and they know where their real refuge is. Theology, therefore, is a "blessed ministry, which is carried out with the most certain purpose, for God himself is at work even through feeble and unworthy men, and he speaks and works through them." Compared to this knowledge, all the difficulties of this calling are of no consequence, and it is from this that the calling of a theologian has its joy.[13] With these words Luther may have also wanted to stabilize Weller, who suffered from depression. But the influence of his statements went beyond that. They permit us to see that Luther understood his profession as the highest of all callings, one that brought confidence and joy.

At the end of October 1535, among other things, Luther was planning more disputations on the topic of justification. They were to treat the understanding of those Bible passages that spoke about justification by works and thus were being introduced into the discussion by the Catholic opponents. Shortly before, he had dealt with Dan. 4:27, "Break off your . . . iniquities [by giving alms]." According to Luther such an action presupposed faith. Another passage that might be cited against Luther's interpretation was 1 Corinthians 13, in which love was regarded more highly than faith. In this case he resisted playing off love against faith. True faith, even if imperfect, was accompanied by love. He advanced the same argument against Luke 7:47, which said of the woman who

130

was a great sinner, "Her sins, which are many, are forgiven, for she loved much." Love is thankfulness for the forgiveness of sins that precedes it. In 1537 Luther dealt with Matt. 22:1-14, in which the marriage garment, i.e., purity, was seen as a requirement for participating in the heavenly marriage, another Bible passage that was difficult for his doctrine of justification. For him, the wedding garment was faith, which clothed one with Christ's righteousness. In a long introduction he once again emphasized the importance of theology for the kingdom of God. The study of theology also included the practice disputations, for through them the theologians could be armed to counter the objections of their opponents.[14]

Among the disputations on the doctrine of justification in the wider sense, the noteworthy *Disputatio de homine* (The disputation concerning man) on 14 January 1536 must be included.[15] In it Luther first took issue at length with the philosophical definition of man "as an animal having reason, sensation, and body." This described man only as a mortal. He acknowledged that reason was the most important and best thing that man possessed, indeed something divine. It is the inventor and mentor of all the arts, medicines, laws, and of whatever wisdom, power, virtue, and glory men possess, and thus it is the essential element distinguishing men from animals. According to the Bible, it is appointed as lord over creation, and it is to exercise this supervision as a divine being. Not even the fall into sin took this dignity from it. Luther thus regarded human reason highly and assigned it a great deal of autonomy, although admitting it might become problematic because of self-chosen legal regulations in certain areas of life that came from it. Nevertheless, reason—and philosophy, which was equated with it—was blind in comparison to theology, because it knew nothing about the origin and purpose of man or about the soul. Only in God could this be comprehended. Reason's definition and understanding of man extended no further than the horizon of this world.

In contrast, theology was able to define a whole and complete human being. A human being is God's creation, made in the image of God, meant to procreate, rule over creation, and never die. Since the fall into sin humans have been subject to the devil and the power of death, incapable of freeing themselves. They can become free and obtain eternal life only through faith in Christ. Even with all their abilities, they remain in the devil's power, subject to sin and death. The philosophical claim that a human's natural powers remained intact after the fall was thus a godless one. The same holds true for the nominalistic affirmation that humans with their powers can obtain grace or use their free will to decide for the good. These false claims about the human condition are once again rebutted with Rom. 3:28, and this conclusion is the result: "Man is justified by faith." Both human sinfulness and dependence upon God are recognized. The present human situation and goal are described as being "the simple material of God for the form of his future life." Here Luther understands humans on the basis of their changeable relationship and experience with God. God's purpose for humans is that they be justified. Here Luther, deliberately following the prevailing Aristotelian tradition of thought—but at the same time critically taking issue with it—identifies the idea of being human with the center of his theology.

Luther continued his discussion of justification on 10 October 1536 with a new series of theses on Rom. 3:28 for the graduation disputations of Jacob Schenk and Philipp Motz.[16] He first discussed the different sorts of justification: Before humankind we are justified by works, but before God by faith alone. God tolerates insufficient righteousness on earth, because here there can be nothing better. The church and the saints thereby experience his forbearance. They are still in the process of becoming righteous and they remain sinners, but God for Christ's sake already regards them as righteous. The righteousness of Christ, which lies outside us, cannot be fashioned by us, but can only be apprehended in faith. Righteousness is thus imputed to us, and accordingly sin is not held against us. Both the realization of the new creature and the struggle against sin begin with faith. This is Luther's very simple and precise description of justification.

The second series of theses dealt with the sinful condition of the man who was to be justified. Humans can never earn anything from God. The truly original or mortal sin, from which all others derive, cannot be recognized by man at all. It consists of not believing in God, or more specifically of not having faith in the crucified Christ who is our salvation. The scholastic definition of original sin as desire, and likewise the assumption that something good remains in man, fails to understand either sin or Christ, although experience with evil ought necessarily to lead one to conclude that human nature is not good. Thus one of the tasks of theology is to "enlarge sin." At the same time it is apparent that the divine work of justification surpasses all human understanding. It is a new creation. In the address that opened the disputation Luther emphasized once more the necessity of constantly dealing with the article of justification, for it alone made someone a theologian. In the disputation itself he made it clear that he was attacking not only scholasticism, but also Erasmus's exposition of Romans and the commentary by Cardinal Jacopo Sadoleto, which had recently been published.

In 1537 another disputation on Rom. 3:28 was held. Like the subsequent disputations against the antinomians, this one also dealt with justification, but it took place in the context of theological disputes within Wittenberg. They will be discussed in chapter 6.

A few years later there were difficulties with the rotating disputations. The students no longer had a mastery of the technique of debating as they had earlier, although there was no longer any dearth of subjects worth discussing. It may not have been easy to debate with the Wittenberg coryphaeus. Luther was willing to be patient when the students argued in an unsatisfactory way. One should not criticize them too hastily as Melanchthon did. Their well-intentioned efforts should be acknowledged. In his opening address at the rotating disputation on 11 January 1539, Luther reminded everyone of the mandate issued shortly before by the elector that had emphasized, among other matters, the disputations. Evangelical theology, which was suspected of heresy and of being a new teaching, especially had to be in a position to reply convincingly to its critics. Luther's preference, if his stamina permitted, would have been to debate every week, so that the students might be equipped to confront their foes and future false teachings.[17] For him, theology, in addition to being instruction, also was and remained a battle for the truth and a defense against the assaults of the devil. In one of his final speeches at the opening of a disputation he lapsed from Latin into German: "It will always be this way; we will always have to fight."[18] Luther's theology was fated to have to fight and defend itself.

The disputation on 11 January 1539 dealt with John 1:14: "The word became flesh."[19] In this context Luther impressively showed that the claim made by the Sorbonne in Paris, that truth was identical in philosophy and theology, was impossible. Rather, reason had to obey Christ. Theology and philosophy repeatedly came into conflict because of their respective rules of thought. This was apparent in the doctrine of the Trinity and in the incarnation, God's coming into the world. Truth was not always uniform in the different disciplines of philosophy. Thus theology drew the conclusion that philosophy should be limited to its own sphere and that in the realm of faith one had to speak with a new language. God was not subject to reason and logical conclusions.

At the graduation disputation of Erasmus Alber in 1543 Luther stated that it was impossible for philosophy to reconcile the unity of God with the trinitarian distinctions of the divine persons, and he rejected all attempts at doing so. He also deliberately did not offer his own explanation. One had to hold fast in faith to the Son of God revealed in flesh. In this way one would be touched and illuminated by the splendor of God's majesty. Following the actual act of graduation, it was customary for a boy to ask the new doctor a question in order to learn something from him in the exercise of his new calling. In Alber's case, the question was formulated by Luther himself. It had to do with whether faith in Christ could coexist with error without endangering one's salvation. Suggestions of good reasons for answering negatively were given, but the line of argument based on faith's weakness and its capacity to grow hinted that the questioner expected an affirmative reply.[20]

The prerequisite for George Major's assumption of the professorship left vacant by Jonas's departure was the possession of a doctorate. The disputation for this purpose took place on 12 December 1544. Once again the theme was the doctrine of the Trinity, a topic that utterly confounded mathematics. Luther took issue with the arguments of the scholastics, but he was more concerned about defending the trinitarian dogma against the modern objections being raised by Campanus and Michael Servetus.[21]

The last time Luther presided at a disputation was the graduation of Petrus Hegemon on 3 July 1545. Preparing the theses had exhausted him. The scope of the theme was broader than usual, extending from the doctrine of the Trinity to the incarnation, from redemption from sin to the problem of how original sin was transmitted. As had Augustine, Luther considered original sin an inheritance from Adam and thus spoke critically against contrary papal doctrinal definitions that seemed to make the Creator partly responsible for the defect of humankind.[22]

4. THE FINAL LECTURES

In March 1532 Luther began to interpret selected Psalms in his lectures, because he believed his health would not permit him to expound the whole Psalter. He did, in fact, have to interrupt his lecturing frequently. From 20 August until 4 November he lectured on Psalm 45.[1] Like the psalmist, he understood himself to be doing the work not of a prophet, but of someone who wrote down the interpretation. Because of its imagery, the royal psalm was interpreted in relation to Christ and his kingdom and thus as comfort for a church afflicted by persecution and sin. The Wittenberg church, where people preached, baptized, and celebrated the Lord's Supper, could be understood as the king's ivory palace in the psalm.

Finishing it, Luther then attempted a longer segment, lecturing on Psalms 120–134—known as psalms of ascent from their use in Israelite worship—until 27 October 1533, with a lengthy interruption from January until June. He was no longer concerned about presenting something new, for by then his theology was well enough known, and he did not want to appear brilliant in comparison to his colleagues. He wished to reiterate what was necessary and continue to offer admonitions. He considered teaching and learning the Psalms as worship, as a necessary spiritual exercise, a fulfillment of the First Commandment, and one in which no one should grow weary. One could never learn enough theology.[2] Psalm 120 dealt with the *Anfechtung* of true doctrine, which drove one to pray: "Praying must go along with teaching." Luther was speaking out of more than enough experience. Only because he had continually brought his cause before God had he been able to survive: "The ultimate wisdom is this: Flee to the Lord God as fast as you can." There are echoes of how much the enthusiasts and Anabaptists—specifically Müntzer, Karlstadt, and Zwingli—had burdened him, and also how much trouble had been caused by the nobles, burghers, and peasants who disdained the Word, but, in contrast, in his interpretation of Psalm 124 he also articulated the experience of God's preservation. As before, Luther continued to have little regard for human attempts at creating security, such as building the Wittenberg wall. It was of no more use than the hut of the shepherd along the Elbe that had been carried away when the river flooded its banks.

Luther had high regard for Psalm 127, which was brief but filled with wisdom, because of its great value for the state and the family. Likewise, the hymn of marriage in Psalm 128 showed that the Holy Spirit was the "best poet and speaker."[3] It made a definitive statement about relationships: It is God who is the Creator and Preserver; human beings are only his instruments. Confusion reigned wherever this was not recognized, as might easily be seen in the regime of bailiffs or in the estate of marriage: "Wittenberg is an anarchy; Duke George, a tyrant." One should not flee from the world into a monastery because of this, but rather should acknowledge God as the chief politician, the governor, the Lord. Here, as well, he saw the home, in which God had placed man, as the nucleus of all human community. The Creator therefore must remain the ruler in this sphere as well. Only with God could home and state be managed. For this, Luther appealed to the example of Frederick the Wise. In the long run, one's own self-chosen works would have no success in politics or commerce either. Duke George of Saxony proved that. Even in procreation God is the Creator who blesses us with children and tends to their preservation. Man and woman are his instruments. Likewise, God creates and preserves political peace. In this exposition one is impressed by how one's natural and political existence must also be lived out in faithful dependence on God. Thus both the family and the community are seen unreservedly as fields for a Christian's activity. The role of a woman was limited to her household, but there she was regarded highly for her gifts. Naturally she had her weaknesses—as, admittedly, did a man as well.

Psalm 130 was for Luther one of the most important psalms because it dealt with the chief article of justification, which alone preserved and enlightened the church.[4] He praised it for its rhetoric, which spoke of *Anfechtung*. Its instructions about forgiveness demolished any self-made sanctity. At the conclusion of the lecture Luther could label it with some justification as the sum of almost all articles of the Christian faith, especially emphasizing preaching, the forgiveness of sins, the cross, love, marriage, and government.[5]

After lecturing on the psalms of ascents Luther took an entire year off. Then he concluded the series of lectures on the Psalms with an exposition of Psalm 90.[6] After the first five lectures in October 1534 there was a long break. The last two lectures were delivered rather sporadically on 8 March and 31 May 1535. Luther saw the message of the psalm as the tyranny of death and the wrath of God, along with the way of salvation from the despair this produced. It saw the fate of death not as a mere infirmity, the way Zwingli had defined it. But the whole psalm served as a setting for hope in the God who raises the dead. God's actions, of course, are experienced in a gripping manner. He is the Creator, but in his wrath he also lets men die after a brief life. A Christian associates death with God's judgment. The positive aspects of life are ultimately completely overshadowed by the fact of its limitations. Unlike the heathen, however, the Bible assuredly knows that God works for people's salvation or condemnation beyond this life. He is moved to be gracious through prayer. According to Luther's understanding, the conclusion of the psalm already foreshadowed salvation through Christ. Thus the psalmist's prayer concluded with a petition for aid in secular life and especially in the life of the church, "that doctrine might remain pure . . . so that the gospel be not corrupted."

Despite the poor condition of his health, which up to then had enabled him to carry out his teaching only with interruptions, Luther began to lecture on Genesis immediately after concluding his exposition of Psalm 90, probably on 1 June 1535.[7] He did not expect to complete it before his death. Except for the two short lectures on Isaiah 9 and 53 delivered in 1543 and 1544, the lectures on Genesis did in fact mark the conclusion of his teaching career. For more than ten years, albeit with numerous interruptions, he was engaged in these lectures, finally completing them on 17 November 1545. In July 1535 he had to make the first pause for half a year when the university was moved to Jena because of the plague. From December 1536 until March 1537, Luther was ill or away on journeys. From February 1538 until March 1539, he progressed only from Genesis 17 to Genesis 19. In 1541 he apparently lectured hardly at all. In December he had reached chapter 26, at the beginning of 1543 he was at chapter 31, and at the beginning of 1545 at chapter 45.[8]

These great lectures are unquestionably monumental documents of Luther's mature theology, and they also reflect his participation in the developments, problems, and conflicts of the last decade of his life. Unfortunately the manuscripts of the notes taken by Rörer and Cruciger for this massive work have not been preserved; only those begun by Veit Dietrich, who published them in a four-volume commentary between 1544 and 1554, are extant. When Dietrich died in 1549, the work was completed by the Nurembergers Michael Roting and Jerome Besold, the latter a sometime resident of Luther's house. They are responsible for the repetitions that it contains, a result of their using different students' notes. They likely also added some things. Above all, their own theology crept into the work, so that one cannot always be sure of reading the genuine Luther. Therefore, we must be very cautious in making use of the lectures on Genesis. Nevertheless, the bulk of this commentary, with its amazing richness of features and allusions, undoubtedly does come from Luther, and his spirit is evident in it. Despite the subsequent alterations, this monumental work may still be regarded as primarily his work and thus as a useful source.

Luther himself had not planned on publishing the lectures. When the idea was presented to him in 1538 he rejected it. He considered the lectures unorganized and imperfect, and felt that although they might be sufficient to stimulate further reflection, they were not complete enough. His other tasks left him no time to concentrate on preparing a polished interpretation. In the summer of 1543, when Rörer presented him with the first printed pages, he still maintained this critical opinion, which was not inaccurate in regard to some portions. In Veit Dietrich's opinion, however, Luther's commentary deserved to be published because there would otherwise be no complete exposition of Genesis. Rörer referred to it as an invaluable treasure.[9]

In the preface to the first volume[10] Luther once again stated that the lectures had not been prepared for publication, but were to be thought of only as exercises in God's Word for the Wittenberg students and the author himself. He did not want to spend his old age unproductively in idleness. He had permitted their publication, but he doubted that the resulting exposition corresponded with his intentions. Then he himself characterized his lectures: "Everything was said freely and in a way that was understandable to all, just as the words came to my mouth, frequently also mixed with German expressions, certainly more verbose than I wished." Naturally he was not aware of having said anything false. He had tried to achieve as much clarity as possible. Although he had done his best, he was not satisfied with the results. No one was able to exhaust the riches of the Bible or master it. No one was able to understand everything, everyone made mistakes. It was enough to love the Bible's wisdom and meditate on it day and night. The inadequacy of commentaries was apparent in the church fathers, but even more so among contemporary exegetes, among whom Luther was probably thinking primarily of Erasmus, not to mention the Jewish commentators whom he frequently and sharply criticized. There were always different gifts being offered in the Lord's temple. Luther did not consider his as one made from precious metal, only simple goat's hair. Despite his humility, he still proudly boasted that he had given his opponents and the devil opportunity enough to take issue with him, "as I have done from the very beginning and am still happy to do." He concluded his preface with a heartfelt plea that the Lord might come and bring redemption.

It is apparent that the interpretation of the first three chapters was difficult for Luther, and he breathed a sigh of relief when he had crossed this "sea." He had had an easier time than his predecessors, however, because he had stuck to the literal text and avoided allegories.[11]

This was occasionally difficult to do, because much of the traditional material had to be discarded. It was obvious for Luther that it was the triune God who was at work in creating the world. God's image in man consisted of living like God, free from fear of death, and having authority over the rest of creation. Man and woman are equal in regard to their potential for attaining eternal life, but woman is subordinate to man in dignity. For Luther, the church, one of the human orders of creation (hierarchies) that was oriented to the Word of God, had been created in paradise when the admonition not to eat of the tree of knowledge was given, a command which included the "worship" of God. Man's original righteousness consisted simply of obeying God. With the creation of Eve a second order of creation, that of the family (*oeconomia*), was added. In its realm man and woman were absolutely equal. The union of man and woman was originally a pure act of living, devoid of the later turmoil. Eve was the partner given Adam by God. On this basis he again criticized celibacy. Government, the third of the orders of creation, was not established until after the flood, when punishment was instituted (Gen. 9:6).

The devilish aspect of the temptation was that the Word was opposed to the Word, something that the church of the Reformation also had to experience. After sin came self-justification, and it was accompanied by accusations against God. Thus it became impossible to plead for forgiveness. Luther saw parallels of this in the piety of the monks. Christ, not Mary, is the one who crushes the serpent. The story of hope began with the promise that looked forward to Christ. The burden of toil was noticed first by the peasants, then it increased among politicians, but it was strongest among ministers of the church who were being attacked by all sides.

Cain and Abel, later Esau and Jacob, were for Luther the representatives of the false and the true church, where it was the constant fate of the true church to be persecuted by the false. The lectures often picked up this distinction, a sign of how strongly Luther was concerned with the theme of the church at that time.[12] God's gracious acceptance and man's recognition of this are not identical. Peace between the two churches was impossible, and could not be achieved by religious negotiations.

The genealogies in Genesis with their enumeration of years inspired Luther to prepare a table of history divided into decades that extended from creation to the year 1540; it was first published in 1541 as *Computation of the Years of the World*.[13] He based it upon existing chronicles. Although he occasionally went his own way in dating biblical events, in general he remained entirely within the Jewish-Christian historical understanding of the Old Testament, which assumed the world was less than six thousand years old. Here, too, there were attempts to show that the two churches were opposed to one another, although this was not consistently carried through. The history of the papacy, in part, was related to the prophecies of Daniel and of John's Apocalypse. According to Luther's reckoning, 1540 was the year 5500 of the world's history. He therefore expected that the world would soon end, for he assumed that the sixth millennium would not be completed. Here there was no hint that a new age is dawning.

When he lectured on Noah's drunkenness (Gen. 9:20-22), Luther thought he himself should get drunk the night before, so that he could speak as an expert about this wickedness. The story showed him that even the righteous and the saints could fall. This was true of the evangelicals as well, and their lapses were eagerly recorded by the Catholics, but Luther solemnly warned against rejoicing over the failings of others and jumping to hasty condemnations. God could tolerate the errors and failings of those who were his own.[14]

The real heart of the lectures on Genesis was obviously the story of Abraham, interpreted in Pauline categories. Although he used the Old Testament texts, Luther here developed his theme of righteousness by faith. For him, Abraham had no qualities of his own. He was "merely the material that the divine majesty seizes through the Word and forms into a new human being and into a patriarch." The story of Abraham was understood on the basis of the promise that was made to all people, and for this reason it deserved to be engraved in golden letters. Abraham was the father in faith, and none of the pious monkish fathers could be compared to him. One should imitate his faithful obedience and follow his call, which was indeed accompanied by *Anfechtung* and the cross. Luther partially excused Abraham's questionable acts, such as telling lies or fathering Ishmael with Hagar, by connecting them with the history of the promise. Because Luther was primarily occupied in October 1537 by the court and engaged in ecclesiastical affairs, he was not able to give adequate preparation to chapter 15, which was important for the New Testament in view of righteousness by faith, and therefore treated it only grammatically and cursorily. Nevertheless, in it the lineaments of his doctrine of justification can be clearly seen. At the end of March 1539 he was unable to exegete the close of chapter 19 thoroughly and had to be content with a "simple and true" explanation.

At the end of May or the beginning of June 1540, Luther had reached chapter 24 and had thus almost finished the story of Abraham. When he completed it, he wanted to discontinue his lecturing. In the three hours each morning when he was in a position either to lecture or write, he planned to write brief commentaries on the entire Bible. When Rörer urged him to continue his teaching, Luther saw the only purpose of his lectures as providing an opportunity for young theologians to listen to a famous personality. In August he gave a somewhat different reason for resuming his teaching: There were several people available whom he considered better qualified than himself. Nevertheless, he would continue, in order that he might weaken the papists and show them he was not going to stop attacking them or proclaiming the gospel. There were, in fact, not many classes in Wittenberg from which to choose. When Melanchthon and Cruciger were absent in November 1540, Luther had to fill in, although he found it difficult: "I am flailing at Moses, and he in turn is flailing at me." Apparently the story of Jacob and Esau had given him difficulties, and he wished to retire. During the entire year of 1541 he lectured hardly at all.[15]

The story of Isaac and Jacob was understood as a continuation of the miraculous history of the promise. To be sure, it was more profane than the edifying stories of the monks, and even offensive because of its human weaknesses; but the significant thing about it remained that God had spoken to the patriarchs. The promise made to Jacob at Bethel (Gen. 28:14), for example, was an especially precious jewel. The account of Jacob's wrestling with God (Gen. 32:25-33) was traditionally regarded as one of the most obscure passages of the Old Testament. Luther's exegesis offers a glimpse into the depth of his understanding of God, for he knew something about how a man in his *Anfechtungen* might have to deal directly with God. From this story came a new proverb: "When you think that our Lord God has rejected a person, you should think that our Lord God has him in his arms and is pressing him to his heart."[16]

Among the stories of the patriarchs, Luther gave a special place to the final one, the history of Joseph with its unhappy beginning, which made it difficult for Jacob to keep hoping until everything finally turned out well. In October 1543, however, he felt unable to do justice to the material and would have preferred to leave it to someone else. Nevertheless, he continued the exposition he had begun, although he considered it more of a mere recitation of the text than an appropriate treatment of the subject.[17] This evaluation was too modest. Once again we are impressed by his insight into situations of *Anfechtung*. The story of Joseph thus also has a deeply psychological meaning. Again and again Luther showed a confident faith in God's guidance. Melanchthon spoke with complete accuracy about how Luther's exegesis, like that of other spiritual men, grew simpler and more lifelike with advancing age. He therefore insisted that Veit Dietrich undertake its publication.[18] Luther himself, in contrast, thought that his commentary was too verbose and not substantial enough. At the beginning of 1545 he was longing to die after he finished the lectures, or even sooner.[19]

Now that we have considered the massive undertaking of the lectures on Genesis, we need look only at the two brief lectures that were interpolated within it. In both their themes and contents they also belong among the important statements of Luther's mature theology. At Christmas 1544 he undertook a treatment of the messianic prophecy of Isa. 9:1-6 in order to deal with the incarnation of God's Son, "the greatest work of all works and the most exalted of all miracles." If the magnitude of this blessing for humankind were fully comprehended, people would perish from the very joy of it, but, to Luther's sorrow, the deed itself and the mystery that the Son of God assumed the closest union imaginable with the believer was not properly articulated or accepted. He wanted to let his students taste at least a few drops of it.[20] The lectures, which were occasioned by the church year, were initially concentrated on preaching. At the same time, he took issue in them with the Jewish interpretation of the Messiah. For Luther, the text of the Old Testament was the gospel. Its contents dealt with Christ freeing a person from death, sin, the law, and hell, and transferring that person into the kingdom of life, righteousness, and peace. He thus emphatically rejected any application of the text to the time of Isaiah, appropriate as this was. If freedom and reconciliation were not to be hoped for from Christ, but merely morality and political wisdom, then Luther wanted no Christ like that; he would prefer to depend on law-books and pagan philosophers. His hope was not only in the immortality of the soul; "I also want the body." Luther again found the messianic promise of freedom in Paul, and therefore referred to him as a "careful Isaiahist."

The counterpart to the lectures on Isaiah 9 were the ones on Isaiah 53, the song of the suffering servant, delivered in the 1544 Lenten and Easter season.[21] Their actual topic was "that Christ is God and man." More than the suffering, he strongly stressed the divinity and exaltation of Christ, "the arm of the Lord." He held firmly to the unity of God and man in the person of Jesus Christ, so that the entire breadth of Luther's Christology appeared once again: The son of the Virgin is the one who preserves the world, and the Son of God dies. Not only did God have the highest sympathy for us, but he also suffered the punishment for our transgressions, enduring the hell of being abandoned by God. This involved much more than guiltless suffering, for it was precisely in this way that he was able to bring peace and salvation.

When we look at Luther's activity as a teacher, the two highpoints are the first and second lectures on the Psalms (1513 to 1521), which began his significant rise, and the complex of lectures in the 1530s and 1540s on Galatians, selected Psalms, and Genesis.[22] No decline at the end of his life is discernible. Until the end, Luther was able to develop his theology from its center in the doctrine of justification and Christology by continually using new biblical texts in new and original formulations, and thus to give his theology a startling richness and mature form. In no sense was the taxing activity of teaching in his final years merely routine, for he was performing his assigned task as a theological educator, and his activity did not fail to produce fruit among his students and readers.

5. THE COLLECTED WORKS

There had been collections of Luther's writings, sermons, and theses ever since 1518.[1] They served to bear witness to the doctor of theology and teacher of the gospel. A "catalogus or index" of all of his books and writings was published in Wittenberg in 1528, and then expanded in 1533. Luther himself took note of the second edition by writing a preface for it.[2] The need for a list of his writings apparently was presented frequently to him. Luther himself was not interested in having his literary activity preserved. He had only produced these works in order that "the Holy Scriptures and divine truth might come to light." This had happened, and therefore they could dispense with his books. Nevertheless, he acknowledged that they did have historical significance. People could learn from them "what has happened to me, yes, what has happened to the precious Word of God, what it has had to suffer from so many great enemies in these past fifteen years until its power became known, and how this happened, and also that I have daily and yearly gotten to know it more deeply and more thoroughly. . . ." Luther knew that he himself had undergone a development; Cochlaeus and Faber were showing that he had made conflicting statements in doing so, but he was not ashamed of it.

Understandably enough, the plans for a collected edition of Luther's works were thus not initiated by him. In 1528 Stephan Roth was the first to pursue a project of this sort, but it did not materialize. Presumably it was the "catalogus" of 1533 that gave Count Ludwig XV of Öttingen the idea of getting Jonas's support for a collected edition. Jonas pointed out that there were difficulties because of Luther's excessive workload, but he did not think that the project was unrealizable.[3] After the agreement on the Wittenberg Concord, Capito energetically worked together with the Strasbourg printer Wendelin Rihel to produce a collection of Luther's works. It was intended to strengthen the solidarity among the evangelicals; moreover, because of financial losses, Capito was interested in the income such an edition might be expected to produce. Luther responded cautiously in July 1537. For him, only *The Bondage of the Will* and the catechism were worthwhile books. He turned the matter over to Cruciger. A few months later he rejected the proposal even more strongly: Theological books had always led the church farther from the Bible. He again claimed that his books had only a historical significance as documents of the conflict with the pope. Whether it was this that ultimately led in 1538 to abandoning the Strasbourg edition is unknown.[4]

In a preface to the drafts of his sermons, which were printed in 1537 without his knowledge, Luther forbade the unauthorized publication, both during his lifetime and after his death, of the notes in which he had recorded his thoughts. They were spontaneous, unfinished, and unguarded statements, or even angry arguments in which he acted like a court jester in trying to instruct God. Even if there were nothing wrong with these notes, they did not belong to the public. Some things, upon later, cooler reflection, were seen to be foolish. Luther had difficulties enough with his best writings, and thus such publications were not helpful. In 1540 he also refused to permit the publication of his letters. He did give careful attention to his correspondence, of course, but it was naturally conditioned by specific situations.[5]

Probably encouraged by the Strasbourg plans, the Augsburg and Wittenberg printers also wanted to produce a collected edition, and one was finally published in Wittenberg. Luther continued to object, but he did nothing to hinder the project. His earlier writings, which he now considered weak, should be forgotten.[6] The chief editors were the experienced Rörer and Cruciger. Rörer resigned from the Wittenberg diaconate in 1537 in order to devote himself full-time to editing Luther's works. He continued to receive his salary. In that way, the elector signified public interest in the edition of Luther's works. Before the end of 1538, work began on the first volume of German writings, which was to contain commentaries on the New Testament epistles. In the fall of 1539 the volume was published.[7]

Luther himself had written the preface.[8] He repeated his old reservations: The numerous books should not and must not compete with the study of the Bible, although a moderate number of them might be preserved as historical documents. In no way could they supersede the Holy Scriptures. The prophets and apostles had to remain "on the professor's lectern" and all others must be their hearers. Because Luther had been unable to prevent the publication of his collected works, he comforted himself with the thought that it, like other books, would soon be forgotten, "since it had begun to rain and snow books." People should use them like the papal decretals, conciliar decisions, church fathers, and scholastic theologians, that is, for historical information, but in no way as the norm or object of real theological study.

Luther used this opportunity to indicate "a correct way of studying theology," through which—according to his self-conscious experience—one might produce books as good as those of the church fathers and the councils. From Psalm 119 he derived three significant rules for doing so: "*Oratio* [prayer], *meditatio* [meditation], *tentatio* [*Anfechtung*]." The Bible turned the wisdom of all other books to foolishness. In order to understand the Bible one needed the Holy Spirit, and should pray for this gift. The Bible could not be mastered by reason, as the dreadful example of the fanatics showed. To meditate meant to have the biblical Word constantly in one's heart, but also to read, reread, compare, take note of, and think about what the Holy Spirit meant by it. One dare never become weary in doing so, or think that he already understands everything: "You will never be a particularly good theologian if you do that, for you will be like untimely fruit which falls to the ground before it is half ripe." God will give his Spirit through constant association with the external Word. Strangely enough, it is *Anfechtung* that adds knowledge and understanding to the experience of "how right, how true, how sweet, how lovely, how mighty, how comforting God's Word is, wisdom beyond all wisdom." It drives one to the Word, and in so doing the devil makes someone a "real doctor." Luther himself was indebted to the papists, "that through the devil's raging they have beaten, oppressed, and distressed me so much. That is to say, they have made a fairly good theologian of me. . . ." One becomes competent to deal with revealed wisdom, in comparison with which the books of one's opponents, and even those of the church fathers, taste stale. But this must be combined with true humility. Anyone who thinks that he is successful and flatters himself about his own teaching and writing will find that he is an ass with long ears and on the way to hell. The preface, therefore, was anything but a recommendation of Luther's writings. It was also, however, more than self-effacement. Once again he used an opportunity to make a statement of his own about his unmistakable way of dealing with the Bible, one that showed the spiritual, scholarly, and experiential manner in which his work developed out of the Scriptures. Here a teacher of theologians was speaking, yet someone who was more than a professor.

The second volume of the German works was not published until 1548, after Luther's death. It contained primarily the writings against his evangelical opponents. Luther had been involved in it at least to the extent that he approved excluding his polemic works against Bucer, with whom he had meanwhile come to an agreement.[9] The publication of the collection proceeded slowly because, as Luther had feared, the large volumes were difficult to sell. Accordingly, Elector John Frederick intervened forcefully with the printers and publishers several times after 1542, for he was concerned that it appear during Luther's lifetime.[10] In 1545 the first volume of the Latin writings was published, which contained primarily the works from the beginning of the Reformation conflict and the theses from the disputations. In part these were precisely the statements that Luther would have most preferred people to forget, especially now that proven textbooks like Melanchthon's *Loci Communes* were available for instructing theologians. Nevertheless, the elector wanted them published, and it seemed advisable to do so while Luther could still make a statement about his earlier work, rather than issue them later without taking their context into account. In the preface, therefore, Luther had to deal with the beginnings of his Reformation, and it thus became an important historical personal testimony.[11] Luther had already dealt with this topic in the preface to the edition of his theses, and he may have reviewed it because of the plan to reprint it. In addition, at the beginning of 1545 he apparently gave attention to his first writings.[12] He asked the reader to read judiciously, and also with commiseration, what he had written at the beginning, when, as he acknowledged, he was still "a monk and a most enthusiastic papist." In order to make this understandable, he related his story of the beginning of the indulgence controversy up to the year 1519; he concluded with the significant report of his reformatory discovery.[13] The reader should be clear that Luther had changed. He would discuss his later controversies with the sacramentarians and Anabaptists in the prefaces of the following volumes, which, however, were never written. In his conclusion, Luther appealed for prayer for the success of the work and against the devil's raging. God would confirm the work and bring it to completion, just as he had begun it. Melanchthon wrote a second preface for this volume.[14] He included Luther in the line of witnesses to the truth that extended from Abraham to Zechariah, from John the Baptist, Christ, and the apostles to Augustine. They had been called forth by God in order to restore the true doctrine. The conflict that was touched off by the indulgence controversy was not one that should be regretted, but seen as God's way of improving things after a period of great darkness. For Melanchthon, there was no need to explain Luther's development.

Luther thus wanted to have his collected works seen primarily as historical documentation. He had expressed his general view of history in 1538 in a preface to Galeatius Capella's *Description and History of the Milan War of 1522–30*, which Link had translated.[15] For Luther "the histories" were an example, "a demonstration, recollection, and signs of divine action and judgment, how [God] upholds, rules, obstructs, prospers, punishes, and honors the world, and especially men, each according to his just desert, evil or good." He had a high regard for the writing of history. What was needed for such a responsible task was "a first-rate man who has a lion's heart, unafraid to write the truth." People like this were rare, of course, and most histories displayed considerable dynastic or national considerations. Therefore, histories had to be read critically.

In a similar way he valued poetry and proverbs, such as Aesop's fables, for their experience and instruction. By 1535 Luther had asked Link in Nuremberg to collect German pictures, poems, songs, and masterful lyrics, which would be of assistance in writing good German books, something Luther confidently thought he himself had done thus far. He was particularly interested in collecting German proverbs, because they were able to convince people through their linguistic power and obvious truth. Mere ludicrous pranks, like those in John Agricola's collection of proverbs, had no place in a careful collection such as Luther envisioned. Probably by the 1530s he had already assembled his own collection of 489 short proverbial statements. It was never published. Luther regarded the striking imagery and focused pithiness that characterized proverbs as useful in what he himself as preacher, teacher, and author intended to accomplish.[16]

VI

Theological Controversies
in Wittenberg

From its very beginning, Reformation theology was not completely uniform and homogeneous. Luther's impetus was adopted by people who came from varied theological traditions, e.g., from late medieval mysticism or from humanism, and they gave accents to the new material that corresponded to their interests. This led to the sharp conflicts among the evangelicals in the 1520s. As we saw with Karlstadt, such differences could appear in Wittenberg as well. Even Luther and Melanchthon did not always agree. Their opinions diverged on an evaluation of Erasmus and on the Lord's Supper. On major issues they may have felt themselves united, but they had to accept a certain tolerance in theological convictions on each side and refrain from attempting to achieve complete unanimity.

The process of drawing theological distinctions also continued in Wittenberg in the 1530s. In the meantime, to be sure, there was now a doctrinal basis in the Augsburg Confession of 1530 to which they could refer, but in developing evangelical theology and translating it into ecclesiastical practice new problems surfaced that demanded new solutions. They became acute because the Religious Peace of Nuremberg of 1532 had reduced the external pressure from the Catholics that had demanded internal unity. The Wittenberg Concord of 1536 noticeably lessened the opposition within the evangelical ranks. Moreover, the second generation of Reformation theologians was now arising. Both Luther and the elector were troubled with the question of if and how the genuine Reformation heritage would be preserved after Luther's death. Efforts at preserving the pure, orthodox doctrine, a sign of the confessionalism that was already beginning, started during Luther's lifetime and with his participation. This process of clarification introduced conflict. The necessary task of reaching precise understandings could also lead to narrowness and one-sidedness. Where no agreement could be achieved, however, the unresolved unclarities themselves could impair the atmosphere. These problems were a considerable burden during the last years of Luther's life and the later phase of the Reformation that was then getting underway. Sometimes provisional solutions could be found, but other times, justifiably or unjustifiably, theological and human divisions occurred.

1. ON THE SIGNIFICANCE
OF REPENTANCE IN JUSTIFICATION—
THE "CORDATUS CONTROVERSY"

On 24 July 1536, Conrad Cordatus, at that time pastor in neighboring Niemegk, attended a class in Wittenberg on 1 Timothy taught by Caspar Cruciger (1504–48), who was lecturing on the basis of Melanchthon's notes. Cordatus may have been harboring certain theological suspicions. In his lecture Cruciger maintained the view that, in addition to the work of Christ, human repentance was also necessary in justification. In saying this, he apparently wanted to explain the process of justification more precisely. Cordatus, however, saw this as a threat to the doctrine of justification by faith alone, because repentance would involve a human accomplishment. Therefore, on 20 August he wrote a letter to Cruciger, requesting an explanation. Receiving no reply, he wrote more sharply on 8 September. He demanded a public correction of this "papistic or philosophical" teaching that was incompatible with Luther's doctrine. If necessary, he would appeal to the theology faculty. He refrained, however, from contacting Luther directly. Although Cordatus was not one to shrink from conflict, as his earlier activity in Zwickau had shown, he was seeking to resolve the matter directly. Cordatus harbored the fear that those pupils of Melanchthon who sympathized with Erasmus would carelessly destroy Luther's theological achievement.[1]

At first, Cruciger delayed because of other obligations, and also in order to let the matter cool down, but he replied immediately to Cordatus's second letter. He denied that he was questioning righteousness by faith in any way, but he continued to maintain that in some way the significance of repentance in the process of justification had to be acknowledged.[2] Among Melanchthon and his pupils this usual psychological view was completely appropriate, for they understood repentance more as a human act than something wrought by the Word. When Cordatus could not be convinced in a discussion on 18 September, Cruciger maintained that he was only reproducing Melanchthon's statements, and he combined this with a critique of Luther's way of speaking. This showed not only that Cruciger did not precisely understand Luther's doctrine of justification, but also that there was possibly a serious difference between Luther and Melanchthon. Apparently Melanchthon was flirting with Erasmian ideas. Presumably this had been one of the factors behind Luther's attack on Erasmus the previous year. Because Melanchthon was in southern Germany at the time, Cordatus insisted on informing Luther.[3]

Even before this, Amsdorf and Stifel had informed Luther in a letter that Melanchthon was saying that good works were necessary for salvation, which was in clear contrast to what Luther was preaching at the time. Cordatus was not the only one to object to this, and people began to choose sides as either "genuine Lutherans" or Melanchthonians. In talking with Cordatus, Luther criticized the terminology employed by Cruciger, for scholasticism had taught him the serious implications it had. Moreover, he was offended that the existing differences of opinion had not been addressed openly. He prepared for a new controversy. Cordatus encouraged him to do so. Significant differences of this sort should best be clarified while Luther was still alive.[4]

On 10 October the graduation disputation of Jacob Schenk and Philipp Motz was held. The theses prepared by Luther on Rom. 3:28 did not deal directly with the new conflict. Cruciger, however, who was presiding at the graduation, addressed the controversial point several times in the disputation. He labeled new obedience as a partial cause of justification. Luther pointed out that this was the opinion of Erasmus and Cardinal Sadoleto. For Luther, new obedience was indeed an essential validation of justification, but not its cause. Cruciger did not give in, but rather advanced his thesis directly: The forgiveness of sins depended on the prerequisite of repentance, and to this extent faith did not justify by itself. For Luther, this was a relapse into the scholastic doctrine of penance. Self-evidently, both repentance and contrition belong to justification, but they are not human accomplishments; they are worked by the Word of God that judges a person. In this respect it is improper to call them a necessary cause (*causa sine qua non*) of justification. Cruciger's graduation address was an appeal for unity among the Wittenberg theologians. Personal accusations should stop. A certain leeway in theological statements should graciously be tolerated. Any errors should be corrected fraternally.[5] The conflict that had broken out could not be swept away so easily. At another visit from Cordatus, when he officially brought charges against Cruciger, Luther stated that he was determined to call Melanchthon to account, and to demand a public retraction from Cruciger.[6]

Immediately after returning, Melanchthon circumspectly defended himself on 1 November before the members of the theology faculty. Any divergence from Wittenberg doctrine was the farthest thing from his mind, but there were questions about the new obedience that needed to be clarified. They had to be explained in precise theological terminology. He did not keep silent about his interest in good works, and denied that he had given incorrect reasons for them. If they were going to harbor suspicions and make accusations against him and thus cause an estrangement, he would rather leave Wittenberg. Following this, the theologians held a discussion with Melanchthon in Bugenhagen's house to clarify the matter. Melanchthon formulated the questions that were at issue, and Luther gave a written response. They agreed: Justifying faith is trust in the Word of the gospel. Man is justified by God's mercy alone. From this come good works, which in this life are always imperfect. They cannot, however, be called a partial cause of righteousness alongside God's mercy. Justification takes place entirely and only by faith, from which also comes the fulfilling of the commandments. Faith is worked by the promise or gift of the Holy Spirit. This is what makes the new man, who then does good works. The sequence of good works as something that follows faith was strictly maintained. These clear statements by Luther were apparently accepted by Melanchthon as well. At the end of the month the controversy seemed to him essentially to have been resolved.[7]

However, when Bugenhagen declared from the pulpit that the entire affair had been a dispute about words, Cordatus protested to Luther; for him, the new formulation missed the point. He was dissatisfied that the theological teachers had settled the matter among themselves, especially because it had also been discussed among the students. Melanchthon's second edition of the *Loci Communes* of 1535 should be recalled because it was too close to Erasmus's views. Cordatus wanted to bring a complaint against Cruciger before the theology faculty. When he failed to get a hearing from Luther, he planned to present his complaint to the rector of the university or, if necessary, even to the elector. At the end of December, Jonas, rector at the time, was able to dissuade him from doing so, mentioning the unforeseeable consequences of such an action. Instead, at a private meeting, Jonas would ascertain whether Cruciger was prepared to retract his claims. Cordatus was consumed with the task of defending true Lutheranism, although he was aware that this was beyond his powers. God, after all, had once spoken through an ass. . . .[8]

For a time the matter rested while Luther and Melanchthon attended the meeting of the Smalcald League. When Cruciger had made no retraction by the beginning of April and Melanchthon had apparently identified with him, Cordatus attacked again. He accused Melanchthon of having long since deviated from Luther's doctrine in several points. Melanchthon naturally denied this, but he did support Cruciger. He declared that he was prepared to engage in a debate or defend himself before an ecclesiastical tribunal. He assumed that the real point of issue was his support for philosophy.[9] At the same time, Cordatus demanded that Jonas as rector procure Cruciger's recantation, which was still outstanding. As a licentiate of theology he could not keep silent, but was obligated to object. In this case his personal stubbornness, of which he was well aware, was justified. Jonas sought to use the entire weight of his office as rector to deter Cordatus, the pastor of tiny Niemegk, from undertaking public action, and to persuade him to deal with the matter privately with Luther. As in the following conflicts, Jonas resolutely supported Melanchthon's party and thus contributed considerably to the personal animosity of the controversies. Neither Jonas nor Melanchthon could intimidate Cordatus, although the matter was affecting him so deeply that he feared he was about to suffer a stroke. After the matter had gone from Luther, the dean of the theology faculty, to the rector of the university it could no longer remain a private matter, but had to be dealt with officially.[10]

At this stage, Cordatus also informed Chancellor Brück about the doctrinal differences in Wittenberg. Because of his concern for doctrinal unity in Electoral Saxony, Elector John Frederick wanted to be informed about the dispute personally in Wittenberg on 5 May, so that, if necessary, he himself could undertake appropriate measures. In all probability this discussion, of which there is only one preliminary note of Brück extant, did take place. It may have resulted in a plan to transfer Cordatus from the vicinity of Wittenberg to Eisleben, in which Luther was very cordially encouraging him a little later.[11]

Luther had been planning, probably already before this, a public theological airing of the controversy, which would spare the elector from stepping in. At the graduation disputation of Peter Palladius and Tilemann on 1 June 1537 the works of the law and grace were to be treated.[12] In his theses Luther skillfully conceded the necessity of works and the law, as well as grace: The works of the law, however, are always impaired by human egoism. They do not therefore justify a person, although at the same time they are necessary for maintaining public order. The works of grace are done in faith by those who are justified, and they thus have nothing to do with justification. In this life the law is fulfilled in faith through the imputation of Christ's righteousness. Its fulfillment in love, however, will take place first in the perfection of the life to come. The new creature only begins to be manifested in the one who is justified, and the same is true of good works. A sinful nature always clings to a justified person in this life, but faith is never without good works.

Luther began his introduction to the disputation with the thematic sentence: "The article of justification is the master and sovereign, lord, leader, and judge of all sorts of doctrine. . . ." In the disputation he dealt with the concept of "necessity." Not everything that is necessary, e.g., the law, also contributes to justification. The same is true of good works, which are solely a result of justification and yet in a certain sense are necessary. Nevertheless, it would be false to say they are necessary for salvation. The word "necessary" in this context is ambiguous, and is thus unsuitable. The only "necessary" element is the mercy of God. In Palladius's concluding address, which had been drafted by Luther, he emphasized that in theology not only was the mastery of terminology important, but also the wisdom given by God; it was upon this that everything really depended.[13]

In Melanchthon's opinion, Luther's theses were more moderate than Cordatus would probably have wished. After the disputation Melanchthon reported with relief that Luther did not appear to be ill disposed toward him and his pupils. For the sake of unity, however, he refrained from emphasizing the differences. He did clearly tell Veit Dietrich that he would have wanted to emphasize the human contribution to salvation more strongly. He also considered this to be Luther's own view. Only certain uneducated spirits would appeal to the reformer's exaggerated statements. Melanchthon did not want to argue with them and therefore kept his opinion to himself.[14] At most, however, the antitheses were not fully aired; they continued to exist, surfacing again after Luther's death. Melanchthon thought that he understood Luther better than Luther understood himself. Thus Melanchthon could let him speak without himself having to correct him.

Cruciger was happy that Luther had at least granted that good works were a necessary result of justification, but he disagreed with his rejection of philosophical terminology, which, of course, he kept to himself. Cordatus had participated in the disputation only as a silent observer. Luther treated him cordially, something that Cruciger could not understand. He learned from a note that was slipped to him in the church that there still were people who were expecting a retraction from him, or else they planned to denounce him as a papist and a teacher of the devil. Cruciger therefore did not dare to demand a thorough investigation.[15] The atmosphere in Wittenberg had thus hardly been cleared. The affair of Simon Lemnius again brought Melanchthon under suspicion. In October 1538 he feared that the controversy would break out anew, because Veit Dietrich had introduced the new terminology into Luther's exposition of Psalm 51.[16] In 1539 Luther did acknowledge that his position and that of Melanchthon complemented each other. He compared Melanchthon to James, Jesus' brother who was zealous for the law, and himself to Peter, who declared that the heathen were free from the demands of the law (Acts 15). Melanchthon, in his theological testament from the same year, had a somewhat different nuance. He expressly stood by his *Loci Communes* of 1535. Cruciger and his pupils should preserve this form of his teaching. It was not a concession to the old believers, but rather a necessary development and clarification of the Augustinian doctrine of justification. Melanchthon was convinced that it corresponded entirely with Luther's view. Even more than to the elector, Melanchthon owed his first thanks and the assurance of his enduring affection to Luther, from whom he had learned the gospel.[17] In the controversy with Cordatus, Luther had indeed maintained his view and achieved a temporary pacification, but he had not convinced his co-workers. They secretly maintained a different opinion. It was their fault that a complete theological settlement was not reached, but this also revealed the limits of Luther's authority. This naturally impaired the intellectual and human climate in Wittenberg.

2. THE REPUDIATION OF JACOB SCHENK

Among the opponents from his own camp against whom the old Luther nursed an abiding anger was Jacob Schenk (ca. 1508–46), or "Jeckel," as he was contemptuously called. This animosity was based on secondary theological differences, which were more Luther's suspicions than anything specific. He was happy to have others encourage him in these suspicions. Schenk understood himself to be a faithful theologian in the Wittenberg tradition, but he appeared very self-confident and independent. This came fully to light after he became the court preacher to Henry of Saxony in Freiberg in the spring of 1536. The two of them undertook to introduce the Reformation in Freiberg without consulting Luther, Wittenberg, or Electoral Saxony. As in other territories, the Reformation in the area of Freiberg had its own peculiarities. In this particular case, however, those in Wittenberg reacted critically to them. Tensions in the church and considerations of ecclesiastical politics added to the personal animosities. To Luther's annoyance, Henry had not been convinced in 1536 of the innocence of the Freiberg card painter, Matthes Lotther, who had been accused of being an Anabaptist. Luther transferred his annoyance about this to Schenk, although the latter had been only peripherally involved with the matter. He even wanted Schenk removed from Freiberg. Nevertheless, Schenk was granted the Doctor of Theology degree in October 1536. Even Luther was aware that one had to give the young theologian time to gain experience.[1]

The controversy with Cordatus was not yet at an end when Schenk became—albeit unintentionally—the means whereby another of Melanchthon's doctrinal deviations came to light during 1537. Schenk had inquired first of Jonas about allowing the laity to receive the cup, and then also of Melanchthon. Melanchthon, with his cautious attitude toward the old believers, thought as before that a communion service in which only the bread was given might be permissible in certain situations. He had, of course, previously come into conflict with Luther over this view. Therefore, his reply to Schenk was to be kept confidential. The *Instructions for the Visitors* in 1528, however, had allowed such an exceptional procedure in the case of the "weak." In Freiberg the Catholic opposition appealed to this provision in order to prevent innovations. Schenk informed the elector of this problematic situation. In the new printing of the *Instructions* the pertinent passage was then removed.[2] In July the difference of opinion between Melanchthon and Schenk became known in Wittenberg. On this account Hans Metzsch, the high bailiff, filed a complaint with the elector, showing in it his clear sympathy for Schenk. This must have added to the difficulties of Schenk's relationship with the Wittenberg theologians. Melanchthon saw that a new conflict was going to involve him. He was asked very specifically by Schenk under what conditions it was permissible to deviate from Christ's institution of the Lord's Supper. After the cup for the laity had been introduced in Freiberg, Melanchthon was concerned about letting the matter rest and not creating a new cause for controversy. He was offended that Schenk had made his confidential opinion public and referred to him as a demagogue.[3]

Luther probably first learned of Melanchthon's statement from Chancellor Brück, who had been sent to Wittenberg by Elector John Frederick, who was concerned and angered about the new discord. Luther felt that he had been bypassed, and his distrust reappeared about Melanchthon's further development of the doctrine of the Lord's Supper since his discussions with Bucer in Kassel in 1534. Luther did not want to lose him, however. Moreover, he disapproved of the sharp tone of Schenk's questions, flatly declared that he was crazy, and sought an amicable resolution of the conflict. On the whole, the elector agreed with this procedure. Schenk was to come to Wittenberg for discussions. Schenk did not comply with the demand, for he recognized that Luther would want to protect Melanchthon as much as possible. Obviously

153

incompletely informed, Luther without justification accused Schenk of presenting his criticisms in order to further his own ambitions, and he forbade him to write any more letters against his Wittenberg teachers, because they would disturb the peace of the church. Thus no real settlement of the matter was achieved, although the elector renewed the pressure in September. Because Schenk would not come to Wittenberg, the elector demanded that he dismiss the matter in the future.[4] Schenk yielded. He became the real victim of the controversy, although he was in the right in the matter. He may have presented it too sharply. There are objective and personal reasons for Luther's attitude that are understandable, but there is no justification for the way he let Jonas and Melanchthon cloud his judgment in this case. The elector and Chancellor Brück saw things more clearly here. Melanchthon, who had originally feared that he might be exiled from Saxony for his advice to Schenk, was only to be given a reprimand. Because of Luther's illness, not even this occurred. Melanchthon, however, took revenge on Schenk with an oration, *On the Ingratitude of the Cuckoo*, that tried to vie with the Wittenberg nightingale.[5]

Schenk himself must have soon regretted starting a quarrel with Melanchthon and Jonas as well. Already at the end of August, Jonas, the dean of the castle church, doubtless with Luther's knowledge, ordered Schenk's brother Michael not to preach practice sermons. Some students, including Jacob Schenk himself when he had been a student, were accustomed to practice their preaching in Wittenberg; they did so without remuneration and under the supervision of the castle preacher. Until then this practice had not offended anyone. Jacob had also advised his brother, who earlier had studied in Wittenberg, then had become an overseer in Joachimsthal, and at this time was preparing for the ministry, to preach this way. There were no real reasons for the prohibition. Jonas obviously wanted revenge on Jacob Schenk. Schenk asked Luther, Jonas, Melanchthon, and then Metzsch and Brück to rescind the ban. The request had no result. Luther freely acknowledged that the measure was directed against Jacob Schenk, who had sent his brother back to Wittenberg.[6]

Schenk was also seriously compromised in Wittenberg a little later by two clergymen who were close to him. He had sent a former priest to the castle preacher, George Karg, with whom he was on friendly terms. Karg was to examine him and see whether the priest could be employed in Freiberg. The priest was a secret adherent of Sebastian Franck, the spiritualist. He won Karg over to his views, among which was a denial of the true humanity of Christ. When Karg did not keep his new convictions to himself, but rather distanced himself from Luther with strong words, he was cited before the elector, probably by Schenk himself. Accordingly, Luther had to interrogate him on 1 January 1538; following this, he was imprisoned in the castle. He soon confessed and declared that he was ready to be better instructed. Luther and

Melanchthon interceded for him; at the beginning of February he was released. Karg later became a general superintendent in Brandenburg-Ansbach, but there he again became involved in a doctrinal controversy. The Wittenberg theologians held Schenk responsible for the episode, although he had immediately taken issue with Karg and clearly repudiated him and the priest. In this case, their accusations were understandable. Schenk had again engaged in his personal politics by informing the elector, but not the Wittenbergers, when he became aware of the false teaching.[7]

In November 1537 Melanchthon had already expressed the suspicion that Schenk shared the antinomian views of John Agricola, who wanted to eliminate the law from the context of justification, which were just touching off another controversy in Wittenberg. From all that can be determined, this suspicion was hardly justified. Nevertheless, at the beginning of 1538, when Luther saw a letter from Schenk to the pastors of Freiberg in which he declared that it was more important to preach the gospel than the law, it was enough to brand Schenk an antinomian.[8] On the basis of rumors—not from Freiberg itself, but only from the vicinity—he accused him a few weeks later of wanting to set up an arbitrary church administration. He had little use for Schenk's explanation, for he no longer trusted him; instead he wanted visible steps of a conversion. This time, too, Schenk sought the mediation of the elector, but this time Chancellor Brück took Luther's side.[9]

In the meantime, Schenk himself had experienced difficulties in Freiberg. The council wanted to continue permitting the distribution of bread alone in communion, as the *Instructions for the Visitors* had permitted. Moreover, the council felt that it had been bypassed in appointing people to ecclesiastical positions. The worst problem was that Schenk had quarreled with Duke Henry's court preacher, the likewise difficult Paul Lindenau. Spalatin was asked to mediate. In June he recommended to the elector that both Schenk and Lindenau should be transferred. Lindenau persuaded Luther to discuss the matter with Brück. Luther had no objections to the plan to make Schenk the Electoral Saxon court preacher, for this would better prevent a complete break with him. As Schenk's possible successor in Freiberg he named several candidates, even including Agricola, whose appointment he then considered too risky. While she was visiting Wittenberg, Duke Henry's wife, Katherine, endorsed Schenk, although without obtaining much support. In contrast, Luther was only too happy to have his mistrust confirmed by representatives of the Freiberg council who reported on Schenk's allegedly libertine, but in fact absolutely correct, statements. Contrary to Luther's expectation, Schenk at once accepted the position of court preacher offered him.[10]

Luther and those around him observed Schenk in his new office with a great deal of mistrust, although he showed no actual doctrinal deviation. They were outraged when they learned that Schenk had succeeded in arranging permission for his brother Michael, who was not yet ordained, to preach.

Luther was not at all satisfied with a sermon by Schenk, which he heard in September at the court in Lochau. An attempt at reconciliation at that time, according to which Schenk would accept the authority of his Wittenberg teachers, bore no fruit. Not even sharing a meal could restore a natural relationship. When Schenk reportedly tried to reconcile with Luther, Luther left the table. Luther attributed Schenk's ability to gain favor with people to his antinomian teaching, and said this would not last. After a while he had to grant that he merely had suspicions. Nevertheless, he continued to regard Schenk as his enemy and warned people about associating with him.[11]

After the Reformation was introduced into Ducal Saxony, Schenk became interested in a position there. Luther attempted to prevent this. In 1541 Schenk became a professor of theology in Leipzig. At that time Luther also delayed the printing of Schenk's sermons for months, so that the elector himself had to press him to come to a decision. As before, Luther believed that Schenk was not preaching the law correctly, and also that he lusted for power. In 1544 Schenk became court preacher in Berlin. Luther noted that Schenk spoke well of him there. He also learned that Schenk soon got into difficulties with the elector of Brandenburg, but he did not advocate that Schenk be placed elsewhere.[12] Schenk, without a position at the time, died in 1546 under circumstances that are not completely clear.

Undoubtedly Luther's relationship with this gifted Wittenberg doctor and his work with him could have taken a more productive form, although the self-assured Schenk was a difficult person. Luther's personal dislike and theological prejudice, fomented by Jonas and Melanchthon, prevented this. This was only one of the reasons Schenk was frustrated.

3. JOHN AGRICOLA AND THE ANTINOMIAN CONTROVERSY

The most bitter and stubborn theological conflict in which the old Luther was involved with one of his former students and supporters was that with John Agricola about the law, the so-called antinomian controversy. Like Luther, Agricola (1492 [1496?]–1566), later contemptuously called "Grickel," came from Eisleben, and therefore was also known as Master Eisleben. The concept of judgment and the strict demands of late medieval piety appear to have oppressed him. After having studied in Leipzig and serving as a teacher in Brunswick, he came to Wittenberg, probably in 1516. Luther became his mentor (*Seelsorger*), and Luther's theology was liberating for him. Like so many others, however, he may have understood Luther one-sidedly from the very beginning. The basic content of Agricola's views, insofar as it is reflected in his writings, always remained the same. He believed the law's demands belonged in the past; a believer is converted, justified, and instructed through the proclamation of the gospel of Christ. The continuing divine demand of the law—or even of ecclesiastical regulations—was no longer of interest in this context. In

IOHANNES ·
DOCTOR · /
GENANT ·
VRFVRTN
ZV · CÓLN
SPRE·IM ·

AGRICOLA ·
EISLEBEN
DESS · CH ⁄
PREDICANT
AN · DER⊃
THVM · Seliger

1 · 5
B:

6 · 5
1:

Die Stubenten in Franck
furt an der Oder gaßen
wider mich geschriben
von hoh vn vnbvoend
keit der werck. So
Ronno ich Reimen
heiligen der so heist

VIL·SPRICHWÖRTER·HAB·ICH·ENTEGKT
DISELBEN·GAR·SCHÖN·AVSGELEGT ⊙⊙
AVF·DAS·DAS·BÖS·SOLT·WERDN·VERMID
DOCH·HALF·ICH·DAS·INTERIM·SCHMID⊓
WART·ABR·IM·GEIST·WIDRVM·SO·STARK
THET·DBEST·PREDIGTE·IN·DER·marck

John Agricola
Woodcut, 1565

criticizing and repudiating Catholic legalism, Agricola correctly knew that he was completely in accord with Luther. Next to Melanchthon, he was initially one of Luther's closest associates. After 1521 he delivered exegetical lectures, and, in addition, he took part in the catechetical instruction of the youth and, after 1523, in the weekday worship services in the Wittenberg city church, from which the office of the diaconate then developed. He must have been a highly respected preacher. Elector John and his son used him as a court preacher when they traveled, especially to meetings of the diet, although he was no longer formally in the service of Electoral Saxony. In 1525 Agricola, in furthering Luther's attempts at establishing schools, had become director of the school in Eisleben and, in addition, had assumed a position as preacher. When Melanchthon, during his first visitation in 1527, demanded a clear increase in the preaching of the law, Agricola protested against this relapse. The compromise achieved by Luther only glossed over the contrasting views.[1]

In the long run, the position of schoolmaster in Eisleben could not satisfy Agricola. The compensation was meager for his growing family and promised raises were not granted. The relationships in the Eisleben church, where the old believer, George Witzel, was an opponent whom Agricola thought he constantly had to attack with his polemics, were also unpleasant. Agricola himself was responsible for some of the friction in the city, for not infrequently after imbibing alcohol he would start a fight with someone. Not least he desired to return to Wittenberg, where he could again work directly with Luther. In the fall of 1536 Luther gave him hope that a position would soon be available. In December, when Agricola received a somewhat cryptic invitation to participate in a consultation about whether the upcoming meeting of the Smalcald League should send representatives to a council, he misunderstood it as a request that he move. He immediately announced his resignation to Count Albrecht of Mansfeld in a letter, which contained all his pent-up dissatisfaction about the situation in Eisleben, and he asked Luther to support his action with the count. Then he moved to Wittenberg with his wife and children. At first, however, there was neither a position nor a place for him to live. For the time being the Agricola family lodged in Luther's house.[2]

The Onset of the Conflict

At first there was pure unity. At the end of January 1537, when Luther left for several weeks to attend the meeting of the league in Schmalkalden, he asked Agricola to look after his house and substitute for him in his preaching and teaching. When he returned in March, Luther learned for the first time that Agricola was teaching peculiar views. Agricola had preached at a meeting of the evangelical princes in Zeitz at the conclusion of the meeting of the league. At that time he attracted attention with his favorite opinion, that God's wrath was revealed not through the law, but through the gospel, i.e., the fate of Christ upon the cross. Presumably Luther at first thought only that such a statement was absurd, because for him everything that confronted a person with judgment was law. At the same time Luther became aware of anonymous theses that asserted that the law should not be preached in the church because it did not justify. He immediately recognized that these were Agricola's views. Luther knew that he and Melanchthon were agreed that the law was essential for revealing sin.[3] The controversy on the importance of repentance and works in justification that Cordatus had initiated was not yet at an end, and now Luther had to deal on the other flank with a disparagement of the continuing demand of God's law.

At first the conflict mounted behind the scenes. The controversial theses were known only by a few. Not until after the beginning of July, when three printed sermons by Agricola appeared, could his views be ascertained more clearly. Melanchthon and Cruciger initially withheld their criticism, but they made no secret that they thought little of Agricola's views. Bugenhagen, who shortly before had left for Denmark, had recommended that Agricola not substitute for him in the pulpit. Luther, nevertheless, did let him preach occasionally so that he would not be at too much of a disadvantage.[4]

In May, Agricola showed Luther a writing he wanted to have published—which no longer can be identified with certainty—and Luther approved it. At the beginning of September, however, Agricola learned that Luther had changed his mind, and he sent him—at that time he was no longer living in Luther's house—an irritated letter.[5] He considered his teaching apostolic and in agreement with Luther. Its chief content was that the proclamation of the death of Christ was a judgment of one's conscience and that the resurrection was the forgiveness of sins. This was not wrong, but it did not address the disputed question about the meaning of the law. Agricola was not aware of any deficiency in his teaching. He was prepared even to let Jonas, who was not at all kindly disposed to him, to mediate between him and Luther. Luther's reaction is unknown. In this context, Agricola presented a catalog of his previous teaching.[6] In it, he expressly affirmed the importance of the law for civil order. Thereby, apparently, he wanted to allay the suspicion of Count Albrecht of Mansfeld that with his antinomianism he was close to Müntzer. In contrast, he wanted to keep the law entirely out of the context of justification, and permit it to exercise no function as a judge of consciences.

On 30 September, in a clear and very pointed sermon, which was immediately published, Luther presented his view of law and gospel. The law, as God's binding demand, made man recognize that he was a sinner. The opinion that someone could be saved without the law was clearly rejected. Christ offers himself as the mediator only to the man who knows that he is a sinner. Not only does he forgive him, but he helps him to begin fulfilling the law, which is then perfectly accomplished in the life to come. Without the law, Christ's work would have no significance, because thereby the law is satisfied and fulfilled. In his weekly sermon on 6 October on John 1:17, Luther expressed himself in the same vein.[7] In October, Melanchthon informed his friends about the controversy with Agricola and sent them the printed version of Luther's sermon. In doing so, he remarked with both satisfaction and resignation: "I would be beaten if I could preach so clearly about the law."[8]

In the second half of October an understanding with Luther must have been reached. Agricola could report to the elector, on whom he was financially dependent, that they were agreed in substance and that, previously, there had been only a misunderstanding between them. John Frederick, who was concerned about doctrinal unity, thereupon dryly advised him to teach not only the substance, but the same words as Luther. As a precaution, he asked Chancellor Brück to have Luther confirm this. Above all, Luther was to explain if he had approved the publication of Agricola's *Summaries* of the Sunday gospels, which was then being published.[9] Throughout these *Summaries*, Agricola's theology appeared, including his exclusion of the law from the process of justification. As a result of Brück's mission, Luther forbade the continuation of the printing. He kept a copy of the fragment for himself and later made critical notes on it concerning Agricola's view of the law. The alleged agreement had thus been only of short duration. Agricola's Mansfeld opponents, along with Rörer, and, once again, Jonas, apparently had propagandized against him.[10]

Disputations and Reconciliations

Following this, Agricola wrote to Luther at the end of November, raising serious criticisms against him. He accused him of teaching two ways of justification, one through the law and faith and another solely through the gospel, which was what Luther had originally taught. He now pressed for a statement that would indicate which one was the apostolic way of teaching. Agricola later remarked: "This letter . . . set the Rhine on fire."[11] Luther must have regarded the letter as a demand, and he now took vigorous action. He published the antinomian theses, which had been known since the spring, expressly distancing himself from them, and prepared countertheses of his own. In no way was the position against Agricola merely a declaration of his own standpoint: "I would have died from sheer fear, before I made these theses." At this time, or perhaps somewhat earlier, there was consideration of revoking Agricola's authorization to teach and thus his livelihood. On the advice of Melanchthon, who worked surprisingly hard to reach an agreement, Agricola tried at the last moment to dissuade Luther from publishing the antinomian theses. As before, of course, Agricola denied his authorship, but he was aware that he was being held responsible for them. In contrast to his earlier criticism, he declared that he was prepared to submit fully and that he acknowledged Luther's authority as an evangelical theologian without any limitation. Nevertheless, the antinomian theses and, somewhat later, Luther's countertheses were published. As a result of Agricola's letter a reconciliation must have taken place in the church sacristy.[12] Despite their differences, it was a long time before the two parted company.

The theses of the antinomians that Luther published contained, in addition to the well-known views of Agricola on the law, a comparison between the "pure" doctrinal statements of Luther and Melanchthon and those that were regarded as "impure" because they insisted on preaching the law.[13] Included in the impure statements was the emphasis on the Decalogue from the

Instructions for the Visitors, which had already produced controversies in 1527. The allegation that Melanchthon and Luther had contradicted themselves and in part had taught incorrectly was naturally an affront. A concluding group of theses seemed like a collection of statements taken out of context. Some of them probably came from Jacob Schenk, who was said to have met with Agricola. The thesis, "The Decalogue belongs in the city hall, not in the pulpit," at any rate, was a coarse slogan from Agricola's circle.

In his countertheses,[14] Luther advocated the position that law and gospel must work together in repentance. The law brings contrition for sin, but it is the gospel that first converts a person and brings comfort. The one-sidedness of the antinomians was something that could certainly be explained as coming out of their opposition to scholasticism's false doctrine of penance, but in spite of the false legalism of scholasticism, the law remains necessary to reveal sin and man's enslavement to death. In the Bible the sequence is always that the gospel's word of comfort is preceded by the law's word of judgment.

Luther hoped that the disputation would bring about a resolution of this conflict with his former friend, which was personally painful to him.[15] He believed that it was really he and not Melanchthon who was being challenged, and thus he functioned as the sole defender of his theses. Agricola, however, did not appear at the disputation on 18 December. Nevertheless, the basic problem was discussed. In his opening address Luther stated that what was at stake was the preservation of the pure doctrine, which had to be expounded as both law and gospel. The argument that the gospel required something impossible was of no effect. The demand for obedience still remained in effect. More substantial was the objection that the law had been abolished by Christ, but without turning to Christ, the law remains in effect in human existence. Grace does not exclude the work of the law, but rather presupposes it. The Holy Spirit works not only through the gospel, but through the law as well. The law has not been abolished by Christ, but fulfilled, and thus it retains its continuing significance. This applies also to the existence of the believer, who is always both righteous and sinner at the same time. In the two-front war, in which the Melanchthonians had made law, repentance, and works necessary for salvation, while the antinomians wanted to eliminate the law, Luther was already indicating that he wanted to explain more clearly the law's necessary contribution to justification. Meanwhile, he stated clearly that the law remained a judgment that always brought death and that was never able to bring life. One of the most impressive claims of the antinomians was their deriving repentance from a recognition that the sin of unbelief really did injury to Christ and not to the law. As touching as that sounded, for Luther defaming Christ was only a special case of violating the First Commandment. Naturally, he also knew that the gospel and Christ punish sin, but in that case they exercise the function of the law. Not even the earlier incorrect legalism could lead to abolition of the law in the church, for that would threaten the serious-

161

ness of repentance and open the door to false security. Luther had no intention of giving up the connection between the law that condemned and the gospel that comforted, for he had experienced both of them deeply and then had put them in their proper order. In this first disputation against the antinomians he had convincingly demonstrated their dangerous theological one-sidedness and presented the validity of his own alternative model.

After the disputation, Luther was annoyed that Agricola had not appeared. He would not accept his excuse that he was criticizing not Luther but Cruciger and Rörer, for in fact his critique was also directed at Luther's catechisms and at the Augsburg Confession. Agricola would turn the comfort of the gospel into a false security and a freedom of the flesh, because he did away with the demand of the law. Luther would take steps to ensure that Agricola would have to defend himself at the next disputation, which was already being planned.[16] Melanchthon again urged Agricola to write a letter on 26 December in which he referred to the agreement he and Luther had achieved in the meeting in the church sacristy, and to his admission of his error. Luther at first refused to read the letter. After a day or two he did bring himself to read it one morning—before, as Agricola maliciously noted, "he became flushed with wine"—and reportedly allowed him to resume his teaching activity. The influential Katy, and Jonas himself, interceded on Agricola's behalf. For unknown reasons Luther revoked this permission on 6 January 1538 and referred the matter to the university senate. The "Agricola Affair" was no longer a matter only for Luther as dean of the theology faculty. The appended warning against secret allegations leads one to suppose that Agricola had previously expressed himself too candidly.[17]

As planned, a second series of theses by Luther against the antinomians appeared before the end of December, followed by a third and fourth at the beginning of January.[18] As mentioned above, in the second series of theses Luther dealt with the essential distinction between law and gospel. The function of the law is limited to revealing sin and in no circumstance can it be extended to justification. Wherever sin is revealed, even in the New Testament, it is the work of the law. In understanding Christ to be the one who fulfills the law, the tension between law and gospel can be maintained. Without the law, sin—and redemption, too—would be irrelevant. The third series of theses, not unintentionally, picked up the famous theme of the first thesis against indulgences from 1517: A Christian's entire life is repentance, i.e., it remains confronted with the demand of the law. This was demonstrated, as in other places, by the petitions of the Lord's Prayer. Here a serious aspect of the Christian life was emphasized in an almost one-sided way. Probably in order to return to the historical roots of the difference of opinion, Luther dealt in the fourth series of theses with the papal doctrine of penance. It was false because it did not teach the certainty of the forgiveness of sins and demanded that a person accomplish something himself, both of which led to despair. In fact, abolishing the law along with penance was even more incorrect, of course, for God's demand continues to exist. What was important was fulfilling it. This took place through Christ; it begins to happen in the life of the believer; and it will be perfected in the life to come. Thus the result: The law does nothing in justification, but justification is necessary in order to fulfill the law.

The disputation on the second series of theses was to be held on 12 January 1538. Shortly before, at Melanchthon's advice, Agricola sent his wife, for whom Luther had a high regard, to ask Luther to make another attempt at reaching an understanding. The request bore fruit. It was agreed that Agricola would participate in the disputation and undertake to clarify some points.[19]

In his opening address, Luther first referred to the original position taken against the Pelagian legalism of nominalism and its significance. The disputation's subject was to be the question of "whether the law is necessary or useful for justification."[20] Naturally, this was to be answered negatively, but then one had to ask what function was ascribed to the law. Every revelation of God's wrath, even in the gospel, is wrought by the law. This was the diagnosis that was the precondition for any healing. This imagery was pursued further: This grave diagnosis brings forth a fierce reaction that ultimately leads to despair, one that is directed even against the physician. Nevertheless, it is necessary to trust the physician's healing power and give the patient comfort, hope, and healing. The law's accusation also continues in the life of a Christian, which is always imperfect. Thus it is necessary to turn permanently to Christ, so that fear will be removed from one's relationship with God and love can replace it. This necessary transition from law to gospel is the critical point in the process of justification. The fear of God dare not drive someone to despair, but must be accompanied by love. Accordingly, law and gospel are to be preached in such a way that the law is limited by the gospel. In justification man is only the material creatively fashioned by Christ. The law only prepares the way for this by pointing out perversity and false self-righteousness; it contributes nothing essential to justification. The entire course of the disputation went beyond the limitation of the law, and thus it went against Agricola, while Luther again clearly distanced himself from the Melanchthonian doctrine of repentance. Nevertheless, it was declared that it was impossible simply to do away with the law. Even if we were to abolish it, the law would remain inscribed on our conscience. Answerability to God's demand is part of man's very nature.

At this point,[21] Luther challenged Agricola to make a statement that agreed with his remarks and correct his teaching of the law. Agricola shrewdly stated that the necessary basic critique of righteousness according to the law occurs only through the gospel. This said nothing about the continuing spiritual significance of the law. Luther, in his reply, was the one who had first introduced this subject. It was he and not Agricola who had stated that Christ as the exemplary norm was on the side of the law, while his work of salvation was a gift of the gospel. These two aspects of Christ's work had played a role in

Luther's beginning of the Reformation and at that time had become significant for Agricola. They had been incorporated in the schema of law and gospel that Luther continued to develop. Agricola did not declare his explicit agreement. Nevertheless, Luther said that he was satisfied; the old suspicion had been removed, and there was no longer any difference of opinion, only friendship. They also appealed to those who were present to be of one mind. Luther was visibly relieved that the dispute had been resolved. Whether this would be a lasting understanding only time would tell. For the time being it appeared as if further controversies were superfluous. No disputations took place over the third and fourth series of theses against the antinomians, which had already been prepared.

The Wittenberg theologians, however, were in no way convinced that Agricola had changed his mind. Nevertheless, at the end of January, Luther secured permission from the elector for Agricola to preach and teach. He was not required to make an explicit recantation, but the Wittenberg theologians were to keep close watch over his statements. Agricola's arrogant behavior had not been forgotten. Luther was relieved that the painful conflict had been resolved and the irritation it caused had come to an end, but probably even he was not convinced that a genuine solution had been found.[22] Agricola, in fact, probably mentioned his old views in the pulpit during the week of Easter. Luther was very dejected and annoyed about this, and let even Katy feel it.[23]

Against the Antinomians

In August 1538 the Mansfeld castle preacher, Michael Coelius, denounced Agricola, saying he was only waiting for Luther to die, and then he would teach whatever he pleased. Now, for the first time, Luther classified the antinomians together with Müntzer, the sacramentarians, and the Anabaptists as sects that opposed him. He informed Chancellor Brück, who was then residing in Wittenberg, of the new accusations. Thereupon, Melanchthon and Jonas were instructed to speak with Agricola. While Melanchthon sought to resolve the issue, Jonas was interested in exacerbating it. Agricola himself complained to Brück that they wanted to force him out of Wittenberg.[24] At that time, Luther added a warning against the new sect of the antinomians to the preface of the second edition of his commentary on Galatians.[25] On 3 September he demanded a public retraction from Agricola, or else he would take action against him. Agricola declared that he was ready to submit.[26]

An opportunity for renewing the theological controversy with Agricola was presented by Cyriacus Gericke's licentiate disputation, which was scheduled for 6 September. Luther wrote a lengthy series of new theses for the occasion.[27] In them, he demonstrated the continuing significance of the law during the whole of human life, and also in the church. Because sin remains a lifelong reality, even in the life of the pious, the law, by which this is recognized, also cannot be abolished. Eliminating the law, which is what the antinomians were

164

teaching, would result in false security. Without the law, the saving act of Christ was meaningless and the situation of sinful man, who was subject to death, was veiled.

The lengthy opening address and the ensuing disputation itself reemphasized these aspects.[28] Experience itself taught that sin is still a reality in the Christian, and that the church was not yet pure. In their laxity the antinomians were altogether blind to this. One had to work out the coexistence of sin and righteousness in the Christian life, i.e., the transitional character from the old to the new. In this situation, one dare not turn the certainty of faith, which had to be maintained, into false security. In this life the struggle continues, and the Christian is still susceptible; the victory is not yet won. The antinomians were irresponsibly overlooking this. When Melanchthon brought up one of the objections of the opposing side for discussion, Luther snapped at him: "You are conceding too much to the antinomians." One should give the "enemies" no assistance.

Remarkably, Agricola later claimed that at this disputation peace had been achieved once again. But no trace of this can be seen in the notes or in Luther's statements shortly after the disputation. Privately and from the pulpit, Luther continued his criticism of the antinomians. Although old and tired, he felt himself as a youth in the battle with a new sect. Melanchthon noted with satisfaction that Luther had again drawn closer to him theologically as a result of this controversy.[29]

Still in September, Agricola drafted a retraction in order to comply with the Mansfeld accusations. It was reworked by Melanchthon, presumably because the original version hardly met expectations. Agricola, however, refused to show it to Luther, and instead asked him how he would formulate a retraction. Apparently he was hoping that, theologically, Luther would meet him halfway. But Luther now decided to attack Agricola publicly with a work of his own.[30] He considered him a hypocrite and was no longer interested in a reconciliation with him. Agricola protested to Jonas, Cruciger, and Melanchthon once again in December, saying that he had not wanted to take issue with the venerable Luther and that he had complied with all his conditions. Because he had been unable to dispel Luther's mistrust, he could only turn his cause over to God. At the same time he asked the elector not to reduce his salary. This he was granted. Any further expenditure, however, would depend on the stilling of the controversy.[31]

In January 1539 Luther's *Against the Antinomians* appeared.[32] It was deliberately dedicated to Caspar Güttel, the preacher in Eisleben who was Agricola's opponent, and was intended to combat the antinomian doctrine. Luther was concerned with making an unambiguous statement against Agricola's claims, so that no one could appeal to him in support of antinomianism. What Agricola had written against the law had to be unmistakably revoked. Luther could easily refute the claim that he had earlier shared this view by referring to his writings and his practice, and not least to the printed, illustrated, and sung catechism. Nevertheless, this accusation bothered Luther. He repeated his most important arguments in a form that was easy to understand: All knowledge of sin comes through the law, even when this knowledge is wrought by the suffering of Christ. The law cannot simply be eliminated, for it is written in man's heart. Christians are always attacked by sin. The fact that the antinomians no longer felt this and thus taught a completely different piety made Luther very suspicious of them. Even the church was a sinner for Luther. The ties between the law's demand and Christ's saving act dare not be separated. The new method of preaching first grace and then the revelation of God's wrath reversed the order of Pauline theology. Luther hoped that Agricola would unambiguously recant these perverted views.

In conclusion, Luther included the "new spirits" among the false teachers he had otherwise experienced. Whenever the Word of God shone forth in the history of the church, the devil began to blow it out. During Luther's time it was first the papacy, and then Müntzer, the peasants, Karlstadt, the Anabaptists, and the anti-Trinitarians. He dispassionately drew the conclusion that he would not be able to protect his posterity against such controversies, although this was actually the goal of the theological politics of Electoral Saxony and Wittenberg at that time. Despite his appearance of resignation, Luther maintained his imperturbability. The devil might blow at him with puffed cheeks, but Christ would strike the devil with his fist. "For after all, we are not the ones who can preserve the church, nor were our forefathers able to do so. Nor will our successors have this power. No, it was, is, and will be he who says, 'I am with you always, to the close of the age.'" Agricola said the book was a libelous work and a book of lies; even Melanchthon called it passionate.[33] But Luther had not simply given free rein to his polemic. When Agricola claimed that Luther supported his views, Luther was personally offended, and he revealed the depth of his theological opposition to the antinomians. For him, in fact, the conflict with the antinomians was one of the greatest controversies he had to endure.

Agricola had to submit to Luther if he wanted to keep his position in Wittenberg. He therefore prepared theses that were to be debated in the liberal arts faculty on 1 February 1539. The first group of these theses did not deal with this subject but referred allegorically to Agricola's situation. He compared himself to Jonathan who, disobeying the command of his father Saul (Luther), had eaten honey but had nevertheless not sinned (1 Sam. 14:24-27). In a roundabout way he presented a justification of why he had bowed to pressure. Then he correctly reproduced Luther's doctrine of the law but stated only that God's wrath was revealed through the gospel. Luther immediately saw that this was not a real retraction and commented on it in his own marginal notes on the theses. Whether Luther took part in the disputation is unknown. He did, however, make note of two objections that should be presented there. The first contradicted Agricola's presentation of his relationship to Luther. The second pointed out that Agricola had only appeared to abandon his false view. Agricola seems to have met forceful opposition at the disputation. Luther now regretted having dealt with him so gently in *Against the Antinomians*. However, an open break was avoided. Agricola received a new position in the Wittenberg consistory, which was reorganized as the central office of the church.[34]

Since the beginning of 1539, antinomianism had also made its presence felt outside Wittenberg and Eisleben. Agricola's friend Caspar Aquila apparently also shared his theological opinions. A controversy about it arose in his congregation in Saalfeld, and Luther had to attempt to settle it.[35] Reports were circulating that statements minimizing sin in the believers had been made in Lüneburg. Although Agricola was not directly responsible, he was blamed, especially since his own life style gave some cause for it. Again and again in his lectures, sermons, and discussions of the following months, Luther criticized the antinomians and their moral laxity.[36] In April he energetically and apparently successfully worked to prevent Agricola's election as dean of the liberal arts faculty. A bit later he was planning to impose the ban on him because of his hypocrisy. It was presumably in this context that Agricola then considered himself a martyr. In no way did this agree with Luther's views. Luther later was happy that a new attempt at reconciliation initiated by Bugenhagen failed because he had not found Agricola at home. For his part, Agricola was no longer interested in a reconciliation as long as the accusations raised in *Against the Antinomians* were not revoked.[37]

The Final Split

In August 1539 Agricola switched to an aggressive defense. He filed complaints against Luther with the rector of the university and with Bugenhagen as the pastor. Later, at the end of January 1540, he lodged a complaint with the Mansfeld clergy and the Eisleben congregation. When this also accomplished nothing, he turned to the elector on 1 March. In a lengthy enumeration, he complained of the personal and theological accusations that Luther, egged on by others, had brought against him. With a good conscience he could deny the dogmatic and moral consequences Luther had invented in his own mind. He did not mention that in fact a theological difference did exist between them, but instead stated that he gratefully acknowledged what he had received from Luther. For the sake of his reputation and his existence he now demanded a public hearing and protection from the false accusations, or else he would appeal to an ever-widening public, even the scholars of all Europe.[38] The elector naturally would have preferred a direct settlement of the controversy between Agricola and Luther, and he certainly could not have been interested in having the conflict taken to the public. The elector initially asked for an opinion from Melanchthon, Jonas, Bugenhagen, and Amsdorf. Accordingly,

Melanchthon gave an account of the conflict and pointed out that Luther's polemic against the antinomians was directed not against Agricola alone, and that he could not repudiate its substance. Luther could hardly be induced to retract it. Agricola should come to an agreement with Luther directly.[39]

Meanwhile, Luther had received a copy of Agricola's Mansfeld complaint from Caspar Güttel. He had Fröschel, the Wittenberg deacon, ask Agricola what he intended to do, and thus learned of his plans to bring the matter before the public. Agricola had asked Luther not to react too quickly, i.e., to await a possible resolution of the matter by the elector. Luther, in fact, at first did nothing, and asked Güttel only for evidence against Agricola.[40] The preacher in Seeburg, Wendelin Faber, collected the material. Moreover, Count Albrecht of Mansfeld counseled the elector to arrest Agricola in Wittenberg. John Frederick also considered it such a serious matter that Agricola had already extended the controversy beyond Electoral Saxony by complaining to the Mansfelders that he forbade him to leave Wittenberg. This also indicates that an investigation of Agricola was underway.[41] The complainant had become the accused.

At the end of April or somewhat later, Luther gave Chancellor Brück the material from Eisleben along with his own opinion of Agricola's complaint.[42] He pointed out the political consequences it would have in the empire if the Wittenberg doctrine were denounced as impure. Agricola was showing that he was an enemy of the Wittenbergers. This was also revealed by his machinations behind the scenes in Eisleben and Wittenberg. Luther's efforts at reaching a theological solution instead of a legal one had been unsuccessful. Luther retracted none of the theological accusations he had made nor the conclusions he had drawn, and he was incensed that Agricola claimed to be innocent. His arrogant, malicious attitude toward the Wittenbergers was now used as an argument to prove that he knew nothing about the law, which humbles a person. Agricola's premises were incompatible with sound evangelical doctrine. Even after Luther's death, people used this work to incite opposition against Agricola.

Jonas, Cruciger, Bugenhagen, and Melanchthon declared in June that Agricola's complaint against Luther was invalid, and that an apology by Luther was inappropriate. Agricola had no hope of prevailing.[43] The proceedings against him dragged on. In mid-August, before they were completed, he broke his promise, secretly leaving Wittenberg and assuming the position of court preacher to Elector Joachim II in Berlin. For Agricola, this was his liberation from a situation that had become untenable, but, for Luther, it was new proof of his antinomianism, which disqualified him for this new office.[44]

Luther used the graduation disputation of Joachim Mörlin on 10 September 1540 as a final opportunity to settle theological accounts with Agricola.[45] In it he drew radical conclusions from the abolition of the law that he ascribed to his opponent: Where there is no law there is no sin, neither wrath nor grace, also no divine or human government, neither God nor man. Only the devil is left. The protestations of the antinomians to the contrary were nothing but empty confessions of the lips. Neither theology nor politics could be learned from them. They served not Christ but their bellies, and they were driven by their own ambition. It was precisely against drawing consequences like these and such a global condemnation, which could come only from political considerations, that Agricola had defended himself in his complaint. The opponent, in fact, was here being made into a monster or bugbear. This time Luther himself took a relatively minor part in the disputation. He maintained, however, that the antinomians were teaching differently than the Wittenbergers not just in certain points, but in everything.

Even after Agricola escaped to Berlin, he and his new sovereign, Elector Joachim II of Brandenburg, must have had a great interest in clearing up the relationship with Luther and Elector John Frederick. Brandenburg, like Electoral Saxony, also had to be concerned about its theological reputation. At first they did not attempt to approach Luther, instead employing Melanchthon as a mediator. Melanchthon immediately made it clear that they should not expect Luther to retract his accusations. Melanchthon himself occasionally had had to endure Luther's rebukes, and it would be no different with Agricola. In Berlin they soon saw that it was Agricola who would have to submit.[46] On 1 October Melanchthon was able to transmit Luther's conditions for peace to Joachim II: Agricola would have to withdraw his complaint against Luther, acknowledge in writing his error to the Eisleben congregation, and retract his criticism of *Against the Antinomians*. Thus an unconditional surrender was being demanded, while Luther was making no concessions on his side.[47] Agricola immediately accepted, and then withdrew his complaint in a letter to the Electoral Saxon commissioners, Benedict Pauli and Bernhard von Mila, who were familiar with the matter. Melanchthon's assurance that not all Luther's accusations had been personally directed at him helped him to save face. Moreover, he asked Elector John Frederick to forgive him for breaking his promise and leaving Wittenberg. Not until February 1541 did he receive permission to enter the territory of Electoral Saxony without being arrested.[48]

Melanchthon did not want to involve Luther in the reconciliation process until the revocation had been presented to the Eisleben congregation. Although he was skeptical, Luther agreed to this procedure. When Melanchthon had to go to Worms in mid-October to attend the colloquy, Bugenhagen took over his role as mediator. The first draft of the revocation had to be sent back, because it would hardly have satisfied Luther. Joachim II took care to see that it was improved.[49] In mid-December he could send Agricola's printed recantation to Wittenberg and hope that it would settle the dispute. In his *Confession and Affirmation of God's Law*, which essentially followed a proposal by Melanchthon, Agricola explained how he had arrived at his previous way of teaching that had been objectionable. He stated, certainly not entirely accurately, that he had eliminated the law from Christian repentance because of his confrontation with Witzel's Catholic legalism in Eisleben, and now he had been better instructed by Luther. Thereby he had so completely fallen in line with the Wittenbergers that his friends in Eisleben were at variance with him. Bugenhagen soon was able to report to Agricola from Wittenberg that Luther and the other theologians had accepted the recantation. Probably not without reason, he only admonished him to lead a life worthy of his calling.[50]

Unlike the other theologians, however, Luther never gave up his old distrust that had developed during the preceding negotiations. Even on 6 December he characterized Agricola to Jacob Stradner, a Brandenburg church visitor, as vanity incarnate, better suited to be a jester than a preacher. His thirst for glory did not allow him to accomplish anything useful. Luther was not hoping for anything positive from him. The requested apology had been given, although Luther was sure that he had been deceived by Agricola. Apparently he could not prove this, however, and thus let things run their course. Agricola's *Confession* made no change in this judgment. Luther repeated it to Stradner a few months later. His own conclusion was that he would avoid any more contact with the man. Agricola's publications in Berlin did, in fact, show that he was persisting in his old views; there was also no significant change in his life style.[51] In the years following, Luther maintained his negative opinion of Agricola. He only occasionally spoke about the dangers of antinomianism, but it was still acute in the form of moral libertinism. Elector Joachim II, of course, thought it wrong for Luther to snub his court preacher so unequivocally, for this impugned the reputation of the Brandenburg church. When he drew nearer to Electoral Saxony and the Smalcald League in 1545, he also sought to bring Agricola together with Luther, sending him with a message to Wittenberg. Luther did not receive him, however, only Else Agricola, his wife. Luther accepted the fact that this meant insulting Joachim II. What he heard from Berlin confirmed his preconceived opinion that Agricola was still an unrepentant hypocrite. Luther's sovereign was in agreement with this attitude.[52] Shortly before his death, Luther warned the Wittenberg theologians a final time about "Eisleben," who was possessed by the devil. Agricola, despite everything, sincerely mourned the death of his spiritual father.[53]

Antinomianism, in fact, was never a danger that could compare to the others that emerged from Luther's own camp. Within a few years it was put to rest. Agricola remained faithful in great part to the Wittenberg doctrine. He never abandoned Luther, but he also never fully understood him. The difference, however, had to do with the center of Luther's theology and piety, the situation of man before God in judgment and grace. When Luther finally became aware of this, he irrevocably broke with his former friend. Dictated by human disappointment, the final verdict was excessively harsh.

170

When we review the three theological conflicts in Wittenberg during the last half of the 1530s, it can been seen that it was one of Luther's great achievements that they remained limited and, although not without effort and difficulty, that to some extent they could be overcome. As harsh as the controversy with Agricola was, the disagreement with Melanchthon and his pupils was more of a problem in the long run, because it could not be fully resolved and the differences were hidden.

VII

Luther and the Council
(1533–39)

1. INITIAL CATHOLIC PROBES AND
EVANGELICAL REACTIONS

After the Religious Peace of Nuremberg in 1532, Luther had little occasion to concern himself about political matters in the empire or in Europe. The agreement achieved by the emperor, however, could not obscure the fact that irreconcilable differences with the papacy continued to exist.[1] Moreover, the peace was to be in effect only until a council met. In December 1532, Charles V and Pope Clement VII met in Bologna. The emperor again insisted that the proposed council be held soon. The pope agreed, although, as before, he had little interest in one. In advance, however, the approval of the European princes was to be obtained. The task of doing this in Germany was assigned to the bishop of Reggio, Ugo Rangoni, accompanied by the imperial orator, Lambert of Briaerde. The nuncio's instructions stated that the council was in accord with the pope's wishes. It was to be a "free" one, held "according to the usual practice of the church." The participants had to promise in advance to submit to its decisions. At the beginning of June 1533, the mission came to Weimar, and somewhat later to Wittenberg.[2] From then on, the council was a topic that concerned the evangelical estates, and Luther as well, for years. The momentous question was whether it would finally bring about the reform of the whole church or whether the council would simply serve as the pope's instrument for crushing the evangelicals.

After the Wittenbergers became aware of the conditions, Luther and Melanchthon prepared several opinions in which they basically advocated participating. There was no question of any other sort of reaction, since they had been demanding a council for so long. Nevertheless, they did not fail to point out unclarities and problems in the preconditions. The council should be conducted "in accordance with God's Word and work." The mention of the "usual practice" could also include the abuses. It was impossible to accept the decisions of the council in advance. There was no question of the pope's serving as the judge, for he himself was one of the accused parties. Luther assumed that the pope would not allow a council to meet, even under these conditions, but he was quite concerned that the evangelicals not be the ones who refused.

The project of a countercouncil in Wittenberg was immediately rejected.[3] The members of the Smalcald League then on 30 June asked the emperor specifically for a truly free council because the pope's conditions indicated to them that this would not be one. Nevertheless, they did not rule out attending the papal council with reservations. They were shrewdly keeping all their options open. In order to convince the public of their willingness to attend a council under the emperor's auspices, the publicity about the council and the Smalcald League's reply were printed in Wittenberg in German and Latin, along with appropriate prefaces by Luther (to the German version) and Melanchthon (to the Latin).[4]

The supposition in Wittenberg that the pope would not permit a council at all proved correct. In March 1534 Clement VII postponed it until a more propitious and peaceful time. It is very probable that Luther himself wrote the Latin satire, *Convocation of a Holy, Free, Christian Council*.[5] Its alleged author was the Holy Spirit, because the infamous pope was refusing the reform council that had frequently been demanded, especially by the emperor. In order to thwart the machinations of the stubborn pope, he himself was convening a council on the basis of a decision made by the Holy Trinity, bypassing all the papal tricks. The summons had been prepared by the Archangel Gabriel, the heavenly notary. This forged "breve from heaven" gave expression to Luther's serious criticism of the pope's action and his own hope that the Holy Spirit would be the real reformer of the church.

Pope Clement VII died on 24 September 1534. His successor, Paul III, immediately let it be known that he was finally thinking of calling a council. At the beginning of 1535, nuncios were sent to Spain, France, and Germany to sound out the European princes about the pope's intention and the site of the council—Mantua, Turin, Piacenza, and Bologna were under consideration. Pietro Paolo Vergerio, formerly the nuncio at the court of King Ferdinand, was assigned the mission to Germany.[6] It was not until August that Elector John Frederick learned through Margrave George of Brandenburg-Ansbach about Vergerio's mission. When the elector requested a statement about the new plans for a council, Luther recommended that they stand by their demand for a Christian and free council from two years earlier. But, at present, he did not dare to hope that one would really occur. He knew nothing about Vergerio's further efforts until the end of October.[7]

At the beginning of November, the nuncio was staying in Halle and wanted to proceed from there through Wittenberg to Berlin. In Wittenberg he was received on 6 November by Hans Metzsch, the city governor, in a courteous manner appropriate to his status and lodged in the castle. On the next day there was a momentous meeting between the pope's representative and Luther; both parties reported on it, although neither one fully.[8] The invitation came from Vergerio, a fact that he himself later concealed from Rome. On his part, Luther had himself shaved and put on his best clothes, a dark doublet with satin sleeves, over which he wore a short, fur-lined coat made of serge, a light woolen material. He also wore a heavy gold chain and several rings. He declared that his intent was to present a youthful appearance, so that in Rome they would see that more could be expected from him. He accomplished his objective. He made a strong impression on the nuncio, who thought he seemed about forty years old and who did not notice the aged and pale features of Luther's rough face. Like others, Vergerio was impressed by the dark, sparkling eyes. He interpreted them as an expression of fury and wrath, and found that they confirmed his other information about Luther's personality (Plate VII). In part, however, this information was dubious. He thought Luther was the son of a day laborer in the mines and a bathmaid of ill repute. Vergerio's report refers again and again to Luther as a beast who has abandoned the Christian faith. On his part, Luther made sure that his partner in the discussion knew that he had married an honorable nun and had had five children by her, of whom the eldest son would be twice as much a man in the evangelical doctrine as he himself.

Luther took Bugenhagen with him to the meeting. When they left for the castle, he joked: "Here go the German pope and Cardinal Pomeranus, God's instruments." In greeting Vergerio, Luther did remove his hat, but he did not use the nuncio's appropriate titles. In speaking, Luther deliberately favored German, so that Vergerio doubted whether he had really written his Latin works all by himself. This behavior fit in with Luther's first question, which was whether they thought of him in Italy as a German drunkard.

The nuncio first sought to obtain information about the English delegation then visiting in Wittenberg and about events in England because Robert Barnes had himself rejected Vergerio's invitation. Vergerio felt that action against the English king was even more urgent than the council. However, he learned very little from Luther about John Fisher and Thomas More, the supporters of the pope who had just been executed in England, except for a few harsh opinions (*verbis verdriesslicissimis*). The nuncio was also interested in how ordination was practiced in Wittenberg. Naturally, Bugenhagen's exercising episcopal functions in ordination was a point of contention. Vergerio had no understanding at all for the worship service in Wittenberg with its German liturgy and hymns. Luther also favored two fast days a week, but only if they were set by the emperor and not the pope. This rejection of papal authority could not help but irritate the nuncio.

Naturally, the most important topic was the council. Luther doubted that the planned council would deal with anything but externals. There they would not even talk about faith, true repentance, justification, and other crucial features of the evangelical doctrine. But when Luther said that the evangelicals did not need a council, but that those on the other side did, the nuncio abandoned the reserved attitude he had had until then, for this touched upon his real assignment. He was certain that a council assembled under the Holy

Spirit would decide against Luther. This provoked Luther into declaring that he would subject himself to a council, even if it were to burn him, but he would not be made to change his beliefs. With this, Vergerio had secured Luther's agreement to attend a council. To Vergerio's surprise, the place where the council was to meet, which the estates wanted to be on German soil, was immaterial to Luther. He would go to Mantua and, if necessary, even to the more distant Bologna in the Papal States. When they parted, the nuncio again reminded him of this agreement, and Luther declared that he was prepared to come "with head and neck."

The discussion had touched on important points and revealed the opposing positions; but it had hardly gone very deeply, and neither side had been interested in doing so. From the beginning, Luther had deliberately wanted to shock this representative of the opposing side with his ostentatious clothing, his coarse manner, and his statements. Vergerio did not see in Luther the serious and profound personality that others saw in him. He thought Luther seemed to have become increasingly intransigent and frantic because of the attention he had received; the tragedy of this man, in accordance with Christ's will, could only have a bitter end. In the diplomatic and somewhat casual report he made, there is no hint that Vergerio, later bishop of Capodistria in Illyria, would give up his position in 1549 after becoming an adherent of the Reformation.

Vergerio first met Elector John Frederick in Prague on 30 November. The joint reply of the Smalcald League to the nuncio's efforts was issued on 21 December.[9] They again agreed to a free council and promised to participate. The prospective site of Mantua, however, did not meet the demands of the previous diets. The pope's supremacy called the freedom of the council into question. The secular rulers had to make sure that the proceedings against the pope, who was the one accused, were conducted properly. The Smalcald League insisted that secular rulers participate in the council. If this free council could not be obtained, they stated that they were prepared to participate in other efforts at achieving unity.

Luther also continued his literary polemic against the pope in 1535. At Christmas 1534, the devil was reported to have appeared to the pastor of Stassfurt, allegedly to make his confession, but in doing so he blasphemed Christ and then vanished, leaving a foul stench. The account of this was published in Wittenberg. Luther wrote the preface, dedicating it to Amsdorf.[10] The event in Stassfurt showed how the devil was vanquished by God's mercy and how those who were the "footstool" of Christ at the right hand of God (Ps. 110:1) were unable to prevail. Luther asked Amsdorf, the "bishop" of Magdeburg, for his opinion of this story, which might also serve as a reply to the legates of the devil. At the outset, he sought to prevent his friend from pushing this task off on him as the "pope." Bishops were often more learned than the pope. Moreover, "Pope Luther" could no more assemble a council of his own supporters than could the Roman pope, for they were being starved, burned, drowned, murdered, hunted, and scattered. In this unusual case of confession, Pope Luther was thus turning over the authority to Bishop Amsdorf, and he also prescribed a formula for him to use in proclaiming God's wrath against the devil and his legates and condemning them to hell. Luther combined this joke with an appeal for prayer and serious attention to the Word of God, for the event showed with whom the evangelicals really had to deal. The pope was an adherent of hell. His resistance to the emperor, which had again become evident in Paul III's friendship with France, proved this. The pope was still acting as if he were the most holy father, although it was he and not Luther or the Turk who was the real rebel. In the face of this perverse attitude, Luther took comfort in the fact that he had unmistakably opposed this pope.

At that time Luther provided an afterword to a new edition of Melanchthon's *The Papal Ass in Rome* of 1523.[11] The appearance of the monstrosity in Rome had not brought the papists to repentance, but instead had made them worse. They knew God's Word, but still opposed it and persecuted God's followers. But the papal ass was already dead, and those who opposed God almighty would accomplish nothing. Here the final culmination of the antithesis between Luther and the pope was beginning to develop.

In this context belongs "A Song of the Holy Christian Church from the Twelfth Chapter of the Apocalypse," one of Luther's most noteworthy poems.[12] The first stanza sounds so much like a secular love song that it is still unclear whether Luther did not simply borrow it. The next two stanzas are a very faithful poetic rendering of Rev. 12:1-6, the passage about the woman clothed with the sun who bears a son whom the dragon persecutes. But the child and his mother are miraculously rescued. Following the traditional exegesis, Luther interpreted the text in terms of the church and not of Mary. He articulated his confidence in a very few words: Christ is exalted; on earth the church may still be persecuted, but God preserves it.

It was probably in connection with the visit of the papal nuncio that Luther arranged a disputation "On the Power of the Council" in the first months of 1536.[13] Since the apostles, there had been no comparable normative authority in the church. All their successors must be in accord with the apostolic foundation. Anyone deviating from this foundation is either a heretic or the Antichrist. A council of bishops, as such, does not possess the Holy Spirit or infallibility, but only when it follows this norm. The council, as such, is not identical with the true church, but only represents it. History teaches that a single individual can be right in opposition to a whole council. In burning Huss and Jerome of Prague, the Council of Constance burned those who witnessed to the truth. In his opening address to the disputation, Luther stated that he was seriously interested in limiting the authority of the council, because it was through this institution that the church had been laid waste. The council must be subject to the authority of the apostles and dare not decree new teachings on its own. Only a council that acts this way is "assembled in the name of Christ." The church is found only where God's Word is kept. There is no institutionalized possession of the Holy Spirit. Here the whole difference between the evangelical and the Catholic understanding of a council can be seen. Given these presuppositions, it was scarcely imaginable that the evangelicals would participate in a council.

2. SUMMONING THE COUNCIL TO MANTUA, LUTHER'S ARTICLES, AND THE SMALCALD ASSEMBLY IN 1537

On 2 June 1536 Pope Paul III summoned a council to Mantua on 23 May of the following year.[1] It was to fight heresies and errors, improve Christian morals, and restore peace among the faithful. Not only were leaders of the church to participate in it but secular rulers as well. Because it was expected that the elector of Saxony and the Smalcald League would be invited, John Frederick asked the Wittenberg theologians and jurists on 24 July for their opinion, informing them at the same time that the council would not be a free one, nor would it take place on the territory of the empire. He himself was inclined to refuse to accept an invitation at all and, instead, to protest the council called by the pope. Nevertheless, one had to remember that the Religious Peace of Nuremberg was to be in effect only until a council met. For the time being, the scholars in Wittenberg did not think the possible objections were serious enough to refuse an invitation.[2] However, John Frederick was not convinced by their arguments, neither then nor in the following discussions.

At the end of August, Chancellor Brück brought Luther the elector's request that he write his testament "in the matter of religion." Luther had occasionally spoken of the confession he had appended to *Confession Concerning Christ's Supper,* which appeared in 1528, as his testament. In light of Luther's ill health and because of the council, the elector wanted a final and definitive theological statement from Luther. This shows how much the cause of the Reformation was identified with Luther. Otherwise, Brück alone dealt with the Wittenberg theologians about the details of the council, the matters which should be discussed there, and the room for negotiating.[3] During September Luther was summoned to the court in Torgau no fewer than three times in order to participate in discussions with a delegation from King Ferdinand. In his sermons there he emphasized the preeminence of the mercy of God, which surrounds the believers, over works. Nevertheless, he did consider fasting, praying, and giving alms Christian actions. At the time he did not believe the opposing side seriously wanted a council. If one did indeed meet, the discussions would be extremely difficult.[4]

In view of the approaching council, it was important to remind the public of the Council of Constance and the burning of John Huss that happened there, for it showed how the church dealt with its critics. Luther therefore undertook an exhaustive study of the history of that council. He published the letters Huss wrote from prison—translated into Latin by John Agricola—with their bitter criticism of the proceedings of the council and the pope. Unlike earlier, he was not simply concerned with a polemic attack against the Council of Constance, but rather that its example might show the present age that truth ultimately could not be suppressed. The chief objective in Constance had allegedly been only to put an end to the schism in the church, not to eliminate abuses, and thus they were continuing to flourish. At the forthcoming council the rulers and bishops had to ensure that this would not be repeated. The injustice against Huss had its bitter consequences. Several additional German editions of these letters of Huss were published. At the beginning of 1537, Luther wrote an afterword for them, reminding people that Huss's criticism of the pope and indulgences was justified and that his execution had proved to be an injustice. The "spiritless," meaning, naturally, the clergy, should not forget this at the coming council. Huss had prophesied that he would have successors who could not be overcome. In 1537 another large collection of Huss's letters was published in Wittenberg. In Luther's preface the pope was depicted as the one who, by proclaiming saints, issuing indulgences, and condemning heretics, had unjustly made himself Lord and God of heaven and hell; but he would not escape the judgment to come.[5]

On about 1 December 1536 the elector discussed with the Wittenberg theologians whether representatives should be sent to the council. He expected nothing good to come of it. The Lutherans would be made out to be heretics, regardless. Nevertheless, Luther was to write down articles that stated the theological views on which he would ultimately stand and provide biblical support for them, i.e., his theological testament. In addition, he was to indicate the articles wherein one might compromise under certain circumstances. Thereafter, the other Wittenbergers and some of the other theologians of Electoral Saxony were to make a definitive declaration about whether they agreed with them and then sign the articles. Because of the recent events during the Cordatus controversy, the elector would not be satisfied with a mere agreement for the sake of peace. He intended to present the theological confession that resulted to the planned meeting of the Smalcald League in February for adoption. The assembly would also have to discuss whether a countercouncil should be called by Luther, his "co-bishops," and other pastors. Because one could expect that such a council would be attacked, the question of resistance also had to be discussed.[6]

In their opinion on 6 December, the Wittenberg theologians anticipated that they would be cited before the council. In view of the action at the Council of Constance, a strictly legal procedure had to be guaranteed in advance. They advised against a countercouncil, for this would be declared a schism and no one could foresee the consequences of that. They considered it permissible to defend the gospel, even against the emperor himself, for he was

179

not sovereign in matters of religion. Thus, in the meantime, the Wittenberg theologians had adopted the legal arguments of the Smalcald League on this question as their own. Luther expressly confirmed this with his signature: "I, too, will do all I can with prayer, and if need be, also with my fist."[7]

The elector then gave Luther a formal assignment to write the articles, mentioning again that questions regarding the papacy were to be touched upon. The confession was obviously to serve more as a demarcation than as an agreement.[8] Luther set to work immediately. From the beginning he seems to have intended to confront the opposite side with the doctrine of justification. He was still undecided as to whether he should comply with a formal citation from the pope to attend the council, but he was sure that he would in no way be welcome there.[9]

The motto that headed the articles stated that in them was presented the doctrine necessary for eternal life, but not additional onerous laws.[10] Luther first confessed that he was united with the opposing side in confessing the triune God, but the sharp confrontation began immediately with the articles concerning Christ's office and work, or redemption. In accordance with Rom. 3:23-28, Luther confessed: Only faith in the redeeming death of Christ makes one righteous. "Nothing in this article can be given up or compromised, even if heaven and earth and things temporal should be destroyed." This is the article "on which the church stands or falls." Luther made its significance absolutely clear: On it rested his entire critique against the pope, the devil, and the world. This had to be certain, or the opposing side had won. This made the doctrine of justification the key problem. The greatest outrage was thus the papal mass, the propitiatory sacrifice offered by men. Luther did advance arguments for a critical discussion of this theme, but he was clear from the very outset that the opponents would not surrender anything on this point. He would rather let himself be burned than accept the sacrifice of the mass as a competitor of the redeeming death of Christ. Here they were "eternally divided." He could demonstrate impressively what accompanied the concept of the sacrifice of the mass: Purgatory with masses for the dead, pilgrimages, brotherhoods, relics, indulgences. Another thing that competed with Christ's work was monasticism. The pope cannot be the head of Christendom by divine right alongside Christ. It was also impossible to accept him as the church's head even by human ordinance. Luther maintained: The pope is the Antichrist. In these fundamental points there was no compromise to be expected at the council, only condemnation, persecution, and coercion.

Luther did think that it was possible to hold discussions on central theological and practical questions, for he assumed, of course, that he would be able to convince the opposing side of his view. These began with a radicalization of the understanding of sin, in which, unlike scholasticism, he denied that man was able to contribute anything to his own salvation, for this would compete with the work of Christ. Accordingly, the law's only function was to reveal sin.

It was to bring a person to recognize and acknowledge that he was powerless and lost. The penance of the papists was false, therefore, because it was always a function of a person's own work in his conversion. Up to this point, Luther had developed the articles relatively extensively. On 18 and 19 December, however, he suffered one or more heart attacks (*angina pectoris*),[11] and had to dictate the remaining articles and thus keep them brief. The gospel offered help against sin through its preaching of forgiveness, baptism, the Lord's Supper, the office of the keys, and fraternal consolation. In the sacraments, the connection between the words of institution and the elements was strongly emphasized. In the Lord's Supper, both bread and wine had to be given in accordance with its institution. The doctrine of transubstantiation was rejected, although, in contrast, private confession was expressly reaffirmed. The ban should be used only to exclude a manifest sinner from the Lord's Supper. Reasons for the Wittenberg practice of ordination were given and the procedure was justified. Celibacy of the clergy, a tyrannical requirement, was also rejected here. He denied that the opposing side was the church. "For, thank God, a seven-year-old child knows what the church is, namely, holy believers and sheep who hear the voice of their Shepherd." The church was defined on the basis of God's Word and true faith in it. Good works do not justify, but are the result of faith. In this life they are always imperfect. Human traditions contribute nothing to the forgiveness of sins or to salvation.

As the elector wished, Luther concluded very personally: "These are the articles on which I must stand and on which I will stand, God willing, until my death. I do not know how I can change or concede anything in them. If anybody wishes to make some concessions, let him do so at the peril of his own conscience." Luther had thus contented himself with listing the essential articles. In them he left no room for negotiating a compromise. If negotiations with "learned and sensible men" did happen, he would expect them to come over to his point of view. This attitude was essentially derived from the character of the articles themselves. Like no other Reformation confession, they were based on the central doctrine of justification. Thus they taught the exclusivity of the Reformation's "by grace alone."

On 15 December 1536 Luther had invited Agricola, Spalatin, and Amsdorf to come on 28 or 29 December to Wittenberg, where the discussion on the articles that the elector desired with the Wittenberg theologians was to be held.[12] The discussion led to the inclusion of another article, which rejected the invocation of the saints. In a few points Melanchthon had a different opinion than Luther. He would be satisfied if the evangelicals were granted the use of both kinds in the Lord's Supper, even though their opponents continued their old practice. This was consistent with his advice to Jacob Schenk a little later, which stirred up so much trouble. Ordination by bishops, which Luther had not ruled out, was something Melanchthon, in contrast, would not accept. In regard to fasting and specific holy days, however, they could compromise with the opposing side. Luther kept them from adding these points, for two of them would have opened room for negotiating. Comments added by the assembled theologians to their signatures at the end of the articles revealed that there was still another difference of opinion. Melanchthon was willing to concede that the pope had superiority over the bishops, as long as he permitted the gospel. As he had done earlier at the Diet of Augsburg, Melanchthon was willing to grant the Catholics more than Luther was, who was imperturbable in his trust in God.[13]

On 3 January 1537 Luther sent the articles to the elector through Spalatin. Probably because of previous discussions, he stated that the theologians did not want to involve the princes in a political adventure with their firm stand. He left it to the elector to decide how to use the articles. The elector immediately read them twice and accepted them fully as his own. In a very personal letter, written in his own hand and therefore not easy to decipher, he thanked Luther: "But we know, praise God, that the things which you have drawn from the Word of God and we have declared right and godly, are not human but divine things, and we want them to be confessed before the world and not denied. . . ." He hoped to persevere in them. The risk that this involved would have to be left to God. He unmistakably rejected the supremacy of the pope in the church, which Melanchthon thought possible.[14]

On 24 December 1536 Elector John Frederick and Landgrave Philip had invited the members of the Smalcald League to come to Schmalkalden on 7 February 1537 to prepare for the council. The most prominent theologians of the allied estates were also to participate in this assembly. An order to this effect was sent to Luther, Bugenhagen, and Melanchthon.[15] As before, the elector wanted to have the articles signed by the most important theologians of Electoral Saxony and by the Erfurt preachers, in order to submit them to the Smalcald Assembly as a sort of Electoral Saxon confession. Moreover, they should serve to bind the theologians of Electoral Saxony to Luther's theology after his death, which was possibly to be expected shortly.[16] Anticipating the assembly, Melanchthon had serious fears. The intractableness of Luther and the princes could threaten the peace. In addition, he was anticipating theological controversies among the members of the alliance.[17] Before he departed, Luther informed the Wittenberg congregation in a sermon that he was not expecting any worthwhile decisions from the council. He was not worried about the evangelical doctrine; it could be left to God. But one had to guard against wanting to do things better than God himself, as Müntzer, the Anabaptists, and the pope had tried to do. Therefore prayer was important, and especially needed were heartfelt petitions that ingratitude for the gospel might be forgiven. Petitions for the Smalcald Assembly were also ordered throughout the whole electorate.[18]

On the journey to Schmalkalden Luther learned that the papal nuncio Peter van der Vorst would appear there with the summons to the council, and also that the imperial vice-chancellor Matthias Held would be there. Luther was in good spirits on the trip. On 4 February he preached in Weimar and complained in his sermon that the evangelicals were being persecuted by kings and bishops. In the audience were also members of the nuncio's party.[19] The Wittenbergers arrived on schedule in Schmalkalden on 7 February, but the opening of the assembly was delayed for a few more days. In addition to the members of the league, other evangelical estates such as Brandenburg-Ansbach, Liegnitz, Nuremberg, and Nordhausen participated because of the question about attending the council. It appeared that it would become a large meeting with "many mules, asses, and horses." In fact, this assembly became a meeting of thirty-eight evangelical theologians from eighteen territories and cities, an unprecedented number. Among them, in addition to the Wittenbergers, were the significant reformers Urbanus Rhegius from Lüneburg, Erhard Schnepf and Ambrose Blaurer from Württemberg, John Lang from Erfurt, John Aepinus from Hamburg, Andreas Osiander and Veit Dietrich from Nuremberg, Amsdorf from Magdeburg, Brenz from Schwäbisch Hall, and Bucer from Strasbourg.[20]

On the evening of 10 February Melanchthon visited Landgrave Philip and told him about Luther's articles. He informed him that Luther had strengthened the article on the Lord's Supper beyond the one in the Wittenberg Concord by identifying the bread and wine with Christ's body and blood, while the Concord spoke about Christ's body and blood being present *with* the bread and wine. Melanchthon blamed Bugenhagen, the "crude Pomeranus," for this more pointed formulation, which was offensive to the southern Germans. But Luther, at the time he wrote it, was annoyed at the report that he had surrendered to the Zwinglians in the Wittenberg Concord. With this bit of information, which was to be passed on to the southern Germans, Melanchthon intended to keep the assembly from dealing with Luther's articles, but to have it affirm only the Augsburg Confession and the Wittenberg Concord as its confessional basis. He probably did not tell the landgrave that he still had other major reservations about Luther's uncompromising articles.[21]

In those days Luther again spoke emphatically in favor of attending the council.[22] They should not provide their opponents, who were not seriously interested in a council at all, with a reason to say that it had failed because of the evangelicals' refusal. It was true that at the council they would be interested only in rooting out the Lutheran heresy and not in a public hearing, but this was intended only to frighten the evangelicals into not attending. The reply to the legate should therefore not be an unequivocally negative one, for in this way it would be obvious that it was really Rome that did not want the council.

Unlike Luther, the estates of the Smalcald League sustained Electoral Saxony's rejection of the council soon after the assembly opened on 10 February, because it did not comply with their demand for a free, Christian council.

Moreover, the cities were opposed to any statements by the theologians about their own theological position, because in this way dissention could arise and any concessions might become known to the opposing side. It was then agreed that the theologians were to examine the Augsburg Confession and the Wittenberg Concord, give additional scriptural proofs for them, and add to them a critical statement on the papacy. Except for this addition, this task was not an especially significant one. Electoral Saxony was thus pursuing its previous intention of assuring a firm and lasting theological basis for the alliance. No serious attempt was made to use Luther's articles as the basis for discussion, because it was obviously hopeless from the very outset. It can no longer be proven that Melanchthon's agitation against the articles had an effect on this decision, but one may assume as much.[23] On 12 February a committee of twelve leading theologians, including all the Wittenbergers present, was formed. The examination of the Augsburg Confession proceeded easily, especially because they followed Luther's advice to provide additional proofs. The task of drafting the supplementary article on the papacy finally fell to Melanchthon alone. Five days later he presented the theologians with the Latin *Treatise on the Power and Primacy of the Pope*, which also contained a section entitled "The Power and Jurisdiction of Bishops." In accordance with the wishes of those who had given him the assignment, Melanchthon refrained from making any concessions to the papacy and emphasized its anti-Christian character. The treatise was accepted by the theologians. In addition, Luther's articles were distributed to them as sort of a private confession in view of the council.[24]

The second session of the theologians took place on 23 February. They were to continue the discussions of the committee concerning the Augsburg Confession, and thus they had to deal with the Lord's Supper. In this context, Luther's more pointed formulation in his articles was criticized by Bucer on behalf of the southern Germans, and he mentioned that this would put an end to any hope that the Swiss might join the Wittenberg Concord. Osiander, who otherwise was not very tactful—he freely criticized a sentence in one of Luther's sermons at that time, for example—responded sharply. On the other side, Blaurer criticized the Wittenberg Concord. They were on their way to becoming involved in a new sacramentarian controversy. This was something no one wanted. Osiander apologized to Bucer the next day. Luther and Melanchthon saw to it that Blaurer's objection did not endanger the Concord, in which Luther obviously also continued to be interested. The following day the theologians present signed Melanchthon's treatise. Subscribing Luther's articles, which indicated, of course, only that they personally agreed with them, was something some of the theologians, including Bucer and Blaurer, declined to do.[25]

The theological results of the assembly were generally minor, and in part even diffuse. Luther's articles were not adopted. Melanchthon had ultimately been able to keep Luther's articles from becoming an evangelical confession. In place of them, he himself had had to formulate a clear demarcation from the papacy. Nevertheless, the alliance's theological unity was preserved.

3. THE ILLNESS

It is possible that Luther might have been more actively involved at the assembly and might have had his position accepted had he been healthy. This time it was not heart problems, but kidney stones that became evident on 8 February when he passed a stone and experienced bleeding. In the following days he could participate in the discussions only sporadically.[1] On Sunday, 18 February, he was well enough to preach. He freely applied the gospel of Jesus' temptation by the devil (Matt. 4:1-11) to the church that had been tempted by external persecution, heretical perversion of the Bible, and now by the anti-Christian papacy and its mass. Only Christ himself could put an end to this.[2] Later that same day he suffered extreme pains. An enema administered by the landgrave's personal physician understandably not only did not help but caused persistent diarrhea that weakened the patient. Melanchthon was quite concerned about this inept treatment. On 19 February Luther was unable to urinate, and this persisted for eight days. Although there were several physicians of the princes in Schmalkalden, at Luther's request Dr. George Sturtz was summoned from Erfurt with suitable medications on 20 February. Previously, too, they had obtained medicine from Erfurt.[3] The discussions of the theologians were handicapped by Luther's illness. It was presumably for this reason that the committee of theologians did not meet again after its first session on 12 February. Without the authority of Luther, Melanchthon did not want to deal with sensitive problems, so it was not until the theologians met on 23 February in the presence of Luther, who felt better that day, that the Lord's Supper was discussed.[4]

The next day Luther, presumably because of his illness, felt somewhat euphoric, but he did not participate in the final meeting of the theologians.[5] The surgeon (*Steinschneider*) from Waltershausen was summoned. The elector's surgeon had a golden instrument fabricated for an operation. Luther had to suffer even more at the hands of the physicians who were helpless in his case, and, when all was said and done, he would rather have died. "They gave me as much to drink as if I had been a big ox." They offered him broth made from almonds. They also tried, from the *Dreckapotheke* (excrement pharmacy), remedies made from garlic and raw manure. From 25 February onward, Luther's condition grew increasingly critical. Melanchthon could not hold back his tears while visiting him. Their previously substantial differences were now obviously irrelevant. Luther was prepared to accept his fate from God's hand. However, he had an urgent wish to die in the territory of Electoral Saxony. Although hardly in condition to be moved, he wanted to leave Schmalkalden. To his consternation, Melanchthon postponed the departure for a day because,

185

for astrological reasons, he thought the new moon was an unfavorable date for this undertaking.

Before Luther's departure on 26 February the elector visited the patient and wished him God's grace and healing for the sake of the Word. Luther advised him to pray against the devil, the real adversary. The papal legate would be happy about Luther's death—in fact, the status of Luther's health was an important political consideration on all sides—but with Luther's death the pope would also lose an important person who was praying for him and he would not escape the evil to come. Luther thanked his sovereign for all that he had done for the sake of the gospel, and exhorted him to continue to work for it. John Frederick stated his concern that God would take away "his precious Word" along with Luther. Luther, however, mentioned the many theologians who had taken it to heart and understood it very well. The anxious elector took this as an opportunity to admonish all those present to preserve the pure Word. Luther also feared that after his death the gospel would be threatened by controversies. Interestingly, in this context he asked whether all the theologians had unanimously signed the articles, which, as mentioned above, was not the case. Melanchthon was able to tell him only that all of them, even Blaurer, had signed the Augsburg Confession and the Wittenberg Concord.[6] Before leaving, the elector assured Luther that he did not need to be concerned about his wife and children: "For your wife shall be my wife, and your children shall be my children." Nevertheless, Luther was afraid that the city governor, Hans Metzsch, who was at odds with him, would take revenge upon his family. Amsdorf should look after Katy. The patient's pains were so severe that he feared he was losing his mind. He felt miserable and had to vomit. Like Stephen, he felt he was being "stoned." But he held fast: "God still remains wise and Christ, my Lord, my wisdom and God." They should stop praying for him in the churches. God had now been "prayed, importuned, and cried to" enough. God would do the right thing. If Luther surrendered to the devilish pain, Christ would take revenge upon him. In this trust he commended his soul to God.

For the trip a copper basin was specially prepared so that towels could be heated and applied to the patient while traveling. When Luther entered the wagon, he made the sign of the cross and wished those standing around: "The Lord fill you with his benediction and with hatred of the pope." In his deathly illness Luther was aware of the significance of this final unreconciled word. The legate apparently assumed that Luther was already dead and had been taken away secretly. He therefore sent his servant to find out if this were so, but Schlaginhaufen prevented him from seeing Luther: "You will not see Luther in eternity." Bugenhagen, Spalatin, Myconius, Schlaginhaufen, and Dr. Sturtz accompanied the patient. Two men walked beside the wagon in order to moderate the discomfort of the trip on the poor road. Possibly, it was this jolting that saved Luther's life. The trip was excruciating, however. Luther wished that a Turk were there to kill him. That day the carriage went only as far as Tambach, fifteen kilometers from Schmalkalden.

During the night the urinary blockage finally opened. The first one to whom Luther wrote in detail, between two and three o'clock in the morning, was his "heartily beloved" (*herzallerliebste*) Melanchthon. Luther's relief that his "silver stream" had been restored is quite understandable. He attributed his improvement to the direct intervention of God. On the wall he wrote, "Here the Lord appeared to me." Schlaginhaufen immediately brought Luther's letter to Schmalkalden. He could not refrain from crying, "Luther lives!" outside the house of the legate. John Frederick rewarded the bearer of this good news with the princely sum of ten silver *Doppelschaugroschen* that bore his own image. He ordered prayers of thanks for Luther's recovery offered in church. In another letter written that night Luther told Katy about his serious illness and the fortunate improvement. He emphasized that the elector had "ordered people to run, ride, fetch, and with all his might tried his best to help me. But it was not to be. Your manure cure [medication sent by Katy] didn't help me either. This night God has accomplished a miracle in me, and he continues to do it through the intercession of godly people." Luther thought it no longer necessary that Katy come to him, for he was hoping soon to be coming happily to her.[7]

On the evening of 27 February the group arrived in Gotha. Despite the improvement in his health, Luther was in no way out of danger.[8] He had a premonition of death. The next day he made his confession to Bugenhagen and gave him final instructions. He considered his critique of the papacy justified, because the pope had blasphemed God, Christ, and the gospel. He asked "Little Philip [Melanchthon]"—who respectfully called Luther "father" in those days—Jonas, and Cruciger, his colleagues, to forgive him if he had sinned against them. We may think about the past theological tensions. Bugenhagen was to comfort Katy by referring to the twelve years Luther and she had lived together happily. "She served me not just like a wife, but also like a maid. God will reward her!" His friends should take care of her and their children. They should greet the Wittenberg deacons. He acknowledged: "The pious burghers of Wittenberg often served me." There was no mention of his difficulties with the congregation. The elector and the landgrave should pay no attention to the current accusation that they had robbed the church of its property, for they had used it for the church. They should trust in God and work for the cause of the gospel. Luther gave no instructions for how they were to do so. He commended them to God, that he would preserve them from relapsing into papal godlessness. He was aware that in many respects the princes were also sinners, but their sins could not be compared with the misdeeds of their anti-Christian opponents. Luther stated that he was ready to die, but he would have liked to live until Pentecost, the date for the opening of the council, in order to bear witness to the world against the apocalyptic beast

187

of Rome and its rule. Luther spoke with Myconius, the superintendent in Gotha, about being buried in that city.

On 1 March Luther was able to discuss the agreement on the Lord's Supper with Bucer and Bonifacius Wolfhart from Augsburg. In case he died, they should appeal to his desire for peace that he had declared in Schmalkalden. On the evening of that day he passed six stones, one of them as large as a bean. He also suffered from weakness, indigestion, vomiting, and insomnia. Not until after this new attack did Luther begin to improve.

The return journey through Erfurt, Weimar, Altenburg, and Grimma had to be made in short stages and with interruptions. Jonas came to Gotha in order also to accompany Luther. In Weimar Melanchthon, who was coming from Schmalkalden, joined the group. One can see from his reports of Luther's condition that the illness reminded him of what the loss of Luther would mean. Katy went to Altenburg to meet her husband. The physician from Zwickau, Stephan Wild, took over the medical treatment from Dr. Sturtz. Luther was already able to write Latin verses. One of them summarized the good shepherd of Psalm 23 and expressed the preservation he had experienced. On 14 March Luther was back in Wittenberg, still weak and without an appetite; he was still passing stones. But he continued to improve.[9]

In mid-April 1537 the elector asked for an opinion from the Wittenberg theologians and jurists about the decision in Schmalkalden to reject the council. As far as is known, they did not comply with this request in Wittenberg. The theologians, as before, were not in agreement with the strict political position of refusing to attend, which could lead to a violent confrontation. In Schmalkalden, however, they were not in a position to act decisively and prevail with their view. For the subsequent course of affairs neither a refusal nor any positive position of the evangelicals was significant. Before the end of April the pope had to postpone the meeting of the council until November, because difficulties had been encountered in holding it in Mantua.[10] The evangelicals' skepticism about Rome's will to reform was thus confirmed anew.

4. CRITICAL PUBLICATIONS AGAINST THE POPE

It is obvious that after the assembly in Schmalkalden Luther escalated his public controversy with the papacy into what was virtually a new pamphlet war. The course of events repeatedly gave new occasions for doing so. His preface to the account of the Council of Gangra (343) by John Kymaeus, a pastor in Hesse, a work directed primarily against the Anabaptists and probably written in March 1537, was one of the typical occasional writings.[1] Luther praised this provincial council for having dealt with genuine theological issues, and compared it with the pope's claim to be superior to councils and temporal estates. He himself was contemplating publishing such texts that were critical of the pope. In this context, in April he then published *The Lying [Lügend]* (instead of *Legend) of St. John Chrysostom* with glosses, preface, and after-word.[2] In the apocryphal life of this saint, which undeniably read like a novel, the pope, purgatory, and indulgences played a significant role, and Luther wanted to attack this. He dedicated the work to the pope, cardinals, and bishops who were soon to assemble at the council. He, the "dammed, stinking heretic," thereby announced his interest in the council, to which he had appealed as early as 1518 and at which he had promised the nuncio Vergerio he would appear. At present, because of his illness and lack of funds, Luther could send only credentials and this work as his representative. It was intended to demonstrate how the papal idolatry was buttressed with pious lies. The most offensive matter was that not only were the pious being cheated out of their money, but that they were also being led astray into works righteousness. Luther predicted that the council would reconfirm these lies. Nevertheless, the real lie was the claim that the pope was supreme over the whole Christian church. Luther wanted to demonstrate this to the pious fathers of Mantua if the council itself did not prove to be a fiction. Cochlaeus immediately attempted to counteract the effect of this publication by asserting, accurately, that these legends, contrary to Luther's claim, had never been approved by the church. Nevertheless, they were widespread.

As he planned, Luther continued to confront the opposing side with its own questionable tradition by publishing in May or June *One of the High Articles of the Most Holy Papal Faith, Called the Donation of Constantine.*[3] This dealt with the legend, which probably had originated in the eighth century, that Emperor Constantine had granted Pope Sylvester I titles of supremacy and portions of the Roman Empire, primarily in Italy. The document had long been recognized as a forgery. Luther chose this topic in order to "annoy the devil and his papacy." The pope's claim to supremacy over the world in the high Middle Ages, in fact, had frequently been based on the Donation of Constantine. Luther's ingenuous question about what Peter, the poor fisher-man of Bethsaida, had to do with the papacy's politics of world supremacy was naturally impertinent, particularly because he demonstrated how the popes were still practicing their politics down to the present time. The forthcoming council should deal with the position of the pope in the church. The result of that would be ruinous for him and the bishops, but no one should expect this to happen. Only Christ himself would judge the Antichrist. For the time being, the only thing that could be done was to expose the outrage of the papacy.

Pope Paul III's bull of 20 April, which ordered the postponement of the council, became known in Wittenberg at the end of May, where with certainty it was published by Luther himself.[4] It was additional proof for him of how little the pope wanted a council and a reform of the church. Somewhat later the papal bull of 15 June, which appealed for prayer on behalf of the Papal

States that were then being threatened by the Turks, aroused Luther's understandable ire because it contained generous indulgences and thus recalled his original conflict with Rome, something his biting glosses on it also made clear.[5]

Two pamphlets, in all probability written by Luther, are also part of the polemic of that time. The letter of *Beelzebub to the Holy Papal Church* was probably intended as a counterpart to the "breve from heaven" of 1534, in which the Holy Spirit convened a free, Christian council.[6] It contained a warning against any reform or an accommodation of the "new Galileans [Jesus' supporters] called Lutheran heretics." The prince of hell was pleased to note that Rome was not really serious about reform. He promised his support at the council in rooting out the Galileans and could give his assurance that the "spirit of the Galilean" would definitely not be present at the council. The second pamphlet dealt with *A Question from the Entire Order of Karnöffel Players.*[7] Because the pope had allegedly reformed his court and eliminated the Lutheran heresy, the forthcoming council, which was to deal only with useless regulations, should explain why in playing the game of Karnöffel a lower card could take a higher one, so that the emperor, as the ace, could be trumped by the pope. The pamphlet suggested that the answer might be that the pope had stolen too much from the emperor. These satires were not especially important, but with their biting humor they exposed the opposing side to ridicule.

In his controversy with the pope, Luther not only wrote polemic glosses and commentaries on revealing texts, but, as a positive action, he also presented his own confession of faith once again. He did so quite consciously by publishing the symbols of the ancient church, viz., the Apostles' Creed, the Athanasian Creed, and the Te Deum Laudamus. At the conclusion he added the text of the Nicene Creed, which was equal in significance to the Apostles' Creed, for it refuted all the Christological heresies. Luther was busy with this task at the end of April, but it was not published until 1538.[8] In this way he laid claim to his continuity with the true church, something he denied the opposing side possessed. As the history of the church showed, the church's faith was correct wherever it maintained the chief article about Christ. In the pope's church they had not let Christ be the Savior, but had lapsed into works. Because the confession of Christ was continually being called into question, there could be no peace in the church, contrary to the opinion of some irenic people; rather, strife must occur. This was because of the conflict between the devilish "heel biter" and the divine "head crusher" (Gen. 3:15). Therefore, the earlier peace in the church was an empty one. There is no church without the cross and *Anfechtung*. The struggle about which side was in real continuity with the church thus entered a new stage.

At the end of January 1538 they learned in Wittenberg that the pope had again postponed the council for half a year, at the same time moving it to Vicenza. Both the elector and Luther indicated that they were no longer particularly interested in it. From the start the evangelicals had not expected any substantial concessions from a council.[9] A little later, Luther obtained a memorandum on reform of the church, which had been prepared by a papal commission a year earlier. Although it was actually a noteworthy work by people genuinely interested in church reform, Luther had an entirely negative opinion of it, and he issued a German translation of it in his usual style. Even the idea for the woodcut on the title page came from him. It depicted three cardinals cleaning the church with soft foxtails, which were ill suited for this purpose, while the pope, flanked by two devils, sat enthroned upon an altar (Plate VIII).[10] He made fun of how the pope would not be able to get a council to meet and suggested, moreover, that no real reform had ever been intended. The infallible pope certainly could not admit an error. The Antichrist described by Daniel was essentially an autocrat who would surrender nothing. The reforms of the curia that were proposed in the memorandum were nothing but an attempt to prevent a council from taking action. This memorandum, which demanded the abolition of some abuses, could have been evaluated more positively. Luther, however, lacked all trust. At the same time he had a papal seal carved, one designed by him and consequently filled with symbols.[11] Judas and the pope are hanging on the broken papal keys. Instead of keys on its field, Judas's moneybag, filled with bishops' hats and all the things that the pope sold, was intended to portray the real nature of the papacy. Accompanying verses explained the woodcut. Luther said in his Table Talk that the picture was intended as revenge: The pope "banned me and burned me, and surrendered me to the devil; so I will hang him on his own keys." This was not the last time Luther used illustrations in his own polemic.

Another attack on papal supremacy in the church was the publication of a letter by the church father Jerome in which he spoke about the original equality of presbyters and bishops and denied Rome's preeminence.[12] For the same purpose, Luther also had the admission of ecclesiastical abuses presented by Hadrian VI in 1523 at the Diet of Nuremberg and the discussions about it reprinted in Latin and German.[13] He considered even such an impressive statement as this by a pope to be untruthful, for it was still within the offensive system. The further development had indeed shown what Rome's promises of reform amounted to. The imperial estates had done the right thing at that time in having nothing to do with the empty promises, and their example could only be commended to the present. One could forget the pope's tyranny no more than Israel could forget its bondage in Egypt.

On 25 April 1538 Pope Paul III postponed the council summoned to Vicenza, this time for an indefinite period. Luther took this as an occasion to publish the articles he had written for the assembly in Schmalkalden the previous year, which, contrary to his own assertion, had not been officially adopted there, only subscribed by most of the theologians.[14] In a few places he expanded the text. He demanded freedom to preach against the mass,

Lampoon of the papal seal
Woodcut according to Luther's directions by the monogramist BP, 1538

defended the article on purgatory against objections, and criticized the enthusiasts' false views about sin's continuing reality. Unlike them, he emphasized
the essential connection between the external Word and the spirit. Now that
the council had not occurred, the articles were even more to be seen as
Luther's last will and testament, which would make incorrect interpretations
impossible, both from without and from within. Luther wished for a council
for the sake of the desolate church that existed under the bishops at that time,
although the evangelical churches that had the pure Word, the proper use of
the sacraments, and a correct understanding of works had no need of one.
Moreover, a council might deal with urgent problems of morality, such as
usury, greed, cheating, extravagance, and disobedience. Only thereafter should
it consider secondary ceremonial questions. In his brief articles Luther himself

had deliberately concentrated on the main topic of justification. Because the pope did not want a council, Luther prayed to Christ: "Assemble a council of thine own, and by thy glorious advent deliver thy servants."

Cochlaeus, Witzel, and Johann Hoffmeister, an Augustinian Hermit from Colmar, wrote rebuttals of Luther's articles. They emphasized the demarcation just as much as did Luther, although Witzel did complain about abuses in the church. Informed by his table companions about them, Luther refused to read the bitter and slanderous works, for they had been written in opposition to the Word and conscience, and they were not edifying to the conscience.[15] Elector John Frederick had a new edition of Luther's Smalcald Articles published in 1543 before the Diet of Speyer. He appealed to them in the intra-evangelical doctrinal disputes after Luther's death and he recommended them, along with the Augsburg Confession, in his testament to his successors as a norm of doctrine. In this way the Smalcald Articles ultimately became one of the confessions of the Lutheran church.[16]

5. THE FINAL POSITION:
ON THE COUNCILS AND THE CHURCHES

As before, it was the same old song about the planned council: On 28 July 1538 it was postponed until Easter of the following year. In September Luther thought that there was no more hope, while at the same time the pope was heaping riches and titles upon his relatives. Rome was so rotten that it deserved not reform, but judgment. In December Luther therefore considered it just as senseless to strike against the pope's person as did Duke George; he had to be attacked on a fundamentally theological basis.[1]

In *The Private Mass and the Consecration of Priests*, his little book in 1533, Luther had already announced his intention to write a fundamental work about the church. Occasionally thereafter he mentioned the plan again. During his serious illness in 1537 it was his wish to be able to write one more attack against the pope, and the next summer people were already waiting for the book.[2] Apparently the project underwent considerable changes. After Luther became convinced at the end of 1538 that the pope would not permit a council to meet, he did not let the matter rest with his polemic publications of the past year and a half, but instead began writing the fundamental and exhaustive *On the Councils and the Churches*, a work that is significant in both form and content.[3] He meant "church" in the singular. The lengthy work was completed in mid-March 1539. How much Luther dealt with this topic is evident in the numerous statements in the Table Talk at that time.

He immediately named names.[4] With the council the pope was acting just like a man who holds out a morsel for his dog to eat, and then hits him in the snout when he snaps at it. There had never been serious thought about reform through a council. The emperor and princes ought to know whether they wanted their "muzzles trampled." The alleged heretics, however, could only feel that they were vindicated by this impenitence. The pope's church was letting Christendom go to ruin and persecuting the poor Christians. Real reform could be hoped for only from Christ. His opponents, however, the enemies of Christ, had excluded themselves from the church. Earlier the bishops had let themselves be killed for the church, but now the pope was killing the church for himself. Nevertheless, the church cannot perish; but the pope was showing himself to be its enemy in the perverse last days. This was the root of Luther's hatred of the pope.

Because the pope did not want a reform council and had excluded himself from the church, the question was what should happen next. Those among the old believers who were willing to reform wanted to orient themselves to the standards of the earlier councils, but those councils had been unaware of the horrendous abuses of the present, and the curia would not desist from them, especially because the pope had placed himself above the council. This meant that a change in the papal system was absolutely necessary. In that case the evangelicals would quickly take part in a reform: "We are not such accursed people (praise and thank God!) that we would let the church perish rather than yield even on major points, as long as they are not against God; on the contrary, if it depends on our knowledge and ability, we are prepared to perish . . . rather than to see the church suffer harm or loss." This was a serious offer to participate in a real reform of the church. But it was inappropriate for Rome to impose demands on the evangelicals that it did not keep for itself. Luther sarcastically and yet seriously described the evangelicals as "very poor, weak Christians," who had so much to do in their faith, "what with reading, thinking, writing, teaching, exhorting, and comforting," that they had no time left for detailed conciliar directives, e.g., about ceremonies. Busily working in the mud, they did not possess the splendor of vestments. Alongside the imperative attention to God's commandments, there was no time for other ecclesiastical regulations. The opposing side might be beyond such "civil works," but it should have mercy on the evangelicals until they, too, could be received into its blessedness. In plain words, new churchly regulations by a council were superfluous.

Luther's objections were of an even more fundamental sort: In his experience, councils and church fathers could not be a suitable norm for reforming the church. As was well known, they were not all unanimous, and, in fact, even contradicted one another. Even Augustine was aware that councils and church fathers were relative, and he therefore preferred the Bible as a norm. Luther demonstrated that it was impossible to orient one's self to the councils by using the example of the apostolic Council of Jerusalem (Acts 15:28), which, appealing to the Holy Spirit, had forbidden the eating of meat sacrificed to idols. This had long since not been observed by anyone. This proved that conciliar decisions could be changed. Even the famous Council of Nicaea (325) had issued decrees that lasted only for a while. For example, it had decreed that Christians who served as soldiers should be punished, which was incompatible with the situation of Luther's day. Moreover, this council knew nothing about any preeminence of Rome within the whole church. Finally, it had decreed the problematic celibacy of priests. The decisions of the councils and church fathers were shown to be human works that could also be fallible; therefore, they could not be equal to the Bible. The first section of Luther's discussion thus led to the conclusion that it was impossible to reform the church according to traditional criteria.[5]

Luther attempted on the basis of thorough, independent, and critical historical studies of the first four ecumenical councils to understand the real purpose of a council. In doing so, he used not only the histories of the ancient church, but also, along with modern presentations, the two-volume collection of conciliar sources by the Franciscan Peter Crabbe, which had just appeared in 1538, although he had reservations about it because it represented the papal view of councils.[6] The Council of Nicaea primarily defended the belief in the divinity of Christ against Arius. Luther denied that it was the business of a council to establish new articles concerning faith or works. It could issue regulations about ceremonies, of course, but these had to be left free, and, in any case, they were of secondary importance.[7] At the Council of Jerusalem the central article had been that the Gentiles were free from the Mosaic law and circumcision, not the ceremonial or moral regulations. The Council of Constantinople (381) dealt with the divinity of the Holy Spirit. The contemporary dispute about the rank of the patriarchs had unfortunate consequences, of course, but it was a subsidiary question. At the Council of Ephesus (431) the question was the relationship of the human and divine natures of Christ. Luther had understandable difficulties in determining the real point of the controversy, for views were attributed to the accused patriarch Nestorius that he hardly would have held. The problem in Ephesus appeared to be that Nestorius was a proud, unlearned man who would not draw the necessary consequences of his true convictions. In some ways he reminded Luther of the way Zwingli argued about Christology. Luther had a difficult time with the Council of Chalcedon (451) because he had available only presentations and publications from the papal side.

Not only did reading the history of the councils make Luther morose, but his increased knowledge about improper procedures and bishops' intrigue also magnified his skepticism about councils in general.[8] If councils could not decree any new articles of faith, but only confirm the Bible, and if their other definitions were conditioned by circumstances, the question Luther asked himself once again was the central one of his entire investigation: What was a council and what was it to do? Its task could only be a restrictive one, i.e., it had to protect against false new articles of faith, and, in addition, against works, ceremonies, and legal mandates insofar as Christians were oppressed by them. Only regulations that served the good order of the church could be allowed. That meant that a council was to do nothing other than what pastors and schoolmasters also did in faithfully teaching God's Word in their congregations. The essential work of the church took place on this basis. The council had the function of a supreme court in the church, but it was just as bound to the norm of God's Word as were the lower courts of pastors and schoolmasters. Unlike the constantly developing secular law, the norm of God's Word did not change. A council had to combat the gross excesses and abuses on a case by case basis, but the real planting, the instruction in God's Word, takes place in the parishes and schools. "They preserve the church," and, "small though they are, they are eternal and useful councils," and better than the great assemblies of the church.[9]

In that day the subject of a council had to be the abolition of the oppressive papal laws that were directed at destroying the article of justification. Against the arch-arsonist of the church and the slayer of Christians, Luther appealed to the council to make a clear, not an equivocal decision. As in the Smalcald Articles, the doctrine of justification with all its consequences for the church's practice should be emphasized. If necessary, the emperor should force the pope to attend such a council, as had been done before. Not all the prelates needed to be present, but competent scholars and interested laity had to be invited. Luther, of course, had long been convinced that such a council was unattainable. If necessary, they should be content with a provincial council in Germany. He did not fear the danger of a schism. A provincial council of this sort could also have an exemplary character. If holding a council proved to be impossible altogether, there were still always the small councils in the parishes and schools. Luther had sharply limited the role of the council by binding it to the norm of the Bible. On this basis he had also stated that the article of justification was the most important subject for the council that he desired. It became evident that the church was not ultimately dependent on a council. Luther's studies had thus led to a quite independent, realistic, and theologically clearly focused concept that challenged the earlier definition of councils.

In the second part of his book it was already apparent that for Luther the church was manifested primarily in the congregation and not in the hierarchical organization. In a concluding section he turned expressly to the topic of the church and picked up the project he had been planning for years.[10] He still continued to have reservations about the expression "church."[11] He called it a "meaningless word," because it could be misunderstood. He would prefer to speak about "God's people" or the "Christian people." According to the Apostle's Creed, Christendom is holy because the Holy Spirit within it works to fulfill the Ten Commandments. This holiness is different from the ceremonial one of the pope.

Luther then listed at length the marks by which a Christian, holy people could be recognized. Luther was concerned about a certain completeness in this, because he wanted to present his church as the true one. First of all, he named the proclamation of the Word of God, the means of salvation. Where it is preached it can never be without fruit, but it needs people who confess it. God's Word and God's people are thus inseparable. This Word works all miracles, puts things right, and preserves everything. It drives out all the papal devils and also new heretical devils. People such as Emser, Eck, and Cochlaeus, like mouthpieces of the devil, raise a hue and cry about this. Baptism and the sacrament of the altar are the next signs, and they do not depend on papal ceremonies. The people of God can also be identified by the use of the keys, through which, privately or publicly, sins are forgiven or retained. The keys do not belong to the pope; he has only the "two skeleton keys to the treasure chests and crowns of all kings." The church calls specific people into its ministry. More strongly than before, Luther excluded women and children from office, except in emergency situations. Here, too, the ministry is understood on the basis of its function of preaching and administering the sacraments. Celibacy, therefore, is not one of the prerequisites for the ministry. The Christian people are also known by prayer. The cross, *Anfechtung*, and persecution for following Christ are also their lot. These are the real relics, and one need not be concerned about any others. Alongside these seven real marks, he also mentioned obedience to God's commands, something that cannot be demonstrated unambiguously. Participants in a council should be selected from the people of God who demonstrate these marks.

Alongside this church the devil, as was his wont, had now built his chapel with all sorts of papal consecrations and rites. Somewhat later Luther criticized a poem that encouraged the use of holy water and an allegedly especially effective Agnus Dei by adding verses of his own.[12] The chapels and supporters of the devil were bigger than God's church and people. But God had bound himself to the external Word, the sacraments, and the ministry of the church; everything else was an invention of the devil. One had to hold fast to God's institution; all actions on one's own part lead only to disobedience to God. Aside from these, there are external ornaments in the church, such as altars, pulpits, baptismal fonts, candles, bells, and vestments, that pertain to good order, but they are really free. Canon law had far too many regulations. In conclusion, Luther did not miss the opportunity to mention once again the important connection between church and school.

Here the church appears, along with family and government, as one of the three hierarchies, or ways in which God governs; they are related to one another: From the family come people, government offers them external protection, and through the church they become children of God. In this order there was no room for a special government of the pope, and it could only be rejected. Here we see the real reason Luther's understanding of the church is based on the congregation. Thus in the final section of the book it was not by accident that the council scarcely played a role any more. A little later Luther considered a council convened by the pope meaningless.[13]

Although the argumentation of each of the book's three sections is impressive, Luther was not satisfied, "because it is too weak and verbose." It was not that he was unable to state the "unique truth," and that he could not elaborate on it and document it; rather, in the limited amount of time he had available, he thought he was no longer capable of the physical exertion needed to do so.[14] Nevertheless, he had at least presented a final statement about the council and a fundamental description of the church.

In 1533 a council seemed to the evangelicals to be a great, risky undertaking. Now, as a result of papal politics, they no longer believed that one would meet, although they had not absolutely rejected a free, Christian council. Luther was convinced that the subject of a council had to be the preservation of the doctrine of justification. Otherwise, the function of a council now seemed to him more limited than before. The people of God were not dependent on one. But if a council did occur, the crucial question would be how it would deal with the ecclesiastical division within the empire.

VIII

The Right of Resistance,
Attempts at Peace,
the Defection of the Landgrave,
and Religious Colloquies
(1538–41)

1. NEW DISCUSSIONS ON THE
RIGHT OF RESISTANCE

Occasional statements by Luther during the 1530s show that, as before, he was opposed to a war for the sake of the gospel or the faith. He thought that a politically based resistance was the only thing acceptable. Even the Smalcald League was acceptable only as a political alliance.[1] When the Wittenberg theologians had to take a stand about a possible defensive war in connection with the discussions about the forthcoming council in December 1536, a noteworthy change of opinion took place.[2] At that time the duty of Christian authorities to protect religion was affirmed. Philip of Hesse had previously appealed to this protective function, but the Wittenbergers had not at first followed him. In fact, such protection was being provided by the evangelical authorities at that time. In their reasoning the theologians now obviously drew closer to the princes' understanding of independence vis-à-vis the emperor and the beginning development of a system of territorial churches. If the emperor moved against the evangelicals before the council met, that would be an obvious breach of the Religious Peace of Nuremberg, and resistance would be permissible. Even a war by the emperor after the council made a decision against the evangelicals would be nothing but an unjust one, and defense would be justified.

When the council was postponed repeatedly, the evangelicals had to anticipate that the religious problem might be solved by force. In April 1538 Luther and Melanchthon were at the court in Torgau for consultations in connection with the Smalcald Assembly, which was then taking place in Brunswick. Not by chance did the conversation also deal with possible resistance to the emperor.[3] Interestingly, Luther would not regard such a conflict as a religious one, but a political one, for the emperor was interested in seizing church property, and the evangelical princes would not tolerate this. In this sort of legal situation the permissibility of resistance was not a problem. Luther himself would issue a call to defense. At that time he was not anticipating an actual religious war. King Ferdinand was occupied with the Turks, and the emperor was residing in Spain. Nevertheless, the fear did surface that this arming against the Turks might be directed against the Lutherans.[4] The Smalcald League had just decided to make its approval of aid in the struggle with the Turks contingent upon a stable religious peace. On the elector's inquiry, Luther said at the end of May that the Turks' attack was a punishment for blaspheming God in Germany, and for this reason King Ferdinand would have little success with his defense. Yet the elector should not refuse to provide assistance because of his feud with the tyrannical Ferdinand. Luther believed that the troops would not be used against the evangelicals after they defeated the Turks, for the soldiers would not act against them. He was convinced, however, for reasons of conscience, that in no case could aid be refused. The future had to be left to God. The present emergency situation took precedence over the previous agreements among the allies. Luther qualified his position by calling it strictly "theological opinions," which he had ventured in the dark while trusting in God, not as competent political advice. He was placing the common good of the empire above the political interests of the evangelicals. The elector, however, did not let this change his earlier stand.[5]

In sermons during the fall of 1538 Luther spoke earnestly about the twofold threat to Germany from the Turks and the pope.[6] In July the emperor and a number of Catholic estates had formed the Nuremberg League, a counteralliance against the Smalcald League. On 9 October the ban of the empire was imposed on the city of Minden, a member of the Smalcald League. An attack by the Catholic side against the Smalcald League in the following year seemed imminent. In mid-November the Wittenberg theologians, along with Bucer who was there at the time, had to make another statement about the question of resistance in this situation.[7] They reaffirmed the right of the government to defend itself even in matters of religion. This applied also in the case of the emperor, if he acted illegally, but now the question of whether a preemptive war was permissible also arose, which the Wittenbergers had previously decisively rejected. It seemed to the theologians that one might strike if the ban were imposed upon one or more of the allies. Yet one still had to consider whether such action was desirable or whether other possibilities existed. In any case, there should be an appeal for prayer and amendment of life. Elector John Frederick referred specifically to this opinion in the discussions with his allies. In January 1539 Luther was expecting military action by the emperor in Germany on behalf of the old believers. In fact, however, Charles V had no such plans at the time.[8]

Probably at the behest of Elector Joachim II of Brandenburg, Johann Ludicke, the preacher in Cottbus, requested an opinion from Luther about the legitimacy of resisting the emperor. Luther expressed himself guardedly, for the question had already been decided for the evangelical princes.[9] One can read between the lines of Luther's letter that he still did not agree completely with their view, yet he also did not want to take a position opposed to them. He concentrated on one of the important reasons that spoke in favor of resistance: In the religious conflict the emperor was not acting for his own cause, but as the pope's soldier and defender; he was thus not the sovereign at all. Resisting the emperor was something Luther had previously considered impermissible, but now he could approve it, because, following the Saxon jurists' theological argument that paralleled the argument from imperial law, in a religious war the emperor was no longer the emperor. The anti-Christian tyranny of the pope must not be accepted by Christians, as examples from the Bible showed. As his preliminary thoughts on this letter expressed in the Table Talk indicate, Luther had adopted an understanding of the empire's constitution that saw the empire as ruled collegially by the emperor and electors; therefore, an attack by the emperor on the electors was unconstitutional. As a comment made a few weeks later revealed, however, Luther himself, as before, was still not completely convinced by this legal argument: Christians were permitted to resist robbers, but resistance against imperial authority was forbidden: "There are great misgivings."[10]

In light of the threat of war from the Turks and papists, Luther published *Warning to All Pastors*, probably at the beginning of March 1539.[11] He left no doubt that in a religious war one could defend himself against "mad dogs." Such a war could certainly destroy Germany. Luther saw in it the threatening punishment of God for both sides, for he was not blind to the ingratitude, disdain for God's Word, and stinginess among evangelicals. Pastors should therefore encourage people to repent and pray in order to avert the punishment. As in the Peasants' War, he regarded a breakdown of political order as one of the worst evils imaginable. Only the widespread disinterest in a war had kept the papists from initiating one before this. Human actions could not prevent this doom, only God alone, and the evangelicals, unlike their opponents, were in a position to pray that he would. As before, Luther basically did not place his hope simply in resistance measures. On 16 March he exhorted the Wittenberg congregation to pray for peace.[12] To be sure, because of Christ, death was not to be feared, but there was a responsibility owed to the coming generation and the church of the future. The princes would do their duty, and the people would have to help them. Anyone who died in doing so died for a good cause. Along with this appeal for defense, however, they were admonished not to forget to love their enemies.

In April 1539 Luther also intended to address the difficult question of resistance in a circular disputation.[13] His theses placed the topic in a much larger context, however, which at first glance appears to be forced: Jesus' demand to sell and abandon everything (Matt. 19:21), which was usually used to support monasticism, presupposed, first of all, living in the world. Monasticism only appeared to comply with this demand, for the monks lived at the expense of others. Jesus' demand applied to everyone's relationship with God and to confessing one's faith, but not to normal relationships with one's fellow human beings. Helping the authorities resist injustice was an obligation of citizenship. If a ruler persecutes his subjects for the sake of Christ, they are to endure it in accordance with Christ's command and are not permitted to offer armed resistance. No other political authority exists than that of government. This seemed to reject any sort of right of resistance. Yet Luther did find a bridge to further consideration of the matter. To Luther the pope was neither an ecclesiastical, nor a political, nor an economic authority, because he condemned the gospel, overturned civil laws, and forbade priests to marry. This proved that the pope was a monster without parallel in human society, like a werewolf that destroys everything. All villages, cities, and men are summoned against him, for the political, economic, and ecclesiastical order of the world must be defended. The authority of a council is not necessary for this, only the existence of an emergency situation. One's conscience need not be troubled by this persecution, quite the contrary. Action against any defenders of this monster is also permissible. Thus if the pope starts a war he must be resisted, for he is not simply a heretical bishop or a tyrannical prince, but the beast of the Apocalypse. This applies also to princes, including the emperor, when they act as his agents, although they may claim to be defenders of the church. This resistance against the pope was an exception to the law, and Luther sharply distinguished it from obedience that was due even to an unjust government, which, as before, he affirmed. In this respect he had not abandoned his earlier political ethics. Against the pope, however, everyone had the obligation to resist, not merely certain estates.

After an extension of the religious peace had been obtained in April, the topic of this disputation was no longer timely. It was therefore postponed until 9 May and expanded with twenty-one additional theses. In them Luther challenged the pope's right to legislate for the church, because he did this only for his own benefit and did not follow biblical norms, which intended that there should be no new laws. His encroachments into the political sphere were sheer arrogance. Finally, the pope had also put the ordinance of marriage and the family into complete confusion. "In sum, there is no divine nor human order that this beast has not devastated."

During the disputation Luther several times emphasized anew that the conflict with the pope was of an exceptional sort and therefore required corresponding action: "Before I would let my soul be carried into hell, I would prefer to do what I could and cause a revolt. We alone as individuals are obligated to requite such blasphemy." The pope was regarded as a demon, a "mixed God" or devil, or possessed by the devil, as lawlessness personified. Here Luther's image of the pope seems to have lost its inner-worldly reality.

Nevertheless, it would be too easy to assume that he had constructed a straw man in order to justify the right of resistance, for his theory was not easy to put into practice politically. The insight that there was no place for including the pope in the order of the world and that he could therefore only be a great disturber of the peace had already been developed by Luther; it was now merely incorporated into his concept of resistance. The Christian right of resistance, as Luther now taught it, applied only in an extreme emergency in which salvation was at stake because of totalitarian claims. For him, at least, this was not a theologically abstract situation or one that was divorced from his world, as it might initially appear. He had not lost his sense of reality. Even on the day of the disputation he mentioned again in the Table Talk that the princes' right of resistance to the emperor was based on constitutional rela-tionships within the empire. Luther, however, was not thinking about resisting the emperor, whose injustices he would tolerate if necessary; instead, he was denying the power of the pope because the pope could not be an authority at all and certainly not a tyrant.[14] His explanation of the right of resistance owes its force to this more pointed argumentation, and in it Luther set aside his own constantly recurring reservations. At the same time, it magnified the contrast with the pope more than ever, and this had an effect upon Luther's later attitude.

2. THE PEACE NEGOTIATIONS IN FRANKFURT, 1539

As dangerous as the political tensions between the old believers and the mem-bers of the Smalcald League may have appeared at the beginning of 1539, the interests in a compromise proved to be stronger. Elector Joachim II of Brandenburg had been working to this end since 1538, King Ferdinand partici-pated not least because of his interest in obtaining help against the Turks from the evangelicals, and the emperor named Archbishop Johann von Weeze, who had been driven from Lund in Sweden, as his representative in this matter. The negotiations were to take place on 12 February 1539 during the assembly of the Smalcald League that was scheduled for Frankfurt am Main. Thus the search for a peaceful solution intersected strangely with the deliberations about the right of resistance.

Luther initially distrusted these efforts. On one side he considered them camouflage for an attack by the Catholics, and on the other he feared that Landgrave Philip would strike. In this situation Luther earnestly appealed for prayers for peace in the worship services.[1] At the beginning of March, Melanchthon could report from Frankfurt that the emperor had offered a genuine peace. Going beyond the Religious Peace of Nuremberg, the mem-bers of the Smalcald League had demanded that such a peace apply also to those evangelical estates that had not joined the alliance. In addition, they wanted the actions quashed that were pending against the evangelicals before the imperial supreme court. Although Luther rejoiced at the good news, he was still skeptical about whether their opponents would extend the peace to the new evangelical estates, which they had previously refused to do. In his opinion, developments were still leading toward a confrontation.[2] In fact, it soon appeared that another temporary peace, a so-called standstill, would be granted, during which discussions aimed at reaching an understanding about religion were to be held. Luther expected the Frankfurt negotiations to collapse. When an agreement with the opposing side appeared impossible, the only refuge in the face of the threatening war lay in prayer. But Luther also stated that he would understand if the landgrave attacked. Because of the continuing religious differences Luther—unlike before—considered a mere new "standstill" as no solution. If a war were to occur, the opposing side would be against God. As such the evangelicals could be confident of their cause, if there were not also so much ingratitude and wickedness among them.[3] At the beginning of April the members of the Smalcald League were offered a standstill for eighteen months, but during that period they would not be permitted to accept any new members and they could not defend any non-members. Luther concluded from this that there was no real hope for peace.[4]

Finally a general promise to keep the peace for fifteen months was achieved. The Religious Peace of Nuremberg was to apply to the current members of the Smalcald League until the next diet. On their part, the allies declared that they would keep the peace and stated that they were prepared to offer assistance against the Turks. Before the end of the summer theological conversations were to be begun in Nuremberg. Luther was thankful that the immediate danger of war had passed. God had thwarted the evil schemes of the papists. On the first Sundays in May he admonished the congregation to give thanks and repent.[5]

Luther did not want to participate in the discussions in Nuremberg. Impartial scholars were needed there. In mid-May Elector John Frederick asked him for advice concerning any possible concessions. As before, Luther would allow ordination by bishops, so long as they abjured the pope and were pious people who were devoted to the gospel. The examination of clergy should continue to be done by the university. In doctrine he would not deviate from the Augsburg Confession and the Smalcald Articles. He shared the rejection of priority for the papal side at a colloquy, on which the evangelicals had insisted in Frankfurt, but he would acquiesce to a provincial council in Germany convened by the emperor, although the evangelicals had no need of one for themselves.[6] Again in October the world situation seemed perilous. The evangelicals were being blamed for the defeat by the Turks in the Mediterranean. They would have to expect an attack. In Luther's opinion, the emperor's political failure was instead due to his having allied himself with the pope whom God hated. After a long pause for peace, the opposing side would deliberately start a war against the evangelicals that could lead to a bloodbath in Germany.[7]

Luther's statements about the course and the results of the Frankfurt negotiations show how he himself was being tossed to and fro between the desire for peace and the view that conflict with the pope and the emperor as his henchman was unavoidable.

3. THE CALAMITOUS BIGAMY
OF LANDGRAVE PHILIP

The situation of the evangelicals, which was already complicated, was additionally burdened in 1539 by an extraordinarily serious problem in their own ranks. During the Frankfurt negotiations Landgrave Philip fell ill with the aftereffects of syphilis and had to leave early to seek necessary treatment. The absence of the politically active landgrave weakened the evangelicals' position. A little later Luther even assumed that because of this a preemptive war would not occur.[1] At that time syphilis was widespread in higher circles of society. The marriage of Philip to Christina, the daughter of George of Saxony, which had taken place in 1523, was an unhappy one, although the couple had seven children. Philip was unfaithful to his wife, but this so troubled his conscience that for years he had communed only rarely. In the late summer of 1539 he met the seventeen-year-old Margaret von der Sale, a Saxon noblewoman. Her mother, Anna, was lady-in-waiting to Philip's sister Elizabeth, the duchess of Rochlitz, to whom John, the son of Duke George, was married. Anna von der Sale would consent to her daughter's relationship with Philip only if it were legitimated as a second marriage. Genuine second marriages were prohibited by church law, however, and the punishment prescribed for bigamy was death; so the landgrave was embarking on a perilous adventure.

The Confessional Advice

Philip initially sought to obtain the approval of Luther, Melanchthon, and the elector of Saxony for the planned second marriage. He got Bucer, who also had considerable reservations, to act as intermediary. The landgrave gave him extensive instructions.[2] In these he confessed his adulterous life that kept him from going to the Lord's Supper and made him anxious about his soul's salvation. He blamed his actions on his unhappy marriage. He mentioned that he could not punish those who indulged in vice when he himself did not live uprightly. The anxiety about the salvation of his soul also robbed him of courage to fight for the evangelical cause. He then sought to produce arguments in favor of a second marriage. It was permitted in the Old Testament, and in the New Testament it did not seem to be prohibited. He recalled that the Wittenbergers had advised against divorce for Henry VIII of England, but they had raised no significant objections to a royal concubine. Therefore, Luther and Melanchthon should publicly, if possible, or at least secretly, give their approval for the bigamy, although for various reasons Philip thought it would be difficult to keep such a liaison a secret. He promised that self-evidently the children from his first marriage would inherit the succession. He imagined that the Wittenbergers might state in their expected reply that the second marriage was an ethically indifferent matter. In his opinion, there needed to be no special concern for the world, the emperor, or the papists. The landgrave did not mind applying pressure to the Wittenbergers. If they did not approve, he would seek permission from the emperor, which perhaps might be contingent on receiving a dispensation from the pope. Of course, the emperor's approval would involve concessions regarding Philip's role in the evangelical alliance, although he protested that he did not want to defect from the gospel. The instructions' conclusion made it quite clear that in any case Philip was prepared to proceed with the second marriage. Under these circumstances, the Wittenbergers should have denied his request from the beginning.

On 9 and 10 December 1539 Bucer discussed the matter with Luther and Melanchthon in Wittenberg. The result was a common recommendation formulated by Melanchthon.[3] The theologians first congratulated the landgrave on his recovery. The embattled church needed pious rulers. They did not think it advisable to make a general rule about a second marriage. Thus they rejected the landgrave's request for an official and public statement. God originally intended monogamy, while polygamy was only a subsequent concession. If they were again to permit multiple marriages by law, it would have unforeseen consequences for the evangelicals and for Philip personally. The theologians showed an understanding for Philip's moral plight, but this did not prevent them from speaking frankly to his conscience. If the landgrave was unable to abandon his immoral life, the theologians were interested, for the sake of his salvation and of his land, in finding a solution with which Philip could in good conscience appear before God. The only possible solution was a secret marriage that would be known only to a very few under the seal of the confessional. The second wife should be kept like a concubine, the way other princes did. This solution was compatible with the gospel, which was concerned about salvation, obedience, and improving depraved nature. As a pious prince, the landgrave should not make the bigamy an object of political concern with the emperor, whose morality was without scruples.

The theologians thus clearly indicated that they could give Philip nothing but extraordinary, pastoral advice in his predicament of conscience, and in no way was it to be made public. This sort of pastoral counsel, which declared that action that deviated from the norm was conscientiously permissible, was not all that unusual. Luther, too, in his pastoral counseling had occasionally done the same, particularly when it involved complicated relationships between the sexes. He was acquainted with predicaments in which a pastor had to disregard the law without fundamentally calling a valid norm into question. Such action was neither immoral nor a matter of double standards, but it was rather exercising Christian freedom, which a pastoral counselor, unlike a judge, could do. In the case of the landgrave, of course, the circumstances were more complex than with a private citizen. First, the landgrave was a public personality. Second, it could be assumed that he would make public use of the secret advice given him. Thus there was a danger that the public would hold the theologians responsible along with him. Therefore this counsel was extremely risky and in all probability wrong from the very beginning. By accommodating Philip, Luther and Melanchthon, as the two most important evangelical theologians, caused themselves very serious difficulties. Elector John Frederick, whom Bucer visited in Weimar on the return trip, was insistent that the landgrave avoid any public offense; he should, however, comply with the confessional advice of the theologians.[4] But even the elector did not seem to have recognized fully the considerable implications of this case that might at least have been expected.

On 4 March 1540 the marriage of Philip and Margaret von der Sale took place in Rotenburg on the Fulda River. Witnesses to the wedding included Bucer and Melanchthon, who had been summoned there from the assembly in Schmalkalden without explanation; in this way Melanchthon became much more involved in the affair than Luther. Eberhard von der Thann, the commander of the Wartburg, took part as the representative of Elector John Frederick. At that time Melanchthon referred in several opinions to the exceptional character of the second marriage, which therefore was to be kept a secret. In no case could it be regarded as something ethically indifferent, as was already being claimed at that time by the Hessian theologians Johannes Lening and Dionysius Melander.[5] At the beginning of April the landgrave wrote Luther a letter thanking him for the advice of the theologians and informing him of the marriage. He emphasized how much freer his conscience felt, and this would also be to the advantage of the evangelical side. He would keep the new marriage as secret as possible; if this should prove impossible, he believed that he could justify it, and then he would seek advice from Luther, Melanchthon, and Bucer. This already indicated that the Wittenbergers would not be rid of this matter quickly or easily. The elector instructed Luther not to answer this letter until the Wittenberg theologians had returned from the assembly in Schmalkalden; in addition, he wished to be informed about the contents of the reply. Luther learned in this way that the landgrave himself was planning to make the second marriage public. Moreover, he also wanted to grant the children of this union the right of inheritance, which would bring them into conflict with the already existing rights of inheritance of the two Saxon princely houses. Luther was unable to give the landgrave's letter to the elector; for safety's sake he had burned it immediately, "for such a secret, God willing, will not be revealed by me." He also urgently asked the landgrave to keep it a secret, for otherwise "the crude peasants" would possibly appeal to his example.[6]

In May the landgrave sent Luther a cask of Rhine wine. It was immediately seen as thanks for approving the bigamy.[7] Rumors about it spread. At the beginning of June, Anthony Lauterbach in Pirna wanted to know from Luther whether there was any truth to it. Luther did not say that there was nothing to the rumor, but he did state that he had not seen any public evidence of a marriage. One should not say anything about princes and their affairs without being fully informed. Luther had not told his friend an untruth, but had kept the secrecy of the confessional inviolate. Somewhat later, however, he did confirm to Lauterbach that the evil rumors were persisting. In fact, they had already become a certainty.[8] At this time, Luther, too, made frank comments in the Table Talk. He feared that the landgrave would ultimately come to an understanding with the emperor to the detriment of the evangelicals, although until then he had remained true to their cause. In the long run he would be seen to be right. By this time Luther had also become aware of earlier high-handed political actions of the landgrave that had irritated his allies, for example, the conquest of Württemberg in 1534. He conceded that Philip had had success with his politics, but he lamented that once again a new offense had arisen in his own camp. Nevertheless, he anticipated that somehow the matter would fade.[9]

Because the bigamy had become known in Ducal Saxony through Philip's sister, the duchess of Rochlitz, and had stirred up considerable dust at the court in Dresden, the landgrave began to think about requesting Luther and Melanchthon to issue a clarification of their confessional advice for Duke Henry of Saxony, which would have involved the Wittenbergers even more deeply in the matter. He apparently changed his mind about this action.[10] Instead, Luther became aware that Duke Henry was asking the elector uncomfortable questions. Therefore he explained to John Frederick once more how he had arrived at his advice. Obviously, he had never thought of it as legal justification, but only as counsel in the confessional, which was not easy for theologians to give. "It was a heavy matter on our hearts, but since we were unable to prevent it, we sought to save his conscience the best we could." Luther now openly admitted that he had been faced with similar cases as a pastor in the confessional and that he had solved them not legalistically, but pastorally. In some respects, of course, he felt that he had been deceived by the landgrave. By this time he had learned that Philip had also had other affairs. His pangs of conscience could thus not have been as great as Bucer had presented them. If Luther had known this in advance, "not even an angel would have gotten me to give such advice." Moreover, there had never been any mention of a public marriage ceremony or of Margaret von der Sale's acting like a princess, something that certainly would have provoked the scandal. He freely dismissed the objection that in his earlier sermons on Genesis he had not forbidden bigamy (apparently out of reluctance to criticize the patriarchs): "If I now had to defend everything that I said or did years ago, especially at the beginning, I would have to worship the pope." Luther was not ashamed of his confessional advice, even after it became known, although he would have preferred that it remain a secret in light of the difficulties that might arise.[11] In spite of everything, Luther was imperturbable, or acted that way; there had been worse scandals before. The landgrave's lapse into sin, over which the opposing side was rejoicing, did not as such endanger the evangelical cause. There had always been failings among God's people, but those who belong to God are forgiven, while his opponents are condemned. Even if the landgrave fell, Christ was still beside them. Luther would not trouble himself about this to the delight of the devil; instead, he would leave the matter to God. He did lament about himself and Melanchthon: "All this mess falls on the two of us!"[12]

Melanchthon's Illness

Melanchthon, unlike Luther, was very disturbed by the scandal. He had serious reservations when he took leave of Luther to travel to the colloquy in Hagenau. There was fear that he would not return home. Luther had prayers said for him in the worship service. Already from Weimar, Melanchthon wrote Luther that he was sick because of the bad news about the landgrave's situation and that he doubted he could continue the trip.[13] At that time Luther was once again aware of the difference between Melanchthon and himself. Melanchthon was more sensitive than he and was more easily disturbed by the course of things. Despite his keen way of thinking, Melanchthon was more moderate in form, so that Luther appeared coarse. In no way was he blind to Melanchthon's failures—his need to compromise, for example—but he thought that his own directness also had its virtues.[14] At first he blamed himself for letting Melanchthon go to the difficult Hagenau negotiations, where he would not have an easy time because of his mild and nervous nature. There was no sense in letting the matter of the landgrave trouble him any more, now that it had happened. Christ, who had judged the devil, would take care of this, and in the future there would be new scandals. One of Melanchthon's concerns apparently was that the landgrave's bigamy might lead to a change in the laws about marriage, but the emperor could prevent this, and the Wittenbergers had never intended any change in imperial laws. They could not be accused of any crime except compassion and "very human thoughtlessness." In the meantime Luther had become aware of his own mistake, but things were hardly as confused as once they had been with David, and in David's case they finally came to a good end. Thus Melanchthon should not torment himself; he should not doubt Christ's victory. Katy also wanted Melanchthon to be fearless and rejoice. His friends would pray for him earnestly and effectively.[15]

Luther learned from Brück that Melanchthon had been greatly weakened by a tertian fever (a fever that persisted for three days). He correctly surmised that this was connected with Melanchthon's emotional state and therefore wished that he could be with him personally. In his class lecture Luther appealed for prayer on Melanchthon's behalf. On 16 June the elector asked

Luther to come to Weimar and bring with him Cruciger, who might possibly go to Hagenau in Melanchthon's place. Luther himself was to participate in Eisenach in the discussions about the Hagenau colloquy. The messenger also brought another letter, which the seriously ill Melanchthon had been able to write only with interruptions. It contained grave new fears about the matter of the landgrave.[16]

Luther arrived in Weimar on 23 June. He found Melanchthon deathly ill, changed almost beyond recognition, unable to hear or speak. According to the account of the physician Matthew Ratzeberger, Luther's first reaction was: "God forbid! How the devil has assaulted this man." He then turned to the window and assailed God in an impudent way that was extraordinary even for him: "Our Lord God had to bear the brunt of this, for I threw my sack before his doors, and wearied his ears with all his promises of hearing prayers that I knew from the Holy Scriptures, so that he had to hear me if I were to trust any of his other promises." After this, he took Melanchthon's hand and encouraged him: "You will not die." God did not desire the death of a sinner, and therefore he would not let Melanchthon perish in sin and melancholia. The patient should not succumb to the spirit of sorrow and in effect commit suicide. At first Melanchthon refused to come back to life and eat. Then Luther applied pressure: "You must eat, or I'll excommunicate you." Luther was firmly convinced that he had prayed Melanchthon back to life, just as he himself had experienced in Schmalkalden.[17] He joyfully informed Katy: "I eat like a Bohemian and drink like a German; thanks be to God for this. Amen. The reason for this is that Master Philip truly had been dead, and really, like Lazarus, has risen from death. God, the dear father, listens to our prayers. This we see and touch, yet we still do not believe it. No one should say Amen to such disgraceful unbelief of ours." On 10 July he could then report from Eisenach: "Master Philip is returning to life again from the grave; he still looks sick, yet he is in good spirits, jokes and laughs again with us, and eats and drinks with us as usual." They should also give thanks for this in Wittenberg.[18] Despite the difficulties Luther had had with Melanchthon during those years because of occasional theological differences of opinion, in the extreme situation in Weimar we see not only a Luther who prayed fervently but a Luther who also had an extraordinarily great affection for Melanchthon, who, as before, was his indispensable co-worker.

Successfully Preventing Publication of the Confessional Advice

The storm touched off by the bigamy was far from abating. After the matter, including the Wittenberg confessional advice, had become known, primarily through the efforts of the Dresden court, the landgrave wrote to Luther on 20 June. He did not ask Luther to sanction two marriages as a general rule, to be sure, but he did want him to confirm that this arrangement was permissible by way of exception. This would have made public the confessional advice that was intended to be purely personal. On the next day the landgrave sent another letter to Luther and Melanchthon. In it he protested that the bigamy had become known through his sister and that he himself was not to be blamed for it. He asked whether he should now make a public statement about how the second marriage had come about, or whether it would be better to wait until he was attacked openly. It was also possible that some representatives of the nobles and the cities knew about it. The Wittenbergers should bear part of the responsibility, regardless. If they tried to evade it, the landgrave would publish their confessional advice. To the Saxon elector he appealed not only to every possible example in the Bible and to the confessional advice, but also to Luther's earlier statements. Moreover, he also mentioned possibly withdrawing from the Smalcald League if the theologians would not protect him fraternally. In this same vein, Feige, the chancellor of Hesse, and some Hessian theologians also contacted Luther and Melanchthon.[19]

Luther asked Eberhard von der Thann to deliver his reply to the landgrave.[20] In case the emperor called Philip to account, he should admit that he had taken a concubine, i.e., not a second wife, and say that he would put her away if other princes set him a good example. This would put an end to the rumors about a second marriage. In no case should Philip explain in writing how the second marriage had occurred. This meant that he should not mention his request for confessional advice that Bucer had brought to Luther. Luther would assume the responsibility for this concession that had meanwhile become known, along with all the considerable consequences for himself resulting from this mistake, without explaining the details, because revealing the landgrave's scruples of conscience and breaking the seal of the confessional would be a greater wrong. Whether the bigamy could be claimed as concubinage was questionable. That Luther, as Philip's pastoral counselor, was willing to accept the responsibility for his questionable advice bears witness to his selflessness and autonomy. In July he again explained, probably to one of the Saxon counselors, his position on publishing the confessional advice.[21] It was essentially a private, secret accommodation that was irrelevant to public life, and no one should try to establish or base public policy on it. Law could not be made on the basis of an emergency decision; emergencies transcended legality. The landgrave, too, had to maintain publicly that bigamy was forbidden. This did not mean that he would have to put away Margaret von der Sale. His confessors could soothe his conscience about his secret relationship, but he himself would have to bear the public responsibility for a bigamous marriage. This presented the conditions in which the confessional advice had been given in precise terms.

Luther continued to maintain this position during the heated discussions with the Hessian counselors and theologians during the Eisenach assembly in mid-July.[22] This was no longer only a private scandal; the bigamy affected land

and people, body and livelihood. Therefore the landgrave had to "tell a good, strong lie" and deny the second marriage; otherwise, Luther foresaw grave consequences for him and the church, and in this he was to be proved correct. Repeatedly, even to the present, Luther has been portrayed as unscrupulous because he advocated lying in this case. In fact, however, it was in no way an opportunistic morality that motivated him. As a confessor, he could do his client no better service than to protect his confidence under all circumstances. To this extent his position was consistent and ultimately also convincing. Meanwhile, the Hessian side thought it unacceptable to call the relationship concubinage; the matter could also no longer be denied. They challenged the secret character of the confessional advice; it had always been intended for public use as well. The second marriage should be recognized as a possible extraordinary arrangement. The landgrave himself, who was not present in Eisenach, wrote Luther at length on 18 July in response to his statements.[23] He charged him not to go back on his confessional advice, and once more listed all the arguments in favor of a possible second marriage. He refused to deny it or claim that it was concubinage. He recognized, of course, that what the Wittenbergers had given him had been advice for his conscience, but he demanded that, if necessary, Luther should stand in Christian solidarity with him, by which he meant that Luther should defend him publicly.

As is evident in the subsequent discussions with the Electoral Saxon counselors, Luther was not impressed by the landgrave's letter and insisted on his own position. In the highly charged atmosphere, in which the Hessian side especially did not hesitate to issue threats and offensive suggestions, Luther once more calmly and thoughtfully explained his position to the landgrave himself.[24] He was seriously trying to help Philip, not cause him difficulties. He would not try to evade his own responsibility, but this could not take place by publishing the confessional advice, for this would only exacerbate the problem. No public recognition of the second marriage could be achieved in this way, because there was no bridge leading from the forum of pastoral care to the forum of law. According to law Margaret von der Sale could be only a concubine. If the landgrave did not accept the confessional counsel as such, it would be of no use at all. Philip should also listen to the counsel of those upon whom he had placed this unusually burdensome shared responsibility. The landgrave's action was credible only if it remained within the sphere of a moral dilemma and confessional advice. This meant that, as before, the bigamy should resolutely be denied in public. The letter did not fail to make an impression on the landgrave. He recognized Luther's good intentions and assured him of his high regard: "I consider you, without flattery, the most distinguished theologian. . . ." Nevertheless, he believed it impossible to deny the second marriage, particularly because the marriage certificate had been made public. He would keep the confessional advice as secret as possible, but a situation might arise in which that would be no longer possible.[25]

In the following period the landgrave hewed to the line Luther recommended. Representatives of Duke Henry of Saxony and Elector Joachim of
Brandenburg disputed Philip's claim to the estate of the deceased Duke
George, his father-in-law through his first wife, by referring to the second
marriage. He abruptly dismissed any doubt that something was wrong with
his marriage. His conscience and his relationship to his wife were clear, and his
confessor did not consider him "a non-Christian." He informed Luther and
Melanchthon that this was the stand he had taken on the matter, about which
Elector Joachim had likewise asked them, but he received no specific advice
from them. This reply was completely acceptable to Luther. The landgrave
should not admit the second marriage, so that no one could put pressure upon
him because of it. Luther stated that he was generally in agreement with a
book that Justus Menius, superintendent in Eisenach, had written against
polygamy after the Hessian pastor Johannes Lening had called it something
morally indifferent. He did not think it advisable to publish it, however,
because it would provide additional fuel for the rumors that were circulating.[26]

Contrary to Luther's expectations, the talk about the bigamy did not die
down. Duke Henry of Brunswick, the landgrave's bitterest enemy, saw to this
with his pamphlets. In defense of Philip, Johannes Lening, under the pseudonym of Hulderichus Neobolus, wrote his *Dialogus . . . on Whether It Is in
Accord or Contrary to Divine, Natural, Imperial, and Spiritual Law to Have
More Than One Wife at the Same Time: And Whether Anyone at This Time
Who Does Should Be Condemned As a Non-Christian or Not* in March 1541. In
the late summer this *Dialogus* was printed with the landgrave's approval.
Luther had repeatedly spoken against Lening's view of the acceptability of
polygamy. At the end of the year he was considering whether he should attack
the "insane and frivolous" *Dialogus* with a work of his own.[27] A little later,
although reluctantly, he had begun writing. He now knew that Lening was the
author of the *Dialogus* and that Bucer had helped in publishing it, which gave
new nourishment for Luther's old reservations about him. He could not have
known that Bucer had originally spoken against its publication. In the meantime Menius had written a book against Lening and sent it to Wittenberg to be
printed, but it was not to appear until after Luther's.[28] Melanchthon was
opposed to initiating the discussion about the bigamy once again from Wittenberg. When the elector learned of Luther's intention, he had his chamberlain
Hans von Ponickau forbid him, and then also personally wrote him about it on
31 January 1542. He did not want to place any constraints upon Luther in
publishing what he considered necessary for the praise of God and the edifica-
tion of Christian people, but such a book would offend the landgrave. Unless
Luther insisted for spiritual reasons on continuing, the sovereign ordered him
to surrender what had already been printed and discontinue the printing for
the time being. This was, in fact, prohibiting him from publishing for political
reasons.[29]

The fragment of Luther's unpublished *Reply to the Dialogus of Hulderichus Neobolus* has been preserved.[30] Luther several times rendered the first name of the alleged author as "Tulrich," deriving it from *toll* (crazy), and this gives an indication of what he thought of the concoction. He was only writing against it because many people had asked him to do so. Its author was obviously afraid of the light or he would not have hidden behind a pseudonym. Luther still remained firm: Secrets from the confessional, marriage intimacies, and secret advice do not belong to the public. The appeal of the *Dialogus* to polygamy in the Old Testament did not apply to Christians. Because its author perverted passages of the Scriptures in any way he wished, he belonged in the same category as those who were opposed to the sacrament. The real offense for Luther, this time also, was that Lening had stated that polygamy was ethically neutral. He declared tersely: "Anyone who follows this fellow and his book and takes more than one wife, and thinks that this is right, the devil will prepare for him a bath in the depths of hell. Amen." Polygamy could not be made into a legal principle. Luther sought to show that even in the Old Testament it was only an emergency solution for a social problem and not a license for carnal pleasure. As much as can be seen in this fragment, Luther continued to maintain his previous position that secrets of the confessional are to be kept inviolate and that a second marriage can be permitted only as confessional advice.

In April the landgrave inquired of Melanchthon whether Luther would write against the *Dialogus*. Melanchthon could report to him that the printing had been stopped and that he and Bugenhagen, the censors, had refused to permit the printing of other writings, undoubtedly including the one by Menius. At Melanchthon's suggestion the landgrave then also approached Luther himself. Somewhat brashly he assumed that no critical statement at all against the second marriage was to be expected from Luther. Luther assured him that he would naturally protect the landgrave, but Lening's pernicious book had almost provoked him. On 5 May the landgrave visited in Wittenberg and had a discussion with Luther about the *Dialogus*. On the basis of Luther's criticism, Philip had the book withdrawn from sale.[31] In fact, the elector's intervention in Luther's relationship with the landgrave prevented a new crisis. Rumors in the spring of 1543 that Luther was still planning to write a book against the *Dialogus* were based on old information and could easily be quelled.[32]

As had become apparent and as Luther recognized, giving confessional advice for Philip of Hesse was one of the worst mistakes Luther made, and, next to the landgrave himself, who was directly responsible for it, history chiefly holds Luther accountable. Let it be noted that in this case Luther did not evade his duty as a pastoral counselor; the broad-mindedness of his decision is truly impressive. Nevertheless, this was not something he did simply to please a prince. In other situations Luther also gave unconventional advice to troubled consciences. Theologically, too, he had nothing for which to apologize. The mistake was in misjudging the circumstances and his client. Luther at once admitted his error and thereby became free to deal with the problems that arose from it. He was willing to accept his part of the responsibility. He stubbornly and convincingly resisted the demand—which appeared opportune in the short term but would have been perilous for conventional morality—to make a general principle out of counsel given to an individual in the confessional. He helped decisively in limiting the ethical damage that came from the landgrave's mistaken action and his own error, but not even he could stop the fatal political consequences that resulted from the bigamy.

4. THE RELIGIOUS COLLOQUIES AND THEIR EXPECTED FAILURE

The Futile Meeting in Hagenau

Charles V had canceled the colloquy in Nuremberg that had been planned for August 1539 by the Frankfurt Standstill. In December, however, Johann von Weeze, after returning from a visit to the imperial court in Spain, informed the elector of Saxony that religious negotiations would be held the following year. They were to be a subject of discussion at the assembly of the Smalcald League in Schmalkalden in March. For this purpose it was again necessary for the evangelical theologians to state their position—thinking of the Augsburg Confession and the Apology—as well as to indicate any possible room for negotiations. Elector John Frederick asked the Wittenberg theologians to take the lead in doing this. If it appeared necessary, the evangelical theologians would also be invited to the assembly. If Luther's health permitted, he should go at least as far as Eisenach in order to be available for consultation.[1] Luther had little use for discussions with the stubborn papists and maintained the theologically based negative attitude that he had assumed before the Frankfurt discussions. He also thought a new meeting of the theologians was superfluous; their opinions could be obtained in writing. Nevertheless, he stated his willingness to make himself available in Eisenach. The opinion of the Wittenberg theologians was drafted by Melanchthon. It recommended that they consistently hold to the Augsburg Confession and the Apology. On the basis of long experience, it stated the points where the opposing side would probably raise objections. In general, the tenor of the opinion was uncompromising. Any supremacy of the pope was rejected. It made scarcely any significant concessions. Ordination by bishops, with reservations, seemed conceivable only if they would accept the evangelical teaching.[2] This determination corresponded with the elector's plans. Because the elector feared that in Nuremberg the theologians would be more willing to make concessions, he asked the Wittenbergers to convince the Nuremberg theologians to agree with their position. In line with their opinion, the Wittenberg theologians then warned against compromises in a lengthy work, once again written by Melanchthon.

215

Clear positions were better than a false unity. The Electoral Saxon theologians promised at that time that they would not compromise for the sake of peace. The Nuremberg theologians agreed with this view.[3]

With the elector's permission, Luther then did stay at home, and he probably did not miss much. He learned from Schmalkalden that the emperor was expected to take unfriendly measures against the evangelicals. This could not help but confirm Luther's opinion that Charles V was the pope's tool. Luther was sure that God would hear the prayers of the evangelicals and help them escape these threats, and he hoped that peace would come instead of the anticipated war. He was surprised to hear from Melanchthon at the beginning of April that the emperor was proposing a religious colloquy, and he interpreted this as a sign of insecurity. It seemed a miracle to him that God had previously prevented Charles V from attacking the evangelicals. This proved that the salutary course of events was being guided by prayer, and the condemned and lost papists had nothing with which they could counter prayer. The evangelicals were also sinners, of course, but they had no blood on their hands.[4]

Like his sovereign, Luther also did not expect much from the religious colloquy that was to begin in Hagenau in June. Charles V was undertaking many things, but he was not in a position to complete them successfully. His brother Ferdinand was firmly in the hand of his confessors. Luther again favored the same action as at the Diet of Augsburg. The Augsburg Confession should be presented anew. Contrary to all expectations, there was nothing in it to discuss and certainly nothing that could be compromised. This was what the previous Smalcald Assembly had decided, and Luther urged Elector John Frederick to hold to that decision. For much too long the papists had not been willing to talk about it, and God would bring his cause to completion. Melanchthon shared this opinion completely. Thus Luther did not regret it when it appeared that Melanchthon might not go to Hagenau, for there he would encounter sharp animosity if he did not display the expected willingness to make concessions. At the beginning of July Luther appears to have been thinking about defending his viewpoint in Hagenau in person, but Elector John Frederick understandably did not allow this because of the risks involved.[5]

The discussions in Hagenau showed that they could not agree on a starting point. The evangelicals insisted on the Augsburg Confession, while the Catholics wanted to begin with the committee discussions at Augsburg. The evangelicals ultimately prevailed, but the next discussions did not take place until the subsequent colloquy in Worms at the end of October. The first dispute concerned the norm on which the theologians participating should base their discussions. The Catholic side proposed that the norm be the "Holy Scriptures according to the true and pure understanding of the whole apostolic and Christian church." Luther and the Saxon theologians who were present in Eisenach for the Hagenau discussions had reservations about this formula, which might in itself have been possible, except that it would permit an appeal to the tradition of the church. Any return of church property, which had likewise been demanded in Hagenau, was rejected, as was also the proposal that their decisions be confirmed by the pope. At the end of July Luther expressed his personal opinion to Katy: "Nothing was accomplished at the diet at Hagenau; effort and labor are lost, and expenses have been incurred for nothing."[6]

Worms—A Deceptive Hope

Luther thought the colloquy in Worms was at best a waste of time. What the opposite side really had in mind was revealed by the numerous cases of arson at that time in evangelical cities of central Germany, for which Duke Henry of Brunswick was rightly believed responsible. Melanchthon, who was to go to Worms with Cruciger and Menius as theological representatives of Electoral Saxony, anticipated that a confrontation would soon occur because Eck, Cochlaeus, and Friedrich Nausea, the coadjutor bishop of Vienna, were the spokesmen for the other side.[7] None of these were compromise-minded theologians. As usual, the opening of the discussions was delayed for almost a month because important participants had not yet arrived, but the situation already appeared gloomy to the evangelical theologians: Albrecht of Mainz had taken three of the twelve votes in the negotiating commission for himself. Meanwhile, the evangelical city of Goslar had been placed under the imperial ban. Bishop Tommaso Campeggio, the brother of the legate at the Diet of Augsburg, was to come as the pope's nuncio. The evangelicals had to protest the participation of a representative of the pope. In addition, they were not at all sure about the unanimity of the evangelical representatives.[8]

Luther was at first impressed by the large number of participants. From this assembly might come the imperial provincial council that the evangelicals had demanded. This meant, however, according to the agreements already made, that the pope's representative could not be allowed to preside. In the interest of obtaining mutual concessions, the evangelicals could offer everything in their power for the sake of peace, but nothing that God had reserved for himself. On the other hand, the opposing side could not offer as concessions anything that the Word of God had already granted. In order to avoid quibbling about words, which was to be expected from people like Eck, it would be better to negotiate in writing and not orally. As at the Diet of Augsburg, it was important to confess the cause of the church.[9]

Except for the fact that a theological understanding appeared hopeless, the first reports from Worms sounded somewhat more positive. Granvella, the imperial chancellor, was reportedly interested in preserving the peace even if an agreement could not be achieved. The preliminary discussions of the evangelical theologians proved unanimous. Nevertheless, Luther expected nothing good from the politics of the emperor and his brother, and certainly no lasting peace. If need be, the prayers of the church could hinder or moderate their aggressive plans.[10] Even before the negotiations, it was noted that there were some among the Catholic theologians, such as Johann Gropper from Cologne, who were working for an agreement. Granvella's opening speech was an appeal for unity. In contrast, however, an imperial edict from Brussels that was sharply opposed to the Reformation had just become known. Furthermore, Luther was convinced that nothing would be accomplished in Worms, and he wished that Melanchthon and Cruciger would soon return.[11]

The actual discussions also did not begin in December, because the Catholic side was no longer united. The Palatinate, Electoral Brandenburg, and Jülich were showing clearly evangelical tendencies at that time. Thus there was a danger that the Catholics would be outvoted. They therefore demanded that the vote be taken according to confessional groups, which led to a protracted discussion about rules of procedure. In order to avoid these difficulties, Granvella proposed that a small committee should handle them, which the evangelicals initially would not accept. For Luther, this was a dubious procedure that indicated they were afraid of the truth.[12] Between 14 and 18 January 1541, however, a genuine religious colloquy on the basis of the Augsburg Confession did take place between Melanchthon and Eck. All they could accomplish, however, after difficult discussions, was to come to an agreement about the second article, which dealt with original sin. On 18 January Granvella adjourned the colloquy until the coming Diet of Regensburg. He believed that a basis for further agreement had been established. This had been developed since mid-December in secret discussions conducted by Gropper and the imperial counselor Gerhard Veltwyk with Bucer and Capito, primarily on original sin and the doctrine of justification. Some things were very conservative, e.g., retaining the seven sacraments, and a few questions were still left open. They sought to achieve a common basis in the spirit of Erasmus. Landgrave Philip and the *Stättmeister* of Strasbourg, Jacob Sturm, both of them, like the imperial side, now interested in an agreement, supported these negotiations, while the Wittenberg theologians did not participate in this important episode of the meeting in Worms.[13]

These articles, the first draft of the so-called Regensburg Book, were sent by Bucer through the landgrave to Elector Joachim II so that he could give them to Luther for his opinion. This procedure, which avoided a direct and open contact, was surprising at the least. Presumably this route through Joachim II was chosen because the evangelicals were agreed upon the Augsburg Confession as the basis for discussion, but the elector of Brandenburg, who was just now drawing closer to the Reformation camp, was not bound to it. Joachim adopted Bucer's arguments in favor of an agreement, but he did not fail to mention that some proposals needed to be improved and others went too far, because for the time being they were concerned about the old believers. He also reassured Luther about the Brussels edict, for which the

218

emperor himself was not responsible and which was also not being strictly enforced.[14] Luther recognized the good intentions of the authors, who were unknown to him, but he thought the proposals were unrealizable. The Catholic hierarchy would not allow itself to be subjected to a strict church discipline in the sense of the ancient church, as the authors, who were influenced by pious humanism, hoped. Some proposals were also unacceptable to the evangelicals. Luther referred again to his earlier reformatory work. One first had to be clear about where God's Word was. Only after one had made it one's own could there be discussions about reform measures. Melanchthon's terse comment on the articles was: "A Platonic republic," a utopia. To Joachim II's disappointment, Luther did not deal at all with the doctrinal articles on original sin and justification, where a real rapprochement had been achieved.[15] An agreement on the religious question was hardly to be expected from Wittenberg.

Against Hanswurst

Before the discussions about an agreement could be continued at the Diet of Regensburg, which opened in April 1541, Luther, provoked by other circumstances, issued a statement on this problem. Since 1538 the conflict had grown increasingly intense between Duke Henry of Brunswick, who meanwhile had become one of the most important supporters of the emperor in northern Germany, and the Smalcald League concerning, among other places, the evangelical cities of Goslar and Brunswick. In addition to the general mutual animosity, this battle was also waged with lengthy pamphlets full of the harshest accusations. In addition to the political and personal attacks, e.g., about the bigamy of the landgrave, the question of religion played a role. In the summer of 1540 Elector John Frederick had denied Duke Henry's accusation that he was disobedient to the church and was pursuing political measures that were directed against the emperor. Henry responded with a long-winded *Duplik* (rejoinder) full of the most vehement insults against the elector of Saxony. The *Duplik* not only accused the elector of turning against the church and becoming a heretic, but also labeled him the "drunkard of Saxony." In one point it made a quite incidental reference to John Frederick as the one "whom Martin Luther has called his dear and revered Hanswurst."[16] Although Luther had previously only taken passing note of the controversy with Duke Henry, he could hardly remain silent in the face of a charge that he had made a public statement insulting his sovereign. Luther first intended to write the official Saxon response, but this was published separately so that Luther had a free hand. His "brief and mild booklet about our cause" appeared in February 1541. In fact, it was very lengthy and in no way mild, but, rather, even in comparison with Luther's other polemic writings, a work of caustic vehemence and crudeness, as shown in the title itself, *Against Hanswurst*, which Luther applied to Henry.[17]

219

Duke Henry's polemic obviously gave Luther a certain pleasure, yet it was also a thoroughly spiritual one: "It makes me tingle with pleasure from head to toe when I see that through me, poor wretched man that I am, God the Lord maddens and exasperates both the hellish and worldly princes, so that in their spite they would burst and tear themselves to pieces—while I sit under the shade of faith and the Lord's Prayer, laughing at the devils and their crew as they blubber and struggle in their great fury." Henry's claims could be easily turned away with: "Devil, you lie." From here onward, the duke was systematically identified as a devil, and this gave the book its particular polemic vehemence. Luther had occasionally used the common expression *Hanswurst* in general, but he had never meant a specific person and certainly not the elector. Also groundless were Henry's characterizations of the elector as a heretic and a rebel, charges which had also been applied to Luther. Evil slanders are part of a Christian's lot. As such Luther himself knew the opposing side better. Persecution was a mark of the true church. Here Luther already touched on the real theme of his book. The accusation that John Frederick was a drunkard did have at least some measure of truth, but Henry, with his well-known questionable life style, had no cause to exaggerate the weaknesses of other men in such a devilish way.[18]

Soon after the publication of his *On the Councils and the Churches,* Luther took Henry's accusation of heresy as an occasion to address the topic of the church once again.[19] Here, too, he used Augustine's distinction between Cain's false church and Abel's true church. The criteria are once again the marks of the church: Baptism, the Lord's Supper, the office of the keys, the ministry, confession of the faith, acknowledgement of government and marriage, persecution, and peaceableness. This listing was intended to prove that the evangelicals were the true church. Its hungering pastors truly fast. In contrast, the papists do not fulfill the criteria. With them, works of satisfaction, indulgences, pilgrimages, and brotherhoods compete with baptism. The Lord's Supper and the office of the keys are perverted. The teachings of men are added to the Word of God. With the pope the church receives a worldly head. Worship of saints and celibacy has been introduced. The church exercises temporal sovereignty. Thus the papists were the apostates and innovators. It made sense that one could see popes, bishops, priests, emperors, and princes in medieval depictions of the horrors of hell.

Luther did not dispute at all that the true marks of the church were also to be found among the Catholics and that the evangelicals had received them from the Catholics, but he accused the papists of having apostatized. The bride of Christ, like the old Israel, had become a whore. Nevertheless, God had preserved a remnant as his people. The leadership of the church had turned into the Antichrist that presumed to set up new regulations. The evangelicals knew that they were bound to the Word of God and thus they could make no concessions, for the true church is constant and exclusive. It could not permit any false teaching alongside the truth. Naturally Luther was aware that the church is not sinless, but it must be pure in regard to doctrine. The norm had to stand firm. Here the identity of the church was objectified in its doctrine. If the papists did not meet these criteria, they should not have the church property. The conflict between the true and false church could not be solved on earth, for both sides were partisan. Therefore the two would have to exist side by side. In no way did this mean that Luther thought the truth could not be ascertained. Even the opposing side had acknowledged the abuses time and time again, not least with the call for a council. The evangelicals were demanding a council not in order to reform their church, but so that the truth might come to light. "You bats, moles, horned owls, night ravens, and screech owls who cannot bear the light do all in your guile and power to prevent, by all means, the truth from being heard and discussed in the light." Thus it was clear which side had the truth and to whom the church property belonged.

Luther next discussed Henry's specific accusations.[20] His charge that Elector John Frederick was rebellious was untrue. He had always been obedient to the emperor, as far as the Word of God permitted. "God cannot be a vassal of the emperor." The church's bridegroom is Christ alone. Luther had already conceded that the reality of the Christian life frequently left much to be desired: "The peasant is wild, the burgher covetous, the nobleman acquisitive." Luther denied the claim that the Reformation originated in a dynastic controversy between Frederick the Wise and Albrecht of Mainz. He took this as an occasion to report his view of how the "Lutheran rumpus" had begun with the dispute about indulgences, for which Albrecht of Mainz was responsible. The pope had then initiated heresy proceedings against Luther, and out of this came the great conflict in the church. It revealed indulgences as a deception and a scheme for making money.

Luther returned to the designation of John Frederick as a drunkard. He made no excuses for the fact that "my gracious lord sometimes takes a glass too many at the table, especially with guests. We do not like to see that either, though he can hold his liquor better than others." This did not make the elector a drunkard who was no longer able to govern his land, however. Nothing but good could otherwise be said about his life: "We have here (God be praised) one whose way and manner of life is modest and honorable, whose tongue is truthful, and whose hand is gentle in helping churches, schools, and the poor; one whose heart is earnest, constant, and true to honor God's Word; one who punishes the wicked, protects the pious, and maintains peace and good government. And his marriage is so pure and praiseworthy that it is a fine example to all princes, lords, and indeed everyone." Here Luther balanced this delicate criticism, which did not overlook the German vice of drinking, with his genuine high regard for his temporal sovereign. This could easily be contrasted with Henry's questionable morality, his murder and arson, and his theft of church property. Luther regarded the bigamy of the landgrave, which Henry had enjoyed criticizing in his pamphlet, as unsubstantiated, but he did not deny that princes set bad examples, and that applied to Henry as well. Luther said this about the "evil, slanderous, and deceitful books" of "Harry the devil": "He knows that throughout the world he has a most infamous name and that he stinks like devilish filth flung into Germany." For this reason he was quarrelsome and cowardly, and stabbed others in the back. His appeal to the papal condemnation and the emperor's edicts did not make his accusations any more justified, for those high officials also were unable to annul God's manifest law. The emperor was responsible only for how people lived together in this world, not for their relationship to God. Henry himself had already been exposed as an arsonist and therefore unqualified to make accusations. No Christian should listen to this damned man; pastors and preachers had to rise up publicly against him and make God's verdict about him known. This justified Luther's aggressive polemic. The princes attacked by Henry should have patience. God's judgment had already begun for him and for the papists.

At the conclusion Luther appended an exposition of Psalm 64, a lament against one's foes, which applied very well to Henry's crimes. He wrote a parody of the late medieval song, "O, You Poor Judas, What Did You Do?" applying it to the damned duke and the papists.[21]

Against Hanswurst caused a stir at the Diet of Regensburg. The Augsburg representatives thought the work detracted from Luther's reputation, for in their opinion the controversy with Duke Henry had nothing to do with the question of religion.[22] Luther, of course, like his sovereign, had a different opinion. He had used Henry's literary attack as an occasion to present anew his understanding of the true church as the Regensburg discussions approached. This was the theological significance of this polemic work. The direct argument with Henry, who after the death of George of Saxony was exposed as the most dangerous of the imperial Catholic princes after Albrecht of Mainz and a tool of the devil, also was part of the controversy. In *Against Hanswurst*, however, Luther appears to have laid down no prerequisites for a theological or a political agreement. Contrary to today's impression, he considered the book moderate and blamed his poor health for not having written more vehemently. Nevertheless, he hoped that with it he had helped the church a little.[23]

Regensburg—Chance or Patchwork?

It is scarcely surprising that Luther expected nothing good from the Diet of Regensburg, but he assured Prince Wolfgang of Anhalt, who was part of the delegation from Electoral Saxony, that Christ would also reign there in the midst of his enemies and that God would not abandon his cause. "For God cannot lose, and even though we are hemmed in, we will ultimately triumph with him." The elector did not accede to Luther's request to spare Melanchthon and Cruciger from attending. The true religion had to be represented competently at the diet. As he had done with Prince Wolfgang, Luther strengthened Melanchthon in Regensburg with a letter. There would be angels, legates, archangels of the church, yes, God himself there, and therefore their cause was invincible. The lion of Judah had won the victory before the foundation of the world.[24]

At the beginning of April, Brück informed Luther about a change of course by the landgrave, who now was cooperating with the emperor. Philip of Hesse would continue to hold fast to the central article of faith, of course, but he would make concessions in neutral matters and those concerning church property. Luther was probably not especially surprised at this change of mind, for in the meantime it had become known in Wittenberg that Bucer and the landgrave had claimed Luther's support for the Regensburg Book. Luther immediately rejected the landgrave's plans for agreement and then also made a written statement. He began very angrily and clearly: "First, I will never again trust the landgrave or Bucer." They must adhere to the Smalcald Articles, which of course were not intended as conciliatory. They had to be united in the central article of faith and then deal with neutral things, not vice versa; if not, such a reform would be a hopeless patchwork. Luther would no longer let himself be led by the landgrave, whom he now considered a false brother, but would rather stand alone. The neutral issues were not important. The worship service in Wittenberg was so conservative that a visitor from the Romance lands did not even notice that he was not in a Catholic church. Church property could be returned only if it was to be used for genuine churchly purposes. Luther was sure that Melanchthon would also reject such a procedure.[25]

On 5 April the emperor informed the imperial estates that he wanted to appoint a committee for the religious question. The evangelicals were fundamentally in agreement and proposed that the Worms discussions be continued. From Wittenberg they could only support the "legates, disciples, and martyrs of the Lord" with their heartfelt prayers. When the landgrave learned how critically even Melanchthon thought about him, he gave his assurance that he did not intend to depart from the standpoint of the evangelicals.[26] The emperor named Eck, Julius Pflug, and Gropper as theological representatives on the one side, along with Melanchthon, Bucer, and the Hessian pastor Johann Pistorius on the other. There were fifteen discussion topics, beginning with the eucharist, the office of the pope, and the sacrifice of the mass, and concluding with the doctrine of justification. The evangelical theologians, like Luther, saw this enumeration, which deviated from the order of the Augsburg Confession, as an evil subterfuge of the opposing side. Sarcastically, and perhaps also somewhat concerned, Luther predicted that the emperor would appeal to

Melanchthon's love of peace and Melanchthon would promise him his best, while Eck and his party would steadfastly defend the pope.[27] This impossible agenda, which had been rumored, quickly turned out to be a false report.

The colloquy began on 27 April. It began on the basis of the Regensburg Book that had been produced during the secret discussions in Worms. This meant that the imperial side was really interested in an agreement. Its efforts were supported by the papal legate himself, Gasparo Contarini, who was one of the curial theologians who favored reform and who had a certain understanding for the Reformation doctrine of justification on the basis of his own religious experiences. They rather quickly reached the article on justification. To Melanchthon's surprise, even Eck cooperated so that the discussion did not come to the abrupt end that might have been expected.[28] One after another, Eck, Melanchthon, and also Contarini proposed their own drafts. On 2 May, to everyone's surprise, they reached a provisional agreement on a formulation that accommodated the interests of both sides. This stated that faith depends entirely on the imputed righteousness of Christ; this was important for the evangelicals. At the same time this faith is active in love; this accorded with the Catholic view of effectively becoming righteous. In the compromise formula imputed righteousness was placed first, to be sure, and on their side the evangelicals emphasized the significance of good works that come from faith, but the relationship between faith and works of love in the process of justification was not unmistakably clarified. The central formula "through faith alone" was used only in a qualified way. Nevertheless, they had come closer together than ever before. Contarini joyfully reported the result to Rome, but there the formula was rejected.[29]

Elector John Frederick immediately sent the formula to Luther and Bugenhagen for their opinion, but he did not disguise his own reservations concerning those concessions that appeared to acknowledge an error on the part of the evangelicals and the possible qualification of "justification through faith alone." The elector warned incidentally about Catholic spies in Wittenberg. In another letter he asked the theologians for advice about whether he should comply with Charles V's demand that he personally come to Regensburg. John Frederick did not want to be embarrassed by having to take a stand against the landgrave's and Bucer's problematic attempts at reaching a settlement. In addition, he feared that he might be compelled to make political concessions to King Ferdinand, Archbishop Albrecht of Mainz, Duke Henry of Brunswick, and the bishop of Meissen that were not in the interests of Electoral Saxony. It could also be assumed that the emperor would make the peace contingent on his not supporting a further spread of the Reformation.[30]

Luther immediately recognized that the Regensburg compromise formula was a patchwork of different conceptions. Both sides would claim that they had preserved the truth. He predicted—accurately—that the agreement would fall apart as soon as the consequences of the doctrine of justification were applied to the other articles. The correct, clear, and brief formula for Luther was Rom. 3:24, 28: "They are justified by his grace as a gift. . . . For we hold that a man is justified by faith apart from works of law. . . . Let the devil, Eck, Mainz, Heinz, and anyone else rage against this. We shall see what they win." There had to be a clear distinction between the cause of justification and its evidence in life, i.e., good works. Before God only Christ's righteousness was valid, not the righteousness within a person. God regards works as holy only for Christ's sake. Naturally, Luther advised the elector against going to the diet and taking the risks there. As before, he doubted that the intentions of the emperor were honorable, and therefore John Frederick should not obey his order. He expressly asked the elector not to reprimand Melanchthon too severely for his provisional approval of the justification formula, "so that he does not once again die of grief." Nothing definite had been decided, but the discussion about justification would not fail to bear fruit. Christ does his work with the weak and in this way also takes care that his own do not become too proud. Unlike during the Diet of Augsburg, Luther now reacted calmly and tactfully to Melanchthon's style of negotiating, but he forcefully told Melanch- thon about the ambiguity of the Regensburg Book: "The Holy Scriptures and God's commandment are by nature not ambiguous." Teachings that were pre- viously false could not subsequently be interpreted in a correct way.[31] On his part, Melanchthon also stated that he was not completely satisfied with the justification formula. From the very beginning it had been interpreted differ- ently by each side. This was intolerable on such a central topic. The common basis was too narrow, and there was no mutual trust. In this respect there had probably never been a genuine chance for an agreement in Regensburg.

In the meantime discussions were continued in May. No advances were achieved on the other articles. Even Melanchthon did not give in. He wanted to leave because the emperor, who was still interested in positive results, incorrectly believed that he was being inflexible because Luther and the king of France had told him to make no compromises. On 19 May Melanchthon was expecting the discussion to collapse, which happened three days later, but he was also aware of rumors that armed action against the evangelicals was not to be expected. Luther was grateful for this development. Christ and Belial could not be reconciled.[32] To Prince George of Anhalt, Luther also rejected the doctrine of transubstantiation as a philosophical construct that was not in the Bible. One could not appropriately express the union of Christ's body and blood or of the human and divine natures in Christ in Aristotelian categories.[33]

Luther advised the elector to be cautious about the emperor's statements of interest in peace and reform. The emperor was very concerned about reaching an agreement. When the theologians made no progress in Regensburg, there was even thought of inviting Luther himself to Regensburg. This plan was ultimately modified: Princes John and George of Anhalt, along with two Bran- denburg representatives appointed by Elector Joachim II, should visit Luther in Wittenberg and persuade him to approve the four articles on original sin, justification, free will, and faith and works that had been agreed upon in Regensburg. Regarding the articles of the Regensburg Book that had not yet been reviewed, he should declare that he was willing to tolerate them. Apparently they had a false understanding of Luther's willingness to reach an understanding. Luther was surprised at the notice of the delegation because he had already made a very reserved statement about the Regensburg Book to the elector of Brandenburg. It seemed to him to be a repetition of his earlier experience in Worms when the imperial estates wanted to extract unacceptable concessions from him.[34]

The discussions took place on 10 June. Luther's written reply was made even more pointed by Chancellor Brück and the elector, who had come to Wittenberg himself, in order to give their opponents no critical room in which to maneuver. Luther recognized that the emperor desired peace and unity, which was also the intention of the evangelicals. The only one of the articles he knew they had examined was the one on justification. Nevertheless, the unity was not credible, because they had not drawn any conclusions from the article on justification for the articles that had not been compared. In addition, the article on justification was itself ambiguous. In Luther's opinion, there could be no declaration that the articles that had not been studied were to be tolerated, for this would permit what Luther rejected and attacked. The additions by the elector declared that such a toleration was unacceptable, for it would involve justifying religious coercion and abuses. The emperor should be content with enforcing the four articles that had been compared without changing them; as a result, consequences for the other articles would then arise and later an agreement on them would be possible. If the opposing side was not serious about the four articles, however, that would show what their intentions of unity were worth.[35] Despite all his skepticism, Luther had not refused to participate in efforts at reaching an agreement. His proposal was aimed at a Reformation that began with the proclamation of justification. This was in accord with his original intention, but he saw no real chance for this in Regensburg and therefore hoped that Melanchthon would soon return from his fruitless work there. Luther hated the emperor, for he thought his politics were untrustworthy; he had not brought charges against the troublemakers Henry of Brunswick and Albrecht of Mainz, he was not seriously battling the Turks, and he was enriching himself by confiscating church lands in the Netherlands. He considered the emperor accursed. Luther's own cause had to be left to Christ.[36]

At the end of June, Elector John Frederick asked Luther and Bugenhagen for a specific statement on the Regensburg Book. This left no doubt about their position. Before an agreement could be reached, the pope would have to admit that he had led many souls astray, and the emperor would have to acknowledge his persecution of the evangelicals and the humiliation that he had caused the elector. Likewise, the Catholic theologians would have to recant their errors. Otherwise, the elector should insist on the Augsburg Confession and the Apology. Even the articles that had been compared were acceptable only if the former errors were also retracted at the same time. Making distinctions is part of confessing. Luther's reply contained a colossal demand: "In sum, in these articles they must retract, condemn, and curse all their theology, their sentences, decretals, all the summists, bulls, letters [papal breves], all foundations' and monasteries' doctrine and life, all popes', cardinals', and bishops' offices and character, along with everything that they have gained with this error, idolatry, blasphemy, and lies." Otherwise, the agreement was only a deception. Condemning the devil went along with faith and confessing one's sins. Nevertheless, Luther did not execute his plan of publishing the Regensburg Book with an "unlaundered preface" and appropriate glosses. The reply of the evangelical estates on 12 July, which was written by Melanchthon, was naturally more moderate, but even in it the articles that had been reviewed were said to need clarification, and they insisted on their own position in respect to the ones that had not been discussed. Thus the colloquy in Regensburg produced virtually no results.[37] Because of these disappointing consequences, Luther expected sharp action by the emperor against the evangelicals.[38] Charles V, however, extended the Religious Peace of Nuremberg until the council they anticipated would soon meet. The evangelicals had once again gained time, but experience had also shown that a religious colloquy was no more able to achieve an agreement than was a council. The means for a peaceful resolution of the conflict were almost exhausted.

We also confront Luther's vehement anti-papal attitude—conditioned by his expectation that the last day was near, which made him uninterested in a compromise—in an expanded introduction to the prophet Daniel written in May 1541, which was primarily a commentary on Dan. 11:36.[39] Here the pope was again portrayed as the great tyrant and a God-like man, who was subject to no law and to whom even the emperor had to submit. He was the great seducer and oppressor of Christians, the destroyer of the three hierarchies of government, marriage, and church. He had introduced the worst outrage in the church, the mass, a worship service that God did not want. Ever since the time of Emperor Louis the Bavarian (1324), Christ had been preparing the downfall of the papacy. In this process a special significance was ascribed to John Huss, who reportedly had prophesied that Luther would arise. The pope was no longer able to suppress the cries of the evangelicals. The archangel Michael stood alongside the embattled Christians. Luther was convinced that the last day was coming soon, although no one could say precisely when. He believed that his exposition had deciphered the mystery of Daniel. This he had achieved, of course, only by a questionable allegorical interpretation, about which he himself was not completely sure: "Someone else may do it better." Luther wanted to interpret the current situation on the basis of the Bible, but

227

at the same time he also interpreted the Bible on the basis of the situation. The two were interrelated and conditioned one's view of history. The actions of the papacy and of some of the Catholic princes gave reason to identify the pope with the Antichrist. In this context the emperor's political efforts at reaching an agreement, which had little hope of success, could not be evaluated objectively. In the last years of his life, Luther's opinion of the religious conflict was buttressed by an indefensible exegesis that was colored by an apocalyptic view of his own age. This had momentous consequences. It is questionable whether a realistic evaluation of the situation in light of the insurmountable differences could have altered the course of events, but Luther's view of history was not helpful in relieving tension.

The Regensburg disputes had continuing effects. On 3 February 1542 for conferring the doctoral degree on Johannes Scotus Maccabeus, who had been called to a professorship in Copenhagen, Melanchthon prepared theses on the subject of the church that dealt primarily with the conflicting views that had been expressed in Regensburg. In the disputation Luther clearly stated that it is not ministerial succession that constitutes the church, but obedience to the gospel.[40] In the theses for conferring the doctorate on 7 July 1542 on Heinrich Schmedenstede, who had been called to Wismar, Luther picked up the same theme. Since the beginning of the world the true worship of God has consisted of believing in the promised Christ, although the form of this faith may have varied. Justification by faith alone is decisive. Therefore, as in the critique of the Regensburg Book, he once again rejected any qualification of faith, such as faith active in works of love. The importance that the Catholics placed upon human achievement showed this was by no means merely a dispute over words between the two religious parties, as some "sad mediators" pretended.[41] Luther wrote a preface to a collection of Franciscan legends published by Erasmus Alber in 1542 under the title of *The Barefoot Monks' Eulenspiegel and Alcoran.*[42] The book proved that all of this was still taught in the papacy, although they had not wanted to admit it in the recent colloquies. Neither had there been any recantation or repentance; rather, the result of the discussions had been to leave everything just as it was. In this way nothing but a useless patchwork resulted. One could only pray God to preserve the new light that had been kindled, so that people would not again fall into darkness.

IX

Personal Affairs
(1537–46)

1. ILL, OLD, AND TIRED OF LIVING

Most of the information we have about how Luther fared personally in the last years of his life has to do with his health. He had not become a hypochondriac, but he was troubled with many illnesses and his strength had obviously diminished, while his work load was not reduced in the same measure. His attitude toward what was happening around him and his opinion of what confronted him could not have been unaffected by this. Of course, one must guard against too hastily explaining Luther's actions in the last years of his life as the grumpiness of an old man.

Luther recovered slowly from the severe illness that afflicted him in Schmalkalden in February 1537. At the end of April or the beginning of May he suffered a fainting spell during the worship service. He saw this as a renewed attack of the devil, and said one had to turn to Christ the true physician against it. He was aware that everything could quickly come to an end for him. Not until the beginning of July did he resume his lecturing and preaching. Even then he did not feel in complete possession of his strength,[1] although he appears to have been in reasonably good health in the months following. In November he celebrated the Lord's Supper in his home because his kidney stones were troubling him again. At the end of the year he frequently had to cut his sermons short because of weakness. At that time the physician Augustine Schurf predicted that Luther would die of a stroke. This made little impression on the patient. Only a blessed death interested him.[2]

Luther blamed the pain of his stones—they were in his kidneys and bladder—on drinking bad wine. He only reluctantly complied with the strict diet prescribed by the physicians, for it seemed as bad as death to him. He had little use for preventive measures. He did not want to starve to death: "I'll eat what I want, and die when God wills." The more harmless version of this statement was: "I'll eat what tastes good and endure what I can." He liked his rich, "good, ordinary household food" and a good drink. He much preferred tender pork to dry venison and wild game. He considered it appropriate to take a short afternoon nap following lunch. The elector once said the sick Luther was not "always an agreeable medicine-man," i.e., he was an impatient

patient. Luther did not deny this at all. He had his own opinions about the physicians; some of them needed a "new cemetery" because of their risky treatments, while others made their patients impatient with their caution. The physicians paid attention only to the natural causes of illness, but not to the devil who brought them. Therefore Luther considered faith and prayer the most important medicines. He thought it right that the physicians had their rules, but he would not always follow them because he thought of himself not as a fixed star, but as a moveable planet. For example, in the summer of 1540 he would not let them forbid him from bathing. He saw that the difficulties of a physician's profession were caused by the unfathomable differences between people. Therefore, only in humility and fear of God could one practice such a vocation.[3]

At the beginning of July 1538 Luther, like his whole family, suffered with severe dysentery and had to submit to the physicians' arts. At mid-month his condition was serious. He confidently entrusted his fate to God's hand. He was aware that even the most elementary things of life were not at all sure. Subsequently he had to use a cane because of pain in his legs caused by gout associated with the kidney stones. Along with these pains came serious spiritual *Anfechtungen*, but he knew that Christ, who was tempted in Gethsemane, was his intercessor. He considered that year an especially unhealthy time, especially after the kidney stones themselves recurred at the beginning of August. Not until 5 August was he again able to go out for a ride, and he praised God for this in order to spite the devil. The miracle of creation caused him to refer to eternal life. The serious attacks of gout returned. Luther writhed in pain. He could not thank God enough for a drink of water to refresh an exhausted man. It was not always easy for him to accept God's will patiently during the period of serious illness.[4]

In mid-September Luther felt old and exhausted. Only the controversy with the Antinomians, he remarked sarcastically, kept him young. The feeling that he was old and worn out continued in the following months. He had trouble dealing with his correspondence. The "letter days," when the mail was delivered and picked up, made him "morose." It became increasingly difficult for him to read anything in the mornings. Because of the great quantity of his business, his friends frequently had to be content with brief letters.[5] After an interruption of several months, Luther resumed his lecturing at the beginning of March 1539, although his health was not stable. On Palm Sunday he had to stop preaching because he became dizzy. He wanted to die. He no longer had the strength to continue the fight against heresy. He wanted at least to "torment the pope a little more." Otherwise, he thought he had done enough; "Only to go to sleep in the sand!" During Holy Week he did not preach, but at Easter he felt much better. In the following days the painful kidney stones returned.[6]

Then, until the end of 1540, there was again a period of time in which

Luther's health was comparatively satisfactory. The overwork continued, however. He said his life was entertaining because he had to accomplish in one hour what other people did in three. He even occasionally wrote letters during meals because he had been unable to do so earlier.[7] During an epidemic in September 1540 he also took over the responsibilities of Bugenhagen, who was sick. At that time he could also accept bad news with equanimity and good spirits, for this only proved that the inevitable battle with the devil was still going on.[8]

In January 1541 Luther first suffered from an abscess on his neck. In February he experienced a serious fainting spell as a result of circulatory disturbances. In March he had an inflammation of his nasal cavity that developed into an inner ear inflammation and caused a perforated eardrum, which festered for a long time. Despite great pain he kept on working during the illness. He attributed the moderation he claimed he displayed in *Against Hanswurst* to this ailment. In late April he was still thinking, "once to live, once to die." The solicitous elector sent his personal physician, Matthew Ratzeberger, and the surgeon Andrew Engelhard, but when they arrived the patient was already improving and could even walk about in his garden once again. He credited his improvement to Bugenhagen's intercession in the worship service. At the beginning of May his hearing returned, but the annoying ringing in his ears continued. Even weeks later he was hardly able to concentrate while reading or speaking. In July he still felt so exhausted that he did not want to write even essential letters. Once again he stated his longing to go home to God.[9]

No more physical complaints are mentioned until March 1542, but then the effects of the old man's exhaustion returned. He felt "old, cold, misshapen," and he was allowed no rest; instead, he had to deal with everything that was going on in Germany, where things were worse than ever, and he was unable to do anything except pray, "Thy will be done!" He had had enough of life. The devil was weary with him, and he was weary with the devil.[10] His health improved in the second half of the year.

In January and February 1543 Luther was hardly able to read or write because of headaches. He thus was unable to deal with some matters or could spend only a short time on them. In the following months he again said that he was tired of living, which had to do with his disgust with the depressing situation of the world. Handicapped by the pain of his stones, he felt overloaded by correspondence, writing, and lecturing. Because of new circulatory problems, in July he again had to postpone a trip to Zeitz that had been planned for months.[11] In order to counteract the headaches and dizziness, a sore on Luther's lower left leg was artificially kept open on the advice of Ratzeberger, the elector's personal physician. Countess Dorothy of Mansfeld did not agree with this treatment. She sensibly advised more exercise and sent her own medicine, including sneezing powder. White aquavit should be used to treat fainting. Yellow aquavit helped to relieve tightness in the chest and stomach trouble. This was not the only time that the countess offered medical advice. Among other things, Luther employed one of Katy's household remedies against his stones and also recommended it to others. The artificial sore naturally had no effect on the headaches, which were pronounced in November. Luther himself blamed his sickness on his age or on the assaults of the devil, like those Paul had experienced (2 Cor. 12:7). No medicine helped against them. Nevertheless, the patient complied with the doctors because he did not want to be blamed for being careless with his health.[12]

At the beginning of 1544 Luther was able to preach and lecture once more, but at the end of February he again had to interrupt his preaching because of severe headaches that had begun at the beginning of the month, and he did not resume until Easter. When Sibylle, the wife of Elector John Frederick, inquired about his health, he told her that he was well enough under the circumstances. He blamed the headaches on his age: "I have lived long enough; may God grant me a blessed death, so that this miserable body may return to its home in the ground and be consumed by worms." In view of the bleak future Luther was no longer interested in living.[13] Others were also concerned about his health. Duke Albrecht of Prussia sent white amber to treat the stones, so that Luther would not have to use an amber rosary, a previous gift from the duke, for purposes other than originally intended. Luther used the amber in a mixture made with special pulverized fish bones. Johann Magenbuch, the Nuremberg city physician, had already sent Luther medicines in 1543. It was more than a year later that Luther thanked him for them with the first part of his commentary on Genesis.[14]

When Anthony Lauterbach, the superintendent in Pirna, asked Luther to write a book about church discipline, probably in July 1544, he responded irritably. As an exhausted and idle old man he did not know where he would get the spare time and health to do so. He was endlessly inundated with letters. He had promised the Saxon princes a sermon on drunkenness, and others a book on secret engagements and one against the sacramentarians. Others were demanding summaries and glosses on the whole Bible. Each one of these was preventing him from completing the others. Luther had thought that in retirement he would have free time when he could rest, live in peace, and sleep, but they were forcing him into an active life. Yet he promised to do what was within his power.[15] Luther's response to Lauterbach is noteworthy both for his desire to rest as well as for the actual achievements that he was still able to accomplish. Although he felt so tired, he continued to be creative as before. He had to turn down the request of Prince John of Anhalt to visit him in Dessau at the conclusion of his trip to Zeitz, which he finally made in August 1544. He was so tired from traveling "that I cannot walk or stand, and even sitting wearies me; I am noticing my age and my body is giving way and will be lowered into the earth. May God soon help me with his grace. Therefore I must be quiet and rest until things are different with me, whether life or death, as God wills."[16]

In the months following, Luther appears to have been spared from serious bouts of illness. In March 1545 he received an Italian pamphlet, which reported that he had died and the circumstances surrounding his death. Among other things, it alleged that he had asked that his body be worshiped, although no one complied with this. Because of great rumors, his grave had been reopened and found to be empty because the devil had taken him away. Luther had the "Italian lie" reprinted. He gave it a motto by using a Latin poem that articulated a statement he had made before: If the living Luther had been a plague to the pope, the dead one would be his death. In an afterword he confirmed that, except for its blasphemy, he had enjoyed reading the news of his death. The pope and papists were the ones who would have to go to the devil with their lies and blasphemies.[17] Luther said nothing at the time about his expectations regarding his own end.

In the week after Easter, Chancellor Brück heard Luther preach a "lovely sermon." He noticed how pale and unenergetic he was. After the sermon he had to fan himself with his beret. The chancellor informed the elector that they might have to be prepared for Luther's sudden death. Luther himself had asked the congregation to pray that God would take him from this world, "for he had had enough of the world and had done all the work he could do."[18] On 15 June Luther was in agony with the pain of his stones. He wanted to die rather than have to endure this pain. If he could not die an easier death, he prayed that God would give him the necessary courage. He wished the pope and the cardinals would have his acute pains. After he passed several stones a week later he improved somewhat, but a few days later there was another severe attack. In August Luther again felt that he was "full of stones"; but this time the pains were not as great.[19] In October 1545, in one of the last comments on his health, he said quite characteristically that he was very busy, listless, old, and longing for death. In January 1546 he described himself in a letter to James Propst in Bremen as "an old man, done with life, lethargic, exhausted, cold, and one-eyed." He could not see with the other eye. He was hoping for a well-deserved rest. Nevertheless, just as if he had never done, written, or said anything, he was inundated and occupied with all sorts of affairs (Plate IX).[20] The tired, old man was not granted the rest he longed for. It is questionable whether it would have made him feel better. He had to remain at his post until the end.

Luther's illnesses obviously made it difficult for him to continue to deal with the demands placed upon him, and this increased his desire for rest. The continually new difficulties and developments in the church could provoke concern, annoyance, and resignation and could lead to sharp reactions. Yet Luther's latter days were not filled only with ill humor, and he was able to

The aged Luther
Woodcut by Lucas Cranach the Younger, 1546

maintain some distance from his own situation. Despite the illnesses, he did not fear death, and he had no apprehension about his life. He had long since committed it into God's hand.

2. MARRIAGE, CHILDREN, FAMILY, AND GUESTS

For Luther, his marriage to Katy (Plate X) was an involvement in one of the elementary divine ordinances. In 1537 he considered sending a portrait of her and himself to the council that had been called in Mantua. In a preeminent way, the title of Eve as "mother of all living" (Gen. 3:20) described for him the role of a wife in general. This transcended any possible weaknesses Katy had.[1] Little is known about the personal relationship between the two marriage partners. They were so self-evident that not much was written about them. Luther insisted that Katy read and study the Bible. Once she complained about this; she thought she knew it and had read and studied enough.[2] We read virtually nothing about marital spats, but Luther once hinted in his commentary on Genesis that they were not entirely avoided.[3] In January 1540 Katy was seriously ill after a miscarriage. Luther later claimed that it was the power of prayer that kept her alive and allowed her to recover relatively quickly. The severity of the condition is seen in the fact that she did not start to walk again until the beginning of March. Two weeks later she sent word to Luther's absent colleagues, who had inquired about her health, that she had resumed the reins of the household and was learning how to scold and reprimand their lazy and disobedient maid.[4] This statement also contains a measure of self-irony. Because of Katy's leading role in the house, Luther occasionally described her as his lord or as Moses.[5] His concern for his wife can be read in a letter from September 1541. At the time, Katy was at her farm in Zöllsdorf when it was rumored that the Turks were approaching. Luther sent his own messenger to her: "Sell and arrange what you are able to, and come home. For it appears to me that it will rain dirt."[6]

Today's reader would probably like to know something about the marital relationship between Luther and Katy, although here we must respect this sphere of intimacy. Luther addressed many of his letters to Katy with "my dearest," or concluded them with "your loved one." One of his last letters ended with "your old loved one."[7] This was certainly not merely following the conventions of letter writing. In addition, in his lectures on Genesis the old Luther frequently spoke indirectly in a very concrete way about married love. Genesis 26:8 reported that Isaac had "fondled" Rebekah. Luther did not interpret this as a shameless display of affection in public. The couple were comforting one another in the face of external tribulations by being together. "With the woman who has been joined to me by God I may jest, have fun, and converse more pleasantly. . . ." Luther considered it also proper for a man to display love for his wife. That showed that the marriage was a happy one. For him, a good marriage involved not only physical attraction, but intellectual companionship as well. It also required mutual forgiving and forgetting. All of this was expressed in the way the two partners dealt outwardly with one another. Marriage is also a "godly union" as far as the physical relationship is concerned, and God is pleased with it. Although Luther shared the biblical image of the woman as the weaker partner, he knew enough about man's deficiencies not to speak about male superiority. The partners in marriage appeared to him to be equal. He did not deny that physical attraction and its needs also involve weaknesses and even vile things, but God takes all of this into account. In contrast to what he had experienced in his earlier confessional practice, he regarded enjoying one another's love within marriage not as a sin, but as something that was part of human sexuality. Here, too, of course, moderation was called for. As in all situations in a person's life, there is also sin in marriage; but it is under God's forgiveness.[8] In his interpretation of the story of Jacob, Luther expressly affirmed that Jacob, although already aged, had taken pleasure in Rachel's appearance. Luther also showed understanding for the ugly Leah's need for love. God accepts those who are scorned. He expressly defended Jacob against the charge that he had an overactive libido because he had four wives.[9] Occasionally, Luther has been accused of only acknowledging sexuality, while eroticism was foreign to him. But the lectures on Genesis show in a beautiful way another image of the relationship between married people, in which eroticism definitely has its place.

Marriage, however, is not something that concerns only sexual relationships. In the ideal sense it is for Luther a conscious and articulate relationship of faith. In this spirit children are also to be raised. Therefore, marriage can be called the origin and nursery of the church. In such a marriage relationship, Christ is present and protects it from the devil's assaults. Thus, in conscious contrast to its ridicule and devaluation among the Catholics, marriage was highly regarded.[10]

Luther's children are mentioned relatively infrequently. This does not mean that he was indifferent to them. He thought children were the "most beautiful joy" parents had. When Luther was on an extended trip in the summer of 1540, he received letters from his children. On his part, he sent them a silver apple the elector had given him, probably one that could be taken apart. Katy was to pay the children for it with cherries and early apples. The remainder was intended for her.[11] The willingness to make up and forgive that he observed in his children, together with their childlike faith, was something he regarded as a model. He also admired the intense and earnest way the eight-year-old Martin played with his doll as an example of genuine innocence.[12]

The children were tutored privately by older students. Luther was very strict with his oldest son, Hans. Unlike the younger Magdalene (b. 1529), he hardly ever "made merry" with him, for he thought boys should be raised more strictly than girls. He did not want Hans to have too much freedom. The father probably had special expectations in mind for his oldest child, but they were too demanding for Hans, and disappointments were inevitable. In some respects, Hans probably suffered most because of his great father. It was undoubtedly to honor his father that the boy was enrolled at the university at the age of seven in 1533 and awarded the bachelor's degree in 1539. After this, Luther no longer considered him a child. It may say something about Luther's expectations for his son that Hans received a letter from the eleven-year-old Duke John William, John Frederick's son—undoubtedly dictated by his preceptor—that encouraged Hans to imitate his great father. An exercise in logic that Luther drew up for Hans in 1540 has been preserved.[13]

In 1542 Hans, together with his cousin Florian von Bora, was sent to the director of the highly regarded school in Torgau, Marcus Crodel, to continue his education. Crodel was to keep Luther informed about his progress. The father thought it better at this time to have the children educated at school than to have them tutored privately. He commended him to John Walther for musical training. When it came out shortly thereafter that Florian von Bora had stolen some small item and then also lied about it, Luther ordered that he be whipped as punishment, "and the thrashing should draw blood." Hans suffered from homesickness in Torgau, but his father did not want to give in to this weakness. Hans was to study in Torgau and become strong. Only in case he fell seriously ill did Luther want to be informed. A single letter from Luther to Hans is known, probably from 1544. In it he stated his satisfaction with his son's studies. At the same time, Hans was strictly admonished to obey his parents and to fear God. In 1544 he was invited, along with Crodel, to the so-called "kingdom," a celebration in Luther's house on Shrove Tuesday.[14]

Hans had just moved to Torgau when he was summoned home by his father because his sister Magdalene was critically ill. Apparently the brother and sister had been very close, and Luther did not want to deny his daughter's request to see her brother. The father spoke plainly with his sick child about the possibility that she would go to be with God. This held no terrors for Magdalene. Her father was prepared to submit to God's will, although it was difficult for him. He consoled her grieving mother by saying that the child would go to heaven and that she trusted in God and had no fear of dying. He prayed for her in her struggle with death, weeping bitterly. On 20 September 1542 she died in his arms. Katy stood somewhat aside because of her grief. After death had come, Luther said, "I am rejoicing in the spirit, but I am very sad according to the flesh." Despite all his hope, the parting was painful. Her funeral was held the same day. The university also took part in it, for the Luther family belonged to that social class. In his announcement the rector did not fail to mention Magdalene's blessed end. As they laid the body in the coffin, the father said that it was well with his beloved child. Then he was overcome with sobbing. But his hope did not let sorrow get the better of him. As they closed the coffin he said: "Close it! She will rise again at the last day."

At the burial he confessed: "There is a resurrection of the body." After returning from the burial he did not want to complain. Death was for him a human
fate that had to be accepted, and he was convinced of the certainty of eternal
life. He willingly surrendered his grief over the girl to God. There are different versions of the inscription for Magdalene's tomb that Luther himself wrote.
It described her as Luther's daughter—there was no mention of Katy. It told
the fate of the deceased: The child sleeps here in the earth as one born to die
and someone lost because of sin, but thanks to Christ's blood and death she
lives.[15]

As a result of Magdalene's death Luther once again mentioned his own
longing for death. He would have preferred it if he and his whole family had
died like Magdalene, for he thought the future held nothing good. Despite all
the thankfulness for Magdalene's blessed death, in the letters he wrote telling
people about it one can see just how much the parents' pain persisted. He
admitted openly that even the remembrance of Christ's death was unable to
take away the pain. His indignant complaining about death helped Luther to
overcome his tears, but Katy was still weeping and her eyes were wet. Along
with the consolation that Magdalene had been taken from this evil world, the
sorrow over their loss remained.[16] In no way did Luther ignore the pain of this
death, but he also did not allow it to shake his hope.

Luther's family included not only his wife and their children, but also
relatives. Until her death, which was reportedly in 1537, Katy's aunt,
Magdalene von Bora, "Aunt Lene," lived with them. Luther was at her side
when she died.[17] The four children of Luther's sister Margarete Kaufmann,
who had died in 1529, also lived in the house. In addition, there were his
nephews John Polner and James Luther, and also Anna Strauss, one of Katy's
grandnieces.[18] It was not always easy for Katy to rein in the family. The head
of the household thought it would take a regime as harsh as that of the Turks to
do so.[19] As time went on, the grown-up girls like Lene Kaufmann and Anna
Strauss were to marry. Lene married Professor Ambrose Berndt in 1538. The
marriage was celebrated in the Luther house, and musicians were hired for
the event. For Luther this was once more an occasion to sing the praises of
marriage. He did mildly criticize the expense of the bridal gown with its
fashionable gold lace. After Berndt died in 1541, Lene moved back into
the Luther house. In 1545 she wanted to marry Ernst Reuchlin, a medical
student. Luther did not think his intentions were honorable and objected to
him, but he was unable to separate them. Reuchlin later did wed Lene.[20]

Occasionally, Luther also was concerned about his family who lived in other
places. In 1538 he interceded with Duke Albrecht of Prussia to get his brother-
in-law Hans von Bora reinstated in his position in the duke's service after a
leave of several years. When he was unsuccessful in this, he sought a position
for Katy's brother in Ducal Saxony, emphasizing that Hans von Bora did not
belong to the type of *Scharrhansen* among the nobility who were not well

liked. He later applied again to the government of Electoral Saxony on his behalf. Then Hans von Bora was employed as administrator of the dissolved Cronschwitz monastery. When this position was discontinued, Luther once again had to try to help his brother-in-law.[21] Luther also once obliged his cousin Heinz Luder in Möhra by giving him a recommendation.[22]

The Luther house was open to others besides his relatives and the students who lived there. The most prominent guest was the Electress Elizabeth of Brandenburg, who had separated from her husband, Joachim I. She had previously stayed in Wittenberg in 1534. In the summer of 1537 she lay critically ill in Luther's house. Luther supported her with fervent prayer, as he evidently did in all cases of sickness: "O Lord God, hear our prayer according to your promise! Let us not cast our keys before your feet, for if we become angry with you and do not give you honor and pay you your due, whither will you go?" It was extraordinarily difficult to care for her, because Elizabeth was out of her mind at least some of the time. Katy had to sit beside her and keep her calm. When Elizabeth's daughter, Princess Margaret of Anhalt, wanted to visit her mother, Luther had to provide quarters for her. He could not find any and therefore advised her not to visit. Nevertheless, the princess came without notice, and Luther treated her rather abruptly and rudely. The months of caring for the electress, who had become childlike, became more and more burdensome, so that Luther had to seek help from Elector John Frederick. Elizabeth was then to be housed in Lichtenburg, but Luther would not simply turn her out before acceptable accommodations had been prepared for her there. Occasionally, he also later visited Elizabeth in Lichtenburg.[23]

In 1539 when first the wife of the jurist Sebald Münsterer and then Münsterer himself died of the plague, their four children were taken into Luther's house. Later they lived with Melanchthon's family.[24] In 1542 Prince George of Anhalt wanted to stay in the Luther house during a visit to Wittenberg, but his confidant George Helt described the situation there to him. A mixed crowd of students, girls, widows, and children was always living there, and therefore there was a great deal of commotion, which many people regretted for Luther's sake. If all the residents possessed Luther's spirit, his house would be a comfortable and suitable lodging for the prince where he could enjoy his conversations with Luther. Under the existing circumstances, however, Helt had to advise him against staying there. The prince did attend one of Luther's sermons in his house in 1544.[25] The head of the house himself never complained about the situation that Helt described.

Luther was frequently deceived and taken advantage of by ne'er-do-wells and swindlers, primarily monks and nuns. On the basis of such experiences he seems to have become more cautious with his aid in later years, but in 1541 he reported half in jest how an alleged nun had smuggled herself into his house under the false name of Rosina von Truchsess. In fact, she was the daughter of a burgher from Münnerstadt in Franconia who had been executed in the Peasants' War. They trusted her completely, until it was discovered that she lied, stole, and was pregnant, whereupon she disappeared and successfully plied her scheme in other parsonages. Years later she appeared in Leipzig, which caused Luther to warn the *Stadtrichter* there about her. Luther was aware that one took a chance of being deceived when exercising charity, but no one would become poor by doing so.[26] Likewise, in 1541 an English beggar left a foundling in Luther's house. Although he had a recommendation from Osiander in Nuremberg, no place could be found for the small child in Wittenberg, which was being overrun with the needy; therefore, Luther hoped that the child would be taken by the Nuremberg foundling hospital.[27]

3. HOME, HOUSEHOLD, GARDEN, AND PROPERTY

Luther's large house could not be operated without servants. His own servant was still Wolfgang Seberger. The elector had awarded him a small income from an ecclesiastical benefice, but Luther occasionally had to intervene to see that it was paid. Seberger took care of the cellar, the garden, and business affairs. Luther continually complained about his laziness, but Seberger compensated for it with his great faithfulness.[1] We do not know how many domestic servants there were. Luther thought there were too many, however, and blamed this for his lack of money. Occasionally, there were also troubles with the servants. After one servant left, a rumor surfaced that he had had a relationship with a girl in the city. Luther wrote a poem in which he stated that a household was in order only if the master and mistress of the house looked after things themselves.[2] The greater portion of this responsibility was Katy's.

They were always building and remodeling in the house. The construction work extended from the cellar, the stairway, several rooms, including the living room on the second floor, which today is called the "Luther room" (Plate XI), to the roof. In addition, there were the brewhouse, the stables, a fountain in the garden, and a new house next to the garden. Some of the building material was furnished by the city without charge. At Katy's request, in 1540 the new entrance was constructed from Elbe sandstone, which Lauterbach had to obtain, and it remains today (Plate XII). The two medallions depict Luther's likeness and his seal with the word *vivit* (Christ lives) encircling it. Luther also took part in planning the installation of windows in the roof. In 1541 a new bathroom was installed, which likewise was built of sandstone. The construction expense of more than eighteen hundred gulden was a considerable sum and ate up part of their available cash. Excavations for the building of the defenses caused damage in several places to Luther's property and house. He thought he was being cheated and complained fiercely to the master of ordinance, Friedrich von der Grüne, who was responsible. He called him a godless servant who deserved hell because he wanted to cheat Luther out of the property that the elector had given him. The tensions must have been substantial, for scarcely ever did Luther defend his private interests so energetically.[3] He also reacted angrily around the end of 1543 when the city wanted to prevent him from brewing beer and also created difficulties concerning a piece of property. These arguments were resolved at once.[4] Katy probably encouraged her husband to react forcefully.

Katy carried out her role as housewife with self-confidence. Possibly she was demonstrating some of the characteristics of a noblewoman landholder. Luther joked about this in addressing his letters to her, calling her the owner of the garden at the pig market, or more frequently the "lady of Zulsdorf [Zöllsdorf]" after the couple purchased the Bora family estate from Katy's brother in 1540, which probably fulfilled Katy's heart's desire. In addition, Luther used the terms "brewer," "gardener," and, surprisingly, "judge," all of them undoubtedly expressions of respect for his competent wife.[5] Katy kept her own livestock as a way of defraying the expenses of the large household. For years she tried to lease the small farm of Boos near Wittenberg. Chancellor Brück opposed this. In 1539, however, Katy prevailed with *Landrentmeister* Hans von Taubenheim and bought the farm for a relatively small amount. Then, to Katy's considerable displeasure, Brück kept her from getting the manor of Wachsdorf near Wittenberg. Not until after Luther's death could she obtain it.[6]

Katy actively undertook the farming of Zöllsdorf, and she and her horse-drawn vehicle were frequently found there "in her kingdom." With the elector's help, the obligation to provide compulsory labor, which was a duty of the small estate, was lifted. She also requested oak firewood from him and then saw to it that a good quality was delivered. She obtained grain from a neighboring nobleman. Several times Spalatin had to intervene before Katy received the building lumber that was also promised her, which was needed for constructing a barn and other purposes. Luther had to write the letters regarding this.[7] The Wittenberg property was also enlarged. In 1544 Luther purchased a garden near the Specke, a small wooded area northeast of the city, and, a little later, a field that enlarged the garden in the Kabelhufen outside the Elster gate, which had been obtained in 1532.[8] Because of the investment necessary, Katy's farming may have returned very little profit or none at all, but she enjoyed it.

Luther also enjoyed gardens in other ways than did the practical Katy. He was not at all an indoor person, for he had a relationship with nature. In April 1538 he complained about being overloaded with work to the point of weariness, for as an old man he would rather have been enjoying himself with the buds and the things growing in the gardens, if he were not getting something else that he deserved because of his previous sins. There were many fish that spring, and he thought that a bad sign. He prayed for rain because of the drought at the time. When considerable precipitation occurred on 26 May he encouraged people to give thanks: "Now it is raining pure corn, wheat, oats,

241

cabbages, barley, wine, onions, grass, milk. But we think it is all nothing."
Despite the earlier fears, 1538 was a fruitful year, but people did not appreciate the miracle and act accordingly. During a trip to Lochau in September he
commented on the livestock in the fields, which as "milk-bringers, butter-
bringers, cheese-bringers, wool-bringers" preached faith in the heavenly
Father. When the children enjoyed a peach at the table, he said they were a
model of true joy at the last day. Compared with the fruits of paradise the
peach was more like a crabapple, and, like it, nature and men were totally
rotten.[9] In February 1539 Luther grafted his trees himself. He regarded it as a
miraculous work of God that the trunk divided into small branches and not the
reverse. He also enjoyed the growth of vegetation in his garden. He saw the
eclipse on 18 April as a warning to repent. He was grateful for the thunder-
storm with its warm rain that occurred the same day.[10] The beginning of May
with its greening trees was an image for him of the resurrection of the dead,
and the rose was a miracle of the creator. The swarms of bees—Katy also kept
an apiary—in which the bees gathered around the queen, was compared to
the church's relationship to Christ. If the queen were taken away, all sem-
blance of order disappeared. In July Luther ate cherries as dessert. He enjoyed
them, for they cleansed one's head and stomach. Among the fruits that flour-
ished in the garden were grapes. In early summer 1542 Luther said that the
blue color of the iris represented the flood, while the yellow color indicated
the flames of the world's destruction.[11] No more of his comments about the
garden are preserved from his later years. Possibly it had become too difficult
for Luther to get to it. Two aspects of Luther's experience of nature are noteworthy. First, he repeatedly emphasized how natural events and products were
useful or harmful for humankind. Second, these natural elements were frequently parables to him of how God acted.

As before, Katy occasionally had acquaintances obtain provisions. Luther
complained to James Propst in Bremen that since the regulations on fasting
had been removed, no more fish were being delivered, viz., herring, trout,
plaice, and salmon. The princes of Anhalt sometimes sent venison, or it could
be requested for special occasions. Gabriel Zwilling in Torgau had earlier sent
Luther a trunk, which had become worm eaten. Kathy asked him for a
replacement. She was simply requesting an ordinary trunk for linen clothing,
one that had no iron fittings so that the clothes would not get rust spots on
them. "For we already have a safe and it is a thousand times too large for our
treasures." Lauterbach often sent apples, trout, and butter. He obtained a fur
for Margaret, their daughter. Katy also secured poles and graftings for the
grapevines. Luther had difficulty repaying Lauterbach's generosity. Link sent
quince juice from Nuremberg. Luther received wine from Margrave George
of Brandenburg-Ansbach and from Amsdorf, and beer from the Torgau council.[12] The most generous contributor of supplies to Luther's household was the
elector. The accounts mention pike, carp, frequently beer and wine, ox meat,

grain for brewing, and wood as part of Luther's salary, in addition to hay, venison, and chickens. Sometimes these were gifts because of Luther's or Katy's illness.[13]

The couple also frequently received special gifts. Prince George of Anhalt sent Luther a valuable silver pitcher in 1541. Amsdorf gave him silver coins. The golden rings with jewels that Luther received were occasionally displayed to those at table. The silverware was an ultimate reserve when money ran out.[14]

Occasionally Katy complained that her husband, unlike some of his colleagues, was not interested in increasing his income. Luther continued to refuse any honoraria for his books and advice. He thought he had enough. In trust that God would make everything come out right, he helped others as God had helped him.[15] It could sometimes happen that difficult times arose. In the summer of 1540 Luther had to do without beer for forty days, presumably because there was no more grain available for brewing.[16] In 1541 the elector set aside one thousand gulden from which Luther was to receive the interest of fifty gulden, and he reserved the right to continue to pay interest to Luther's heirs after his death or to pay them the principal.[17] Beginning in 1542, King Christian of Denmark regularly sent Luther, Melanchthon, and Bugenhagen each a cask of butter and of herring. Because there were difficulties in delivering these products, he switched in 1544 to an annual payment of fifty gulden. In his letter of thanks in 1546 Luther expressed his hope that the king would not have to pay out this amount much longer. When Christian III replied on 3 March 1546, against Luther's expectation, that God "will keep you healthy and alive for a long time in order to help and encourage the Christian church and our true religion," Luther was already dead.[18]

For the Turkish tax, which was levied in 1542, Luther had to provide an inventory of his property, but the tax itself was paid by the elector. It was impossible for Luther to estimate the value of the former monastery building. He referred to the high expenditures required to keep the structure in repair. Luther had only paid part of the cost of the house in front of the monastery, which he had bought from Bruno Brauer the previous year, but he included it in the inventory of his property. In contrast, however, Luther wanted to pay the tax that was due for his garden properties. He wanted to provide no more cause for envy than already existed as a result of Katy's accumulation of property in Wittenberg, and he was also willing to pay his share to stop the Turks. He estimated his Wittenberg property was worth 1,030 gulden. In addition, there were the taxable animals, and on this occasion we learn something about them: Five cows, nine calves, one goat with two kids, eight swine, two sows, and three piglets worth a total value of fifty gulden. Although Luther rounded off the totals, it was difficult for him to calculate the tax of sixteen gulden, eight groschen, and three pfennigs, and he miscalculated by one groschen.[19]

The will that Luther dictated in Gotha in 1537 when he was critically ill was of a theological nature and contained no bequests of property. When Melanchthon wrote his will in 1540, Luther refused to make one of his own. Katy would become his sole heir. The children were to have his books. He did not think it necessary to provide guardians.[20] Nevertheless, at the beginning of 1542 he did write a will. It was relatively unconventional and was designed primarily to assure Katy's inheritance, for otherwise according to Saxon inheritance laws she would have been ill provided for. He bequeathed her the Zöllsdorf property. She was to have a residence in the small house in front of the monastery that shortly before had been purchased from Brauer. It had initially been thought of as a bequest to his servant Wolfgang Seberger, who now was to remain with Katy. In addition, Katy was to receive the beakers and valuables, such as rings, necklaces, and gifts of coins in the value of about one thousand gulden. Luther based these bequests on the fact that "as a pious and faithful spouse she has at all times held me dear, worthy, and fine," and also that she was the mother of his five children. She should be able to pay the indebtedness remaining on the house purchased from Brauer. Above all, she was to be independent of her children, and Luther was certain that Katy would use her property for the best interests of the children. The elector was to see to it that these provisions were carried out, which he did after Luther's death. He asked his friends to defend Katy. In order to prevent any possible jealousy, he certified that there was no other ready cash available. The money that had been set aside had already been used for construction and purchasing land. The unconventional legal form of the instrument, which was not witnessed by a notary, was something Luther explained by saying that he was a person known in heaven and in hell as a trustworthy teacher of the gospel, i.e., "God's notary and witness," and that he was also to be believed in this trifling matter.

Two years later, in an expanded form, Luther had this testament recorded in the Wittenberg legal register, probably to make it incontestable. Now the former Brauer house was bequeathed to Katy for her unrestricted use and not just as a residence. In addition, the four pieces of property in Wittenberg were to belong to her.[21] Luther had provided for his wife as best he could. The "household reckoning"[22] in the first testament was probably intended as a sort of accounting to the city of what had become of the former monastery property and the gifts of material that had been provided by the city. In this respect, too, Luther wanted to stop any ungrateful mouths at the very beginning.

4. SOCIAL LIFE, FESTIVALS, AND MUSIC

In the course of time the regular companions at Luther's table naturally changed, and many of them recorded conversations that took place there. One of the most reliable recorders and concerned friends was Anthony Lauterbach (1502–69). He was a deacon in Leisnig until 1536, and then became a deacon at the Wittenberg city church until assuming the parish and superintendency in Pirna in 1539. His notes frequently make possible an exact identification of the people and guests with whom Luther was speaking. From 1540 to 1542 John Mathesius (1504–65) returned to study in Wittenberg, after having been a schoolmaster in Joachimsthal. He assembled a vast collection of Luther's Table Talk. In a series of seventeen sermons, which he then published, he was one of the first to give a comprehensive life of Luther. One of the last recorders in 1545 and 1546 was the considerably younger John Aurifaber (1519–75), Luther's famulus in those years. He worked at editing Luther's works and letters, among them the German version of the Table Talk, which was not always exact but became very influential. One of the most highly regarded and stimulating conversational partners at Luther's table was the learned Austrian nobleman Wolfgang Schiefer (Severus) in 1539 and 1540. Naturally, Melanchthon, Bugenhagen, and Jonas were also principal participants in the conversations during their frequent visits in the Luther house.[1]

A conversation that took place in 1542, but in Cruciger's house, appears to have been fully recorded and therefore gives us an impression of the unstructured nature of these table conversations.[2] Melanchthon began with the weather. Then they discussed military and political news about Maurice of Saxony and Duke Henry of Brunswick. Because of a Hungarian who was to be ordained in Wittenberg, the conversation switched to the meaning of ordination. This caused Luther and Melanchthon to talk at length about the significance of the former canonical hours. Recent news that Deacon Fröschel shared brought the topic back to politics. Following that, Luther argued with Melanchthon about his exact age. Then Melanchthon changed the subject to the history of the Cistercian monastery of Doberlug. Luther concluded by commenting on the lies contained in the Koran.

One can assume from a reference that St. Nicholas Day was celebrated in the Luther household. At Christmas Luther spoke at table about his joy over the miraculous birth of Christ. Probably Christmas hymns were also sung.[3] The hymn "From Heaven on High I Come to You," which was written no later than 1535, is modeled after the nativity plays of the medieval church. "From Heaven the Angel Troop Came Near" of 1543 is also an exposition of the angels' Christmas message.[4] On 1 January they wished each other a mutually happy new year. On this occasion the children and servants received modest gifts. Their total value in 1539 was more than two taler, and Luther was regarded as generous. The giving of gifts was accompanied by exhortations to piety, faithfulness, and obedience.[5]

On the Thursday before Shrove Tuesday the millers' apprentices marched through the city, collecting sausages from burghers' houses for their evening festival. On Shrove Tuesday Luther also celebrated the so-called "kingdom," a long-discontinued custom that originated in the celebration of Epiphany, in which a king of the festival was chosen. It was celebrated in the Luther house with a festive dinner at which hymns were sung and texts from the Gospels, the catechism, and prayers were recited. Some of the family members were nervous about their recitation, which Luther compared to the way the ungodly would quake at the final judgment. At the kingdom celebrated in 1544, which lasted until midnight, Bugenhagen, Melanchthon, Rörer, Major, and the Torgau schoolmaster Marcus Crodel took part, among others. On this occasion Luther denied the rumor circulating in Wittenberg that he allowed his wife to influence his preaching. It was true that he endured her rule in the household, but in matters of conscience and exposition of the Scriptures he acknowledged no other authority than the Holy Spirit.[6] Another regular time for celebrations was 11 November, Luther's name day. In 1541 the two fat geese for the banquet were a gift from Jonas. The last celebration of this sort, in 1545, he concluded, after their happy fellowship, by earnestly admonishing his colleagues to remain faithful after his death, which was soon going to occur. He was more afraid of a departure from the faith in his own camp than he was of the war against the evangelicals that was already being anticipated.[7]

In Luther's house, as before, they liked to sing in several-part harmony, for example, on New Year's Day in 1537 after the meal. On this occasion Luther reflected on how many good composers had died during the previous year: Josquin de Prez, Pierre de La Rue, and Heinrich Finck. Duke Albrecht of Prussia exchanged songs and compositions with Luther.[8] During a visit to Torgau Luther heard the cantorei directed by John Walther with great appreciation. He did not have a very high regard of his own musical ability, but he would not do without it, for he regarded music as a special gift of God next in importance to theology. The youth should be trained in it, so that they would become "fine, skillful people." When motets were played in Luther's house on 17 December of the same year, it was again an indication of the future for him: "If our Lord God has given us such noble gifts in the outhouse of this life, what will there be in that life eternal where everything will be perfect and delightful?"[9]

Also from 1538 come Luther's two greatest encomiums to music. One is the preface to the *Symphoniae iucundae* published by the Wittenberg printer and composer George Rhau, fifty-two motets by various composers.[10] Luther did not feel competent to praise God's gift of music. He felt he was a prosaic and deficient eulogist. At the very beginning music was part of creation. Even the invisible air made a sound. David had marveled at the singing of the creatures, especially the birds. Nothing is like the human voice. It is proof of God's overflowing and incomprehensible generosity and wisdom. Not even philosophers are able to fathom it. Its value exceeds that of any art of speech. Next to the Word of God, music can most strongly affect human emotions. It is able to comfort the sad, terrify the happy, encourage the despairing, humble the proud, calm the passionate, or appease those who are full of hate. The Holy Spirit makes use of it, and one can cast out Satan with it. It is not by chance that the Word of God is associated with music in the Psalms and biblical hymns, for music belongs to the praise of God. It reaches its perfection in artistic music.

Luther was thinking of the polyphonic style of music, in which the tenor was accompanied by other voices. He compared it to a heavenly dance. Music was recommended to the youth as a salutary and joyous gift of creation that could aid them against evil desires and bad company. God should be recognized and praised in it. He warned against misusing it as did shameless poets like Lemnius, who satanically perverted it for their foolish love songs. For Luther, music was not an art that could be employed as one chose. As one of God's best gifts it had to be associated with God's relationship with man.

In 1538 Luther also wrote the rhymed *A Preface for All Good Hymnals* as a preface to John Walther's poem in praise of music.[11] The conventional heading indicated that "Dame Music" was speaking in the poem. Here we find essentially the same thoughts as in the other preface, although the poetic description of birdsongs, especially that of the nightingale, is much more attractive. The two prefaces indicate anew how much Luther was a man of the ear, who reacted especially sensitively to tones and words. This had to do with more than musicality; his feelings were directly affected by hearing. Music worked deep inside him: "If one sings diligently, the soul, which is located in the body, plays and derives special pleasure from it."[12]

Fraw Musica.

Fur allen freuden auff Erden /
Kan niemand kein feiner werden.
Denn die ich geb mit meim singen /
Vnd mit manchem süssen klingen.
Die kan nicht sein ein böser mut /
Wo da singen Gesellen gut.
Die bleibt kein zorn / zanck / has noch
Weichen mus alles hertzeleid. (neid
Geitz / sorg / vnd was sonst hart anleit.
Fert hin mit aller trawrigkeit.
Auch ist ein jeder des wol frey /
Das solche Freud kein sünde sey.
Sondern auch Gott viel bas gefelt /
Denn alle Freud der gantzen Welt.
Dem Teuffel sie sein werck zerstört /
Vnd verhindert viel böser Mörd.
Das zeugt Dauid / des Königs that /
Der dem Saul offt geweret hat /
Mit gutem süssen Harffenspiel /
Das er jnn grossen Mord nicht fiel.
A iij   Zum

Frau Musica
Luther's rhymed introduction to John Walther's poem, "Glory and Praise of the Laudable
Art of Music," Wittenberg, 1538

X

Luther's Congregation—
Wittenberg
(1537–46)

1. THE PREACHER AND PASTOR

Luther's relationships to the Wittenberg church centered primarily in his office of preacher (Plate XIII). In his sermons he made announcements to the congregation and took stands on situations within it. Luther substituted as pastor when Bugenhagen was absent. Bugenhagen was in Denmark introducing the Reformation from July 1537 until July 1539. Luther took over his weekday sermons and preached on Matthew 18–24, normally on Wednesdays. When Bugenhagen returned, Luther continued this series of sermons on Sundays from the fall of 1539 until September 1540. In the Saturday sermons he treated John 1–4.[1] With this series of sermons Luther completed his serial expositions of the Gospels. When Bugenhagen was in Schleswig-Holstein from February until May of 1542, and in Hildesheim and Brunswick-Wolfenbüttel from August to November, Luther again filled in for him as pastor, but this time he was unable to handle the weekday sermons for health reasons. In 1542 Luther preached only a single time in Wittenberg, and the next year he was in the pulpit only four times.[2] The number of Luther's Sunday and festival sermons also dropped in the other years. The most were in 1537 when there were fifty-two, and in 1538 when there were sixty-three. In 1539 he preached thirty-nine sermons; in 1540, thirty-three; and in 1541, only ten. In 1544 he was able to preach forty times, and in 1545 he delivered thirty-three sermons.[3]

Luther was able to speak about the Wittenberg congregation as "my congregation," and he felt accountable to God for it, since as a preacher he had the highest office committed to him. Because of this position, he would tolerate no abuses in his church. This had nothing to do with vanity or an authoritative attitude. He could also say: "You have enough thoughtful and excellent preachers," and he considered himself only one among the rest.[4] He wanted his sermons to be understandable by the simple people and the young. He loathed his colleagues who sought to impress the intellectuals. One had to speak to the people as simply as a mother speaks to her child while nursing it.[5] A preacher must be certain that his task is to proclaim the true doctrine and he

249

should conclude after no more than an hour—something Bugenhagen, especially, found difficult to do in Wittenberg—and even in his old age Luther was not loquacious in his sermons. In the pulpit one should speak thoughtfully. Preachers whose speech bubbled over as from a full barrel might impress some, but they did not instruct.[6] Luther conceived of the office of a preacher and pastor not as one of power but one of service, through which a congregation meets God and has God's Word brought to it. In order to remain independent in this task, Luther would take no money for doing so. The congregation as such was responsible for supporting the preacher, however.[7] True preaching always had to deal with faith and works. The sermon texts ensured that there would be different emphases. Luther understood that there had to be a rich variation in one's basic rhetorical style. In preparing a sermon, he would plan for it to flow in a particular direction, but in the pulpit he might then deviate completely from it. Afterward he would be upset, even if others praised the sermon. Possibly God had led the preacher in a different direction in such a case. In his preaching Luther does not seem to have tried to address specific listeners, but rather to address the subject: "When I climb into the pulpit I look at no one, but think of them as pure blocks who stand there before me, and I speak my Word of God to them."[8] This did not mean that his preaching was not addressed to the hearers. When it criticized social classes, economic practices, or sexual activities it immediately provoked a considerable negative reaction. A preacher could not let the desire to please the people divert him from his task, even if he were vilified as a blasphemer for it. He was not speaking as a mere man; God put his own Word in the preacher's mouth.[9]

Nevertheless, resignation became noticeable in the old preacher. In 1537 he began a sermon on Matt. 5:20ff. this way: "I have been preaching this gospel for nearly twenty-five years, and we see how we have improved. The older we get, the stingier; the longer we live, the more wicked." Similarly, a little later he began a sermon on the Good Samaritan: "We preach this gospel every year, because we cool down every year." There were few who improved because of preaching, but a preacher must not therefore let himself be deceived. The message of Christ is such a "glorious thing" that it must be repeated.[10] A preacher, like every Christian, is dependent upon prayer. In a *Trostzettel* (comforting pamphlet) Luther encouraged people to pray.[11] Even in the midst of despair, or because of the feeling of unworthiness, one should not be dissuaded from this "most noble, most difficult work on earth, the greatest service to God and the exercise of faith." One who is tempted should say, I am worthy, for God has created me, redeemed me, and given me a desire and love for the gospel: "God considers me worthy, and he has given me the holy office of the ministry." Then even the temptation becomes a way through which he is strengthened. All of this means that anyone who is so honored by God can confidently turn to God. A pastor's prayer from the lectures on Genesis has been widely circulated. Its beginning fittingly states Luther's understanding of the office: "Lord God, thou hast appointed me in the church as bishop and pastor. Thou seest how unfit I am to attend to such a great and difficult office, and if it had not been for thy help, I would long since have ruined everything. Therefore I call upon thee. . . ."[12]

Individual sermons by Luther were occasionally still printed if they had been delivered to princes or dealt with specific topics. There continued to be a demand for the postils. In 1540 Luther improved the winter portion, shortening it by removing particularly the outdated portions, and republished it. He declined, however, to write a new preface to a Latin edition of his postils in Strasbourg in 1539 because he was no longer accustomed to writing in Latin.[13] This was not entirely true, but in fact the old Luther now did write his works intended for publication predominately in German. He was dissatisfied with the summer portion of the postils that Stephan Roth had put together in 1526. This may have had less to do with their contents than with Luther's dislike of the Zwickau city clerk, which had developed in the meantime. In 1535 he wanted Caspar Cruciger to prepare a revision. At that time, before the Cordatus controversy, he had great confidence in his younger colleague as a "man of peace," and was thinking of entrusting the Wittenberg church to him after his death. Cruciger had proved himself by years of editing Luther's sermons. Today we can see that Luther himself had begun to revise the summer postil but soon turned it over to Cruciger. As a result of other obligations, Cruciger made slow progress, and the new version of the summer postil did not appear until 1544. As Roth had done earlier, Cruciger also had to assemble the sermon collection from printed sermons or from notes, primarily those taken by Rörer. He mainly used ones from the 1530s and thus offered an alternative to Roth's collection. He was freer in editing than Roth, and therefore in some places the result was more polished or toned down, but Luther took no objection to this.[14] In his preface Cruciger emphasized that he intended to present the true doctrine and the holy gospel as Luther had again rightly understood and taught it. Luther himself said in his preface that he was gratified that the Word of God had now been richly proffered in the German language. He referred principally to the catechisms as well as to the postils that expounded the sermon texts in a way the laity could also understand. They no longer contained the legendary material that was previously useless. The false prayerbooks had been replaced by pure prayers and good Christian hymns, primarily by the Psalter. It was even more important, however, that the German Bible was available to the laity as well. Now one had to use these gifts thankfully.[15]

A little later, at his own initiative, Veit Dietrich published another complete postil. It was composed principally of sermons that Luther had preached in his home between 1532 and 1534, and was intended to be read in the home. Dietrich also thought it might be used by uneducated country pastors. He had filled in gaps with other sermons by Luther, or, as he openly admitted, with his own expositions. Thus, for example, he himself wrote the twelve Lenten ser-

251

mons. In a short preface Luther acknowledged that these remaining "morsels, scraps, and crumbs" were being given to the people.[16] In 1543 he had already written a preface to a postil by the Nordhausen pastor Johann Spangenberg, which was divided into questions and answers and intended for use in instructing the youth. In this preface he used the remarkable term "mystery" to identify Christ, although sermons were constantly preached about him. In the meantime Luther had learned that one never understood this mystery, although many people believed that they could quickly deal with it. He therefore welcomed Spangenberg's work, but he criticized pastors who simply depended on such books and then repeated them like a parrot or jackdaw because they were too lazy to study the Bible themselves. Thus this preface ultimately became an appeal from him not to grow weary in studying and teaching the Bible: "Therefore, dear sirs and brothers, pastors and preachers, pray, read, study, be diligent! Truly in this evil, disgraceful time there is no time for lazing, snoring, and sleeping. Use the gifts that you have been given, and reveal the mystery of Christ."[17]

Aside from his preaching, there is relatively little known about Luther's activity in the parish and the congregation. As pastor he had to issue a summons to a husband who had left his wife. The man was threatened with divorce if he did not appear. In a similar case, Luther declared a divorce when the man did not appear.[18] Not as the representative of the pastor, but out of concern for the student Johannes Schneidewein who lived in his house, Luther sought to secure Schneidewein's mother's permission for him to marry the daughter of the goldsmith Christian Düring. When the mother had not replied to three letters, Luther regarded this as an improper refusal of parental permission and gave Schneidewein permission to marry without her blessing.[19] Once he criticized the bad singing in church: "If they want to growl and grumble, they should go to the cows and pigs, who will surely answer them. . . ." When things were no better the following Sunday, Luther left the service, whereupon Bugenhagen accused the congregation of having driven "our father Doctor Martinus" out of the church.[20]

In 1539 Luther complained to the burgomaster about the increasing commercial use of the churchyard, which was encroaching on the repose of the dead. He would permit the community brewing kettle, which had stood there for a long time, but it was intolerable that the carpenters had taken over the square so that people were unable to understand the sermon because of their sawing and hammering.[21]

According to existing regulations, the pastor was to have one of the three keys to the common chest. In Wittenberg, however, the administration of the chest was in the hands of representatives of the council and the pastor had no say over it. Luther attempted to correct this situation, but it is not known whether he had any success.[22]

Only occasionally do we see anything about Luther's performing pastoral care in the congregation; presumably, this was usually left to the deacons. One noteworthy example is his visit to the sick wife of Burgomaster Hohndorf, Hans Luther's godfather. There were other instances. In 1537 Hans Cranach, Lucas Cranach's son, died in Italy. Luther visited the parents. He tried to stop them from blaming themselves for letting their son go there. They should know that their obedient son was with God. When the wife of the jurist Bleikard Sindringer suddenly died during childbirth Luther comforted him. He himself was deeply affected by this death: "Our Lord God is the greatest adulterer [*Ehebrecher*, lit., marriage-breaker]."[23] Possibly these visits were not to ordinary members of the congregation, but to dignitaries or university colleagues with whom Luther was otherwise associated. As much as can be determined, however, he did not participate actively in such social relationships.[24] In 1538, as Bugenhagen's representative, Luther may have performed the wedding of the daughter of the printer Hans Lufft.[25] In 1542, his short *Comfort for Women Who Have Had a Miscarriage* grew out of his pastoral care.[26] For them, sorrow over a miscarriage was connected with concern for the salvation of the unbaptized child who had died. They should not be additionally burdened with this concern; they should be helped to accept their lot as God's good will. Instead, they should trust that their prayer for their child was a substitute for baptism.

2. THE CONGREGATION

The circumstances within the Wittenberg congregation are reflected primarily in the admonitions with which Luther concluded his sermons. For years the attitude of the congregation had been a problem for him in many points, and this did not leave his relationship to it unaffected.[1]

General Criticism of Morality and Moral Discipline

Weeks before the plague epidemic reached Wittenberg in the fall of 1538, Luther had to counter the fear of the disease. It was no different with Amsdorf in Magdeburg. Despite the evangelical preaching and the certainty of faith, the fear seemed greater than previously under Catholicism, which for Luther was a symptom that Christianity had grown old. When the first cases of illness appeared in Wittenberg he warned against panicking and fleeing, which would leave the sick to their fate. The plague should be accepted as God's chastisement. City authorities had to make sure that personnel were available in the hospital. Luther would confiscate the firewood and provisions of those who had fled and have them distributed to the poor. This time, too, as a pastor there was no question of his fleeing himself. He had no fear of death. Nevertheless, one should not thoughtlessly put himself in danger. The colleagues of one of the deacons who heard confessions of the sick wanted to isolate the man. Luther opposed this at the time. It was his experience that those who gave pastoral care (*Seelsorger*) were usually spared from sickness. Later he also thought it sensible to appoint only some of the clergy to care for the sick. He would have preferred to discontinue communion of the sick, because it was done when no congregation was assembled.[2] A year later the plague struck Wittenberg anew. Once again people fled from the disease, and family members abandoned the sick. In this situation Luther openly took into his house the children of the Münsterers, who had succumbed, and was then blamed for spreading the disease. Luther was correct in believing that this epidemic was a limited one. For him, the real plague was the destruction of social relationships caused by fear of the disease, and not even the evangelical preaching was effective against this.[3]

He constantly had to encourage parents to send their sons to school, because this above all was important for the future of the church. Here parents had a responsibility for the church. In inviting people to attend a school festival, Luther sought to encourage respect for education in general, a possession that could not be lost. To counteract the disdain for schooling that still existed, he encouraged support of the school, for pupils were the tiny plants from which the church grew.[4]

Infrequent mention is made about crime. At the beginning of 1538 a man who had killed a burgher was executed in Wittenberg. Luther thought the punishment justified, although the victim had been a godless man who despised the Word of God and thus had suffered a fate he deserved. Somewhat later a day laborer, whom Katy occasionally employed, got drunk, committed a murder, and fled. The episode was painful for Luther, because it was said in the city that the criminal was his servant.[5] Considerable attention was aroused in 1537 by the case of the master Paul Heintz, who was married to the widow of the physician Heinrich Stackmann. In order to obtain his stepson's inheritance, Heintz claimed the boy had died in 1535 during the plague and even staged his burial, although the boy was sequestered with a peasant in Jüterbog. Another dead child had been buried instead of the stepson. It was reported at first that there had been a dog in the coffin. Heintz himself admitted during the hearing that he had buried a dead toad as a magic spell to ward off the plague. Because he was able to dispel the suspicion that he was stealing the inheritance, the sentence was only that he be dismissed from the university. Luther was incensed that the punishment did not take into account the sacrilege of feigning a church burial. The jurists should know that "they were dealing with Luther in this case." He asked the elector to overrule the verdict; otherwise, he would denounce the jurists from the pulpit. He contradicted their opinion that he was bloodthirsty by pointing out that he had appealed for mercy for some pious offenders. He gave no credence to pious letters from the accused that he found in the pulpit. Heintz, however, appears to have had strong support in the city. Luther's protest came too late; the elector had already confirmed the verdict and moreover could only banish him from the territory.[6] In this unusual case, the jurists had had to render a judgment according to their own discretion, and they had imposed a mild punishment upon their colleague. Several factors show that Luther better understood the facts of the case than they did.

Magic was practiced in the world around Luther, and he himself had no doubt that there were evil machinations of this sort. More energetic action should be taken against magic than the jurists, in light of the uncertain evidence, were accustomed to taking. In 1538 Luther himself had to deal with a legal matter concerning a marriage in which a wife allegedly had tried to poison her husband. The evidence was that the man had vomited lizards. The woman was tortured but admitted nothing. In Luther's opinion, the devil would not let her speak. Even without her confession, an example should be made of her. Women who stole milk, butter, and eggs by magic tricks—as Luther, along with Bugenhagen, uncritically believed to be true—should be burned.[7] Luther was convinced that the devil and witches brought bad weather and other harmful things. He also thought it possible that incubi and succubi, who had sexual relationships with women or men, could exist. Nevertheless, he regarded stories of witches riding brooms as a deception of the devil. In 1541 Luther warned Melanchthon, who was then in Regensburg, about poisoners sent by the devil who were practicing their wiles everywhere.[8] Magic, witchcraft, and other occult practices occurred only on the periphery of Luther's experience. They were self-evidently rejected but hardly examined critically. It was impossible to do so because of Luther's concrete conception of how the devil worked. He therefore favored punishing witches. Consequently he did not oppose the excesses of witch-hunts.

Luther considered severe depressions, against which physicians were powerless, as *Anfechtungen* of the devil. In a unique way he attempted to help people who suffered from this sort of illness. Together with the chaplain and a few other men Luther sought them out, laid hands on them, and prayed with them, reminding the triune God of his promise to answer prayer. This was not an exorcism; the devil was not mentioned at all. Basically, many of Luther's visits of the sick were similar. He also recommended this procedure to other pastors.[9]

Normally, Luther's critique of morality was concerned with less serious, everyday abuses, and from it we learn something about the condition of the community. He vehemently attacked students who brought certain young women into disrepute through insulting letters. Either the young women should be confronted in private or they should be cited before the authorities. As before, Luther considered dances that were chaperoned by dependable men and women a suitable opportunity for the sexes to meet. Once he even thought about appearing there himself in order to keep the young men from dances that were too wild.[10] At Pentecost in 1543 Luther warned about prostitutes possibly infected with syphilis who were coming from other places. If necessary, the sovereign should step in and clean out the favored meeting places in the Speckwald and the fishermen's quarter outside the city. Students who could not live without prostitutes should leave Wittenberg: "Here there is a Christian church and school, where one should learn God's Word, virtue, and discipline." Luther would have preferred to see prostitutes who infected the youth executed. The young men should learn to control themselves.[11] Although Luther could indeed be this plain on questions of sexual morality, in general these issues did not occupy a prominent place in his exhortations.

The congregation did not like preachers making specific moral criticisms. In view of the external threat to the evangelicals in the fall of 1538, Luther called for repentance. This made an impression, of course, but it also met with resistance: "Now the snot-lords [*Rotzherrn,* instead of *Ratsherrn* (councilors)] will not permit someone to preach about how they booze, rob, steal, carouse, and feast." Nevertheless, a "preacher of light" cannot be silent about whore-mongering, greed, profiteering, lying, and deception. The criticism became specific; for example, when the bakers were accused of baking loaves of bread that were too small, they said he brought all trades into disrepute.[12] Luther saw the flooding of the Elbe at the beginning of April 1539 as God's justifiable punishment for godlessness, ingratitude, and greed, and not even prayer could prevent it.[13] The sermon on the epistle for Exaudi Sunday on 1 Pet. 4:7-11 gave an opportunity to speak against the German vice of drunkenness, which was widespread among all classes, even the princes, among both sexes, and among the children as well. "Germany is a land of pigs and filthy people who are destroying their body and life." Luther would say nothing at all against someone who, because of fatigue or sadness, drank a bit more than necessary to quench his thirst, but said the authorities and not just pastors had to take action against those who caroused all the time. Drunkenness was incompatible with the Christian life. One had to be sober in order to pray, and had to possess reason in order to serve God in one's daily life. Not even at baptisms, weddings, Christmas, or Pentecost were people moderate. Luther did not carry out his intention of writing another sermon against drunkenness, which he mentioned in this sermon, but the first sermon was published a few years later. Several times Luther reminded people about the elector's regulation against visiting taverns during the sermons. Whether he had any success in this is unknown.[14]

The complaints at that time about servants who refused to obey and neglected their duties led to the conclusion that there were tensions between the social classes. Luther even went so far as to claim: "Virtually all servants are thieves." If such dereliction was established, the person should not be permitted to receive the Lord's Supper nor be comforted in sickness. If people could not be made to obey, perhaps the Turks would restore order. It was probably no coincidence that Luther again took up this same theme a year later.[15]

The people probably became immune to the constant exhortations. An admonition to repent in the face of imminent foreign danger, which the elector issued in 1544, accomplished nothing. No consciousness of injustice existed in any social class. Luther sought to make it clear that people had to listen to him and the other pastors not because of their personal authority, but because they were Christ's servants who were responsible for their souls. A few months later he complained: "Our work is almost done, because the world is now completely holy; there are no more sinners." A preacher of the gospel has to deal with sinners and those who are contrite; there are no others to whom he can proclaim his message. Apparently the necessary insight was lacking among all classes. No one wanted criticism. The pastors therefore had to convince people that it was part of their responsibility. For the sake of love, they could not refrain from calling sins and sinners by name, and Luther himself did so in his final years.[16] Such statements reveal that there was something almost like a crisis of authority or a crisis of the ministry.

In addition to preaching, the clergy could have an effect on members of the congregation by hearing confessions. In 1538 it was noted that the student Valerius Glockner, the son of the burgomaster of Naumburg, lacked any fear of God or of men. It was discovered that he had made a pact with the devil. After the young man had truly repented for this step and confessed his sins, Luther, in the presence of the deacons and his teacher, absolved him by laying hands upon him in the sacristy and admonished him to live a pious, obedient life.[17] Obviously, a confessor was pledged to silence. This meant that even in a criminal case he could make no statement to the court. Luther gave an example of a mother who had confessed to him that she had murdered her child and whom he had absolved. In 1540 he opposed citing before the authorities an adulterer from Zeitz, who had confessed his sins and had repented in the church. The elector, however, decided appropriately that reconciliation with the church did not preclude temporal punishment.[18]

In an extreme case the clergy could exclude a member of the congregation from the Lord's Supper and from serving as a sponsor at baptisms. This was the form in which the ban or excommunication continued to be practiced. In 1538 Luther excluded the Wittenberg high bailiff (*Landvogt*), Hans von Metzsch, from the communion of the church for a second time, after Metzsch would not change his intolerable attitude against the clergy, the university, and the city magistracy, even after Luther's frequent admonitions. Metzsch, as much as can be ascertained, had not committed any tangible errors, but had simply obstructed the common work, which was essential. Luther would not accept his claim of repentance so long as no real reconciliation took place. Metzsch was later transferred and became bailiff in Colditz. Almost simultaneously Luther excommunicated the nobleman Heinrich Rieder for usury because he had loaned money at an interest rate of 30 percent.[19] Luther would allow a man who had committed manslaughter to receive the Lord's Supper again after he had made his peace with the church and had also paid the civil punishment.[20]

The application of the ban was not well liked in the congregation. Luther occasionally had to justify it in his sermons. The ban was not punishment for committing a crime, because the civil authorities were responsible for administering punishment; rather it was directed against moral failings, which of course were not punished publicly but were nevertheless intolerable within the community of the church. Feuding members of the congregation could be admitted to the Lord's Supper only after they were reconciled with one other. The Metzsch case had been handled this way. The congregation as such would have to agree with this practice, particularly because such a ban was not a permanent measure. Active repentance was a prerequisite for reinstatement in the fellowship of the church. Usurers, for example, had to repay their unjust profits, but if a pastor could not prove that a miser was guilty, he could not exclude him from the Lord's Supper. Luther was also aware that many people received the Lord's Supper without having confessed their sins. The presence of such hypocrites in the congregation had to be tolerated.[21] At that time, usurers, whoremongers, drunkards, and blasphemers also removed themselves by not taking part in the life of the church at all. In Wittenberg they were forbidden a Christian burial in which the clergy and the student choir participated.[22] Because of his own experience with the Catholic practice of excommunication, Luther did not employ the evangelical ban with pleasure. Nevertheless, for the sake of the church's credibility one could not dispense with it.[23]

The Chief Evil: Greed and Usury

Luther had earlier seen stinginess, greed, and usury, i.e., not using one's possessions in a Christian way, as one of the most acute problems in the evangelical congregations, and not least in Wittenberg. He seems to have applied the ban a number of times against usurers. The greed that was rampant in all classes of society, however, continued to be the moral failing that he attacked most extensively.[24]

In the fall of 1538 when prices rose because of a plague of mice, he considered it punishment for the action of the peasants and usurers who were driving up prices.[25] The following spring he again had to inveigh against the peasants who were holding back wheat and causing famine among the poor. The pious should pray that these robbers would either perish or be converted. In fact, the difficulties in providing food must have been considerable. Students left the city; the government failed to act. Together with the council and the custodians of the common chest, Luther as pastor allowed the schoolmasters, one of the deacons, and the sexton additional supplies of rye because of the increase in prices.[26] In April the famine grew worse. There was no more bread for sale. In one of his admonitions Luther held the city magistracy responsible, but then he had to be informed by Lucas Cranach, one of the burgomasters, that grain consigned to Wittenberg had been impounded in the Mark Brandenburg. By this time he no longer thought it was the peasants who were responsible for the emergency situation, but the nobility, e.g., the former high bailiff Hans von Metzsch, with their grain speculation. He personally begged a few scheffel of wheat for the poor from the *Schosser* (an administrative official). Effective help could be provided only by the territorial sovereign, and ultimately Luther appealed to him. His letter shows that he knew the complex causes of the famine: Wittenberg had to feed the surrounding countryside, and the castle mill could not operate because of high water in the Elbe. The elector should forbid the nobles to sell and export wheat. In a letter Luther accused the nobleman Friedrich Brandt of speculating in wheat, which Brandt denied. Luther does not appear to have been totally convinced by his excuses, however.[27] Self-evidently, Luther also criticized the wheat speculators from the pulpit and called them robbers and murderers. According to Prov. 19:17, a Christian who shows mercy to the poor does a good thing, for God will reward his alms with life eternal. This was not meant in the sense of merit. For Luther, the root of economic evil was unbelief.[28]

The experiences of 1529 led to Luther's basic *Admonition to the Clergy That They Preach against Usury*.[29] Usury had become so established a practice that Luther, after fifteen years, felt that it was necessary for pastors to take an unequivocal stand against it. First he commented on a noteworthy change in concepts. "Renting" was now understood as a profit-making business, but the word really meant only letting someone use property for a limited time. Pastors should speak against such a change in terminology. They should not let themselves be impressed by a claim that the practice was widespread. Renting for profit was nothing but forbidden usury. The objection that no one would lend anything to someone else if there were no profit involved did not impress Luther, and he certainly did not want such machinations to be continued. He also could not be convinced that thereby a charitable service was being performed. Many allegedly charitable acts did not in fact help one's fellow men, and therefore they were to be called sins. A miser's action has nothing to do with charity. At most Luther would allow compensation, the so-called *Schadewacht*, in case a lender suffered a loss when a debtor did not return money in a timely fashion, but this did not justify the current practice of profitable lending.

Luther did not at all dispute the objection that "there cannot be a world without usury," but said that was also true for other crimes, like adultery or theft. One had to try with weak human laws to control this evil to some extent. Historical examples showed that the state had always had to take action against usury. It was time to do so again, now that interest of 30 or 40 percent was being demanded in Saxony. The demand of lenders that contracts had to be fulfilled did not apply to their immoral agreements. As far as consequences for the church were concerned, usurers were to be excommunicated. Even more strongly than before, Luther attacked the usual commercial practice that permitted interest of no more than 6 percent. It was clear to him that there would be objections to pastors getting involved in economic life, but they could not deviate from the norm set by God. Luther, however, did not consistently apply his legal principle. A widow who was dependent on the return from her property had to be allowed "a little emergency usury" on the grounds of fairness, with which all law had to be practiced. Here the jurists should seek solutions. In general, however, usury tended to promote capital accumulation, in which an owner earned more than he needed.

A Christian had to give to someone who asked, without having an eye for profit, but not to swindlers and loafers, who were a virtual plague and who did not hesitate to steal. Acts of love were also limited by one's own needs. One had to give simply and could not exploit the recipient, as noble patrons often attempted to do with pastors. Supporting the needy was nothing other than service to other human beings, which was required of every Christian. In contrast, the fat misers and usurers were the most monstrous enemies of God and humankind. Even if the government did not take appropriate action against usurers, pastors and schoolmasters should consider them the most wicked of devils and monstrous werewolves, and thereby should proscribe them. Using one's possessions in an unchristian way was a normal practice, however. In an entire territory all the peasants who were truly Christian taken together would not equal the population of a single, small village. Few burgomasters and city councilors were disposed to the gospel, and it was no different among the nobility and government officials. From the attitude toward possessions it was obvious how Christianity was practiced in society. Therefore it was inevitable that relationships between society and pastors would be tense. The proverb "One should not let pastors become lords" betrayed this attitude, although no one could talk about poor Lazarus being a lord in the rich man's house. One should forestall the uncomfortable criticism of the pastors. This was nothing new. People of God had always been persecuted by their own people, and this was one of the *Anfechtungen* of the few pious people in the world. It was false to claim that business dealings with capital funds involved only those who had property and did not affect the poor. The price increases caused by these business practices naturally affected the poor most heavily. Because greedy people and usurers made themselves guilty of the "chief mortal sins" of murder and theft, they had to be excluded from the congregation by the pastors. Seldom was the anti-godly aspect of serving mammon and its destructive consequences for society diagnosed more sharply than here.

In a brief concluding comment, Luther indicated that he excluded the honest use of ground-rents from his criticism, something he had previously approved. He later held the same opinion. In contrast, he rejected starting a business with nothing but borrowed capital.[30]

In general, Luther's criticism of commercial behavior increased considerably, and it extended to all property-owning classes. This changed it into a diagnosis of a deep crisis within Christian society. One might qualify this by commenting that Luther had no understanding of economic necessity, were it not for his accurate observation of how society had been perverted by the desire for profit. Only the state could have dealt to any extent with the social obligations of property ownership and thus relieved the worst abuses, but even in Electoral Saxony this hardly happened. Luther did not speak as a lawgiver. Specific regulations were not the concern of pastors, but of jurists. He wanted only to emphasize the simple and clear Word of God that had been obscured and concealed by the personal interests of property holders. Thus his admonition was ultimately not just a suggestion that language and terms be purified as a necessary prerequisite for a specific reform. Even today, the radical nature of these late statements by Luther on economic questions has not yet been fully apprehended.

The problem with the food supplies was still tense in 1540. In January the Wittenberg theologians requested Elector Joachim II of Brandenburg to lift his prohibition on exporting grain from the Mark Brandenburg and permit the nobleman Dietrich von Rochow to deliver the relatively small amount of approximately five hundred scheffel of wheat to the community and the poor in Wittenberg.[31] The admonition of 1542, which Luther had printed because he was unable to preach, generally demanded an improvement. It was depressing for the old Luther that after thirty years of evangelical preaching conditions were worse than before. He advised the council to punish the offenders. His most specific demand had to do with putting a stop to greed. Although grain was cheap, the prices of bread in the city remained as high as during the period of high prices. Greed was also apparent among the traders and artisans, and they would not escape God's punishment for it.[32] When Spalatin asked for detailed charges against the grain speculators in 1544, Luther declined to provide them because of the fluctuating circumstances. One should generally orient one's self to the good of one's neighbor and the obligation to use one's possessions for the benefit of society.[33] He once appealed to the master of the hunt and officials to allow people to fell their own timber for construction. In this case, therefore, he preferred private industry to a government undertaking.[34]

His critique of commercial behavior had little success. In 1544 Luther had to protest several times against unjustified price increases. People accepted high prices. "Beer, wine, cloth, iron, spices are all of poor quality, wages are also increased, the world is full of thievery." Involved were "the big shots who wear the golden yellow necklaces and ride stallions." The noble officials also aided them, but the peasants did basically the same thing. The greatest evildoers, in their coats of marten pelts, went unpunished as usual. Luther did not fail to mention that there were also lazy parasites who were supported from the common charity. The government had to prohibit this just as it did economic crimes.[35]

When he dealt with the famine in Egypt in his lectures on Genesis (chap. 47) in 1545, Luther again had an occasion to make a statement about economic questions. Using barley in brewing beer was in itself an extravagance. The consumption of wine and luxury clothing took a great deal of money, as did the great commercial fairs in Frankfurt and Leipzig. "The usurers have certainly instituted a very harsh reformation," he commented sarcastically in view of the current shortage of money. He praised Joseph for his fair way of fixing prices. If necessary, the state would ultimately have to feed the poor. Luther naturally did not fail to mention expressly how support was provided for the priests in Egypt. Finally, he discussed the problem of taxes. He considered them too high and estimated them, presumably exaggerating, as half or a third of one's income. Possibly the state was even claiming everything. In this context he also complained: "The tax on beer has been in force for a long time, and there is no end to the skinning." Next to the increasing consumption of the family, taxes had to be added to the expenses caused by the usurers and by the cheating and thieving otherwise common in economic life. Luther considered the generally tight situation in regard to income as God's punishment for not properly supporting the clergy.[36]

The Crisis

In a sermon on 14 June 1545 Luther again complained passionately about stinginess in the evangelical church. Moreover, hatred and envy were widespread. "What are we preaching? It would be better if we would quit. . . . It seems that everything is lost." Instead of offering mutual help, people take from one another. Preaching did nothing to stop this. The pious who listened to God's Word were a small minority, and judgment was threatening the others. The hangman would have a lot to do in Wittenberg. "You are reviling my Word." In the graveyard and whorehouse that was the world, preaching could gather only the few who belonged to God.[37] If we take these statements seriously, and there is reason to do so for they are not isolated ones, the Wittenberg preacher must have been suffering a deep resignation because faith was not producing love for the neighbor. We should not let ourselves be deceived by the fact that Luther did not pick up this theme again in his next sermon, delivered five weeks later.

On 25 July Luther left on a several-week trip to Zeitz and Merseburg, during which he also came to Leipzig, Halle, and other places. Three days later he sent word to his wife that he did not want to come back to Wittenberg. "My heart has become cold, so that I do not like to be there any longer." Katy should sell the Wittenberg property. Luther would give the monastery back to the elector. He was thinking about living with Katy at the Zöllsdorf estate, assuming that the elector would continue his salary for at least one more year. It would also be better to move away because Katy would not have an easy time in Wittenberg after his death. Here is another hint that she was not exactly beloved in Wittenberg. The reasons for this abrupt decision are only partially apparent. Luther must have been aggravated because of the immoral dances and ridicule of God's Word against which no one took any action. "Only away and from this Sodom." There had also been trouble with one of Luther's maids, who had been seduced by a man who then abandoned her. During his trip Luther had received additional negative information about Wittenberg that ultimately provoked his harsh decision. "Consequently I am tired of this city and do not wish to return. May God help me with this." He would rather "eat the bread of a beggar than torture and upset my poor old age and final days with the filth at Wittenberg. . . ." Katy was to inform Melanchthon and Bugenhagen about his decision.[38]

As abruptly as Luther may finally have reached his decision, it did not come without warning. In 1530 he had already gone on strike and ceased preaching; no real resolution of his relationship to the Wittenberg congregation was subsequently achieved. In connection with the conflict with the jurists in 1544 he thought once more about leaving. Cruciger may have been right at the time in observing that this action was indeed touched off by an acute cause, but behind it was a deeply rooted resentment also directed against theologians. In addition, Luther may have occasionally felt discriminated against socially in the city.[39] But the real problem was surely the preacher's inability to create a Christian life style, which in large measure corresponded to the failure to realize his theological program.

As might have been expected, the news about Luther's decision exploded in Wittenberg like a bomb. The university at once appealed to the elector to persuade Luther to stay. If Luther was dissatisfied "with anyone's life or teaching in this university or city," they would help in correcting this and also in improving discipline among the young people. Melanchthon, and probably also Bugenhagen and George Major, went immediately to the court in Torgau, and from there they wanted to continue on and locate Luther himself in order to convince him to return. Melanchthon did not find the elector in Torgau; all he could do was inform Chancellor Brück. Melanchthon thought Luther's reasons were misplaced. Perhaps he supposed that the differences that had arisen between the two of them were the real cause of his irritation; however, there is no other evidence for this. Brück instantly saw that his departure from Wittenberg could not take place so quickly because there would not immediately be buyers—here we see the chancellor's reservations about Katy's purchases—for the "expensive houses and property." But it was also instantly clear to him how damaging the rumors would be of Luther's intended departure, which were already beginning to spread. Moreover, without Luther it might also be impossible to keep Melanchthon in Wittenberg. Thereupon the elector delegated his personal physician, Matthew Ratzeberger, to change Luther's mind. He was discretely to order Melanchthon, who meanwhile had left to follow Luther, to come to Torgau to meet with the elector, although Luther was not to know of this. Nicholas von Amsdorf in Zeitz was to influence Luther to return to Wittenberg. Luther himself received a letter from the elector brought by Ratzeberger. In it Luther was gently reproved for not informing his sovereign about the trip to Zeitz, which was not without its dangers. The elector was also troubled about Luther's aggravations in Wittenberg. If he had been notified of them he would have taken remedial measures. The rumors of Luther's departure from Wittenberg could only bring joy to the Catholic enemies. Ratzeberger's real task was to persuade Luther to meet with the elector. This meeting took place on 17 August in Torgau. Almost nothing is known about what went on, but Luther returned to Wittenberg the next day.[40]

Luther resumed his preaching. His moral admonitions were no less specific than before. They were again directed first of all against greed, then against immorality or drunkenness, but he apparently refrained from emphasizing the sort of criticism that turned into resignation.[41] His annoyance seems to have continued, although he may not have displayed it openly. The elector did indeed try to deal with Luther's complaints by issuing an ordinance at the end of 1545—planned already in 1544—against extravagance at weddings and baptisms, excesses at dances, and crying out in the streets in Wittenberg. The elector had already made promises of this sort to Luther in Torgau in August. Luther doubted that the government would take serious enforcement measures, and he did not participate in drafting the ordinance. Nevertheless, he stated again: "If they do not do something reasonable, he will leave; you can count on it."[42] Thus a complete settlement of the relationship between Luther and his city was never achieved. To be sure, it was always clear to him that there could never be a sinless community on earth, but he expected a Christian city to take more energetic action against abuses than it actually did. This proved to be difficult in the context of a people's church (*Volkskirche*). The situations in Wittenberg were definitely not a special case, but rather typical. We also cannot pass off the Wittenberg preacher's sufferings over this as the grumpiness of an old man. Evangelical preaching certainly was not without results, but there were limits in changing the social conditions of broad classes in a Christian way because of egoism, self-interest, and human weakness. The evangelical church has also had to deal with this problem since Luther. Either the church includes the whole society and must therefore tolerate its contradictions and deficiencies, or it must withdraw into being only a voluntary church. There were good reasons to maintain the *Volkskirche*. It was then inevitable, however, that it would have to confront the difficulties that went along with this. Luther did not consider possible differentiations within the congregation.

Luther did not become absorbed in bitter resignation against Wittenberg. Even in August 1545 he published a woodcut of the city of Wittenberg with a poem he had written.[43] It first related how God always chose the lowly. Tiny Jerusalem had become a world city that was to encompass all people. Wittenberg was a part of Jerusalem. The poor, small city had become famous "by God's Word that streams from it and creates many souls for heaven." Luther had no doubt about the significance of the message that went out from Wittenberg or of its claim. This was not a chauvinistic local patriotism. The city's status was not automatically assured. His concluding wish stated:

> God grant she may be thankful
> And forever more be so;
> Thus do abundant for her name,
> So blest she may become. Amen.

He meant by this "a city set on a hill," recognizable to all.

XI

Luther's Church—
Electoral Saxony
(1537–46)

1. THE RELATIONSHIP TO ELECTORAL
SAXON SOCIETY

The relationship between Luther and Elector John Frederick continued to be an enduring and good one. When it seemed desirable to the elector and Luther's health permitted, he was, as before, summoned, sometimes with Melanchthon, to conferences at the court, primarily to Torgau.[1] In addition, the two met together when the elector was residing in Wittenberg. They also carried on an active correspondence, which frequently also involved Luther's colleagues. The sovereign was Luther's most frequent correspondent, which is explained not only by the fact that, naturally, their correspondence has been particularly well preserved. Although the initiative in their personal contacts was almost always on the side of the elector, Luther did write to him whenever he thought it necessary. The scope of their relationship was extraordinarily broad. It ranged from great political considerations of church affairs to requests concerning individual cases. Each partner shared with the other what seemed important to him. Their common interests far exceeded their occasional differences of opinion. Each partner respected the other and knew that he was dependent on the other. From the start, neither the sovereign nor the theologian claimed a predominant role. The elector maintained his independent decisions in the light of higher political considerations, and Luther was in no way a docile tool who could automatically be assumed to support the politics of Electoral Saxony. To be sure, sometimes there were boundaries between state and political interests and those of the church and theology, but the men attempted to deal with these needs and demands as much as possible. Luther once stated the relationship generally: "If the government tolerates me as a teacher of the Word, I will honor it and recognize it as my ruler with all respect."[2]

John Frederick frequently let Luther know personally of his generous solicitude concerning his salary, supplying additional financial and other support or medical treatment. Nevertheless, the difference in status and two decades in

The Baptism of Christ with Luther and the family of Elector John Frederick as observers, the city of Wittenberg in the background

Woodcut by Jacob Lucius, 1556/58

age did not permit a very intimate relationship between the two. It was an exception for them to have a relaxed conversation at table about comets, history, and theology in 1538 when Luther made an unannounced visit to Torgau. Afterward, John Frederick took Luther to visit his wife, who was bedridden after giving birth, and then personally showed him the new construction in the Torgau castle.[3] Luther admired John Frederick's honesty and steadfastness, but he hoped that the prince would take forceful action against public officials.[4] In *Against Hanswurst*, Luther, responding to the accusations of Henry of Brunswick, resolutely defended the way his sovereign discharged his duties and lived his life, as well as his piety.[5] The fact that John Frederick himself encouraged drunkenness at the court was not concealed. Luther and Melanchthon learned of this during their visits in Torgau. Luther's efforts to encourage moderation had no results. He openly criticized the bad example given by the court. The campaign against widespread drunkenness had to begin with the court. In a sermon delivered in 1544 before the elector in the Wittenberg castle, Luther sharply attacked the morality prevailing at court.[6]

The first new evangelical church built was the castle church in Torgau. It is a rectangular hall (*Saalbau*) with two galleries. A free-standing altar is at the front; the pulpit is located on the side wall of the nave (Plate XIV). In deliberate contrast to the Catholic practice, it was dedicated in 1544 with a sermon by Luther and prayers of the congregations. A bronze tablet from 1545 commemorates this special event of the first dedication of an evangelical church. Luther made it clear that evangelical worship is not bound to holy spaces, times, or persons, although for practical reasons certain conventions may be followed. The castle church was also not a special place. Before God, the class distinctions that are necessary in the world count for nothing. He can humble the mighty and raise up the lowly. A higher rank obligates a person to serve those below him. No one has reason to be arrogant or to hold others in contempt. This is true for lords as well as servants. The most important example of condescension and humiliation is Christ himself. Luther accepted the existing social order and yet relativized it.[7] Such a sermon that criticized social classes was not an isolated occurrence. In 1537 Luther had also been very clear in a Saturday sermon: "If you are a nobleman, take no pride in your nobility and do not plague your peasants and treat them like dogs. Do not think you are better before God because of your nobility than a preacher, burgher, or peasant, for now all other people stink in comparison to the nobility. God gave you your nobility not so that you might be arrogant, but only so that you might use it for good. But the world cannot tolerate this; it must abuse this gift. A nobleman is a tormenter and pest of the peasants, a rich burgher bleeds the poor, and so do the peasants who also oppress and shave the burghers. This is what people in all classes are now doing. . . ."[8]

Luther usually criticized the other classes from his own standpoint of preacher, theologian, and churchman, and from the interests associated with these roles. Relatively infrequently did he say anything against other specific abuses, as, for example, the so-called "riding in" of the nobility, in which a noble would take up residence with his retinue in an inn at the expense of a debtor or guarantor until he paid. Luther was opposed to this ruinous collection practice, but he did not promise to write against it himself; instead, he demanded intervention by the government.[9] Again and again encroachments on the office of the ministry by the government, the nobility, and also by village judges had to be hindered. These officials, in order to avoid uncomfortable criticism, attempted to prescribe how pastors should preach. This combination of the spiritual and secular office could only be destructive and could not be accepted. Such a necessary demarcation could easily be misinterpreted as an aversion to the jurists or the nobility.[10] It was not easy to obtain a hearing for ecclesiastical interests at court. One could not appear like a meek Christ, but rather had to call attention to himself in an unpleasant way by complaining loudly, like a Moses with his horns. Luther therefore advised pastors to appeal to the court about injustices they had suffered. He publicly told the elector that he thought he was personally pious and honorable, but that government officials did whatever they pleased. Luther accepted the unpleasant attention that such sermons caused. He was critical of Spalatin for not defending the interests of his pastors more vigorously, even before the elector. It had to be made clear to the nobility that, especially if they paid poorly, they would not get sincere pastors like Luther or Melanchthon. The elector also had to accept that alongside the few genuinely gifted noble officials there were many *Füllsteine* (filling stones).[11]

Luther generally presented the relationship of the nobility and the city councilors to the church as a tense one. One of the most significant points of friction was the compensation of pastors, for which the nobility and cities were responsible. It was usually paltry and was reduced at every opportunity. In Electoral Saxony they achieved no satisfactory overall solutions that would have eliminated this problem. Often the taxes due the church were not paid. Luther interpreted this as ingratitude for the gospel. It was a special work of the Holy Spirit that the sovereign was responsible for maintaining the church, for all other groups of people were robbers. Pastors were frequently not even in a position to buy a shirt for their children. Not only did the nobility enrich themselves with monastery properties, but they also seized the pastors' properties on which the clergy were dependent. Contrary to the New Testament's admonition, they did not regard the servants of the church as worthy of their hire. In view of the widespread ingratitude, they could only do their duty and hope that God would be their reward.[12]

Some officials in fact mistreated the pastors. The communities of Plötzky and Pretzin, for example, complained that the governor Sigismund Pflug, contrary to existing agreements, withheld from their pastor a residence, salary, and payments in kind in the monastery there. The pastor had to live in a cabin "where a swineherd would hardly dwell." The members of the congregation were in no position to help the pastor, and they feared that they might lose him. Luther and Bugenhagen sent these complaints to the elector, who then took measures to remedy the situation. Pflug was not an isolated instance. Even the court marshal Asmus Spiegel, with whom Luther had a friendly relationship, had to be admonished not to burden the pastor in Gruna with taxes.[13] In Luther's eyes, the secular officeholders, without exception, were opponents of God, the church, and the pastors. Keeping pastors short of money and criticizing them brought public officials respect. Only with difficulty could the public officials be forced to change. The surprising exception was the elector, but things were different at court. There was great difficulty in convincing the officials in the country to deliver what the elector had provided. For Luther, the real help was in prayer; other means, like counsels and relationships, all too frequently proved deceptive.[14] Luther thought the rule of the powerful nobles was scarcely less severe than the government of the Turks. If the elector were to die, the schools and parishes would need to fear these nobles.[15] It may have been an exception when once in 1544 Luther defended dispersing church properties among the nobles.[16] At that time tensions between the secular and ecclesiastical organizations were immense. The sovereign seemed to be the only one concerned about the interests of the church, but this did not result in any change in the actions of the lesser officials. Under these circumstances the burden of the church was not easy to bear.

Sometimes Luther was also induced to appeal to the elector in matters for which he was not officially responsible. In 1537 the relatives of the Zwickau counterfeiter Wolf Schalreuter asked him to advocate a commutation of his sentence of life imprisonment. Wisened by bad experiences, Luther formulated his request cautiously, but it produced no results.[17] In 1528 Heinrich von Queiss attempted to defend his rights in a feud with the bishop of Lebus, but without success. Until 1540, in contrast to other nobles involved, he had not yet achieved a settlement. At that time Luther interceded for Queiss, who by then was well up in years, asking that he be permitted to settle in Herzberg. The elector, however, did not want to be bothered with this matter.[18] Luther supported the appeal of a few nobles for the release of Pankraz von Pöllnitz, who had been imprisoned for violating the electoral hunting laws, because he thought the imprisonment was a hasty reaction by the officials, which was causing more damage instead of serving the cause of justice.[19] Luther was in somewhat of a quandary in 1544 because of the case of Andreas Gutjahr, who was accused of counterfeiting. Gutjahr's wife appealed to Luther, to whom she was related. He had always advocated severe punishment for all economic crimes, however, and thus could not now act differently. Nevertheless, it appears that Gutjahr, unlike his accomplice, was not executed.[20] Luther's appeals concerning punishment for crimes were apparently not especially effective. Nevertheless, they indicate something about his sense of justice.

In addition to criminal cases, Luther was also active in financial emergencies. Together with Jonas and Spalatin he appealed to the *Landrentmeister* Hans von Taubenheim to support the family of an electoral fisherman who had died. At the request of King Christian III of Denmark he sought to help a creditor obtain a judgment against his slow debtors. Luther also assisted a young noble whose hereditary property, on which he was dependent, had been taken by the electoral *Schosser* (administrator).[21] The wife of the physician Basilius Axt had to be helped to get her inheritance, which had been withheld from her by her brother because as a former nun she was not entitled to inherit. The widowed Margaret von Staupitz stubbornly sued for her parents' estate. Luther supported her in this out of gratitude to her brother-in-law John von Staupitz, "my father in this (evangelical) doctrine," who had given him birth in Christ.[22] The aged physician Peter Schör had lost his position in Halberstadt because of his support of the Reformation and was in great need. Luther and some of his colleagues sought to convert his temporary support from the elector into a lifelong one, and also to ensure the later livelihood of the family. After sixteen years of service, the schoolmaster Bernhard Zettler had become unable to discharge his duties because of failing eyesight, but he was still helpful in preparing people for ordination examinations. Luther and Bugenhagen finally obtained a permanent allowance for him.[23] An exquisite glimpse into Luther's motivation for this sort of social involvement is offered by his letter of thanks to Anton Unruhe, the judge in Torgau, after Unruhe on his own initiative had prevented a poor woman from having what was hers taken by the "noble big shots": "You know that Doctor Martinus is not only a theologian and a defender of faith alone, but also a supporter of the rights of poor people who flee to him from all places and points in order to obtain from him help and assistance from the authorities, so that he would have enough to do even if no other work were piled on his shoulders. But Doctor Martinus likes to serve the poor, as you, too, are accustomed to doing. . . ." That the judge had also remembered Luther with a vat of Torgau beer was more than enough.[24]

2. PASTORS AND CONGREGATIONS

Luther's chief concern was for the pastors. This was not just because of his interests as a professor of theology and a preacher. Pastors were the most important mediators of God's Word; if they did not do their job, the church would be in danger. But the professional needs of the pastors, viz., compensation and authority, were frequently ill provided. The church's income from its own property and from gifts had decreased even more sharply than the number of clergy. The church was thereby being threatened with ruin. Pastors and their families often suffered want. If they had debts they were in no position to repay them.[1]

Not only was there a lack of money, but also of suitable and qualified theological candidates. Despite the large number of students, the university at Wittenberg could not supply the need, particularly because many of the young theologians were not seeking positions in Electoral Saxony. Moreover, the inadequate pay discouraged people from entering the ministerial profession. Here there was a vicious circle: Only an improvement in pastors' compensation could bring about a positive change in the situation in the congregations, but pastors were already having a difficult time there. Luther was clearly acquainted with the lack of personnel, because congregations frequently appealed to the Wittenberg theology professor when a pastoral position had to be filled.[2] At this time the organization of the church administration was not yet developed, so he had to assume this responsibility. Several times Luther advocated making schoolmasters pastors and preachers, even superintendents. This was not strictly a solution born of necessity. The schoolmasters possessed professional experience that was also valuable for the tasks of preaching and teaching. Even in the pre-Reformation period they had performed a respectable service for the church.[3]

Providing pastors and schoolmasters was not a routine matter. Special circumstances of the applicants and the congregations often had to be considered. For instance, a pastor who had harassed his peasants, and who also could not farm successfully himself, had to be transferred. Possibly he was a drinker. Luther did not conceal these problems when he recommended him to Gabriel Zwilling in Torgau.[4] Because of the need to support his family, a position had to be found quickly for John Cellarius, a preacher coming to Saxony from Frankfurt am Main. He then became pastor and superintendent in Dresden.[5] Luther had intended Wolfgang Wagner, the deacon from Jessen, for the parish of Seyda. His pastor had sent him to Wittenberg with a letter of recommendation for this purpose. The letter also stated that at first Wagner had been theologically indolent. He had improved but still he needed additional stimulus. Nevertheless, he was more qualified than many other pastors in Saxony.[6] This also sheds light on the situation in the pastorate. Stephan Agricola, pastor in Hof, a city in Brandenburg-Ansbach, encountered difficulties because of his publicly displayed sympathies for Electoral Saxony and therefore was seeking a position in the electorate. Luther believed that a Christian had to endure such suffering, however, and did not support his request.[7]

When George Spenlein, the former Wittenberg Augustinian, was to take over the parish of Gräfenhainichen, Luther asked that some pieces of property and rentals that had been confiscated for the common chest be returned to the pastor's use, as they originally had been, because the pastor's salary there was not high.[8] Spenlein's transfer was planned because he had been in conflict with his previous congregation of Creuzburg and with the local bailiff over his abusive sermons, which were, in fact, excessively crude. The visitors, however, found nothing amiss in the way he conducted his office. Luther thus wanted to keep Spenlein in Creuzburg. He therefore energetically warned bailiff and council not to attack their pastor, for thereby they would be assailing Christ himself, "the supreme pastor and bishop." Those responsible for this would lose their salvation and the church would become devastated. Luther was very clear in this letter, which aroused interest beyond Electoral Saxony: "You are not lords over the parishes and the ministry, did not create them, but God's Son alone . . . , and should neither control nor instruct them, also not restrain them from punishing." Bailiff and council did not have the right to attack the pastor for serving another lord. This was not Luther's admonition, but God's. If the Creuzburgers did not follow it, they would thereby be excommunicating themselves. They should therefore reach an agreement with their pastor. The bailiff, George von Harstall, was deeply affected by this and protested that he was thoroughly in favor of moral criticism, but the pastor ought to moderate his language and his personal attacks. Luther then turned the matter over to Justus Menius, the assigned visitor, and presumably he also admonished Spenlein personally.[9]

In 1541 Pastor Philipp Schmidt, who had caused controversy in his congregation of Kahla, was dismissed by the elector. Luther was able at first only to keep him from being expelled from the territory. Later the elector agreed to reinstate him, but Schmidt then found a position at the Dominican church in Erfurt.[10] In 1543 the pastor of Ernstroda was in dire straits because of his dismissal by Superintendent Myconius, and he therefore appealed to Luther. Luther did not question the dismissal, but sent the pastor back to Myconius so that he might be helped in some way. He probably interceded for him again two years later.[11] Caspar Schaller, whom Luther had recommended to Colditz as a schoolmaster, must have been in acute need, for initially he needed an advance on his salary for clothing and household furnishings.[12] Luther may have written some recommendations only to dispense with the petitioners. Occasionally he also said this clearly.[13]

The elector was usually the only official able to give assistance in financial emergencies. For example, he was to aid a former monk from the Lichtenburg monastery in getting an increase in his salary so that the man, now a poor pastor, could leave something behind for his family. The person responsible in this case was Wolfgang Reissenbusch, the preceptor of the monastery. After some persistence, Luther appears to have achieved his goal. He was also able to get a salary for Wolfgang Wagner, mentioned above.[14] Occasionally compensation for pastors was due because of the expropriation of church property, and Luther had to complain to the elector anew, although not always successfully.[15] It was especially critical when a pastor became unable to work, because there was not yet any provision for such cases. One pastor, for example, became mentally ill, in Luther's opinion because of poverty. The suffering of his family with its six children was great. Here one could only appeal to the mercy of the elector, who then provided minimal support. Unfortunate people, like a former priest who was handicapped by poor eyesight and also had a sick wife, had to be cared for in some way, and therefore Chancellor Brück and Luther appealed jointly on his behalf.[16] In a relatively orderly procedure, the Wittenberger Johannes Mantel, who was ill, was allowed alms from a Gotha benefice, from which Rörer also received an allowance. But after the reform of church property, continued payments had to be approved once again. Luther later also interceded for the support of Mantel's widow.[17]

Johannes Weiss, the Eisenach deacon, received a salary that as such was not too small, but he was unable to support his nine-member family on it. In 1540 Luther had already supported a request for an increase, but it is not known if it was granted. Three years later, however, he rejected new attempts from Weiss because he had so many petitions to write. If they were repeatedly rejected at court, there would be nothing more that could be done in the future, especially because Luther frequently had not prevailed with his petitions. In his view, the climate had worsened at court, because the number of "robbers" there had increased and the elector himself could not oversee all their intrigues.[18] The attempt of a family from Salzungen permanently to receive the income from a benefice originally given by them was only reluctantly supported by Luther, and then without result.[19]

Luther was not concerned only about pastors' outward needs. Some of them used him as a pastoral counselor (*Seelsorger*). For example, he invited Bernhard von Dölen, who suffered from inner *Anfechtungen,* to come to Wittenberg, because he was unable to get a picture of his condition from afar. He comforted Cordatus with a letter.[20] Frederick Myconius in Gotha was seriously threatened by tuberculosis. Luther told him that as a Christian he already had part in the resurrection; now only the curtain needed to be drawn away. Luther himself earnestly hoped that he would die before Myconius and not be left behind by him. In 1544 he admonished Myconius, who had difficulty in speaking, to take care of himself. The church depended on "veteran Christian soldiers" like the Gotha superintendent. For Luther, all men were sick unto death, but this fate had been transcended by the resurrection. Therefore he could react imperturbably to acute illness. As far as the stones that were threatening the Altenburg pastor Eberhard Brisger were concerned, Luther was himself an expert. He did not minimize the danger that the physicians had diagnosed, but his advice was still: "You must pray an Our Father against all this." Not infrequently, a long period of time was granted to someone threatened by death.[21]

Luther had to deal not only with the elector and his officials on behalf of pastors, but frequently also directly with the congregations. In addition, other problems from the congregations were brought to him. He asked the council of Torgau to provide a lot on which Gabriel Zwilling, the local pastor, could build a house. It was to be used for the care of old people and widows.[22]

Luther sharply reprimanded the Niemegk schoolmaster for his intrigues against Cordatus, the pastor there. This sort of disobedience should not be tolerated. The schoolmaster had probably criticized the pastor's drinking.[23] As had already been seen many times, the pastors easily offended people with their criticisms of immorality. This was the experience of Johannes Reimann in Werdau (Vogtland). Luther first encouraged him to do his duty. At the request of the elector, the congregation gathered its complaints about Reimann's confused sermons, which contained wild accusations. Luther reacted to this quite indignantly. Next to Zwickau, there was no city that treated its pastors as badly as Werdau. The congregation did not have a good reputation. Spalatin, the visitor, should quiet it, or else it should present a proper complaint about its pastor. Otherwise, Luther would see to it that there would be an end to the unrest. He was also considering removing Reimann and then not providing a successor. The elector, too, favored his removal, but without the consequences threatened by Luther. Luther himself supported Reimann. He should not leave until he had a new parish, and until then he should continue to speak against immorality. Reimann then received the parish of Grossenhain near Dresden but was removed from it in 1543 because of his preaching style. Thus, in this case, Luther had not made an objective decision. But at the time he had the impression that cities and towns wanted arbitrarily to remove their pastors and control them, although they would not even pay them. He would not allow this.[24] Luther already knew from his own experiences in Wittenberg how unpopular it was for a pastor to criticize morals, but he was also not unaware that occasionally pastors acted unskillfully in doing so. In such cases the members of the congregation should also be prepared to accept it, arrange a discussion to clarify the matter, or bring the matter before the superintendent. It was often the case that certain congregational members could not get along with any pastor. They deserved to be excommunicated. In no case should a deserving pastor be harassed on their account. It was part of a pastor's office to work for the improvement of life. Anyone unwilling to accept this should be left to his own devices.[25]

Pastors had to be protected against congregations that were too demanding. The peasants in the village of Lissen did not want Pastor Conrad Claudius because of his weak voice, although he was otherwise fully qualified. Luther put it to the elector in this way: "If the peasants are to choose as they please, asking that he [the pastor] be learned, pious, handsome, young, eloquent, perhaps also does not shout, eat and drink, says what people like to hear, carouses and plays with them, etc., then we will never be able to get any pastor in this way."[26] From the very outset, it did not prove simple to bring a congregation's wishes into line with a person's qualifications in selecting a pastor. When the pastor in Barby had difficulties in his congregation, Luther was prepared to remove him, but he preferred to have him stay with "the little flock" who liked him and not bother with the others.[27]

In 1539 the Torgau council disputed the right of a pastor's widow to receive his estate because according to city law it belonged to his relatives. But Luther protested that the property of pastors should be treated no differently than that of other burghers, since pastors now had civil rights. Presumably, he wanted to assure the support of the widow. He sought to obtain increased brewing rights for Pastor Gabriel Zwilling. Zwilling could increase his income by selling beer. Incidentally, he once criticized the creation of the Torgau taproom, because it promoted drunkenness and other vices. Luther considered the expropriation of a garden, which was needed by the city in order to enlarge the hospital cemetery, as proper, so long as the owners were compensated.[28]

In 1537 Luther instructed the Coburg pastor, Johannes Langer, to reconcile two feuding noblewomen. In the controversy one of the women had appealed to Langer's accusations of the other. It was therefore a matter for the pastor to eliminate this discord in the world.[29] Two years later serious accusations were raised against the other Coburg pastor, Johannes Fesel. A newborn infant had been drowned. Fesel's maid was allegedly the mother, and he himself the father. The investigation before the council, which was initiated by the electoral conservator (*Pfleger*) Hans Schott, showed that the charges could not be substantiated, but this did not adequately satisfy Fesel. Luther had Fesel come to Wittenberg and subsequently determined that the incident was an evil intrigue by Schott, who did not enjoy a particularly good reputation and from whom the city should clearly distance itself. Luther announced that he would report this to the elector. Schott explained to Luther that he had proceeded only on the basis of suspicion after Pastor Langer had first spoken about the child's murder from the pulpit. The burgomaster and council defended themselves in a similar fashion, although they presented Fesel as quarrelsome. There is no indication of regret, however, that the way the case was handled seriously injured the pastor. Because of Luther's excessive workload, the subsequent reply to the council was written by Melanchthon. He would have preferred for Fesel not to have brought the matter to Luther, but the Coburgers also should have spared Luther their sharp letter, for he had enough "trouble, care, work, and *Anfechtung*" in his high office. Melanchthon assumed that the Coburgers knew how to treat the servants of the church.[30] Luther himself would hardly have been satisfied with such a solicitous resolution of the case.

The elderly Spalatin increasingly got into difficulty with the Altenburg council. The council complained to Luther in 1542 that Spalatin had personally attacked members of the council, and that they had stopped receiving the Lord's Supper because of this. Spalatin wanted the council to compel them to commune. Until then the Wittenbergers had assured Spalatin of their support, but at this point even Luther recognized that he was responsible for the tensions. Luther advised the council to have patience with the old man until he had an opportunity to speak with him personally, for Luther did not want to reprimand him in a letter. It appears that the matter was then resolved, but a few months later Luther had to admonish Spalatin to be reconciled with the Alten-burg schoolmaster. The Altenburg preacher, Eberhard Brisger, was asked to be patient with his old colleague, who could no longer be changed.[31] Spalatin dedicated to Luther a collection of words of comfort from the tradition of the church for those in need, and Luther wrote a preface for it in 1544.[32] In the same year Spalatin himself fell into a deep depression. He had allowed a pastor to marry the stepmother of his deceased wife. Luther, in contrast, considered this an incestuous marriage that had to be dissolved. Spalatin despaired because of his improper decision. Luther sought to help him with one of his great letters of comfort. Although Spalatin may have failed seriously, forgive-ness would not therefore be withheld from him. It was precisely as a sinner that he could appeal to the Savior. Luther extended a hand to him in brotherly fashion to lift him up. Spalatin should know that he was being supported in his need. Luther's greatest thanks would be for Spalatin to accept the forgiveness declared to him. The entire letter is permeated with solidarity with his afflicted friend.[33] Spalatin died at the beginning of 1545. Luther informed the elector that it would not be easy to find a suitable successor for the important Alten-burg position. Too many competent people had had to be sent to other places, even as far away as Hungary. With both regret and pride he said: "Wittenberg certainly cannot furnish pastors for the whole world. But it is doing more for the church than Rome and the papacy are now doing." It was months before a successor for Spalatin was found in the pastor of Colditz, Augustine Himmel.[34]

The parish of Belgern had belonged to the monastery of Buch. The assets of the congregation were insufficient to pay the pastor and deacon. The congre-gation's legitimate request for a subsidy from the monastery property was supported by Luther and Jonas. In Grimma the salaries of the clergy were so inadequate that the pastor had to contribute from his own resources and one of the deacons had to leave his position. In this case, too, Luther encouraged a betterment from the assets of the local Augustinian monastery.[35] The Zwickau school, which had grown to about six hundred students, was to be moved to a new location in the former commercial building (*Wirtschaftshof*) of the Grün-hain monastery. Luther naturally supported this with the elector. The city schools of Zwickau and Torgau were two gems in the land. He recalled with gratitude that in Zwickau they accepted the task of education, while in other cities ne'er-do-wells, rascals, and godless misers abounded. For example, Luther had to intercede in Gotha and Eisenach in order even to keep the schools open so that there would be no gaps in the educational opportunities in Thuringia. In order to support the schools, a benefice in Zwickau was not to be taken for the common chest, but to remain with the family that had given it and be used as a stipend for students.[36]

The inadequate compensation and the pastors' criticisms of morals clearly appear as the two chief problems in Luther's relationship with pastors and congregations. The difficulties in regard to paying the pastors were obvious.

Occasionally they were exacerbated by the action of the congregations. Not infrequently, the moral criticism of the pastors may have been exaggerated, although the circumstances in certain congregations may have been unpleasant. Despite his partisan support for the pastors, Luther was not blind to this. Emphasizing their solidarity, he may have tried too little to provide adequate mediation in the situations existing between ministers and congregations.

3. CHURCH ADMINISTRATION AND CHURCH ORDER

Only very infrequently did Luther himself still participate in ongoing visitations. In 1538 he and the other visitors arranged for the pastor of Sausedlitz to be arrested in Wittenberg because he was leading a life style that was inappropriate for a pastor, abusing his wife and children and keeping bad company. Luther did not neglect the opportunity to appeal on behalf of the wife and children. In contrast, however, he would not protect the pastor, because he had caused a scandal. The case occupied the visitors and the elector for a long time, until the pastor was finally exiled from the territory in 1539.[1]

Added to the usual duties of the visitors was the responsibility of persuading the elector to provide subsidies from expropriated church property for inadequately endowed parishes. These were cases that had become more critical because of the officeholder's illness or age.[2] Normally, Luther referred petitioners to the assigned visitor, occasionally supporting the appeal. In 1537, when Pastor Caspar Glatz in Orlamünde was to be removed from office, Luther deliberately did not want to intervene, but instead directed Glatz to the Thuringian visitors Menius and Myconius, who, if necessary, were also to arrange a hearing before the elector. Later he asked Vice-chancellor Francis Burchart to ensure that Glatz, who was still in Orlamünde, would not make trouble for his successor. In this case Luther did not approach the elector directly, for on that day he had already burdened him with two letters.[3] When the deacon Jacob Siegel in Saalfeld was to be removed because of conflicts with his pastor, the Thuringian visitors requested an opinion from Luther, who considered this superfluous in view of the clear-cut case. They should perform the duties of their office. He advised against involving the elector in the matter, citing an interesting reason: "For we should not trouble our most gracious lord—our sole emergency bishop [*Notbischof*], because otherwise no bishop will help us—with such distasteful matters unless you, who have been appointed to do so, want to be perceived as doing nothing and putting everything on his electoral grace's shoulders, which already, especially now, are much too heavily burdened without this." Menius was able to reconcile Siegel with his pastor, and Luther was naturally satisfied with this change of events.[4] The Siegel case shows that Luther did not want a centralized church administration where all decisions would be made by the sovereign, although in fact often enough the elector did have to do so. Moreover, Luther's own attitude toward the visitation proves that he did not claim any position in the administration of the church for himself. He did not understand himself to be *the* bishop, or even *a* bishop, in Electoral Saxony. That task was to be performed by the visitors.

Matters dealt with in the marriage courts had long been a particular burden for Luther. He would have preferred to pass them on to the sovereign. In 1537 he did reply to a pastor's important question, but he asked pastors to spare him these matters, for he was overburdened with work, "so that I can scarcely read a book or write anything. I cannot employ secretaries, for that would reinstitute a papacy, and it is impossible for me to do everything myself."[5] Luther did not want to become the supreme marriage tribunal. In May 1537 a committee of the territorial estates requested that four consistories be established to deal with disputes between pastors and congregations, but they would primarily have jurisdiction over matrimonial matters. The territorial estates thus recognized that a special supreme ecclesiastical court was needed, especially for dealing with legal affairs. It was certainly no coincidence that the initiative did not come from Luther. The discussions about establishing the consistory were lengthy ones. The deliberations first became specific in November 1538. The nobility wanted the offensive excommunications to be imposed only with the approval of the consistory, and no longer by pastors alone. Luther, in contrast, appears to have insisted on a thoroughgoing application of moral discipline by the government, alongside which ecclesiastical excommunication should be diligently practiced.[6]

The basic opinion concerning the establishment of the consistories was certainly written by Jonas, who was experienced in church law. Luther had given his comments verbally and at least had not raised any fundamental objections.[7] In part, the consistory should replace the earlier jurisdiction and oversight of the bishops. The visitation commissions had not proved suitable for this, because they were not permanent bodies. The superintendents would be overloaded with this task. The electoral chancellory could not continually handle it. The church needed its own supervisory body, which could also function as a marriage tribunal. This institution was set up by the sovereign, and this was another step toward the establishment of a church government under the territorial prince. The consistory was to have the right to cite people before it, to interrogate, and to punish them. Luther and the Wittenberg theology and law faculties, together with some of the superintendents, had to take care that the same abuses did not develop with these consistories as had earlier happened with the episcopal courts. At first, only the Wittenberg consistory was set up, which included Jonas and John Agricola as theologians and Kilian Goldstein and Basilius Monner as jurists. In 1542 a constitution for the consistories was prepared, which was based on the earlier opinion, but it was not expressly put into force.[8]

Luther was happy that there was a consistory, especially to deal with the burdensome marriage matters. He hoped that the new establishment might achieve an effective moral discipline and thereby support the pastors. The beginnings of the new body appear to have been difficult, especially because no ordinance was in effect. Luther advocated a gradual development of this constitutional question, one oriented toward the evangelical doctrine, so that the new establishment could avoid an "oppression" like that of the episcopal courts.[9] Occasionally, we can see how Luther worked practically with the consistory. In April 1539, as the Wittenberg pastor, he attempted to persuade a young man to honor his promise to marry, which would also avoid turning the case over to the consistory. This was not because Luther disliked the higher authority, but because he was concerned for the engaged couple. In view of the languishing morality, the church was urgently in need of support from the consistory.[10] It was no coincidence in 1541 that Spalatin feared he might lose his responsibility as a visitor to the consistory. Luther allayed his fears. The consistory was to handle marriage matters, with which the Wittenberg theologians no longer wanted to deal, to restore moral discipline among the peasants, and to assure the payment of church taxes. These were precisely the matters for which the visitors had previously also been responsible. Nevertheless, Spalatin was assured personally that the new body would not handicap him in his duties. Luther himself was not afraid of any competition between the consistory and the visitation,[11] but the two bodies overseeing the church did not quite fit together. In 1542 when some new appointments to the consistory were necessary, the elector made sure that Luther, Bugenhagen, and Melanchthon approved. At that time, the theologians in the consistory were given the task of examining ordinands, which previously had been a matter for the university.[12] The consistory thereby gained an additional function in the administration of the church.

As had been foreseen in difficult questions, Luther and Bugenhagen cooperated with the consistory in dissolving the engagement of Duke Ernest the Younger of Brunswick-Grubenhagen to the noblewoman Anna von Starschedel, whom he had met at the electoral court. The union would not have been suitable to his station. The duke's promise to marry her could be declared invalid because his father had not given his consent. This is what the consistory and Wittenberg theologians concluded.[13] The situation was reversed for one of Melanchthon's maids. She had become engaged to an artisan, and her parents had given their consent. When the artisan returned from a lengthy absence, she no longer wanted him. The joint decision of Luther and the consistory was: "She must have him or leave the city."[14] The case of the former abbot of Pegau, Simon Blick, was extremely complicated. For a long time he had already had a lover, a married woman, but her husband had left her. In order to marry her, Blick sought to have her previous marriage dissolved.

Before this was accomplished, he became engaged to a young woman from Naumburg. At this point, Luther declared that this second engagement was legally valid. In the meantime, however, a divorce of the first woman's marriage was granted, and she demanded that Blick's second engagement be withdrawn. Blick was forbidden to marry the second partner in Naumburg, but he celebrated the marriage in a village. The consistory decided in favor of the first woman and ordered that Blick be punished. Luther and Bugenhagen concurred with this verdict.[15]

It sometimes happened that the consistory was unable to function because its members were away resolving other matters. In such a case, Luther, in place of Bugenhagen, joined with the Wittenberg clergy in invalidating the engagement of Franz Zulsdorf, the son of a wealthy Wittenberg burgher, because the groom's father had not given his approval. Luther had assured himself of this by questioning the dying father. The son was to pay a considerable fine for his frivolous action. The matter was brought before the elector, because the dying father had not made his refusal before the consistory in the proper way. John Frederick ultimately confirmed Luther's decision. As this shows, Luther recognized engagements only when the parents approved. This makes his displeasure understandable when the jurist members of the consistory made contrary decisions in 1544.[16] Luther referred a marital dispute, in which he was approached by a woman from Torgau, to the council there. He turned over to the consistory the task of informing an adulterer's wife about the law.[17]

A question of law once had to be clarified. In Electoral Saxony marriages between grandchildren of siblings were prohibited, but Luther had previously declared they were permitted. They were also prohibited in Ducal Saxony. Chancellor Brück had difficulty in reaching an agreement with Luther, until the latter declared that with his theological view he did not want to annul the prevailing law. In a specific case, however, a dispensation was granted.[18] The Zwickau pastor, Leonhard Beyer, involved the Wittenberg theologians in a complicated matter. Beyer suspected that the Zwickau cantor had had a relationship with a woman whose daughter he later wanted to marry, which would have been incest. The council thought that there were insufficient grounds for suspicion. The Wittenbergers recommended a more through investigation. When it could not reach a decisive conclusion, it could not prohibit the marriage. The council decided to tell the cantor what a grievous sin he was possibly committing. The marriage ceremony should not take place in Zwickau, and, if possible, the cantor should leave the city.[19]

Only after 1543 can it be determined that the consistory assumed tasks that earlier had been the responsibility of the visitors. For example, Luther, together with the consistory, asked the elector for an increased salary for a pastor. The Wittenberg theologians and the consistory made joint efforts for the support of the poor and feeble pastor of Hohenbucko.[20] In 1545 Luther and Bugenhagen, as visitors, together with the consistory, approved the planned sale of a church's silver so that the proceeds could be used for construction work on the church buildings. Earlier, Luther had made a similar decision by himself.[21] If we exclude the serious conflict in 1544, Luther's work with the consistory was performed in a businesslike manner without serious conflict.

Luther was repeatedly asked questions about church order and worship practices. Probably in 1538–39, he corresponded with Leonhard Beyer in Zwickau concerning the baptism of children who were not yet born. Luther maintained his view, which he had developed in 1531, that such a baptism was invalid and that the child had to be baptized after birth.[22] Baptisms that the midwives in Kahla performed by invoking the triune God but without using water were naturally invalid. Emergency baptisms that were accidentally performed with wine instead of water were originally accepted by Luther. Later, the Wittenberg theologians agreed that in such cases the baptism should be performed properly with water. Luther had no reservations about baptizing with warm water. This interest in the proper way of performing baptisms was connected with the repudiation of Anabaptist activities.[23]

In Wittenberg bread and wine remaining after the celebration of the Lord's Supper were immediately consumed by those present. The basic understanding was that bread and wine were the body and blood of Christ only during the communion service. Luther had no objection, however, if such bread were used to commune the sick.[24] The elevation—lifting up the consecrated communion elements and letting them be seen—which could be misunderstood as a sacrificial act, was handled in different ways in Electoral Saxony. Luther had originally retained it as a protest against Karlstadt's criticism. Bugenhagen wanted to abolish it in 1542, and Melanchthon shared this view. In the Wittenberg castle church it was no longer being practiced in 1539. Although Luther would have preferred to keep the traditional practice, he would not argue about it but would allow freedom. The abolition of the elevation aroused attention in Wittenberg, but Luther, in response to a query from Chancellor Brück, declined to write on the subject. Ceremonies did not have to be uniform, and the elevation was one of those practices left free. In no case could it be made into an article of faith, and in this respect its abolition made sense. He maintained this view even after he was accused in 1544 of drawing closer to the Swiss by abolishing the elevation.[25]

Luther would have been happy to omit the statement "Be fruitful and multiply" when marrying older couples, but he refrained from making any arbitrary changes in the order for marriage, because this would lead to the casuistry in liturgical matters that previously had prevailed.[26] When a pastor was troubled in conscience for having performed a church funeral for a suicide, contrary to the usual custom, Luther consoled him. It had not really been the suicide victim himself who had done the deed, but the devil. The victim was therefore not responsible for his action. Nevertheless, in order to warn others against doing so, Luther insisted that attempted suicide should be punished.[27] Again and again his statements on various questions of church order show that Luther was conservative, but that as much as possible he avoided making a rigid law out of an order of worship.

Luther himself was still involved in enlarging the repertoire of evangelical hymns. To the Christmas hymn published in 1535, "From Heaven on High I Come to You," he added, "Herod, Why Dreadest Thou a Foe," no later than 1541, a translation of a hymn from the early church, and "From Heaven the Angel Troop Came Near," in 1543. At Christmas in 1542 Luther exhorted: "Sing, dear children, sing about the newborn child! For if we do not sing about him, about whom will we sing?" Most men might have been silent, but the angels sang of this birth.[28] In 1539 another catechism hymn was completed: "Our Father in the Heaven Who Art." The completed manuscript is still extant. Except for the sixth stanza and a few word changes and transpositions, the hymn appears to have been ready as first written down.[29] The baptismal hymn of 1541, "To Jordan When Our Lord Had Gone," with its precise doctrinal statements, is directed primarily against the Anabaptists. This also makes it one of the most ponderous of the Luther hymns.[30] The Trinity hymn, "Thou Who Art Three in Unity," is a translation of a hymn of the early church, which the Torgau schoolmaster Marcus Crodel probably requested from Luther in 1543. Luther, however, missed the great statements of salvation in the hymn.[31] At the time Luther would have liked the Reformation production of hymns to be richer. He asked the question: "Why is it that we have so many fine poems and so many beautiful songs of the flesh, but of the spirit we have such worthless, cold things?"[32]

Christian Hymns, German and Latin, for Burial, which appeared with a preface by Luther in 1542, was intended not for congregational singing, but for the choir that took part in the funeral. It offered an enrichment of the burial liturgy. Luther had taken over the melodies from the Catholic burial liturgy for the seven Latin hymns, but had given them central biblical texts containing the hope of the resurrection. In the *Deutsche Messe* of 1526 he had rejected such a procedure, but now he was able to combine the old tunes with the new text to form a unity. The preface made it clear that an evangelical burial with its articulated hope of the resurrection should definitely rise above the earlier requiem masses with their fear of purgatory. Gravestones and epitaphs should also express this hope. Luther gave suggestions for Bible verses that could be used for this purpose, either in prose or in rhyme. Thus old forms were given new contents. The Reformation brought about considerable changes in this sphere.[33] In 1545 the Leipzig printer Valentin Babst brought out what was until then the most beautiful edition of an evangelical hymnal and thus introduced the successor to the Wittenberg hymnal. Luther's last hymnal preface was written for this book. He used this opportunity to correct an incorrect phrase in one of his hymns, which shows how well considered were his texts. He especially welcomed the attractive format of the book, which should encourage people to rejoice in the faith. The new song and the service of God in the New Testament should be one of joyful praise for God's redeeming act.[34]

In some respects, Luther's activity in the church of Electoral Saxony was just as tiring and arduous as his work in the Wittenberg congregation. In the larger sphere no critical conflict occurred, but we must always be aware that the sources reveal difficulties more strongly than areas in which there were no problems. Nevertheless, the tensions at that time with nobles, burghers, and peasants cannot be overlooked. With the elector's help they could be confronted in part. Some areas could be put in order rather easily. In order to make a concluding evaluation of Luther's effectiveness in Electoral Saxony we must make some distinctions, as in the case of his relationship to the Wittenberg congregation. To administer the church there should be faithful bishops and inspectors to keep watch over purity of doctrine and the use of the sacraments, and to guard against heretics and the pope.[35] Here he was not referring to functions within the church. In his lectures on Isaiah 9 in 1543, Luther mentioned ingratitude and wickedness, which had to be dealt with by those who bore responsibilities. In view of the difficulties appearing everywhere, there was nothing gratifying in the world to be seen: The political situation was nothing but anarchy. People despised the preachers, booed God's Word, and mocked God, their creator and redeemer. The threats and admonitions, which God gave through his servants, were considered mere empty words. In such a situation all that could be done was to pray that the Lord would come.[36] Almost simultaneously, however, Luther could also claim that there existed for the preacher of the gospel, as once for St. Paul, reason to give thanks for the riches of God's Word and for God being known in Germany.[37] In looking back over his life's work, Luther had written this to Link in Nuremberg just a few months earlier: "I do not leave behind a sad face of our congregations; they flourish in pure and sound teaching, and they grow day by day through many excellent and most sincere pastors."[38] Once again, the viewpoint was decisive. Ultimately, it was not the difficulties that counted, but the true proclamation. Luther had no doubt that this was the basic prerequisite for the church.

XII

The Progress of the
Lutheran Reformation in the
German Empire and in Europe

From 1539 onward, a rapid expansion of the Reformation occurred, primarily in central and northern Germany, but also beyond. This was caused by the force of Reformation ideas and the favorable political situation. Although Luther and his colleagues were involved in it in many ways, this development was not planned from Wittenberg. Therefore, circumstances differed from territory to territory. In Wittenberg there was no strategic plan for spreading the Reformation. Had there been one, it would have been difficult to implement because of the differing conditions. The Wittenbergers attempted, as best they could, to help and give advice when they were approached. They supplied pastors and schoolteachers, sought to have them paid adequately, gave opinions on ordinances, encouraged, criticized, and resolved conflicts. Their contribution to the German Reformation—aside from their theology—consisted of numerous campaigns, letters, opinions, and discussions. They were repeatedly confronted by the same problems, not only when the Reformation was introduced, but also with regard to its expansion and preservation. Sometimes in this context they also had to make a statement on major political questions. In addition, the serious controversy over the Lord's Supper among the evangelicals was still not at an end. In order to present an appropriate and comprehensive picture of Luther as a reformer, the following chapter must deal with broad topics, serious problems, and many small, banal matters. All of them together belong to Luther's activity.

1. THE REFORMATION IN DUCAL SAXONY

The death of Duke George of Saxony on 17 April 1539 meant that one of Luther's most vehement opponents no longer existed. The accession of Duke Henry presented the prospect of introducing the Reformation into Ducal Saxony. Luther was well enough acquainted with the situation to know that this would not be an easy venture. The competition between the two Saxon states continued, and it could easily lead to strife between Elector John Frederick and Duke Henry of Saxony. In the duchy there were opposing forces that did not want simply to submit to the leadership of Electoral Saxony.[1]

The introduction of the Reformation began in Leipzig. On 22 May Luther, Jonas, Melanchthon, Cruciger, and Lauterbach traveled there in the retinue of the elector. Myconius also came from Gotha. Duke Henry was also in the city. Luther's arrival naturally stirred up interest. The Wittenbergers received the customary honorary gift from the university, but, in contrast, Ägidius Morch, the Catholic burgomaster, pointedly did not greet them, which reinforced Luther's preconceived idea that mammon was the god of the Leipzigers. On Whitsaturday (24 May) Jonas preached in the St. Thomas church and Luther at the Pleissenburg castle. It is no longer possible to determine if he was required to appear before the court or whether he preferred a smaller auditorium for reasons of health. Luther's sermon dealt with the difference between the evangelicals and the papists over the understanding of the church. For Luther, the church was constituted by God's Word. From it, the sacraments, absolution, and prayer receive their power, when people trust God's Word and promise. The human regulations of the pope, in contrast, have no place in the church. Luther then preached in the St. Thomas church at noon on Pentecost, where he was led to the pulpit by the Leipzig bailiff, the jurist Dr. George von Breitenbach, who had previously not been favorably disposed toward him. During the stay in Leipzig, consultations took place about introducing the Reformation into the duchy. The theologians and the elector left on Whitmonday; only Cruciger and Myconius stayed in Leipzig.[2]

In the following period the Wittenberg theologians were much occupied with the Reformation of the duchy. The bishop of Meissen, John VIII of Maltitz, attempted to prevent this by initiating his own reform. His cause was also to be helped by *Instruction in Religion,* a catechism that Luther thought had been written by one of the Meissen cathedral canons, Julius Pflug. Duke Henry sent it through John Frederick to the Wittenberg theologians for their examination. This so-called Meissen Book (*Liber Misnicus*) breathed the spirit of reform Catholicism, but it distanced itself from the evangelicals as schismatics and heretics and omitted critical issues like the marriage of priests, private masses, and both kinds in the Lord's Supper. It did attempt to accommodate the evangelical doctrine of justification, but, in so doing, left many things problematically imprecise. As a whole, therefore, the Wittenbergers refused to approve this document as an interconfessional compromise. In a separate opinion, they refuted its denial of the right to resist the emperor in matters of religion.[3] Thereby the attempt to achieve a Catholic reform in the duchy was blocked, although, as before, adherents of the old faith remained.

Luther proposed to Duke Henry that one of the first reformatory measures should be the abolition of the mass in the monasteries and churches of the bishop of Meissen, for it was the sovereign's task to take action against idolatry. In addition, Henry should also order a visitation in the areas of the monasteries and the bishop. The visitation began in Meissen in mid-July. Jonas and Spalatin were members of the visitation commission. The difficulties caused by the bishop and the cathedral chapter were confirmation for Luther that they were on the right track. The visitation was completed within a few weeks, and thus was done too quickly. On 25 July Luther was already complaining to the duke, who was the authority in charge, about it. Luther believed that this was not enough time for a thorough examination of the Catholic pastors. The financial matters of the parishes could not quickly be modified in this way in order to assure adequate compensation for pastors. Luther also asked the energetic Duchess Katherine to see that the visitation—against which opposition was appearing, in Leipzig, for example—did not come to a standstill. Duke Henry replied to Luther that for the present they would have to be satisfied with temporary measures, but that a second visitation was already being planned.[4] Luther was in agreement with this, but, on the basis of Jonas's experiences as a visitor, he urged the elector to see that the second visitation included theologians from Electoral Saxony. Otherwise no removal of the numerous country pastors who were old believers could be expected and there was hardly any reasonable way in which evangelical clergy could help out. Again in mid-November, just as the second visitation was about to begin, Luther sought to involve the theologians of Electoral Saxony, but the visitation took place without them. The primary reason for this was probably less one of economy than of a desire to demonstrate the duchy's independence of Electoral Saxony.[5]

As happened in every place where the transition to the Reformation took place suddenly, there was also an acute shortage of evangelical pastors and preachers in Ducal Saxony. Wenceslaus Link in Nuremberg was asked by Melanchthon to become a pastor in Leipzig. Luther was very reticent about this plan. He doubted that the city and its council were serious about adopting the Reformation, and the prospects for paying Link were uncertain. Cruciger, who himself was a native of Leipzig, had had uncomfortable experiences with old believers in his hometown, and because of this Luther wished that he would soon return to Wittenberg. In the fall, when Cruciger was to become superintendent in Leipzig, Luther successfully asked the elector to refuse to release him, for he could accomplish more as a professor in Wittenberg.[6] The beginnings of the Reformation went better in other cities. The former Wittenberg deacon, Anthony Lauterbach, was called to become pastor and superintendent in Pirna. It was difficult for him to leave his former place of work. Luther encouraged him and formally assured him of his prayers for him.[7] Luther suggested the Torgau deacon, Johann Buchner, as superintendent of the city of Oschatz, but there were reservations about him because he did not possess a master's degree. The duchy apparently did not automatically accept people recommended by the Wittenbergers. Luther, however, was not interested in exercising any sort of government over the church in this way. The cities in Ducal Saxony were simply unaware of how limited the supply of competent pastors was.[8]

In his new field of service, Lauterbach sometimes sought advice from Luther. Luther advised him if possible to do away with communion of the sick, for in times of epidemics this was a severe burden on the church, and, moreover, it was requested by those who previously had contempt for the church. Lauterbach should have patience with women who continued to receive only bread. A question from Jerome Weller in Freiberg about whether deacons who distributed communion were obligated to receive it was one that Luther preferred to have answered by evangelical freedom. He told Weller that he categorically opposed reintroducing the bordello that had been abolished by the Reformation. It was incompatible with the preaching of the gospel and the government's obligation to suppress vice.[9]

Except for his relationship with Lauterbach, Luther had few contacts with Ducal Saxony. This was no coincidence. In March 1540 he thought that arrogance and avarice were rampant at the Dresden court. The old Duke Henry was no longer able to control the government, and his sons did not have the necessary competence. Luther was obviously dissatisfied with the inadequate way the court was supporting the second visitation in the duchy, so the visitors would be unable to accomplish much. Several times Luther ridiculed the Dresden court, calling it a stall. He therefore thought it proper that John Lang in Erfurt had refused to accept a position in the duchy. He continued to nurse a special dislike for the city of Leipzig, which, with its pride, arrogance, greed, and usury, did not deserve an evangelical preacher. As before, the reason for his ill will was the compensation of the local pastors, which was, in fact, shameful.[10] In June Luther had to turn down a request from Weller that he appeal to the Dresden court. Luther thought he was in such disrepute there that he would be unable to accomplish anything. He felt that the reason for this was the duchy's fear of coming under the tutelage of Wittenberg or Electoral Saxony; he himself regarded this attitude as ingratitude. This was not the only time that Luther refused for this reason to intercede within the duchy. Nevertheless, he approached Duchess Katherine at that time with a request to encourage churches and schools. He told her directly that he heard and saw many things that did not please him. Those who supposedly loved the Word of God were in fact its great, secret enemies.[11] Luther's efforts on behalf of the duchy were based on his previous experiences and problems. He was not acting as an agent of the political concerns of Electoral Saxony. He may have paid too little attention to the sensitivities of the Dresden court. After Duke Maurice (b. 1521) succeeded his deceased father, Henry, in August 1541, conditions appeared to change for the better. Luther wished that God would strengthen him in the true faith and in governing in a salutary way.[12] At first, no one could see that a serious new conflict would soon arise.

IMAGO ILLVSTRISSIMI PRINCIPIS MAVRICII
DVCIS SAXONIAE, ELECTORIS, LANDGRAVII TVRINGIAE,
Marchionis Mysniæ, & Burggrauij Meideburgensis.

Maurice of Saxony
Woodcut by Lucas Cranach the Younger, ca. 1553

Protecting the diocese of Meissen was a joint responsibility of the Saxon princes. Elector John Frederick therefore claimed that a portion of the Turkish tax should be sent through him to the empire, so that it would not go directly to the Catholic side. When the bishop of Meissen, Johann von Maltitz, refused this, the elector had the area of Wurzen occupied in March 1542, collected the tax, and introduced the Reformation there. This occurred without the approval of Duke Maurice, the other protector of the diocese, who, for his own inter-ests, could not have wished Electoral Saxony to get a foothold in Wurzen. Responding to an appeal for help from the bishop, Maurice prepared to move militarily against the elector.[13] The Wittenbergers learned of the impending conflict at the beginning of April. Luther, to be sure, had thought the elector's action premature, but he believed the persons at fault for the threatened confrontation were Maurice's councilors and the Meissen nobility, who were unkindly disposed to the evangelical church. He considered the duke's action one of ingratitude, for it had only been because of the intercession of Elector Frederick the Wise that Duke Henry had been allowed to marry. Thus Duke Maurice owed Electoral Saxony nothing less than his very existence. He seemed determined to bring about his own destruction. This evaluation was one-sided and naive. It did not take into account the duke's special interests. Luther first attempted, in a letter that is no longer extant, to dissuade Maurice from his action, but he received no reply.[14]

On 7 April Luther addressed a letter to the two feuding princes that was intended for publication.[15] Because of subsequent developments it was not printed, but both sides knew of the letter. In this case Luther did not want to intervene in secular affairs, and he did not presume to form an opinion about them. Nevertheless, it was the concern of a preacher and of the church to pray for peace and, moreover, in obedience to God's command, to admonish the evangelical princes to keep the peace. To this extent the letter claimed ulti-mate authority. It appealed to Jesus' commandment about peace. The contro-versial issue, which as such was a minor matter, did not justify breaking the peace. Neither of the two sides should enforce its right with force; rather, they should submit the matter to the common tribunal for a decision. Thus in this conflict, as in the Peasants' War and in other instances, Luther held to the maxim: "No one may sit as judge in his own case." Wurzen was not worth fighting over. This way of putting it may have underestimated the interests of Duke Maurice. Luther surely had reason to fear that such a conflict would damage the credibility of the gospel. He warned against the horror of a civil war between the two Saxon principalities "for the sake of a louse or nit," meaning Wurzen. He could accurately refer to the tradition of peace in Fred-erick the Wise's political concerns. The princes, and with them their two territories, should turn to God so that God might change their minds. Luther himself, without regard to personalities, would be on the side of the one who offered justice and peace. He alone could have a good conscience. The one attacked could defend himself, because he was in an emergency situation, and he could thereby be confident of forgiveness. In that case he would die blessed. Luther had once said something similar to the authorities about suppressing the Peasants' War. God's judgment and wrath, in contrast, were forecast for the aggressor. No one was obligated to support him in an unjust war, not even his own subjects.

The letter to the Saxon princes is undoubtedly one of Luther's most significant statements on the subject of peace and war. With its principles and love of peace, it fits into the sequence of earlier statements. At first glance Luther appears to be attempting to maintain a position of neutrality with respect to the contending parties, but we cannot overlook the fact that in this specific situation it was Maurice who was playing the role of the aggressor. Luther's further correspondence shows clearly that he did in fact hold this opinion. He would have been glad if Maurice, "whom the whole world, even his own people, now considers crazy," had suffered a bloody beating. However, the Wittenberg jurists also questioned the legitimacy of the elector's action. Luther was happy when the hastily initiated mediation by Landgrave Philip soon promised success, and because of this he had already given up his plan of publishing the letter to the Saxon princes by 8 April.[16]

On his part, the landgrave simultaneously sought to have Luther and Melanchthon convince the elector to give in. Duke Maurice should be granted free passage through the territory of Wurzen, which was important for his access to portions of his own land surrounding it. The landgrave also pointed out how detrimental a conflict would be for the evangelical side. Luther immediately responded to this request. Although Luther thought the duke's legal claims were doubtful, the elector, as much as possible, should deal with him like a mad dog. On the other hand, the landgrave should convince his son-in-law Maurice that it was irresponsible for him to resort to force.[17] The landgrave already informed Luther on 9 April that there was hope for an end to the controversy. In his reply, Luther did not repress his resentment over the ungrateful duke, whom God would visit with his wrath for having risked a civil war "for the sake of rubbish." In case, as was expected, Maurice took part in the war against the Turks, Luther anticipated that the soldiers accompanying him would regret it, for punishment of the one who broke the peace would be delivered by the Turks.[18] Even more clearly he spoke to Chancellor Brück about the "crazy bloodhound" Maurice, whose youthful inexperience was also being exploited by those around him. Luther had transferred his earlier animosity toward Duke George to his nephew. As once he had done for Duke George, he would now pray for Maurice's death.[19] Because of his preconceived opinions he was unable to remain objective. His decision about Maurice was unjust and incorrect. The only thing correct was the sense of an estrangement that would be detrimental to the Reformation. In a letter to Weller, Luther also held the Meissen nobility and the Leipzigers responsible for the conflict.

Thereby the extremely bitter accusations of the past years were brought up again (e.g., only feigned support for the gospel, usury, greed, arrogance, disloyalty, hate, and all sorts of evil), for which God's punishment would not be withheld. Presumably, it was this letter that became known to the government of Ducal Saxony, something, incidentally, that Luther learned later and then accepted with relative equanimity. Maurice reacted surprisingly coolly: People were used to having Luther attack not only nobles, but also great potentates, "so this does not mean very much." The young duke did not think the polemics of the aged reformer were important any more and thus ignored them. Here we see one of the first signs that a change in generations was occurring.[20]

Luther had no relationship with the Dresden court. The duke was not interested in Luther's advice and cooperation in ecclesiastical affairs. Luther had to send a petition to him about supporting a pastor's widow through the Leipzig superintendent Johann Pfeffinger. After the end of 1543, occasional pious wishes for Maurice indicate that Luther was again thinking more positively about him.[21] The Leipzig theology faculty, however, thought cooperation with Wittenberg was important and invited the theologians there to attend the first granting of an evangelical doctorate in October 1543. Because of calendar conflicts, the Wittenbergers arranged for Cruciger and Master Paul Eber to represent them.[22] Luther's contacts with the duchy were then primarily limited to his friend Lauterbach, who seems generally to have been in agreement with him in his opinion of the conditions of the church there, and probably also kept him informed about them. Luther warned him in May and June 1542 to be on guard against supporters of the bishop of Meissen, the duke's councilors—among them the chancellor Simon Pistorius and the Erasmian George von Carlowitz—and the Meissen nobility, until they clearly repented. Concerning the duke himself, Luther made allowance for his youth. This enmity continued in the years following. Luther no longer expected any change for the better. Despite his reservations, he was only interested in helping the church in Ducal Saxony and strengthening Lauterbach in his service.[23] After John Cellarius died, Daniel Greser from Giessen succeeded him in May as superintendent in Dresden, although with serious inward reservations. Luther encouraged him in his office, despite the external difficulties and his inward reluctance. The much afflicted and weak church needed people like him.[24]

When the Freiberg superintendent, Caspar Zeuner, appealed to Luther in 1543 about differences in the orders of worship in the two Saxon territories, Luther placated him with the opinion he had previously stated: As long as unity in doctrine existed, there did not need to be uniformity in ceremonies; rather, their variety showed that they were not to be understood legalistically. He also repeated this conviction to Lauterbach. He would approve if the Hessian church order of 1538 were introduced into the duchy, but he did not believe that it would be accepted.[25] He considered it an encroachment into the affairs of the church when the Dresden court set up regulations for how

Superintendent Greser was to employ the ban in specific cases. Luther also denied Lauterbach's wish, expressed several times, for a book on church discipline.[26] In January 1546 he complained once again about the animosity against the elector in Electoral Saxony. Luther was incensed that Christoph von Türk, Albrecht of Mainz's former chancellor, had been retained by Duke Maurice, for Türk had ultimately been equally responsible for the politics of one of his worst opponents.[27]

The Reformation in Ducal Saxony did not bring Luther any significant expansion in his direct influence. Duke Maurice pursued a political program independent of Electoral Saxony, and he did not allow religion the same influence on it as Luther was accustomed to from his own sovereign. To be sure, the duke never considered reversing the Reformation in his land, but he no longer needed the reformer. Ducal Saxony is an example of how much the Reformation had become an autonomous movement even during Luther's lifetime.

2. THE REFORMATION IN THE ELECTORATE OF BRANDENBURG

At the end of 1539 the government of Elector Joachim II, who had come to power in 1535, introduced the Reformation into the Mark Brandenburg. Joachim II sent the Wittenberg theologians a draft for a church ordinance that had been prepared in line with his conservative attitude by, among others, Prince George of Anhalt and Melanchthon, but also by Witzel, an old believer. Luther was pleasantly surprised at this step by Joachim, and naturally welcomed it. He advised against retaining the Corpus Christi procession. He had no fundamental objection to extreme unction and communion of the sick, but he did not believe that anointing was a sacrament, and any change in the practice would be very difficult. He also indicated his well-known reservations about continuing the communion of the sick.[1] In general, Luther's attitude to a very conservative new ordinance is not surprising, but because the Catholic ritual was retained to such a degree in Brandenburg the Berlin dean, George Buchholzer, raised objections to Luther's ideas. Luther mollified him. Mass vestments and processions could be accepted if the gospel were proclaimed purely without additions, baptism and the Lord's Supper were celebrated according to their institution, and the invocation of saints, the Corpus Christi processions, and requiem masses were discontinued. In supreme sarcasm Luther let his freedom be known: If one mass vestment was not enough for the elector, Buchholzer, like Aaron, should put on three robes, and if necessary, like Joshua, should hold not one procession but seven, or even, like David, jump and dance before the ark of the covenant. As long as ceremonies like these were not made necessary for salvation, Luther would even allow the pope to perform them. This freedom also applied to the elevation.[2] Regarding Cordatus, who in 1540 wanted to go to Stendal and become the superinten-

Elector Joachim II of Brandenburg
Woodcut by Lucas Cranach the Younger

dent, Luther declared that the numerous festivals and fasts were acceptable. Retaining compulsory confession, however, was a problem. One should deal with it by instructing people about the freedom of confession, and thus remain in agreement with justification by faith. Luther informed the pastor in Tangermünde, Gregory Solinus, that in his opinion the old customs would not last much longer. Until then, they could be practiced. If Solinus had reservations about them, however, he should do as the pastor of Spandau, who had told the elector that he would perform his duties only if he were not obligated to the old rituals.[3]

The appointment of Agricola as Joachim II's court preacher undoubtedly helped to keep Luther's relationship to the prince distant.[4] Luther sought to provide protection in Brandenburg for Erasmus Alber, whom the council there wanted to dismiss. He tried to secure an improvement in income for one of the poor pastors in Brandenburg. When Cordatus encountered difficulties with the old believers in Stendal, Luther tried to encourage him. He advised Pastor Christoph Fischer in Jüterbog in the same matters.[5] In 1545 Joachim II sent Dean Buchholzer to Wittenberg regarding the plans to establish a consistory and had him convey his surprise that Luther had never written him. Luther assured the elector that he bore no ill will against him and was praying for him in his difficult office, for it was not easy to be a prince, considering unfaithful advisors and the power of the court devil, but he had never had a specific reason to write. He took the opportunity to warn the elector about the Jews and alchemists whom he was encouraging. Joachim then became suspicious of the alchemists. Luther's request at the close, that the elector not consider him an enemy, clearly signaled how distant the relationship was between the two.[6] Luther had given space for the conservative Reformation in the Mark Brandenburg, but he had not strongly put his stamp upon it.

3. HALLE—BETWEEN ALBRECHT OF MAINZ AND ELECTORAL SAXONY

After Ducal Saxony went over to the Reformation, Cardinal Albrecht of Mainz's position in the arch-foundation of Magdeburg, which had long been weak, became even more difficult. After the Magdeburg territorial estates assumed responsibility for his debts in February 1541, he turned over the arch-foundation to his cousin Johann Albrecht of Brandenburg-Ansbach as coadjutor, left Halle, and returned to the archdiocese of Mainz. The citizens of Halle were unwilling to pay the additional taxes unless evangelical preaching was allowed. Elector John Frederick saw to it that Jonas went to Halle, and there, over the coadjutor's protests, he preached for the first time on Good Friday (15 April) in St. Mary's Church.[1] Thereby this close co-worker of Luther entered a new sphere of activity. As a rule, the intimate contact between the two was maintained through letters, especially because Luther continued, as before, to take an active interest in ecclesiastical developments in Halle. Sometimes this correspondence became almost too much for him. Occasionally he also complained about a lack of information. He soon advised Jonas to give the Lord's Supper only to those who requested it, but not to make a general ordinance of it. He should pay no attention to any possible government prohibitions of evangelical preaching, for God's Word was free.[2]

As burgraves of Magdeburg, the electors of Saxony possessed a few rights in Halle that were not particularly significant. In a lengthy legal interpretation, John Frederick had claimed that he had jurisdiction over the city. In order to eliminate the influence of Electoral Saxony, Cardinal Albrecht had attempted to purchase these rights from John Frederick, but the cathedral chapter and the territorial estates had thwarted this intention. Albrecht nevertheless kept pursuing this goal in order to be able to exercise his authority in Halle without having to share it. The evangelicals in the city were interested in having the protection of the elector of Saxony, and Luther supported their request that the elector not sell the burgrave's rights. John Frederick agreed, but he had to inform Luther that the rights of the burgrave in Halle were limited. This did not prevent Luther from making promises for the Reformation in Halle from this position. He also advised Jonas about obtaining an evangelical syndic for the city, but he was in no position to send additional theologians to Halle.[3] In August 1542 the Wittenberg theologians also forced the holding of an evangelical worship service in the church of the St. Maurice monastery because Albrecht of Mainz had been brought to nought, and there was nothing more to fear. The evangelicals soon prevailed over the objections of the council and forcibly took over possession of the church.[4]

The situation at the time was favorable for the evangelicals, because Duke Henry of Brunswick-Wolfenbüttel, the old believer, had just been defeated. This fortunate combination of events made John Frederick think about using his army to occupy Halle. He asked Luther about this.[5] By using the law and negotiations, he had been unable to sustain the burgrave's legal rights and secure the Reformation in Halle, so he proposed to occupy Halle. This, however, would contravene the assurance he had given to the imperial estates that the campaign was only directed against Henry of Brunswick and his supporters. The elector wanted Luther to advise him what to do, because in conscience he was answerable to those outside.

Luther's advice[6] was considered and clear: If peace were concluded after the Brunswick campaign, then it would also assure the Reformation in Halle. In any other case, the war would definitely have to be continued and thereby not only Halle but also the entire territory of the Magdeburg foundation would be occupied. The opposing side, behind which, ultimately, the pope was standing, would again try to alter any peaceful solution to its advantage. This rotten peace would have to be accepted, however, and future developments would have to be entrusted to God. Thus Luther spoke against occupying Halle, which would be advantageous but also illegal, and it did not occur. This did not mean that the elector should abandon his rights in Halle, no matter how attractive the coadjutor's offer to purchase them might appear. Without Electoral Saxony's support the Reformation would not endure there. This the elector had to consider, although his direct negotiations with the city about acknowledging Electoral Saxony as the city's protector were complex.[7] Nevertheless, the elector determinedly pursued his own interests and demanded that Halle be separated from the archdiocese of Magdeburg and that it recognize the territorial sovereignty of Electoral Saxony, which would have cost the city its previous independence; otherwise, he would agree to the sale of the burgrave's rights. On the basis of impassioned complaints from Halle, Luther once again interceded for the city. He enumerated for John Frederick why the sale would not be profitable, either economically or politically. It would make it difficult to achieve a peaceful relationship with the neighboring archdiocese. Even more serious would be the loss of the elector's good reputation as an evangelical ruler, were he to abandon the evangelicals in Halle. John Frederick followed Luther's advice. The elector gave up his plan of enlarging the territory of Electoral Saxony, and in November, in exchange for an annual indemnity of one thousand gulden, promised not to sell the burgrave's rights and to defend Halle against an attack on the evangelical religion.[8] A few years later the question of whether this decision had been politically correct was debated at the electoral court. It undoubtedly helped to preserve the Reformation in Halle, but the Reformation probably would have survived even if Electoral Saxony had withdrawn from the city. In any case, the episode is an example of how Luther at least occasionally could influence the politics of Electoral Saxony.

When Cardinal Albrecht left Halle, he transferred his rich collection of relics, which carried extensive indulgences, to Mainz, where they were displayed annually at the end of August. Luther took note of this news by publishing anonymously a masterful satire, *New Newspaper from the Rhine.*[9] He did not fail to mention the collection's reported new acquisitions: "A beautiful piece of Moses's left horn," three flames from the burning bush, "two feathers and an egg of the Holy Spirit," "half a wing of the archangel Gabriel," "two yards of music from the trumpets on Mount Sinai," etc. The cardinal had already willed to the collection "an entire fifth of his faithful, pious heart and his whole truthful tongue." The indulgence that could be won with them applied not only to the past, but ten years into the future. The *New Newspaper* contained no word of criticism. It depended on the effect of its grotesque exaggerations. Before Luther, the criticism of venerating relics had employed the same literary style.

The printer Hans Frischmut in Halle, who reprinted the *New Newspaper,* was accused of publishing a prohibited libelous work and imprisoned by the coadjutor. Luther in a letter to Jonas, which was designed for publication, confessed to its authorship, which in his opinion Albrecht of Mainz should have known immediately. He protested that the *New Newspaper* was not a libelous writing, but he would not forbid such publications "against the cardinals, pope, devil, and all their hordes." If the printer Frischmut were punished, Luther would go after the "enemy of God and blasphemer at Mainz" in a very different way. Because of concern for the imprisoned Frischmut he postponed preparing a defense of the *New Newspaper*, and finally gave up the idea entirely.[10]

On 26 December 1542 Luther had to comfort Jonas on the death of his wife. She had been one of Luther's and Katy's close acquaintances, and one can see the genuine personal esteem in the letter. Luther told his friend that the separation would not be a permanent one, for he should believe in a future reunion.[11] Only a few weeks later, Jonas was complaining that he could not live without a wife. In June 1543 he married the twenty-three-year-old Magdalene Heusner. Such a speedy remarriage naturally aroused attention. Luther had advised Jonas to delay it. When he was unsuccessful, he raised no further objections, as long as Jonas felt strong enough to endure the rumors. Jonas's friends defended him against malicious gossip. For Luther, there were more serious moral conditions in Wittenberg, and no one was disturbed about them. His wedding present was small because of large debts he had just incurred and his numerous other gift obligations.[12]

Originally, Jonas was to work in Halle only a few weeks, but his stay there was extended many times. At the end of 1543 it was finally decided that he was to remain in Halle as superintendent and pastor of St. Mary's church. His position as dean and professor in Wittenberg remained to be resolved. Not unreasonably, he preferred to keep it and simply pay a substitute. He hoped that Luther and Melanchthon would support his desire. The university opposed it, and Chancellor Brück, angered by Jonas's presumption, improperly spoke disparagingly of his service. Luther finally proposed paying Jonas 140 gulden for the next eight or nine years, on condition that he would be available for the Wittenberg theology faculty when needed. The elector ultimately granted him one hundred gulden, but clearly forbade him from making any more requests.[13] Halle was well supplied by the experienced Jonas, so that Luther no longer needed to be concerned about the evangelical church there.

4. THE REFORMATION EXPERIMENT
IN THE DIOCESES OF NAUMBURG
AND MERSEBURG

The bishops of the Saxon dioceses of Naumburg and Merseburg, like the bishop of Meissen, had rejected the Reformation. It nevertheless had found its way into the Naumburg cities of Naumburg and Zeitz, assisted by the powerful support of the Wittenberg theologians and Elector John Frederick, chiefly when it came to appointing pastors.[1] A completely new situation arose when Bishop Philipp von Freising, previously the administrator of the Naumburg diocese, died on 6 January 1541. Understandably enough, Elector John Frederick was extremely interested in further developments. Apart from the matter of introducing the Reformation into the diocese, the bishop's successor could be selected only with approval of the "territorial prince and protector," and he had to be an evangelical. Under these circumstances, the elector wanted the bishop to be elected not by the Catholic cathedral chapter but by the congregation. He therefore determined to impose his political and confessional interests without regard for Duke Maurice, or for existing regulations, which raised doubts for Chancellor Brück. In accordance with the elector's instructions, Brück met with the Wittenberg theologians in Luther's house on 22 January. They, too, were unclear concerning the source of the elector's decisive right of codetermination, but they accepted his claim. The conclusion was that the elector would seek the election of a competent person and simultaneously introduce the Reformation into the diocese. In case the cathedral chapter denied the elector's legal claim, as was to be expected, the only remaining course would be to negotiate forcefully, although this also might produce no results. The theologians unmistakably advised against using force. One should be concerned about preaching the gospel, and, if necessary, a new appointment to the bishop's chair should be delayed. Rejecting any implementation of the Reformation by political means was in accord with the Wittenbergers' theological principles, and they thereby distanced themselves from the intentions of their sovereign. All of these considerations were outdated on 23 January, when it became known that three days earlier the cathedral chapter had already secretly elected Julius von Pflug, the dean of the foundation in Zeitz.[2]

Because Pflug delayed accepting the election for a long time, the elector was still able to intervene in the Naumburg diocese. In September 1541 he entrusted the bailiff of Electoral Saxony, Melchior von Creutz, with the secular administration of the foundation. A little later he had Brück negotiate again with the Wittenberg theologians about reforming the diocese and appointing an evangelical bishop. The theologians spoke in favor of maintaining the bishopric but reforming it. The Reformation transformation of a diocese could have exemplary significance in the empire. A momentous comprehensive concept emerged: Bishop and cathedral chapter should form a consistory and undertake to administer the church in a new way, deal with marriage matters, be a body for examining and ordaining clergy, and function as a synod and as visitors who were responsible for doctrine and discipline. Possibly, the cathedral chapter could be persuaded to elect Prince George of Anhalt, who as cathedral dean of Magdeburg was a representative of the clerical estate and also enjoyed Luther's complete confidence. In 1538 Luther had already spoken to Prince George in favor of keeping bishoprics and large monasteries so that the church might be supported. He thought people like George were competent to effect a Reformation of the dioceses. In contrast, the Wittenbergers did not believe that Nicholas von Amsdorf, who was intended by the court for this office, could be secured. In addition, the theologians wished that evangelical preaching and worship services should be introduced, the mass abolished, and both the cathedral chapter and the Zeitz foundation filled with suitable persons who could assume the functions of church administration.[3]

On 20 October the cathedral chapter informed the elector that it would stand by its right to elect and support Pflug. For political and confessional reasons John Frederick did not want to accept this and therefore sent Brück to Wittenberg for more discussions. The question was how to appoint an evangelical bishop for Naumburg when the cathedral chapter refused to cooperate. John Frederick and Brück were thinking of an assembly of evangelical representatives of the Naumburg estates and the local preachers, also including some neighboring clergy from Electoral Saxony. The councilors of Electoral Saxony should nominate a suitable candidate to this body, and it would then elect him and install him into office. Once again the person they intended was Amsdorf, who was a suitable candidate not least because he was unmarried and thus would not offend the old believers. The bishop should continue to be assisted by the Electoral Saxon governor, who would administer secular matters. In this way the bishopric would be largely incorporated into the state of Electoral Saxony. This also was in accord with the separation of ecclesiastical and political functions as understood by the Reformation.[4]

The Wittenberg theologians had a different opinion. They thought deposing Pflug and introducing an evangelical bishop was politically risky. The elector should use his governor to administer the secular affairs of the foundation. In addition, a consistory could be established, evangelical pastors appointed in the foundation's territory, and evangelical worship be introduced. For the time being, however, there should be no attempt to reorganize the foundation completely. The theologians believed it would be difficult to find a suitable solution. They thought it impossible to combine secular government and ecclesiastical offices and that this could not be implemented, because in that way the officeholders would continue to become corrupt. They desired adequate financial support for the church, but also showed a realistic understanding of the fact that the nobility wanted to profit from the church property. The leadership of the proposed consistory could be turned over to a bishop. The theologians' proposal was a change at this point, for, remarkably, this bishop was then also to be in charge of the secular administration of the foundation, which was inconsistent. In both functions, however, he was to be subject to the elector. The method of election needed special consideration.[5] The theologians thus had not found a clear way of separating spiritual and secular functions. In fact, they were much more reticent about a new order than the elector was, and wanted to be content with introducing the Reformation into the foundation and establishing a consistory.

The electoral councilors thought a provisional solution was impossible, for it would create friction between the electoral governor of the foundation (*Stifts-*

hauptmann) and the cathedral chapter. Moreover, they needed to fear Pflug's intrigues. The bishop should be subject to the sovereign, as had already been done in England, Denmark, Sweden, Prussia, and even by the emperor in the Netherlands. The councilors expected that Amsdorf would agree to this, but they had reservations about George of Anhalt.[6] As a member of a princely house he would be less submissive to the interests of Electoral Saxony. From 16 November 1541 onward, Luther, Melanchthon, Bugenhagen, and Cruciger were at the court in Torgau for the final deliberations on the matter. At this time they agreed to the appointment of a bishop. Because the cathedral chapter had forfeited its right of election, the elector as patron should nominate a candidate to the territorial estates and they should elect him. Then the ordination would follow, performed by a few preachers. This proposed procedure was generally similar to the appointment of a pastor. For the time being, no participation of clergy in the election was foreseen. Not without reason did the theologians think it important that the bishop be superior to the electoral administrator of the foundation (*Stiftsvogt*), and that ecclesiastical and secular funds be kept separate. An accounting should be made to the sovereign. Finally, specific details had to be determined concerning grants to clerical positions, the consistory, stipends for students from the nobles and burghers, and the allotments that were due the sovereign.[7] The theologians had thus generally acceded to the elector's views, and thereby accepted the integration of the diocese into the state of Electoral Saxony. Whether their wishes provided for a clear distinction of authority between state and church remained to be seen.

Amsdorf agreed, though not without reservations, to become bishop of Naumburg. His installation into office was set for 20 January 1542. A few days earlier, Pflug had informed the chapter and the estates of the foundation that he accepted the election of the previous year. This must have made the situation in the foundation difficult, although Pflug still remained in Mainz. The elector naturally did not let Pflug's announcement deter him from his plan to make Amsdorf the bishop. The negotiations with the estates of the foundation concerning the election began on 18 January. They expressed concern, because the oath of loyalty the estates had taken in accepting the previous bishop had also bound them to the cathedral chapter, which was being bypassed. Luther arrived in Naumburg on the afternoon of 19 January, accompanied by Melanchthon and Amsdorf. On the evening of the same day the estates visited him in order to get his opinion of the validity of that oath. His argument was simple, but convincing: A bishop who persecutes the gospel is to be deposed. The same is true of the chapter, if it does not carry out a proper election. The patron (the elector) and the estates have to void such an election and themselves elect a bishop. In this way the true interests of the chapter would be preserved. Even the oath of subjection—which could be called political— to the bishop, who was to be removed for spiritual reasons, was not binding. A bishop's power and possessions were only means by which he exercised his spiritual office. On the morning of 20 January the estates ratified the election of Amsdorf.[8]

Participating in the subsequent ordination in the Naumburg cathedral were the elector and his brother as guardians and patrons, and the estates of the foundation, along with two representatives of the cathedral chapter, the evangelical clergy of Naumburg headed by Superintendent Medler, the superintendents Spalatin and Wolfgang Stein as outside "bishops," and a large congregation as well. Medler delivered the sermon. He also presented the new bishop. The actual ordination address, a "very powerful and comforting" one on Acts 20:28, was delivered from the altar by Luther. He deliberately mentioned Amsdorf's difficult situation, and spoke about a bishop's responsibility for the congregation that was entrusted to him and the anxiety that this task produced. But God would grant his power to his weak servant. The Catholic bishops with their arrogance, miserliness, tyranny, debauchery, and whoring had not been Christ's true officeholders. In closing, the congregation was admonished to remain steadfast, for it would not be spared from *Anfechtung*. Despite all obstacles, the victorious journey of "God's chariot" could not be stopped. The ordination itself was performed by Luther, assisted by the Naumburg abbot Hebenstreit and the superintendents Medler, Spalatin, and Stein. The liturgy was virtually the same as that used in Wittenberg for the ordination of pastors. Only the admonition to stand before the church and to care for it, along with the enthronement at the close, were added to it. Really, a bishop was nothing more than a pastor, and the content of a "consecration of a bishop" was the same as ordination.[9] On the same day, at the request of the elector, Luther and Melanchthon accompanied the new bishop to his residence in Zeitz. They wanted to discuss with him reforming the cathedral chapter and establishing a consistory. On the following Sunday Amsdorf preached in his foundation church for the first time. Luther delivered the afternoon sermon on the power and force of God's Word, also in Zeitz, mentioning Amsdorf's installation and guaranteeing that the cathedral chapter would continue to exist.[10]

The elector was also interested in seeing that Luther's instructions to the Naumburg estates of the foundation, about the legitimacy of appointing a bishop, were published as soon as possible. The book *Example of How a True, Christian Bishop Is to Be Consecrated: Done at Naumburg, 20 January 1542* appeared at the end of March.[11] Even the title picks up Luther's earlier idea that the installation of the Naumburg bishop should serve as an example. The opening sentences sound defiantly self-confident and sarcastic: "We poor heretics have once again committed a great sin against the hellish unchristian church of the most hellish father the pope, in ordaining and consecrating a bishop in the Naumburg foundation without any chrism, and also without butter, lard, fat, coal-tar, grease, incense, charcoal . . . against its will, but not without its knowledge." The sin was gladly confessed, and the penance for it was the decade-long persecution by the old believers. The circumvention of the cathedral chapter's decision in electing Amsdorf was then justified on the basis of Christ's command not to follow false prophets. A "wolf" cannot be a bishop of the true church. In principle, the pope acted no differently in his church. With Pflug, the cathedral chapter had secretly and against the will of the sovereign elected an adherent of the pope and an enemy of God's Word, and thereby had disqualified itself. Action had to be taken against this. In this conflict it was not merely one opinion against another, but the Word of God spoke against the old believers, and thereby all civil legal claims like that of the cathedral chapter were invalidated. The loyalty oath applied only to a true bishop who acted in accordance with the Bible; thus they could not be accused of breaking their oath. Luther emphasized that reforming the cathedral foundation and giving it a Christian administration were at stake, not dissolving it. Its real task was to support pastors and preachers in their ministry, a responsibility that now had to be assumed by the secular rulers as emergency bishops. He referred to the elector's promise to let the foundation continue to exist, and emphasized John Frederick's spiritual intentions in taking action against the cathedral chapter. Finally, Luther spoke again of the legitimacy of consecrating Amsdorf a bishop, which allegedly had been done by heretics. As a sinful man he assumed no special authority for himself, except for his competence as a theologian. The imposition of hands at the ordination was to be understood as an act of confirmation, similar to that at a wedding. Otherwise, they had followed the church's order, for neighboring superintendents, who were understood to be bishops, participated in the ordination. This was a makeshift situation that could be altered if a reform took place in the elevations of Catholic bishops, which at that time were irregular in many respects. No objections could be raised against Amsdorf as the new bishop. He was from the nobility, theologically educated, led an irreproachable life, and was even unmarried. Luther expressly rejected Pflug's accusations, which even then were being raised, that the cathedral foundation had been compromised and had lost its imperial freedom. Luther sincerely favored the foundation's independence. He denied that there were expansionist tendencies in the politics of Electoral Saxony. He categorized Pflug's protestations that he was not opposed to the gospel as unbelievable. The Scriptures offered a model for the transformation of a bishopric by the Reformation. The criteria for an evangelical bishop were consistent. The transformation itself, like the Reformation, was otherwise possible only with the help of secular power. Whether and how the protecting power of Electoral Saxony would respect the spiritual principality, which had now become an evangelical one, remained an open question.

From the beginning Amsdorf did not feel at all comfortable in his new role, which involved courtly ceremonies. Luther had to encourage him pastorally. One had to accept the role that went with any office. Even the church had a role to play in this world. God, however, looked not at the role but at the person. It is noteworthy that Amsdorf did not want Luther to address him as bishop or prince. Luther agreed to this, with the provision that no one else was to know of it, so that the impression would not be given that Luther thought little of the dignity of the bishop's office. Amsdorf should therefore destroy Luther's letters. In order to strengthen his friend, Luther wrote him more and more frequently and also planned to visit him, but had to postpone this intention for years because of his health.[12] One can also see from Luther's letters that Amsdorf's office was a difficult one. Luther was annoyed that the court of Electoral Saxony delayed establishing the planned consistory in Zeitz, as well as a theological lectureship. In January 1543 he intended to complain about this to Chancellor Brück or even to the elector, because a significant part of the planned reform of the foundation had not been carried out. As anticipated, Amsdorf had a difficult position as bishop alongside the Electoral Saxon governor of the foundation, who ruled arbitrarily. Luther himself saw how the governor, contrary to promises, was acting solely in the interests of Electoral Saxony.[13] In addition, the relationship between Medler, the Naumburg superintendent who performed episcopal functions, and Amsdorf, who was his superior, had not been clarified. This inevitably led to additional difficulties in making appointments and imposing excommunications. At the beginning of 1543 Luther was able to mediate between the two, and he and Melanchthon advised against sending Medler to be superintendent in Brunswick.[14]

Nothing changed the bitter reality that the politics of Electoral Saxony were not serving the ecclesiastical interests in Naumburg. The planned visitation was not begun in August 1543, nor was the consistory established. The governor of the foundation, Melchior von Creutz, was also not recalled. Amsdorf was not free of the "tyrant" until the following spring. In general, the ecclesiastical affairs of Naumburg were handled by the court at a snail's pace.[15] Luther's frequently postponed trip to Zeitz finally took place in August 1544. Amsdorf did not let him pay the costs of the trip, and presented him with a silver tankard and spoon. As Luther's letter of thanks shows, the meeting must have been favorable.[16] In January 1545 he encouraged Amsdorf to undertake the long-delayed visitation, at least in the districts of his diocese where he could. He himself would also rewrite the *Instructions for the Visitors* for this purpose.[17] In October the Wittenbergers had to intervene in a new dispute in Naumburg. Superintendent Medler had become suspicious of the cathedral preacher George Mohr because of the latter's too friendly attitude toward the Catholic cathedral chapter. Although no doctrinal deviation could be proved, Mohr was dismissed. Luther attempted to console him and gave him hope of getting another position.[18] A little later Luther looked back and stated his satisfaction that the elector had put forward Amsdorf as bishop to oppose Pflug. He did not mention that Amsdorf's position was as difficult as before.[19] Ultimately the Naumburg model of a diocesan Reformation failed because of the old believers' resistance and the evangelical prince's own political interests.

Merseburg was handled differently than the diocese of Naumburg. Duke Maurice was the protector of this bishopric. When Bishop Sigismund von Lindenau died on 4 January 1544, Maurice appointed his brother August as secular administrator and in that way satisfied August's territorial claims. Prince George of Anhalt was to work with him as coadjutor for spiritual matters. Maurice sought to integrate Merseburg into Ducal Saxony, although in doing so he had to take into account the needs of the church to some extent. Luther initially disagreed with this solution.[20] Nevertheless, he wished God's good spirit to Prince George in the visitation that was soon planned and urgently needed because of the desolate circumstances of the parishes. On 2 August 1545 he even ordained George in Merseburg. Two days later he married the cathedral canon Sigismund von Lindenau, who had long lived in concubinage. This was no longer to be tolerated. In one of his Merseburg sermons Luther indicated that, as before, he had a reform of the bishop's office and the cathedral foundation in mind.[21]

Luther frequently advised the conservative Prince George in his office as coadjutor. After the death in 1545 of his former teacher and advisor, George Helt, Luther consoled him with one of his letters about God's miraculous way of acting. He also participated in the discussions about finding a suitable successor for Helt, who should be unmarried if possible.[22] He warned Prince George against prescribing orders of worship too specifically. "I do not like the necessary ceremonies, and the unnecessary ones I hate." Everything depended on pure preaching and suitable people to do it, and then an agreement on ceremonies would also be possible. Uniformity was not necessary, but rituals that were clearly godless should be eliminated. Altars and vestments could be retained for the time being. Luther was opposed to any legalism. Practices should be regulated through oversight, the sort a father or teacher exercises. A prerequisite for preparing effective people was the educational system. In contrast to Prince George, who was still tied to traditional ecclesiastical ordinances, Luther, exercising freedom, clearly emphasized the real needs of the church.[23] Luther added clear marginal notes to the drafts of the Merseburg church ordinance and the consistory ordinance, which were submitted to him in the summer of 1545, calling them "intolerable, godless, superstitious, useless." The superintendents Lauterbach and Greser made complaints about this in Wittenberg. It is no longer possible to determine to what extent Luther's criticism bore results.[24] Yet in February 1546 Luther replied to a number of questions about marriage law that Prince George had submitted to him.[25] In fact, the Merseburg solution with its separation of the bishop's ecclesiastical and political functions stood the test better than the Naumburg model. Certain problems were caused by George's conservative attitude, but, like the Reformation in the electorate of Brandenburg, they were not taken all that seriously by Luther.

5. RELATIONSHIPS WITH SMALLER NEIGHBORING TERRITORIES

The smaller territories bordering on Electoral Saxony, after accepting the Reformation, frequently appealed to the electorate or to the Wittenberg theologians about certain matters. These issues were usually the same as in Electoral Saxony. In 1541 Luther had to recommend a pastor and superintendent for Gera. He replied to the elector that there was already a shortage of qualified people in the electorate. He did propose a few candidates, but none of them was immediately available.[1]

The Arnstadt superintendent, Joachim Mörlin, was another cleric who sharply criticized immorality and thus also caused offense. In 1543 he sent the Wittenberger theologians a strict ordinance concerning excommunication. Luther said that he was in agreement with it, but it would run into opposition. A few months later he had to advise Mörlin to leave. In this case, too, he completely supported the side of the pastor, who had one-sidedly informed him, and he did not want to help the "unworthy" congregation get a successor. Mörlin was not without support in Arnstadt. The burghers sent two petitions objecting to his removal by Count Günther von Schwarzburg and the council. Luther specifically defended four of these burghers against the accusation that their submission was seditious. Ultimately, Myconius from Gotha and John Lang from Erfurt were able to put an end to the controversy. Myconius told Luther frankly that the church's illness could not be cured with drastic treatment and excessive force, as Mörlin had employed, for example, in excommunicating the entire council. Myconius wanted to restore the relationship between Arnstadt and Luther with his letter. Luther immediately reciprocated and conceded that Mörlin had been guilty as well. His previous experiences with actions of cities and nobles against their pastors had biased him against them. When a new dispute erupted between the deacon and a burgher a little later, he asked George Spenlein, Mörlin's successor, forcefully to urge each side to give in. He expected that a congregation as such would also accept a critical word from its pastor.[2]

In 1539 Luther recommended a pastor for Nordhausen and also insisted on an appropriate salary for him. In 1542 a disagreement arose with the burgomaster, Michael Meienburg, over a former monk, now blind, whom, in Luther's opinion, the previous abbot and the burgomaster had not supported. He may have evaluated the case of this troublemaker in a one-sided way. The case involved reservations about Meienburg's life style. Despite Melanchthon's efforts, Luther's relationship with Meienburg remained strained from then on. In 1543 the council of Nordhausen also sent Luther a letter, seeking to prevent their pastor, Johann Spangenberg, from being called to Magdeburg. The letter emphasized that the pay in Nordhausen was not as good as in Magdeburg but was still adequate. Church finances were obviously an intricate problem in this city. In the same year, Luther also had to admonish Spangenberg and the preacher Anton Otto to come to an agreement.[3]

After the Reformation had been introduced into Mühlhausen under pressure from Electoral Saxony, Justus Menius became superintendent there. In 1544, however, Menius wanted to return to Eisenach. He therefore explored in Wittenberg the possibility of finding a successor. Subsequently, the council applied officially to the Wittenberg theologians, and in so doing eloquently distanced itself from the Müntzer episode and the Catholic period that had followed. As was anticipated, the Wittenbergers sent Sebastian Boetius. They admonished the council to be diligent and emphasized the responsibility it had for the church.[4]

Luther at this time had only occasional contacts with Erfurt. In 1539 he sought to keep the preacher Mechler there. A year later he was happy that John Lang had not moved to Ducal Saxony. Luther and Lang were in agreement on rejecting secret engagements.[5]

In his home county of Mansfeld, Luther took an interest and became involved not only in church affairs, but also in economic and political situations. These will be discussed later. Luther spoke to Count Albrecht about his concerns over predestination and about absenting himself from Word and sacrament. It seems that the count, believing in predestination, had become indifferent to human action. Luther sought to make distinctions: One had to believe in God's revelation, promise, and commandment. Beyond this, there was also God's unfathomable decree, which was not for humans to decide. The count was not the only one whom Luther had to call to account on this difficult question, which could involve anxiety as well as despair.[6]

In Eisleben, even after Witzel left in 1538, there was still a small group of old believers, who had not joined the evangelical congregation but wanted to await the decisions of a council. For this reason their members were called Expectants. On the occasion of an Expectant's funeral in 1541, the superintendent Caspar Güttel declared that they were no longer to be regarded as Christians. The sermon was printed with a preface by Luther. In Luther's opinion, one should allow those who wished to rely on human statutes to go their own way. Those who recognized the gospel and yet rejected it or even persecuted it, like Duke George, would suffer God's judgment.[7]

In 1543 the pastor Simon Wolferinus caused a scandal in Eisenach by keeping the excess hosts and wine consecrated for the Lord's Supper with the unconsecrated supplies until the next communion. This was in accordance with Melanchthon's view that the elements used in the Lord's Supper were the body and blood of Christ only during the celebration. Luther favored consuming the consecrated gifts of bread and wine during the service. He advised Wolferinus to follow this practice and thus forestall any controversy in the congregation.[8]

A little later Luther was asked by a delegation from Mansfeld, among them Luther's brother James, whether it was permissible to deal in mortgages. In accordance with his view, which had become more negative in the meantime, he declared this to be usury and thus impermissible.[9] The Mansfelders— James Luther again among them—also tried to enlist the aid of the Wittenberg theologians in obtaining a replacement for their pastor who had become old and feeble.[10]

Luther's relationships with the principality of Anhalt remained active. In 1537 he had to console the suffering Prince John because his wife, Margaret, had left him. For Luther, such "disobedience" was close to adultery. In a discussion with the princess he clearly told her his opinion and advised her, for the sake of her own reputation, to burn the list of complaints she had brought with her. Difficulties in a marriage should be endured by both parties in Christian patience. A few months later, to Luther's satisfaction, a reconciliation took place.[11] He consoled the aged Princess Margaret, Prince Wolfgang's mother, in her illness, saying, whatever happened to her, she should know that she was in God's keeping.[12] In June 1538 Luther visited Princes George and Joachim. In 1542 he was also invited to Dessau.[13] Luther was also asked to be one of the godparents for Bernard, Prince John's son, born in 1540. On the occasion of the baptism he preached three times in Dessau at the beginning of April. His baptismal gift was a promise to pray for the child and his mother, and it was gratefully accepted.[14] When a conflict arose in 1543 between Prince Wolfgang and his cousins, Luther exhorted them to make peace and sought to mediate between them.[15] The gifts that Luther constantly received from the Dessau princes show that the relationship between them was very friendly.[16]

Luther's correspondence with Anhalt was also concerned with the usual church matters. In 1538 he supported lending Jonas to Zerbst for a few weeks. He was also otherwise helpful in securing clergy. During the epidemic in 1538 Prince John asked for a preacher who had to be unmarried. Luther proposed a compromise, suggesting that someone come for the period of time in question but not bring his wife. He did not think that John Zechariah Petzensteiner, a member of his former order, was sociable enough to be recommended to Dessau as Hausmann's successor.[17] The good relationship with the princes of Anhalt permitted Luther to turn to them frequently with requests. A widow with many children, whose husband had drowned during a hunt, probably while serving as a beater, should be supported "because this is really performing good works." A creditor of Prince Wolfgang should receive his money back as promised, without any loss for inflation. The aged and weak pastor Johannes Rosenberg in Zerbst needed relief; a student, a stipend.[18] In 1539 Luther insisted that the blasphemous old cultus in the München-Nienburg monastery be abolished. Later he warned Prince Wolfgang not to undertake to reform the monastery on his own without his cousins.[19] A Palm Sunday play written by the Dessau schoolmaster, Joachim Greff, was rejected by the local pastor as "a foolish work and dissolute rhymes." For Luther it was an adiaphoron, which a pastor should not simply condemn out of hand. Thus he supported the schoolmaster.[20]

6. THE OTHER GERMAN TERRITORIES AND ADJACENT LANDS

Luther's contacts with the remainder of German Protestantism were very different—sometimes dealing with a specific point, sometimes coincidental; sometimes sporadic, sometimes intensive. This depended on whether there were people with whom he had a relationship or on how great an interest the people had in establishing a connection with Wittenberg.

Since 1535 Luther had known that the Bohemian Brethren were in harmony with him. Occasionally, however, there were tensions. In 1540 he rejected their criticism for retaining confession and absolution. A year later he protested that they appealed to him when they denied the presence of Christ's body and blood in the Lord's Supper. In a letter in 1542 to Johann Augusta, the bishop of the Bohemian Brethren, he thanked him for his prayers and encouraged him to maintain fellowship in the Spirit and doctrine.[1] Close connections existed with the city of Joachimsthal, where Luther's former table companion and later biographer, John Mathesius, had been active since 1542. In 1542 a mandate of King Ferdinand ordered the expulsion of all married clergy. Luther thereupon wrote Mathesius an encouraging letter in which he expressed, accurately, his opinion that the mandate would not be implemented in Bohemia.[2]

In Austria Luther still had contacts with the Jörger family of nobles in Tolleth. Dorothea Jörger sent students to study in Wittenberg, her own grandson among them. Her son Christoph had scruples about participating in Catholic worship services in Vienna. Luther knew no other advice to give him than to obey his conscience. Taking part in a worship service that one knew was wrong was not part of the obedience one owed to government. When Christoph Jörger was relieved of his office at the Vienna court in 1545, Luther congratulated him. To him, King Ferdinand was a person suffering from misfortune because of his persecution of the Word of God.[3]

In southern Germany, Luther's most intensive contacts were with Nuremberg. Characteristically, the reasons for this lay in the personal sphere. Link, above all, but also Veit Dietrich were among his close acquaintances, and they were interested in not having their connection with him severed. Link frequently demonstrated his support by sending Luther gifts. Despite his overwork and exhaustion, Luther wrote a preface recommending Link's commentary on Genesis.[4] When the Nuremberg city councilor Jerome Paumgartner

(Baumgartner), who once had studied in Wittenberg, was taken prisoner by the notorious Franconian knight Albrecht von Rosenberg in 1544, the Wittenbergers took an active interest in his fate. Luther wrote a consoling letter to Paumgartner's wife, stating that God's faithfulness endured even in misfortune. The Wittenberg theologians asked Philip of Hesse to intercede with Rosenberg on Paumgartner's behalf. Apparently they had better relations with the landgrave than the Nurembergers did. Philip, however, had already taken action in the matter on his own. Paumgartner's imprisonment dragged on because the high ransom that was demanded could not be paid. He was not freed for fourteen months. He combined his thanks to Luther with a lengthy, impressive report of how he had dealt inwardly with his fate, which shows how deeply Paumgartner was imbued with evangelical piety.[5] The Wittenberg theologians sent condolences to Osiander when his first wife died. In 1545 Luther had to console him on the loss of his second wife and a daughter. He tried to help Osiander in the great tension between the harshness of fate and faith in God's good will, which he himself had experienced in the death of his own daughter Magdalene.[6]

In Wittenberg they also took note of events in the Nuremberg church. Luther was annoyed that a dispute about the elevation occurred there in 1538.[7] Osiander's independent attitude on theological matters was also regarded as troublesome in Wittenberg. Luther did not fail to recognize Osiander's theological giftedness, but he accurately perceived the danger that his self-possessed, pedantically arrogant, and contentious attitude threatened.[8] In 1540 Luther and Melanchthon sought to solve the controversy that was still raging about so-called public confession (in which absolution was declared after a confession of sin was recited by the whole congregation, not by an individual), which Osiander rejected. They presented their own formulas for absolution. Despite his high regard for individual confession, Luther did not think it could be introduced as the exclusive form of confessing sins, and he was probably correct in this.[9] The differences between the two of them did not keep Luther from recognizing and acknowledging the theological unity he and Osiander shared.[10] Thus, during his lifetime, no break occurred between Wittenberg and the Nuremberg reformer.

The custom of the *Schembartlaufen* (a masked celebration by artisans) was resumed on Shrove Tuesday in Nuremberg in 1539 after a lapse of fifteen years. On that occasion the preachers, who had objected to it, were ridiculed, and Luther was filled with indignation.[11] After Link—apparently very disturbed—complained in 1541 about the disdain for pastors in Nuremberg as "priests," something with which Luther could identify on the basis of his own experience, he stated his view of the situation of the church there. The threat from papal tyranny and the sectarians had been overcome. But now the enemy within was revealing himself through moral laxity and a weariness with God's Word. As when John the Baptist and Jesus had done it, criticizing immorality caused offense, and the use of excommunication was not accepted. The Nuremberg clergy should present their case to Erasmus Ebner and Jerome Paumgartner, who were favorably disposed councilors, and ask for protection. If necessary, Luther himself would contact the council, and he still had some hope that it would take action, although the devil was constantly fanning the antigodly conflict between the political order and the church. If Link were unable to stay in Nuremberg, Luther would find another position for him. At present, however, confident that the church would not be destroyed, he recommended that the best weapon against this hellish opposition was prayer.[12] The difficulties of the church of the Reformation are clearly contained in this letter, and yet it is filled with confidence.

Luther recommended that Margrave George of Brandenburg-Ansbach encourage the new generation. To this end he advised in 1542 that the Heilsbronn monastery should be converted into a school of higher learning.[13] When the city of Amberg in the Upper Palatinate wanted to introduce the Reformation in 1538, the local council asked Luther and Melanchthon for a preacher. They could recommend only Andreas Hügel from Salzburg, who was qualified but "not good looking" and who did not have a powerful voice. The Ambergers still accepted him. Already in 1539 Hügel was forced to leave Amberg by Elector Louis of the Palatinate because he was married. In 1543 the preacher Laurentius Rudel also wanted to leave the city because he was forbidden to use the German language in baptisms. At Hügel's insistence, Luther urged him to stay. For the sake of continuing to preach the gospel, it was justifiable to leave baptism to the Catholic pastors. The confessional transformation occurred in the Upper Palatinate in 1544 under Palsgrave Wolfgang. Thereupon, the Amberg council requested the return of Hügel and the former rector there, Johannes Faber. Faber was to become the preacher and Matthew Michael from Torgau would take over the school.[14]

Luther had few direct relationships with the other evangelical churches in the area of southern Germany, including Hesse. They were not supplied personally or theologically from Wittenberg, and Luther had no trusted acquaintances there. Only because of the controversy on the Lord's Supper, which was threatening anew, were there occasional contacts that will be presented later. It was different in the area of western Germany and especially in northern Germany.

In March 1542 Luther became aware of the intention of the Archbishop of Cologne, Hermann von Wied, to reform his diocese. In view of the difficulties of the church in his own area, this advance in a distant territory, an ecclesiastical one, seemed to him an act of God.[15] Luther, nevertheless, remained more of an observer of this initially promising plan, which eventually failed because of the resistance of the Catholics in Cologne. In introducing the Reformation the archbishop sought assistance from the evangelical side, primarily from Martin Bucer. In the spring of 1543, Melanchthon was also invited to come to

313

Bonn in order to overcome the stalemate in the negotiations with the opposing side and to provide theological assistance in preparing a church ordinance. Luther encouraged him to make the trip. Luther was aware that the cathedral chapter in Cologne was blocking the Reformation.[16] Melanchthon published a rebuttal of the attacks of the Cologne clergy against the work of the Reformation, and Luther wrote a preface for it in which he interpreted the stubbornness of the pope and his supporters as God's righteous judgment.[17] Based on Melanchthon's reports, Luther hoped that the resistance of the Cologne clergy might be overcome, since the other dioceses supported the archbishop. At the beginning of 1544, however, it was clear that the archbishop was in a difficult position against his opponents.[18]

The so-called "Cologne Reformation Proposal," on which Melanchthon had worked, was the result of a confessional compromise. Luther did not deal with the proposal until the summer of 1544, after Amsdorf had sharply criticized it. His own objections did not pertain to the remnants of Catholicism, but were concentrated on the article on the Lord's Supper because it did not seem to express the presence of Christ's body and blood clearly enough, and the proposal therefore accommodated the enthusiasts. This was directed against Bucer's mediating position, although Melanchthon, too, had approved its formulations. A new intra-evangelical conflict on the Lord's Supper was emerging. Melanchthon was deeply hurt that Luther had not rejected Amsdorf's criticism. He thought there was a possibility that he would be driven out of Wittenberg, to the joy of their opponents, especially because the court of Electoral Saxony had also become involved in the dispute.[19]

Luther and Melanchthon were incidentally involved in 1543 with the prospect of introducing the Reformation into the territory of Duke Wilhelm of Jülich-Cleves-Berg. Through his marriage to Sibylle, Wilhelm's sister, Elector John Frederick had been granted by treaty a right of inheritance of Jülich-Cleves-Berg. The territorial estates there, however, made their approval dependent upon a pledge from the elector not to introduce any new measures in the church. Luther, like Melanchthon and also Chancellor Brück, resolutely rejected making religion a subject of politics: "God's Word is our Lord and creator, to which we are subject, and it is not a matter of indifference to us how much less subject we can be."[20]

Luther recommended the schoolmaster George Ämylius for Siegen.[21] The church ordinance of the county of Lippe was sent to the Wittenberg theologians in 1539 and approved by them, with the exception of slight changes proposed by Melanchthon to the marriage law.[22] Luther corresponded with his friend James Propst in Bremen only when there was a specific reason to do so. For example, he sent him two Dutchmen who could not be used in Wittenberg because of their language. In case they could find no support in wealthy Bremen, however, Propst should send them back and Luther would then share what he had with them. He did the same with a refugee who probably had come from Ghent.[23]

In 1543 the Lübeck superintendent Hermann Bonnus helped to introduce the Reformation into Osnabrück. At that time it seemed that the dioceses of Münster and Osnabrück were receptive to the Reformation, along with the archbishopric of Cologne. When it became apparent that it would be necessary for Bonnus to stay in Osnabrück longer than the leave he had been granted, he appealed to Luther. Luther implored him to stay. Bishop Franz von Waldeck, who was favorable to the Reformation, could not be left in the lurch. Lübeck would have to release Bonnus for a time.[24]

In 1544 Luther wished God's blessing in his new office for Joachim Mörlin, who had been called from Arnstadt to Göttingen. A few months later he had to console him because of the meager results of his preaching. He did this in a very wise, pastoral way. Mörlin, as a doctor of theology, could not be unaware of what he had to preach, namely, law and gospel as judgment and grace, but he should not expect that everyone would hear and love the Word. Luther, probably correctly, could not exclude the possibility that Mörlin was preaching too legalistically. But he told Mörlin to be satisfied if one-fourth of his auditors accepted the Word; Christ himself had done no better than that.[25]

In the duchy of Mecklenburg the Reformation did not make any progress, primarily because Duke Albrecht, in contrast to his brother Henry, opposed it. As administrator of the bishopric of Schwerin, Duke Magnus, Henry's evangelically disposed son, demanded in 1538 at the *Landtag* in Parchim that the two ruling dukes introduce the Reformation, because as Schwerin's bishop he himself was responsible only for a portion of the church within the duchy. When he accomplished no appreciable results with his appeal, he had doubts about whether he should undertake a reorganization of the church himself, and he contacted Luther about it. Luther thought that Magnus had acted properly. He did not consider the possibility of initiating the Reformation in Mecklenburg from the diocese of Schwerin.[26]

In 1537 Duke Barnim of Pomerania asked Luther and Bugenhagen to convince Paul von Rode, the pastor of Stettin who had accepted a call to become superintendent in Lüneburg, to remain in his previous position. The Wittenbergers flatly rejected this wish, because Rode's demands that a church ordinance be introduced and that he be better paid had not been heeded. In Stettin the city itself was apparently seeking to expropriate church property. It had confiscated the church silver and refused to give it to the church treasury. In 1541 it sought Luther's approval for using these funds to discharge the debts of mortgaged villages and estates. In order to predispose him to agree, they had previously sent him a shipment of fish. His reply, which is no longer extant, must still have been a negative one.[27] A serious controversy arose between the city of Stolp and Duke Barnim in regard to the considerable property of the church, which the city wanted to transfer to the church treasury and the duke wanted for himself. When the emperor decided in favor of the city, the duke occupied it and had the burgomaster, Peter Suave, arrested. Simon Wolder, a refugee who belonged to the nobility and who was also responsible for taking the church property, was arrested in Danzig at Barnim's request. The Wittenberg theologians interceded with Barnim and Duke Philip of Pomerania on behalf of those who were persecuted. They should not have to suffer for their well-intentioned advocacy of the interests of the church. Barnim, however, could not be dissuaded from his regal harshness.[28]

For the proposed election of a new bishop for Kammin in 1544, Duke Barnim and his nephew Philip were to nominate a candidate, but initially they could not agree. Barnim had proposed Count Ludwig of Eberstein, just seventeen years old, who hardly would have been suitable for such an office. The Wittenberg theologians therefore reminded the dukes of their responsibility for the church. The new bishop should be able to teach, to visit, to supervise the schools, to administer the marriage tribunal, and to enforce church discipline. The Wittenbergers were thus pursuing the same goals here as in Naumburg. The count of Eberstein did not meet the qualifications St. Paul required of a bishop. The dukes would incur God's punishment for such a nomination. The Wittenbergers also tried in the same way to influence the councilors charged with continuing the negotiations. They then agreed on Bugenhagen. Understandably enough, Elector John Frederick was also involved in the negotiations with Bugenhagen. Chancellor Brück proposed that Bugenhagen should agree to serve for a brief time, and during that period recommend a suitable successor. In this context Bugenhagen was initially induced to agree by being told that a war between the dukes would occur if he refused, but later he withdrew because he did not want to leave his Wittenberg pastorate. As before, it appeared desirable to the elector that Bugenhagen go to Kammin for a limited time, and Luther should work together with Melanchthon to persuade him. Bugenhagen explained to them his personal and objective reasons for refusing. He recommended that a Pomeranian pastor be selected, and this was finally done.[29]

In St. Mary's church in Danzig evangelical preaching was permitted, but the pastor, Pankratius Klemme, was forbidden to administer the sacraments. Luther encouraged him in 1543 to celebrate the Lord's Supper also, but he thought preaching the gospel was more important.[30]

Duke Albrecht of Prussia contacted the Wittenbergers relatively frequently to seek advice and encouragement. The letters were also an opportunity to exchange both political and ecclesiastical news. In 1538 Albrecht was interested in including Prussia, which did not belong to the empire, in the religious peace. At the same time he inquired about the degrees of relationship permitted in solemnizing marriages in Wittenberg. Luther made a note on a slip of paper: "I, Dr. Martinus, have neither the strength nor the time to answer

Prussia, but I'll do it as soon as I can." Melanchthon undertook to reply for him, and Luther's slip of paper was sent along with it, certainly unintentionally. Albrecht responded to the slip of paper with a concerned question about Luther's health. Luther was in agreement with discontinuing the elevation in Prussia.[31] Again and again the duke sent students to Wittenberg with personal recommendations, which indicated his responsibility for educating the next generation, which Luther constantly encouraged the sovereign to do. The establishment in 1542 of a special school (*Partikularschule*) in Königsberg, a preliminary stage of the university there, must have been entirely in accordance with his intention. Conversely, Wittenberg students were recommended to Prussia. Occasionally, the duke asked for the return of a student whom he needed in Prussia.[32] One cannot characterize Luther's relationship to Duke Albrecht as close, but undoubtedly it was good and not encumbered by serious problems.

Since 1539 Duke Albrecht's brother Wilhelm had been archbishop of Riga. Because there was a question of whether he had to let himself be consecrated and become a member of the order of Teutonic Knights, the duke turned to Luther and Melanchthon. Luther was determinedly against a Catholic consecration and seeking confirmation from Rome. They should avoid having anything to do with the horror of the papacy. Wilhelm should fill the office as an administrator. Occasionally, people were sent from Wittenberg to Riga. In 1540 Heinrich Bock was sent to Tallinn to be the future superintendent. The Wittenberg theologians linked this with an expectation that his compensation would be improved. At the same time they warned against Anabaptists and sectarians who were infiltrating from the Netherlands.[33]

Luther's influence in evangelical territories was frequently dependent on his personal relationships with theologians or the authorities. These connections could continue, or they could be isolated ones that happened only by coincidence. The initiative was usually taken more by the partners than by Luther himself; he himself hardly developed relationships. His declining strength and the number of claims upon him also limited his correspondence. The subjects treated in the letters varied and usually dealt with specific concerns. The same problems recur: Personnel matters, concerns about compensation, questions of church order, marriage matters, church discipline, controversies, opposition to Catholics and sectarians. This catalog was not imposed by Luther; it mirrored the reality and the everyday activity of the Reformation churches at that time. Both light and shadow were closely related.

When Luther had to prepare a preface in 1542 to a collection of Old Testament prophecies about Christ written by Urbanus Rhegius, the Lüneburg superintendent, who had died the previous year, he took the death of this "bishop" as the occasion for reviewing the situation of the churches "that I include in my prayers."[34] He deplored the lack of suitable clergy. Even among the outstanding ones there was a great deal of weakness and sometimes also

317

perversity. Among the people he saw no concern for the church, no support for maintaining pastorates, no fear of God's wrath, and no improvement in morality. Among the youth in the schools, who in the future would have to assume the leadership of church and state, he criticized irresponsibility, ignorance, and arrogance. He was pained and indignant about the princes and their courts. It was their responsibility to support the church, protect morality, establish schools, provide a good example, and with diligence perform all righteousness, punish with severity, and protect brave burghers and allies. But where was this happening? Finally, he mentioned blasphemers in all the estates. It was no coincidence that death had taken away pious people like Rhegius before the impending judgment came. Luther thus regarded the situations in the evangelical territories as questionable. In this, he was not just being pessimistic. His opinion was based point by point on specific experiences.

7. THE REFORMATION IN EUROPEAN LANDS

Needy foreigners occasionally appeared in Wittenberg. Luther sent a Pole and likewise a Greek on with letters of recommendation.[1] Just as relationships between German territories and Luther usually developed when initiated from outside, the same was true with non-German lands. In Luther's later years there were no contacts with France, the Netherlands, and England, or virtually none.

His closest contacts were with King Christian III of Denmark, who, as duke of Schleswig-Holstein, was also a prince of the German empire. Luther had welcomed the removal of the Danish bishops that Christian effected in 1536, but at the same time exhorted him to leave the church enough property to support them.[2] Nevertheless, church property was extensively expropriated by the king. Strangely enough, Luther took no more exception to Christian's strong encroachment in the Danish church; perhaps he was not accurately informed about it. In 1537 the king applied not only to Elector John Frederick but also to Luther about Bugenhagen's move. At the same time he submitted the Danish church ordinance to the Wittenberg theologians for examination, and they gave it their approval. At the end of that year Luther could see that Bugenhagen's work in Denmark was going well. Like a true bishop, he had crowned the king and reorganized the university of Copenhagen.[3] In 1540 Christian sought a court preacher. The Wittenbergers, however, had no suitable candidate available at first.[4] At the beginning of 1542 the king asked again for Bugenhagen in order to implement the church ordinance. This time it was the elector who wanted Luther to convince Bugenhagen to accept the call. He was aware that the Reformation had not yet been firmly established in Denmark. At that time King Christian began sending Luther, Melanchthon, and Bugenhagen annual shipments of butter and herring, which were later changed to monetary contributions.[5] The continuing correspondence between Luther and the king dealt primarily with stipends and recommendations of Danish students studying in Wittenberg.[6] Bugenhagen kept Christian regularly informed about Luther's publications. In January 1546 he told him: "The gentlemen, our dear father Dr. Martinus and Philippus [Melanchthon], along with me, are extremely grateful that your majesty so graciously cares for us in deed, and we cannot thank your majesty enough, because we know that thereby your majesty honors the dear gospel of Christ."[7] This shows how strongly the relationship between the Wittenbergers and Denmark was oriented toward the king.

Sweden had already turned to the Reformation in 1531 under King Gustavus I Vasa. In 1539 he sought a tutor for his son. One was found in George Normann, who in the years following gained considerable influence over the king. Luther gave him a letter of recommendation. In it, he encouraged the establishment of schools, primarily cathedral schools for the education of future pastors. This same letter also contained praise for Michael Agricola, the future reformer of Finland, who was returning home from the university of Wittenberg.[8] The king sent his thanks the next year for recommending Normann. He praised Luther and Melanchthon as those who had led people out of error and darkness into the salvific Word of God, also calling himself one who followed that Word. Luther should give no credence to rumors, presumably coming from Denmark, that characterized the king as unevangelical. He justified the sentence that had been imposed upon the old reformers, Olaus Petri and Laurentius Andreae, for high treason.[9] Gustavus also entered into conversations with the emperor because of the strained relationships with Denmark. Luther told him of his displeasure over this. The king, however, could report that he had unsuccessfully attempted to join the Smalcald League. Luther should notify him what obstacle prevented such a step. Moreover, he justified the divorce of the Swedish chancellor Conrad Peutinger, which Luther had criticized.[10] After 1541 the correspondence seems to have been broken off.

The Reformation in Transylvania was able to put down roots under King John Zápolya. In 1543 the pastor of Sibiu (Hermannstadt), Matthias Ramassy (Ramser) contacted Luther about a church ordinance. Luther referred him to the church ordinance by Johannes Honterus in Brașov (Kronstadt), which Ramassy already knew, and with which the Wittenberg theologians were in complete agreement, for it followed the Wittenberg model. Honterus had visited Wittenberg in 1535.[11] A year later Honterus himself wrote to Luther. With the letter was enclosed a gift from the judge Johann Fuchs in Brașov, a gold coin of Emperor Theodosius. In his reply Luther praised the advances made by the Brașov church and exhorted them to be vigilant against enemies without and within. At the time the influence of the Swiss Reformation was beginning to appear in Transylvania. Its adherents rejected the elevation, images, and private confession. The clergy of Sibiu also complained about this and asked the Wittenbergers to write their city council, because it was partly supporting the innovations.[12] Luther's later conflicts with the Swiss were fore-shadowed here. These also played a prominent role in his relationships with Hungary and Italy. They will be discussed separately later.[13]

As a whole, it will be seen that Luther's Reformation had spread beyond Germany's borders in several places. This was not a result of Luther's deliber-ate planning or an interest in all of Europe. He did not have the strength for that, and he probably also did not think it advisable in view of his expectation that the world was soon coming to an end. The successful spread of the Lutheran Reformation was inherent within itself. It was helped by political circumstances and not least by the education and training offered by the pop-ular Wittenberg university.

8. THE ACTION AGAINST DUKE HENRY OF BRUNSWICK-WOLFENBÜTTEL AND THE REFORMATION IN BRUNSWICK-WOLFENBÜTTEL

In discussing Luther's relationships with German territories we passed over the duchy of Brunswick-Wolfenbüttel because it was a special case in which politics and Reformation formed a unique mixture. After the death of George of Saxony in 1539, Luther now considered Duke Henry the Younger of Bruns-wick-Wolfenbüttel, the most agile Catholic prince of the empire and opponent of the Smalcald League in northern Germany, as his greatest enemy and attacked him as such, primarily in *Against Hanswurst*. In this he was fully in accord with Elector John Frederick.[1] The acts of arson and murder that Henry perpetrated in the territories of his neighbors in 1540 had already raised ani-mosity against him on all sides, and Luther was also incensed about them. The duke's actions were regarded as a threat. At the end of 1541 Luther suspected that the emperor and King Ferdinand were in league with Henry, something that proved to be false, as were his fears of the last times that were connected with this.[2]

Contrary to the decisions of the emperor and his brother, Henry continued his attacks on Brunswick and Goslar in 1542. Because Goslar was a member of the Smalcald League, this provided a legal reason for Electoral Saxony and Hesse to strike against the duke, who was isolated within the empire, and in July they decisively took advantage of it. The Wittenberg theologians were not asked by Elector John Frederick about this attack, only informed in order to pacify them, and they, like the people, were called upon for prayer. Luther sent this request on to Amsdorf. He believed that a war was necessary in order to defend the many people who were oppressed. God's grace was also needed for the undertaking, of course, and God would not hold the sin in their own camp against them.[3] The victory over the unprepared duke was surprisingly easy for the allies. Henry had to flee his land. Luther told the elector that the success was an act of God against his foes, but he immediately warned against arrogance. He rejoiced primarily over the report that the people and the land were being dealt with graciously. Bugenhagen was immediately assigned to introduce the Reformation into the duchy of Brunswick-Wolfenbüttel in August. Luther soon took up the cause of Christoph von Schulenburg, one of Henry's creditors, whom Henry had treated unjustly.[4] The news of a peaceful occupation quickly proved to be a false report. Nobles as well as soldiers looted unscrupulously, and the princes, despite their good intentions, were unable to maintain discipline over them. Luther was enraged at this. In this way the God-given victory had been defiled.[5] Luther had not advised this war, but he had considered it a just one and therefore had urged that it be fought justly.

Luther regarded Duke Henry, who had fled, as a continuing danger, as Germany's "Turkish enemy." Henry understandably did all he could, with the emperor's help, to take back his land. At the end of 1543 Elector John Frederick informed the Wittenberg theologians that Duke Maurice of Saxony had been charged with carrying out negotiations with the Smalcald League about a settlement. If Henry were to return, the Reformation in Brunswick-Wolfenbüttel would likewise be in danger. Therefore, the question was whether the continuation of the Reformation in the duchy should be made a non-negotiable condition of peace, thereby risking a new war. On the basis of previous experiences, Luther doubted that the Smalcald League was ready to defend itself, for its members were interested only in enriching themselves personally. Accordingly, the Wittenbergers' opinion was a very realistic one. They were in favor of defending the Reformation to the extent it would be done—which was something of which the theologians were not so sure—and if there was a chance of military success. The duchy could not be surrendered to idolatry again and the evangelicals left defenseless. If the risk were too great, the church had to be prepared to suffer. In that case the government was not obligated to protect it. In view of the disinclination toward a new war within the Smalcald League, the theologians were in fact advising against defending Brunswick-Wolfenbüttel. The elector's councilors rejected this. The cause of the Smalcald League was just, and therefore they had to continue to defend it. Weakness would only encourage the opposing side and inflict severe injury on the evangelicals. The elector shared the opinion of his councilors, but he had heard the critique of the theologians about introducing the Reformation and helping the church in Brunswick-Wolfenbüttel well. Bugenhagen should contact the superintendent there and inform him of this.[6] Luther himself had been directly involved only in appointing the superintendent in Brunswick. In 1545 Nicholas Medler moved there from Naumburg.[7]

The Smalcald League's problem of what to do with the conquered duchy, which had existed from the outset, grew worse in 1544. The southern German members of the league favored following a proposal from the emperor that would turn the administration of the territory over to a neutral prince like Duke Maurice or Elector Joachim II until a final decision was made. The city of Constance spoke emphatically against this so-called sequestration plan, primarily for the sake of preserving the evangelical confession. Luther, in contrast, favored it, because the Brunswick undertaking was too costly for Electoral Saxony. In a reply to the Constance opinion, the Wittenberg theologians maintained their earlier realistic view. The willingness of the members of the Smalcald League to become involved seriously in preserving the Reformation in Brunswick-Wolfenbüttel was not great, and they also could not be expected to perform such an act of love for a foreign territory. Everyone was responsible only for his own house. Especially if the alternatives were sequestration or war, the preachers could hardly advise going to war. The concern for the gospel in other areas would have to be left in God's hands. This deliberately narrow position was in line with the earlier ideas of the Wittenberg theologians. They never favored a political policy of defending the Reformation in a vast area, but always advocated keeping the peace.[8] The Smalcald League finally consented to the sequestration. Before that happened, however, things took an unexpected turn.

In September 1545 Luther incidentally mentioned indefinite rumors of war. At the beginning of October, Elector John Frederick informed Luther that Duke Henry was preparing to reconquer his land. The elector, Philip of Hesse, and Duke Maurice planned to oppose him. Luther was again asked for his intercessions.[9] At first the Wittenbergers had only vague information about the war. Luther was aware, however, that Duke Henry was outnumbered by the allied princes. He expected that now, after twenty years, the feared priests' war would break out. Later he acknowledged: "Never before did I sleep less over a war." Even though their own cause might be good, there was still a great deal of ingratitude and weakness among the evangelicals.[10] Without any major battles, however, Duke Henry surprisingly fell into the hands of Philip of Hesse on 21 October. This development came so unexpectedly for Luther that he initially suspected there had been a secret reconciliation between Henry and his opponents. But then his belief in a direct intervention by God was restored, and he praised the victory over this opponent with his whole heart. The elector ordered that thanks be given in the prayer of the church.[11] Their joy over the victory did not prevent the Wittenberg theologians from interceding for the city of Helmstedt, which had been forced to support the advancing Duke Henry and now was to pay a heavy indemnity for this breach of loyalty to the allies. The Wittenbergers sympathized with the city's action and asked the victors for mercy. When they initially had no success, they appealed to the elector again. They combined this with the request that the pastor of Helmstedt should finally be paid his salary, which had not been done since the occupation.[12]

The elector requested a work from Luther on the subject of Henry's capture as soon as possible, for he wanted to use it against the members of the Smalcald League. Chancellor Brück was apparently charged not only with seeing that it was prepared speedily, but also that nothing undesirable was contained in the politically relevant publication. Brück was well satisfied with the text, but he wanted to eliminate a reference to the emperor's support of Henry, which in fact was incorrect. Luther, who at the time was otherwise not in the court's high favor, was unhappy with this censorship. Brück later believed that he had gone too far in his regimentation.[13]

Luther's open letter, *To the Elector of Saxony and the Landgrave of Hesse on the Imprisoned Duke of Brunswick*, appeared on 19 December 1545.[14] Its purpose was to prevent a release of the dangerous duke, which possibly even the landgrave was considering. Luther admitted publicly that at first it was not apparent to him why he should write, but the duke of Brunswick had many friends who might support him, and therefore it was fitting to strengthen the resolve of the elector and the landgrave. To be sure, Luther favored mercy and forgiveness, but it did not appear advisable to release the duke if he did not change his mind. Luther supported this with a biblical example. Henry was an exponent of the tireless anti-evangelical coalition, which would not cease its animosity. Preventing him from exercising his tyranny and protecting other people from him was the real mercy that was commanded. One could show mercy to the duke personally after he had repented of his many crimes. Luther urgently admonished his own side not to become arrogant over the victory God had given it. The fortunes of war could also have favored the other side. The evangelicals had certainly not deserved the victory because of their piety, for among them there were many papists and those who despised God's Word, and in all estates there were arrogance, usury, and greed. Nevertheless, the evangelicals did have the pure Word of God, which would not remain without fruit, while works and prayer were perverted in the papacy. Giving God the glory did not mean eliminating weapons, but, rather, it meant not placing one's trust in them, rather than in God alone. Luther intentionally appended Psalms 64 and 76 to this letter, for they set this tone and he understood them in this sense. This letter is one of the few things Luther wrote that speaks directly to a political question. One cannot say that he thereby made theology a means of politics. The theological reasons for imprisoning Henry were consistent. There is no hint that he was improperly intoxicated with victory; on the contrary, critical admonition of the victors is not missing.

9. RENEWED CONTROVERSY ABOUT THE LORD'S SUPPER

The Wittenberg Concord had in part ended the sacramentarian controversy but in part only suspended it, for the Swiss waited years before declaring that they would not accept the Concord.[1] In addition, it became apparent that the view attacked by Luther had widespread adherents. It was only a question of time until the sacramentarian controversy erupted anew, and once again Bucer and even Melanchthon were drawn into it. This complicated development of a number of factors was climaxed by a definitive confession by Luther.

A turbulent figure on the periphery was Caspar von Schwenckfeld, who caused difficulties with his conventicles and his spiritualism primarily for the southern German Reformation, which was in agreement with Luther in rejecting Schwenckfeld.[2] In Silesia there were also numerous supporters of Schwenckfeld. In 1537 Luther wrote a preface to a book by the Breslau pastor Ambrosius Moibanus against the contempt of the proclamation of the Word and the sacraments, which he regarded as a sign of the last days. In 1542 he spoke with consternation about how in his opinion the Schwenckfelders were despising his (Luther's) Savior by rejecting his Christology. Beyond Silesia, there were problems in Prussia with the Schwenckfelders and other sacramentarians.[3]

As early as March 1542 the theologians of the Smalcald League had taken a position against Schwenckfeld's Christology. Luther had not participated in this assembly, but his significant disputation *On the Divinity and Humanity of Christ*[4] belongs in this context. In it Luther defended his doctrine of the unity of the divine and human natures of Christ (*communicatio idiomatum*) that he had developed in the previous controversy with Zwingli. Based on this doctrine, he could make the paradoxical statement: "This man created the world, and this God suffered, died, etc." At the same time, this subject, which transcended the bounds of human thought, needed to be expressed in precise language, which would best be confined to that of the Bible and the established fathers of the church. Questionable statements by the church fathers were to be interpreted in an orthodox sense. Schwenckfeld was interested only in the divinized humanity of Christ, which had put off all that was creaturely. Therefore he had criticized referring to the exalted Christ as a creature according to his humanity. In Luther's view, it was essential to call the human Christ a creature, no matter how problematic this might be in relation to Christ's true divinity. In his preface to the disputation Luther explained that he was dealing with the topic because of the attention Schwenckfeld's views had stirred up in northern Germany. In the disputation, Luther constantly returned to the unity of the two natures in the person of Christ. He admitted that Christology broke the normal rules of grammar and philosophy. It could not be otherwise where the finite and infinite are one.

Against the rejection of the theologians of the Smalcald League Schwenckfeld wrote a lengthy book, *Confession and Declaration of the Knowledge of Christ*, which he sent to Melanchthon at the beginning of 1542 with a request for an opinion on it, mentioning his gratitude toward him and Luther.[5] In an incidental reference in 1543 Luther accused Schwenckfeld of the heresy of separating Christ into a divine and a human person.[6] Schwenckfeld would not let this dangerous accusation pass; he therefore wrote directly to Luther in October 1543 and sent him a few of his own relevant publications. He believed that Luther was on his side, and supported this by a collection of appropriate citations, but, in contrast to Luther, he was only secondarily interested in Christ's humanity. Anticipating Luther's reaction, Melanchthon did not even want to give Luther the letter, because his polemic attack, which was to be expected, could result in an increase in the number of Schwenckfeld's supporters against Luther. Luther was content to deliver a harsh reply to the messenger. He mentioned that Schwenckfeld was responsible for the controversy over the Lord's Supper that was still continuing in Silesia, and he expressly repeated the accusation of heresy. Schwenckfeld should leave him alone with his writings. He concluded with a curse upon Schwenckfeld and his followers as false prophets. Schwenckfeld did not respond again to this during Luther's lifetime.[7] In the following year, in a larger context, Luther himself came back to his condemnation of Schwenckfeld.

For years a growing number of Hungarian students had studied in Wittenberg, and they naturally also sought personal contact with Luther. In 1538 they asked Luther to celebrate the Lord's Supper in Latin for them, since they did not understand the German worship service. Luther did not grant their exceptional request, for he was unwilling to deviate from the current church ordinance. In 1539 Leonhard Stöckel from Bartfeld in present-day Czechoslovakia was summoned home by the council of his hometown in order to assume the position of rector there. Through him and others, the Reformation there spread beyond the cities. In response to an inquiry from the Bartfeld council, Luther advised them not to compel the distribution of bread and wine in the Lord's Supper.[8]

One of the highly placed advocates of the Reformation in Hungary was Count Franz Réway. In 1538 he had, by letter and through a student, told Luther of his doubts concerning his own doctrine of the Lord's Supper, which he had developed under the influence of the Swiss views. Luther attempted to dispose of them in two letters,[9] but the Swiss doctrine of the Lord's Supper remained virulent in Hungary. In 1544 the clergy from the area of Eperies, to which Bartfeld belonged, complained that Matthias Biro Dévay had fallen prey to it. He had studied in Wittenberg and had lived in Luther's house during later visits. Luther was amazed at the news of Dévay's change of mind, and he unmistakably assured the Hungarians that, as long as he was in his right mind, he would not share the views of the enemies of the sacrament and would not tolerate them in the church entrusted to him. After the last confrontation with Schwenckfeld, the news from Hungary was another reason for him to add a new confession about the Lord's Supper as soon as possible to his numerous earlier ones.[10]

In 1538 news reached Wittenberg of the spread of evangelical preaching in

Italy.[11] In November 1542 Baldassare Altieri, who was then the secretary of the English orator in Venice, contacted Luther and Melanchthon on behalf of the evangelicals in Venice, Vicenza, and Treviso. He first eloquently praised Luther's service in bringing Christ out of darkness into light. The evangelicals in Italy also knew they were his children and had taken comfort from him. Altieri apologized that he had not previously dared to attempt to contact him. He described the vicious persecution that was raging against them, and asked that the evangelical princes intercede with the Venice council on their behalf. The second problem of the evangelicals in Venice was that they had also become involved in the sacramentarian controversy. Through Bucer they had been informed about the Wittenberg Concord. Altieri therefore asked Luther to instruct them on the Lord's Supper and to suggest a way of reconciling the contending parties.[12]

Veit Dietrich, at whose hand Luther had received the letter, was interested in having him reply promptly. In May 1543 Luther apologized to Dietrich that because of illness he was not able to do so and said that he had asked Melanchthon to reply, but that in the meantime Melanchthon had been summoned to reform Cologne. Although he was still not feeling well, he promised to write Venice as soon as he possibly could. There was an additional reason for Luther's delay, as we learn from one of Melanchthon's letters. Luther was not in agreement with Bucer's minimizing explanation of the Wittenberg Concord, but at first he hesitated to make a critical statement against it.

A month later Luther did write the promised letter. He declined the praise bestowed upon him, for he had written little in Latin and was only a "German preacher and uneducated teacher" who thus could be of little help to the Italians, but he was happy that the mystery of the Christ who brings salvation had also become known in Italy, the land of the Roman Antichrist. Luther also thought it desirable that the princes of the Smalcald League write the council of Venice, which was supporting the evangelicals, but he informed them that this would take some time. Then he reported that an agreement had been reached with the southern Germans, which he hoped would endure, although the old leaven had not been cast out entirely. In Switzerland, however, it was primarily the Zurichers who were stubbornly maintaining their position. They had a different spirit than the Wittenbergers and should be avoided. In great detail, and stating his own point of view, he pointedly informed them of how the Wittenberg Concord had been achieved and what it contained, clearly stating that in it he had not accepted Bucer's minimizing compromises. Finally, he gave an unembellished picture of the situation in the church in Germany. Veit Dietrich would take care of supplying the Italians with the theological literature they had requested.

Altieri at once replied that the letter of the princes had arrived, but that the council had taken objection to it because of certain formalities. The council of Venice shared Luther's view on the Lord's Supper, but Altieri mentioned that there were also other opinions circulating in Italy. Luther does not seem to have responded to the urgent request that he write to those imprisoned for the evangelical faith.[13] He also did not reply to Altieri's letter until November 1544, and then at the urging of Matthias Flacius Illyricus. Surprisingly, aside from the existing personal obstacles, he does not seem to have considered it necessary to intensify contacts with the evangelicals in Italy. Nevertheless, Flacius persuaded Luther to have the princes write another letter to the Venice council on behalf of the imprisoned evangelicals. Because Luther's opponents in the renewed sacramentarian controversy were also agitating in Italy and France, Luther wanted Latin translations made of his pertinent German works. Here Luther's interest in a European presence of his theology can be seen. It is remarkable that in this context he did not mention his *Brief Confession Concerning the Holy Sacrament,* which had just been written, and there was no provision made for its translation into Latin.[14]

It was apparent in Luther's correspondence with the Italians that he no longer fully trusted Bucer on the doctrine of the Lord's Supper. The estrangement involved more than this, and it had already begun in 1541 when Luther thought Bucer had gone too far in accommodating the Catholics with the Regensburg Book. Luther had subsequently become distrustful of Bucer's action in the matter of Landgrave Philip's bigamy. By 1542 this distrust had already spread to Bucer's attitude on the question of the Lord's Supper. It grew into rage when Luther became involved in the Cologne Reformation Proposal in August 1545. At that time he called Bucer a "blabbermouth," and he would have nothing more to do with his proposals of mediation. "I will consider him as damned. . . ." The foundation of personal trust, which had made the building of the Wittenberg Concord possible, was showing cracks. Its permanence appeared threatened.[15] The danger of a new sacramentarian controversy increased.

The real opponents in this conflict remained the Swiss. After it was seen in 1538 that they could not be won over to the Wittenberg Concord and were going to continue to follow Zwingli's line, Luther's old animosity revived. A little later, in *On the Councils and the Churches,* he denounced Zwingli for the heresy of Nestorianism, i.e., separating the two natures of Christ. On 30 August 1539 the Zurich clergy protested against this accusation, which must have affected their mutual relationship. Luther, however, would not be turned from his polemics. In 1541 he said that Zwingli, along with Müntzer and the Anabaptists, were seditious theologians.[16]

On 24 December 1541 Karlstadt died in Basel. Luther was very interested in knowing whether he had repented. He was quite willing to believe the reports from Basel and Nuremberg that before he died Karlstadt had been visited by the devil and that he had then died in fear of death. It fitted Luther's expectation that this opponent, like Zwingli and Oecolampadius, would also have to die a wretched death. Nevertheless, this did not prevent

Luther from interceding with the Basel council to see that Karlstadt's widow and children were supported.[17]

The real declaration of war in the renewal of the sacramentarian controversy came from Luther on 31 August 1543. Christoph Froschauer, the Zurich printer, had sent him a Latin translation of the Bible made by the theologians there. Luther regretted this and asked that he be sent no more works of the Zurich preachers, with whom neither he nor the church could be in fellowship. He considered them lost because his warnings to cease their errors and stop leading people astray had been fruitless. Luther wanted nothing to do with them; instead, he would pray and teach against them until his end. He expected that the judgment of God that Zwingli had experienced would swiftly be visited on them as well. The Swiss theologians were understandably incensed. Bucer sought to pacify Bullinger in Zurich and promised to persuade Melanchthon to moderate Luther. Melanchthon advised Bullinger to ignore Luther's attack in silence for the sake of unity. Bullinger, however, believed a confrontation was unavoidable if Luther insisted on his unjust condemnation of the Zurich clergy.[18] With the same intention as Bucer, John Calvin in Geneva also contacted Melanchthon and found understanding with him. The Genevan reformer had already entered Luther's field of view in 1539. Only a year later Luther was accurately noting Calvin's learnedness, but also that there were differences between them on the Lord's Supper. In this respect he remained suspect for Luther.[19]

In a letter in January 1544 to Landgrave Philip, Bucer advocated on one hand that they should remain firm in the forthcoming negotiations between the religious parties at the Diet of Speyer, and on the other that they should acknowledge deficiencies in their own camp. He specifically mentioned Luther's polemics against George of Saxony, Albrecht of Mainz, and Henry of Brunswick, along with the attack on the Zurichers in the letter to Froschauer. Luther saw Bucer's letter and it so enraged him that Melanchthon was terrified. In this context Luther was probably again aware that Bucer had never categorically repudiated the sacramentarians and had not retracted his own errors. The separation was unavoidable, and for this purpose Luther wanted to write a new confession concerning the Lord's Supper. In May he sharply attacked the "sacramental enthusiasts" from the pulpit, because they were basically denying God's omnipotence.[20]

The complex development of the sacramentarian controversy induced Luther to write *Brief Confession Concerning the Holy Sacrament,* which appeared in September 1544. For this purpose he had once again reviewed his earlier publications on the sacramentarian controversy.[21] The work was dedicated to an unknown friend who had become aware of Luther's letter condemning Schwenckfeld.[22] Luther expressly confirmed "that I have earnestly condemned and rejected the fanatics and enemies of the sacrament—Karlstadt, Zwingli, Oecolampadius, Stenkefeld [sic], and their disciples at Zurich and wherever they are." He thereby repudiated Schwenckfeld's claim that he and Luther were in agreement. Luther now indicated the separation very sharply. At the Marburg Colloquy in 1529 no agreement had been reached on the Lord's Supper, only an armistice. Zwingli's final work published after his death proved that he had held to his false view. Because Zwingli's followers praised it highly, they had broken the Marburg armistice. Luther emphasized the unmistakable repudiation: "As for a man who is factious, after admonishing him once or twice, have nothing more to do with him [Titus 3:10]." Luther returned once again to the old argument, that the different ways the opponents interpreted the words of institution proved that these seven spirits—Karlstadt, Zwingli, Oecolampadius, Schwenckfeld and his friends, and Campanus—had nothing to do with the Holy Spirit. In this context he included the Strasbourgers, although not mentioning them by name, who minimized the conflict. The commonality among the opponents consisted in their denying that Christ's body and blood were present in the Lord's Supper. Luther then referred to the way he had refuted their other arguments. In doing so he mentioned in passing that he had never agreed with Bucer's acceptance of Christ's spiritual presence. Finally, the opponents had not taken God's judgment of Zwingli's death as a warning. The argument, also raised again by the Strasbourgers, that the Swiss theologians were faithful servants of their congregations counted for nothing with Luther. He regarded the errors of the opponents as refuted, and they had been warned three times about them. According to biblical teaching the only thing to do was to separate from them. Luther appealed to Rom. 4:21 in support of his own position: "God was able to do what he promised." This referred to all the articles of the Christian faith. Arbitrarily interpreting even one article according to human reason was heresy. Given this rigorous attitude, Luther was no longer prepared to see and acknowledge what he and his evangelical opponents had in common. In the final section of the confession Luther discussed the questions concerning the elevation that had come from Hungary.

With this, the church fellowship with Schwenckfeld and the Zurich theologians was declared at an end, and the Strasbourgers were at least given an unmistakable warning. Contrary to expectations, Melanchthon was unscathed. In April 1544 Luther had already expressly told the Hungarians that he harbored no suspicion against him. To be sure, the formulation of the doctrine of the Lord's Supper in the "Cologne Reformation" had also aroused Luther's distrust, but this distrust was directed against Bucer and only very indirectly against Melanchthon, insofar as he sympathized with Bucer's views. But even though Melanchthon wanted to emphasize the presence of the person of Christ and not that of his body and blood in the Lord's Supper, his explanations must have satisfied Luther so that the sensational event that Melanchthon feared, in anticipation of which he already was thinking of leaving Wittenberg, never came to pass.[23] The extent of Melanchthon's uncertainty is revealed by the fact that in the last ten days of September he did not dare to deliver one of Bucer's letters to Luther. The letter might have helped to solve things, for in it Bucer had distanced himself from the Zurichers and declared again that he accepted the Wittenberg Concord. But Bucer's continuing interest in limiting the conflict and preventing the issuance of new polemical writings was unmistakable. The elector was aware of the controversy looming between Luther and Melanchthon, which would have been very damaging to the Wittenberg university. Chancellor Brück was therefore delegated to speak to Luther. All the Wittenberg theologians were sent a stag to put them in a good mood. Through Brück, Bucer's letter came into Luther's hands. What the two talked about is unknown, but even in advance Brück suspected that Melanchthon's fears had been exaggerated, since Luther probably had never intended to attack him in his confession. In November, to the Italians, he denied the intense rumors that Melanchthon or he agreed with the "madness" of the Zurichers.[24]

After Luther's confession appeared, Melanchthon still feared a new controversy with the Swiss and thought his ten-year efforts at settling the conflict had been in vain. He hoped that the Zurichers would not reply to Luther's confession.[25] Calvin thought as Melanchthon did, and he sought on his part to placate the Zurichers. But he was no less interested in an association with Luther. In January 1545 Calvin sent him two books against the so-called Nicodemites, secret adherents of the evangelical faith who continued to participate in Catholic worship services. Calvin rejected this attitude and asked for Luther's opinion. He had left it up to Melanchthon whether to give the letter to Luther. Melanchthon, because of not understandable, despondent fear of Luther's distrust, declined to give him the letter.[26] Although this did not result in an open breach between Luther and Melanchthon, it shows that at the end of their common activity the relationship, especially from Melanchthon's side, was greatly impaired.

In December 1544 Bullinger had already expressed his surprise to Melanchthon that the Zurichers had not been sent Luther's confession. He informed Melanchthon that they could not keep silent about Luther's repeated attacks, and placed the blame on the collapse of Bucer's attempts at agreement, which obviously had failed. The lengthy counterconfession of the Zurich clergy appeared in March 1545. It emphatically rejected Luther's historical presentation, his theological understanding, and his condemnations, in which he was acting like a pope. Although recognizing that Luther had done great things by God's grace, they accused him of arrogance. Especially bad, they noted, was his propensity for invective.[27] Bucer immediately wrote to Melanchthon, distancing himself from the Zurichers in order to divert Luther's expected wrath from the Strasbourgers. Calvin believed that the Zurich confession was a poor defense of Zwingli, but he also thought Luther's vehemence was dangerous. In thinking that an explanation from Melanchthon on the Lord's Supper could offer a solution, he was not accurately evaluating the situation.[28] Bullinger hoped that after Luther's death the true doctrine of the Lord's Supper could be restored. He was even more critical than Luther of Bucer's role as a mediator, and thought it would be better if Bucer were already dead.[29]

Luther himself was still undecided in mid-April about whether he should answer the excessively long work of the "fanatic, proud" Zurichers in which they had turned on the person who once had set them free. At least there should be a brief announcement that the verdict condemning them had been imposed. Perhaps Luther was thinking of having the Wittenberg theologians prepare a common statement, as the Zurich theologians had done with their confession. Cruciger and Melanchthon were already afraid that they might have to join in signing harsh condemnations with which they were not entirely in agreement. Melanchthon expressed his great concern to Brück that Luther was now going to call the Wittenberg Concord into question and also attack Melanchthon himself. Brück, as the elector's representative, should at least convince Luther not to undertake any action against Melanchthon that would cause a scandal. This time, as well, his fears proved to be without foundation.[30]

At the beginning of May Luther had decided to reply only briefly and incidentally to the Zurichers. He did not want to waste his time with these bawlers and dignify their writings by reading them. In the countertheses he published in September against the theologians of Louvain he then included a condemnation of the "Zwinglians and all those who pervert the sacrament" and deny the oral reception of Christ's body and blood in the Lord's Supper, labeling them "heretics and estranged from the holy Christian church." The massive formulation of the bodily presence of Christ in the Lord's Supper led to an inquiry from Luther's supporters in Rome at the end of the year, but it no longer reached him.[31] Luther had not yet given up the plan of writing a new work against the Zwinglians, but he lacked the time and strength. At that time the Wittenberg theologians also refused to permit the Swiss to become members of the Smalcald League for confessional reasons. When Luther learned in January 1546 how much the Swiss had condemned him, he could only rejoice because this confirmed their opposition, which he had wanted to reveal in his confession. Referring to Psalm 1, which he treasured, he said: "Blessed is the man that walketh not in the counsel of the sacramentarians, nor standeth in the way of the Zwinglians, nor sitteth in the seat of the Zurichers." At that time he appeared finally to be thinking of having his Wittenberg colleagues examine their doctrine of the Lord's Supper, now that their noticeable reluctance on this point had raised his doubts about them. Even in one of his last sermons he mentioned "those in Switzerland who disgrace the sacrament."[32]

The later sacramentarian controversy had European dimensions for Luther. He sought to deal with it not by searching for an agreement, but by sharply drawing a distinction between himself and Zwingli's supporters and like-minded friends, with whom he long had known he was not in agreement. This threatened his relationship with Bucer, and even with Melanchthon, because they wanted to maintain those bonds that Luther rejected. Despite their reservations concerning Luther's attitude, Bucer and the southern Germans did not break with him. Luther himself stated his satisfaction with Melanchthon's declaration that he agreed with him, although he could not have failed to see the differences that existed between them. Thus although the sacramentarian controversy was not put to rest, the unity of German Protestantism that had been achieved in the Wittenberg Concord remained intact, thanks to the force of Luther's theological personality and the reasonableness of all involved.

The emphasis of Luther's direct work on behalf of the Reformation was naturally in the central and northern areas of Germany. An evaluation of it produces a complex picture. His influence on the Reformation in Ducal Saxony and Electoral Brandenburg was limited. Only inadequately could his ideas about reforming the dioceses be implemented. The Reformation introduced into Brunswick-Wolfenbüttel as a result of conquest proved very questionable. The Cologne Reformation failed. In Scandinavia the Reformation that was initiated primarily by the princes had to be accepted. One success was the effort at securing the Reformation in Halle. The relationship with the princes of Anhalt and Albrecht of Prussia must also be evaluated positively. The historical effect of the many people he supplied and the opinions he gave is difficult to assess, but it was certainly not insignificant on a local level, where it not infrequently determined the course of the Reformation. In detail, Luther's effort on behalf of the Reformation was anything but a triumph, and yet, viewed from a distance, it is unmistakable that in this way Lutheran churches came into existence and began to gain stability. A final result was caused by Luther's explicit separation in the sacramentarian controversy. It contributed to the long-lasting division of European Protestantism.

XIII

The Enemies of Christ and of His Church: Jews, Turks, and the Pope

In his final years Luther lived increasingly with the expectation that the world was soon coming to an end. This was connected with his impression that conditions were generally growing worse and that the church was beset by ever more dangerous threats.[1] In 1540 he expected that either he himself or the next generation would experience the last day. The signs of the final time appeared to be fulfilled. The pope had been revealed as the Antichrist, and the world raged and did not improve. Luther did not let this disturb his own equanimity. He longed for the Lord's return and, unlike during his Catholic beginnings, he no longer feared that event.[2]

In the sermons on Matthew 24 in 1539 and 1540, Luther dealt extensively with the signs of the last days that were presently appearing.[3] It seemed significant to him that the pope was not particularly concerned about Turks, Jews, sacramentarians, Anabaptists, and their errors. For him, the Turks and the pope were the powers that would introduce the final affliction. Moreover, along with the Jews, they no longer let Jesus Christ be the Savior but errone-ously depicted him as a severe judge. The pope himself behaved like the lord of Christendom. There could be no agreement or compromises with these false leaders. This was the reason for the harshness of Luther's later theology. For him, the Antichrist was a living reality personified in the pope. Christ is there only where his Word is present. The pope's teachings, in contrast, did everything to lead people away from this center.

Among the signs of the last days for Luther, and against which he preached, was the unwillingness to repent—especially for the sins of usury and greed—which he confronted in those around him. In 1542 he had to admit resignedly that he had been unable to change the contempt for God's Word in Germany and would have to let the destruction run its course.[4] In the following year he stated that all the classes lacked a consciousness of injustice and sin, and that the only complaints people raised were about injustices that they themselves experienced, which Luther considered a perverse situation. The only comfort offered by the fact that the world had forgotten Christ was that this presaged

333

the imminent coming of the Lord.[5] To Luther, the peace treaty concluded by the "most Christian emperor" and "most holy pope" with the Turks in 1544 was a criminal and insane action that signified a collapse of the world's order, and this could only be the beginning of the end.[6] Set within this context of the end of the world, it was the conflict with the Jews, the Turks, and the pope that showed Luther who the people of God really were.[7] It was a foregone conclusion that he would attack this tooth and nail.

1. THE JEWS (1525–46)

Luther's relationship to the Jews must be discussed here in a larger context. In 1523 in his book *That Jesus Christ Was Born a Jew,* he had attempted to win some of the Jews for the message of the gospel, and in that context he also advocated humane treatment for them.[1] Aside from the hope of converting the Jews, his relatively positive attitude toward them at that time was also a reaction against Catholic charges that he had too closely adopted their views. The subsequent development of his relationship to the Jews is a problem that has been much discussed, and—for obvious reasons—with much passion, and the answers are sharply contradictory. One view is that there was a lamentable disjunction in Luther's attitude, while the other contends that there was a basic continuity in his position, but that it was modified as a result of specific circumstances. Alternatives like this may not entirely address the subject. Obviously Luther's statements were strongly conditioned by specific situations and by the biblical texts to which he related them.

Exegetical Differences
and Occasional Disappointments

The pertinent text of John 8:46-59 prompted Luther to mention in the Lenten Postil of 1525 the perpetual stumbling block for the Jews—that the man Jesus was God. Conversely, Christ still eluded them. In this the Jews were simply the prototype of blinded humans in general.[2] Among the four psalms whose expositions Luther dedicated to Queen Mary of Hungary in 1526 was Psalm 109, a persecuted person's prayer for punishment of his enemies.[3] For Luther, the psalm was directed primarily against Judas, but likewise against all those "who take Judas's part." Faith curses them, for it cannot allow the error of the Jews to prevail against the gospel. This applies to the Jewish Talmud, but just as much to Catholic canon law and to the Turkish Koran. The psalm foretold the dispersion of the Jews and their homelessness as punishment for this attitude. It stated that they would be treated mercilessly like dogs; nevertheless, they would persist in their hardness of heart and not abandon it. It had become their nature. For contemporary Jews, Christ had become the man who was executed, and the impious attitude of Christians confirmed them in their hardness of heart. Luther's statements were obviously provoked by the text he was exegeting. They are more descriptive than polemic, and in general they apply to more than the Jews. Nevertheless, the hardening of the Jews and the judgment that followed were incontestable facts. The exposition of Psalm 24 in 1530 argued that the Jews, like the pope, did not belong to the people of God, because the former persecuted the prophets; the latter, the evangelical Christians.[4]

In 1530 Luther advised a pastor on how the baptism of a Jewish girl should be performed. He coupled this with a warning that he should make sure the girl's intention was honorable. To be sure, he did not doubt that there was a remnant of Israel that belonged to Christ, but it also happened that Jews were baptized to mock the Christian faith. In 1532 Luther reported the baptism of a Jew in Wittenberg who had not taken it seriously. In the future, therefore, he would take such candidates to the Elbe bridge and dunk them in the water. Later he spoke out in opposition when Amsdorf wanted to baptize a Jew, for "they are rogues."[5] It is difficult to determine whether Luther was here generalizing on the basis of individual experiences. He continued to support the baptized Jew Bernard (Jacob Gipher). When Bernard had to leave his family in 1531 because of his debts, Luther and Melanchthon each cared for one of his children. Bernard was unable to escape poverty for years, and with his needs he was a constant burden to Luther. At the same time, Luther felt obligated to do good to Bernard as a member of the Jewish church. Bernard occasionally served as Luther's messenger.[6]

We also find critical and disappointed statements in 1532 about the Jews, about their rejection of Christ and the resulting inward and outward bondage, about fruitless discussions with them concerning the question of whether those who were uncircumcised also belonged to the people of God.[7] Although the stem of the Jewish people had brought forth prophets, apostles, and Christ, it no longer seemed productive. Nevertheless, the conversion of Israel mentioned in Rom. 11:25-26 compelled Luther to say that the Holy Spirit was more learned than he.[8] He acknowledged in his comments on the Gospel of Matthew (ca. 1534-35) that the Jews were God's chosen and called people. But this did not apply exclusively to them; the Gentiles also belonged to the church. Conversely, it was not only the Jews, but also the papists who had cut themselves off from the children of God by their arbitrary laws and worship practices.[9]

From 1535 onward Luther lectured on Genesis. In so doing he was constantly aware of the contrast between his interpretation and that of the rabbis. In his opinion, their legalism was not in accord with the Holy Spirit and therefore had to be criticized.[10] For Luther, it was none other than the triune God who spoke in the story of creation; he emphatically rejected Jewish interpretations that did not correspond with this. Without Christ, neither the Jews nor the scholastics could understand what gospel and law, sin, grace, and righteousness were.[11] The effort required to correct the rabbinic interpretation was often annoying to Luther. But he considered it valuable to have read the

Jewish exegetes, e.g., the commentary on the Pentateuch by Rabbi Raschi (1040–1105)—although with a "critical authority" that did not permit Christ to be obscured or God's Word deformed.[12] In part he was correct in his criticism, but in part his Christian interpretation reflected the original sense less than did that of the rabbis. The exegetical controversy added fuel to Luther's disdain and hate for the rabbis. He saw them as his foes, because they "crucified Moses" and in their own darkness, like Turks and papists, they did not let Christ and the prophets call them to repentance. Not least were the conflicts over whether the promise to Abraham (Gen. 12:3), which for Christians had been fulfilled in Christ, also applied to Gentiles and over who could claim to be the true people of God. With their false interpretation of Abraham's righteousness (Gen. 15:6), the papists and rabbis showed that they were enemies of Christ and his promised salvation who did not understand the way God acted.[13] Luther's theological controversies were always a struggle over the interpretation of the Bible. Seldom were they matters of mere philology or professorial desire to be right; they almost always concerned the true understanding of revelation, and therefore the conflict was frequently a relentless one. This theological and exegetical difference was a significant element in Luther's conflict with the Jews. He remained in part within the traditional Christian tradition of interpretation of a Nicholas of Lyra (ca. 1270–1349) or the Jewish Christian, Paul of Burgos (1351–1435), but in part the points of contention for him were emphatically Pauline and Reformation.

Luther also dogmatically determined the exegetical difference. In his explanation of the three Christian creeds in 1537 he attacked not only heretics and papists, but also the Jews' shrewd rationalistic denial of the divinity of Jesus and the Trinity, and he confessed his faith explicitly in these articles, which transcended reason and could be believed only with the help of the Holy Spirit. Luther would not let his faith in the triune God be taken from him, especially not by the apostatized Jewish people.[14]

In 1533 Luther showed an understanding of why the Jews had not been won by the papacy, and he hoped to convince many of them by preaching the gospel. In contrast, however, he thought debating with them held no promise.[15] Since 1432 Jews had been forbidden to take up permanent residence in Electoral Saxony. It is unclear why Elector John Frederick issued a mandate at the beginning of August 1536 that prohibited them from staying there, engaging in business, or passing through. There is no evidence that Luther was involved in this, although he had met with the elector in Wittenberg on 23 and 24 July. He appears to have approved the mandate because of the Jews' unwillingness to repent and because of their usury. He also occasionally criticized usury among the Jews, but this was not the real offense. He reported in this context that three rabbis had visited him previously. They knew about Luther's interest in the Hebrew language and hoped to reach some agreement with him. They were not in agreement on the interpretation of messianic prophecies in the Old Testament, however, and Luther left no doubt that he could not approve of the Jews. He then gave his visitors a letter of introduction in which he asked "for Christ's sake" that they be granted free passage. Because of his mention of Christ they refrained from using the letter.[16]

Rejecting the Judaizing Sabbatarians: An Attitude Fundamentally Unchanged

In 1537 Josel of Rosheim (Alsace), who at the time served as sort of a spokesman for Jews in Germany, tried to persuade Elector John Frederick to rescind the mandate of the previous year. A recommendation from Luther would gain him an audience with the elector. Wolfgang Capito interceded with Luther on Josel's behalf. This may not have been the first time that Josel had written to Luther. Luther declined to support Josel's cause with the elector because his advocacy of the Jews in *That Jesus Christ Was Born a Jew* had been misused and the Jews had called Christians apostates. Luther was still in favor of benevolent treatment of the Jews, in order to win them for the Messiah, but he would do nothing to confirm them in their error. He mentioned that he was intending to write a new pamphlet for this purpose. He had been asked to do so years earlier.

Luther attempted to explain to Josel that the Gentiles, who were enemies of the Jews, would not worship the Jewish king, not to mention a crucified Jew, if God had not done this. The Jews' suffering would come to an end only if they joined with the Gentiles in accepting this Christ, their "cousin and Lord." Luther mentioned the rejection of Christ in the rabbinic writings. For him, this was a continuation of the persecution of the saints and prophets in the Old Testament by their own people. It was unmistakable for Luther that the messianic prophecies could refer only to Christ. Finally, Luther maintained: "For the sake of the crucified Jew, whom no one will take from me, I gladly wanted to do my best for you Jews, except that you abused my favor and hardened your hearts."[17]

Luther's letter to Josel has been seen as a turning point in his attitude toward the Jews, but this is hardly accurate. A little later Luther praised the advantages of the chosen people, although he did not fail to mention that they were of no avail before God.[18] In the letter to Josel itself he stated his positive interest in winning the Jews to the Messiah. Alongside this was a polemic against the rabbis who rejected the Messiah. He also mentioned negative experiences of Jewish agitation against Christians. This situation must have existed for several years. Thus the letter to Josel did not indicate a break. Incidentally, the elector's mandate of 1536 was modified in 1539 through Josel's intervention, so that Jews were again permitted to travel through Electoral Saxony.

In the fall of 1532 Luther had already learned, probably from Joachimsthal, that a new sect had arisen in Moravia, which insisted on keeping the Sabbath instead of Sunday. Presumably, its adherents came from circles of the bibli-cistic Anabaptists. Nothing is known about a direct connection between the Sabbatarians and the Jews. Neither can any proselytizing by the Jews be established. It is possible that Luther may have received exaggerated reports. For him, the action of the Sabbatarians was a relapse into Jewish legalism. His rejection of Josel of Rosheim's request for support with the elector was con-nected with the spread of the Sabbatarians in Moravia, who reportedly were practicing circumcision as well. This was significant proof for Luther of the aggressive obduracy of the Jews.[19] In February 1538 Luther was lecturing on Genesis 17, the institution of circumcision. The significance of this eternal covenant of God with Israel was a problem for him. In this context he had to take issue with the Sabbatarians in order to respond to their agitation.[20] Out of this exegetical work grew his letter *Against the Sabbatarians*, published in March.[21] It was intended for Count Wolf Schlick of Falkenau (near Karlsbad), who had asked Luther to supply arguments with which to refute the Sabbatar-ians. Luther advised against a direct exegetical confrontation with the Jews, which could hardly win the Jews, for in Luther's experience of years past,[22] they would when necessary retreat from the text of the Bible to the rabbinic interpretations. What was necessary, therefore, was to strengthen Christians. Luther employed the argument from salvation history, used by Nicholas of Lyra, of why the expulsion of the Jews had lasted for fifteen hundred years. There must be a reason for this puzzle of why the divine promise had not been fulfilled. He mentioned, on the Jewish side, the sins of Israel, among them the worship of the golden calf, but said God still had done good things for Israel, and no other specific sin could be mentioned. Moreover, in Jeremiah 31 there was the promise that God would put his law in his people's heart, that they would know the Lord, and that he would remember their sin no more. Here Luther's exposition became a deep, fundamental presentation of how God acts. God's promise is not conditioned upon human guilt or achievement, but he is the one who makes righteous. This leads to the conclusion that it is precisely in Christ that God's covenant with David must be fulfilled. There-fore the history of the Jewish people cannot continue. He explicitly did not speak about a conversion of Israel to Christ. Luther hoped that this argumen-tation would convince reasonable Jews, that it would at least irritate those who were obdurate, and that it would strengthen Christians in the controversy.

In the second part of the letter Luther dealt with the eternal validity of the law. He sought to refute this on theological, historical, and exegetical grounds, by attempting, among other things, to distinguish what was human and rela-tively "eternal" from what was divine, but his arguments varied in plausibility. He did not understand circumcision to be a universal commandment. The covenant of the law prevailed only until the coming of the Messiah. The Decalogue in its biblical form is initially a Jewish law, which for the most part corresponds to the universal natural law. The commandment about the sabbath was acknowledged only as a general instruction about teaching and hearing God's Word. Luther hoped that thereby he had given the recipient of his letter adequate arguments against the Sabbatarians. If the Jews were not converted by this, it was just like their hardness of heart in relation to their own prophets. He was resigned about this. Because the Jews had not repented in the fifteen hundred years of their diaspora, one should not expect them to do so in the present. God had abandoned his people. In conclusion, Luther said that he still had more to say on this subject, although the open letter had already become inordinately long.

Against the Sabbatarians was intended to be used by Christians as a theological and apologetic argument against Judaism. Not all its arguments are equally convincing, but some are still impressive. Aside from occasionally revealing a general criticism and annoyance with the Jewish interpretation of the Bible, it does not go beyond the bounds of a theological treatise. The letter was reprinted only once, and was also translated into Latin by Jonas. The preface to the Latin translation stated that the reason the Jews had been scorned was the disdain for study of the Bible in the papacy. It emphasized Christianity's heritage from Judaism. The task of Christians, therefore, was to lead Jews out of their errors and show them the right way. Jonas believed that Luther's work did this, and it had even impressed Duke George of Saxony. Jonas therefore wanted the work to be regarded as serving a missionary purpose, not an apologetic one. Nevertheless, Luther fails to demonstrate the positive interest in the Jews that Jonas expressed in his preface.[23]

Sentiments of this sort were not unknown to Luther at that time, but he emphasized in this context that the Jews had condemned themselves by rejecting the Messiah. For him, Jesus' prophecy of the destruction of the Temple was proof that the worship of the Jews and their reign had come to an end, but the Jews would not accept this.[24] In 1539 Luther read a book published in 1530 by the Jewish Christian, Anthony Margaritha, *The Whole Jewish Faith, Together with a Thorough and Truthful Account of All the Regulations, Ceremonies, and Prayers Both for Family and Public Worship, as Observed by the Jews throughout the Year, with Excellent and Well-founded Arguments against Their Faith*, out of which in part he drew his critical arguments against the Jews. Reading it confirmed for him their blindness, which wanted nothing to do with faith and justification through faith, thus making them like the papists. He thought it dangerous for Christians to have Jewish doctors treat them. He insisted that a divorce involving a baptized Jew could not take place in the Jewish form, but had to be performed in accordance with the regulations of the Christian government, because no one could trust Jews.[25] Michael, a Jew from Posen who wanted to be baptized, came to Luther in 1540. As in earlier cases, Luther questioned him intently in order to make sure

339

that his intentions were pure.[26] Luther once stated that he admired—indeed, loved—the Jewish people. Their great men were superior to the church fathers of the Christians. Christ was the flower that grew from the beautiful plant of this people. Nevertheless, the fact that the angel Lucifer and the seed of Abraham had been cast down should frighten Christians out of their complacency.[27]

Nothing changed concerning Luther's rejection of rabbinic biblical exegesis. In his opinion, it was impossible to interpret the suffering servant (Isaiah 53) as referring to the Jewish people. He was thinking about writing a new preface to the Bible that would warn against the blinded and obdurate rabbis.[28] To some extent he carried out this intention with his *New Preface to the Prophet Ezekiel* of 1541.[29] In it he accused the rabbis of "tearing the Scripture apart and tormenting it with their commentaries, like filthy sows rooting up and overturning a pleasure garden." For Luther, the vision of the throne and wheels in Ezekiel 1 could refer only to the kingdom of Christ and thus it had to be interpreted in terms of the cessation of the Jewish worship services. This nullified the promise of a land to Israel and the Jews' hope of returning to it. The new covenant was fulfilled in Christ, but the Jews did not accept it and therefore were scattered. The Christians became the true Israelites. The Jews injured themselves in not accepting the new covenant. This preface, in fact, was a total repudiation of Jewish hopes.

In the Bible revision of 1541, a new gloss was added to Matt. 27:15, which concerned the choice between releasing Christ or Barabbas: The Jews "would rather have worshiped the devil himself than let God's Son go. This is also true today and always." But entirely different is the gloss on Rom. 15:8: "In sum, this epistle says that both, Jews and Christians, will be saved."[30] The extensive protocol from 1541 on the revision of Romans 11 confirms this several times: "The Jews are not denied life, and the door of grace is not closed." Grace stands open to Jews and Gentiles until the end of the world. "The Jews are not to be abandoned entirely, this is his [Paul's] earnest affirmation." The papal church is held equally answerable for the fact that few Jews have been won. The outcome (Rom. 11:33) remains open. There God says: "Go, preach, baptize; who knows what I will do with Jews, Gentiles. I do not share my will with you. Let God alone, we cannot fathom his decree."[31]

In these years, as before, Luther's attitude toward the Jews was not uniform. To be sure, he left no doubt about his rejection of the Jewish exegesis of the Bible and their expectation of salvation, but he did not abandon the Pauline expectation that a portion of the Jews might be won for Christ. The confrontation with rabbinic exegesis and the appearance of the Sabbatarians caused him to note clearly his demarcation from the Jews, without thereby fundamentally changing his previous view. Even the vacillation in Luther's statements shows that there was no discontinuity in his view, even though some scholars wish to claim that there was.

Advocating Expulsion of the Jews Because of a Violated Faith

Reportedly in May 1541, but probably not until a year later, Luther learned that the Jews had been expelled from Bohemia. In his opinion, they had brought this on themselves by their impenitence. At that time, probably again from Count Wolf Schlick, he received a (no longer extant) rabbinic writing that attacked his *Against the Sabbatarians.* He was reminded in this context of the offense the hymn "Christ Is Arisen" caused for the Jews, for it testified that the Crucified One still lived.[32] In the summer or fall Luther developed a plan to write once more against the Jews because they were being tolerated in some evangelical territories—which territories were not mentioned. Luther wanted to advise expelling them. The reason given was their evil calumnies against the Virgin Mary and Christ, which the authorities should not tolerate. This shows that the escalation of Luther's Jewish polemic was not occasioned by following the anti-Jewish politics of some sovereign; quite the contrary, because he felt they were doing violence to his faith, he advocated that the government take action against the Jews.[33] In preparation for his task, Luther reread Anthony Margaritha's *The Whole Jewish Faith,* which renewed his awareness of the relationship between Jewish and Catholic legalistic piety. The action of the Jews was proof for him that conditions had gotten dangerously worse. He reacted to this with the prayer: "Come therefore, dear Lord! Come and strike about thee with thy day of judgment, for no improvement is any longer to be expected!"[34]

On the Jews and Their Lies was completed at the end of December 1542. On 21 December Luther was "immersed in the madness of the Jews." On 17 January 1543 Melanchthon sent "the pamphlet, which truly contains many useful teachings" to Landgrave Philip.[35] Luther had not intended to write against the Jews again. With his new book he was thus not executing the plan he had frequently mentioned earlier, although this became his great and problematic attack against the Jews, the one that eclipsed all his other statements. It was not until Count Schlick sent Luther the rabbinic rebuttal of his *Against the Sabbatarians,* with its misinterpretation of central Bible passages about Christ and Mary, that he grasped his pen. Like *Against the Sabbatarians,* this work was not intended for the Jews, because there was nothing to learn from them, nor could they be converted or refuted. One should not debate them but at most ask anew how their dispersion for nearly fifteen hundred years could be reconciled with God's promises. There was no sense in debating the articles of the Christian faith with them, until they gave in to their suffering and confessed that Jesus was the Messiah. Thus Luther wanted, first of all, to strengthen the faith of Christians and refute the blasphemies of the Jews for them. That is why the title was not "Against the Jews" but *On the Jews.*[36]

The first part dealt with the advantages of which the Jews boasted.[37] In it Luther referred to the Jewish prayers he knew from Margaritha's *The Whole*

341

Jewish Faith. Their first boast was that they were children of Abraham. He could show convincingly with several biblical passages that this in itself did not guarantee an unbroken relationship with God. This climaxed in the decisive argument of Luther's anthropology: The sinner has nothing that he can present before God. The same was true of circumcision. According to the biblical witness, it is not limited to the Jews and does not guarantee salvation. The uncircumcised can also be chosen by God. Luther understood circumcision as an analogy to baptism, which as an outward sign or work was also of no avail if one did not believe in the promise of one's acceptance as a child of God that accompanied it. The Jews also boasted that God had spoken directly to them in revealing the law and thereby established a covenant similar to marriage. By referring to the prophets' condemnations, however, it could be asked whether the human partner in this covenant was not a whore instead of a pure bride. Restricting this at most to pious Jews was something Luther would not grant, for in his spiteful opinion there were none such. Luther also did not recognize as superior the Jewish law that went beyond the Decalogue. For Luther, it was just as much a document of a legalistic piety as was the Catholic canon law. He then focused on the question of the meaning of the law. In unison with the penitential psalms, its meaning lay not in its fulfillment, which was impossible for men, but in its revelation of sin and acknowledgement of the one upon whom God had laid all sin (Isa. 53:4-5). One could thus only warn Christians against being led astray by Jewish legalistic piety. Finally, Luther dealt relatively easily with the boast that they had been promised a land, for this had become meaningless when the Jews were driven out of Palestine. Luther's opposition to the Jewish piety resulted centrally from his doctrine of justification, and this sharply defined the insurmountable differences. As in the later parts of the book, this was accompanied by a penetrating critique, which in its generalizations was also exaggerated and vicious. The emphasis, however, lay in the noteworthy theological argumentation.

As important as this first part of *On the Jews* was, the main portion was the following section, which dealt with the promised Messiah. This was explicated not dogmatically but rather as a thoroughgoing, renewed controversy with the rabbinic interpretation of the Scriptures of four central promises. Interestingly, it was this section that especially impressed Landgrave Philip.[38] First, Luther dealt again with the obscure word to Judah in Jacob's blessing (Gen. 49:10): The scepter, the rule, shall not depart from Judah until Messiah comes. Luther believed that he could prove that the Messiah had come fifteen hundred years earlier, at the same time Judah lost the scepter. In regard to the covenant with David (2 Sam. 23:1-5), he maintained the same thesis: The Davidic rule lasted, although with limitations, until the time of Herod and then was taken over by Christ. Luther later wrote *The Last Words of David* on this subject, another separate work. In the messianic prophecy of Hag. 2:6-9 the Vulgate differed from the original text.[39] Following it, Luther had translated: "The consolation of the Gentiles [viz., Christ] shall come." The Jewish version, in fact, was correct: "The treasures of all nations shall come in," although Luther denounced it as motivated by the greed of the Jews. He saw the greater glory of the Temple embodied in Christ. His messianic interpretation of the passage was a foregone conclusion, and he himself should have recognized it as incorrect. Luther also saw the seventy weeks of years until the beginning of the time of salvation in Dan. 9:24 as precisely referring to Jesus as the coming Messiah. Despite the incorrect exegesis of Haggai 2, Luther's understanding of salvation history, in which the messianic prophecies were fulfilled in Christ, was considered more plausible at that time than the Jewish interpretations. It was not until the Enlightenment that the problems of messianic interpretation were considered extensively.

Although the first two parts of *On the Jews and Their Lies* are scarcely known any longer, the concluding third part,[40] sadly, has achieved infamy in connection with modern anti-Semitism. For a proper understanding, it is once again necessary to look closely at its context. While previously questions of theological fact were at stake, in this part it is Jewish "lies" about people, viz., Christ, Mary, and the Christians.

Luther regarded these polemics as personal attacks on what was holy for his faith, and accordingly he reacted vehemently. Here he dealt with the legend that Jesus was a cabalistic magician. Luther declared that he would take issue with this in a separate publication. Then he mentioned the Jewish curses against Jesus, which in part were likewise initiated by a cabalistic manipulation of the letters of the alphabet. Mary was treated no better than Jesus, for she was called a whore or a dung heap. She was also accused of having conceived Jesus while menstruating, and for this reason he was a freak. According to Luther, the reason for such abuse of the "poor man Jesus" could be only a madness and blindness inflicted by God. Christians were affected by these blasphemies, for they reverenced Christ and Mary. In addition, the Jews expected that their Messiah would slay the Gentiles. In this context Luther accepted the horror stories about Jews poisoning springs and abducting children for ritual murders. He rejected the claim that the Jews were even then being held captive: "We surely did not bring them from Jerusalem. . . . We would be glad to present gifts to them . . . it would be good riddance." Luther also made economic arguments. In a grotesque perversion of the facts, he depicted Jews as loafers, while Christians had to work. The Jews were a plague, a sickness one had contracted.

This posed the question of what measures should be employed against the Jews. The madness worked by God could not be cured, nor was a conversion possible. Luther rejected any sort of vengeance, for it was certainly coming upon the Jews anyway. "With prayer and the fear of God we must practice a sharp mercy," in order, perhaps, to rescue a few from the flames of wrath. The concept of "sharp mercy," which Luther also used in referring to the peasants and to Henry of Brunswick, appears here in all its contradictoriness and precariousness, for it can justify the use of force. Luther made seven specific proposals. Synagogues should be burned and destroyed, because in them Christ and Christians were reviled. No "churches" should be available for the idolatry caused by rabbinic legalism. Here Luther was arguing with concepts taken from the sacred law of the Old Testament and from the laws against heretics, which provided that blasphemy was a criminal offense. Both of these were inappropriate in the context of his theology. In addition, the houses of the Jews should be destroyed, because similar blasphemy was committed in them. Instead, Jews should be provided emergency shelters like that of the gypsies. For the same reason, the Talmud and prayerbooks should be confiscated and the rabbis forbidden to teach.

Luther argued that for economic reasons the Jews should be denied free passage, prohibited from practicing usury, and have their possessions of money and precious metals confiscated, for they had stolen them from Christians. This money should be used to provide a minimum standard of living for baptized Jews and to support aged Jews. It should therefore be used for a specific purpose and not simply be put into the treasury. The Jews, like everyone else, had to obey imperial laws in conducting business. They should earn their living by performing a sort of compulsory labor for Christians. If this implementation of "sharp mercy" seemed too dangerous, they should be exiled, as had happened in other lands. The indemnities that the authorities had imposed upon the Jews were no proof of their value to the state, for these funds had previously been extorted from those under them. Moreover, these indemnities could not be a license for blasphemy and animosity. These proposals were addressed to the authorities, who, along with their subjects, were not to become a party to the sins of others. In light of the existing enmity, Luther believed that coexistence of the Christian and Jewish religions was impossible; at best, a symbiotic relationship was acceptable, predicated upon a lowering of the Jews' social position. What Luther really intended was the expulsion of the Jews, not their deaths. The proposals were the unavoidable consequence of the preceding analysis and the evaluation of the relationship between both parties. If this animosity of Jews against Christians existed—and, for Luther, there was proof for it in the rabbinic interpretation of the Scriptures, their polemics, and their agitation—there could then be no coexistence. He gave no thought to the possibilities of a common modus vivendi or mutual toleration.

Besides the authorities, Luther addressed the pastors and preachers, who, even if the authorities did nothing, had to warn against the Jews, for on every Sabbath they cursed Christ the Redeemer and the Christians. To be sure, one could not force Jews to adopt the Christian faith, but one also should not encourage their behavior by allowing them to live together with Christians. Accordingly, pastors had to instruct the authorities either to follow the proposals or else to banish the Jews. Luther soberly assumed, however, that pastors would be able to accomplish little because of the "indulgence of the perverted world." All that was left was the conviction of the New Testament that Jews were "a brood of vipers and children of the devil," which could again be proved with horror stories. Then Luther dealt even more deeply with the problem. Even if it were granted that the Jews did not accept the New Testament, Christians were not to tolerate their public cursing of Christ and Mary, and thereby God himself, or else they would become party to their sin. Jewish polemics could not be accepted, but rather had to be forbidden, especially because God unmistakably had revealed his Son in the New Testament. Luther again specifically mentioned his proposals about burning the synagogues, confiscating Jewish books, and prohibiting Jewish worship, and he also wanted to forbid Jews to speak the name of God. He did not accept the excuse that the Jewish polemic was not meant seriously. Even if these proposals were carried out, the Jews would continue to curse in secret, and thus the only thing to do was expel them. The authorities should not let themselves be deterred from doing so by offers of money. One of the most offensive issues Luther held against the Jews was their claim that Christians worshiped more than one God. Luther would have preferred to have the Jewish scholars forced "on pain of losing their tongues" to prove this. He understood, of course, that they had difficulties with the doctrine of the Trinity, but the accusation of tritheism was an insufferable lie for him. The only thing that would avail against it would be sharp mercy that purged the evil away.

What concerned Luther most deeply is seen in his reason for rejecting Jewish messianism, which displays similarities to his renunciation of Erasmus:[41] "If God were to give me no other Messiah than such as the Jews wish and hope for, I would much, much rather be a sow than a human being." These alternatives, which at first glance are uncouth, are more deeply based than initially apparent. Luther wanted nothing to do with a Messiah as a worldly ruler who simply slew Christians. This would be the same whether he acknowledged the Turkish sultan or the Jewish Messiah. There would still be the fear of an inevitable death and God's judgment. In contrast, a sow can live free and easy in the day. "However, if I had a Messiah who could remedy this grief, so that I would no longer have to fear death but would be always and eternally sure of life, and able to play a trick on the devil and death and no longer have to tremble before the wrath of God, then my heart would leap for joy and be intoxicated with sheer delight; then would a fire of love for God be enkindled, and my praise and thanks would never cease." This was the Messiah the Christians had in Christ. With their earthly expectation and their legalistic piety, the Jews did not know what to do with him. The Christian Messiah claimed no earthly power. In accordance with the promises of the prophets, swords would be turned into plowshares in his kingdom. He had extended and established his reign without force, and the Gentiles had submitted to him. In him and in no other were the messianic prophecies fulfilled. Although Luther thought that Jews were possessed by all the devils, in the conclusion he yet expressed the wish: "May Christ, our dear Lord, convert them mercifully and preserve us steadfastly and immovably in the knowledge of him, which is eternal life. Amen."

It is obvious how Luther was ultimately contending in this book for his faith in Christ. At the same time there is a deep contradiction in his argumentation that is apparent: He wanted to defend his non-violent Christ with the power of the Christian state. His bias in favor of the existing political and social system of evangelical Christianity of that time induced him to suggest completely inappropriate, even dangerous measures. Because of his fear and hate there was little room for confidence and love. The weaknesses and false consequences of Luther's piety, which drew sharp distinctions, are nowhere more clearly visible than here.

As he had announced, Luther soon continued his pertinent literary activity during the first months of 1543. In preparation for *On the Jews* he had read, in addition to Margaritha's *The Whole Jewish Faith,* the *Victoria adversus impios Hebraeos* (Victory over the godless Hebrews) by Salvagus Porchetus, a Carthusian monk from Genoa, which had been written about 1300, and he had made critical marginal notes in it.[42] In both books he found Jewish legends of how Jesus had craftily gotten control of the *Schem Hamphoras* (the ineffable name of God, derived from cabalistic speculation about the letters in Exod. 14:19-21) and thereby had been able to perform miracles until he was exposed and executed. Luther took issue with this vilification of Jesus, and also with a criticism of the differing genealogies of Jesus in Matthew and Luke, which was contained in the Jewish response to *Against the Sabbatarians,* by writing *On the Tetragrammaton and the Genealogy of Christ.*[43] It was no coincidence that it once more dealt with the person of Jesus. The intention was again to instruct Christians, not to win Jews, which Luther considered a hopeless undertaking, "for a Jew or a Jewish heart is as hard as a stick, a stone, as iron, as a devil, so that there is no way it can be moved." In no case could conversion of all the Jews be expected. Luther initially presented a translation of the legend of Jesus and the *Schem Hamphoras* by Porchetus. Then he subjected this "devil's dung that the Jews eat" to a critique, which was not difficult in light of the legend's fantasies. In this context he unmistakably and with great ridicule rejected the cabala's manipulation of the alphabet as magic, which was irreconcilable with a proper exegesis of the Bible. This applied also to its beloved speculations about the name of Yahweh. He depicted the origin of these ideas in an extreme fashion by referring to a medieval caricature of the Jews that to this day is located on the Wittenberg city church (Plate XV): "Here at Wittenberg on our parish church is a sow carved in stone, and lying under her are young piglets and Jews who suckle there. Behind the sow stands a rabbi, who lifts up the sow's right leg and with his left hand pulls the sow's rump toward him, bends down, and with great interest looks at the Talmud under the sow's rump, as if to read and learn something difficult and special." One could not perceive God's promises through the cabalistic arts of manipulating letters of the alphabet, but in this way could only become a servant of the devil. Because of, among other things, the inclusion of the Wittenberg caricature, the Zurich theologians thought the book worthy only of a swineherd (*Schweinehirten*), not of a great shepherd of souls (*Seelenhirten*), and this can hardly be denied. Andreas Osiander in Nuremberg, who was otherwise also favorably disposed toward the Jews, had a different opinion of the cabala and therefore criticized *On the Tetragrammaton*. Melanchthon made sure that his criticism did not reach Luther, for he would presumably have reacted harshly to it.[44]

The fact that Jesus' genealogy in Matthew was traced through Joseph (Matt. 1:16) and not through Mary had long been regarded as a problem. For Luther, however, it was clear from Old Testament prophecy that Mary was also of David's line, and if the Jews had not been hardened they would have had to believe this. In addition, there was a clear statement in Matt. 1:1 that Jesus was David's son. Luther then made an extensive attempt to clarify the complex relationships of Jesus' lineage. He also tried to prove that the virgin birth had been prophesied in Isa. 7:14, although it spoke only of a young woman, not of a virgin, and thus his proof cannot be conclusive. That Luther called the Jews' objections "Jewish piss and shit" did not make matters any better. Nevertheless, for him both Old and New Testaments testified to the virgin birth, and people had to submit to this Word of God instead of believing in the rabbinic glosses. Thus the work was more than a warning against the "Jewish piss" of the rabbinic interpretation of the Scriptures, like the one Luther at that time also issued against the philology of the Hebrew scholars.[45] He declared that he was going to make a new Christian translation and explanation of 2 Sam. 23:1-7, an important passage for the study of messianism.

This work, *Treatise on the Last Words of David*,[46] first presented the critique by rabbis and Hebrew scholars of the Christian interpretation of the Bible. Luther did not let this disturb him. For him, the premise that the Old Testament also bore witness to Christ was unshakable, for otherwise the Bible could not be rightly understood. The Old Testament was to be interpreted on the basis of the New. Luther placed this fundamental principle above philological findings, and therefore he was unwilling to accept rabbinic criticism at face value: "Now I will be stubborn and follow no one but my own spirit." God would reveal who was right. Because of this he prepared a new commentary and translation of the last words of David, which was then included in the Luther Bible. According to Luther, in these words David appealed to a promise of the anointed one (Messiah). He thus was living—entirely in accord with the schema of Lutheran theology—on the basis of the promise. According to the actual text, David himself was speaking as the anointed one (king), but for Luther it was really the triune God, in whom the humanity of Jesus was involved, who was speaking in David. Luther reached this conclusion, which was important for him, by altering somewhat the order of the elements of the sentence. God's covenant with David (2 Sam. 7:11-16 and 1 Chron. 17:10-14) did not, as the sense of the words indicated, refer to Solomon and the Temple, but pointed beyond: to the Messiah and his kingdom. It was irrefutable that the Messiah was God and man at the same time. David was said already to have learned from Moses of the witness to the divine Trinity. According to him, the creation of the world was the work of the triune God. Luther's work thus became a profound treatise on the doctrine of the Trinity and the divine sonship of Jesus, which also used the Old Testament extensively, so that the traditional Christian interpretation of the Old Testament with its many interesting aspects can be fully seen. Luther believed that with this amount of material he had proved there was no value to the grammatical interpretations and commentaries of the rabbis. Christian theologians should take the Bible away from them, so that its testimony to Christ could be sharply and clearly seen.

As impressively as he presented all of this, Luther was still aware that he had interpreted and transformed the biblical text of David's final words in his own sense, and that he had offered a "stubborn" interpretation. The literal understanding of the rabbis was not infrequently more accurate. Luther deliberately violated exegetical methods for the sake of what were for him higher theological principles. This occurred at the expense of the convincing power of his interpretation, which could not be maintained in the long run. None of the theologians among Luther's associates was in a position to correct him. Melanchthon called *The Last Words of David* a "shining work."[47] That the God of the Old Testament and the Father of Jesus were one and the same could have been explained in a different way, and his controversy with the Jewish interpretation might have been conducted differently. Then it would not have been possible for Luther to reject it so harshly out of hand. On the contrary, points of contact for a common discussion might have arisen.

The two short lectures, on Isaiah 9 in 1543–44 and Isaiah 53 in 1544, again dealt with central messianic prophecies. It was not unintentional that in them Luther took issue with the Jewish exegesis. He vehemently rejected the correct interpretation of Isaiah 9 as a reference to the time of the war between Syria and Ephraim. For him, this was not about a war on earth. The text had to refer to Christ, and the Jews, "the crucifiers of Christ," had garbled it, as they were otherwise wont to do.[48] The Jews denied that the song of the suffering servant of God (Isaiah 53) referred to Christ, but in this case the text itself (Isa. 52:14-15) appeared to speak about their blindness. The Jews understood the mystery of the union of the divine and human natures in Christ no more than they did the suffering of the Son of God. For them, the suffering servant of God was the Jewish people. In Luther's opinion, their murderous hatred for Christ and those who belonged to him extended into the present, and he again referred to alleged horror stories as proof of this. Nevertheless, he did not fail to mention that the suffering servant of God had prayed for his torturers.[49] In a sermon in the summer of 1544 Luther once drew sharp distinctions between Christians and Jews. The latter were still waiting for the Messiah as an earthly ruler, who would rebuild the Temple and slay the Gentiles. Christians expected forgiveness of sins and resurrection from the coming Christ. There was no longer any basis for the hope of the Jews.[50]

In his lectures on Isaiah 53 the Jews were occasionally held responsible for the death of Christ, although he also emphasized that they were merely carrying out the will of God. But in regard to the old accusation that the Jews had killed the Son of God, Luther unmistakably gave a different interpretation in a revision of the hymn, "O, You Poor Judas, What Did You Do," which was published in Wittenberg in 1544 and certainly is to be ascribed to him:

> T'was our great sins and misdeeds gross
> Nailed Jesus, God's true Son, to the cross.
> Thus you, poor Judas, we dare not blame,
> Nor the band of Jews; ours is the shame.[51]

Any other interpretation would hardly have been compatible with Luther's theology. In the revision of the Bible in 1544 he noted again: "There are always a few Jews who will be saved."[52]

Luther's writings against the Jews were reprinted relatively seldom. This may lead us to the conclusion that they had little effect during his lifetime, but he himself did attempt to see that his proposals for harsh action against the Jews were implemented. Thus it is clearer than perhaps has previously been noted that his specific proposals were not mere theory. The harsh mandate against the Jews in Electoral Saxony on 6 May 1543, which forbade any Jew to settle or to pass through the land and also ordered the confiscation of their property, referred specifically to *On the Jews and Their Lies*. Luther was a guest of the elector on the day it was issued.[53] Luther thanked Prince George for expelling the Jews from Anhalt in June 1543.[54] Influenced by Luther's book, Margrave Hans of Brandenburg-Küstrin also expelled the Jews, who, however, were taken in by his brother, Elector Joachim II. When George Buchholzer, the dean in Berlin, preached against the Jews and advocated that Elector Joachim take action against them, this corresponded entirely with the intention of Luther, who, regarding Buchholzer, again referred to the Jews' calumnies against Christ and Mary. Thus it aroused his ire that much more when John Agricola in Berlin defended the Jews with Bible passages. In February 1544 Luther mentioned that Joachim II and also King Ferdinand in Prague were accepting the Jews for financial reasons. He hoped that Christ, who soon would be coming in judgment, would punish such love of money. A year later he warned Joachim once more about the tricks of the Jews and praised Buchholzer's agitation against them.[55] When Friedrich Bachofen, the preacher in Hammelburg, demanded that the Jews there attend his sermons, the mayor, on advice of the prince-abbot of Fulda, rejected this demand. Luther complained that the abbot was "the patron of the Jews," who liked Christ's enemies and blasphemers more than the true servants of Christ.[56]

When Counts Philip and Hans George of Mansfeld were favorable to the Jews in the spring of 1543, despite Luther's writings, it provoked his rage, which so mounted that he said that in his rage he would kill a blaspheming Jew—that would sooner be allowed against a blasphemer than against a robber.[57] During his last journey to Eisleben, Luther suspected that the cold wind that blew against him in Rissdorf was the fault of the Jews there. Several times in his sermons in Eisleben he attacked the Jews. He realized, of course, that they were the firstborn, and that Christians had to thank them for the law, the prophets, and even Christ himself, but this gave the Jews no right to set themselves up against God and to kill Christ and Christians.[58] He appended *An Admonition Against the Jews* probably to his last sermon but one. He wanted people initially to deal in a Christian way with them and call upon them to accept the Messiah, their "cousin," and to be baptized, but the Jews blasphemed Christ daily. This could not be tolerated, or people would be participating in the sins of another. The princes should expel such Jews, but in case they converted, abandoned usury, and accepted Christ they should be considered brothers. There was no other option. This time as well, Luther did not fail to mention the well-known invectives of the Jews, as well as to accuse Jewish doctors of being poisoners. In the obdurate Jews he saw blasphemers, leeches, and potential murderers. There could be no fellowship with them. One last time the motive for Luther's hostility was apparent: "I am still praying daily and I duck under the shelter of the Son of God. I hold him and honor him as my Lord, to whom I must run and flee when the devil, sin, or other misfortune threatens me, for he is my shelter, as wide as heaven and earth, and my mother hen under whom I crawl from God's wrath. Therefore I cannot have any fellowship or patience with obstinate blasphemers and those who defame this dear Savior." Those who converted should gladly be forgiven, but those Jews who refused "we should neither tolerate nor suffer among us."[59] Luther's inward piety of Christ also had the harsh result of condemning those who were enemies of his faith.

In conclusion, an evaluation of Luther's relationship with the Jews must be made. Like all Christian theologians of his time, he regarded the Jewish religion and its adherents in a negative way and wished that they would convert to Christianity. He became increasingly pessimistic about the possibilities and prospects of this happening, but he never denied them entirely. His opposition to the Jews, which ultimately was regarded as irreconcilable, was in its nucleus of a religious and theological nature that had to do with belief in Christ and justification, and it was associated with the understanding of the people of God and the interpretation of the Old Testament. Economic and social motives played only a subordinate role. Luther's animosity toward the Jews cannot be interpreted either in a psychological way as a pathological hatred or in a political way as an extension of the anti-Judaism of the territorial princes. But he certainly demanded that measures provided in the laws against heretics be employed to expel the Jews—similarly to their use against the Anabaptists—because, in view of the Jewish polemics against Christ, he saw no possibilities for religious coexistence. In advising the use of force, he advocated means that were essentially incompatible with his faith in Christ. In addition, his criticism of the rabbinic interpretation of the Scriptures in part violated his own exegetical principles. Therefore, his attitude toward the Jews can appropriately be criticized both for his methods and also from the center of his theology. Luther, however, was not involved with later racial anti-Semitism. There is a world of difference between his belief in salvation and a racial ideology. Nevertheless, his misguided agitation had the evil result that Luther fatefully became one of the "church fathers" of anti-Semitism and thus provided material for the modern hatred of the Jews, cloaking it with the authority of the Reformer.

2. THE TURKS

The Turks advancing through southeastern Europe were a source of anxiety throughout Luther's lifetime.[1] He frequently spoke in his Table Talk and letters about the latest news of the Turks, but he was more than just an interested contemporary. Luther associated the threat from the Turks with the end of history and connected the possibility of repulsing them with the situation of the church. Therefore he himself had to deal with the Turkish danger in different respects.

In 1532 Luther took note of the cautious advance of the Turks in Hungary, where they were avoiding a decisive battle. He thought King Ferdinand's loss of territory was punishment for his persecution of the gospel.[2] In August 1537 he was anticipating a divine visitation of Germany by the Turks, against which the pope, "the Antichrist in Rome," could offer no help. The evangelical Christians were likewise threatened, but they had the comfort of having a gracious God, and they would go to heaven if they died.[3] From December onward, there was news in Wittenberg of a severe and ignominious defeat that King Ferdinand had suffered. There was a rumor that Katzianer, the commander of the army, had been taken prisoner by the Turks. The Germans seemed unequal to the antigodly strength of the Turks. One could only hope that their power would finally be broken.[4] Luther viewed the stockpiling of arms against the Turks in 1538 with suspicion, for he feared that they were really intended for an attack on the evangelicals. He advised his elector to contribute assistance against the Turks, even though he doubted King Ferdinand's leadership qualities and his chances of success. One was not required to come to Ferdinand's aid, but rather to the aid of the fatherland and those who were suffering. Moreover, Luther assumed that there would be serious consequences if the imperial army were to attack the evangelicals. In everything else, one had to trust God. Luther's distrust of Ferdinand continued, of course.[5] The confused situation—whether the threat was of an attack by the Turks or by Ferdinand against the evangelicals—lasted into 1539. Under these circumstances Luther addressed an admonition to the pastors, probably at the end of February. They should call attention on one hand to blasphemy and persecution among the Catholics, and on the other to ingratitude, disdain for God's Word, and moral failings among the evangelicals. They should pray that God's punishment would be limited and not lead to a breakdown of the political order or to a religious war in Germany, such as the pope wanted. In these circumstances God alone could help, and only the evangelicals were able to pray to him in hopes that he would hear them. In the months following nothing changed this view.[6]

Süleyman I took advantage of the death of King John Zápolya of Hungary in 1540 to occupy large sections of Hungary in August of the following year. At the beginning of September he marched into Buda. Once again, this increased the threat to Germany posed by the Turks. The chamberlain of Electoral Saxony, George Weiss, wanted to take part in a campaign against the Turks and asked Luther for his advice about this. Luther replied in mid-August with a very pessimistic evaluation of the undertaking. Impenitent people, among them papists with their bloodstained hands, had little prospect of success. Luther therefore opposed having good people sacrifice themselves to no avail. He did not see that he was in a position to pray for a victory over the Turks, but only that as many people as possible might be spared. A requirement for participating in the Turkish war had to be one's recognition of his own sin, for which the Turks were the punishment. The legitimate motive for taking part in a war was to help those in distress, and one's inner equipment had to be faith in God.[7] Germany was going to be punished either for its animosity toward the evangelicals or for its sins. Luther, nevertheless, saw his task as praying for his Christian opponents.[8]

After the conquest of Buda, which now seemed to put Vienna in danger, Elector John Frederick asked Luther and Bugenhagen to send preachers an *Appeal for Prayer Against the Turks*.[9] Luther's thoughts went in the same direction as before. The new enlightenment through God's Word that the Reformation had brought had been met with persecution. God could not be pleased about this, for God was not a "puppet." There was also great ingratitude among the evangelicals with sectarians like Müntzer, Zwingli, and the Anabaptists, with greed and usury in all the estates, and also widespread underpayment and persecution of pastors. Here Luther's entire criticism of the political, ecclesiastical, and social circumstances was repeated. Germany was thus ripe for judgment, just like humankind before the flood, but no word of despair should be uttered. The Turk should rather be seen as a schoolmaster teaching the true fear of God. This meant to repent and put away the existing abuses; otherwise, no help should be expected. But it might also happen that no repentance took place; Christians then would have to trust that God would not abandon them in their misfortune. Meanwhile, everyone was admonished, each in his own calling, to offer resistance. For true Christians this meant to pray fervently. In that time, to be sure, there were no charismatics who were strong in prayer, but God would hear the cries of his church as he always had, and in the past he had miraculously helped it even against the pope, whom Luther regarded as worse than the Turks. Thus preachers had to call people to repent, even though they might not like doing it. Those who did not want to suffer showed only that they did not belong to the church, but to the Turks, the pope, and the devil. Likewise, cursing should be stopped in the army. Along with repentance there should be constant prayer. One should have confidence in God's goodness, not in one's own worthiness. God's freedom could not be limited, of course.

Luther then suggested a liturgy for prayer against the Turks, appending a prayer of his own. After a confession of sins, it emphasized that confronting the Turks and Mohammed was God's own affair, and also Christ's. Luther's praying was anything but naive. He knew that there could be situations in which one could no longer pray because of the perversity that existed, but he did not see this as one. It might be, however, that prayer would not be answered because the danger from the Turks was one of the apocalyptic events of the last days. Then the end of the Turks, like the pope, would not be far off. Luther expressly warned against a fatalistic Turkish-like determinism, such as he had frequently encountered in his pastoral care, which regarded one's own fate as unchangeable. One should not investigate God's eternal decree, but trust in him and accept what one has been given. Regarding the war against the Turks, one had to remember that it really concerned the devil. With God on their side they had nothing to fear, not even death, not even if the Turks and the pope were to be the two apocalyptic enemies. In an appendix Luther specifically excluded from God's protection the Catholic opponents like Henry of Brunswick and Albrecht of Mainz, as well as the tyrannical nobles, usurers, and misers in his own camp. Unlike them, Christians did not depend on wisdom and power, and, also unlike them, they had no fear. "Our solace, boldness, self-confidence, security, victory, life, joy, our honor and glory are seated up there in person at the right hand of God the Father Almighty. Satan, we dare you to touch a single hair of his head. His name is and always will be *Sheblimini* [he who sits at God's right hand, Ps. 110:1]."

Luther's skepticism about the Turkish war continued. He feared that everything would be in vain as long as Christians venerated the wild and true "Turks," namely, greed, usury, arrogance, arbitrary morality, tyranny of those in high places, unfaithfulness, evil. In addition, there was satanic disdain for God's Word, ingratitude, and ridicule of Christ's blood that was shed for us. A victory over the earthly Turks would have no purpose, as long as one worshiped the spiritual and eternal "Turks," who were more of a danger to Germany than the Turkish army itself could ever be. This showed the apocalyptic character of the existing abuses. That Christ was ruling despite the Turks and the emperor was a certainty for Luther that could not be shaken, despite all the bad news.[10] At the Diet of Speyer in February 1542 it was decided to mount a campaign against the Turks, to be financed by a special Turkish tax. Luther naturally did not share the arrogance toward the Turks that existed in circles of the nobility. Nevertheless, he had to accept it. One could do nothing but pray for success. The world did not know that it was being preserved only for the sake of the church and the Word of God, not vice versa.[11]

The sharp criticism of conditions in Germany did not deter Luther from attacking Islam. Until then, knowledge in Germany about Islam had been inadequate. Not until February 1542 did Luther see a Latin translation—although a poor one—of the Koran. It confirmed for him the information he had already learned from the Latin *Refutation of the Koran* that had been written before 1300 by a Florentine Dominican, Ricoldo da Monte Croce, but which Luther had not believed credible. At this time he translated this *Refutation of the Alcoran by Brother Richard, Dominican* into German. He did so very freely and, for example, eliminated Ricoldo's scholastic argumentation and supplemented his criticism of Islamic marriage law and the sensual understanding of paradise. In marginal notes he passionately expressed his own position.[12] As with the Jews, he was concerned not about converting the Turks, whom he believed obdurate, but about informing Christians. He understood Islam's aggression as God's well-deserved punishment of Christians. In addition, suffering and martyrdom belonged to the church's fate. He thought that possible seduction by the Turks, like that by the pope, was one of the plagues of the last days. In his own refutation at the conclusion,[13] in order to prove that no one should believe such a book, Luther underscored the Koran's admission (which, however, he had misunderstood) that only parts of its contents were true. He did not fail to mention that a majority of Christians also worshiped the devil or mammon, so that there were two kinds of Turks, "Mohammedan" and "Christian," both of them "sows" and not men, who confronted each other. Turks and papists both trusted in fabricated traditions instead of God's Word. Both of them could experience only God's wrath. Luther wanted to enlighten people about the dual seduction by false prophets—on one side by Mohammed; on the other, by the pope. Yet God still mercifully preserved the church. For Luther it was not Mohammed with his deception who was the Antichrist, but rather the pope within the church, no matter how much some of their monstrosities might resemble one another. Only if people rejected the pope, Christendom's internal foe, and honestly repented could there be hope for a victory over Mohammed, its external foe. Otherwise, there was no hope that prayer would be heard. In the following period Luther also complained about the failure to repent even in the face of this danger.[14]

In the fall of 1542 Luther contributed to a better knowledge of Islam in yet another way. At the beginning of 1542 the Zurich theologian Theodore Bibliander had produced a translation of the Koran that for the first time was satisfactory for scholarship. It was to be published by the Basel printer Johannes Oporin, but it had to be subjected to the required censorship. When the project became known, the Basel council prohibited its printing in August and imprisoned Oporin for a time. Luther learned of this from the Wittenberg booksellers returning from the Frankfurt book fair, and he approached the Basel council about it. He referred to his struggle of more than twenty years against false books and his efforts on behalf of a clear understanding of the Bible and the right use of the sacraments. Just as he had previously seen to it that the works of his opponents were printed, so he now thought that one could cause the Turks no worse harm than publishing the Koran with its lies, fables, and outrages. Thereby pastors would be in a position to strengthen people in their Christian faith and resistance. Luther therefore asked that they allow the publication of the translation, which otherwise he gladly would have done at Wittenberg, for it could help in hindering the Turks' seduction and perhaps convert some Turks. In case the Basel council could not decide to do so, they should leave the printing to the Wittenberg booksellers. Luther was in favor of making the false doctrine accessible, for otherwise it could not be overcome. The appeal, which the Strasbourg theologians also supported, produced results. The Basel council submitted to Luther's arguments and permitted the printing under condition that neither the printer nor the place of publication would be mentioned, and that it would not be sold in Basel.[15]

Along with an admonition by Melanchthon that had been written earlier, Luther contributed a preface.[16] He referred to the parallel useful knowledge about the "Jewish absurdity" that was possible because of Nicholas of Lyra, Paul of Burgos, and Anthony Margaritha. Not until one knew what was in the Koran could it be refuted. He was not afraid that members of the true church would be led astray. They had a clear orientation in the Bible, and in prayer the church distinguished itself from Jews and Turks. The teachers of the church had to take up the struggle against Mohammed as they had done against the pope, the Jews, and the Anabaptists.

The command of the imperial army against the Turks was given to Joachim II of Brandenburg, because he was a moderate man on whom evangelical and Catholic imperial estates could agree. Before accepting in May 1542, he asked Luther and Melanchthon to pray for him. Luther promised that he would, for in view of the sins in Germany much depended upon the prayers of the church. The elector had to be concerned about good discipline in the army, for otherwise no one could count on God's support but rather on his wrath. Despite all his reservations about the sins of his own side and the malice of the papists, Luther considered it his duty to support the elector in prayer. He also acted accordingly, but he was greatly concerned about whether the imperial army would be supported by the empire and by King Ferdinand in such a way that it would be a match for the Turks. He had nothing but critical ridicule for news about alleged successes.[17] Duke Albrecht of Prussia was required by his cousin Joachim to participate in the Turkish war. He therefore inquired of Luther whether he had to obey this call. Because Albrecht was not a prince of the empire, Luther thought that he was under no obligation. Albrecht could in good conscience remain at home.[18] In October it became evident that Luther's fears that the campaign would only waste money and deserve ridicule were correct. Nevertheless, it was important to keep praying for God to put an end to the Turkish beasts, as he had done with the pope and his frightful hypocrisy and outrage. In connection with the deliberations of the Smalcald League in November concerning resisting the Turks, Luther declared that the previous campaign had only made the Turks more arrogant. Sins and unwillingness to repent on their own side were the Turks' allies. If God did not help them, they would be a laughingstock for the Turks.[19] In December he began to suspect that only the Lutherans were sending troops against the Turks, for King Ferdinand had not supported the campaign, but he was confident that these machinations would prove unsuccessful and that they could be countered by prayer. A renewed appeal for prayer by Luther and Bugenhagen in January 1543, which the elector had requested, struck a similar tone. It spoke openly of the failure of the previous campaign and did not refrain from raising the suspicion of whether treason had played a part. Along with the lack of repentance, greed within all the estates had made prayer powerless. Nevertheless, pastors were still to pray as well as make use of the Word of God. It had to remain open whether God would help or whether he would punish. It was important to Luther that even children pray, for their future was at stake. Prayer should be offered for the diet in Nuremberg, that it might finally take common action against the Turks before it was too late. The appeal induced Elector Joachim II of Brandenburg to send the Wittenberg theologians his apology for the failed campaign against the Turks and to deny responsibility for it.[20]

Midway through 1543 Luther was still praying against the Turks, although he was uncertain against whom he should specifically pray. He thought the oppression of the church by the nobles was scarcely less severe than that by the Turks, and this he regarded as a symptom of the decay of the last days. His petition was: "God punish us graciously." Because of ingratitude for the suffering of Christ and disdain for his Word, punishment could not be long in coming.[21] Before the coming Diet of Speyer in 1544 the elector again decreed an appeal for repentance in February 1544. Luther accepted it with great resignation. No one repented, for no one thought he had done wrong, and therefore all appeals fell on deaf ears. Luther complied with this assignment only because he was required to do so. He was not expecting results in large numbers. Because people would not listen to him, the Turks and the Catholic emperor would have to lecture them.[22] In all these years it had been impossible to create a serious and pious attitude on an extensive scale within society that would have been appropriate in the face of the danger threatened by the Turks. To Luther, the future therefore looked gloomy.

The danger from the Turks was incorporated into Luther's total view, which included powers evangelical and Catholic, time and the end of time. Because he considered the Turks the penultimate enemies of God, he could deal realistically with them to some extent. This problem was thus not overexposed in the same way as was the contrast with the pope or with the Jews. Consequently, triumphalism in regard to the Turks was lacking, and under the given circumstances there was also no reason for it. Instead, in the light of the external threat, Luther functioned as a severe critic of the moral and religious conditions within Christendom that made a successful defense at least questionable. Despite the bad internal situation and the fruitlessness of appeals of this sort, he felt he was obligated to undergird the defense against the Turks with the power of prayer. Whether God would deal mercifully with Christendom or whether he would punish it still had to be left an open question, but Luther had no doubt that the true church and those who believed would be preserved both in time and in eternity.

3. THE POPE (1542–46)

Luther had already clearly stated his theological rejection of the papacy in what he had written for the proposed council, and this never changed fundamentally. Nevertheless, the action of the pope, which he regarded as a sign of the last time, provoked him to issue one last polemic against him. Probably in 1542 he wrote "a children's hymn to be sung against the two archenemies of Christ and his holy church, the pope and the Turks." It was the hymn that is quite well known in confessional polemics:

> Lord, keep us steadfast in thy Word
> And curb the Turks' and papists' sword
> Who Jesus Christ, thine only Son,
> Fain would tumble from off thy throne.[1]

In his works against the Turks Luther had repeatedly said that the pope was the real enemy of the church, even worse than the Turks. At the time, however, he was not confronted directly by the pope, but rather by the emperor and his brother Ferdinand. Luther was a skeptical and critical observer of their politics. In their egotism King Ferdinand and the Catholic princes appeared to make common cause with the Turks at the Diet of Nuremberg in the spring of 1543; moreover, the greed of the princes and nobles also amounted to the oppression of Germany. With his attitude Ferdinand was bringing destruction upon himself.[2] When the pope remained neutral in 1544 in the conflict between the emperor and the French king who was allied with the Turks, this, according to Luther's information, was complicity with the Turks, and it revealed the pope—with his earlier Turkish indulgences and taxes—in all his perversion. Luther could only pray: "Come, come, Lord Jesus, come! It is time to step in, Lord. Amen."[3]

Reconciling the religious division was a task for the long-awaited council. Because it was just as uncertain as before if one would ever be held, the recess of the Diet of Speyer in June 1544 placed the topic of a religious agreement on the agenda of the new diet that was planned for the coming fall or winter. The imperial estates were to prepare proposals. In November 1544 the elector assigned this task to the Wittenberg theologians.[4] For this purpose Melanchthon wrote the so-called Wittenberg Reformation,[5] to which the Wittenberg theologians affixed their names. It was formulated "leniently," i.e., it was more interested in compromise than in division. For the pure doctrine of the gospel by which the church was constituted, it appealed essentially to the Augsburg Confession of 1530. It made proposals for a rational form of confirmation, ordination, and confession that agreed with the evangelical understanding and practice, and at the same time incorporated an offer of agreement. As far as the mass was concerned, however, a host of old differences appeared. The office of the ministry (*Predigtamt*) was considered constitutive of the church. Episcopal administration of the church was regarded as logical, so long as it was normed by the true doctrine. Here once again we see the Wittenbergers' consistent ideas regarding a reformation of the bishoprics. They considered this an accommodation of their opponents' side. Even more pointed than the opinion of the Wittenberg theologians was Bucer's, which demanded a formal indictment of the pope and the bishops before the diet. Its intention was to have the emperor initiate a general Reformation. The Wittenbergers had just as many reservations about Bucer's harsh attitude as they had about the grand solution of an imperial Reformation. As before, they were interested in an external peace that would make it possible to proclaim the gospel. They did not believe that a council would occur, nor would they participate in one. At most, the religious question should be adjudicated before an impartial court.[6]

The intention of the recess of Speyer that discussions about an agreement on religion be held at the coming diet met with serious resistance in Rome. It was regarded as an incursion into the pope's prerogatives. In addition, the emperor should have nothing to do with those the church had already declared heretics. Moreover, negotiations of this sort would compete with the council that had now been called to meet in Trent in 1545. Pope Paul III therefore censured Charles V's intention in a breve of 24 August 1544, which, however, was a somewhat more moderate version of a harsher draft.[7] It called upon the emperor to extirpate heresy, i.e., to initiate a war against the evangelicals. The breve as well as the draft itself were known in Germany at the end of 1544, and thus in Wittenberg as well. Luther at first thought the draft was a forgery, but its authenticity quickly became apparent. In rejecting religious discussions, the pope appeared to be allying himself with the Turks, even with the devil himself, in order to avoid a Reformation through God's Word. Luther expected that Christ himself would visit his judgment upon the pope. Nevertheless, he planned to make the breve's evil intentions public. If the emperor were serious about religious negotiations in Germany, it would be bad for the pope's cause. Luther did not exclude the possibility that all this was nothing but a trick to force the evangelicals to attend the council.[8]

The political interests of Electoral Saxony were concentrated on religious negotiations, not on a council. Therefore the elector and Chancellor Brück wanted Luther to take issue with the papal breve. Their urging was hardly necessary, however, for Luther had already decided to reply. In February he was engaged in writing *Against the Roman Papacy, an Institution of the Devil,* which was printed at the end of March.[9] It was written in an extremely vehement manner, full of crude statements and vulgar expressions. He was probably unable, because of his declining abilities, to organize it in as well-balanced a manner as he planned. To this extent, it is not one of Luther's best works, but its offensiveness and formalistic weaknesses need not divert us from seeing that once again he was dealing with essential matters in his conflict with the papacy.

Luther began with the pope's claim to have the right to convene a general or a national council and to determine whether the council's decisions were to be granted, i.e., the pope's superiority over a council. This was more than a question of mere power, for the pope was embodied as the "abomination," the principle of perversion in the church. Luther engaged in a great historical review. Since the Diet of Worms in 1521 there had been talk of a "free, Christian council in Germany," and in his breve to the emperor the pope had once again contemplated one. At the Council of Constance in 1415 the council's supremacy over the pope had been established, but the papacy had been trying to reverse this, as the most recent breve about calling the Council of Trent showed. Thus the council would be neither free nor Christian, but rather papal, i.e., subject to the laws of the pope. No questions could be raised about indulgences, purgatory, the sacrifice of the mass, celibacy, or many other issues. The pope made the council in Germany dependent upon such political preconditions that one could scarcely imagine the emperor being able to comply with them. This was the sort of evil game the popes had always played with German emperors. The pope was shown to be "a desperate scoundrel, the enemy of God and man, the destroyer of Christendom, and Satan's bodily dwelling," a werewolf who brought only destruction to ecclesiastical and political order. Luther presented the pope and the curia as unscrupulous atheists, and there was no sense in holding a council with them. He repeated that he himself was no longer interested in a council. The pope's claim that he could call a council and determine who participated in it could easily be refuted from history. Luther was especially incensed that the pope had nullified the attempts at a peaceful resolution initiated by the Diet of Speyer and was instead risking a bloodbath in Germany. Nothing could more clearly reveal the devilish character of papal politics. The pious protestation of the breve that the pope could not be a party to the sins of others was revealed as sheer hypocrisy. One had to deal with the pope and the entire Roman curia as with people who were insane. Out of consideration for his health, Luther would concentrate on only three problems dealt with in the papal breve or in the draft: Whether the pope was the head of Christendom over emperor and councils, whether any-one could judge or depose him, and whether the Roman empire had been passed on to the Germans. Thus he was dealing with themes similar to those in *To the Christian Nobility* of 1520 and the controversy with the papacy at that time.[10]

It was not difficult to prove that the primacy of the pope had not existed from the church's beginning. For Luther, the continuing growth of the claims of primacy was a perverted development that neither the emperor nor the church wanted, but instead had been desired by the devil. The papacy was not a divine institution, but a human invention. Thus he also rejected the alleged biblical basis for the papacy, for the church had no other head than Christ. The thesis compelled Luther once again to undertake a thorough exegesis of Peter's words in Matt. 16:13-19. He held fast to his earlier interpretation: The rock on which the church is built must be spiritual in nature; it consists of faith in Christ. Rome's claim to be the head of the church competed with Christ himself and exposed the papacy as "an antichristian, papal school of scoun-drels." In confessing Christ, Peter was nothing more than a spokesperson for the believers. The object of faith could only be Christ. Saving faith in Christ and Christ's work was diametrically opposed to the pope's claim of authority. The office of the keys had to do only with forgiveness of sins, and, according to Matt. 18:18 and John 21:21-23, it was not restricted to Peter alone. There was no proof of an exclusive authority of Peter or of the papacy, not in ancient Christianity or in the early church. Also, no authority to exercise temporal or spiritual power was bestowed in the passage about the keys. This was a denial of the papal system of law-making, which had led the church astray from within. The system had become so perverted that even catechumens were more learned than the pope. Canon law had succumbed to blasphemy and idolatry; its arbitrary legalism was the true Antichrist in the papacy. That Luther could not convince the pope of this did not trouble him. He was satisfied to have God's Word on his side and in good conscience to consider the pope a "fart-ass and enemy of God." Luther believed that with his exeget-ical interpretations, which had become too lengthy, he had proved that the pope could not be the head of the church, but instead that he was the worst antithesis imaginable, even the Antichrist.

Luther had to deal more briefly with the other two aspects of his intended topic. The pope could be judged by any baptized Christian who had renounced the devil, and any rational person also had the ability to pass judgment upon papal statements. As the verdict of the church, indeed of Christ himself, Luther declared that the papacy "who will not and cannot listen, has been damned by God and thrown out of his church because of his decretals, those sheer pagan, heathenish, sinful things; that is, he is of the devil and of an unchristian realm, before which everyone should bless himself, flee, and against which everyone should pray and act." The political rulers should not let the pope make fools of them, but treat him as he deserved. Thus they should declare themselves free of their associations with him, and attack him like they would a werewolf that had invaded the church. The pope and the cardinals had forfeited their lives because of their crimes. A true bishop was needed in Rome, one who would preach the gospel purely, leave the secular kingdoms alone, and not be lord over the other bishops. This was a judgment on the basis of spiritual independence, which every Christian possessed. They had no lord but Christ. Luther sought to refute the claim that the pope had given the Roman empire to the Germans by referring to historical facts and events.

At that time the gulf between Luther and the pope, between the evangelical and the Roman church, was seen by both sides as unbridgeable. Luther specifically attacked the pope's claim—also contained in the breve—to superiority within the church and the world, and the pope's demand that the emperor support him in establishing it. For Luther, this stated the alternatives as salvation or condemnation, and thus either God or the devil. No longer was it possible to have certain nuances, differentiations, and relativizations. As well-grounded as his criticism was, Luther's evaluation of the conflict as an absolute and eschatological one, and one in which the opposing side was made out to be demonic, certainly did not do justice to reality. As Luther himself admitted, he had written in anger about the pope's appalling actions, and because of them his rage could not be ameliorated; the horror was too great. He now understood himself as the final trumpet preparing the way of the Lord. Although it might find little resonance in the world, he believed it was otherwise with the angels. They would follow his trumpet and hasten the coming of the end. Amsdorf and the elector were pleased with the book, but others were not. This made no difference to Luther. He did not hold it against them. Either they were afraid, or they did not understand the nature and traits of what in fact was the unspeakable abomination of the pope. His own intention to send the book in German and Latin to the Council of Trent was thwarted by death.[11]

In *Against the Roman Papacy*, Luther had already announced another "pamphlet" on the same topic, and it was also known in Wittenberg that he was working on several appropriate works. This intention was mentioned several times as late as June, always with the provision that Luther's health would permit him to do so. Not until September did he abandon it; he lacked the strength.[12] Nevertheless, two more antipapal publications were produced, probably in the spring of 1545. One was *Papal Fidelity of Popes Hadrian IV and Alexander III toward Emperor Frederick Barbarossa.* This was essentially a translation of the section of Robert Barnes's *Lives of the Popes,* which depicted the pope's treacherous action against Barbarossa.[13] It was to attack the popes "as the archenemy of our Lord and Savior and the destroyer of his holy Christian church." Even if this emperor had been a heretic, the popes should not have treated him in such an arrogant way. Luther was not aware that a similar criticism might have been addressed against his own attitude toward the pope. The translation and work's marginal notes can scarcely have come from Luther.

During his writing of *Against the Roman Papacy* and closely related to its contents, Luther designed a series of ten caricatures of the papacy, which Lucas Cranach produced as woodcuts with Latin titles above them and German verses, along with Luther's name, underneath them.[14] The series began with the "Origin and Source of the Pope." A female devil is giving birth to pope and cardinals. The newborn "Antichrist" is tended by three furies.[15] The second picture depicts the papal ass of 1523 once again.[16] On one side of a dual picture the pope is giving Germany a council. He is riding on a sow and holds in his hand a pile of dung at which the sow is sniffing greedily. Germany has to eat the dung the pope offers it.[17] The other side shows an ass playing a bagpipe, thus personifying the pope as an incompetent doctor of theology and teacher of the faith. Luther undoubtedly primarily had in mind the deficiencies of the pope as an interpreter of the Bible. The execution of Conradin of Hohenstaufen by Pope Clement IV was intended to demonstrate how grateful popes were toward emperors. The scene, like that of the pope placing his foot on the neck of Emperor Frederick Barbarossa, was intended to illustrate how the pope despised people. The proper worldly reward that the pope and cardinals deserve is shown by a gallows on which they were hanging. Because of their blasphemies their tongues have been nailed to it. Devils are receiving their souls. The best known of these caricatures is the papal throne in the jaws of hell, which, in accordance with 2 Thessalonians 2, depicts its occupant as the Antichrist. This illustration was used on the title page of *Against the Roman Papacy.* The last two pictures are designed primarily to ridicule the pope. In one the pope is holding in his hand a bull from which emanate the rays of his ban. Two peasants are running away, exposing their rears to him and breaking wind.[18] The other shows people worshiping the pope as a God on earth. On a podium decorated with the papal keys (pictured, however, as skeleton keys) stands an inverted tiara in which peasants are defecating.

These caricatures are extraordinarily vulgar, but frequently so were also Luther's written statements about the pope. Luther, however, did not intend them to be obscene. He criticized Cranach as a "rough painter" for his picture of the pope's birth; he should have been more considerate of the female sex. He asked that this woodcut be changed.[19] Otherwise, the caricatures fully expressed Luther's view of the papacy. In August 1545 he expressly stated that he approved of them and was prepared to answer for them. They contained

DIGNA MERGES PAPAE SATANISSIMI ET CARDINALIVM SVORVM.

Wenn zeitlich gestrafft solt werden:
Bapst vnd Cardinel auff Erden.
Jr lesterzung verdienet hett:
Wie jr recht gemalet steht.
Mart.Luth.D.

Execution of the pope and his cardinals
Woodcut by Lucas Cranach the Elder, Wittenberg, 1545

the opinions he wanted to express in the work he was planning against the pope, and in this sense he referred to the pictures as his testament.[20] Luther had no word of apology concerning the pope and his "devilish kingdom." Judging by their contents, his satirical parody of the two table prayers, the Benedicite and the Gratias, as well as the Our Father and the Ave Maria, may well belong in the time of this final controversy.[21]

In the middle of April 1545 Luther was aware that the negotiations at the Diet of Worms were proceeding slowly and that the Council of Trent that had been summoned for March was moving at a snail's pace, i.e., it had really not yet begun. When the opening was postponed until September, it merely confirmed Luther's opinion that the pope did not want the council at all. The news in May that a few prelates had already arrived in Trent was something Luther considered an unfounded rumor. At the beginning of June he informed Amsdorf: "I do not care about diet and council, I do not believe anything about them, I do not expect anything from them, I do not worry about them. Vanity of vanities."[22] Luther did not trust the emperor because of his action against the evangelicals in the Netherlands. Although Charles should have known the truth, he was fighting against it. Luther had rightly observed that the emperor was following a dual political goal in Worms. On one side he was seeking to convince the evangelicals to attend the council, and on the other he was still offering them a new religious colloquy. That these concessions were intended to disguise the emperor's preparations for war against the evangelicals was something that was hidden from Luther at the time. On the basis of his previous experiences, he emphatically rejected sending a delegation to the council.[23] In July he mentioned the contradiction between the emperor's desire to have the evangelicals participate in the council and the pope's rejection of this. For Luther such participation could not even be considered unless the pope would first acknowledge that the council had authority over him. Otherwise, the evangelicals could already have submitted to the pope in 1520. By this time Luther was aware of rumors that the emperor was seeking peace with the Turks in order to attack the evangelicals.[24]

At the end of December 1544 the theology faculty of the University of Louvain issued a series of theses dealing with Catholic dogmas and the heresies of the Lutherans, the Oecolampadians, and the Anabaptists that deviated from them. Charles V confirmed these theses in March 1545 and made them obligatory for the Catholic church in the Netherlands.[25] Luther learned of them at the beginning of May. He regretted that the emperor had adopted the disgraceful teaching of the Louvain theologians as his own. Initially, Melanchthon was to write a rebuttal, but he declined to do so because he did not want to exacerbate the discord among the evangelicals, nor that between the evangelicals and the Catholics.[26] Luther himself then wrote the countertheses *Against the Thirty-five Articles of the Louvain Theologians*, which appeared in September in Latin and somewhat later also in German.[27] In contrast to the Louvain theologians, he stated at the outset that the doctrine of the church

Wider das Bapstum zu

Rom vom Teuffel gestifft/
Mart. Luther D.

Wittemberg/1545.
durch Hans Lufft.

Papal throne in the jaws of hell

Title woodcut by Lucas Cranach the Elder for *Against the Papacy in Rome, Established by the Devil*, Wittenberg, 1545

must be based on the Word of God, or else it was falsehood, godlessness, and heresy. This was true for the opposing side's claim that there were seven sacraments. Luther took care to refute the Anabaptists' view of baptism. Apparently, the men from Louvain were unable to do so. Their weapons "of the spirit," with which they were fighting the Anabaptists, were fire and sword. Regarding the Lord's Supper, Luther rejected the doctrine of transubstantiation, withholding the cup from the laity, the sacrifice of the mass, and masses for the dead as unscriptural, as well as the sacramentarians' denial of the presence of Christ's body and blood. He dealt with the other sacraments in the same way. The true church was sharply distinguished from that of the werewolf pope and of the Louvain murderers. Here the demarcation from the papacy became evident once more. Purgatory and monastic vows were rejected as devilish, blasphemous, and idolatrous. In Luther's opinion, the very thesis of the Louvain theologians—that faith's assurance of forgiveness was not taught in Scripture—exposed them as unqualified. Luther doubted that these theses had truly been confirmed by the emperor, yet they brought shame on the emperor's name. Confirming the teaching of the church was not the task of the emperor at all; he should rather submit to it and serve it. Much less should he protect such godless doctrine, but instead had to resist it. Apart from the political aspect, the example of the Louvain theses taught one to guard against doctrines made by men and to adhere that much more closely to the Bible. It was relatively easy for Luther, using the criterion of Scripture as his principle, convincingly to refute these officially endorsed Louvain theses. How strongly this controversy affected him is seen in his sermons and primarily in his last lectures, in which he referred repeatedly to the Louvain theses.[28] He had already declared in the conclusion to his countertheses that he would reply to the Louvain theologians at greater length. On 23 September he was occupied with them, but he made slow progress because of his health and then discontinued the work. Not until January 1546 did he resume it. The ignorance of the Louvain theologians had once again enraged him, which was inappropriate for a theologian and old man. The devil was handicapping him with illness, but Luther considered it his duty to devote his last breath to this task.[29] In fact, until the last days of his life in Eisleben he was working on another work, *Against the Asses of Paris and Louvain*, but he never completed more than the introduction.[30] He once again recalled his controversies with the Louvain theologians from 1520 and those a year later with the theologians from Paris.[31] Since then these opponents had been silent, but under the protection of the emperor and king they had again ventured forth with the old scholastic monstrosities and thus confirmed Luther's criticism. The approach he intended to use with them is shown by his forced derivation of the names of Paris and Louvain from the Hebrew words for robber and fool. He did not regard the theologians of Paris and Louvain as fit to live in such famous cities, nor would he even want to let his pigs be in the same stall and eat from the same trough.

At the end of November the Wittenberg theologians thought, accurately, that the religious colloquy announced by the emperor at the Diet of Worms in 1545 was nothing but a subterfuge to mask the imperial preparations for war. If the imperial theologians from Louvain and Cologne took part in it, an agreement was no more to be expected than on the question about the authority of councils in the church.[32] In January Luther spoke against sending Melanchthon, who was ill, to the Regensburg meeting. It would be satisfactory to have Wittenberg represented by George Major, especially because only time and effort would be wasted there. Luther never received any further information about the course of the religious discussions.[33] In contrast, however, he did learn about the opening of the Council of Trent in December 1545, which he thought would last for a long time and never reach a conclusion. He was right about this in the short term, but ultimately incorrect. He himself prayed, "The Lord arise and scatter his enemies. Amen. Amen. Amen." His last appeal for prayer had to do with the cause of God and his gospel, "for those at the council in Trent do not mean well for him."[34] On 3 February 1546 Luther mentioned the arming of the emperor and the pope against the evangelicals.[35] He did not live to see the outbreak of the Smalcald War.

Although Luther did not consider using force against the pope—unlike against the Jews—among his last great battles the one against the pope was the fiercest, for the pope embodied for him the eschatological principle of the Antichrist. This evaluation was understandable on the basis of the renewed experiences with the pope's attitude toward reform of the church and his behavior against the evangelicals during Luther's last years. Although the manifestation of Christianity in the papacy was a pollution to Luther—theologically, juridically, ecclesiastically, and politically—his reaction was still inappropriate, for, conditioned by his anger and eschatological bias, he could scarcely see any positive alternative in the controversy that concerned him until his end.

XIV

The Final Journey

1. THE UNITY NEGOTIATIONS
IN EISLEBEN

Luther never lost contact with his homeland of Mansfeld or his interest in it. In addition to connections with the families of his brothers and sisters in Mansfeld there were also contacts with the counts of Mansfeld. He had close relationships with the evangelical Count Albrecht until 1536, when Albrecht, because of his increased need for funds, sought to bring the copper mining industry, which owed him taxes, under his own control. Up to then the smelters had been run by smeltermasters who had hereditary or term leases. The ruler's efforts at concentrating this in his own hands posed a threat to Luther's brother James and his brother-in-law Paul Mackenrot, and this caused Luther concern. Several times in 1538 he criticized Albrecht's greed at the expense of his subjects.[1] In order to accomplish his objective, the count was endeavoring to convert the inherited smelters into ones that were leased for a period of time and consequently would be subject to additional taxes. When Paul Mackenrot was affected by this effort in 1540, Luther appealed to Albrecht. He told Albrecht that because of this action toward his subjects he would not receive God's blessing. Anyone who showed no mercy to others could not hope for God's grace. A year later he asked the Mansfeld preacher Michael Coelius to admonish the count in the same way.[2] In a pastoral letter to Albrecht, probably written in February 1542, Luther related Albrecht's *Anfechtungen* over predestination to the economic oppression of his Mansfeld subjects. As one who knew that he was approaching the grave, Luther spoke to the count's conscience. The letter is said to have made Albrecht so angry that he threw it to the floor and trampled it underfoot.[3]

Luther later asked Duke Maurice of Saxony to intercede with Count Albrecht on behalf of Bartholomew Drachstedt, an Eisleben mining entrepreneur. He argued on the principle of fairness, which did not permit the nobility to act like tyrants and oppress their fellow Christians. He was willing personally to take the chance of incurring Albrecht's displeasure and likewise appeal to him on Drachstedt's behalf. Moreover, it was as a native of Mansfeld and because of his responsibility as a preacher that Luther was writing to Counts Philip and John George, asking them to convince Albrecht to discontinue his unjust economic policies. This had no results; instead, Philip and John George joined in support of Albrecht's action.[4]

Luther also objected to Albrecht's action against his brother Gerhard, who was heavily in debt and had to transfer his financial obligations and payments to Albrecht. Albrecht then unconscionably sought to increase the revenues from Gerhard's possessions and thus to force him from his throne. Luther asked Elector John Frederick to take action against this. He also approached Philip of Hesse about mediating the quarrel between the two brothers. When Duke Maurice imprisoned Albrecht in 1543 because of this, Luther thought the punishment was just.[5] Luther must have considered Count Albrecht a representative of the nobles whose greed he was constantly criticizing as one of the vices of the time. It must also be mentioned that, in addition to the economic quarrel between the members of the ruling lines, there was a dispute in 1542 about filling the position of pastor and preacher of St. Andrew's church in Eisleben. Luther sought to involve both sides in negotiating a compromise, and initially he had some success, until new disputes occurred in 1544 concerning the preacher Johann Libius, who had criticized Albrecht's financial dealings.[6]

The disunity among the counts was an unfavorable situation for the long term. Therefore Luther's relatives persuaded him to attempt to reconcile them. For this purpose, "although old and weak," he traveled to Eisleben at the beginning of October 1545 with Melanchthon, who accompanied him only reluctantly. Luther did not act as an arbitrator, but he wanted to assist the counts in reaching an agreement through his sermons, admonitions, and suggestions. An initial success occurred when the family members, including Count Albrecht, agreed to seek a settlement. However, the negotiations could not begin immediately because Counts Philip and John George were away on the Brunswick campaign. Luther attempted by letter to gain their support for his action. Combined with the attempts at reaching a settlement was also Luther's family's interest in the situation of the smeltermasters, whose operations the counts had taken over in the meantime. As before, Luther was skeptical about this change, but he considered it unchristian and inhumane for the counts not to assume the debts of the previous owners as well. In addition, he made a request on behalf of his brother and the Kaufmanns, to whom he was related through his sister, asking that they be allowed to operate their smelters for two more years in order to pay their debts, because they had few assets.[7]

After Counts Philip and John George also declared their willingness to participate in the negotiations, it was finally decided that they would start in December 1545. Despite his other concerns, Luther wanted to take time to achieve a reconciliation, which he was already viewing as one of his final tasks. Melanchthon again accompanied him, although he was not feeling well. Melanchthon's illness compelled Luther to return to Wittenberg at the beginning of January 1546, before an agreement had been reached. Thus another session in Eisleben had to be scheduled for 25 January.[8]

On 17 January Luther preached on Rom. 12:3. He spoke of the fruits of faith with which a Christian confronts the sins that still cling to him in this earthly "hospital." In contrast to all the clever heresies, he exhorted people to have a simple, childlike faith in Christ.[9] This was the last time Luther functioned in his office as a preacher in Wittenberg. Melanchthon took leave of Luther with the prayer that God's angels, who once had protected the patriarch Jacob on his journey, would also "guard our Doctor Luther," and aid in bringing about a permanent agreement among the Mansfeld counts.[10] The journey, on which Luther's three sons accompanied him, encountered many obstacles. Because of floating ice and flooding they could not cross the Saale at Halle on 25 January or the two days following. In a letter to Katy, Luther graphically described the Saale as a huge female Anabaptist. He preferred to quench his thirst with Torgau beer and Rhine wine, but he specifically mentioned that for once he was carefully following all of Katy's advice. The letter shows that Luther was in good spirits. This was a comfort to Katy and Melanchthon.[11] On 26 January, the day after the festival, Luther preached in Halle on the conversion of St. Paul. He took this as an opportunity to speak about the proper way to honor the saints, which was to listen in faith to Paul and the Word of God. He did not do so without criticizing the Catholic cult of the saints, especially the veneration of relics Albrecht of Mainz previously had encouraged in Halle, and not without criticizing the monks in the city. Luther hoped that God with his love might preserve Halle in the Word of God.[12]

Then on 28 January sixty Mansfeld horsemen, who had been sent to meet Luther, succeeded in bringing him across the Saale. Jonas had joined Luther. While underway Luther suffered a dizzy spell, probably caused by a circulatory problem as a result of the cold, which he blamed on the Jews in Rissdorf. A few days later he could reassure Katy that he had recovered, but he told her that beautiful women were no temptation for him, undoubtedly meaning that he still felt weak. He enjoyed some Naumburg beer that helped his digestion. He had sent his sons, who understandably were afflicted with boredom, on ahead to relatives in Mansfeld. Luther himself stayed in the elegant house of the city clerk Johann Albrecht, which belonged to the city of Eisleben, next door to St. Andrew's church (Plate XVI).[13]

Luther preached in St. Andrew's church in Eisleben four times, viz., on 31 January, 2 and 7 February, and on 14 or 15 February. Twice he received the Lord's Supper.[14] In his sermons he emphasized the uniqueness of faith in Christ in comparison to the religions of the Turks and Jews, which consisted essentially for him in the certainty that God was gracious and accepted the hard-pressed little band of Christians. In the face of the devil's *Anfechtung* one had to cling to Christ. The parable of the weeds among the wheat (Matt. 13:24-30) again gave him an opportunity to say something basic about the church. There was no such thing as a pure church, such as the Anabaptists wanted, any more than there was a pure body without sickness and odors. The church always had heretics and evil people in it. A Christian was dependent upon forgiveness and was engaged in a lifelong battle against sin. The process of perfection had not yet been completed. Therefore, one had to live alongside heretics, papists, and Jews, and one could not stamp them out or convert them. Therefore it was necessary that preaching and the sacraments remain pure.[15] On Sunday, 14 February, Luther ordained two ministers. Possibly it was at this time that he delivered his last sermon on Matt. 11:25-30, although the sources indicate that it was on the following day.[16] It warned chiefly against false wisdom in dealing with the Word of God. It closed with the appeal to hold fast to Christ's Word: "Thou alone art my beloved Lord and Master, I am thy disciple. This and much more might be said concerning this gospel, but I am too weak and we shall let it go at that."

Accompanying Luther was also John Aurifaber (1519–75), his last theological assistant. He recorded the table conversations at that time. Some of them deal with the usual topics of the never-ending struggle of preachers against usury, theft, adultery, and fornication, which of course could not be eliminated, but which still had to be attacked. As before, Luther advocated harsh punishment for adulterers. Occasionally he mentioned stories about the devil.[17] Luther repeatedly mentioned his firm confidence that, despite all persecution, God's Word would not perish. He even thought a war against the evangelicals was unlikely, for the emperor would not spend any money on the pope. On the basis of his long years of experience, Luther did not believe that the Word of God and the church could be suppressed by political machinations.[18] Several times Luther spoke about the nearness of his end, as he had already done in the years before. He knew that he could not finally be rid of the "mobs and stormy winds" because the devil was still alive and reigning. He warned those who were to come after him about the devil, but he did not consider himself indispensable in this great struggle. At sixty-three years of age he considered himself a very old man. For him, his sense of age came from having "seen the devil's ass" and from being able to testify to his wickedness. He had no illusions about his own wisdom: "A Christian is only certain about the devil when he believes that Christ is his wisdom, salvation, righteousness, and redemption." This echoes one of the key passages (1 Cor. 1:30) of Luther's Reformation discovery. On one of the last days of his life he wrote in a Bible that the Father was not angry, for he let himself be perceived in the sweet words of his Son: "Who then can be against us, if the Son is for us?" Luther was ready to die, and two days before his death he spoke graphically of what this meant: "If I go back home to Wittenberg, I'll lie down in a coffin and give the maggots a fat doctor to eat."[19]

The negotiations took place every second or third day. Except for 17 February, Luther took part in them for an hour to an hour and a half each time, for his condition would permit nothing more.[20] The negotiations were difficult. Secular matters were foreign to Luther, and in his condition he was annoyed with them. On 1 February, after the sharpest arguments, it appeared that the controversial issue concerning the new town of Eisleben, "a porcupine with more quills than a porcupine," had been "slaughtered." Count Albrecht had brought in people to work in the mines and settled them in the new town, giving the settlement municipal rights, something that affected the old city adversely. During the negotiations Luther soon became irritated with the hair-splitting and pompous bombast of the Wittenberg jurist Melchior Kling, who was also present, and he started a fight with him.[21]

In the subsequent round of negotiations the reports of success were already proving to be premature, and Luther doubted that things would turn out well. On 6 February he wrote to Katy: "We are sitting here allowing ourselves to be tortured," and his return would be delayed another eight days. He blamed the damned lust for wealth for this. Therefore he wanted to be patient, in order still to achieve something good with God's help. Luther was having good days as such and there was enough to "eat and drink," if it had not been for "this disgusting business." In a letter to Melanchthon at the same time he described his frequently futile attempts at mediation. The controversy about the new town was not settled. This was because of the deep-seated mistrust between the participants and especially because of the attitude of the jurists. In their quibbling over words they did not want to understand one another, and thus Luther's great anger over these "plagues of the human race" was aroused once again. His respect for their profession disappeared. In order to apply pressure on the negotiations, the elector should have Chancellor Brück order Luther to return home, for the feuding parties could hardly allow him to leave without having accomplished anything. The next day the stalemated situation had not changed at all. Hell seemed to have been emptied of all its devils, for all of them had congregated in Eisleben.[22]

Katy was understandably concerned about her husband because of the dangerous trip, and then about a fire in the stove in Luther's room on 2 February. Luther chided her lack of faith, as if God could not create "ten Doctor Martins" if one of them died: "Free me from your worries. I have a caretaker who is better than you and all the angels; he lies in the cradle and rests on a virgin's bosom, and yet, nevertheless, he sits at the right hand of God, the almighty Father. Therefore be at peace. Amen." Here, once again, the immediate relevance for Luther's piety of the great affirmations of Christology is evident. In his next letter he also sought to dispel Katy's cares with his confidence that God was protecting him. The council of Eisleben provided Luther with a half *stübig* (ca. 1.8 liters) of Italian wine for each meal, and occasionally he shared some with his companions. In addition, he again praised the Naumburg beer, although he blamed the congestion in his chest on it. Nevertheless, he reported that he was chipper and healthy. He complained only about the unpleasant negotiations and wished that he could return home.[23]

Luther made a contribution to the agreement not only by participating in the discussions. He also invited the participants to visit him, e.g., Count

Albrecht and Count John Henry of Schwarzburg, one of the mediators, and tried to change their minds. He argued on the basis of examples from history, nature, and the Bible. Wherever reconciliation was at stake, justice had to be set aside. The attitude in which he wanted to see the negotiations conducted was expressed in a phrase that he wrote on the wall of his bedroom in the last days of his life: "We cannot do what everyone wants; but we can certainly do what we want." At the time he praised Aristotle's concept of prudent equity, which he saw lacking among the jurists.[24] His elementary interest in peaceful solutions to worldly conflicts was also something Luther displayed in this last matter, one that, even though foreign to him, he undertook once again only for the sake of love.

On 14 February Luther could finally report to Katy that fortunately the negotiations were almost complete. In order to achieve a reconciliation between the two feuding brothers, Albrecht and Gebhard, he was going to invite them to come to him. At that time Luther had received the summons to return that he had requested from the elector and he himself was pressing to leave. He asked Melanchthon to send him the medication necessary to keep the artificial wound on his leg open, a sign that he did not feel entirely well.[25]

The results of the negotiations were incorporated in two treaties. One document prepared by Luther on 16 February and also signed by Jonas, to which all the counts agreed, regulated the rights of patronage as well as the compensation of clergy and schoolmasters in the county, including the authority of the Eisleben superintendent and the Mansfeld castle preacher. Luther was happy with this sound ordering of church affairs in the county, and it also endured.[26] On the following day, in another lengthy treaty, the "secular and temporal matters" were established. Although Luther was unable to take part in the closing sessions because of his weakness, he was listed, along with the other participants—Prince Wolfgang of Anhalt, Count John Henry of Schwarzburg, and Jonas—as one of the issuers. Because not all the controversial questions had yet been settled, 2 May was set as the date for new negotiations.[27] Even before that, the controversies among the counts broke out again. Thus Luther's efforts had not been able to bring about a lasting peace between his real territorial sovereigns.

A slip of paper from 16 February, which John Aurifaber copied, was Luther's last written statement.[28] It concerned the difficult task of understanding things, which was thoroughly characteristic of its author. It first referred to the classical texts that Luther had cherished his entire life: "Nobody can understand Virgil in his Bucolics or Georgics [poems about the life of a shepherd and a farmer], unless he has been a shepherd or ploughman for five years. Nobody can understand Cicero in his epistles unless he has lived for twenty-five years in a large commonwealth." Understanding cannot be simply theoretical, but requires practical experience. The more complex situations are, that much more is the demand for experience. Luther's great respect for the competence of farmers and even of politicians, and for their importance for understanding, becomes visible here. All these statements were surpassed by a third about the Bible: "Let no one think he has sufficiently grasped the Holy Scriptures, unless he has governed the churches for a hundred years with the prophets." Luther possibly also mentioned John the Baptist, Christ, and the apostles along with the prophets, but perhaps this reference to them applies to the following statement: Understanding the Bible is presented here as a task that transcends human capabilities and "therefore is a mighty wonder." Luther quoted a corresponding statement of the Roman poet Statius about Virgil: "Don't venture on this divine Aeneid, but rather bend low in its footprints!" The first three words of the often quoted final sentence were originally written in German: "We are beggars, that is true." This final confession of one of the greatest interpreters of the Bible is not meant as resignation about his life's work. The miracle of understanding had happened, but the expositor, who was fully and completely oriented toward the praxis of the people of God, knew that in his efforts he was humbly, reverently, and prayerfully dependent upon the miraculous help of God. Like his whole life, interpretation was a gift of grace.

2. "NOW LETTEST THOU THY SERVANT . . ."

Even as a young Erfurt master, thoughts about his own death had not been foreign to Luther. Thereafter he had always thought he would soon die from illness or martyrdom. With his faith he had overcome his original anxiety about death and the following judgment. He first found himself in acute danger of dying as a result of his heart trouble in 1527. Ten years later in Schmalkalden, he seemed to be facing imminent death because of his kidney stones. From at least this time onward, the old Luther constantly anticipated that death would strike soon. He believed the peace mission to Mansfeld, which he undertook despite his poor state of health, would be one of the last tasks he would accomplish.[1]

There are numerous reports and accounts of Luther's death, the most important of which are the ones offered by the eyewitnesses Justus Jonas and the Mansfeld castle preacher, Michael Coelius.[2] They were aware that the reformer's death would also have an impact on the controversy between the parties, and therefore they took care to present accurate information.

As mentioned above, Luther had not participated in the final negotiations on 17 February 1546 because he had not felt well. But he did take supper with his companions that day. The conversation turned to the question of whether they would recognize one another in the life to come. For Luther this was not a banal question. He thought that those who were renewed in Christ would know one another spiritually better than did Adam and Eve in Paradise. After the meal, he went as usual to his room at about eight o'clock to pray at the window. Shortly thereafter he suffered pains and tightness in his chest, undoubtedly symptoms of an attack of angina pectoris. Aurifaber obtained, from Count Albrecht, a medication made of grated unicorn. Thereafter, Luther was able to sleep for an hour on the day bed. At about ten o'clock, he wanted to lie down in his bed in the bedchamber adjoining the room. He committed his soul to God with the words of Ps. 31:5, which were often used by those who were dying. With supreme irony he exhorted those present to pray "for our Lord God and his gospel, that all might be well with him, for the Council of Trent and the accursed pope are very angry with him."

At about one o'clock Luther awakened with another attack of pain. He expected matter-of-factly that he would die in the city where he had been born and baptized. He moved again from the bedchamber to the day bed in the room and once more commended his soul to God. They sought to warm him with hot towels. His hosts, the city clerk Johann Albrecht and his wife, were summoned, along with the two physicians of the city and finally Count Albrecht himself and his wife, Anna, who was familiar with drugs. The pain and fear continued. When he began to sweat, Luther saw it as a symptom of death. In a prayer he gave thanks to the God of all comfort, the Father of Jesus Christ, that he had revealed to him his Son, "whom I have believed, whom I have loved, whom I have preached, confessed, and praised, whom the pope and all the godless revile and blaspheme." Here once again he named the content of this life in a positive and definitive way. Luther commended his "little soul" to the Lord Christ. He was sure that death would not be able to snatch him from God's hand. He based this on John 3:16: Anyone who believes in the Son, whom God gave in love, will not perish, but have eternal life. He stood firm on the words of Ps. 68:20: "Our God is a God of salvation; and to God, the Lord, belongs escape from death." Echoing the words of the aged Simeon (Luke 2:29) he said with confidence: "Lord, now lettest thou thy servant depart in peace. Amen."[3] Finally, he repeated Ps. 31:5 three more times, and then became silent.

Countess Anna especially tried to revive Luther by rubbing him with rose vinegar and aqua vitae. Jonas and Coelius shouted loudly, "Reverend father, are you ready to die trusting in your Lord Jesus Christ and to confess the doctrine which you have taught in his name?" A distinct "Yes" was his reply. With his final word Luther had made a confession of his cause. This was significant. After this he fell asleep and responded no more. His face became pale; his feet and nose grew cold. At about a quarter to three he took a deep breath and gave up his spirit. The reporters emphasized that Luther had died peacefully. An attempt to revive Luther by having the apothecary Johann Landau, who had been summoned, administer an enema was futile.[4]

The accounts of Luther's death show again how deeply piety had been altered by him. All sacramental elements were missing. Of course, there was no extreme unction, but neither did Luther make any last confession, although he treasured the practice of confession itself. Understandably, no last communion was offered, for Luther had otherwise had great reluctance about this practice. He had received the Lord's Supper the Sunday before. Thus there were no priestly ministrations at all at his death. It was almost exclusively Luther himself who spoke, not the others present. This may have been a mark of respect in the face of his authority. His last statements consisted primarily of brief, confident prayers to God and Christ, including the traditional deathbed prayer from Ps. 31:5. The recitation of Bible passages served to reassure him. His confidence corresponded to the confession of God and Christ that was his life's work. Jonas and Coelius asked him expressly to confirm this at the end. Unlike the earlier situations when his life was threatened, nothing is known about any word to his sons, who were present, or a final greeting to Katy. For the dying man, that was obviously not as important as his relationship to God and his vocation.

3. "DEAD IS THE CHARIOTEER OF ISRAEL"— BURIAL AND REMEMBRANCE

Immediately after Luther's death, in the early morning of 18 February 1546, Jonas sent word to Elector John Frederick and the Wittenberg theologians of Luther's death. John Frederick was deeply affected by the loss of "such a dear man, through whom God's Word has again been brought to light." Especially in this difficult time for the Reformation, they urgently needed Luther. In a letter to the counts of Mansfeld he ordered at once that Luther's body be returned to Wittenberg and buried in the castle church. The counts' wish to bury Luther in Eisleben was overridden.[1]

The elector asked Chancellor Brück to inform the Wittenberg theologians of Luther's death, but they had learned of it shortly before. They agreed to a funeral in the castle church, although they themselves had been thinking of a burial in the city church.[2] The sovereign's desire was determinative.

The theologians then had to bring Katy the news of her husband's death. "How easy it is to see that the poor woman is deeply dismayed and in great sorrow." She was especially distressed that she had not been able to be with him to care for him. As a mother, Katy was also concerned how the three sons in Mansfeld had taken the death of their father.[3] A letter Katy wrote a few weeks later to her sister-in-law, Christina von Bora, shows how deeply Katy grieved for her husband and yet how proud she was of his importance: "For who would not be sad and afflicted at the loss of such a precious man as my dear lord was? He did great things not just for a city or a single land, but for the whole world. Therefore I am truly so deeply grieved that I cannot tell a single person of the great pain that is in my heart. And I do not understand how I can cope with this. I cannot eat or drink, nor can I sleep. And if I had had a principality or an empire and lost it, it would not have been as painful as it is now that the dear Lord God has taken from me this precious and beloved man, and not from me alone, but from the whole world."[4] Although the elector promised Katy and her children his support, and actually did provide for her, and even though she also received support from King Christian of Denmark and the counts of Mansfeld, widowhood was difficult for Katy. Chancellor Brück caused difficulties for her concerning the Wachsdorf farm, which she had obtained years before, for in his considered opinion it was not profitable. Nevertheless, Katy had her way. From November 1546 until January 1547, and again from April until June 1547, she had to leave Wittenberg because of the Smalcald War. Her properties were also ravaged in the war. As a result, Katy had to borrow money. In the summer of 1552 Wittenberg was afflicted with the plague once again. The university had to be transferred to Torgau because of it. Katy also moved there in September. While moving there, she fell into a ditch filled with cold water. She never recovered from this accident. She died on 20 December 1552 in Torgau and was buried in St. Mary's church there (Plate XVII).[5]

Luther's body had been clothed in a white "Swabian smock," probably similar to a contemporary farmer's one-piece smock, and laid out on his bed until a pewter coffin could be molded.[6] On 19 February at two o'clock in the afternoon he was taken to the choir of the nearby St. Andrew church in Eisleben. Jonas preached the funeral sermon.[7] He praised Luther as a great expositor of the Bible, a mighty translator from whom the chancellories had learned German, a skilled speaker, preacher, and bishop. The painter Lukas Fortennagel (Furtenagel) from Halle was commissioned to paint the dead Luther, whose face may already have been considerably changed (Plate XVIII).[8] On the next day Michael Coelius delivered a second funeral sermon. On that afternoon the body was moved from the city. The bells were tolled in most of the villages through which the funeral procession traveled. At about five o'clock in the afternoon it reached Halle, where a great number of clergy, the council, the schoolchildren, and a large crowd of people waited at the city gate. The body was brought into the sacristy of St. Mary's church. It was too late in the day to hold the worship service that had been planned. At about noon on 21 February the procession reached Bitterfeld in the territory of Electoral Saxony, where it was greeted by the senior officials Erasmus Spiegel, Gangolf von Heilingen, and Dietrich von Taubenheim, who received it and accompanied it that day as far as Kemberg.

On 19 February Melanchthon had immediately informed the students in his class on Romans about the death of Luther, who had been "called to the heavenly university." Using the words of Elisha, whom Elijah left behind (2 Kings 2:12), he lamented: "Dead is the charioteer of Israel, who has led the church in these last times." It was not human intelligence from which the doctrine of the forgiveness of sins and trust in the Son of God had come, but God who had revealed it to Luther. He exhorted them to uphold Luther's memory and his doctrine, for his death appeared to be an evil omen of what was to come.[9] With his words, Melanchthon stated Luther's central discovery and acknowledged that it had the character of a revelation. His successors would have to preserve his heritage in a difficult time.

Melanchthon also wrote the rector's announcement to the members of the university, calling them to attend Luther's funeral. It mentioned that it had been Luther's divine mission to bring the gospel out of darkness into light again. At the funeral one should remember thankfully that this was the costly pearl that Jesus said was better than all other treasures.[10]

On the morning of 22 February the funeral procession proceeded from the Elster gate through the city of Wittenberg. First came the schoolboys and the clergy. They were followed by the representatives of the elector and Count Hans and Count Hans Hoyer of Mansfeld with about sixty-five horsemen. Then, drawn by four horses, came the wagon that bore the coffin, which was covered by a black cloth on which a white cross had been embroidered. Behind it came Katy, her daughter Margaret,[11] and some other women in a smaller, lower wagon. Luther's three sons,[12] his brother James, and the sons of his sister, along with other members of the family, followed on foot. After the family came the rector of the university and students who were members of the nobility. They were followed by Chancellor Brück, Melanchthon, Jonas, Bugenhagen, Cruciger, and Jerome Schurf as the most distinguished doctors of the university, and after them came the other doctors and masters. Then came the Wittenberg council, the students and citizens, and finally women and children. In the procession one can see again the structured social order within the university city where Luther had lived. In the castle church the coffin was placed perpendicular to the chancel. The grave had intentionally been prepared underneath the pulpit, one of the important places of Luther's activity (Plates XIX and XX).[13]

The funeral sermon on 1 Thess. 4:13-14, the usual text from the Bible, was delivered by Bugenhagen,[14] who had a difficult time speaking because of his grief. He was convinced that God had bestowed unspeakable gifts and grace on Christ's church in Germany and in many other nations through Luther. Luther's support of the gospel had brought him into conflict with the pope, the sectarian hordes, and the tyrants, and because of this he seemed to many to be an excessive polemicist. Bugenhagen, however, characterized him as "a high teacher, prophet, and reformer [!] sent by God to the church." In his grief, he saw Luther united with Christian kings, princes, and cities who had recognized the truth of the gospel. His opponents had no reason to rejoice at Luther's death, for his "powerful, blessed, divine teaching" continued to live. As Michael Stifel had already done in 1522, Bugenhagen identified Luther with the angel in Rev. 14:6 who proclaimed the everlasting gospel, whereupon the fall of Babylon would occur. Bugenhagen was confident that this would be fulfilled following Luther's death. In a letter he wrote to Christian III of

Denmark a few weeks later he mentioned a statement of one of the "great princes" after Luther's death: "Previously we had two great rulers whom we had to obey, Luther in the spiritual realm, and the emperor in the temporal one. . . ."[15] This stated who the two great authorities of that age were. Charles V himself was shown Luther's grave when he occupied Wittenberg in 1547 during the Smalcald War, but he did not disturb it.[16]

The eulogy that followed was delivered by Melanchthon.[17] In this conclusion we must deal more thoroughly with this tribute to Luther. Here, too, Melanchthon referred to Luther as someone called by God to be a servant of the gospel, and whose teachings were not seditious opinions, but a testimony to the true worship of God, the exposition of the Holy Scriptures, and the proclamation of the gospel. Melanchthon deliberately concentrated on Luther's office in the church. For him, Luther belonged to the succession of patriarchs, prophets, Christ, apostles, and church fathers who extended down to Bernard of Clairvaux and John Tauler, and who were to be preferred above all the wise men of the world.

Luther's personality was obviously also a problem for Melanchthon, and he tried to do justice to it, for the deceased was regarded by many as a disturber of the church. But the blame for this belonged to those who did not want to be convinced by the Holy Spirit. He listed Luther's theological insights: True repentance, the strong comfort of one's conscience, the Pauline doctrine of justification by faith, the distinction between law and gospel, spiritual and political righteousness, true prayer that is addressed to God and Christ alone, a new theological foundation of civil life, and the abolition of human regulations. For Melanchthon, Luther's work was in no way limited to theology. He did not fail to mention his translation of the Bible and the exposition of the Scriptures. He skillfully referred to the coexistence of necessary theological polemic alongside helpful and edifying teaching. Abiding gratitude was due for the blessings that God had brought the church through Luther. Here he caught something of Luther's enduring significance as a teacher of the church.

Melanchthon referred to the theological controversies as essential for the sake of clarifying the truth, which through the Bible Luther had on his side. He seriously raised the question of whether Luther had not been sharper than he should have been. Then he defended him with a phrase from Erasmus, who had said that the sickness of the time required a strong physician. God's instruments were not all alike. Melanchthon did not conceal the fact that he himself had not approved of Luther's outbursts, but regarded them as the sin and infirmity that afflicted humankind. This did not diminish his respect for Luther's greatness. He also mentioned that the deceased could be very approachable in confidential dealings. His vehemence was ultimately caused by his zeal for the truth.

The address did not deal with the remainder of Luther's life and only mentioned that many more suitable things could have been said. Only Luther's self-discipline, love for peace, and his disinterest in personal power were mentioned briefly. Melanchthon also described him as one who had prayed fervently for the church, and whose practice of prayer and confidence had been grounded in faith, even in dangerous situations, something the speaker himself had not lacked. Finally he praised the keenness of Luther's spirit, his understanding of the needs of the state and the welfare of his fellow citizens, as well as his interest in theological authors and history that he applied to the present day.

Melanchthon then spoke about Luther's communion with Christ and the prophets and apostles, among whom he was now living in the fulfillment of his hope and having his efforts on behalf of the gospel recognized. There in the heavenly university he was now beholding the nature of God, the union of the human and divine natures of Christ, and God's decrees concerning the church, all mysteries that he had taught on earth, although seeing them through a veil. This section of the address was not merely an edifying excursus; its intention was rather to state that Luther confidently believed that heaven was open and there was direct access to God. For Luther, God's sphere of action was not divorced from the world, for there was a continual and vital exchange that took place between them, particularly in regard to the church. But now Luther could also see the present heavenly reality in which he had believed.

Those who were left behind must certainly have felt like orphans. Now their task was to preserve the memory of Luther's gifts, virtues, and blessings, and to imitate them. This meant his doctrine, his fear of God, his faith and zeal for prayer, his faultless conduct of his office, his painstaking concern not to give occasion for insurrection, and his desire to learn. Melanchthon did not shy from holding up Luther as a model in the line of Jeremiah, John the Baptist, and Paul. This led into a prayer to the Lord of the church, in which he gave thanks for Luther's work and pled for continual preservation and guidance for the church. Here, too, Melanchthon freely interpreted Luther's death as a sign of the punishment that was to come—war and the thoughtless destruction of doctrine. Above all, therefore, he called upon everyone to preserve the pure doctrine of the gospel, for in that way they would remain God's dwelling and the church.

In his eulogy Melanchthon was the first to give an extensive evaluation of Luther's life after his death. Despite certain reservations, he wanted to make a positive statement.[18] The address has therefore become a notable document because it did not simply employ the obvious reasons for praising Luther. As a man, Luther was also a problem for his closest theological co-worker, and he had repeatedly suffered under him until the end. Melanchthon was so honest that he could not refrain from mentioning this, but he tried instead to give a sympathetic explanation. Anyone who thoroughly explores the peaks and valleys of Luther's long and complex life confronts the same problem. Wherever we place him, we are also free to criticize him; this detracts not at all from

Luther's greatness, but rather helps us above all to understand more deeply. Like every biographer, Melanchthon evaluated Luther from his own personal and theological standpoint, and he chose to accent certain things accordingly. Thus he lifted up the significance of pure doctrine, with justification by faith as its center, as the heritage that was scrupulously to be preserved. This inaugurated the new age of "Lutheranism."[19] It was no coincidence that several times Melanchthon emphasized Luther's acceptance of existing political relationships. That he accurately and understandably regarded himself as Luther's epigone was evident from the number of times he compared himself to Luther, thus seeing his own limits. His own political and ecclesiastical interests did not prevent Melanchthon from also perceiving the political and social significance of Luther's thought or certain features of his piety and human qualities. For Melanchthon, Luther's historical dimension and his calling consisted in his action—in the succession of the great teachers of the people of God—of again bringing evangelical truth to light, which inexorably led to a great conflict. In total agreement with Luther, this was for him an event that took place not only within this world. Luther's first biographer had already accurately perceived his person and work (both theologically and historically) as more than something that affected the history of the world—as a continuing challenge.

Abbreviations

In general the abbreviations from Siegfried Schwertner, *Internationales Abkürzungsverzeichnis für Theologie und Grenzgebiete: Zeitschriften, Serien, Lexica, Quellenwerke mit bibliographischen Angaben* (Berlin: W. de Gruyter, 1974), will be used.

(a) Luther's Works

WA	*D. Martin Luthers Werke: Kritische Gesamtausgabe.* 61 vols. Weimar: Hermann Böhlaus Nachfolger, 1883–1983.
WA, DB	*D. Martin Luthers Werke: Kritische Gesamtausgabe, Deutsche Bibel.* 12 vols. Weimar: Hermann Böhlaus Nachfolger, 1906–61.
WA, Br	*D. Martin Luthers Werke: Kritische Gesamtausgabe, Briefwechsel.* 18 vols. Weimar: Hermann Böhlaus Nachfolger, 1930–85.
WA, TR	*D. Martin Luthers Werke: Kritische Gesamtausgabe, Tischreden.* 6 vols. Weimar: Hermann Böhlaus Nachfolger, 1912–21.
St. L.	Walch, Johann Georg, ed. *Dr. Martin Luthers sämtliche Schriften.* 2d ed. 23 vols. in 25. St. Louis: Concordia Publishing House, 1880–1910.
LW	Pelikan, Jaroslav, and Helmut T. Lehmann, eds. *Luther's Works.* 55 vols. St. Louis: Concordia Publishing House; Philadelphia: Fortress (Muhlenberg) Press, 1955–86.

(b) Other works

CR	Bretschneider, Carolus Gottlieb, and Henricus Ernestus Bindseil, eds. *Philippi Melanchthonis Opera.* 28 vols. Halle: C. A. Schwetschke, 1834–60.
MWA	Stupperich, Robert, ed. *Melanchthons Werke in Auswahl.* 7 vols. to date. Gütersloh: G. Mohn, 1951–.

MBW	Scheible, Heinz, ed. *Melanchthons Briefwechsel.* 5 vols. to date. Stuttgart-Bad Cannstatt: Frommann-Holzboog, 1977–.
Benzing	Benzing, Josef. *Lutherbibliographie.* Bibliotheca Bibliographica Aureliana, vols. 10, 16, and 19. Baden-Baden: Heitz, 1966.
Bornkamm	Bornkamm, Heinrich. *Martin Luther in der Mitte seines Lebens.* Göttingen: Vandenhoeck & Ruprecht, 1979.
Bornkamm, ET	Bornkamm, Heinrich. *Luther in Mid-career, 1521–1530.* Translated by E. Theodore Bachmann. Philadelphia: Fortress Press, 1983.
Brecht, *Luther* 1	Brecht, Martin. *Martin Luther,* Vol. 1: *Sein Weg zur Reformation, 1483–1521.* 2d ed.; Stuttgart: Calwer Verlag, 1983.
Brecht, *Luther* 1, ET	Brecht, Martin. *Martin Luther: His Road to Reformation, 1483–1521.* Translated by James L. Schaaf. Philadelphia: Fortress Press, 1985.
Brecht, *Luther* 2	Brecht, Martin. *Martin Luther,* Vol. 2: *Ordnung und Abgrenzung der Reformation, 1521–1532.* Stuttgart: Calwer Verlag, 1986.
Brecht, *Luther* 2, ET	Brecht, Martin. *Martin Luther,* Vol. 2: *Shaping and Defining the Reformation, 1521–1532.* Translated by James L. Schaaf. Minneapolis: Fortress Press, 1990.
Junghans	Junghans, Helmar, ed. *Leben und Werk Martin Luthers von 1526–1546: Festgabe zu seinem 500. Geburtstag.* 2 vols. Berlin: Evangelische Verlagsanstalt; Göttingen: Vandenhoeck & Ruprecht, 1983.
Köstlin–Kawerau	Köstlin, Julius, and Gustav Kawerau. *Martin Luther: Sein Leben und seine Schriften.* 5th ed. 2 vols. Berlin: A. Duncker, 1903.

Notes

I. PEACEFUL BEGINNINGS UNDER ELECTOR JOHN FREDERICK—BUT WITH MOST OF THE OLD PROBLEMS (1532–36)

1. Elector John Frederick

1. Cf. Günther Wartenberg, "Luthers Beziehungen zu den sächsischen Fürsten," in Junghans, 549–71, esp. 554–62. Georg Mentz, *Johann Friedrich der Grossmütige, 1503–1554: Festschrift zum 400jährigen Geburtstage des Kurfürsten, namens des Vereins für Thüringische Geschichte und Altertumskunde,* ed. Thüringische Historische Kommission, Beiträge zur neueren Geschichte Thüringens, 3 vols. (Jena: G. Fischer, 1903–8), vol. 1, pts. 1 and 2.

2. WA, TR 2, nos. 1906b, 1909, 1931–33, 2617. WA, TR 3, no. 2986. Cf. WA, TR 2, no. 1558 = LW 55:156–57. WA, TR 2, no. 1564.

3. WA, Br 6:353–54, 391–92. With some certainty, the letter "to a nobleman" in WA, Br 7:40–42 was written to Rietesel and belongs in this context. The arguments against Enders in the WA can hardly be supported.

4. WA 40³:108, lines 9–10.

5. Wartenberg, "Luthers Beziehungen," 923–24 n. 121.

6. Cf. Eike Wolgast, *Die Wittenberger Theologie und die Politik der evangelischen Stände: Studien zu Luthers Gutachten in politischen Fragen,* QFRG, vol. 47 (Gütersloh: G. Mohn, 1977), 285–99, which has a somewhat different nuance.

7. WA, Br 7:349, line 50—350, line 52 = LW 50:128–29. WA, Br 7:372, lines 15–21. WA 41:xxxi; 516–20. WA, TR 4, no. 4953. WA, TR 6, no. 7054. Roderich Schmidt, "Die Torgauer Hochzeit 1536," in Paul Althaus, ed., *Solange es "heute" heisst: Festgabe für Rudolf Hermann zum 70. Geburtstag* (Berlin: Evangelische Verlagsanstalt, 1957), 234–50. Hans Georg Thümmel, "Der Greifswalder Croy-Teppich und das Bekenntnisbild des 16. Jahrhunderts," *Theologische Versuche* 11 (1979):187–214.

8. WA, TR 2, no. 1255.

9. WA, Br 7:352, lines 1–4 = LW 50:130–31.

10. WA 40³:214, lines 2–11; 230, line 5—231, line 13. WA, TR 1, no. 628. WA, Br 7:182, lines 40–45.

11. WA, TR 1, no. 653. WA, TR 2, no. 1938. WA, TR 3, nos. 3468, 3514 = LW 54:205–6, 218–19. Cf. WA 42:380, line 22—381, line 5 = LW 2:168–69.

12. WA, TR 2, nos. 2721–22. WA, Br 7:393.

13. WA, Br 6:377–78.

14. WA, Br 6:230–31.

15. WA, Br 7:90–91, 122–23, 139–40.

16. *WA*, Br 7:508–9.
17. *WA* 51:197–264 = *LW* 13:143–224. *WA* 53:659–78.
18. *WA* 51:239, lines 22–23 = *LW* 13:194.
19. *WA* 51:258, lines 8–9 = *LW* 13:217.
20. *WA* 51:257, lines 5–10 = *LW* 13:216.
21. *WA* 51:198.

2. Electoral Saxony and Its Church

1. *WA*, Br 6:346–48.
2. *WA*, TR 2, no. 1616b. *WA*, Br 6:384, lines 17–19. Cf. Karl Pallas, ed., *Die Regis-traturen der Kirchenvisitationen im ehemals sächsischen Kurkreise*, 2 vols., Geschichts-quellen der Provinz Sachsen und angrenzender Gebiete, vol. 41 (Halle: O. Hendel, 1906–18), 1:20–44. Emil Sehling, ed., *Die Evangelischen Kirchenordnungen des XVI. Jahrhunderts*, vol. 1¹, *Sachsen und Thüringen* (Leipzig: O. R. Reisland, 1902), 183–86.
3. *WA* 36:304–14.
4. *WA*, TR 1, nos. 393, 954. *WA*, TR 2, nos. 1622b, 2737. *WA*, TR 3, no. 2806b. Cf. also *WA*, TR 2, nos. 1923, 1926, 1932, 1947. *WA*, TR 3, no. 3506.
5. *WA* 37:555–58.
6. *WA* 41:3, line 18—4, line 4; 31, lines 9–12; 293, line 1—297, line 5.
7. *WA* 42:275, line 16—276, line 6 = *LW* 2:19–20.
8. *WA* 38:70–74.
9. *WA*, Br 6:442–43.
10. *WA*, Br 7:50–51.
11. *WA*, Br 6:463.
12. *WA*, Br 7:376–78.
13. *WA*, Br 6:386–87.
14. *WA*, Br 6:513–14.
15. *WA*, Br 6:558–59. *WA*, Br 7:251, lines 3–6 = *LW* 50:98; *WA*, Br 7:431.
16. *WA*, Br 12:170–80. *WA*, Br 7:57, lines 4–13.
17. Gustav Kawerau, ed., *Der Briefwechsel des Justus Jonas*, 2 vols. (Halle: O. Hendel, 1884–85; reprint ed., Hildesheim: G. Olms, 1964), vol. 1, no. 244.
18. *WA*, Br 7:47, lines 6–13; 48, lines 20–31. Cf. Matthias Simon, "Johannes Petzensteiner, Luthers Reisebegleiter in Worms," *ZBKG* 35 (1966):113–37, esp. 126–27. Brecht, *Luther* 1, 444–45, 450 = Brecht, *Luther* 1, ET, 467, 472.
19. *WA*, Br 7:499–501, 502–3, 507–8.
20. *WA*, Br 6:378, lines 5–7; 431–32. *WA*, TR 1, no. 1037. *WA*, TR 2, no. 2769b. *WA*, TR 5, no. 6111.
21. *WA*, Br 6:540–42. *WA*, Br 7:48–49; 151, lines 3–9; 337, lines 3–8; 163–64; 519–20. Cf. *WA* 36:554, lines 4–22.
22. *WA*, Br 6:468–69.
23. *WA*, Br 6:354–55, 467–68, 469–71.
24. *WA*, Br 6:53–55.
25. *WA*, Br 7:47, lines 14–24.
26. *WA*, Br 7:71; 85, lines 5–10.
27. *WA*, Br 7:191–93.
28. *WA*, Br 7:501–2, 578–79. *WA*, TR 3, no. 3489.

29. Cf. the final report of the visitors in the electoral district from November 1535, Pallas, ed., *Die Registraturen der Kirchenvisitationen*, 1:25–33.

30. Viktor Komerell, "Michael Stifel," in Hermann Häring and Otto Hohenstatt, eds., *Schwäbische Lebensbilder*, 5 vols. (Stuttgart: W. Kohlhammer, 1940–50), 3:509–24. Joseph Ehrenfried Hofmann, *Michael Stifel: Zur Mathematikgeschichte des 16. Jahrhunderts*, Jahrbuch für die Geschichte der Oberdeutschen Reichsstädte, Esslinger Studien, vol. 14 (Esslingen: Stadtarchiv Esslingen, 1968), 30–60.

31. WA, Br 4:545–46 = LW 49:210–11. WA, Br 4:584; 593, lines 9–17. WA 27:383–90.

32. WA, TR 2, no. 2756. WA, TR 3, no. 2955. WA, TR 5, 5519. WA, Br 6:364–65. *St. L.* 21:1864.

33. WA, Br 6:495–96.

34. WA, Br 6:514. WA, TR 3, no. 3660b. WA 37:154–67. Georg Buchwald, "Lutherana," *ARG* 25 (1928):56–57.

35. *St. L.* 21:1864–70.

36. WA, Br 6:544–45; 546, lines 21–23.

37. WA, Br 6:555–57. WA, Br 7:61, lines 20–23; 172, lines 16–17.

38. WA, Br 7:9–10.

39. WA, Br 7:61–62.

40. WA, Br 7:152–53.

41. WA, Br 7:178–80.

42. WA, Br 7:408–9.

43. WA, Br 7:180; 243, lines 1–5; 320, lines 1–12; 555.

44. WA, Br 6:459.

45. WA, Br 7:571–72.

46. WA, Br 7:67.

47. WA, Br 7:225–26; 240, lines 1–16.

48. Wolfgang Ribbe, "Hans Kohlhase," *NDB* 12:427–28 (some of the details are incorrect). WA, Br 7:57, line 14—58, line 21; 124–25. Karl Eduard Förstemann, "Mittheilungen aus den Wittenberger Kämmerei-Rechnungen in der ersten Hälfte des 16. Jahrhunderts," in *Neue Mittheilungen aus dem Gebiete historisch-antiquarischer Forschungen*, 24 vols. (Halle: E. Anton, 1834–1910), 3^1:116.

49. WA, TR 4, nos. 4058, 4315. WA, Br 8:558–59.

50. WA, Br 8:362, lines 13–16; 379, lines 16–21. WA, TR 4, no. 4738.

51. WA, TR 5, no. 6120. WA, Br 9:70, lines 14–21.

52. WA, Br 8:362, line 15; 402, lines 12–13. WA, Br 9:3, line 16.

3. Wittenberg

1. WA 40^2:549, line 11—552, line 8 = LW 12:255–57. WA 41:241, line 12.

2. WA, TR 1, no. 496.

3. WA, Br 7:172, lines 6–7. WA, TR 2, no. 1804.

4. WA, TR 3, no. 3472 = LW 54:206–7.

5. WA 36:ix. WA, TR 2, no. 2726b.

6. WA 36:478–696 = LW 28:57–213.

7. WA 37:xiv–xvii. WA 59:260.

8. WA 59:242–310. WA 45:465–733 = LW 24:1–298. WA 46:1–111 = LW 24:299–422.

9. *WA* 37:xiv–xv, xviii–xix. *WA* 59:260.

10. *WA* 41:xi–xvii.

11. *WA* 38:442–605. *WA* 60:20–104. *WA* 45:421–64.

12. *WA*, TR 1, nos. 868, 965. *WA*, TR 3, no. 3421. *WA*, TR 3, no. 3494 = *LW* 54:213–14.

13. *WA*, TR 2, nos. 2642–43. *WA*, TR 3, nos. 3364, 3420, 3422, 3463h. *WA*, TR 3, no. 3494 = *LW* 54:213–14.

14. *WA*, Br 7:209–10, 221.

15. *WA*, TR 2, no. 2801.

16. *WA* 48:708; no. 7201. Cf. *WA*, Br 7:57, line 14—58, line 21.

17. *WA*, TR 1, no. 949.

18. *WA*, TR 3, no. 3612c.

19. *WA*, TR 3, no. 3669.

20. On him, cf. Nikolaus Müller, "Peter Beskendorf, Luthers Barbier und Freund," in *Aus Deutschlands kirchlicher Vergangenheit: Festschrift zum 70. Geburtstage von Theodor Brieger* (Leipzig: Quelle & Meyer, 1912), 37–92.

21. *WA* 38:351–75 = *LW* 43:187–211.

22. *WA*, TR 3, no. 3481.

23. Cf. Brecht, *Luther* 2, 123–24 = Brecht, *Luther* 2, ET, 119–21.

24. *WA*, Br 7:347, lines 3–9 = *LW* 50:123.

25. Müller, "Peter Beskendorf," 65–80. Luther's own contribution is probably contained in *WA* 48:149–52. Cf. also the supplement volume of revisions on this reference.

26. *WA*, TR 2, no. 2724. Cf. *WA* 36:323, lines 22–23.

27. *WA* 41:471, lines 14–19. *WA*, TR 3, no. 3482 = *LW* 54:209–10.

28. *WA*, TR 3, no. 3453. *WA* 37:530–33.

29. *WA*, TR 3, no. 2958 = *LW* 54:184–85.

30. Otto Vogt, ed., *Dr. Johannes Bugenhagens Briefwechsel*, reprint ed. (Hildesheim: G. Olms, 1966), 126–27.

31. *WA* 41:379, line 17—380, line 24; 650, lines 1–27.

32. *WA* 41:471, line 20—472, line 4. *WA*, TR 3, no. 3477 = *LW* 54:207.

33. *WA* 41:683, line 20—684, line 1. *WA*, TR 3, no. 3491.

34. *WA*, Br 6:563–64. *WA*, TR 1, no. 582 = *LW* 54:104. Cf. *WA*, TR 3, no. 2991.

35. *WA*, Br 7:206–8.

36. *WA* 41:380, line 25—381, line 10; 384, line 31—385, line 14; 390, lines 14–33; 433, lines 12–26.

37. *WA* 41:633, lines 30–34.

38. *WA*, TR 3, no. 2880. *WA* 40³:137, lines 5–14; 143, lines 2–10.

39. *WA*, Br 7:12–14.

40. Gustav Kawerau, ed., *Der Briefwechsel des Justus Jonas*, 2 vols. (Halle: O. Hendel, 1884–85; reprint ed., Hildesheim: G. Olms, 1964), 2:359.

41. *WA*, Br 7:384–85 = *LW* 50:135. *WA*, Br 7:487, lines 10–29; 495; 506, lines 20–23.

42. *WA*, TR 3, no. 3395c.

43. Karl Eduard Förstemann, "Mittheilungen aus den Wittenberger Kämmerei-Rechnungen in der ersten Hälfte des 16. Jahrhunderts," in *Neue Mittheilungen aus dem Gebiete historisch-antiquarischer Forschungen*, 24 vols. (Halle: E. Anton, 1834–1910), 3¹:116–17.

4. Home, Family, and Personal Health

1. *WA,* Br 12:498–99. On the following, cf. Helmar Junghans, "Luther in Wittenberg," in Junghans, 11–37, esp. 22–27.

2. *WA,* Br 12:423–26. Georg Buchwald, "Lutherana," *ARG* 25 (1928):86–88.

3. *WA,* TR 2, nos. 2731, 2769. *WA,* TR 3, no. 2972.

4. *WA,* TR 3, no. 2857.

5. *WA,* Br 7:132–33.

6. *WA,* Br 7:87–89.

7. *WA,* Br 7:232, line 25—233, line 33. Cf. Brecht, *Luther* 2, 117 = Brecht, *Luther* 2, ET, 113.

8. *WA,* TR 3, no. 2835. *WA,* Br 9:583–85.

9. Cf. *WA,* Br 12:417. The *Kabelhufen* may have been lands that formerly belonged to the community.

10. Cf. *WA,* Br 9:581, lines 67–74.

11. *WA,* Br 6:396.

12. *WA,* TR 3, no. 2803.

13. *WA,* Br 7:316, line 14—318, line 18 = *LW* 50:108–9.

14. *WA,* Br 7:249, lines 3–13 = *LW* 50:94–95.

15. *WA,* TR 1, no. 798c.

16. *WA,* Br 7:232, lines 14–19.

17. *WA,* Br 7:173, line 23—174, line 27.

18. *WA,* TR 3, no. 3390b.

19. *WA,* TR 1, no. 443 = *LW* 54:71–72. *WA,* TR 1, no. 1090.

20. *WA,* TR 1, no. 1154a.

21. *WA* 38:290–93.

22. *WA,* Br 7:151, lines 14–16; 171.

23. *WA,* TR 2, no. 2754. *WA,* TR 3, no. 1848. *WA,* Br 6:392 top, lines 15–17.

24. *WA,* Br 6:382, lines 11–12 = *LW* 50:72–73. *WA,* TR 2, no. 2764.

25. *WA,* Br 6:425–26 = *LW* 50:73–74. *WA,* TR 3, no. 2946 = *LW* 54:184.

26. *WA,* TR 1, no. 237 = *LW* 54:32. *WA,* TR 3, no. 2963.

27. *WA,* TR 3, no. 3319.

28. *WA,* Br 7:128–29, 131–32. *WA,* TR 3, no. 3541.

29. *WA,* TR 1, no. 476. *WA,* TR 1, no. 508 = *LW* 54:89–90. *WA,* TR 1, nos. 614, 833.

30. *WA,* TR 2, no. 2789. *WA,* TR 3, no. 2804. *WA,* TR 3, no. 2847 = *LW* 54:174–75. Georg Buchwald, *Zur Wittenberger Stadt- und Universitäts-Geschichte in der Reformationszeit: Briefe aus Wittenberg an M. Stephan Roth in Zwickau* (Leipzig: G. Wigand, 1893), no. 120.

31. *WA,* TR 3, no. 2862.

32. *WA,* Br 7:349, lines 15–19 = *LW* 54:126.

33. *CR* 4:887–92 = *MBW* 3, no. 3070. *WA,* Br 7:343–45. Bernhard Klaus, *Veit Dietrich: Leben und Werke,* EAKGB, vol. 32 (Nuremberg: Selbstverlag des Vereins für Bayerische Kirchengeschichte, 1958), 125–28.

34. *WA,* TR 1, no. 344, passim.

35. *WA* 51:265–95. Cf. *WA* 31¹:549–64.

36. *WA,* Br 7:153–54.

37. *WA,* TR 1, no. 869. *WA,* TR 3, no. 2849 = *LW* 54:175.

38. *WA*, Br 6:384, lines 9–17. *WA*, Br 7, no. 301, lines 24–27.

39. *WA*, Br 7:74, lines 15–20.

40. *WA*, TR 3, nos. 3476, 3483 = *LW* 54:207, 210.

41. *WA*, Br 6:365, lines 20–21; 392 top, lines 15–16. *WA*, TR 2, no. 1684 = *LW* 54:162.

42. *WA*, Br 6:392, lines 5–9; 410, lines 3–10; 419, lines 1–8.

43. *WA*, TR 3, no. 2957.

44. *WA*, TR 3, no. 2970. *WA*, Br 6:565.

45. *WA*, TR 1, nos. 461, 469 = *LW* 54:74–77, 78. *WA*, TR 3, no. 2982 = *LW* 54:188.

46. *WA*, TR 3, no. 2980 = *LW* 54:187. *WA*, TR 3, nos. 2988, 3005–6. *WA*, Br 6:437, line 5; 462 top, line 22; 462 bottom, lines 13–14; 508, lines 3–15.

47. *WA*, TR 3, no. 3365. Annemarie Halder, "Das Harnsteinleiden Martin Luthers" (diss., University of Munich, 1969).

48. *WA*, TR 1, no. 613. *WA*, TR 3, no. 2893. *WA*, Br 6:508, lines 11–15. John Aurifaber, *Briefe und Acten zu der Geschichte des Religionsgespräches zu Marburg 1529 und des Reichstages zu Augsburg, nach der Handschrift des Joh. Aurifaber nebst den Berichten der Gesandten Frankfurts a. M. und den Regesten zur Geschichte dieses Reichstags*, ed. Friedrich Wilhelm Schirrmacher, reprint ed. (Amsterdam: B. R. Gruner, 1968), 375 = *MBW* 2, no. 1710.

49. *WA*, Br 7:6, line 7. *WA*, Br 7:24, lines 5–9 = *LW* 50:79. *WA*, Br 7:101, lines 2–3. *WA* 59:299, lines 29–33.

50. *WA* 41:xii. *WA*, Br 7:172, lines 13–15; 239, lines 10–12; 245, lines 14–17 = *LW* 50:87.

51. *WA* 41:xii. *WA*, Br 7:316, lines 8–9 = *LW* 50:108. *WA*, Br 7:348, line 3—349, line 14 = *LW* 50:125–26. *WA*, Br 7:356.

52. *WA*, Br 7:372, lines 15–17; 379, lines 3–5. Buchwald, *Zur Wittenberger Stadt- und Universitäts-Geschichte*, no. 136.

53. *WA*, Br 7:405, lines 8–12, 17–20; 410, lines 6–8; 425, line 3.

54. *WA*, TR 3, nos. 1510–11 (*WA*, TR 3, no. 3510 = *LW* 54:218). *WA*, TR 5, no. 6079. Buchwald, *Zur Wittenberger Stadt- und Universitäts-Geschichte*, no. 124.

II. LUTHER'S ROLE IN THE REFORMATION'S PROGRESS IN OTHER GERMAN TERRITORIES, THE AGREEMENT ON THE LORD'S SUPPER, AND THE RELATIONSHIPS WITH FRANCE AND ENGLAND (1532–36)

1. The Reformation in the Principality of Anhalt

1. On the following, cf. Hermann Wäschke, *Geschichte Anhalts von der Teilung bis zur Wiedervereinigung*, vol. 2 of *Anhaltische Geschichte* (Cöthen: O. Schultze, 1913). Otto Clemen, ed., *Georg Helts Briefwechsel*, ARG, supplementary vol. 2 (Leipzig: M. Heinsius Nachfolger, 1907).

2. *WA*, Br 6:355–56.

3. *WA*, Br 6:384, lines 1–13; 385. *WA*, TR 1, no. 397 = *LW* 54:62–63. *WA*, TR 2, no. 2802b. *WA*, TR 3, no. 2869. *WA* 36:xxvii–xxviii. *WA* 36:352–75 = *LW* 51:257–87.

4. *WA*, Br 6:438–42; 491–92.

5. *WA*, Br 6:536–39.

6. *WA*, Br 7:19–20.

7. *WA*, Br 7:45; 46; 49–50. Emil Sehling, ed., *Die Evangelischen Kirchenordnungen des XVI. Jahrhunderts*, vol. 1², *Sachsen und Thüringen, nebst angrenzenden Gebieten* (Leipzig: O. R. Reisland, 1904), 540–43.

8. *WA*, Br 7:55–57.

9. *WA*, Br 7:65–67.

10. *WA* 38:425–50. *WA* 59:320–23. *WA*, Br 7:70. *CR* 2:738 = *MBW* 2, no. 1463.

11. *WA*, Br 7:73–79.

12. *WA*, Br 7:91–93 (*WA*, Br 7:91 = *LW* 50:79–81). *CR* 2:738, 794 = *MBW* 2, nos. 1463, 1464. *WA* 37:484–504.

13. *WA*, Br 7:190–91, 325–26.

2. Relationships with Other Territories and Their Reformation

1. *WA*, Br 6:412–13. *WA*, Br 7:174–75. *WA*, Br 7:546, lines 3–7 = *LW* 50:148–49.

2. *WA*, Br 6:512–13, 526–27. *WA* 38:128–31.

3. *WA*, Br 7:89, lines 10–12. Cf. *WA*, TR 4, nos. 5046, 5096 (p. 658, lines 2–3) = *LW* 54:382, 389–90. *CR* 2:727–29 = *MBW* 2, nos. 1436–38.

4. *WA*, Br 6:459–60, 471–72.

5. *WA*, Br 6:499–500 = *WA*, Br 12:139–40.

6. *WA*, Br 7:380–81, 385–86, 389–90, 392, 537–38.

7. *WA*, Br 6:521–24. *WA*, Br 7:148, 509–10.

8. *WA*, Br 7:414–15.

9. *WA*, Br 6:428–31.

10. *WA*, Br 6:516–17.

11. *WA*, Br 7:11–12.

12. Cf. Brecht, *Luther* 2, 430–31 = Brecht, *Luther* 2, ET, 448–49. *WA*, Br 6:472–73, 535. *WA*, Br 7:106–8, 112–15. Robert Stupperich, "Das Herforder Fraterhaus und die Reformatoren," *JVWKG* 64 (1971):7–37.

13. *WA*, Br 12:150–56.

14. *WA*, Br 6:497–98. *CR* 2:656–57 = *MBW* 2, no. 1337.

15. *WA*, Br 6:446–68. Cf. *WA*, Br 13:214–15. *WA*, Br 6:453–56. Gottfried Seebass, *Das reformatorische Werk Andreas Osianders*, EAKGB, vol. 44 (Nuremberg: Verein für Bayerische Kirchengeschichte, 1967), 254–62.

16. *WA*, Br 6:502–6. Andreas Osiander, *Gesamtausgabe*, ed. Gerhard Müller, vol. 5 (Gütersloh: G. Mohn, 1983), no. 183. *WA*, Br 6:506–7.

17. *WA*, Br 6:518–21, 527–30, 530–32 = Osiander, *Gesamtausgabe*, vol. 5, no. 188, cf. no. 186. *WA*, Br 6:542–43, 546–47.

18. *WA*, Br 7:181–82.

19. *WA*, Br 7:588–90, 594–95.

20. *WA*, Br 7:319–20, 482–87, 489–90.

21. *WA*, Br 6:382–83, 392–93. Cf. also *WA*, Br 7:95–96, 399–400.

22. *WA*, Br 6:386–89.

23. *WA*, Br 7:81–83.

24. *WA*, Br 7:117–18.

25. *WA*, Br 7:147–48.

26. *WA*, Br 6:273–74, 407–10, 461–62, 546–47. *WA*, Br 7:60, 172.

27. *WA*, Br 6:408–10. *WA*, Br 7:481.

28. Theodor Pressel, *Lazarus Spengler* (Elberfeld: R. L. Friderichs, 1862), 93–99. WA 38:311–14.

3. Defense against the Münster Anabaptists

1. *WA*, Br 6:398–403. On the following, cf. Martin Brecht, "Die Theologie Bernhard Rothmanns," *JVWKG* 78 (1985):49–82. Günter Vogler, "Martin Luther und das Täuferreich zu Münster," in idem, ed., *Martin Luther: Leben, Werk und Wirkung* (Berlin: Akademie, 1983), 235–54. Some details of this article need correction.

2. *WA*, Br 7:87, lines 11–19. Robert Stupperich, ed., *Die Schriften Bernhard Rothmanns*, part 1 of *Die Schriften der münsterischen Täufer und ihrer Gegner*, Veröffentlichungen der historischen Kommission Westfalens, vol. 32 (Münster: Aschendorff, 1970), 195–208, esp. 198–200. The "confession" was thus known at that time.

3. *WA*, Br 7:126, lines 9–11. The date is corrected in *WA*, Br 13:227.

4. Robert Stupperich, ed., *Schriften von evangelischer Seite gegen die Täufer*, part 3 of *Die Schriften der münsterischen Täufer und ihrer Gegner*, Veröffentlichungen der historischen Kommission Westfalens, vol. 32 (Münster: Aschendorff, 1983), 68–73.

5. Robert Stupperich, ed., *Schriften von katholischer Seite gegen die Täufer*, part 2 of *Die Schriften der münsterischen Täufer und ihrer Gegner*, Veröffentlichungen der historischen Kommission Westfalens, vol. 32 (Münster: Aschendorff, 1980), 98–127.

6. Stupperich, ed., *Schriften von evangelischer Seite gegen die Täufer*, 82–137. WA 38:336–40. Cf. above, note 2.

7. Cf. the following paragraph and the work by Cochlaeus mentioned in note 5. It has not previously been recognized that Luther was also attacking him.

8. WA 38:341–50. The information in the *New Newspaper* may have come from the emissaries sent to Soest.

9. WA 38:349, lines 11–12. Luther cites the Low German text.

10. Cf. Günter Vogler, "Das Täuferreich zu Münster als Problem der Politik im Reich: Beobachtungen anhand reichsständischer Korrespondenzen," *MGB* 42 (1985): 7–23.

11. WA 41:448, lines 23–25; 459, lines 7–9; 570, lines 8–9; 621, lines 36–37.

12. *WA*, Br 12:218–24, 236–40.

13. *WA*, Br 7:414, lines 9–12.

14. Stupperich, ed., *Schriften von evangelischer Seite gegen die Täufer*, 220–45. The final word may not yet have been said about the identity of the author (Anton Corvinus?).

15. WA 37:258–67, 271–75, 278–84, 288–93, 299–304.

16. WA 37:627.

17. *WA*, Br 7:84–85.

18. *WA*, Br 7:111–12.

19. *CR* 2:889–90 = *MBW* 2, no. 1586.

20. *WA*, Br 7:346, lines 9–13.

21. *WA*, Br 7:416–18, 427. WA 50:6–15.

22. Cf. Brecht, *Luther* 2, 327–28 = Brecht, *Luther* 2, ET, 338. Hans J. Hillerbrand, "Die Vorgeschichte der hessischen Wiedertäuferordnung von 1537," *ZRGG* 15 (1963):330–47. Gottfried Seebass, "Luthers Stellung zur Verfolgung der Täufer und ihre Bedeutung für den deutschen Protestantismus," *MGB* 40 (1983):7–24.

23. *WA*, Br 7:365–67, 427–28, 583–85. Cf. *WA*, Br 7:72–73. Paul Vetter, "Lutherana III: Luthers Streit mit Herzog Heinrich von Sachsen," *Neues Archiv für Sächsische Geschichte und Altertumskunde* 29 (1908):82–94.

24. *WA* 47:326, line 36—336, line 26. *WA* 46:145–55; 167–85; 194, line 14—201, line 23. *WA* 35:281–85. Markus Jenny, ed., *Luthers geistliche Lieder und Kirchengesänge*, AWA, vol. 4 (Cologne and Vienna: Böhlau, 1985), 117, 299–301.

25. *WA* 46:138, line 19—139, line 15. Cf. also *WA* 46:749, lines 22–28 = *LW* 22:239. *WA*, TR 4, no. 3978. *WA* 50:343–47.

26. *WA*, Br 8:320–25.

27. *WA*, Br 8:503–5. *WA*, TR 5, no. 5232ab.

28. *WA* 54:116–18.

4. The Agreement between the Southern Germans and Luther on the Lord's Supper in the Wittenberg Concord

1. See Brecht, *Luther* 2, 394–95, 432 = Brecht, *Luther* 2, ET, 409–10, 450. On the following, cf. primarily Walther Köhler, *Zwingli und Luther: Ihr Streit um das Abendmahl nach seinen politischen und religiösen Beziehungen*, vol. 2, *Vom Beginn der Marburger Verhandlungen 1529 bis zum Abschluss der Wittenberger Konkordie von 1536*, QFRG, vol. 7 (Gütersloh: C. Bertelsmann, 1953); Ernst Bizer, *Studien zur Geschichte des Abendmahlsstreits im 16. Jahrhundert*, 2d ed. (Darmstadt: Wissenschaftliche Buchgesellschaft, 1962); Martin Brecht, "Luthers Beziehungen zu den Oberdeutschen und Schweizern von 1530/1531 bis 1546," in Junghans, 497–517. As I originally planned, the following discussion is a revised version of pages 501–14 of this article. *WA* 40³: 1–594 (*WA* 40³:484–594 = *LW* 13:73–141).

2. *WA* 30³:554–71.

3. *WA* 30³:555–56. Traugott Schiess, ed., *Briefwechsel der Brüder Ambrosius und Thomas Blaurer*, 3 vols. (Freiburg im Breisgau: F. E. Fehsenfeld, 1908–12), vol. 1, nos. 326, 328.

4. *Martin Bucers Deutsche Schriften*, vol. 4 (Gütersloh: G. Mohn, 1970), 507–14, 312–19.

5. Köhler, *Zwingli und Luther*, 2:302–5.

6. See Brecht, *Luther* 2, 78–82 = Brecht, *Luther* 2, ET, 72–77. On the following, cf. Amedeo Molnár, "Luthers Beziehungen zu den Böhmischen Brüdern," in Junghans, 627–39, esp. 635–37.

7. *WA* 38:75–80.

8. Schiess, ed., *Briefwechsel der Brüder Ambrosius und Thomas Blaurer*, vol. 1, nos. 334, 337.

9. *WA*, Br 7:175–77. CR 2:854–55 = *MBW* 2, no. 1559.

10. *WA*, Br 7:558–63, 585–86.

11. *WA*, Br 8:146–48, 160–61.

12. *WA* 50:375–80.

13. *WA*, Br 12:140–49.

14. *WA*, Br 6:492–94; 508, line 16—509; 510–12. Cf. the criticism of the Augsburg catechism, *WA*, TR 3, no. 2446. *WA*, Br 6:539–40, 547–48.

15. *WA* 38:315–25. Cf. *WA* 60:105–13. *WA* 38:171–372 = *LW* 38:139–214. Schiess, ed., *Briefwechsel der Brüder Ambrosius und Thomas Blaurer*, vol. 1, nos. 400, 402.

16. *CR* 2:641–42 = *MBW* 2, no. 1315. *CR* 2:498–99, 675–76, 710–13 = *MBW* 2, nos. 1355, 1368, 1420.

17. *Martin Bucers Deutsche Schriften*, vol. 5 (Gütersloh: G. Mohn, 1978), 119–258.

18. See Brecht, *Luther* 2, 322 = Brecht, *Luther* 2, ET, 332.

19. *CR* 2:751 = *MBW* 2, no. 1467. *CR* 2:775–76 = *MBW* 2, no. 1468. Heinrich Ernst Bindseil, ed., *Philippi Melanchthonis epistolae, iudicia, consilia, testimonia aliorumque ad eum epistolae, quae in Corpore Reformatorum desiderantur* (Halle: Gustav Schwetschke, 1874), 90–91 = *MBW* 2, no. 1482. WA, Br 7:102–3, 109–10.

20. Schiess, ed., *Briefwechsel der Brüder Ambrosius und Thomas Blaurer*, vol. 1, nos. 499–503. Ernst Bizer, "Martin Butzer und der Abendmahlsstreit," *ARG* 35 (1938):203–37, esp. 219–37.

21. WA 38:294–310. WA, Br 7:127. WA, Br 12:157–63. WA, TR 5, no. 5815.

22. WA, Br 12:167–68. Bizer, "Martin Butzer und der Abendmahlsstreit," 224–29.

23. WA, Br 12:164–66. Gerhard Müller, "Die Kasseler Vereinbarung über das Abendmahl," *JHKGV* 18 (1967):125–36. W. Ian P. Hazlett, "Les entretiens entre Mélanchthon et Bucer en 1534; Réalités politiques et clarification théologique," in Marijn de Kroon and Marc Lienhard, eds., *Horizons européens de la réforme en Alsace: Mélanges offerts à Jean Rott pour son 65e anniversaire* (Strasbourg: Librairie Istra, 1980), 207–25.

24. WA, Br 7:144–46, 149–50, 156–58. WA, Br 12:169. *CR* 2:835–37, 841–42 = *MBW* 2, nos. 1535, 1537.

25. Schiess, ed., *Briefwechsel der Brüder Ambrosius und Thomas Blaurer*, vol. 1, nos. 525, 544, 546, 549, 614. WA, Br 7:183–85.

26. WA, Br 7:195–99; 200; 210–13; 220–21; 239, lines 5–7. Schiess, ed., *Briefwechsel der Brüder Ambrosius und Thomas Blaurer*, vol. 1, no. 616.

27. WA, Br 7:234–37. Theodor Pressel, *Anecdota Brentiana: Ungedruckte Briefe und Bedenken von Johannes Brenz* (Tübingen: J. J. Heckenhauer, 1868), 142–54.

28. WA, Br 7:242–43, 148–49, 252–66, 272–73, 278.

29. WA, Br 7:286–98, 328–29. Köhler, *Zwingli und Luther*, 2:400–1.

30. WA, Br 7:303–5, 306–16, 323–24, 324–25.

31. WA, Br 7:327–28. WA, Br 7:353 = WA, Br 12:197–98. WA, Br 7:355. *CR* 10: 149–50 = *MBW* 2, no. 1675.

32. Schiess, ed., *Briefwechsel der Brüder Ambrosius und Thomas Blaurer*, vol. 1, nos. 660, 665, 668–70, 673, 684, 689, 693. WA, Br 7:357–59.

33. WA, Br 7:378–79, 406–8, 409–14, 418–19. *CR* 3:54–55, 70 = *MBW* 2, nos. 1724, 1736.

34. The primary accounts of the Wittenberg negotiations are those of Myconius (*St. L.* 17:2090–99) and Johannes Bernhardi (Algesheimer), which is essentially the report of the southern Germans drafted by Bucer; cf. Zwick's additions in Ernst Bizer, "Martin Luther und der Abendmahlsstreit," *ARG* 36 (1939):66–87, esp. 66–77. Martin Greschat, "Martin Bucers Anteil am Bericht der oberländischen Prediger über den Abschluss der Wittenberger Konkordie (1536)," *ARG* 76 (1985):296–98.

35. Christopf Friedrich Gayler, *Historische Denkwürdigkeiten der ehemaligen freien Reichsstadt . . . Reutlingen*, vol. 1 (Reutlingen: B. G. Kurtz, 1840), 455.

36. Pressel, *Anecdota Brentiana*, 184–85.

37. Schiess, ed., *Briefwechsel der Brüder Ambrosius und Thomas Blaurer*, vol. 1, no. 720. Bizer, "Martin Luther und der Abendmahlsstreit," *ARG* 36 (1939):127.

38. Theodor Kolde, ed., *Analecta Lutherana: Briefe und Aktenstücke zur Geschichte Luthers* (Gotha: F. A. Perthes, 1883), 216–30 (Wolfgang Musculus's report of the trip). WA 41:591–600.

39. *WA, Br* 12:206–12.

40. Bizer, *Studien zur Geschichte des Abendmahlsstreit im 16. Jahrhundert*, 121–30. Köhler, *Zwingli und Luther*, 2:455.

41. *WA, Br* 7:419–26, 460–64. *CR* 3:96–97 = *MBW* 2, no. 1759.

42. *CR* 3:78–81. Bizer, "Martin Luther und der Abendmahlsstreit," *ARG* 36 (1939): 79–87. Martin Bucer, *Études sur la correspondance avec de nombreux textes inédits*, ed. Jacques V. Pollet, vol. 1 (Paris: Presses universitaires de France, 1958), 36, line 26—39, line 5.

43. *WA, Br* 7:432–37, 466–70.

44. *WA, Br* 7:474–76, 490–93.

45. *WA, Br* 7:471–73.

46. *WA, Br* 7:538–39.

47. Schiess, ed., *Briefwechsel der Brüder Ambrosius und Thomas Blaurer*, vol. 1, no. 713.

48. *WA, Br* 7:514–19, 520–25, 531–37, 556–58. *WA, Br* 12:228–29.

49. *WA, Br* 7:566–68.

50. *WA, Br* 7:572–78. Cf. *WA, Br* 12:213–14. *WA, Br* 7:591–92.

51. *WA, Br* 12:241–75.

52. *WA, Br* 7:595–99, 608–10.

53. *WA, Br* 12:224–35. Schiess, ed., *Briefwechsel der Brüder Ambrosius und Thomas Blaurer*, vol. 1, no. 707. Ernst Bizer, "Die Wittenberger Konkordie in Oberdeutschland und in der Schweiz," *ARG* 36 (1939):214–52, esp. 215–24. Cf. Bernd Moeller, *Johannes Zwick und die Reformation in Konstanz*, QFRG, vol. 28 (Gütersloh: G. Mohn, 1961), 186–200.

54. *WA, Br* 7:618–20.

55. *WA, Br* 8:99, lines 10–25 = *LW* 50:173–74.

56. *WA, Br* 8:43–45. *WA, TR* 3, no. 3544. Bizer, "Die Wittenberger Konkordie," 226–33. *CR* 3:291–94 = *MBW* 2, no. 1858.

57. *WA, Br* 8:149–53, 153–57, 157–58. *St. L.* 17:2148–54.

58. *WA, Br* 8:207–8; 215, lines 32–39. *WA, TR* 3, no. 2868 = *LW* 54:178.

59. Bizer, "Die Wittenberger Konkordie," 233–46. *WA, Br* 8:211–14.

60. *WA, Br* 8:241–42, 281–85. Bizer, "Die Wittenberger Konkordie," 248–52.

61. *WA, Br* 8:268–73, 274–76. *WA, TR* 4, no. 3986.

5. France and England

1. *WA, Br* 7:85–86. *WA, TR* 4, no. 4126. *CR* 2:730–31, 737 = *MBW* 2, nos. 1444, 1460.

2. On the following, cf. primarily Karl Josef Seidel, *Frankreich und die deutschen Protestanten: Die Bemühungen um eine religiöse Konkordie und die französische Bündnispolitik in den Jahren 1534/35*, RGST, vol. 10 (Münster: Aschendorff, 1970). Eike Wolgast, *Die Wittenberger Theologie und die Politik der evangelischen Stände: Studien zu Luthers Gutachten in politischen Fragen*, QFRG, vol. 47 (Gütersloh: G. Mohn, 1977), 230–32. Gerhard Philipp Wolf, "Luthers Beziehungen zu Frankreich,"

in Junghans, 663–75, esp. 666–68, 672–73. *CR* 2:880–81, 879–80, 899 = *MBW* 2, nos. 1578, 1579, 1596.

3. *CR* 2:741–75 = *MBW* 2, no. 1467.

4. *CR* 2:899, 900, 903–5 = *MBW* 2, nos. 1596, 1600, 1603. *MBW* 2, no. 1605.

5. *WA*, Br 7:227–30. *CR* 2:910–13, 915–16 = *MBW* 2, nos. 1610, 1611.

6. *CR* 2:918–19, 936–37, 955–56 = *MBW* 2, nos. 1616, 1619, 1622. *WA*, Br 7:232, lines 5–8; 243, lines 6–8. *WA*, Br 7:245, lines 17–20 = *LW* 50:87. *WA*, Br 7:246, lines 12–15.

7. *WA* 38:386–400. *WA*, Br 7:320, line 14—321, line 19. Cf. Max Lackmann, "Luthers Brief von 1535 an die Soester," *Soester Zeitschrift* 71 (1958):21–41.

8. *WA*, Br 7:527–30.

9. On the following, cf. Friedrich Prüser, *England und die Schmalkaldener*, QFRG, vol. 11 (Leipzig: M. Heinsius Nachfolger, 1929). Neelak Serawlook Tjernagel, *Henry VIII and the Lutherans: A Study in Anglo-Lutheran Relations from 1521 to 1547* (St. Louis: Concordia Publishing House, 1965), 135–219. Idem, *Lutheran Martyr* (Milwaukee: Northwestern Publishing House, 1982). Eike Wolgast, *Die Wittenberger Theologie*, 232–39. James Atkinson, "Luthers Beziehungen zu England," in Junghans, 677–87.

10. *CR* 2:920–30, 1027–28 = *MBW* 2, nos. 1555, 1678. *WA*, TR 4, no. 4699 = *LW* 54:361–62.

11. *MBW* 2, no. 1604. *WA*, Br 7:281–84.

12. *WA*, Br 7:266–70, 281–84 (*WA*, Br 7:266–67 = *LW* 50:100–2).

13. *WA* 50:1–5.

14. *WA*, Br 7:299, lines 2–3. 7:330, lines 3–16 = *LW* 50:114–15.

15. *CR* 2:1027–28, 968–72 = *MBW* 2, nos. 1678, 1679.

16. *WA*, Br 7:340–431; *WA*, Br 7:349, lines 20–25 = *LW* 50:126–27. *CR* 3:22–26 = *MBW* 2, no. 1690. Cf. also *WA*, Br 7:359–62.

17. *WA*, Br 7:352, lines 5–10 = *LW* 50:131. *WA*, Br 7:353, line 12—354, line 20; 355, lines 8–12. Georg Buchwald, "Lutherana," *ARG* 25 (1928):60–61.

18. *WA* 39[1]:134–73.

19. *CR* 3:52–53, 527–29 = *MBW* 2, nos. 1714, 1716. Georg Menz, ed., *Die Wittenberger Artikel von 1536*, QGP, vol. 2 (Leipzig: A. Deichert, 1905). *WA*, Br 7:383, lines 4–22. *WA*, Br 7:400–4 = *LW* 50:138–41.

20. *WA*, Br 8:219–23 = *LW* 50:177–80. Cf. *WA*, TR 3, no. 3873.

21. *WA*, TR 4, no. 4694. *WA*, TR 4, no. 4699 = *LW* 54:361–62.

22. *WA*, Br 8:562–66; 567, lines 23–24. *WA*, Br 8:569, lines 22–26; 572–78 = *LW* 50:189–90, 192–206. *CR* 2:804–19 = *MBW* 2, no. 2298.

23. *WA*, TR 4, no. 5064 = *LW* 54:384. *WA* 51:445–51.

III. RENEWED STRIFE WITH OLD OPPONENTS

1. Duke George and the Repression of the Reformation in Ducal Saxony (1532–39)

1. *WA*, Br 6:352–53. *WA*, Br 13:210.

2. *WA*, TR 2, nos. 2715, 2747, 2798. *WA*, Br 6:370–72. On the following, cf. Brecht, *Luther* 2, 403–5 = Brecht, *Luther* 2, ET, 419–21. Artur Hecker, "Religion und Politik in den letzten Lebensjahren Herzog Georgs des Bärtigen von Sachsen" (diss., University

of Leipzig, 1912). Günther Wartenberg, "Luthers Beziehungen zu den sächsischen Fürsten," in Junghans, 562–66. Mark U. Edwards, Jr., *Luther's Last Battles: Politics and Polemics, 1531–46* (Ithaca, N.Y.: Cornell University Press, 1983), 38–67. Helmar Junghans, "Georg von Sachsen," *TRE* 12:385–89.

3. *WA*, Br 6:411, lines 18–19; 417, lines 16–17. *WA*, TR 1, no. 565. *WA*, TR 3, nos. 2870, 3612b.

4. *WA*, TR 2, no. 2747. *WA*, TR 3, nos. 2925, 3326, 3464o. *WA*, Br 6:421–23.

5. *WA*, Br 6:515. *WA*, Br 7:115–17, 599–600.

6. *WA*, TR 5, no. 6046. Cf. *WA* 38:86–88. *WA*, Br 6:448–50.

7. *WA*, Br 6:465–67, 548–49.

8. *WA*, Br 6:450–52. Cf. Brecht, *Luther* 2, 405 = *Luther* 2, ET, 420–21. *WA*, Br 6:464–65.

9. *WA*, Br 6:456–59.

10. *WA* 38:86–127; cf. esp. 108, lines 7–8.

11. *WA* 38:135–38. *WA*, TR 3, no. 3367. The cited writings by Cochlaeus were examined.

12. *WA* 38:135–70. *WA*, Br 6:517, lines 9–14. Cf. *WA*, TR 3, no. 3357b.

13. *WA*, Br 6:562, lines 3–7.

14. *WA*, Br 7:20–23, 43–44. Cf. Brecht, *Luther* 2, 342–43 = *Luther* 2, ET, 355–56.

15. *WA*, Br 7:136–39, 141–44, 148–49.

16. *WA*, Br 7:201, lines 3–15.

17. *WA*, Br 7:383, lines 23–34 = *LW* 50:134–35. *WA*, Br 7:429, lines 10–17. Cf. *WA*, TR 3, no. 3838 = *LW* 54:282.

18. *WA* 39^1:9–39; cf. esp. 32, lines 1–16.

19. Cf. Wartenberg, "Luther's Beziehungen zu den sächsischen Fürsten," 568–69. *WA*, Br 6:90. *WA* 37:506–26. Cf. also the visit of Henry's wife to Wittenberg in 1538 (*WA* 46:449).

20. *WA*, Br 7:167–68; cf. 365–67.

21. *WA*, Br 7:411, lines 33–42. *WA*, Br 8:118, lines 78–88. See above, pp. 37–38. Cf. Martin Schmidt, "Die Reformation in Freiberger Ländchen (im Albertinischen Sachsen) 1537 und ihre prototypische Bedeutung," in Lewis W. Spitz, *Humanismus und Reformation als kulturelle Kräfte in der Deutschen Geschichte*, VHK, vol. 51 (Berlin and New York: W. de Gruyter, 1981), 104–20. Paul Vetter, "Lutherana III: Luthers Streit mit Herzog Heinrich von Sachsen," *Neues Archiv für Sächsische Geschichte und Altertumskunde* 29 (1908):82–94.

22. *WA*, Br 8:250–51, 308–10, 346–48, cf. 359–61. *WA*, TR 4, no. 4072.

23. *WA*, TR 3, no. 3531. Cf. Georg Buchwald, ed., *Zur Wittenberger Stadt- und Universitäts-Geschichte in der Reformationszeit: Briefe aus Wittenberg an M. Stephan Roth in Zwickau* (Leipzig: G. Wigand, 1893), 125.

24. *WA*, TR 4, nos. 4740, 4380, 4398.

25. *CR* 2:722–26 = *MBW* 2, no. 1433. On the following, cf. Günther Wartenberg, "Die Leipziger Religionsgespräche von 1534 und 1539," in Gerhard Müller, ed., *Die Religionsgespräche der Reformationszeit*, SVRG, vol. 191 (Gütersloh: G. Mohn, 1980), 35–41.

26. *WA*, TR 4, no. 4189.

27. *WA*, TR 4, nos. 3922, 3942, 4172.

28. *WA, TR* 4, no. 4509 = *LW* 54:349–50. *WA, TR* 4, nos. 4522–23, 4527, 4530, 4532, 4552, 4560, 4563–64, 4587.

29. *WA, TR* 4, nos. 4467, 4526, 4547, 4549. *WA, TR* 4, no. 4556 = *LW* 54:352.

2. The Private Mass and the Consecration of Priests

1. *WA* 38:171–256.
2. See Brecht, *Luther* 2, 383, 386 = *Luther* 2, ET, 397, 400.
3. *WA* 38:185–95.
4. *WA, Br* 6:562, lines 9–26.
5. *WA, Br* 7:18.
6. *WA* 38:197, line 19—205, line 31 = *LW* 38:149–58.
7. *WA* 38:205, line 32—250, line 24 = *LW* 38:158–210.
8. Cf. Brecht, *Luther* 2, 372 = *Luther* 2, ET, 386.
9. *WA* 38:247, lines 10–31 = *LW* 38:208–9.
10. *WA* 38:250, line 25—251 = *LW* 38:210–11.
11. *WA, Br* 7:16, lines 14–15. *WA* 38:269, lines 27–33 = *LW* 38:230.
12. *WA, Br* 6:562, lines 10–11. *WA, Br* 7:6, lines 21–23; 15, lines 10–13; 16, lines 3–11; 18; 63, lines 9–15. *WA* 38:179–82. Gustav Kawerau, ed., *Der Briefwechsel des Justus Jonas*, 2 vols. (Halle: O. Hendel, 1884–85; reprint ed., Hildesheim: G. Olms, 1964), vol. 1, nos. 250, 350a (pp. 443–44).
13. *WA* 38:257–72 = *LW* 38:215–33. The assumption of Kawerau, the editor, that John, the brother of George of Anhalt, was the opponent against whom Luther was writing can hardly be reconciled with the course of the Reformation in Anhalt. The objections must have come from old believers in Halle or Dessau. Cf. Otto Clemen, ed., *Georg Helts Briefwechsel*, ARG.E, vol. 2 (Leipzig: M. Heinsius Nachfolger, 1907), nos. 88, 91.

3. Erasmus and Witzel

1. Cf. Brecht, *Luther* 2, 210–34 = *Luther* 2, ET, 213–38.
2. *WA* 60:192–228.
3. *WA, TR* 2, nos. 1597, 2170, 2205, 2308.
4. *WA, TR* 1, no. 817. *WA, TR* 2, no. 1319 = *LW* 54:136. *WA, TR* 2, no. 1605. *WA, TR* 3, nos. 3031, 3039, 3144. Cf. Erasmus of Rotterdam, *Opera omnia, recognita et adnotatione critica instructa notisque illustrata*, vol. 1, part 3 (Amsterdam and Oxford: North-Holland Publishing Co., 1972), 470–94.
5. *WA, TR* 1, nos. 430, 432 = *LW* 54:68–69, 69. *WA, TR* 3, nos. 2866, 2939. Cf. Erasmus, *Opera omnia*, vol. 1, part 3, 453–69 (pp. 454–55 refer to Luther). *WA, TR* 1, nos. 1086, 1193.
6. *WA, TR* 3, no. 2876. *WA, TR* 1, no. 446. Cf. *WA, TR* 3, no. 3010. *WA, TR* 1, nos. 448; 466 = *LW* 54:73, 77–78. *WA, TR* 3, no. 3028. *WA, TR* 1, no. 468.
7. *WA, TR* 3, no. 3033b = *LW* 54:189. *WA, TR* 1, no. 500.
8. *WA, TR* 1, no. 494 = *LW* 54:84–85. Jean Leclerc, ed., *Desiderii Erasmi Roterodami opera omnia*, 10 vols. (Leiden: Petri Vander Aa, 1703–6), 7:289–90. *WA, TR* 2, no. 2297 (from 1531).
9. *WA, TR* 3, nos. 3302, 3316. *WA, TR* 1, no. 838.
10. Winfried Trusen, *Um die Reform und Einheit der Kirche: Zum Leben und Werk*

Georg Witzels, KLK, vol. 14 (Münster: Aschendorff, 1957). Cf. Brecht, *Luther* 2, 428 = *Luther* 2, ET, 446. *CR* 2:677–80 = *MBW* 2, no. 1370. *WA*, Br 7:16, lines 12–13. *WA* 40²:530, lines 8–13. *WA* 38:81–85. Raida's work is printed in *Schriften zur Förderung der Georg-Witzel-Forschung*, vol. 2 (Ludenscheid: P. Jarszombeck, 1976), 1–64. *WA*, TR 1, no. 604 = *LW* 54:107–8.

11. *WA*, Br 6:543–44. *WA*, TR 3, no. 2978b.

12. *WA*, Br 7:100–1. Otto Clemen, "Georg Witzel und Justus Jonas," *ARG* 17 (1920):132–52, esp. 146ff.

13. *WA*, Br 7:169, lines 3–11. *WA*, TR 4, nos. 4051, 4055, 4065, 4086, 4094, 4566, 4605. *WA*, TR 5, no. 5383.

14. *WA*, Br 7:16, line 12—17, line 21.

15. *De sarcienda ecclesiae concordia*, Erasmus of Rotterdam, *Opera omnia, recognita et adnotatione critica instructa notisque illustrata*, vol. 5, part 3 (Amsterdam and Oxford: North-Holland Publishing Co., 1986), 245–313, esp. 302–13.

16. *WA*, Br 7:27–40.

17. Erasmus of Rotterdam, *Opera omnia, recognita et adnotatione critica instructa notisque illustrata*, vol. 5, part 1 (Amsterdam and Oxford: North-Holland Publishing Co., 1972), 177–320.

18. Erasmus of Rotterdam, *Ausgewählte Schriften*, ed. Werner Welzig, vol. 3 (Darmstadt: Wissenschaftliche Buchgesellschaft, 1967), 38–77.

19. *Desiderii Erasmi Roterodami opera omnia*, 6:*4–5.

20. P. S. Allen and H. M. Allen, eds., *Opus epistolarum Des. Erasmi Roterodami*, 12 vols. (Oxford: Clarendon Press, 1906–58), 6:1186.

21. *CR* 2:710–13, 708–9 = *MBW* 2, nos. 1420, 1421. *WA*, TR 3, no. 3392. *WA*, TR 4, no. 4899.

22. *WA*, Br 7:51–53.

23. Erasmus of Rotterdam, *Opera omnia, recognita et adnotatione critica instructa notisque illustrata*, vol. 9, part 1 (Amsterdam and Oxford: North-Holland Publishing Co., 1982), 427–83. One should consult the introduction by Cornelis Augustijn.

24. *WA*, Br 7:79–80.

25. *WA* 38:273–79.

26. *WA*, Br 7:119, line 19—120, line 33.

27. *WA*, TR 4, no. 3963. *WA*, TR 4, no. 4028 = *LW* 54:312.

28. *WA*, TR 3, no. 3795. *WA*, TR 4, nos. 4899, 5119–20. *WA*, TR 5, nos. 5487, 5535, 5670. *WA* 42:596, lines 21–23 = *LW* 3:67.

29. *WA* 54:101–6. Cf. *WA* 43:614, line 35—615, line 41 = *LW* 5:269–71.

4. The Injustice of Archbishop Albrecht of Mainz

1. *WA*, TR 3, no. 3038. *WA*, Br 7:15, lines 2–11. Cf. Brecht, *Luther* 2, 338 = *Luther* 2, ET, 350–51. On the following, see Walter Delius, *Die Reformationsgeschichte der Stadt Halle an der Saale*, BKGD, vol. 1 (Berlin: Union Verlag, 1953), 52–58, 61–65.

2. *WA*, Br 7:59, lines 11–17; 68–70; 142, lines 36–46; 143, lines 14–16.

3. Cf. *WA* 50:387–88. Fr. Hülsse, *Kardinal Albrecht, Kurfürst und Erzbischof von Mainz und Magdeburg, und Hans Schenitz*, Geschichts-Blätter für Stadt und Land Magdeburg: Mittheilungen des Vereins für Geschichte und Alterthumskunde des Herzogthums und Erzstifts Magdeburg (Magdeburg: E. Baensch, 1889), 24:1–82. This

work is full of information, but it is partial to the house of Hohenzollern. The case deserves a new investigation.

4. *WA,* Br 7:202–3, 205, 277–79, 298.

5. *WA,* Br 7:216–19. Cf. *WA* 50:389.

6. *WA,* Br 7:351–52; 368–71; 372, lines 11–15. *CR* 3:42–43 = *MBW* 2, no. 1700. *WA* 50:391. *WA,* TR 4, no. 4018 = *LW* 54:309–10. *WA,* TR 4, no. 4640.

7. *WA,* Br 7:457; 464–65; 511–13; 526, lines 1–8; 553–54. Gustav Kawerau, ed., *Der Briefwechsel des Justus Jonas,* 2 vols. (Halle: O. Hendel, 1884–85; reprint ed., Hildesheim: G. Olms, 1964), 1:322, 324–25, 354–55, 360–61.

8. *WA,* Br 7:610–13. *WA,* Br 8:20–21. Veit Ludwig von Seckendorf, *Commentarius historicus et apologeticus de Lutheranismo,* 2d ed. (Leipzig: Joh. Friedrich Gleditsch, 1694), 251.

9. Kawerau, ed., *Der Briefwechsel des Justus Jonas,* vol. 1, nos. 366, 368. *WA,* Br 8:198, lines 15–26. *WA,* TR 3, nos. 3714, 3750, 3791, 3905. *WA* 47:420, line 36—425, line 13.

10. On the following, cf. Paul Merker, *Simon Lemnius: Ein Humanistenleben,* Quellen und Forschungen zur Sprach- und Culturgeschichte der Germanischen Völker, vol. 104 (Strasbourg: K. J. Trübner, 1908). Lothar Mundt, *Lemnius und Luther: Studien und Texte zur Geschichte und Nachwirkung ihres Konfliktes (1538/1539),* Arbeiten zur Mittleren Deutschen Literatur und Sprache, vol. 14 (Bern and New York: P. Lang, 1983). Franz Wachinger, *Anmerkungen zu den Epigrammen des Simon Lemnius,* Humanistica Lovaniensia, vol. 34b (Louvain: University Press; The Hague: Martinus Nijhoff, 1985), 114–32. Idem, "Lemnius und Melanchthon," *ARG* 77 (1986):141–57. *WA,* TR 4, no. 3908. *WA,* TR 4, no. 4018 = *LW* 54:309–10.

11. Merker, *Simon Lemnius,* 25–26. *CR* 3:543.

12. *WA* 50:348–51. *WA* 46:438, line 14—439. Cf. Merker, *Simon Lemnius,* 46–48. *WA,* TR 3, no. 3896.

13. *WA,* Br 8:287–89.

14. Otto Clemen, "Zur Relegation des Simon Lemnius," in idem, *Beiträge zur Reformationsgeschichte aus Büchern und Handschriften der Zwickauer Ratsschulbibliothek,* 3 vols. (Berlin: C. A. Schwetschke, 1900–3), 1:59–62. Theodor Kolde, ed., *Analecta Lutherana: Briefe und Aktenstücke zur Geschichte Luthers* (Gotha: F. A. Perthes, 1883), 326–27. *CR* 3:545–48, 550, 551–52, 552–53, 559–60, 557–59, 571–73 = *MBW* 2, nos. 2053, 2061, 2062, 2063, 2066, 2067, 2086.

15. *WA,* TR 4, nos. 4032–33. *CR* 3:593–94, 595–96 = *MBW* 2, nos. 2101, 2126.

16. *WA,* TR 5, nos. 4584, 4592. Merker, *Simon Lemnius,* 69–73. *WA* 54:175, lines 5–20.

17. Kolde, ed., *Analecta Lutherana,* 322–23, n. 1.

18. *WA,* Br 8:253–56, 261–62, 299–300.

19. *WA,* Br 8:341; 351, lines 23–30. Kawerau, ed., *Der Briefwechsel des Justus Jonas,* vol. 1, no. 406. *WA,* TR 4, no. 4640.

20. *WA,* TR 4, no. 4188 = *LW* 54:326.

21. *WA* 50:386–431.

22. See Brecht, *Luther* 2, 176 = *Luther* 2, ET, 176, and above, p. 11.

23. *WA,* Br 4, no. 4640.

24. *WA,* TR 4, no. 4445. Seckendorf, *Commentarius.*

IV. COMPLETING THE TRANSLATION
OF THE BIBLE

1. Translating the Prophets and the Apocrypha

1. See Brecht, *Luther* 2, 279 = *Luther* 2, ET, 286. On this entire chapter, cf. Hans Volz, *Hundert Jahre Wittenberger Bibeldruck 1522–1626*, Arbeiten aus der Staats- und Universitätsbibliothek Göttingen: Hainbergschriften, n.s., vol. 1 (Göttingen: L. Hantzschel, 1954). Idem, *Martin Luthers deutsche Bibel: Entstehung und Geschichte der Lutherbibel* (Hamburg: Wittig, 1978). WA, DB 11²:ix–lxvii. WA, Br 3:577, line 15—578, line 19; 578, lines 29–33. WA, DB 8:xlix–l, n. 14.

2. See Brecht, *Luther* 2, 172–93 = *Luther* 2, ET, 172–94. WA, Br 4:168, lines 7–9.

3. WA, Br 4:197, lines 7–11. WA, Br 4:198, lines 6–10 = *LW* 49:165. WA 30²:640, lines 28–32 = *LW* 35:194–95. Cf. WA, DB 11²:cxiii–cxxxiii. Gerhard Krause, *Studien zu Luthers Auslegung der kleinen Propheten*, BHT, vol. 33 (Tübingen: Mohr, 1962), 15–60.

4. WA, Br 4:243, lines 7–13.

5. WA, Br 4:468 top, lines 9–11. *CR* 1:982–83 = *MBW* 1, no. 693. WA, Br 4:484, lines 14–18. WA, DB 11¹:22, lines 14–19 = *LW* 35:277–78.

6. WA, DB 12:xxiv–xxx, 48–107 (WA, DB 12:49–55 = *LW* 35:340–45). WA, Br 5:75, lines 12–15; 86, lines 11–13.

7. WA, Br 5:242, lines 11–13. WA, DB 11²:xxv–lv. WA, DB 11²:2–49, 124–31 = *LW* 35:294–316. WA, DB 11²:376–87. Cf. Brecht, *Luther*, 2, 379 = *Luther*, 2, ET, 393.

8. WA 30²:220, 236.

9. WA, Br 5:285, lines 3–6 = *LW* 49:288. WA, Br 5:309, lines 9–11; 316, lines 7–10; 381, lines 17–19; 382, lines 9–10; 385, line 12; 522, lines 17–20; 548, lines 25–28; 554, lines 8–9. WA, Br 5:608, lines 21–22 = *LW* 49:418. WA, DB 11²:lvii–lxiii.

10. WA, Br 6:269, lines 14–18. WA, DB 11¹:2–15 = *LW* 35:265–73.

11. WA, TR 2, no. 1317 = *LW* 54:135–36. WA, TR 2, no. 2381.

12. WA, DB 12:xxxi–xliii. WA, Br 6:382, lines 10–11 = *LW* 50:72. WA, TR 1, nos. 367, 530. WA, TR 2, nos. 2761, 2771, 2776–78, 2781–82, 2790–91. WA, DB 12:148 = *LW* 35:348–49.

13. WA, DB 12:xliii–lix. Cf. WA, TR 2, no. 2790b. WA, DB 8:34. WA, TR 1, nos. 444, 478, 694–97. WA, TR 2, no. 1880. WA, TR 3, nos. 2987, 3003–4, 3007, 3391. WA, DB 12:416, line 17—418, line 2.

14. WA, Br 7:37, lines 371–72.

15. Elfriede Starke, "Luthers Beziehungen zu Kunst und Künstlern," in Junghans, 531–48, here 542–45. Cf. WA, TR 1, nos. 533, 533a. Kurt Galling, "Die Prophetenbilder der Lutherbibel im Zusammenhang mit Luthers Schriftverständnis," *EvTh* 6 (1946/47):273–301.

16. Martin Brecht, "Luthers Bibelübersetzung," in Horst Bartel, Gerhard Brendler, Hans Hübner, and Adolf Laube, eds., *Martin Luther: Leistung und Erbe* (Berlin: Akademie, 1986), 118–25.

17. WA, Br 12:288–92. WA, TR 2, no. 1459.

18. Volz, *Hundert Jahre Wittenberger Bibeldruck*, 62 n. 21.

19. WA, DB 8:xlv–lxx, 2–5. WA, Br 4:38–39.

20. WA, Br 7:94, line 1—95 top, line 15. Cf. the corrected dating in WA, Br 13:225.

21. WA, Br 12:284–88. WA, Br 8:488–92 = *LW* 50:185–87.

22. *WA*, DB 8:6–9.

23. Volz, *Martin Luthers deutsche Bibel*, 10.

24. *WA*, DB 7:xliv.

2. Revisions

1. See Brecht, *Luther* 2, 63 = *Luther* 2, ET, 56. *WA*, DB 10¹:94–97. *WA*, DB 10¹:98–105 = *LW* 35:253–57. *WA*, DB 10¹:588–90.

2. *WA*, DB 5:1–2. *WA* 23:435–42. *WA*, DB 10²:158–289, esp. 185–88.

3. *WA*, DB 6:lxiii–lxiv. *CR* 1:1073–74, 1082–84, 1092–93, 1112–13 = *MBW* 1, nos. 792, 807, 816, 844. *WA*, Br 5:215, lines 15–16; 242, lines 13–16. *WA*, DB 7:82–87, 406–20 = *LW* 35:380–83, 399–411.

4. *WA*, DB 6:414–17 = *LW* 35:363–65.

5. *WA*, Br 6:17, lines 29–33; 23, lines 16–18. *WA*, DB 3:il–lxii. *WA*, DB 4:507–77. *WA*, DB 10¹:590. *WA*, DB 3:xxx–xlii, 1–666. *WA*, DB 4:419–28. Unfortunately, the editing is unsatisfactory.

6. *WA* 31¹:481–514. Statements that also belong among the preliminary versions are *WA*, TR 2, nos. 1565, 1570, 1576–77, 1662, 1664–65, 1668–71 (Summer 1532). *WA* 38:1–74. *WA*, TR 1, no. 404. *CR* 2:500–1, 625–27 = *MBW* 2, nos. 1152, 1301. *WA*, Br 6:413–14.

7. *WA*, DB 4:xviii, xxiv–xxv. Otto Clemen, ed., *Georg Helts Briefwechsel*, ARG, supplementary vol. 2 (Leipzig: M. Heinsius Nachfolger, 1907), no. 110.

8. *WA*, Br 8:554, lines 19–21. *WA*, Br 9:418, lines 36–39. *WA*, DB 3:xv–xvi. *WA*, DB 4:xxvi–lix. *WA*, DB 3:167ff. *WA*, DB 4:1–418.

9. *WA*, DB 9:165–68.

10. *WA*, Br 9:358, line 25—359, line 27. Hans-Ulrich Delius, ed., *Der Briefwechsel des Friedrich Mykonius: Ein Beitrag zur allgemeinen Reformationsgeschichte und zur Biographie eines mitteldeutschen Reformators*, SKRG, vol. 18/19 (Tübingen: Osiandersche Buchhandlung, 1960), no. 258. *WA*, DB 11¹:394–405, 406–9 = *LW* 35:290–93.

11. Delius, *Der Briefwechsel des Friedrich Mykonius*, no. 258. *WA*, DB 11²:22–30, 50–125.

12. *WA*, DB 8:14–16 = *LW* 35:237–40. *WA*, DB 2:639. *WA*, Br 9:564, line 1—565, line 32. *WA*, Br 10:110, line 4—111, line 13.

13. Hans Volz, *Martin Luthers deutsche Bible: Entstehung und Geschichte der Lutherbibel* (Hamburg: Wittig, 1978), 156.

3. Arguing with the Critics

1. *WA*, Br 4:150, lines 19–32.

2. See Brecht, *Luther* 2, 60 = *Luther* 2, ET, 53. On the following, cf. Kenneth A. Strand, *Reformation Bibles in the Crossfire: The Story of Jerome Emser, His Anti-Lutheran Critique and His Catholic Bible Version* (Ann Arbor, Mich.: Ann Arbor Publishers, 1961). Gottfried Mälzer, "Hieronymus Emsers deutsche Ausgabe des Neuen Testaments," *BiW* 14 (1973):40–54.

3. *WA* 14:40, lines 6–10. *WA* 17¹:153, lines 14–23.

4. Hans Volz, *Martin Luthers deutsche Bibel: Entstehung und Geschichte der Lutherbibel* (Hamburg: Wittig, 1978), 198–99.

5. *WA*, Br 4:295, lines 39–46 = *LW* 49:183–84. *WA*, Br 4:596, lines 8–12.

6. *WA*, Br 5:183–89.

7. *WA* 30²:627–46 = *LW* 35:175–202, esp. *WA* 30²:632–43, line 13 = *LW* 35:175–98.

8. *WA*, TR 2, no. 2382. *WA*, TR 1, no. 312 = *LW* 54:42–43.

9. *WA*, TR 3, no. 3503. *WA*, TR 5, no. 5521. *WA*, TR 5, no. 5533 = *LW* 54:445–46. *WA*, TR 5, no. 5723.

10. *WA*, TR 5, no. 5324 = *LW* 54:408. *WA*, TR 5, nos. 5469, 5723. Cf. *WA*, TR 2, no. 2628b.

4. Praising and Recommending the Bible

1. *WA* 48:1–297, and the supplementary revision. Martin Brecht, "Zu Luthers Schriftverständnis," in Karl Kertelge, ed., *Die Autorität der Schrift im ökumenischen Gespräch*, ÖR.B, vol. 50 (Frankfurt am Main: Otto Lembeck, 1985), 9–29.

V. THE PROFESSOR

1. The University: Its Organization and Constitution

1. Walter Friedensburg, *Geschichte der Universität Wittenberg* (Halle: Max Niemeyer, 1917), 178–88. Idem, ed., *Urkundenbuch der Universität Wittenberg*, part 1, *1502–1611*, Geschichtsquellen der Provinz Sachsen und des Freistaates Anhalt, n.s., vol. 3 (Magdeburg: Selbstverlag der historischen Kommission für die Provinz Sachsen und für Anhalt, 1926), no. 169. Luther's entries in the dean's register, *WA*, Br 12: 440–44.

2. Friedensburg, ed., *Urkundenbuch*, nos. 183–84, 189–93. *WA*, Br 8:379, lines 42–44.

3. Friedensburg, ed., *Urkundenbuch*, no. 212. *WA*, TR 4, no. 4058.

4. *WA*, Br 8:545–46. *WA*, Br 10:509–15. *WA*, Br 9:338–39.

5. *WA*, Br 9:381, lines 20–27. *WA*, Br 10:242–45; 260–61; 300, line 32—301, line 47.

6. *WA*, Br 10:457–61.

7. Gustav Kawerau, ed., *Der Briefwechsel des Justus Jonas*, 2 vols. (Halle: O. Hendel, 1884–85; reprint ed., Hildesheim: G. Olms, 1964), vol. 2, no. 733. *WA*, Br 11:1–6, 7–9.

8. *WA*, TR 4, no. 4638 = *LW* 54:358–59. Cf. Heinrich Bornkamm, "Kopernikus im Urteil der Reformatoren," in idem, *Das Jahrhundert der Reformation: Gestalten und Kräfte*, 2d ed. (Göttingen: Vandenhoeck & Ruprecht, 1966), 177–85. Diedrich Wattenberg, "Martin Luther und die Astronomie," in Joachim Rogge and Gottfried Schille, eds., *Themen Luthers als Fragen an die Kirche heute: Beiträge zur gegenwärtigen Lutherforschung* (Berlin: Evangelische Verlagsanstalt, 1982), 149–69. Gunter Zimmermann, "De revolutione orbium coelestium," *ZKG* 96 (1985):320–43.

9. Cf., e.g., *WA*, TR 1, nos. 320, 349. *WA*, TR 1, no. 431 = *LW* 54:69. *WA*, TR 1, no. 1043 = *WA*, TR 3, no. 2809. *WA*, TR 1, no. 1217. *WA*, TR 2, no. 1261. *WA*, TR 2, no. 1364 = *LW* 54:144. *WA*, TR 2, no. 1419. *WA*, TR 2, nos. 1421–22 = *LW* 54:50–51. *WA*, TR 2, no. 1528. *WA*, TR 3, no. 2831. *WA*, TR 3, no. 3575 = *LW* 54:236. *WA*, TR 3, no. 3584. *WA* 48:691, no. 7120. Albert Stein, "Luther über Eherecht und Juristen," in Junghans, 171–85, esp. 181–85. Hans Liermann, "Der unjuristische Luther," *LuJ* 24 (1957):69–85 (an inadequate perspective in part). Wiebke Schaich-Klose, *D. Hieronymus Schürpf: Leben und Werk des Wittenberger Reformationsjuristen, 1481–1554* (Trogen, Switzerland: Fritz Meilli, 1967), 41–60.

10. *WA*, TR 3, no. 3496 = *LW* 54:214–15. *WA*, TR 5, no. 5663 = *LW* 54:472–74.

11. *WA*, Br 9:236–37. *WA*, TR 4, no. 4872.

12. *WA*, TR 3, no. 3609 = *LW* 54:243–44. *WA*, TR 4, nos. 4308, 4588, cf. 4920.

13. *WA* 47:670, line 16—671, line 4: 676, line 3—678, line 10. *WA*, TR 4, nos. 4382, 4743, 4745. Cf. the significant section in *On the Councils and the Church*, which was written only a little later (*WA* 50:634, line 34—641, line 19 = *LW* 41:156–64). *WA*, TR 4, no. 4393.

14. *WA*, Br 8:373–74. *WA* 43:292, line 19—300, line 9. Cf. Hermann Dörries, "Das beirrte Gewissen als Grenze des Rechts: Eine Juristenpredigt Luthers," in idem, *Wort und Stunde* (Göttingen: Vandenhoeck & Ruprecht, 1966–70), 3:281–326.

15. *WA*, Br 10:498–504. *WA* 49:297, line 14—307; 316–17; 318–24; 340, line 16—343, line 13.

16. *WA*, Br 10:499 = *MBW* 4, no. 3428. *WA*, Br 10:504–9. *CR* 5:292–94, 309–11, 324–25 = *MBW* 4, nos. 3436, 3450, 3472.

17. *WA*, Br 10:599, lines 1–8; 684–88; 693–96. *WA*, Br 11:22–25, 31–32. *WA* 49:682, line 24—684, line 20. *WA*, Br 11:139, lines 26–29.

18. *WA*, Br 6:361–64, 378–80, 462. *WA*, Br 7:161–62, 396–98, 564–65. *WA*, Br 8:113–14; 276–77; 358–59; 383, lines 1–7. *WA*, Br 10:544–45. *WA* 41:11, line 1—12, line 9.

19. *WA*, Br 7:42–43; 60; 89, lines 3–9; 194–95; 213–14; 221; 291; 392–93. *WA*, Br 9:106–9; 212, lines 12–18; 346, line 3—347, line 10. *WA*, Br 10:214–15, 248–49.

20. Friedensburg, ed., *Urkundenbuch*, nos. 205, 229, 248, 257. *WA*, Br 12:431–35. *WA*, Br 10:714, 720–21.

21. *WA*, Br 6:423–25. *WA*, Br 7:80–81, 593. *WA*, Br 8:487–88. *WA*, Br 9:48–50, 465. *WA*, Br 10:266, lines 37–45; 303–4; 586. *WA*, Br 11:218–19.

22. *WA*, Br 9:549–50. *WA*, Br 10:294–96, 324–25.

23. *WA*, Br 11:229–30.

24. *WA*, Br 9:78–79. *WA*, Br 10:540–41. *WA*, Br 8:337, lines 3–7. *WA*, Br 7:169, lines 11–25.

25. *WA*, TR 4, no. 4568 = *LW* 54:353–54.

26. *WA*, Br 10:698–700.

27. *WA* 41:471, line 20—472, line 14.

28. *WA* 47:665, line 14—666, line 15.

29. *WA*, TR 4, no. 4658.

30. *WA* 53:212, lines 19–33.

31. *WA* 54:12–15.

2. The Ordinations

1. Paul Drews, "Die Ordination, Prüfung und Lehrverpflichtung der Ordinanden in Wittenberg 1535," *DZKR* 15 (1905):66–90, 273–321, esp. 288–290. Hellmut Lieberg, *Amt und Ordination bei Luther und Melanchthon* (Göttingen: Vandenhoeck & Ruprecht, 1962). Walter Friedensburg, ed., *NDB*, part 1, vol. 1 (Gotha: F. A. Perthes, 1892; reprint ed., Frankfurt am Main: Minerva, 1968), 544. *WA*, TR 5, no. 6484.

2. Cf. Brecht, *Luther* 2, 277 = *Luther* 2, ET, 284. In my opinion, the question from Johann Sutel in Göttingen (*WA*, Br 6:44, lines 15–20), which has frequently been the subject of research, may have considered whether Sutel should undertake to distribute the sacrament, which, properly speaking, was the prerogative of the Catholic pastor of

the St. Nicholas church. For a contrary view, cf. Rolf Schäfer, "Allgemeines Priestertum oder Vollmacht durch Handauflegung," in Henning Schröer and Gerhard Müller, eds., *Vom Amt des Laien in Kirche und Theologie: Festschrift für Gerhard Krause zum 70. Geburtstag* (Berlin and New York: W. de Gruyter, 1982), 141–67.

3. Georg Buchwald, "Lutherana," *ARG* 25 (1928):81. *WA* 38:409 must be corrected accordingly. *WA* 41:240, line 33—242, line 10.

4. *CR* 3:901–2. *WA* 41:454–59; 762–63. *WA, Br* 7:302–3. Cf. Brecht, *Luther* 2, 73–78 = *Luther* 2, ET, 66–72.

5. *WA* 38:401–33 = *LW* 53:122–26. Cf. also the ordination address, *WA, TR* 4, no. 4655 = *LW* 54:359–60.

6. Georg Buchwald, ed., *Wittenberger Ordiniertenbuch 1537–1560* (Leipzig: G. Wigand, 1894).

7. *WA, Br* 8:511–12, 646–47.

8. *WA, Br* 12:447–85. *WA, TR* 4, no. 4655 = *LW* 54:359–60.

3. Graduations and Disputations

1. *WA, Br* 6:459–61, 471–72. Otto Vogt, ed., *Dr. Johannes Bugenhagens Briefwechsel*, reprint ed. (Hildesheim: G. Olms, 1966), nos. 50–52.

2. Carl Eduard Foerstemann, ed., *Liber Decanorum Facultatis Theologicae Academiae Vitebergensis* (Leipzig: Carl Tauchnitz, 1838), 28–31. *CR* 12:517–20. *WA* 48:701, no. 7168.

3. Hans Volz, "Luthers und Melanchthons Beteiligung an der Tübinger Universitätsreform im Jahre 1538," in Martin Brecht, ed., *Theologen und Theologie an der Universität Tübingen*, Contubernium, vol. 15 (Tübingen: Mohr, 1977), 65–95, esp. 75–78.

4. Cf. *CR* 4:1063–65 = *MBW* 3, no. 2422. *WA, Br* 10:268–69, 583–85. *WA, Br* 11:175. *WA, Br* 12:435–40. *WA, Br* 10:92–95, 270–71, 429–34. Foerstemann, ed., *Liber Decanorum*, 152.

5. Foerstemann, ed., *Liber Decanorum*, 31–34.

6. Walter Friedensburg, ed., *Urkundenbuch der Universität Wittenberg*, part 1, *1502–1611*, Geschichtsquellen der Provinz Sachsen und des Freistaates Anhalt, n.s., vol. 3 (Magdeburg: Selbstverlag der historischen Kommission für die Provinz Sachsen und für Anhalt, 1926), no. 170, p. 155; no. 193, p. 177; no. 212, pp. 203–4. Ernst Wolf, "Zur wissenschaftsgeschichtlichen Bedeutung der Disputationen an der Wittenberger Universität im 16. Jahrhundert," *Peregrinatio: Studien zur reformatorischen Theologie und zum Kirchenproblem*, vol. 2 (Munich: Chr. Kaiser, 1965), 38–51.

7. *WA* 39^1:1–8.

8. *WA* 39^2:xiv–xviii. This enumeration is corrected in part by Gerhard Ebeling, *Lutherstudien*, vol. 3 (Tübingen: Mohr, 1985), 260–61, n. 9.

9. Gerhard Ebeling, "Die Rechtfertigung vor Gott und den Menschen: Zum Aufbau der dritten Thesenreihe Luthers über Röm. 3,28," *Lutherstudien*, 3:223–57, esp. 223–26. Cf. also the *Dialecta, WA* 60:140–62.

10. *WA, Br* 7:222, line 22—223, line 29; 232, lines 7–24; 241, lines 13–16. *WA, Br* 7:244, lines 1–11; 249, lines 1–13 = *LW* 50:85–87, 93–97. *WA, Br* 7:275, lines 25–27.

11. *WA* 39^1:40–59. *WA* 59:702–5.

12. *WA, Br* 7:246, lines 26–36.

13. *WA* 39^1:59–61 = *LW* 34:128–31.

14. *WA*, Br 7:316, lines 12–14. *WA* 39¹:63–75. *WA* 59:705–7. *WA* 39¹:76–77. *WA* 59:708–11. *WA* 39¹:127–33, 265–333. Cf. *WA* 39²:407–14.

15. *WA* 39¹:174–80 = *LW* 54:133–44. Gerhard Ebeling, "Disputatio de Homine," *Lutherstudien*, vol. 2, parts 1–3 (Tübingen: Mohr, 1977–89). Idem, "Das Leben—Fragment und Vollendung," *Lutherstudien*, vol. 3 (Tübingen: Mohr, 1985), 310–36.

16. *WA* 39¹:78–126. Ebeling, "Die Rechtfertigung vor Gott und den Menschen." Idem, "Sündenblindheit und Sündenerkenntnis als Schlüssel zum Sündenverständnis: Zum Aufbau der vierten Thesenreihe Luthers über Rm 3,28," *Lutherstudien* 3:258–310.

17. *WA*, TR 4, nos. 4056, 4193. *WA* 39²:6, lines 5–7; 8.

18. *WA* 39²:266, lines 15–16.

19. *WA* 39²:1–53. On the following, cf. Reinhard Schwarz, "Gott ist Mensch," *ZThK* 63 (1966):289–351, esp. 334–38.

20. *WA* 39²:252–57.

21. *WA* 39²:284–336. The theses for Johann Faber, who graduated at the same time, are beyond the scope of our treatment.

22. *WA* 39²:337–401. *WA*, TR 5, no. 6438.

4. The Final Lectures

1. Cf. Brecht, *Luther* 2, 158 = *Luther* 2, ET, 157. *WA* 40²:471–610.

2. *WA* 40³:1–475; esp. 9—12, line 12, and 63, line 17. *WA*, TR 3, no. 2954.

3. *WA* 40³:202–309.

4. *WA* 40³:335–76.

5. *WA* 40³:469, line 9—470, line 3.

6. *WA* 40³:476–594 = *LW* 13:73–141.

7. *WA* 40³:594, lines 1–2 = *LW* 13:141. *WA* 42–44 = *LW* 1–8. *WA* 59:389–401. Peter Meinhold, *Die Genesisvorlesung Luthers und ihre Herausgeber*, FKGG, vol. 8 (Stuttgart: W. Kohlhammer, 1936).

8. *WA* 59:389–94.

9. *WA*, TR 3, no. 3888 = *LW* 54:288–89. *WA*, TR 4, no. 4845. Dietrich's preface to the first volume is in *WA* 44:xix. Georg Buchwald, ed., *Zur Wittenberger Stadt- und Universitäts-Geschichte in der Reformationszeit: Briefe aus Wittenberg an M. Stephan Roth in Zwickau* (Leipzig: G. Wigand, 1893), no. 206.

10. *WA* 42:1–2. Cf. *WA*, Br 10:443–44.

11. *WA* 42:176, lines 19–26 = *LW* 1:237.

12. Cf. Jaroslav Pelikan, "Die Kirche nach Luthers Genesisvorlesung," in Vilmos Vajta, ed., *Lutherforschung heute: Referate und Berichte des 1. Internationalen Lutherforschungskongresses, Aarhus, 18.–23. August 1956* (Berlin: Evangelisches Verlagshaus, 1958), 102–10.

13. *WA* 53:1–184.

14. *WA*, TR 3, no. 3476 = *LW* 54:207. *WA* 42:377, line 25—383, line 18 = *LW* 2:165–72.

15. *WA*, TR 4, nos. 4959, 4962, 5164. *WA*, Br 9:278, line 31—279, line 34.

16. *WA* 44:93–116, esp. 111, lines 32–34 = *LW* 6:125–55, esp. 149.

17. *WA* 44:233, line 25—234, line 9 = *LW* 6:313.

18. *CR* 5:522–24 = *MBW* 4, no. 3730.

19. *WA*, Br 11:20, lines 16–23.

20. *WA* 40³:595–682, esp. 597, line 20—599, line 13; cf. 652, lines 12–34.

21. *WA* 40³:683–746; esp. 686, line 25—687, line 12.

22. Cf. Brecht, *Luther* 1, 129–37, 277–82 = Brecht, *Luther* 1, ET, 128–37, 289–95 and Brecht, *Luther* 2, 433–39 = *Luther* 2, ET, 451–57.

5. The Collected Works

1. Cf. Brecht, *Luther* 1, 271 = Brecht, *Luther* 1, ET, 283. On the following, cf. Eike Wolgast, *Die Wittenberger Luther-Ausgabe: Zur Überlieferungsgeschichte der Werke Luthers im 16. Jahrhundert* (Nieuwkoop: De Graaf, 1971).

2. *WA* 60:3–15. *WA* 38:232–34 = *LW* 38:190–92.

3. Wolgast, *Die Wittenberger Luther-Ausgabe*, 11–13. Gustav Kawerau, ed., *Der Briefwechsel des Justus Jonas*, 2 vols. (Halle: O. Hendel, 1884–85; reprint ed., Hildesheim: G. Olms, 1964), vol. 1, no. 240.

4. Wolgast, *Die Wittenberger Luther-Ausgabe*, 13–14. Idem, "Der Plan einer Strassburger Lutherausgabe 1536/38," *Archiv für Geschichte des Buchwesens* 7 (1967): 1131–40. *WA*, Br 7:433, line 36—434, line 74. *WA*, Br 8:99, lines 5–9 = *LW* 50:172–73. *WA*, TR 3, no. 3797 = *LW* 54:274–75.

5. *WA* 45:422, line 16—423, line 18. Cf. *WA*, Br 8:354, line 8—355, line 14. *WA*, TR 4, no. 5170.

6. *WA*, TR 5, no. 6439. Cf. *WA*, TR 4, no. 4025 = *LW* 54:311. *WA*, TR 4, no. 4029. Wolgast, *Die Wittenberger Luther-Ausgabe*, 14–15. Cf. also *WA*, TR 3, no. 3572. *WA*, TR 4, no. 4452. *WA*, TR 4, no. 4462 = *LW* 54:342–43. *WA* 43:93, line 40—94, line 7 = *LW* 3:305–6. Bernhard Klaus, "Georg Rörer, ein bayerischer Mitarbeiter D. Martin Luthers," *ZbKG* 26 (1957):103–45.

7. Wolgast, *Die Wittenberger Luther-Ausgabe*, 93–95.

8. *WA* 50:654–61 = *LW* 34:279–88.

9. Wolgast, *Die Wittenberger Luther-Ausgabe*, 134–37.

10. Wolgast, *Die Wittenberger Luther-Ausgabe*, 102–3.

11. *WA* 54:176–87 = *LW* 34:323–38.

12. *WA* 39¹:6–8. Cf. above, p. 128. Cf. the frequent mention of earlier writings in the lectures on Isaiah 9, *WA* 40³:666, line 34—673, line 18.

13. Cf. Brecht, *Luther* 1, 219–20 = Brecht, *Luther* 1, ET, 225–27.

14. *CR* 5:691–96 = *MBW* 4, no. 3829.

15. *WA* 50:381–85 = *LW* 34:269–78.

16. *WA*, TR 4, no. 4085. *WA*, TR 5, no. 5335. *WA*, Br 7:163, line 17—164, line 28. *WA* 51:634–726.

VI. THEOLOGICAL CONTROVERSIES IN WITTENBERG

1. On the Significance of Repentance in Justification—
The "Cordatus Controversy"

1. *CR* 3:159. The significant documents are listed in *WA*, Br 7:541–45. Köstlin-Kawerau, 2:445, 676. On the following, cf. Wilhelm H. Neuser, *Luther und Melanchthon: Einheit im Gegensatz*, TEH, vol. 91 (Munich: Chr. Kaiser, 1961). Martin Greschat, *Melanchthon neben Luther: Studien zur Gestalt der Rechtfertigungslehre zwischen 1528 und 1537* (Witten: Luther-Verlag, 1965), 209–51. In the following presentation the emphasis is placed somewhat differently.

2. *CR* 3:159–61.

3. *CR* 3:161, note. *WA*, Br 7:541–42. Cf. above, pp. 80–83.

4. *WA*, Br 7:540, lines 5–11; 542.

5. Cf. above, pp. 132–33. *WA* 39¹:93, line 17—96, line 23; 102–105, line 9 = *LW* 34:162–66, 171–74. *CR* 11:272–78.

6. Theodor Kolde, ed., *Analecta Lutherana: Briefe und Actenstücke zur Geschichte Luthers* (Gotha: F. A. Perthes, 1883), 264–66. Cf. *WA*, Br 7:568–70.

7. *WA*, Br 7:580, line 1—581, line 36. Cf. Melanchthon to Amsdorf, *CR* 3:181, 185–86 = *MBW* 2, nos. 1805, 1808.

8. *WA*, Br 7:600–2, 606–8. *CR* 3:202–4 = *MBW* 2, no. 1819. *CR* 3:206–8. *WA*, Br 12:189–95. Melanchthon to Camerarius, *CR* 3:193–94 = *MBW* 2, no. 1815.

9. *WA*, Br 7:544, top. *CR* 3:341–42 = *MBW* 2, no. 1887.

10. *CR* 3:347–55.

11. *CR* 3:353. *WA*, Br 8:79–85.

12. *WA* 39¹:198–257. *CR* 11:324–29.

13. *WA* 39¹:258–63.

14. *CR* 3:375, 383–84 = *MBW* 2, nos. 1906, 1914.

15. See above, pp. 150–51. *CR* 3:383–87. Cf. also *CR* 3:396–98. *CR* 3:407–8 = *MBW* 2, no. 1933.

16. See above, pp. 88–89. *CR* 3:593–95 = *MBW* 2, nos. 2101–2.

17. *WA*, TR 4, no. 4577. *CR* 3:825–30 = *MBW* 2, no. 2302.

2. The Repudiation of Jacob Schenk

1. See above, pp. 37–38, 72. *WA*, TR 3, no. 3515. Paul Vetter, "Luthers Streit mit Herzog Heinrich von Sachsen," *Neues Archiv für Sächsische Geschichte und Altertumskunde* 29 (1908):82–94. On the following, cf. idem, "Luthers Stellung im Streite Jakob Schencks mit Melanchthon und Jonas 1537," ibid. 30 (1909):76–109. Idem, "Luther und Schencks Abberufung aus Freiberg im Jahre 1538," ibid. 32 (1911):23–53. Johann Karl Seidemann, *Dr. Jacob Schenk, der vermeintliche Antinomer, Freibergs Reformator: Zum ersten Male aus den unbekannten urkundlichen Quellen dargestellt* (Leipzig: J. C. Hinrichs, 1875).

2. Vetter, "Luthers Stellung," 105–8 = *MBW* 2, nos. 1904–5, 1932–35. Cf. Brecht, *Luther 2*, 260 = *Luther 2*, ET, 266. Cf above, p. 72. Vetter, "Luthers Stellung," 87–103.

3. *CR* 3:392 = *MBW* 2, no. 1922. *CR* 3:396–98. *CR* 3:404–5, 407–8, 410–11 = *MBW* 2, nos. 1930, 1933, 1941. It is noteworthy that many official letters dealing with Melanchthon and Jonas are known only through secondary references. Presumably the files were intentionally purged.

4. Vetter, "Luthers Stellung," 103–4.

5. *CR* 3:419–21, 428–30, 452–54 = *MBW* 2, nos. 1953, 1956, 1968. *CR* 11:335–43.

6. *WA*, Br 8:115–21. Cf. Paul Vetter, "Ein ungedruckter Brief des Justus Jonas 1537," *ARG* 7 (1909/10):121–34. Idem, "Luthers Stellung," 101–2.

7. *WA*, TR 3, no. 3683 = *LW* 54:255–56. *WA*, TR 3, nos. 3713, 3699, 3691. *WA*, Br 8:179–86; 189, lines 10–14. Heinrich Ernst Bindseil, ed., *Philippi Melanchthonis epistolae, iudicia, consilia, testimonia aliorumque ad eum epistolae, quae in Corpore reformatorum desiderantur* (Halle: Gustav Schwetschke, 1874), no. 509 = *MBW* 2, no. 1982.

MBW 2, no. 1984. Vetter, "Luther und Schencks Abberufung," 45–46. Georg Buchwald, ed., *Zur Wittenberger Stadt- und Universitäts-Geschichte in der Reformationszeit: Briefe aus Wittenberg an M. Stephan Roth in Zwickau* (Leipzig: G. Wigand, 1893), no. 150. Seidemann, *Jacob Schenk*, 157–60.

    8. *CR* 3:447–48 = *MBW* 2, no. 1962. Traugott Schiess, ed., *Briefwechsel der Brüder Ambrosius und Thomas Blaurer*, 3 vols. (Freiburg im Breisgau: F. E. Fehsenfeld, 1908–12), vol. 1, no. 789 = *MBW* 2, no. 1966. *CR* 3:452–54 = *MBW* 2, no. 1968. *WA*, Br 8:188, line 8—189, line 10. *WA*, TR 3, no. 3691.

    9. *WA*, Br 8:201–3. *WA*, TR 3, no. 3786. Vetter, "Luther und Schencks Abberufung," 23–28.

    10. *WA*, Br 8:244–51. *WA*, TR 3, no. 3895 = *LW* 54:289–90.

    11. *WA*, TR 4, nos. 4307, 4003, 4311, 4043. *WA*, TR 4, nos. 4048, 4050 = *LW* 54: 313–14, 314. *WA*, TR 4, nos. 4078, 4724, 4727.

    12. *WA*, Br 8:554, lines 11–16. *WA*, Br 9:4–6. *WA*, TR 4, nos. 4952, 5011, 5476, 5478. *WA*, Br 11:51, lines 49–50; 84, line 10—85, line 16.

3. John Agricola and the Antinomian Controversy

    1. Cf. Brecht, *Luther* 2, 259–60 = *Luther* 2, ET, 264–66. On the following, cf. Gustav Kawerau, *Johann Agricola von Eisleben: Ein Beitrag zur Reformationsgeschichte* (Berlin: W. Hertz, 1881; reprint ed., Hildesheim: G. Olms, 1977); Joachim Rogge, *Johann Agricolas Lutherverständnis: Unter besonderer Berücksichtigung des Antinomismus*, ThA, vol. 14 (Berlin: Evangelische Verlagsanstalt, 1960). Following the sources, my presentation occasionally diverges from Rogge. See also Steffen Kjeldgaard-Pedersen, *Gesetz, Evangelium und Busse: Theologiegeschichtliche Studien zum Verhältnis zwischen dem jungen Johann Agricola (Eisleben) und Martin Luther*, AThD, vol. 16 (Leiden: E. J. Brill, 1983). This work goes beyond the scope of Rogge's. See also Ernst Koch, "Johann Agricola neben Luther: Schülerschaft und theologische Eigenart," in Gerhard Hammer and Karl-Heinz zur Mühlen, eds., *Lutheriana: Zum 500. Geburtstag Martin Luthers von den Mitarbeitern der Weimarer Ausgabe*, AWA, vol. 5 (Cologne: Böhlau, 1984), 131–50; Rudolf Hermann, "Zum Streit um die Überwindung des Gesetzes: Erörterungen zu Luthers Antinomerthesen," in idem, *Studien zur Theologie Luthers und des Luthertums*, vol. 2 (Göttingen: Vandenhoeck & Ruprecht, 1981), 145–69; Martin Schloemann, *Natürliches und gepredigtes Gesetz bei Luther: Eine Studie zur Frage nach der Einheit der Gesetzesauffassung Luthers mit besonderer Berücksichtigung seiner Auseinandersetzung mit den Antinomern*, TBT, vol. 4 (Berlin: A. Topelmann, 1961). Despite several publications of sources, the manuscript material left by Agricola is in part inaccessible.

    2. *WA*, Br 7:586–87, 714. Carl Eduard Förstemann, ed., *Neues Urkundenbuch zur Geschichte der evangelischen Kirchen-Reformation* (Hamburg: F. A. Perthes, 1842; reprint ed., Hildesheim: G. Olms, 1966), 1:290–96.

    3. *WA*, TR 4, nos. 4043, 4960. *WA*, TR 3, no. 3354.

    4. *CR* 3:384–87. It is improbable that Luther's sermon on Luke 5:1–11 in Cruciger's house postil, which contains an extensive polemic against the antinomians (*WA* 22:74–92, esp. 86, line 33—89, line 3), was delivered on 1 July 1537, as Kjeldgaard-Pedersen, *Gesetz, Evangelium und Busse*, 256–62, has most recently claimed. It is not included in Rörer's list. On that day Luther preached in the afternoon on a different

text. In all of 1537 there otherwise was never a time when he preached twice on the same day. It is noteworthy that Cruciger said on 10 July that Luther's attitude toward Agricola was not yet entirely clear.

5. *WA*, Br 8:121–22. Whether this already had to do with the printing of the *Summaries* is not entirely clear.

6. Gustav Kawerau, "Briefe und Urkunden zur Geschichte des antinomistischen Streites," *ZKG* 4 (1881):299–324, 437–62, here 304–5. Rogge, *Johann Agricolas Lutherverständnis*, 143, does not consider the political aspect.

7. *WA* 45:145–56. *WA* 46:657, line 20—665, line 29 = *LW* 22:139–48.

8. *CR* 3:390–91, 419–21, 426–27 = *MBW* 2, nos. 1952, 1953, 1954.

9. Kawerau, "Briefe und Urkunden," 205–6. Förstemann, ed., *Neues Urkundenbuch*, 311–13.

10. Förstemann, ed., *Neues Urkundenbuch*, 296–311. *WA* 50:674–75. *CR* 3:454–55. E. Thiele, "Denkwürdigkeiten aus dem Leben des Johann Agricola von Eisleben," *ThStKr* 80 (1907):246–70, here 257.

11. *WA*, Br 8:279; cf. *WA*, Br 13:265. Presumably Melanchthon alluded to this correspondence on 25 November (*CR* 3:452–54 = *MBW* 2, no. 1968). *CR* 3:454–55.

12. *CR* 3:454–55. *CR* 3:459–60, 458–59 = *MBW* 2, nos. 1971, 1972. *WA*, Br 8:158–59. *WA*, TR 3, no. 3729 (p. 573, line 1). Thiele, "Denkwürdigkeiten," 258. Rogge, *Johann Agricolas Lutherverständnis*, 167, dates the reconciliation in the sacristy still in November, although it more likely took place in mid-December.

13. *WA* 39^1:342–45.

14. *WA* 39^1:345–47.

15. *WA*, TR 3, no. 3650ab (*WA*, TR 3, no. 3650a = *LW* 54:248). *WA* 39^1:360–417.

16. *WA*, TR 3, no. 3650cd.

17. *WA*, Br 8:342–43, the date corrected in accordance with *WA*, Br 13:267. *WA*, Br 8:186. Thiele, "Denkwürdigkeiten," 258–59. Rogge, *Johann Agricolas Lutherverständnis*, 174–75, misinterprets Luther's reaction to Agricola's letter.

18. *WA*, Br 8:188, lines 3–18. Theodor Kolde, ed., *Analecta Lutherana: Briefe und Actenstücke zur Geschichte Luthers* (Gotha: F. A. Perthes, 1883), 318. *WA* 39^1:347–54.

19. Thiele, "Denkwürdigkeiten," 259.

20. *WA* 19^1:418–85. The evaluation of the theses by Rogge, *Johann Agricolas Lutherverständnis*, 176–77, ignores the fact that Luther's theses were already written before the reconciliation.

21. *WA* 39^1:457, line 5—468, line 2.

22. Thiele, "Denkwürdigkeiten," 261–62. *WA*, TR 3, no. 3729.

23. Thiele, "Denkwürdigkeiten," 262–63. *WA*, TR 3, no. 3855.

24. Thiele, "Denkwürdigkeiten," 263. *WA*, TR 4, nos. 3966, 3973.

25. *WA* 40^1:3; 36, line 28—37, line 20.

26. *WA*, TR 4, no. 4307. *WA* 50:469, lines 26–29. Rogge, *Johann Agricolas Lutherverständnis*, 186–88, has not correctly understood the chronology or the context. The following section deals with the revocation written for Mansfeld.

27. *WA* 39^1:354–57.

28. *WA* 39^1:354–57. In this disputation, however, it is noteworthy that the occasion of graduating a licentiate was not mentioned in the opening address. Not Gericke, but Luther appears as the respondent. It is also unusual that such a disputation was continued into the afternoon. All of this would be better suited to a circular disputation. It is

also interesting that the theses were not sent out by Luther and Melanchthon until 15 September (cf. the following note), for otherwise this generally took place before a disputation.

29. Thiele, "Denkwürdigkeiten," 263. Cf. *WA, TR* 4, no. 4002 = *LW* 54:308. *WA* 49:111, lines 26–35. *WA,* Br 8:292, lines 18–26 = *LW* 50:182–83. *CR* 3:587–88 = *MBW* 2, no. 2093. Cf. *WA* 43:34, lines 10–17; 46, line 15—49, line 14 = *LW* 3:222, 239–43.

30. Förstemann, ed., *Neues Urkundenbuch,* 325–27 = *MBW* 3, no. 2409. *WA, TR* 4, no. 4030. Thiele, "Denkwürdigkeiten," 263. Rogge, *Johann Agricolas Lutherverständnis,* 194, does not accurately state the context.

31. *WA, TR* 4, no. 4050 = *LW* 54:314. *WA, TR* 4, no. 4156. Thiele, "Denkwürdigkeiten," 263–65. Förstemann, ed., *Neues Urkundenbuch,* 314–15. Kawerau, "Briefe und Urkunden," 312 = *MBW* 2, no. 2131.

32. *WA* 50:461–77 = *LW* 47:99–119.

33. Förstemann, ed., *Neues Urkundenbuch,* 320–26. *WA* 51:425 characterizes the work as "spiteful."

34. *WA,* Br 12:276–79. *WA, TR* 6, no. 6880. *WA,* Br 8:362, lines 21–25. Thiele, "Denkwürdigkeiten," 265–66.

35. *WA,* Br 8:374–76; 379, lines 9–15. *WA, TR* 4, nos. 4724, 4756, 4790.

36. *WA* 43:76, lines 20–34; 100, lines 29–32 = *LW* 3:281–82, 314. *WA* 43:170, line 19—171, line 31 = *LW* 4:49–50. *WA* 47:692, lines 11–13; 741, lines 27–28. *WA, TR* 4, nos. 4395, 4511. Cf. also *WA* 50:627, lines 14–33 = *LW* 41:147.

37. *WA, TR* 4, nos. 4521, 4587, 4692. Cf. *WA, TR* 5, no. 5195. *WA* 47:851, lines 9–11. Thiele, "Denkwürdigkeiten," 265–66.

38. Kawerau, "Briefe und Urkunden," 316. Förstemann, ed., *Neues Urkundenbuch,* 315–20. Thiele, "Denkwürdigkeiten," 267–68.

39. Förstemann, ed., *Neues Urkundenbuch,* 320–21, 325–27.

40. *WA,* Br 9:86–88, 92–93.

41. Förstemann, ed., *Neues Urkundenbuch,* 328–34.

42. *WA* 51:425–44.

43. Förstemann, ed., *Neues Urkundenbuch,* 334–36 = *MBW* 3, no. 2446. Cf. *WA, TR* 4, no. 5021.

44. *WA,* Br 9:230, lines 6–10. *WA, TR* 5, no. 5273. Walter Delius, "Johann Agricolas Berufung als Hofprediger des Kurfürsten Joachim II. nach Berlin (1540)," *ThViat* 7 (1959/60):107–19.

45. *WA* 39^1:358. *WA* 39^2:122–44.

46. Kawerau, "Briefe und Urkunden," 437–38. Kawerau, "Briefe und Urkunden," 439–40, 440–41 = *MBW* 3, nos. 2491, 2501. Förstemann, ed., *Neues Urkundenbuch,* 345–46 = *MBW* 3, no. 2502.

47. Kawerau, "Briefe und Urkunden," 442 = *MBW* 3, no. 2514. Förstemann, ed., *Neues Urkundenbuch,* 346–47 = *MBW* 3, no. 2515. *WA, TR* 5, no. 5311.

48. Kawerau, "Briefe und Urkunden," 442–45, 445–48 = *MBW* 3, nos. 2520–21. Förstemann, ed., *Neues Urkundenbuch,* 347–48, 351–54.

49. *CR* 3:789 = *MBW* 3, no. 2523. Kawerau, "Briefe und Urkunden," 448, 449 = *MBW* 3, nos. 2524, 2525. Otto Vogt, ed., *Dr. Johannes Bugenhagens Briefwechsel,* reprint ed. (Hildesheim: G. Olms, 1966), nos. 87–88. *WA, TR* 5, no. 5338.

50. Vogt, *Bugenhagens Briefwechsel,* nos. 90, 92. Förstemann, ed., *Neues Urkundenbuch,* 349–51. Kawerau, "Briefe und Urkunden," 453–54, 457–60.

51. *WA*, Br 9:285–87, 304–5. *WA* 43:427, lines 6–12 = *LW* 4:405. Rogge, *Johann Agricolas Lutherverständnis*, 219–32.

52. *WA*, Br 10:388, line 4—389, line 15. *WA* 40³:727, lines 6–20. *WA* 49:526, lines 1–2. *WA*, Br 11:81–83; 84, line 10—85, line 16; 86, lines 5–15; 95–100.

53. *WA* 51:443, lines 17–23. Rogge, *Johann Agricolas Lutherverständnis*, 233–35.

VII. LUTHER AND THE COUNCIL (1533–39)

1. Initial Catholic Probes and Evangelical Reactions

1. *WA*, Br 6:394, lines 11–14. On the following, cf. Eike Wolgast, "Das Konzil in den Erörterungen der kursächsischen Theologen und Politiker 1533–1537," *ARG* 73 (1982):122–52, esp. 122–31.

2. *WA*, TR 3, no. 2947. *WA*, Br 6:480–83. Gerhard Müller, *Die römische Kurie und die Reformation 1523–1534: Kirche und Politik während des Pontifikates Clemens' VII*, QFRG, vol. 38 (Gütersloh: G. Mohn, 1969), 223–78.

3. *WA*, Br 6:483–89 = *MBW* 2, no. 1333. *CR* 2:654–56 = *MBW* 2, no. 1334.

4. *St. L.* 16:1879–87 = *MBW* 2, no. 1341. *WA*, Br 6:489–91. *CR* 2:667–70 = *MBW* 2, no. 1354.

5. *WA* 38:280–89.

6. Hubert Jedin, *Geschichte des Konzils von Trient*, vol. 1, *Der Kampf um das Konzil* (Freiburg: Herder, 1949), 232–42. Walter Friedensburg, ed., *Nuntiaturbericht aus Deutschland nebst ergänzenden Aktenstücken*, Part 1, *Nuntiaturen des Vergerio 1533–1536* (Gotha: F. A. Perthes, 1892; reprint ed., Frankfurt: Minerva, 1968), 1:12–34. Anne Jacobsen Schutte, *Pier Paolo Vergerio: The Making of an Italian Reformer*, THR, vol. 160 (Geneva: Librairie Droz, 1977), esp. 93–96.

7. *WA*, Br 7:237–38; 316, lines 8–10 = *LW* 50:81–85, 108.

8. *WA*, Br 7:317–18; 322, lines 5–11. *WA*, TR 5, no. 6384. Friedensburg, ed., *Nuntiaturen des Vergerio*, 539–47. Cf. Köstlin–Kawerau, 371–76. *CR* 2:982–89.

9. *CR* 2:1018–22 = *MBW* 2, no. 1677.

10. *WA* 38:326–35. The introduction dates the publication at the beginning of 1535, but the printing in Zwickau must have been earlier. Otherwise, the legate motif could have referred to the context of Vergerio's visit.

11. Cf. Brecht, *Luther* 2, 102 = *Luther* 2, ET, 102. *WA*, Br 12:186–88.

12. *WA* 35:462–63 = *LW* 53:292–94. Markus Jenny, ed., *Luthers geistliche Lieder und Kirchengesänge*, AWA, vol. 4 (Cologne and Vienna: Böhlau, 1985), 111–13, 292–94. Cf. the preface to *Querela de fide*, *WA* 38:379, lines 2–6. Hans Ulrich Hofmann, *Luther und die Johannes-Apokalypse: Dargestellt im Rahmen der Auslegungsgeschichte des letzten Buches der Bibel und im Zusammenhang der theologischen Entwicklung des Reformators*, BGBE, vol. 24 (Tübingen: Mohr, 1982), 594–603.

13. *WA* 39¹:181–97.

2. Summoning the Council to Mantua, Luther's Articles, and the Smalcald Assembly in 1537

1. Hans Volz and Heinrich Ulbrich, eds., *Urkunden und Aktenstücke zur Geschichte von Martin Luthers Schmalkaldischen Artikeln (1536–1574)*, KIT, vol. 179 (Berlin: W. de Gruyter, 1957), 15–17. On the following, cf. Ernst Bizer, "Zum geschichtlichen Verständnis von Luthers Schmalkaldischen Artikeln," *ZKG* 67 (1955/56):61–91. Hans Volz,

"Luthers Schmalkaldische Artikel," *ZKG* 68 (1957):259–86. Ernst Bizer, "Noch einmal: Die Schmalkaldischen Artikel," *ZKG* 68 (1957):287–94. Despite his claim, Bizer has hardly said the final word in this controversy.

2. Hans Virck, "Zu den Beratungen der Protestanten über die Konzilsbulle vom 4. Juni 1536," *ZKG* 13 (1892):487–512, esp. 507–8. C.A.H. Burkhardt, ed., *Dr. Martin Luthers Briefwechsel: Mit vielen unbekannten Briefen und unter vorzüglicher Berücksichtigung der De Wette'schen Ausgabe* (Leipzig: F.C.W. Vogel, 1866), 256–58 = *MBW* 2, no. 1765. *CR* 3:99–104. *CR* 3:119–25 = *MBW* 2, no. 1769. Eike Wolgast, "Das Konzil in den Erörterungen der kursächsischen Theologen und Politiker 1535–1537," *ARG* 73 (1982):122–52, esp. 131–51.

3. Volz and Ulbrich, eds., *Urkunden,* 18–22. Cf. Brecht, *Luther* 2, 311–13 = *Luther* 2, ET, 320–22.

4. *WA* 41:xxxvii–xxxviii, 663–67, 693–96. *WA,* Br 7:546, lines 16–17 = *LW* 50:150. *WA* 42:276, line 35—277, line 2; 290, line 39—291, line 4 = *LW* 2:21, 41.

5. *WA* 50:16–39, 121–25. *WA,* TR 3, nos. 3502, 3522 = *LW* 54:215–16, 220. *WA,* TR 3, no. 3542.

6. Volz and Ulbrich, eds., *Urkunden,* 22–26 = *CR* 3:139–44. *CR* 3:191–92, 193–94, 194–95 = *MBW* 2, nos. 1813, 1815, 1816.

7. Hans Volz, "Zur Entstehungsgeschichte von Luthers Schmalkaldischen Artikeln," *ZKG* 74 (1963):316–20. *CR* 3:126–31 = *MBW* 2, no. 1818.

8. *WA,* Br 7:612–14 = Volz and Ulbrich, eds., *Urkunden,* 26–29.

9. *WA,* TR 3, nos. 3502, 3504 = *LW* 54:215–16, 216.

10. Volz and Ulbrich, eds., *Urkunden,* 35–69.

11. *WA,* TR 3, nos. 3510–11 (*WA,* TR 3, no. 3510 = *LW* 54:218). *WA,* TR 5, no. 6079.

12. *WA,* Br 7:614–15, 615.

13. Volz and Ulbrich, eds., *Urkunden,* 69–75. *CR* 3:234–36 = *MBW* 2, no. 1831. *WA,* TR 3, no. 3518 = *LW* 54:219.

14. *WA,* Br 8:2–6. *WA,* TR 3, no. 3537 = *LW* 54:224.

15. Volz and Ulbrich, eds., *Urkunden,* 79–83. *WA,* Br 7:620–21.

16. Volz and Ulbrich, eds., *Urkunden,* 87–92.

17. Volz and Ulbrich, eds., *Urkunden,* 92–94 = *MBW* 2, nos. 1836, 1838–39.

18. *WA* 45:9, line 30—10, line 37. Georg Buchwald, "Lutherana," *ARG* 25 (1928):62.

19. *WA,* Br 8:22–24 = *LW* 50:153–57. *CR* 3:266 = *MBW* 2, no. 1843.

20. *WA,* Br 8:39. Volz and Ulbrich, eds., *Urkunden,* 110–11.

21. Volz and Ulbrich, eds., *Urkunden,* 103–7 = *MBW* 2, no. 1845. Cf. *WA,* Br 7:618. See above, p. 51. Here this presentation differs from Bizer, "Zum geschichtlichen Verständnis von Luthers Schmalkaldischen Artikeln."

22. *WA,* Br 8:35–39. Volz and Ulbrich, eds., *Urkunden,* 103–7. Luther's opinion must have come from before the league's refusal to attend the council, which happened at the very beginning of the assembly.

23. Volz and Ulbrich, eds., *Urkunden,* 147–67.

24. Volz and Ulbrich, eds., *Urkunden,* 167–71. *BSLK,* 469–98 = Theodore G. Tappert, ed., *The Book of Concord: The Confessions of the Evangelical Lutheran Church* (Philadelphia: Fortress Press, 1959), 319–35.

25. Volz and Ulbrich, eds., *Urkunden,* 171–73, 139–44, 120–26. *WA,* TR 4, no. 5047 = *LW* 54:382–84. See above, p. 55.

3. The Illness

1. *WA*, Br 8:40, lines 16–21; 42, lines 3–8; 45, lines 32–34. *CR* 3:267–69. Annemarie Halder, "Das Harnsteinleiden Martin Luthers" (diss., University of Munich, 1969), 40–58.

2. *WA* 34:25-47.

3. On the following, cf. *WA*, Br 8:46–48. Georg Buchwald, "Lutherana," *ARG* 25 (1928):12–16. This deals with the elector's considerable expenditures for Luther's health. *CR* 3:296–97 = *MBW* 2, no. 1861. Hans Volz and Heinrich Ulbrich, eds., *Urkunden und Aktenstücke zur Geschichte von Martin Luthers Schmalkaldischen Artikeln (1536–1574)*, KIT, vol. 179 (Berlin: W. de Gruyter, 1957), 117–18 = *MBW* 2, no. 1849. *WA*, Br 8:53, lines 25–31.

4. *CR* 3:270–71 = *MBW* 2, no. 1851.

5. The following presentation is dependent on *WA*, TR 3, no. 3543ab (*WA*, TR 3, no. 3543b = *LW* 54:225–28) and Otto Clemen, "Luther in Schmalkalden," *ARG* 31 (1934):252–63. *WA*, TR 3, no. 3733 = *LW* 54:266. *WA*, TR 5, no. 5368.

6. On 26 February, however, Blaurer had belatedly signed the Augsburg Confession, the Apology, and Melanchthon's Treatise, but not the Wittenberg Concord. Volz and Ulbrich, eds., *Urkunden*, 116.

7. *WA*, Br 8:48–52 (*WA*, Br 8:50–52 = *LW* 50:165–69). *WA*, TR 3, no. 3553 = *LW* 54:232. *WA*, TR 5, no. 5368. Theodor Kolde, ed., *Analecta Lutherana: Briefe und Aktenstücke zur Geschichte Luthers* (Gotha: F. A. Perthes, 1883), 299–300.

8. The following presentation is based on *WA*, Br 8:54–56. *WA*, TR 3, no. 3543b (p. 394, lines 8–31), 3544. *WA*, TR 4, no. 4991 = *LW* 54:373–75. *CR* 3:290–91, 327–28 = *MBW* 2, nos. 1856, 1869.

9. Clemen, "Luther in Schmalkalden," 262–63. *WA* 35:602. *CR* 3:325–27, 328–29 = *MBW* 2, nos. 1867–68, 1871–72. *WA*, Br 8:59 = *LW* 50:169–70.

10. *WA*, Br 8:68. Gustav Kawerau, ed., *Der Briefwechsel des Justus Jonas*, 2 vols. (Halle: O. Hendel, 1884–85; reprint ed., Hildesheim: G. Olms, 1964), 1:253. Volz and Ulbrich, eds., *Urkunden*, 176–77.

4. Critical Publications against the Pope

1. *WA* 50:45–47.

2. *WA* 50:48–64.

3. *WA* 50:65–89. The undated *Disputation on the Monarchy of the Pope* by the Italian Dominican, Giovanni Nanni (1481) probably also belongs in this same context. In it the supremacy of the pope was defended. Luther edited it (*WA* 50:96–105).

4. *WA* 50:90–95.

5. *WA* 50:111–16.

6. *WA* 50:126–30. It may also have been written at the beginning of 1537. Cf. above, p. 174.

7. *WA* 50:131–34.

8. *WA* 50:255–83 = *LW* 34:197–229. Georg Buchwald, *Zur Wittenberger Stadt- und Universitäts-Geschichte in der Reformationszeit: Briefe aus Wittenberg an M. Stephan Roth in Zwickau* (Leipzig: G. Wigand, 1893), 129–30 n. 5. *WA* 46:557, line 17—558, line 12 = *LW* 22:25–26.

9. *CR* 2:77–78 = *MBW* 2, no. 1985. *WA*, TR 3, no. 3732.

10. WA 50:284–308 = LW 34:231–67. WA, Br 8:200, lines 14–17 = LW 59:176. WA 50:206, lines 3–4. Elfriede Starke, "Luthers Beziehungen zu Kunst und Künstlern," in Junghans, 531–48, here 547 and Plate 29.

11. WA 54:346–49. WA, Br 8:200, line 23 = LW 50:176. WA, TR 3, no. 3749.

12. WA 50:338–43 (April 1538). The editor does not appear to have understood the significance of the marginal glosses referred to in the notes.

13. WA 50:352–63.

14. WA 50:160–254. The preface is WA 50:192–96 (WA 50:160–254 = Theodore G. Tappert, ed., *The Book of Concord: The Confessions of the Evangelical Lutheran Church* [Philadelphia: Fortress Press, 1959], 287–318). Hans Volz and Heinrich Ulbrich, eds., *Urkunden und Aktenstücke zur Geschichte von Martin Luthers Schmalkaldischen Artikeln (1536–1574)*, KIT, vol. 179 (Berlin: W. de Gruyter, 1957), 177–83.

15. Hans Volz, ed., *Drei Schriften gegen Luthers Schmalkaldische Artikel von Cochläus, Witzel und Hoffmeister*, CCath, vol. 18 (Münster: Aschendorff, 1932). Volz and Ulbrich, eds., *Urkunden*, 184–85. WA, TR 4, no. 4055.

16. WA, Br 10:438, lines 10–22. Volz and Ulbrich, eds., *Urkunden*, 188–229.

5. The Final Position: *On the Councils and the Churches*

1. WA, Br 8:292, lines 29–34 = LW 50:184. WA, TR 4, no. 4198; cf. no. 4319.

2. WA 38:216, lines 7–9 = LW 38:171. WA 38:279, lines 1–2; WA, Br 7:16, lines 12–14. Otto Clemen, ed., *Georg Helts Briefwechsel*, ARG, supplementary vol. 2 (Leipzig: M. Heinsius Nachfolger, 1907), nos. 110, 114. WA, Br 8:56, lines 29–34.

3. WA 50:488–653 = LW 41:3–178. On the following, cf. Jaroslav Pelikan, "Luthers Stellung zu den Kirchenkonzilien," in Kristen E. Skydsgaard, ed., *Konzil und Evangelium: Lutherische Stimmen zum kommenden römisch-katholischen Konzil* (Göttingen: Vandenhoeck & Ruprecht, 1962), 40–62 = "Luther's Attitude toward Church Councils," in *The Papal Council and the Gospel: Protestant Theologians Evaluate the Coming Vatican Council* (Minneapolis: Augsburg Publishing House, 1962), 37–60. See also Christa Tecklenburg Johns, *Luthers Konzilsidee in ihrer historischen Bedingtheit und ihrem reformatorischen Neuansatz* (Berlin: A. Topelmann, 1966).

4. WA 50:509—514, line 5 = LW 41:9–14.

5. WA 50:514, line 6—547, line 11 = LW 41:13–53. Cf. Luther to Melanchthon, 28 December 1538, WA, Br 8:343–45.

6. WA 50:547, line 12—624, line 3 = LW 41:53–142. WA 50:502–4, WA, TR 4, nos. 4732–34. Cf. Friedrich Wilhelm Kantzenbach, "Kontroverstheologische Methode und Denkform bei Luther," in Leo Stern and Max Steinmetz, eds., *Vierhundertfünfzig Jahre lutherische Reformation, 1517–1967: Festschrift für Franz Lau zum 60. Geburtstag* (Göttingen: Vandenhoeck & Ruprecht, 1967), 154–71.

7. WA, TR 4, no. 4360 = LW 54:332–33 (end of February 1539).

8. Cf. WA, TR 4, no. 4374.

9. Cf. WA, TR 4, no. 4500.

10. WA 50:624, line 4—653 = LW 41:143–78. On the following, cf. Friedrich Wilhelm Kantzenbach, "Strukturen in der Ekklesiologie des älteren Luther: Ein Beitrag zur reformatorischen Lehre von den 'notae ecclesiae,'" *LuJ* 35 (1968):48–77.

11. Cf. Brecht, *Luther* 1, 328–29 = Brecht, *Luther* 1, ET, 345–46.

12. WA 50:668–73.

13. *WA*, TR 4, no. 4601.

14. *WA*, Br 8:391, lines 23–27.

VIII. THE RIGHT OF RESISTANCE,
ATTEMPTS AT PEACE, THE DEFECTION OF
THE LANDGRAVE, AND
RELIGIOUS COLLOQUIES (1538–41)

1. New Discussions on the Right of Resistance

1. *WA*, TR 1, nos. 539, 1023. Cf. Brecht, *Luther* 2, 348–49, 396–400 = *Luther* 2, ET, 361–62, 411–15. See also Hermann Dörries, "Luther und das Widerstandsrecht," in idem, *Wort und Stunde*, 3 vols. (Göttingen: Vandenhoeck & Ruprecht, 1966–70), 3:195–270, esp. 236ff; Cargill Thompson, "Luther and the Right of Resistance to the Emperor," *SCH(L)* 12 (1975):159–282; Eike Wolgast, *Die Wittenberger Theologie und die Politik der evangelischen Stände: Studien zu Luthers Gutachten in politischen Fragen*, QFRG, vol. 47 (Gütersloh: G. Mohn, 1977), 224–30, 239–53; Karl Dietrich Erdmann, "Luther über Obrigkeit, Gehorsam und Widerstand," in Hartmut Löwe and Claus-Jürgen Roepke, eds., *Luther und die Folgen: Beiträge zur sozialgeschichtlichen Bedeutung der lutherischen Reformation* (Munich: Chr. Kaiser, 1983), 28–59.

2. *CR* 3:126–31 = *MBW* 2, no. 1818.

3. *WA*, TR 3, no. 3810 = *LW* 54:278–79.

4. *WA*, Br 8:215, lines 25–32; 227, lines 11–13.

5. *WA*, Br 8:232–36.

6. Georg Buchwald, *Zur Wittenberger Stadt– und Universitäts-Geschichte in der Reformationszeit: Briefe aus Wittenberg an M. Stephan Roth in Zwickau* (Leipzig: G. Wigand, 1893), nos. 165–66.

7. Heinz Scheible, ed., *Das Widerstandsrecht als Problem der deutschen Protestanten 1523–1546*, TKTG, vol. 10 (Gütersloh: G. Mohn, 1969), 92–94 = *MBW* 2, no. 2121. *CR* 3:609–10 = *MBW* 2, no. 2123. Gustav Kawerau, ed., *Der Briefwechsel des Justus Jonas*, 2 vols. (Halle: O. Hendel, 1884–85; reprint ed., Hildesheim: G. Olms, 1964), vol. 1, no. 399.

8. *WA*, Br 8:354, lines 4–6.

9. *WA*, Br 8:364–68.

10. *WA*, TR 4, nos. 4342, 4380. Cf. Wolfgang Günter, *Martin Luthers Vorstellung von der Reichsverfassung*, RGST, vol. 114 (Münster: Aschendorff, 1976), 130–42.

11. *WA* 50:478–84.

12. *WA* 47:684, line 17—685.

13. *WA* 39²:34–91. Rudolf Hermann, "Luthers Zirkulardisputation über Mt 19,21," *LuJ* 23 (1941):35–93.

14. *WA*, TR 4, no. 4582. The opinion of the Wittenberg theologians in July 1539 when Duke Henry of Saxony joined the Smalcald League (*WA*, Br 8:515–18) justified the alliance with the arguments that had been common since 1536.

2. The Peace Negotiations in Frankfurt, 1539

1. *WA*, TR 4, no. 4352 = *LW* 54:330–32. *WA*, TR 4, no. 4744. *WA*, Br 8:382, lines 13–15. Cf. Franz Lau and Ernst Bizer, *Reformationsgeschichte Deutschlands bis 1555*, KIG, vol. 3, fasc. K (Göttingen: Vandenhoeck & Ruprecht, 1964), 104–9.

2. WA, Br 8:383–86; cf. also the letters of Bucer and Myconius, WA, Br 8:386–90. WA, TR 4, no. 4392. WA, Br 8:391, lines 1–18. Cf. Brecht, *Luther* 2, 406–10 = *Luther* 2, ET, 421–26.

3. WA, Br 8:393, lines 4–15; 397, lines 3–10. WA, TR 4, nos. 4429–30, 4460, 4482.

4. WA, Br 8:410, lines 3–16. WA, TR 4, no. 4483.

5. CR 3:698–700 = *MBW* 2, no. 2191. WA, TR 4, nos. 4537, 4563, 4748. Bucer's report, WA, Br 8:413–17.

6. WA, TR 4, nos. 4572, 4595. WA, TR 4, no. 4596 = *LW* 54:356–57. Cf. Brecht, *Luther* 2, 372–73 = *Luther* 2, ET, 386–87.

7. WA, Br 8:566, line 8—567, line 35. WA, Br 8:569, lines 27–29 = *LW* 50:190. WA 47:558, lines 8–20.

3. The Calamitous Bigamy of Landgrave Philip

1. WA, Br 8:393, lines 20–24; 400, lines 16–26. CR 3:698–700. WA, TR 4, no. 4669. William Walker Rockwell, *Die Doppelehe des Landgrafen Philipp von Hessen* (Marburg: N. G. Elwert, 1904). Wilhelm Maurer, "Luther und die Doppelehe Landgraf Philipps von Hessen," *Lu* 24 (1953):97–120.

2. WA, Br 8:628–37.

3. WA, Br 8:636–44.

4. Rockwell, *Die Doppelehe*, 30.

5. Rockwell, *Die Doppelehe*, 40–43. Heinrich Ernst Bindseil, ed., *Philippi Melanchthonis epistolae, iudicia, consilia, testimonia aliorumque ad eum epistolae, quae in Corpore Reformatorum desiderantur* (Halle: Gustav Schwetschke, 1874), nos. 187, 191 = *MBW* 3, nos. 2385, 2387. CR 4:761–66 = *MBW* 3, no. 2404.

6. WA, Br 9:82–85, 90–92.

7. WA, Br 9:117–18.

8. WA, Br 9:123–24; 138, lines 11–14. Gustav Kawerau, ed., *Der Briefwechsel des Justus Jonas*, 2 vols. (Halle: O. Hendel, 1884–85; reprint ed., Hildesheim: G. Olms, 1964), vol. 1, nos. 500–3.

9. WA, TR 4, nos. 5038, 5046 = *LW* 54:379–82, 382. WA, TR 4, no. 5045.

10. WA, Br 9:126–29.

11. WA, Br 9:131–35. Because the letter includes many things that the elector already knew through Bucer, it appears to have been written for use against Henry. Cf. WA 24:144, lines 19–24; 303, line 29—305, line 30.

12. WA, TR 4, no. 5088b. WA, TR 4, no. 5096 = *LW* 54:387–90. WA, TR 4, no. 5063.

13. WA, Br 9:137, lines 7–11. ARG 26 (1929):17, no. 6 = *MBW* 3, no. 2450. Georg Buchwald, *Zur Wittenberger Stadt- und Universitäts-Geschichte in der Reformationszeit: Briefe aus Wittenberg an M. Stephan Roth in Zwickau* (Leipzig: G. Wigand, 1893), no. 184. WA, TR 4, no. 5062.

14. WA, TR 4, no. 5091, cf. no. 5054.

15. WA, Br 9:144–46. Cf. WA, TR 4, no. 5100.

16. WA 43:326, lines 21–26 = *LW* 4:266. WA, Br 9:140–42. WA, Br 14:266n.

17. Georg Buchwald, "Lutherana," ARG 25 (1928):21. Christian Gotthold Neudecker, ed., *Die handschriftliche Geschichte Ratzeberger's über Luther und seine Zeit* (Jena: F. Mauke, 1850), 102–5. WA, TR 5, no. 5407. WA, TR 5, no. 5565 = *LW* 54:453–54.

18. WA, Br 9:168, lines 3–10. 172, lines 22–26 = *LW* 50:208–9, 215. Cf. Melanch-

thon to Bugenhagen, 8 July, Otto Vogt, ed., *Dr. Johannes Bugenhagens Briefwechsel,* reprint ed. (Hildesheim: G. Olms, 1966), no. 84 = *MBW* 3, no. 2459.

19. *WA,* Br 9:146–57.

20. *WA,* Br 9:159–65.

21. *WA,* Br 9:176–80. This letter can hardly have been addressed to Feige, the Hessian chancellor, because the original is in the archives in Weimar. Eberhard von der Thann is likewise probably excluded as the addressee, for his papers concerning this matter later came to Marburg (cf. *WA,* Br 9:159). Possibly the letter is to be dated somewhat earlier.

22. Max Lenz, ed., *Briefwechsel Landgraf Philipp's des Grossmüthigen von Hessen mit Bucer,* vol. 1, Publicationen aus den K. Preussischen Staatsarchiven, vol. 5 (Leipzig: S. Hirzel, 1880), 372–77. Theodor Kolde, ed., *Analecta Lutherana: Briefe und Aktenstücke zur Geschichte Luthers* (Gotha: F. A. Perthes, 1883), 182–91.

23. *WA,* Br 9:182–91.

24. *WA,* Br 9:191–204.

25. *WA,* Br 9:206–10.

26. *WA,* Br 9:225–28, 233–35, 237–41, 248.

27. Rockwell, *Die Doppelehe,* 121–27. *WA,* Br 9:370, lines 16–22; 565, lines 35–39.

28. *WA,* Br 9:588–91. Rockwell, *Die Doppelehe,* 122.

29. *CR* 4:754–55 = *MBW* 3, no. 3878. *WA,* Br 9:607, lines 62–78.

30. *WA* 53:185–201.

31. Max Lenz, ed., *Briefwechsel Landgraf Philipp's des Grossmüthigen von Hessen mit Bucer,* vol. 2, Publicationen aus den K. Preussischen Staatsarchiven, vol. 28 (Leipzig: S. Hirzel, 1887), 75–76 n. 2 = *MBW* 3, no. 2923. *CR* 4:797–99 = *MBW* 3, no. 2931. *WA,* Br 10:44, lines 16–31; 46, lines 18–27; 60, prefatory note.

32. Nikolaus Müller, "Zur Bigamie des Landgrafen Philipp von Hessen," *ARG* 1 (1903/4):365–71 = *MBW* 3, no. 3185. Max Lenz, "Nachlese zum Briefwechsel des Landgrafen Philipp mit Luther und Melanchthon," *ZKG* 4 (1881):148–49 = *MBW* 3, no. 3201.

4. The Religious Colloquies and Their Expected Failure

1. *WA,* Br 8:647–50. On the following, cf. Marion Hollerbach, *Das Religionsgespräch als Mittel der konfessionellen und politischen Auseinandersetzung im Deutschland des 16. Jahrhunderts,* European University Studies, Series 3, History and Allied Studies, vol. 165 (Frankfurt am Main and Bern: Lang, 1982), 123–29.

2. *WA,* Br 9:17–35.

3. *WA,* Br 9:38–40, 50–59, 64–67.

4. *WA,* Br 9:40–41; 60–62; 77, lines 14–34; 89, lines 3–25.

5. *WA,* TR 4, nos. 5040, 5042, 5058. *WA,* Br 9:129–30; 131, lines 1–7. *CR* 3:1052–54. On the following, cf. Hollerbach, *Das Religionsgespräch,* 129–39.

6. Cf. Brecht, *Luther* 2, 387–90 = *Luther* 2, ET, 402–5. *WA,* Br 9:180–82. *WA,* Br 9:205, lines 7–8 = *LW* 50:221–22.

7. *WA,* Br 9:242, lines 22–27; 246–48. On the following, cf. Hollerbach, *Das Religionsgespräch,* 139–54.

8. *WA,* Br 9:254–66.

9. *WA,* Br 9:271–73 (21 November).

10. *WA,* Br 9:269–70; 278, lines 1–19; cf. 280, lines 9–20.

11. *WA*, Br 9:275–77, 281–85, 287–90.

12. *WA*, Br 9:291–99; 303, lines 23–34.

13. *WA*, Br 9:307–9. *CR* 4:33–81. Cf. Robert Stupperich, *Der Humanismus und die Wiedervereinigung der Konfessionen*, SVRG, vol. 160 (Leipzig: M. Heinsius, 1936), 75–94.

14. *WA*, Br 9:322–27. Max Lenz, ed., *Briefwechsel Landgraf Philipp's des Grossmüthigen von Hessen mit Bucer*, vol. 1, Publicationen aus den K. Preussischen Staatsarchiven, vol. 5 (Leipzig: S. Hirzel, 1880), 312–14, 529–38. *ARCEG* 6:21–88.

15. *WA*, Br 9:329–30, 332–34.

16. Friederich Hortleder, *Der Römischen Kaiserlichen und Königlichen Majestäten, auch des Hl. Römischen Reichs . . . Handlungen und Ausschreiben von Rechtmässigkeit, Anfang, Fort- und endlichen Ausgang des Teutschen Kriegs Kaiser Karl V. wider die Schmalkaldischen Bunds Obersten Chur. und Fürsten Sachsen und Hessen . . .* (Gotha, 1645), 1098–1143, 1335–68.

17. *WA* 51:461–572 = *LW* 41:179–256. *WA*, Br 9:330 top, lines 5–10. Hortleder, *Der Römischen . . . Majestäten*, 1457–79.

18. *WA* 51:469–76, line 25 = *LW* 41:185–93.

19. *WA* 51:476, line 26—531 = *LW* 41:193–224. Cf. above, pp. 196–97.

20. *WA* 51:532–65, line 19 = *LW* 41:224–52.

21. *WA* 51:565, line 20—572 = *LW* 41:252–62. Related to *Against Hanswurst* is Luther's preface to Urbanus Rhegius's exposition of Psalm 52, which was likewise written against Henry of Brunswick (*WA* 51:573–76).

22. *WA*, Br 9:360, lines 11–14. Theodor Kolde, ed., *Analecta Lutherana: Briefe und Aktenstücke zur Geschichte Luthers* (Gotha: F. A. Perthes, 1883), 377–78. *WA* 51:463–64.

23. *WA*, Br 9:366, lines 19–23.

24. *WA*, Br 9:335–38; 345, lines 27–33; cf. also 366, lines 1–13. On the following, cf. Hollerbach, *Das Religionsgespräch*, 154–61.

25. *WA*, Br 9:355–57; 358, lines 1–19. Cf. *CR* 4:138–40 = *MBW* 3, no. 2646.

26. *WA*, Br 9:364–65; 368; 370, lines 1–14.

27. *WA*, Br 9:377–79; 383–84; 390, lines 1–20; 394, lines 1–7.

28. *WA*, Br 9:384–85.

29. Cf. *ARCEG* 6:52–54. Walter von Loewenich, *Duplex Iustitia: Luthers Stellung zu einer Unionsformel des 16. Jahrhunderts*, VIEG, vol. 68 (Wiesbaden: F. Steiner, 1972), 23–55. Karl-Heinz zur Mühlen, "Die Einigung über den Rechtfertigungsartikel auf dem Regensburger Religionsgespräch von 1541—eine verpasste Chance?" *ZThK* 76 (1979):331–59.

30. *WA*, Br 9:296–406.

31. *WA*, Br 9:406–11.

32. *WA*, Br 9:413–15. Cf. *CR* 4:318–21. *WA*, TR 4, no. 4796.

33. *WA*, Br 9:419–20; cf. 443–45.

34. *WA*, Br 9:424–26. Cf. *CR* 4:293–96. *WA*, Br 9:433–36. Cf. Brecht, *Luther* 1, 442–47 = Brecht, *Luther* 1, ET, 464–70.

35. *WA*, Br 12:309–13. *WA*, Br 9:436–43.

36. *WA*, Br 9:445–49, 451–53.

37. *WA*, Br 9:456–63. *CR* 4:479–505 = *MBW* 3, no. 2751. *WA*, Br 9:486–87.

38. *WA*, Br 9:474, line 20—475, line 38; 496, lines 8–10.

39. *WA*, DB 11²:lxxxvi–xciv; 50–124, line 20.

40. *WA* 39²:145–84.

41. *WA* 39²:185–203 = *LW* 34:299–321. Cf. the theses *Against Satan and His Synagogue*, which probably belong in the same context (*WA* 59:719–23).

42. *WA* 53:406–11.

IX. PERSONAL AFFAIRS (1537–46)

1. Ill, Old, and Tired of Living

1. See above, pp. 185–88. *WA*, TR 3, no. 3580 = *LW* 54:237. On the following, cf. Annemarie Halder, "Das Harnsteinleiden Martin Luthers" (diss., University of Munich, 1969). Helmar Junghans, "Luther in Wittenberg," in Junghans, 25–26, 33–34.

2. Georg Buchwald, *Zur Wittenberger Stadt- und Universitäts-Geschichte in der Reformationszeit: Briefe aus Wittenberg an M. Stephan Roth in Zwickau* (Leipzig: G. Wigand, 1893), 130n. *WA* 47:133–34 = *LW* 22:415–16. *WA* 47:362. *WA*, TR 3, no. 3655a.

3. *WA*, TR 3, nos. 3684, 3693, 3757. *WA*, TR 3, no. 3801 = *LW* 54:277. *WA*, TR 3, no. 3823. *WA*, TR 4, nos. 4326, 4784. *WA*, TR 5, no. 5378.

4. *WA*, TR 4, no. 3909. *CR* 4:1050–51 = *MBW* 2, no. 2060. *WA*, TR 4, no. 3916 = *LW* 54:294. *MBW* 2, no. 2070. *WA*, TR 4, nos. 4203–4, 3929, 4777, 3933, 3937, 3943, 3945. *WA*, TR 4, no. 3951 = *LW* 54:297–98. *WA*, TR 4, no. 3952. *WA*, TR 5, no. 6303.

5. *WA*, Br 8:292, lines 18–20 = *LW* 50:182–83. Cf. *WA*, Br 8:371, line 18—372, line 22. *WA*, TR 4, no. 4067. *WA*, Br 8:304, lines 6–10; 337, lines 3–4; 344, lines 3–4; 357, lines 12–13. *WA*, TR 4, no. 4736. Cf. *WA*, Br 9:222, lines 8–9.

6. *WA*, Br 8:379, lines 39–40. *WA* 47:716. *WA*, TR 4, no. 4454. *WA*, TR 4, no. 4479 = *LW* 54:346. Cf. *WA*, TR 4, no. 4508.

7. *WA*, TR 4, no. 4696. *MBW* 3, no. 2475. *WA*, Br 8:560, line 1—561, line 13.

8. *WA*, Br 9:230, lines 1–6. *WA*, TR 5, no. 5284 = *LW* 54:405–6.

9. *WA*, Br 9:319, lines 5–11. Gustav Kawerau, ed., *Der Briefwechsel des Justus Jonas*, 2 vols. (Halle: O. Hendel, 1884–85; reprint ed., Hildesheim: G. Olms, 1964), vol. 1, no. 543. Hans–Ulrich Delius, ed., *Der Briefwechsel des Friedrich Mykonius: Ein Beitrag zur allgemeinen Reformationsgeschichte und zur Biographie eines mitteldeutschen Reformators*, SKRG, vol. 18/19 (Tübingen: Osiandersche Buchhandlung, 1960), no. 258. *WA*, Br 9:344, lines 1–5; 366, lines 20–22; 367, line 43. *CR* 4:172–74 = *MBW* 3, no. 2669. *WA*, Br 9:376, lines 28–30. Walter Friedensburg, ed., *Urkundenbuch der Universität Wittenberg*, part 1, *1502–1611*, Geschichtsquellen der Provinz Sachsen und des Freistaates Anhalt, n.s., vol. 3 (Magdeburg: Selbstverlag der historischen Kommission für die Provinz Sachsen und für Anhalt, 1926), no. 230. *WA*, Br 9:380–81; 390, lines 20–25; 417, lines 3–6; 466, lines 3–10; 495, line 4—496, line 7.

10. *WA*, Br 10:23, lines 3–23; 55, lines 7–9.

11. *WA*, Br 10:251 bottom, lines 3–4; 259, lines 2–5; 277, lines 1–3; 309, lines 12–28. *WA*, Br 10:335, lines 4–10 = *LW* 50:242. *WA*, Br 10:344, line 3—345, line 9; 368, lines 3–4; 370, lines 20–21; 388, lines 3–4.

12. *WA*, Br 10:373–74; 396; 442, lines 10–19; 522, lines 20–22.

13. Otto Vogt, ed., *Dr. Johannes Bugenhagens Briefwechsel*, reprint ed. (Hildesheim: G. Olms, 1966), no. 132. *WA* 49:352–53, 37. Kawerau, ed., *Der Briefwechsel des Justus Jonas*, vol. 2, no. 742. *WA*, Br 10:545–49; cf. 581–82.

14. *WA*, Br 10:562, lines 11–24; 575–76.

15. *WA*, Br 10:614, lines 13–21.

16. *WA*, Br 10:642, lines 4–10.

17. WA 54:188–94 = *LW* 34:362–66.

18. WA 59:331.

19. *WA*, Br 11:120–21. *CR* 1:801 = *MBW* 4, no. 3923. *WA*, Br 11:132, lines 27–29 = *LW* 50:267. *WA*, Br 11:168, lines 3–5.

20. *WA*, Br 11:199, lines 4–6; 263, line 3—264, line 8.

2. Marriage, Children, Family, and Guests

1. WA, TR 3, no. 3528 = *LW* 54:222–23.

2. WA, TR 3, no. 3835. On the following, cf. Helmar Junghans, "Luther in Wittenberg," in Junghans, 30–33.

3. WA 42:586, line 7—587, line 9 = *LW* 3:53–54.

4. Gustav Kawerau, ed., *Der Briefwechsel des Justus Jonas*, 2 vols. (Halle: O. Hendel, 1884–85; reprint ed., Hildesheim: G. Olms, 1964), vol. 1, no. 481. WA, TR 4, no. 4885 = *LW* 54:369. WA, TR 5, no. 5407. *WA*, Br 9:68, lines 12–14; 77, line 35—78, line 38.

5. WA, TR 4, no. 4910. WA, TR 5, no. 5202.

6. *WA*, Br 9:518–19 = *LW* 50:223–25.

7. *WA*, Br 9:168, line 37; 174, line 2; 175, line 19; 205, line 24 = *LW* 50:212, 218, 220, 223. *WA*, Br 11:276, line 27; 287, line 50 = *LW* 50:292, 304.

8. WA 43:449, line 8—455, line 12 = *LW* 5:29–38.

9. WA 43:627, line 18—632, line 3; 645, line 27—646, line 36; 650, line 38—655, line 21 = *LW* 5:288–94, 314–16, 322–28.

10. WA 33:410, lines 14–38 = *LW* 23:258.

11. WA, TR 4, no. 4569. *WA*, Br 9:168, lines 19–26 = *LW* 50:210–11.

12. WA, TR 4, no. 3964 = *LW* 54:300. WA, TR 4, no. 4027. WA, TR 4, nos. 4364, 4367 = *LW* 54:334, 335.

13. *WA*, Br 8:383, lines 3–4. WA, TR 4, no. 4353. Cf. WA, TR 5, no. 5500. *WA*, Br 9:168, lines 19–20; 506–7. WA, TR 4, no. 5082b. Cf. WA 60:140–62. Ernst Kroker, *Katharina von Bora, Martin Luthers Frau: Ein Lebens- und Charakterbild*, 2d ed. (Zwickau; J. Hermann, 1925), 140–56.

14. *WA*, Br 10:132–35, 136–37, 228–29 = *LW* 50:230–33, 233–34, 239–40. *WA*, Br 8:18–20 = *LW* 50:151–53 (date corrected in accordance with *WA*, Br 10:133–34). In some details this presentation differs from that of Junghans, "Luther in Wittenberg," and Kroker, *Katharina von Bora*.

15. *WA*, Br 10:146–47. The reports of Magdalene's sickness and death are in WA, TR 5, nos. 5490–5502 (WA, TR 5, nos. 5491–5500 = *LW* 54:428–34). *WA*, Br 12:352–53.

16. *CR* 4:881–83 = *MBW* 3, no. 3067. *WA*, Br 10:149, line 20—150, line 35 = *LW* 50:238. *CR* 5:151–52 = *MBW* 3, no. 3284. *WA*, Br 10:156, lines 17–23; 169, lines 1–14; 176, lines 3–7; 401, lines 16–18.

17. WA, TR 5, no. 6445.

18. Cf. Junghans, "Luther in Wittenberg," 30–31.

19. WA, TR 3, no. 3771 = *LW* 54:270.

20. WA, TR 3, no. 3648. Cf. WA, TR 5, no. 5188. WA, TR 4, nos. 4100, 4138, 4144–45. *WA*, Br 11:200, lines 23–27.

21. *WA*, Br 8:214, line 3—215, line 25; 532, lines 1–11. *WA*, Br 10:224–25, 277–79.
22. *WA*, Br 9:212, lines 8–12.
23. *WA*, Br 7:38–40. *WA*, TR 5, no. 6015. *WA*, Br 8:111–12, 126–27. *WA*, TR 5, no. 6121. *WA*, Br 8:138–41, 161–67, 455–56.
24. *WA*, Br 8:579, line 13—580, line 21.
25. Theodor Kolde, ed., *Analecta Lutherana: Briefe und Aktenstücke zur Geschichte Luthers* (Gotha: F. A. Perthes, 1883), 378. *WA* 49:499, line 2.
26. *WA*, TR 5, no. 5201. *WA*, Br 9:505, lines 11–20. *WA*, Br 10:176, line 14—177, line 19; 519–21. *WA*, TR 5, no. 6165.
27. *WA*, Br 9:527–29.

3. Home, Household, Garden, and Property

1. *WA*, Br 7:151, lines 13–16. *WA*, Br 8:609, line 3—610, line 17. *WA*, Br 9:537–38. *WA*, TR 3, no. 3536. *WA*, Br 9:168, lines 32–35 = *LW* 50:212. On the following, cf. Helmar Junghans, "Luther in Wittenberg," in Junghans, 28–30. Ernst Kroker, *Katharina von Bora, Martin Luthers Frau: Ein Lebens- und Charakterbild*, 2d ed. (Zwickau; J. Hermann, 1925), 77–117.
2. *WA*, TR 4, no. 4408 = *LW* 54:337. *WA*, TR 4, no. 4668. *WA*, TR 3, no. 3691. *WA* 35:592–93.
3. Karl Eduard Förstemann, "Mittheilungen aus den Wittenberger Kämmerei-Rechnungen in der ersten Hälfte des 16. Jahrhunderts," in *Neue Mittheilungen aus dem Gebiete historisch-antiquarischer Forschungen*, 24 vols. (Halle: E. Anton, 1834–1910), 3¹:117–18. *WA*, Br 8:609, lines 16–18. *WA*, Br 9:173, lines 46–53 = *LW* 50:216–17. *WA*, Br 9:520, line 3—521, line 8; 561, lines 58–66; 562, lines 82–106 (household account); 566–68.
4. *WA*, TR 5, no. 6436.
5. *WA*, Br 9:168, lines 1–4; 205, lines 1–3 = *LW* 50:208, 221. *WA*, Br 11:149, lines 1–2; 269, lines 1–2 = *LW* 50:277, 286. Kroker, *Katharina von Bora*, 236–41.
6. *WA*, Br 8:420–21.
7. *WA*, Br 9:266, line 3—267, line 18; 279, lines 3–4; 416, lines 2–8; 593–94. *WA*, Br 10:19, lines 10–14; 99, lines 3–27; 138, lines 22–24; 178 top, lines 9–12; 152, lines 7–11; 462, lines 23–27.
8. *WA*, Br 12:420–22. Cf. above, p. 18.
9. *WA*, Br 8:209, lines 10–16. *WA*, TR 3, nos. 3818, 3820. *WA*, TR 5, no. 6238. *WA* 46:493–95. *WA*, TR 4, no. 4309.
10. *WA*, TR 4, nos. 4741, 4484, 4747, 4517.
11. *WA*, TR 4, nos. 4542, 4593 = *LW* 54:351, 355–56. *WA*, TR 4, nos. 4639, 4766. *WA*, TR 5, no. 5221 = *LW* 54:399. *WA*, TR 5, no. 5403.
12. *WA*, Br 8:216–17; 369, lines 12–23; 372, lines 25–33; 395, lines 30–34. *WA*, Br 9:514. *WA*, Br 10:135, lines 3–6; 446, lines 7–8; 526, line 14—527, line 20; 543, lines 5–11. *WA*, Br 11:21, lines 30–31; 120, line 3; 167, lines 20–23.
13. Georg Buchwald, "Lutherana," *ARG* 25 (1928):88–93. Cf. *WA*, Br 11:215.
14. *WA*, Br 10:419, lines 4–7. *WA*, Br 11:201, lines 3–4. *WA*, TR 3, no. 3557. *WA*, TR 4, no. 5181.
15. *WA*, TR 3, no. 3692 = *LW* 54:257–58. *WA*, TR 4, nos. 4690, 5181, 5186. *WA*, TR 4, no. 5187 = *LW* 54:396. *WA*, TR 5, no. 5340.
16. *WA*, TR 5, no. 5271.

17. *WA*, Br 9:563–64. *WA*, Br 12:489.

18. *WA*, Br 18:206–8. *WA*, Br 10:522, lines 18–32. *WA*, Br 11:9–10; 219, lines 24–26; 260, lines 5–21; 306, line 1—307, line 10.

19. *WA*, Br 10:17–22.

20. See above, p. 187. *WA*, TR 4, no. 5041.

21. *WA*, Br 9:571–78. *WA*, Br 12:349–50. Tibor Fabiny, *Martin Luthers letzter Wille: Das Testament des Reformators und seine Geschichte* (Berlin: Union Verlag, 1983).

22. *WA*, Br 9:579–82.

4. Social Life, Festivals, and Music

1. Ernst Kroker, *Katharina von Bora, Martin Luthers Frau: Ein Lebens- und Charakterbild*, 2d ed. (Zwickau; J. Hermann, 1925), 165–74.

2. *WA*, TR 5, no. 5428.

3. *WA*, TR 4, no. 4180. *WA*, TR 3, no. 3654b = *LW* 54:248–49. *WA*, TR 4, no. 4201 = *LW* 54:326–27. *WA*, TR 5, nos. 5528–29. On the following, cf. Erika Kohler, *Martin Luther und der Festbrauch*, Mitteldeutsche Forschungen, vol. 17 (Cologne and Graz: Böhlau, 1959).

4. WA 35:258–66. Markus Jenny, ed., *Luthers geistliche Lieder und Kirchengesänge*, AWA, vol. 4 (Cologne and Vienna: Böhlau, 1985), 287–91, 306–8.

5. *WA*, TR 4, no. 4720.

6. *WA*, TR 3, nos. 3787–89. Georg Buchwald, *Zur Wittenberger Stadt- und Universitäts-Geschichte in der Reformationszeit: Briefe aus Wittenberg an M. Stephan Roth in Zwickau* (Leipzig: G. Wigand, 1893), no. 109a.

7. *WA*, TR 4, no. 4313a. *WA*, Br 9:548, lines 6–7. *CR* 5:887–88 = *MBW* 4, no. 4064. Christian Gotthold Neudecker, ed., *Die handschriftliche Geschichte Ratzeberger's über Luther und seine Zeit* (Jena: F. Mauke, 1850), 131–33.

8. *WA*, TR 3, no. 3516. *WA*, Br 8:60, lines 17–24.

9. *WA*, TR 3, no. 3815. *WA*, TR 4, no. 4192.

10. WA 50:364–74 = *LW* 53:321–24.

11. WA 35:308. WA 35:483–84 = *LW* 53:319–20.

12. *WA*, TR 5, no. 5408 = *LW* 54:420.

X. LUTHER'S CONGREGATION— WITTENBERG (1537–46)

1. The Preacher and Pastor

1. WA 47:232–627. WA 46:538–789 = *LW* 22:1–274. WA 47:1–231 = *LW* 22: 275–530.

2. WA 49:254–68, 271–93.

3. WA 45:1–362 (WA 45:205–250 = *LW* 12:95–136). WA 46:113–537. WA 47:628–75. WA 49:1–254, 294–805. WA 51:1–106.

4. Cf. above, pp. 11–17. WA 49:318, lines 2–14; 325, lines 2–3.

5. *WA*, TR 3, no. 3573 = *LW* 54:235–36. *WA*, TR 3, no. 3579. *WA*, TR 4, no. 4719.

6. *WA*, TR 4, no. 5171b = *LW* 54:393. *WA*, TR 5, no. 5199 = *LW* 54:396. *WA*, TR 5, no. 5200.

7. WA 47:368, line 32—369, line 37.

8. WA 45:324, lines 19–25. *WA*, TR 4, nos. 4097, 4719.

9. *WA* 49:780, line 16—787. *WA* 51:15, line 11—16, line 12.

10. *WA* 45:109, lines 7–9. The inaccurate reference to thirty-five years has been corrected. *WA* 45:132, line 17. *WA* 46:596, lines 3–7 = *LW* 22:70. *WA* 49:55, lines 3–6.

11. *WA* 51:454–57.

12. *WA* 43:513, lines 9–15 = *LW* 5:123. Frieder Schulz, *Die Gebete Luthers*, QFRG, vol. 44 (Gütersloh: G. Mohn, 1976), no. 515.

13. Cf. Brecht, *Luther* 2, 25–27, 278–79 = *Luther* 2, ET, 15–18, 285–86. *WA*, Br 8:569, lines 18–21 = *LW* 50:189.

14. *WA*, Br 7:329, lines 14–20. *WA* 22:xi–xix. Cf. Brecht, *Luther* 2, 279–80 = *Luther* 2, ET, 286–87. *WA* 21:195–551. *WA* 22.

15. *WA* 22:197–203.

16. *WA* 52. Theodor Kolde, ed., *Analecta Lutherana: Briefe und Aktenstücke zur Geschichte Luthers* (Gotha: F. A. Perthes, 1883), 387 bottom.

17. *WA* 53:213–18.

18. *WA*, TR 6, no. 6923. *WA*, Br 12:282–83.

19. *WA*, Br 8:453–55; 492–93; 499, lines 11–14.

20. *WA*, TR 5, no. 6404.

21. *WA*, Br 8:363–64.

22. *WA*, TR 4, no. 4525.

23. *WA*, TR 3, no. 3644a. *WA*, TR 4, nos. 4787, 4709.

24. *WA*, TR 3, no. 3702.

25. *WA*, TR 3, no. 3755 = *LW* 54:269.

26. *WA* 53:202–8 = *LW* 43:243–50.

2. The Congregation

1. Cf. Brecht, *Luther* 2, 280–85 = *Luther* 2, ET, 287–92, and above, pp. 11–17.

2. *WA*, TR 4, no. 4313. *WA*, Br 8:327–29. *WA*, TR 4, nos. 4789, 4176, 4179. *WA* 47:134, line 3—138, line 14 = *LW* 22:416–19. *WA*, TR 5, no. 5503 = *LW* 54:434–36.

3. *WA*, Br 8:579, line 10—580, line 20; 600, lines 5–16; 604, line 18—605, line 23.

4. *WA* 45:115, lines 9–16; 191, line 11—194, line 20.

5. *WA*, TR 3, no. 3707. *WA*, Br 8:198, lines 27–40.

6. *WA*, Br 8:96, lines 10–13; 102–3. Georg Buchwald, *Zur Wittenberger Stadt- und Universitäts-Geschichte in der Reformationszeit: Briefe aus Wittenberg an M. Stephan Roth in Zwickau* (Leipzig: G. Wigand, 1893), no. 167. *WA*, TR 4, no. 5162. *WA*, TR 5, nos. 6228, 6336.

7. *WA*, TR 4, nos. 3969, 3979. Cf. above, p. 16. Beatrice Frank, "Zauberei und Hexenwerk," in Gerhard Hammer and Karl-Heinz zur Mühlen, eds., *Lutheriana: Zum 500. Geburtstag Martin Luthers von den Mitarbeitern der Weimarer Ausgabe*, AWA, vol. 5 (Cologne: Böhlau, 1984), 291–97.

8. *WA*, TR 4, no. 5027. *WA* 42:269, line 30—270, line 11 = *LW* 2:11–12. *WA* 51:55, line 26—57, line 6. *WA*, Br 9:345, lines 16–34; 375, lines 7–13.

9. *WA*, Br 11:111–12.

10. *WA*, TR 3, no. 3523 = *LW* 54:221. *WA*, TR 5, no. 5265. Cf. Brecht, *Luther* 2, 283 = *Luther* 2, ET, 290.

11. *WA* 49:278–79, line 8.

12. WA 47:110, line 17—111, line 25; 119, line 38—120, line 13. Buchwald, *Zur Wittenberger Stadt- und Universitäts-Geschichte*, nos. 165–66.

13. *WA, TR* 4, no. 4464.

14. WA 47:757–71 = *LW* 51:289–99. *WA, TR* 4, no. 4606. WA 47:756, lines 25–27; 815, line 20—816, line 4.

15. WA 49:385, line 8—386, line 20; cf. 488–91; 716–23, line 3.

16. WA 49:337, line 11—340, line 15; 520–25, line 5; 554, line 18—562, line 2; 770–87. *WA, TR* 5, no. 6406. Cf. *WA, Br* 9:508, lines 17–25.

17. *WA, TR* 3, no. 3739. On the following, cf. Rudolf Hermann, "Die Probleme der Exkommunikation bei Luther und Thomas Erastus," *ZSTh* 23 (1954):103–36. Ruth Götze, *Wie Luther Kirchenzucht übte: Eine kritische Untersuchung von Luthers Bannsprüchen und ihrer exegetischen Grundlegung aus der Sicht unserer Zeit* (Göttingen: Vandenhoeck & Ruprecht, 1958).

18. *WA, TR* 4, no. 5178 = *LW* 54:395–96. *WA, TR* 4, no. 5179. *WA, TR* 5, no. 5205. *WA, Br* 9:102–4.

19. *WA, TR* 4, nos. 4013a–c. Cf. Brecht, *Luther* 2, 420 = *Luther* 2, ET, 436–38. *WA, Br* 8:362, lines 17–21.

20. *WA, TR* 4, no. 4340.

21. *WA, TR* 4, no. 4381. WA 47:669–70, line 15. *WA, TR* 5, nos. 5216, 5270 = *LW* 54:398, 404–5. *WA, TR* 5, no. 5258. *WA, TR* 5, no. 5593.

22. *WA, TR* 5, no. 5438 = *LW* 54:422–23. *WA, Br* 9:594–95.

23. WA 49:556, line 5—558, line 6.

24. Cf. Brecht, *Luther* 2, 282 = *Luther* 2, ET, 289. WA 47:385, lines 2–29.

25. *WA, TR* 4, no. 4046.

26. *WA, TR* 4, no. 4079 = *LW* 54:317. Cf. *WA, TR* 4, no. 4412 = *LW* 54:337. *WA, TR* 4, no. 4746. *WA, Br* 8:397, lines 10–15. *WA, Br* 12:279–81.

27. *WA, TR* 4, no. 4472 = *LW* 54:344–45. *WA, Br* 8:403–5. *WA, TR* 4, no. 4749.

28. WA 47:724, line 20—728, line 7. *WA, TR* 4, no. 4496, cf. 4505, 4545.

29. WA 51:323–424. Cf. Brecht, *Luther* 2, 143–47 = *Luther* 2, ET, 142–46.

30. *WA, TR* 4, no. 4805 = *WA, TR* 5, no. 5429.

31. *WA, Br* 9:6–8.

32. WA 53:211–12, line 18.

33. *WA, Br* 10:532.

34. *WA, Br* 10:599, line 8—600, line 3.

35. WA 49:330–34, line 3; 476, line 28—479, line 13; 541, line 19—542, line 11.

36. WA 44:666, line 34—668, line 11; 670, line 19—673, line 14 = *LW* 8:120–22, 124–29.

37. WA 49:788–93.

38. *WA, Br* 11:148–52 = *LW* 50:273–81.

39. Cf. Brecht, *Luther* 2, 281 = *Luther* 2, ET, 289. *CR* 5:313–14. Carl Eichhorn, "Amsdorfiana," *ZKG* 22 (1901):622–25.

40. *CR* 5:816–17 = *MBW* 4, no. 3979. Buchwald, *Zur Wittenberger Stadt- und Universitäts-Geschichte*, nos. 213–14. *WA, Br* 11:160–65.

41. WA 51:42–106 (especially noteworthy are pp. 50–57).

42. *WA, Br* 11:232; 233, lines 15–30.

43. WA 35:593–95.

XI. LUTHER'S CHURCH— ELECTORAL SAXONY (1537–46)

1. The Relationship to Electoral Saxon Society

1. Georg Buchwald, "Lutherana," *ARG* 25 (1928):16–23.

2. *WA* 43:507, lines 13–14.

3. *CR* 2:777–78 = *MBW* 2, no. 1985.

4. *WA*, TR 4, no. 4045.

5. *WA* 51:546, line 33—549, line 26 = *LW* 41:237–40.

6. *WA*, TR 3, no. 3803 = *LW* 54:277–78. *WA*, TR 3, no. 3804. *WA*, TR 4, no. 4017. *WA* 51:66, lines 3–24. *WA* 59:327–28.

7. Oskar Thulin, *Schloss und Schlosskirche in Torgau* (Berlin: Evangelische Verlagsanstalt, 1963). *WA* 49:588–615, line 3 = *LW* 51:331–54. *WA*, TR 5, no. 6396.

8. *WA* 46:616, line 15—619. *WA* 47:445–47, line 29.

9. *WA*, Br 9:2–4.

10. *WA* 46:734, line 21—738, line 3 = *LW* 22:225–28. *WA* 40³:648, lines 24–37.

11. *WA*, TR 3, no. 3527 = *LW* 54:222. *WA*, TR 3, no. 3549a. *WA*, Br 8:97–98.

12. *WA* 47:411, lines 1–4; 461, line 35—462. *WA*, TR 4, no. 4712. *WA* 44:347, line 5—348, line 5 = *LW* 7:63–64.

13. *WA*, Br 9:11–14, 15–17, 14–15.

14. *WA* 49:12, line 33—13, line 21. *WA* 44:14, line 23—15, line 8 = *LW* 6:20–21.

15. *WA*, Br 10:335, lines 20–26 = *LW* 50:243–44. *WA* 49:622, line 12—623, line 10.

16. *WA*, Br 10:497.

17. *WA*, Br 8:85–87.

18. *WA*, Br 9:249–51.

19. *WA*, Br 10:326–27.

20. *WA*, Br 10:722–28.

21. *WA*, Br 8:141–42, 204, 444–46.

22. *WA*, Br 9:118–19. *WA*, Br 11:60–67.

23. *WA*, Br 10:656–58, 700–3.

24. *WA*, Br 8:237–38.

2. Pastors and Congregations

1. *WA* 46:211, line 18—212, line 7. *WA*, TR 4, nos. 3898, 4036. *WA*, Br 10:375, lines 1–9.

2. *WA*, TR 3, nos. 3747, 3758, 3872.

3. *WA*, TR 4, no. 4701. *WA*, TR 5, nos. 5238, 5252. Cf. *WA* 51:453, lines 18–20.

4. *WA*, Br 8:369, lines 3–11.

5. *WA*, Br 8:443–44, 452–53.

6. *WA*, Br 8:518, line 1—519, line 14.

7. *WA*, Br 10:237, lines 4–22.

8. *WA*, Br 10:246–47.

9. *CR* 5:25 = *MBW* 3, no. 3155. *WA*, Br 10:252–58; 309–13, line 14.

10. *WA*, Br 9:550–52, cf. 522–26. *CR* 10:166 = *MBW* 3, no. 3080.

11. *WA*, Br 10:286–87. *WA*, Br 11:75.

12. *WA, Br* 8:128.

13. Cf. *WA, Br* 8:654, and above, n. 10.

14. *WA, Br* 8:92–94, 145–46, 172–73, 332–33.

15. *WA, Br* 8:137–38, 167–72.

16. *WA, Br* 9:327–28, 249–51. *WA, TR* 4, no. 5186.

17. *WA, Br* 10:56–59, 417–18.

18. *WA, Br* 9:210–11. *WA, Br* 10:313, line 14—314, line 23.

19. *WA, Br* 11:39–41.

20. *WA, Br* 8:231–32; 604, lines 1–17.

21. *WA, Br* 9:302–3, line 22. *WA, Br* 10:539, lines 16–24. *WA, Br* 9:553–54.

22. *WA, Br* 8:112–13.

23. *WA, TR* 4, no. 4010.

24. *WA, Br* 8:337, lines 7–13; 433–38; 449–51; 519–23. *WA, TR* 4, no. 4650.

25. *WA* 21:202–3, line 20.

26. *WA, Br* 11:116–20.

27. *WA, Br* 11:158–60.

28. *WA, Br* 8:394, line 3—395, line 29. *WA, Br* 11:166–67. *WA, TR* 4, no. 4349. *WA, Br* 10:672–73.

29. *WA, Br* 8:142–43.

30. *WA, Br* 8:457–58, 493–96, 500–2. *CR* 3:754–55 = *MBW* 2, no. 2254.

31. *CR* 3:951–52 = *MBW* 3, no. 2363. *CR* 4:860–61 = *MBW* 3, no. 3031. *WA, Br* 10:178–81; 188–89; 234, lines 6–15; 342–43; 375, lines 9–19. Cf. Irmgard Höss, *Georg Spalatin, 1484–1545: Ein Leben in der Zeit des Humanismus und der Reformation* (Weimar: Hermann Böhlaus Nachfolger, 1956), 403–7.

32. *WA* 54:112–15. Cf. *WA, Br* 10:452, lines 3–6; 477–78.

33. *WA, Br* 10:638–41; cf. 609, lines 3–8.

34. *WA, Br* 11:21, lines 27–30; 55–58. Cf. Höss, *Georg Spalatin*, 416–20.

35. *WA, Br* 9:45–48, 59–60, 80–82.

36. *WA, Br* 9:568–70, 618–20. *WA, Br* 11:122–25.

3. Church Administration and Church Order

1. *CR* 3:521–23 = *MBW* 2, no. 2031. *WA, Br* 8:262–67, 442–43. *WA, TR* 3, no. 3710.

2. *WA, Br* 8:497–98, 536–38.

3. *WA, Br* 8:66–67, 203.

4. *WA, Br* 8:396, 411.

5. *WA, Br* 8:136.

6. Cf. Georg Buchwald, *Zur Wittenberger Stadt- und Universitäts-Geschichte in der Reformationszeit: Briefe aus Wittenberg an M. Stephan Roth in Zwickau* (Leipzig: G. Wigand, 1893), no. 153; *WA, TR* 4, no. 4113; Gustav Kawerau, ed., *Der Briefwechsel des Justus Jonas*, 2 vols. (Halle: O. Hendel, 1884–85; reprint ed., Hildesheim: G. Olms, 1964), vol. 1, no. 540; Carl Wolfgang Huismann Schoss, "Die rechtliche Stellung, Struktur und Funktion der frühen evangelischen Konsistorien nach den evangelischen Kirchenordnungen des 16. Jahrhunderts" (diss., University of Heidelberg, 1980).

7. Ludwig Richter, *Geschichte der evangelischen Kirchenverfassung in Deutschland* (Leipzig: Tauchnitz, 1851), 82–96. Otto Mejer, *Zum Kirchenrecht des Reformationsjahrhunderts: Drei Abhandlungen* (Hannover: Carl Meyer, 1891), 1–83, esp. 20.

8. Emil Sehling, ed., *Die Evangelischen Kirchenordnungen des XVI. Jahrhunderts,* vol. 1¹, *Sachsen und Thüringen* (Leipzig: O. R. Reisland, 1902), 200–9.

9. *WA,* TR 4, nos. 4736, 4428. *WA,* Br 8:337, lines 8–10.

10. *WA,* TR 4, nos. 4497–98.

11. *WA,* Br 9:306, lines 5–15.

12. *WA,* Br 10:75–81.

13. *WA,* Br 9:385–89, 412–13, 455–56.

14. *WA,* TR 5, no. 5387.

15. *WA,* Br 10:103–10.

16. *WA,* Br 10:128–30, 183–88. Cf. above, p. 10.

17. *WA,* Br 10:325; 658, line 2—659, line 6.

18. *WA,* Br 10:356–64.

19. *WA,* Br 11:170–73, 234–36.

20. *WA,* Br 10:398–400, 402–3.

21. *WA,* Br 11:174. Cf. *WA,* Br 8:340.

22. *WA,* Br 6:550–55. These letters may also have come from 1533–34. Cf. Brecht, *Luther* 2, 431 = *Luther* 2, ET, 449.

23. *WA,* Br 9:497–500, 502–4. *CR* 10:104–5 = *MBW* 3, no. 2995. *CR* 4:918 = *MBW* 3, no. 3111. *WA,* TR 5, no. 5446 = *LW* 54:425–26. *WA,* TR 5, no. 5893. *WA,* Br 10:64, line 10—65, line 15; 96, line 3—97, line 10.

24. *WA,* TR 5, no. 5314 = *LW* 54:407–8.

25. *WA,* Br 8:626, lines 41–50. *WA,* Br 10:171–72; 178 top, lines 6–8. *CR* 4:840–41 = *MBW* 3, no. 3001. *WA,* Br 10:237, line 23—238, line 33; 265, line 8—266, line 26; 283, line 8—284, line 17. *WA* 49:xlv. *WA* 54:162, line 31—167. H. B. Meyer, "Die Elevation im deutschen Mittelalter und bei Luther," *ZKTh* 85 (1963):162–217, esp. 196–210.

26. *WA,* TR 5, no. 5212 = *LW* 54:397.

27. *WA,* Br 10:691–93.

28. *WA* 35:258–70. Markus Jenny, ed., *Luthers geistliche Lieder und Kirchengesänge,* AWA, vol. 4 (Cologne and Vienna: Böhlau, 1985), 287–91, 302–3, 306–8. *WA,* TR 5, no. 5528.

29. *WA* 35:270–81. Jenny, *Luthers geistliche Lieder,* 295–98, 345–51.

30. *WA* 35:281–85. Jenny, *Luthers geistliche Lieder,* 299–302. Hans-Jürgen Laubach, "Luthers Tauflied," *JLH* 16 (1971):134–54.

31. *WA* 35:285–86. Jenny, *Luthers geistliche Lieder,* 311–12. *WA,* Br 10:486–87. Ernst Kähler, *Studien zum Te Deum und zur Geschichte des 24. Psalms in der Alten Kirche* (Göttingen: Vandenhoeck & Ruprecht, 1958), 131–46.

32. *WA,* TR 5, no. 5603.

33. Jenny, *Luthers geistliche Lieder,* 341–42. *WA* 35:478–83 = *LW* 53:325–31. Marcus Jenny, "Sieben biblische Begräbnisgesänge: Ein unerkanntes und unediertes Werk Martin Luthers," in Gerhard Hammer and Karl-Heinz zur Mühlen, eds., *Lutheriana: Zum 500. Geburtstag Martin Luthers von den Mitarbeitern der Weimarer Ausgabe,* AWA, vol. 5 (Cologne: Böhlau, 1984), 455–74.

34. *WA* 35:476–77 = *LW* 53:332–34.

35. *WA* 44:451, lines 14–20 = *LW* 7:205.

36. *WA* 40³:615, line 32—616, line 11.

37. *WA* 21:200, lines 2–23.
38. *WA*, Br 10:335, lines 14–17 = *LW* 50:242.

XII. THE PROGRESS OF THE LUTHERAN REFORMATION IN THE GERMAN EMPIRE AND IN EUROPE

1. The Reformation in Ducal Saxony

1. *WA*, TR 4, no. 4558. See above, pp. 73–74. On the following, cf. Günther Wartenberg, "Luthers Beziehungen zu den sächsischen Fürsten," in Junghans, 568–70.

2. *WA*, TR 4, nos. 4615, 4620–24. *WA* 47:772–79 = *LW* 51:301–12. Gustav Kawerau, ed., *Der Briefwechsel des Justus Jonas*, 2 vols. (Halle: O. Hendel, 1884–85; reprint ed., Hildesheim: G. Olms, 1964), vol. 1, no. 429. Georg Buchwald, "Lutherana," *ARG* 25 (1928):19–20.

3. *WA*, Br 8:458–62, 469–81, 515–18. *WA*, TR 4, no. 4797. On the following, cf. Albrecht Lobeck, *Das Hochstift Meissen im Zeitalter der Reformation bis zum Tode Herzog Heinrichs 1541*, Mitteldeutsche Forschungen, vol. 65 (Cologne and Vienna: Böhlau, 1971), 90–131.

4. *WA*, Br 8:482–84; 499, lines 4–9; 505–7; 509–10; 513, lines 1–23; 524–26.

5. *WA*, Br 8:551–53; 553, line 4—554, line 10; 610–11. Kawerau, *Der Briefwechsel des Justus Jonas*, no. 470.

6. *WA*, TR 4, no. 4643. *WA*, Br 8:513, lines 4–7; 465–69; 526–27; 579, lines 1–10. *WA*, TR 4, no. 4675 = *LW* 54:360. *WA*, Br 8:585–87; 600, line 25—601, line 40.

7. *WA*, TR 4, nos. 4702, 4713, 4717.

8. *WA*, Br 8:538–44, 555–58.

9. *WA*, Br 8:609, lines 3–16; 627–28. *WA*, Br 9:113, lines 2–4; 222, line 7—223, line 14; 228–29; 464, lines 3–13. Cf. *WA*, Br 10:597, lines 11–26.

10. *WA*, Br 9:68, lines 3–8; 72–75; 109, lines 6–16; 111 top, lines 7–9; 145, lines 54–55. *WA*, TR 4, nos. 5138, 5149.

11. *WA*, Br 9:157–59, 223–25.

12. *WA*, Br 9:521, lines 9–15; 547, lines 6–7; 557.

13. On the following, cf. Hermann Kunst, *Evangelischer Glaube und politische Verantwortung: Martin Luther als politischer Berater seines Landesherrn und seine Teilnahme an den Fragen des öffentlichen Lebens* (Stuttgart: Evangelisches Verlagswerk, 1976), 369–74; Eike Wolgast, *Die Wittenberger Theologie und die Politik der evangelischen Stände: Studien zu Luthers Gutachten in politischen Fragen*, QFRG, vol. 47 (Gütersloh: G. Mohn, 1977), 262–69; Karlheinz Blaschke, "Moritz von Sachsen," in Martin Greschat, ed., *Die Reformationszeit II*, Gestalten der Kirchengeschichte, vol. 6 (Stuttgart: W. Kohlhammer, 1981), 295–314; Günther Wartenberg, "Martin Luther und Moritz von Sachsen," *LuJ* 42 (1975):52–70; idem, "Luthers Beziehungen zu den sächsischen Fürsten," 571.

14. *WA*, Br 10:29, lines 9–24. *WA*, TR 5, nos. 5428, 5428a.

15. *WA*, Br 10:31–37.

16. *WA*, Br 10:37–38.

17. *WA*, Br 10:38–43.

18. *WA*, Br 10:44, line 1—15; 45, line 1—46, line 17.

19. *WA*, Br 10:46–47. *WA*, TR 5, nos. 5428 (p. 135, lines 2–22), 5428a (p. 144, lines 15–22).

20. *WA*, Br 10:51–52; 113; 135, lines 6–17. Erich Brandenburg, ed., *Politische Korrespondenz des Herzogs und Kurfürsten Moritz von Sachsen*, vol. 1 (Leipzig: B. G. Teubner, 1900), 452, line 31—453, line 4.

21. *WA*, Br 10:277; 323–24; 446, lines 10–11; 543, lines 3–5; 596, lines 3–4.

22. *WA*, Br 10:403–9, 412–15.

23. *WA*, Br 10:62–63; 91–92; 283, lines 3–7; 401–2; 440–41; 613, line 3—614, line 12.

24. *WA*, Br 10:83–85.

25. *WA*, Br 10:259–60; 283, line 6—284, line 23. *WA*, Br 11:199, line 6—200, line 19.

26. *WA*, Br 10:436–37; 596, line 4—597, line 10; 614, lines 13–14.

27. *WA*, Br 11:251–54.

2. The Reformation in the Electorate of Brandenburg

1. *WA*, Br 8:620–24. Cf. Walter Delius, "Die Reformation des Kurfürsten Joachim II. von Brandenburg im Jahre 1539," *ThViat* 5 (1953/54):174–93. Idem, "Die Kirchenpolitik des Kurfürsten Joachim II. von Brandenburg in den Jahren 1535–1541," *JBBKG* 40 (1965):86–123. Bernd Moeller, "Luthers Stellung zur Reformation in deutschen Territorien und Städten," in Junghans, 583–84.

2. *WA*, Br 8:624–26.

3. *WA*, TR 4, no. 5146. *WA*, Br 9:243–46, lines 14–22.

4. See above, p. 168.

5. *WA*, Br 10:74–75. *WA*, TR 5, no. 5506. *WA*, Br 10:114, 644–45, 682–84. *WA*, Br 11:6–7.

6. *WA*, Br 11:49–52.

3. Halle—Between Albrecht of Mainz and Electoral Saxony

1. Gustav Kawerau, ed., *Der Briefwechsel des Justus Jonas*, 2 vols. (Halle: O. Hendel, 1884–85; reprint ed., Hildesheim: G. Olms, 1964), vol. 2, no. 557. On the following, cf. Walter Delius, *Die Reformationsgeschichte der Stadt Halle an der Saale*, BKGD, vol. 1 (Berlin: Union Verlag, 1953), 66–100. Idem, *Lehre und Leben Justus Jonas, 1493–1555* (Gütersloh: C. Bertelsmann, 1952). Bernd Moeller, "Luthers Stellung zur Reformation in deutschen Territorien und Städten," in Junghans, 586–88.

2. *WA*, Br 8:381–82. *WA*, Br 10:25, lines 3–10; 54, lines 3–7.

3. *WA*, Br 8:393–94; 395–96; 417, lines 8–24. *WA*, Br 10:5, lines 3–15. Eike Wolgast, *Die Wittenberger Theologie und die Politik der evangelischen Stände: Studien zu Luthers Gutachten in politischen Fragen*, QFRG, vol. 47 (Gütersloh: G. Mohn, 1977), 253–62.

4. *WA*, Br 10:117–18.

5. *WA*, Br 10:119–23.

6. *WA*, Br 10:125–28.

7. *WA*, Br 10:140; 141, lines 3–11; 142–47.

8. *WA*, Br 10:153–55.

9. WA 53:402–5.

10. *WA*, Br 10:172–76, 225–26.

11. *WA*, Br 10:226–28.

12. *WA*, Br 10:252, lines 5–8; 304–6; 333–34. Cf. Kawerau, *Der Briefwechsel des Justus Jonas*, vol. 2, no. 688.

13. Kawerau, *Der Briefwechsel des Justus Jonas*, vol. 2, nos. 715, 731–32. *WA*, Br 10:677–79.

4. The Reformation Experiment in the Dioceses of Naumburg and Merseburg

1. *WA*, Br 8:1–2, 73–74, 129–30, 133–34, 593. *WA*, Br 9:36–38, 111–12, 113–14, 120–23.

2. *WA*, Br 9:310–20. *WA*, Br 10:48, lines 6–7. On the following, cf. Peter Brunner, *Nikolaus von Amsdorf als Bischof von Naumburg: Eine Untersuchung zur Gestalt des evangelischen Bischofamtes in der Reformationzeit*, SVRG, vol. 179 (Gütersloh: G. Mohn, 1961). This study has been superseded in part by an analysis of the sources (see the following notes). Hans-Ulrich Delius, "Das bischoflose Jahr: Das Bistum Naumburg-Zeitz im Jahr vor der Einsetzung Nikolaus von Amsdorfs durch Luther," *HerChr* 8 (1973/74):65–95. Irmgard Höss, "Episcopus Evangelicus: Versuche mit dem Bischofsamt im deutschen Luthertum des 16. Jahrhunderts," in Erwin Iserloh, ed., *Confessio Augustana und Confutatio: Der Augsburger Reichstag 1530 und die Einheit der Kirche*, RGST, vol. 118 (Münster: Aschendorff, 1980), 499–516.

3. *WA*, Br 12:314–47. Cf. *WA*, Br 8:304, line 25—305, line 28; 432, line 12—433, line 29.

4. *WA*, Br 9:539–40. *WA*, Br 12:328–32.

5. *WA*, Br 12:332–39.

6. *WA*, Br 12:340–44.

7. *WA*, Br 12:344–47.

8. On the following, cf. Brunner. *Nikolaus von Amsdorf als Bischof von Naumburg*, 51–60. *WA*, Br 9:596–99.

9. Brunner, *Nikolaus von Amsdorf als Bischof von Naumburg*, 60–76. WA 49: xxvi–xxix.

10. *WA*, Br 12:350–51. Brunner, *Nikolaus von Amsdorf als Bischof von Naumburg*, 76–78.

11. *WA*, Br 12:351, lines 13–17. *WA*, Br 9:606, line 55—607, line 61. WA 53:219–60. The introduction is outdated in part. *WA*, Br 10:15–17, 20, 53–59.

12. *WA*, Br 9:608–13. *WA*, Br 10:1–2, 30, 39–42, 48–50, 169–70, 344–45.

13. *WA*, Br 10:97, line 3—98, line 14; 196, lines 1–7; 241, lines 13–21; 288, lines 7–15.

14. *WA*, Br 10:235–36; 241–42; 282, lines 3–13; 287, line 3—288, line 6; 291–93; 300, lines 5–31.

15. *WA*, Br 10:370, lines 3–19; 542, lines 11–12; 609, lines 8–16.

16. *WA*, Br 10:590–92, 623–24.

17. *WA*, Br 11:12, lines 3–18.

18. *WA*, Br 11:194–97.

19. *WA*, Br 11:215–19.

20. *WA*, Br 10:576, lines 8–9. Franz Lau, "Georg III. von Anhalt (1507–1533), erster

evangelischer 'Bischof' von Merseburg: Seine Theologie und seine Bedeutung für die Geschichte der Reformation in Deutschland, Festschrift Albrecht Alt," *WZ(L).GS* 3 (1953/54):93–106. Höss, "Episcopus Evangelicus," 509–12.

21. *WA*, Br 10:641–42. *WA*, Br 11:155–58. *WA* 49:l, 792–805. Cf. *WA*, Br 11:145, line 13—146, line 29. *WA* 51:11–22, esp. 20, lines 16–39.

22. *WA*, Br 11:44–49, 52–54, 89–90, 109.

23. *WA*, Br 11:132–35.

24. *WA*, TR 5, no. 6354. Cf. Emil Sehling, ed., *Die Evangelischen Kirchenordnungen des XVI. Jahrhunderts*, vol. 1¹, *Sachsen und Thüringen* (Leipzig: O. R. Reisland, 1902), 291–92, 297–304. It is no longer possible definitely to determine the document to which Luther's comments apply. It is also uncertain whether *WA*, Br 11:145, lines 5–12, belongs in this context.

25. *WA*, Br 11:292–95 (*WA*, Br 11:292 = *LW* 50:309–10).

5. Relationships with Smaller Neighboring Territories

1. *WA*, Br 9:361–63, 369.

2. *WA*, Br 12:353–54. *WA*, Br 10:397–98; 447–51; 516–18; 518, line 3—519, line 7; 525, lines 7–10; 533–39. Cf. *CR* 5:320–21 = *MBW* 4, no. 3464. *WA*, Br 10:594–96.

3. *WA*, Br 8:611–12. *WA*, Br 10:100–3. *WA*, Br 18:204–5. *WA* 48:667–68, no. 6868. *WA*, Br 10:486.

4. *WA*, Br 10:610–13.

5. *WA*, Br 8:45–46. *WA*, Br 9:109. *WA*, Br 10:622–23. *WA*, Br 11:137–38.

6. See below, pp. 369–75. *WA*, Br 9:624–30. *WA*, Br 10:488–95. *WA*, Br 11:165.

7. *WA* 51:626–33. See above, p. 80.

8. *WA*, Br 10:336–42, 347–49. See above, p. 283. Luther took the same position in a similar situation in Weida (*WA*, Br 11:259, lines 3–20).

9. *WA*, Br 10:349–52. See above, pp. 282–83.

10. *CR* 5:459–60 = *MBW* 4, no. 3650.

11. See above, pp. 25–28. *WA*, Br 8:108–10. *WA*, Br 8:200, lines 4–11 = *LW* 50:175. *WA*, TR 3, no. 3675. *WA*, TR 5, no. 6327.

12. *WA*, Br 8:189–91.

13. *WA*, Br 8:218, lines 1–17; 225, lines 1–4; 226–27; 227, lines 1–10; 236–37. *WA* 49:xxx.

14. *WA* 49:111–60. *WA*, TR 4, no. 4903.

15. *WA*, Br 10:439–40, 446–47.

16. Cf., e.g., *WA*, Br 8:200, lines 1–3 = *LW* 50:175. *WA*, Br 8:327, lines 11–14. *WA*, Br 9:419, lines 4–10; 514.

17. *WA*, Br 8:173–75; 305, lines 39–51; 319–20; 326, line 3—327, line 10. *WA*, Br 9:119–20.

18. *WA*, Br 8:313. *WA*, Br 10:147–49, 279–80, 586.

19. *WA*, Br 8:529–31. *WA*, Br 10:53.

20. *WA*, Br 10:284–86.

6. The Other German Territories and Adjacent Lands

1. See above, pp. 40–41. *WA*, TR 4, no. 5165. *WA*, TR 4, no. 5176 = *LW* 54:394. *WA*, Br 9:218–20, 382–83. *WA*, Br 10:150–52.

2. *WA*, Br 9:500–2. *WA*, Br 10:372–73.

3. See above, p. 33. *WA*, Br 8:87–88. *WA*, Br 10:95–96, 484–86. *WA*, Br 11:79–80.

4. *WA*, Br 8:425–26. Gustav Kawerau, ed., *Der Briefwechsel des Justus Jonas*, 2 vols. (Halle: O. Hendel, 1884–85; reprint ed., Hildesheim: G. Olms, 1964), vol. 1, no. 424. *WA*, Br 8:462, line 3—463, line 23. *WA*, Br 9:495–96. *WA*, Br 10:111, lines 13–22; 334, lines 4–14. *WA* 54:1–4.

5. *WA*, Br 10:604–7, 696–98. *WA*, Br 11:10–11, 38–39, 43–44, 184–88.

6. *CR* 3:398–400 = *MBW* 2, no. 1929. *WA*, Br 11:113–14.

7. *CR* 3:487–89 = *MBW* 2, no. 1997.

8. *CR* 3:893–96, 902 = *MBW* 3, nos. 2337–38. *WA*, TR 4, nos. 4763, 5004. *WA*, TR 5, nos. 5465, 5825.

9. See above, pp. 31–32. *CR* 3:954–58 = *MBW* 3, nos. 2369, 2373–75. *WA*, Br 12:298–300. *WA*, TR 5, no. 5290.

10. *WA*, Br 11:21, 26–27.

11. *WA*, TR 4, no. 4407.

12. *WA*, Br 9:510–12.

13. *WA*, Br 9:48–50. *WA*, Br 10:215–17.

14. *WA*, Br 8:310–12, 318–19, 330–31. *WA*, Br 10:232–33, 661–63.

15. *WA*, Br 10:3, lines 30–34. On the following, cf. August Franzen, *Bischof und Reformation: Erzbischof Hermann von Wied in Köln vor der Entscheidung zwischen Reform und Reformation*, KLK, vol. 31 (Münster: Aschendorff, 1971), 69–93. Mechthild Köhn, "Martin Bucers Entwurf einer Reformation des Erzstiftes Köln" (diss., University of Münster, 1966), esp. 124–29.

16. *CR* 5:54–55 = *MBW* 3, no. 3187. *WA*, Br 10:306, lines 4–7, 316–18.

17. *WA* 54:5–11.

18. *WA*, Br 10:371, lines 31–37; 456, lines 53–58; 527, lines 22–24.

19. *WA*, Br 10:600, lines 3–12. *CR* 5:448–49 = *MBW* 4, no. 3631. *WA*, Br 10:614–18. *CR* 5:458–59, 462 = *MBW* 4, nos. 3646, 3652. Cf. Hermann von Wied, *Einfältiges Bedenken: Reformationsentwurf für das Erzstift Köln von 1543*, ed. Helmut Gerhards and Wilfried Borth, SVRKG, vol. 43 (Düsseldorf: Presseverband der Evangelischen Kirche im Rheinland, 1972), 139–66. Otto Albrecht and Paul Flemming, "Das sogenannte Manuscriptum Thomasianum," *ARG* 13 (1916):163–65. Wilhelm H. Neuser, *Luther und Melanchthon: Einheit im Gegensatz*, TEH, vol. 91 (Munich: Chr. Kaiser, 1961), 25–27.

20. *WA*, Br 10:320–23.

21. *WA*, Br 9:101–2.

22. *WA*, Br 8:590–92. Robert Stupperich, "Melanchthoniana inedita," *ARG* 52 (1961):91–93.

23. *WA*, Br 8:291, line 3—292, line 18 = *LW* 50:181–82. *WA*, Br 8:371, lines 1–8.

24. *WA*, Br 10:354–55.

25. *WA*, Br 10:525, lines 3–6; 660–61.

26. See above, p. 28. *WA*, Br 8:426–30.

27. *WA*, Br 8:61–66. *WA*, Br 12:306–9.

28. *WA*, Br 11:125–29, 153–54.

29. *WA*, Br 10:566–75, 587–90, 704–6, 716–20.

30. *WA*, Br 10:273–75.

31. *WA*, Br 8:314–16, 330, 370. *WA*, Br 10:219–20, 265–67.

32. *WA*, Br 9:328–29, 373–75, 453–54, 478–80, 519–20, 592–93. *WA*, Br 10:220–23, 364–67, 410–16, 444–45, 452–54, 561–63, 690–91. *WA*, Br 11:63–64, 106–7.

33. *WA*, Br 18:201–2. *WA*, Br 9:242, lines 3–21, 142–43, 220–21. *WA*, Br 12:302–3.

34. *WA* 53:397–401.

7. The Reformation in European Lands

1. *WA*, Br 8:422–24, 228–29.

2. *WA*, Br 7:602–4. On the following, cf. Martin Schwarz-Lausten, "Luthers Beziehungen zu Skandinavien," in Junghans, 689–92.

3. *WA*, Br 8:69–72; 158, lines 19–21.

4. *WA*, Br 9:96–97.

5. *WA*, Br 9:605, line 1—606, line 53. Otto Vogt, ed., *Dr. Johannes Bugenhagens Briefwechsel*, reprint ed. (Hildesheim: G. Olms, 1966), no. 203. See above, p. 243.

6. *WA*, Br 10:616–17. *WA*, Br 11:70, lines 11–14 = *LW* 50:252. *WA*, Br 11:101–2, 218–19.

7. Vogt, ed., *Dr. Johannes Bugenhagens Briefwechsel*, nos. 154, 165.

8. *WA*, Br 8:411–13. Cf. Schwarz-Lausten, "Luthers Beziehungen zu Skandinavien," 694–97.

9. *WA*, Br 9:213–16.

10. *WA*, Br 9:426–33, 530–31. Cf. *WA*, Br 12:313–14.

11. *WA*, Br 10:391–93. On the following, cf. Tibor Fabiny, "Luthers Beziehungen zu Ungarn und Siebenbürgen," in Junghans, 641–46. Oskar Wittstock, *Johannes Honterus, der Siebenbürger Humanist und Reformator: Der Mann, das Werk, die Zeit*, KO.M, vol. 10 (Göttingen: Vandenhoeck & Ruprecht, 1970), 131–38, 227–48.

12. *WA*, Br 10:564–66, 715–16, 732.

13. See below, pp. 323–32.

8. The Action against Duke Henry of Brunswick–Wolfenbüttel and the Reformation in Brunswick–Wolfenbüttel

1. See above, pp. 219–22. *WA*, TR 4, no. 5105. On the following, cf. Friedrich Koldewey, *Heinz von Wolfenbüttel: Ein Zeitbild aus dem Jahrhundert der Reformation* (Halle: Verein für Reformationsgeschichte, 1883), 44–66. Franz Petri, "Herzog Heinrich der Jüngere von Braunschweig-Wolfenbüttel," *ARG* 72 (1981):122–58. Hermann Kunst, *Evangelischer Glaube und politische Verantwortung: Martin Luther als politischer Berater seines Landesherrn und seine Teilnahme an den Fragen des öffentlichen Lebens* (Stuttgart: Evangelisches Verlagswerk, 1976), 375–97. Eike Wolgast, *Die Wittenberger Theologie und die Politik der evangelischen Stände: Studien zu Luthers Gutachten in politischen Fragen*, QFRG, vol. 47 (Gütersloh: G. Mohn, 1977), 275–84.

2. *WA*, Br 9:242, lines 27–37; 270, lines 3–4; 289, lines 25–26; 559, line 26—560, line 52.

3. *WA*, Br 10:88–91; 98, lines 15–19.

4. *WA*, Br 10:120, lines 2–5; 123–25; 131–32; 138, lines 15–32.

5. *WA*, Br 10:141, lines 12–19; 156, lines 1–12.

6. *WA*, Br 10:275–76; 454, line 3—456, line 52; 467, lines 40–49; 469–76; 483.

7. *WA*, Br 10:282, lines 14–16. *WA*, Br 18:212–14. *WA*, Br 11:140–41, 180–81.

8. *WA*, Br 10:600, line 13—601, line 16; 626–37.

9. *WA*, Br 11:177, lines 8–9; 182–84.

10. *WA,* Br 11:198, line 19—199, line 42; 201, lines 12–26. *WA* 48:238–39. The date must be corrected.

11. *WA,* Br 11:206–9, 223–25. *WA,* Br 12:360.

12. *WA,* Br 11:209–14, 217–18, 227–29.

13. *WA,* Br 11:233, lines 2–14. Theodor Kolde, ed., *Analecta Lutherana: Briefe und Aktenstücke zur Geschichte Luthers* (Gotha: F. A. Perthes, 1883), 419–24. Hans-Ulrich Delius, ed., *Der Briefwechsel des Friedrich Mykonius: Ein Beitrag zur allgemeinen Reformationsgeschichte und zur Biographie eines mitteldeutschen Reformators,* SKRG, vol. 18/19 (Tübingen: Osiandersche Buchhandlung, 1960), no. 427. *WA* 54:382.

14. *WA* 54:374–411.

9. Renewed Controversy about the Lord's Supper

1. See above, pp. 39–59. On the following, cf. Ernst Bizer, *Studien zur Geschichte des Abendmahlsstreits im 16. Jahrhundert,* 2d ed. (Darmstadt: Wissenschaftliche Buchgesellschaft, 1962), 229–33. Martin Brecht, "Luthers Beziehungen zu den Schweizern und Oberdeutschen (1530/1531–1546)," in Junghans, 514–17.

2. Cf. Brecht, *Luther* 2, 292–95 = *Luther* 2, ET, 300–3. Cf. Olivier Millet, "La correspondance du réformateur strasbourgeois W. F. Capiton avec Jodocus Neuheller, compagnon de table de Luther (1536–1538)," *BSHPF* 128 (1983):81–83. Horst Weigelt, "Luthers Beziehungen zu Kaspar von Schwenckfeld, Johannes Campanus und Michael Stiefel," in Junghans, 473–76.

3. *WA* 50:117–20. *WA,* Br 9:630, line 9—631. Cf. Horst Weigelt, *Spiritualistische Tradition im Protestantismus: Die Geschichte des Schwenckfeldertums in Schlesien,* AKG, vol. 43 (Berlin and New York: W. de Gruyter, 1973), 159–77. *WA,* Br 10:211, line 15—212, line 44; 219–20.

4. *WA* 39^2:92–121. *CR* 3:983–86 = *MBW* 3, no. 2396. *CSch* 6:119–36. Cf. Brecht, *Luther* 2, 302–15 = *Luther* 2, ET, 310–14.

5. *CSch* 8:27–34 = *MBW* 3, nos. 2870, 2885. *CSch* 7:451–884.

6. *WA* 54:88, lines 7–8; 90, line 35—91, line 16 = *LW* 15:338, 341–42.

7. *WA,* Br 10:420–29. *CR* 5:248–29 = *MBW* 3, no. 3391. *WA,* TR 5, no. 5659 = *LW* 54:469–71.

8. *WA,* TR 4, no. 3947, 4008. *WA,* TR 4, no. 4020 = *LW* 54:311. *WA,* Br 8:406–9. On the following, cf. Tibor Fabiny, "Luthers Beziehungen zu Ungarn und Siebenbürgen," in Junghans, 643–46.

9. *WA,* Br 8:258–61. The editor has redated the letter from 1539 to 1538, but the reasons for this are not convincing. The fact that there were Hungarian students with Luther on 4 August 1538 (*WA,* TR 4, no. 3947) does speak in favor of the transposition. *WA,* Br 8:296–98. The sequence of the letters is not significant for this presentation.

10. *WA,* Br 10:555–56. Cf. *WA,* Br 13:327.

11. *WA,* TR 3, no. 3736. *WA,* TR 4, no. 3907 = *LW* 54:291–92. *WA,* Br 8:198, lines 11–14.

12. *WA,* Br 10:196–208.

13. *WA,* Br 10:262, lines 3–9. *MBW* 3, no. 3195. *CR* 5:61–63 = *MBW* 3, no. 3197. *WA,* Br 10:307–9, 327–33, 376–84.

14. *WA,* Br 10:679–82.

15. *WA,* Br 9:355–57; 474, lines 24–27; 590, lines 7–8. *WA,* TR 5, no. 5461. Cf. above, pp. 205–15, 218–19, 313–14. *WA,* TR 5, no. 5390 = *LW* 54:417–18. *WA,* TR 5,

nos. 5522, 5729. Otto Albrecht and Paul Flemming, "Das sogenannte Manuscriptum Thomasianum," *ARG* 13 (1916):163–65.

16. See above, p. 195. *WA* 50:591, lines 9–21 = *LW* 41:105. *WA*, Br 8:546–47. *WA*, Br 13:276. *WA* 51:587, lines 26–31 = *LW* 43:220.

17. *WA*, Br 9:620–22 = *LW* 50:225–30. *WA*, Br 10:13, line 1—14, line 12; 24, lines 30–31; 29, lines 24–30; 35; 49, lines 55–59; 71–72.

18. *WA*, Br 10:384–88. *CR* 5:342–43 = *MBW* 4, no. 3487. Heinrich Ernst Bindseil, ed., *Philippi Melanchthonis epistolae, iudicia, consilia, testimonia aliorumque ad eum epistolae, quae in Corpore Reformatorum desiderantur* (Halle: Gustav Schwetschke, 1874), no. 261 = *MBW* 4, no. 3596.

19. *CR* 39 (*Calvini opera*, vol. 11):696–98 = *MBW* 4, no. 3531. *CR* 5:415–16 = *MBW* 4, no. 3588. *WA*, Br 8:569, lines 29–34 = *LW* 50:190–91. *WA*, TR 5, nos. 5303, 6050.

20. Max Lenz, ed., *Briefwechsel Landgraf Philipp's des Grossmüthigen von Hessen mit Bucer*, vol. 2, Publicationen aus den K. Preussischen Staatsarchiven, vol. 28 (Leipzig: S. Hirzel, 1887), no. 188. *CR* 5:292–93 = *MBW* 4, no. 3435. *WA*, TR 5, no. 5370. *WA* 49:404–15.

21. *WA* 54:119–67 = *LW* 38:279–319. Albrecht and Flemming, "Das sogenannte Manuscriptum Thomasianum."

22. See above, pp. 324–25.

23. *WA*, Br 10:556, lines 33–34. *CR* 5:460–62 = *MBW* 4, nos. 3652–53. See above, pp. 313–14. *CR* 5:473–74, 481–83, 498–99 = *MBW* 4, nos. 3667–68, 3689, 3705. Albrecht and Flemming, "Das sogenannte Manuscriptum Thomasianum." Wilhelm H. Neuser, *Luther und Melanchthon: Einheit im Gegensatz*, TEH, vol. 91 (Munich: Chr. Kaiser, 1961), 25–41. This presentation of the conflict may indeed correspond to Melanchthon's view, but it is somewhat exaggerated.

24. *WA*, Br 10:650–55, 660. *WA*, Br 13:357. *WA*, Br 10:681, lines 51–58.

25. *CR* 5:488–89, 491–92, 495–96, 525 = *MBW* 4, nos. 3695, 3696, 3701, 3729.

26. Bindseil, ed., *Philippi Melanchthonis epistolae*, no. 279 = *MBW* 4, no. 3803. *WA*, Br 11:26–29. Bindseil, ed., *Philippi Melanchthonis epistolae*, no. 281 = *MBW* 4, no. 3885.

27. Bindseil, ed., *Philippi Melanchthonis epistolae*, no. 273 = *MBW* 4, no. 3748. Cf. *WA* 54:126–33.

28. *MBW* 4, nos. 3854, 3906. Bindseil, ed., *Philippi Melanchthonis epistolae*, no. 284 = *MBW* 4, no. 3928.

29. *WA* 54:134–35.

30. *WA*, Br 11:71, line 12—72, line 24; 78–79. Theodor Kolde, ed., *Analecta Lutherana: Briefe und Aktenstücke zur Geschichte Luthers* (Gotha: F. A. Perthes, 1883), 413–14.

31. *WA*, Br 11:94, lines 25–31. *WA* 54:427, lines 8–10. *WA* 54:434, lines 14–17 = *LW* 34:356. *WA*, Br 11:238–40.

32. *WA*, Br 11:177, lines 12–13; 236–37; 264, lines 9–16. *WA*, Br 12:361–63. *WA* 51:140, lines 14–15. On the basis of these sources, the secondary information is untrustworthy. Before his final journey to Eisleben, Luther told Melanchthon his view of the Lord's Supper was exaggerated (cf. Th. Diestelmann, *Die letzte Unterredung Luther's mit Melanchthon über den Abendmahlsstreit* [Göttingen: Vandenhoeck & Ruprecht, 1874], 362–67).

XIII. THE ENEMIES OF CHRIST AND OF HIS CHURCH: JEWS, TURKS, AND THE POPE

1. WA 50:665–66 (1539).
2. WA, TR 4, no. 5130. WA, TR 5, no. 5237. WA, TR 5, no. 5239 = LW 54:402.
3. WA 47:554, line 9—627.
4. WA, Br 10:23, lines 7–23.
5. Cf. Gustav Kawerau, ed., *Der Briefwechsel des Justus Jonas*, 2 vols. (Halle: O. Hendel, 1884–85; reprint ed., Hildesheim: G. Olms, 1964), vol. 2, no. 681 (25 April 1543). WA, Br 10:370, lines 9–19; 442, line 22—443, line 39.
6. WA, Br 10:553, lines 3–14.
7. WA 43:6, lines 9–15 = LW 3:182–83. WA 53:448, lines 19–30 = LW 47:175.

1. The Jews (1525–46)

1. Cf. Brecht, *Luther* 2, 116–17 = *Luther* 2, ET, 112–13. On the following, cf. Reinhold Lewin, *Luthers Stellung zu den Juden: Ein Beitrag zur Geschichte der Juden in Deutschland während des Reformationszeitalters*, NSGTK, vol. 10 (Berlin: Trowitzsch & Sohn, 1911); Wilhelm Maurer, "Die Zeit der Reformation," in Karl Heinrich Rengstorf and Siegfried von Kortzfleisch, eds., *Kirche und Synagoge: Handbuch zur Geschichte von Christen und Juden*, vol. 1 (Stuttgart: Klett, 1968), 363–452; Heiko Augustinus Oberman, *Wurzeln des Antisemitismus: Christenangst und Judenplage im Zeitalter von Humanismus und Reformation* (Berlin: Severin und Siedler, 1981); Walther Bienert, *Martin Luther und die Juden: Ein Quellenbuch mit zeitgenössischen Illustrationen, mit Einführungen und Erläuterungen* (Frankfurt am Main: Evangelisches Verlagswerk, 1982); C. Bernd Sucher, *Luthers Stellung zu den Juden: Eine Interpretation aus germanistischer Sicht*, BHRef, vol. 23 (Nieuwkoop: de Graaf, 1977); Heinz Kremers, ed., *Die Juden und Martin Luther. Martin Luther und die Juden: Geschichte, Wirkungsgeschichte, Herausforderung* (Neukirchen: Neukirchner Verlag, 1985); Johannes Brosseder, *Luthers Stellung zu den Juden im Spiegel seiner Interpreten: Interpretation und Rezeption von Luthers Schriften und Äusserungen zum Judentum in 19. und 20. Jahrhundert vor allem im deutschsprachigen Raum*, BÖT, vol. 8 (Munich: M. Hueber, 1972); Kurt Meier, "Luthers Judenschriften als Forschungsproblem," *ThLZ* 110 (1985):483–92. In part, my presentation goes in a different direction.
2. WA 17²:236, line 36—237, line 11.
3. WA 20:320, lines 31–33. WA 19:595–615 = LW 14:257–77.
4. WA 31¹:370, line 26—371, line 10.
5. WA, Br 5:451–52. WA, TR 1, no. 1060. WA, TR 2, no. 2634. WA, Br 6:427, lines 1–2.
6. See Brecht, *Luther* 2, 117 = *Luther* 2, ET, 113. CR 2:514–16 = MBW 2, no. 1167. WA, Br 7:232, lines 25—233, line 33; 463, line 38. WA, Br 7:503, line 3 = LW 50:145.
7. WA 36:183, line 4–6. WA, TR 1, no. 369 (p. 161, lines 2–13). WA, TR 2, no. 1743. WA, TR 3, no. 2863.
8. WA, TR 1, no. 746. WA, TR 2, no. 1610.
9. WA 38:595, line 16—597, line 19.
10. WA 59:705, lines 12–20.
11. WA 42:10, lines 17–35; 43:18–44, line 4; 195, lines 14–21; 298, line 27—299, line

10; 218, lines 10–26; 240, lines 5–14 = *LW* 1:12; 3:200–35; 4:83–84, 227–28, 115, 145. *WA* 43:31, line 33—32, line 7; 306, lines 1–4 = *LW* 3:219, 237.

12. *WA* 42:222, line 36—223, line 40.

13. *WA* 42:257, lines 9–21; 259; 16–24, line 39; 262, lines 7–19; 271, line 17—273, line 2; 298, line 40—299, line 8; 450, line 12—451, line 17; 484, lines 24–27; 563, lines 21–36; 596, lines 11–37 = *LW* 1:349–50, 352–53, 19–32, 356–57; 2:13–16, 52, 264–65, 311; 3:21; 67. *WA* 44:6, lines 9–15; 157, line 32—158, line 4; 217, lines 9–29; 339, line 9; 459, lines 28–31 = *LW* 6:9, 212–13, 291–92; 7:52, 216.

14. *WA* 50:268, lines 8–15; 273, lines 22–38; 279, line 20—282, line 29 = *LW* 34:209, 216, 224.

15. *WA*, TR 3, no. 2912.

16. The text of the mandate is no longer extant. Cf. C.A.H. Burkhardt, "Die Juden-verfolgungen im Kurfürstentum Sachsen von 1536 an," *ThStKr* 70 (1897):593–98, esp. 596–97. Maurer, "Die Zeit der Reformation," 370. Georg Buchwald, *Luther-Kalendarium*, SVRG, no. 147 (Leipzig: M. Heinsius Nachfolger, Eger & Sievers, 1929), 108. *WA*, TR 3, no. 3512 (December 1538). *WA*, TR 4, no. 5026. *WA* 42:494, line 39—495, line 2 = *LW* 2:326–27.

17. *WA*, TR 3, no. 3596. *WA*, Br 8:76–78, 89–91. Selma Stern, *Josel von Rosheim: Befehlshaber der Judenschaft im Heiligen Römischen Reich Deutscher Nation* (Stuttgart: Deutsche Verlags–Anstalt, 1959). Cf. *WA* 48:644, line 13 = *WA*, Br 4:590, line 63 (1528 or 1530).

18. *WA* 46:615, line 18—619, line 19 = *LW* 22:92–96.

19. *WA*, TR 1, no. 356 = *LW* 54:51–52. *WA*, TR 1, no. 385. *WA*, Br 8:371–75 also probably belongs in this context. *WA*, TR 3, no. 3597 = *LW* 54:239. Cf. *WA* 42:520, lines 22–30 = *LW* 2:361. William Klassen and Gerhard Hein, "Sabbatharier," *MennLex* 4:3–4.

20. *WA*, TR 3, nos. 3731, 3768. *WA* 42:602, line 40—632, line 36 = *LW* 3:76–118.

21. *WA* 50:309–37 = *LW* 47:57–98.

22. Cf. *WA* 25:185, lines 24–26.

23. Gustav Kawerau, ed., *Der Briefwechsel des Justus Jonas*, 2 vols. (Halle: O. Hendel, 1884–85; reprint ed., Hildesheim: G. Olms, 1964), vol. 1, no. 428.

24. *WA* 47:418, line 40—420, line 35; 545, line 25—554, line 7. *WA*, TR 4, no. 3988.

25. *WA*, TR 4, nos. 4401, 4485. *WA*, TR 4, no. 4493 = *LW* 54:348. *WA*, Br 8:419–20.

26. *WA*, TR 5, no. 5354; cf. no. 5843.

27. *WA*, TR 4, no. 5089. *WA*, TR 5, no. 5281.

28. *WA*, TR 5, no. 5263. *WA*, TR 5, no. 5324 = *LW* 54:408.

29. *WA*, DB 11²:394–404.

30. *WA*, DB 6:125. *WA*, DB 7:75.

31. *WA*, DB 4:340–45.

32. *WA*, TR 4, no. 4795. The year 1541 is only a possibility.

33. *WA*, TR 5, no. 5462 = *LW* 54:426. This invalidates the thesis in Bienert, *Martin Luther und die Juden.*

34. *WA*, TR 5, no. 5504 = *LW* 54:436–37.

35. *WA* 53:412–552 = *LW* 47:121–306. *WA*, Br 10:226, lines 19–20. *CR* 5:19–21 = *MBW* 3, no. 3148.

36. *WA* 53:417—419, line 21 = *LW* 47:137–40.

37. *WA* 53:419, line 22—448 = *LW* 47:140–76.

38. *WA* 53:449—511, line 24 = *LW* 47:176–254. Cf. *WA*, Br 10:258–59, line 10.

39. Gerhard Krause, " 'Aller Heiden Trost' Haggai 2,7," in Paul Althaus, ed., *Solange es "heute" heisst: Festgabe für Rudolf Hermann zum 70. Geburtstag* (Berlin: Evangelische Verlagsanstalt, 1957), 170–78. Cf. *WA*, TR 4, no. 4019.

40. *WA* 53:511, line 25—552 = *LW* 47:254–306.

41. Cf. Brecht, *Luther* 2, 229–30 = *Luther* 2, ET, 233–34.

42. *WA* 60:236–39.

43. *WA* 53:573–648.

44. Maurer, "Die Zeit der Reformation," 433–34. *CR* 5:728–29 = *MBW* 4, no. 3870.

45. *WA*, TR 5, no. 5535.

46. *WA* 54:16–100 = *LW* 15:265–352.

47. *CR* 5:164–65 = *MBW* 3, no. 3305.

48. *WA* 40³:600–7, line 4; 610, line 31—611, line 2; 615, lines 6–12; 614, line 22—643, line 5; 648, line 38—649, line 5; 662, line 16—663, line 19; 668, line 21—669, line 21; 670, lines 5–21; 681, lines 1–9.

49. *WA* 40³:695, line 29; 697, line 11—700, line 9; 702, line 18—706, line 12; 713, line 21—715; 718, line 7—719, line 6; 725, lines 2–13; 730, line 6—731, line 36; 735, line 19—736, line 22; 746.

50. *WA* 49:452, line 2—453, line 8.

51. *WA* 35:576–77. Markus Jenny, ed., *Luthers geistliche Lieder und Kirchengesänge*, AWA, vol. 4 (Cologne and Vienna: Böhlau, 1985), 123–24, 312–13.

52. *WA*, DB 4:339, lines 18–21.

53. Burkhardt, "Die Judenverfolgungen," 596–98. *CR* 5:100–2.

54. Otto Clemen, ed., *Georg Helts Briefwechsel*, ARG, supplementary vol. 2 (Leipzig: M. Heinsius Nachfolger, 1907), no. 206.

55. *WA*, Br 10:368, lines 16–34; 526, lines 8–13. *WA*, Br 11:51, lines 24–36.

56. *WA*, Br 11:108, lines 7–11.

57. *WA*, TR 5, no. 5576.

58. *WA*, Br 11:275, line 5—276, line 2 = *LW* 50:290–91. *WA*, Br 11:286, line 15—287, line 24. *WA* 51:172, line 32—173, line 2.

59. *WA* 51:195–96. Possibly this admonition did not come until 15 February 1546.

2. The Turks

1. See Brecht, *Luther* 2, 351–55 = *Luther* 2, ET, 364–68. On the following, cf. Stephen A. Fischer-Galati, *Ottoman Imperialism and German Protestantism, 1521–1555* (Cambridge, Mass.: Harvard University Press, 1959); Carl Göllner, *Turcica*, vol. 3, *Die Türkenfrage in der öffentlichen Meinung Europas im 16. Jahrhundert*, BBAur, vol. 70 (Bucharest: Editura Academiei; Baden-Baden: Heitz, 1978); Mark U. Edwards, Jr., *Luther's Last Battles: Politics and Polemics, 1531–46* (Ithaca, N.Y.: Cornell University Press, 1983), 97–114; Rudolf Mau, "Luthers Stellung zu den Türken," in Junghans, 647–62.

2. *WA*, TR 2, no. 2706. *WA* 36:577, line 34—578, line 18 = *LW* 28:131.

3. *WA* 46:609, line 13—610, line 10 = *LW* 22:85–86.

4. *WA*, TR 5, nos. 6155, 6158. *WA*, TR 3, nos. 3687, 3753, 3764. *WA*, TR 3, no. 3765 = *LW* 54:269. *WA*, TR 3, no. 3766.

5. *WA*, Br 8:227, line 11—228, line 14; 232–36. *WA*, TR 4, no. 3997.

6. *WA* 50:478–87. *WA*, Br 8:566, line 11—567, line 30.

7. *WA*, Br 9:491–92.

8. *WA*, Br 9:515, lines 8–17.

9. *WA*, Br 9:512–14. *WA* 51:577–625 = *LW* 43:213–41.

10. *WA*, Br 9:548, lines 9–25; 559–62.

11. *WA*, Br 9:622, lines 30–38 = *LW* 50:228–29. *WA*, Br 10:5, lines 16–32.

12. *WA*, Br 10:23–25. *WA*, TR 5, no. 5428 (pp. 139, line 28—140, line 10). *WA* 53:261–396. In addition to the literature cited in note 1, cf. Walter Beltz, "Luthers Verständnis von Islam und Koran," *WZ(H).GS* 32 (1983):85–91. Hartmut Bobzin, "Martin Luthers Beitrag zur Kenntnis und Kritik des Islam," *NZSTh* 27 (1985):262–89.

13. *WA* 53:388–96.

14. *WA* 43:545, lines 30–36 = *LW* 5:170. *WA*, Br 10:48, lines 50–54.

15. *WA*, Br 10:160–63, 217–19.

16. *WA* 53:561–72. To be sure, there are similarities between Melanchthon's *Praemonitio* (*CR* 5:10–14) and Luther's preface, but Beltz, "Luther's Verständnis," 85, overemphasizes Luther's dependence on Melanchthon.

17. *WA*, Br 10:65–67. *WA*, TR 4, no. 4803. *WA*, Br 10:111, lines 25–34.

18. *WA*, Br 10:68–69, 72–74.

19. *WA*, Br 10:169, lines 20–24; 196, lines 9–14.

20. *WA*, Br 10:230, lines 8–28. *WA* 53:553–60. *WA*, Br 10:271–73.

21. *WA*, Br 10:335, lines 20–26 = *LW* 50:243–44. *WA*, Br 10:365, lines 12–18; 467, lines 33–39.

22. *WA* 49:337, line 11—343, line 5. Cf. *WA*, Br 10:59–67.

3. The Pope (1542–46)

1. Cf. above, pp. 188–203. Markus Jenny, ed., *Luthers geistliche Lieder und Kirchengesänge*, AWA, vol. 4 (Cologne and Vienna: Böhlau, 1985), 118–19, 304–5. On the following, cf. Ernst Bizer, *Luther und der Papst*, TEH, vol. 69 (Munich: Chr. Kaiser, 1958), esp. 41–56. Hubert Kirchner, "Luther und das Papsttum," in Junghans, 441–56, esp. 451–56.

2. *WA*, Br 10:275, lines 3–10; 288, lines 18–21; 306, line 14—307, line 16; 370, lines 21–25.

3. *WA*, Br 10:525, lines 17–22; 527, lines 30–39; 542, lines 19–26; 553, lines 18–22.

4. *WA*, Br 10:688–90.

5. *WA*, Br 11:14–15, line 21. Emil Sehling, ed., *Die Evangelischen Kirchenordnungen des XVI. Jahrhunderts*, vol. 1¹, *Sachsen und Thüringen* (Leipzig: O. R. Reisland, 1902), 209–22.

6. Veit Ludwig von Seckendorf, *Commentarius historicus et apologeticus de Lutheranismo*, 2d ed. (Leipzig: Joh. Friedrich Gleditsch, 1694), 539–43. *WA*, Br 11:16–19.

7. *CT* 4, nos. 276–77.

8. *WA*, Br 11:12, lines 19–28; 20, line 24—21, line 26; 29–31.

9. *WA* 54:195–299 = *LW* 41:257–376.

10. Cf. Brecht, *Luther* 1, 302–6, 327–31, 352–55 = Brecht, *Luther* 1, ET, 317–21, 343–48, 369–72.

11. *WA*, Br 11:59, lines 1–9; 71, lines 3–12. Gustav Kawerau, ed., *Der Briefwechsel des Justus Jonas*, 2 vols. (Halle: O. Hendel, 1884–85; reprint ed., Hildesheim: G. Olms, 1964), vol. 2, no. 792.

12. *WA* 54:236, lines 27–29; 299, lines 4–8; 300–1 = *LW* 41:300, 376. *WA*, Br 11:72, lines 24–25; 91, lines 17–19; 120, lines 11–12; 177, lines 12–13.

13. *WA* 54:300–54. Cf. above, p. 61.

14. *WA* 54:348–73; plates 1–11. Cf. above, 190–92. Erwin Mülhaupt, "Vergängliches und Unvergängliches an Luthers Papstkritik," *LuJ* 26 (1959):56–74. Elfriede Starke, "Luthers Beziehungen zu Kunst und Künstlern," in Junghans, 546–48.

15. *WA*, Br 11:94, line 3—95, line 25, offers an explanation of the picture, but the editor did not mention it.

16. Cf. Brecht, *Luther,* 2, 102–3 = *Luther,* 2, ET, 98–99.

17. *WA*, TR 6, no. 6528.

18. The heading, "Kissing the Foot," does not fit the picture.

19. *WA*, Br 11:115, lines 17–20 = *LW* 50:264; *WA*, Br 11:120–21.

20. *WA* 54:353. *WA* 48:239–40.

21. *WA* 60:175–79.

22. *WA*, Br 11:70, lines 6–7. *WA*, Br 11:83, line 13—84, line 18; 88, lines 11–21; 115, lines 11–12 = *LW* 50:254–55, 256–57, 263.

23. *WA*, Br 11:85, lines 24–25. *WA*, TR 5, nos. 6311, 6388 (incorrectly considered by the editor as relating to the 1544 Diet of Speyer).

24. *WA*, Br 11:131–32 = *LW* 50:264–67.

25. *WA* 54:412–22.

26. *WA*, Br 11:85, lines 23–25. *WA*, Br 11:88, lines 5–11 = *LW* 50:255–56. *CR* 5:758–59 = *MBW* 4, no. 3904.

27. *WA* 54:412–43 = *LW* 34:339–60. The proposal in *WA* 59:394, that they are to be dated in July 1545 cannot be considered certain.

28. *WA* 51:54, lines 22–23; 89, lines 35–37. *WA* 44:717, lines 21–26; 753, lines 34–38; 773, lines 17–23; 775, lines 23–28; 778, lines 34–36; 787, lines 30–34; 790, lines 20–24; 807, lines 20–30; 808, line 38—809, line 5 = *LW* 8:189, 238–39, 264–65, 267, 272, 284, 288, 310, 312.

29. *WA*, Br 11:177, lines 11–12. (The editor's reference to the second work against the pope is incorrect.) Otto Vogt, ed., *Dr. Johannes Bugenhagens Briefwechsel,* reprint ed. (Hildesheim: G. Olms, 1966), no. 165 (p. 349). *WA*, Br 11:264, lines 21–24; 265, line 21—266, line 23. Cf. also the following note.

30. *WA* 54:444–58.

31. Cf. Brecht, *Luther* 1, 322–25 = Brecht, *Luther* 1, ET, 338–41, and Brecht, *Luther* 2, 19–20 = *Luther* 2, ET, 9–10.

32. *WA*, Br 11:219–22.

33. *WA*, Br 11:254–56; 265, lines 3–11.

34. *WA*, Br 11:273, lines 14–18 = *LW* 50:289. Christof Schubart, *Die Berichte über Luthers Tod und Begräbnis: Texte und Untersuchungen* (Weimar: Hofbuchdruckerei, 1917), no. 28 (p. 31), lines 6–8.

35. *WA*, Br 11:180, lines 13–14.

XIV. THE FINAL JOURNEY

1. The Unity Negotiations in Eisleben

1. *WA*, Br 7:349, lines 38–47 = *LW* 50:128. *WA*, TR 3, no. 3783 = *LW* 54:272. *WA*, TR 3, no. 3812. *WA*, TR 4, no. 3948 = *LW* 54:297. On the following, cf. Arno Sames, "Luthers Beziehungen zu den Mansfelder Grafen," in Junghans, 591–600.

2. *WA*, Br 9:114–16, 334–35.

3. *WA*, Br 9:628, line 80—629, line 119, and the introduction, pp. 624–26.

4. *WA*, Br 10:7–12.

5. *WA*, Br 10:27–28, 60–61. *WA*, TR 5, no. 6127.

6. *WA*, Br 10:81–83; cf. 659, lines 7–21.

7. *WA*, Br 11:189–92.

8. *WA*, Br 11:225–26 = *LW* 50:281–84. *CR* 5:910–12, 912–13 = *MBW* 4, nos. 4102, 4104 (*MBW* 5, no. 4105). *WA*, Br 11:242–43, 254–55. *MBW* 4, no. 4121. *WA*, Br 12:375, line 1—376, line 27.

9. *WA* 51:123–34 = *LW* 51:369–80.

10. *CR* 6:19–20. Cf. *WA*, Br 11:274–75.

11. *WA*, Br 11:268–70 = *LW* 50:284–87. *WA*, Br 11:274–75.

12. *WA* 51:135–48. *WA*, TR 5, no. 5633b–5634.

13. *WA*, Br 11:273, lines 5–13 = *LW* 50:288–89. *WA*, Br 11:275–76; 278, lines 18–26 = *LW* 50:290–92, 294. *WA*, Br 11:280, n. 7.

14. *WA* 51:148–96 (*WA* 51:187–94 = *LW* 51:381–92), in the following, esp. 148–63. *WA* 54:488, lines 3–8.

15. *WA* 51:173–87.

16. *WA* 51:xiv–xv. *WA* 51:187–94 = *LW* 51:381–92.

17. *WA*, TR 6, nos. 6576, 6934–38, 6809, 6816.

18. *WA*, TR 6, nos. 6508–9, 6526–28, 6796.

19. *WA*, TR 5, no. 5899. *WA*, TR 6, nos. 6565, 6635, 6975. *WA* 48:182–83, nos. 240, 242.

20. Christof Schubart, *Die Berichte über Luthers Tod und Begräbnis: Texte und Untersuchungen* (Weimar: Hofbuchdruckerei, 1917), no. 1 (p. 3), lines 6–7.

21. *WA*, Br 11:277, line 3—278, line 17 = *LW* 50:293–94.

22. *WA*, Br 11:279–80 = *LW* 50:295–97. *WA*, Br 11:283–84. *WA*, Br 11:285–86; 286, lines 13–15 = *LW* 50:297–99, 302.

23. *WA*, Br 11:286, lines 3–12; 287, lines 39–45; 290–92 = *LW* 50:302, 303–4, 305–8.

24. *WA*, TR 6, nos. 6962–94, 7031.

25. *WA*, Br 11:299–302 = *LW* 50:310–15. See above, p. 231.

26. *WA*, Br 12:367–74.

27. *WA*, Br 12:374–77.

28. *WA* 48:241–42. *WA*, TR 5, nos. 5468, 5477. *WA*, Br 12:363–64. The exact text has not been preserved. Heinrich Bornkamm, *Luthers geistige Welt*, 2d ed. (Gütersloh: C. Bertelsmann, 1953), 330–50. A similar tradition, but somewhat different from the one on the "slip of paper," is already to be found in the graduation address for Peter Palladius in 1537 (*WA* 39[1]:262, lines 6–14). Certain echoes may also be seen in Luther's last sermon (*WA* 51:187–94 = *LW* 51:381–92).

2. "Now Lettest Thou Thy Servant . . ."

1. Cf. Brecht, *Luther* 1, 54–58, 126, 237 = Brecht, *Luther* 1, ET, 45–50, 125, 246; Brecht, *Luther* 2, 196, 203–5 = *Luther* 2, ET, 197, 204–7; above, pp. 185–88, 246.

2. Christof Schubart, *Die Berichte über Luthers Tod und Begräbnis: Texte und Unter-*

suchungen (Weimar: Hofbuchdruckerei, 1917), esp. nos. 1 and 28. *WA* 54:478–96 conflates the first reports.

3. Schubart, *Die Berichte über Luthers Tod und Begräbnis*, no. 2 (p. 9), lines 5–6; no. 4 (p. 10), lines 19–20.

4. Schubart, *Die Berichte über Luthers Tod und Begräbnis*, no. 78 (pp. 77, line 35—78, line 11).

3. "Dead Is the Charioteer of Israel"— Burial and Remembrance

1. Christof Schubart, *Die Berichte über Luthers Tod und Begräbnis: Texte und Untersuchungen* (Weimar: Hofbuchdruckerei, 1917), nos. 1, 7, 11, 16–17.

2. Schubart, *Die Berichte über Luthers Tod und Begräbnis*, nos. 13, 25.

3. Schubart, *Die Berichte über Luthers Tod und Begräbnis*, no. 25. Ernst Kroker, *Katharina von Bora, Martin Luthers Frau: Ein Lebens– und Charakterbild*, 2d ed. (Zwickau: J. Hermann, 1925), 224.

4. Kroker, *Katharina von Bora*, 223–24.

5. Schubart, *Die Berichte über Luthers Tod und Begräbnis*, nos. 26, 32. *MBW* 4, no. 4165. *CR* 6:81–82 = *MBW* 4, no. 4185. *MBW* 4, no. 4193. Theodor Kolde, ed., *Analecta Lutherana: Briefe und Aktenstücke zur Geschichte Luthers* (Gotha: F. A. Perthes, 1883), 432–33, 433. Kroker, *Katharina von Bora*, 224–76.

6. The following is in accordance with *WA* 54:492, line 38—495, line 13.

7. Karl Eduard Förstemann, ed., *Denkmale dem D. Martin Luther von der Hochachtung und Liebe seinen Zeitgenossen errichtet und zur dritten Säkularfeier des Todes Luthers herausgegeben* (Nordhausen: Ferd. Förstemann, 1846), no. 14.

8. Schubart, *Die Berichte über Luthers Tod und Begräbnis*, nos. 69 (p. 65), lines 5–8; 78 (p. 79), lines 14–34. Alfred Dieck, "Cranachs Gemälde des toten Luther in Hannover und das Problem der Luther-Totenbilder," *Niederdeutsche Beiträge zur Kunstgeschichte* 2 (1962):191–218.

9. *CR* 6:57–59.

10. *CR* 6:60–62.

11. Margaret, who married Erhard von Kunheim, a Prussian civil servant, died in 1570.

12. Hans Luther became a jurist and died in 1575. Martin studied theology, but died at an early age in 1565. Paul Luther became a physician and died in 1593.

13. *WA* 54:495, line 14—496. Schubart, *Die Berichte über Luthers Tod und Begräbnis*, nos. 64 (p. 56), lines 34–36; 80. The bronze grave inscription gives Luther's age incorrectly. The bronze memorial tablet was not brought to Wittenberg because of the Smalcald War, and it was later placed in St. Michael's church in Jena. The one in the Wittenberg castle church is a copy.

14. We use the 1546 printing by George Rhau in Wittenberg (Georg Geisenhof, *Bibliotheca Bugenhagiana: Bibliographie der Druckschriften des Joh. Bugenhagen* [Leipzig: M. Heinsius Nachfolger, 1908], no. 350).

15. Otto Vogt, ed., *Dr. Johannes Bugenhagens Briefwechsel*, reprint ed. (Hildesheim: G. Olms, 1966), no. 169.

16. Christian Gotthold Neudecker, ed., *Die handschriftliche Geschichte Ratzeberger's*

über Luther und seine Zeit (Jena: F. Mauke, 1850), 170–71. I am grateful to Helmar Junghans for this reference.

17. *CR* 11:726–34. In some respects Melanchthon's preface to the second volume of Luther's Latin works in June 1546 (*CR* 6:155–70) forms a counterpart to his eulogy.

18. Cf. *CR* 6:80 = *MBW* 4, no. 4184.

19. Already on 28 February 1546 Elector John Frederick called upon the theology faculty of the Wittenberg university to preserve the pure doctrine that Luther had brought to light. *MBW* 4, no. 4169. *CR* 6:72–73 = *MBW* 4, no. 4179.

Index

There is no entry for "Luther, Martin."
Page numbers in *italics* refer to illustrations.

445

Leipzig, 11, 14, 21–22, 65–69, 73, 80, 84,
100–101, 122, 156, 240, 262, 284,
288–90, 294
Leipzig Colloquy (1534), 73; (1539), 73,
80
Leisnig, 7, 71, 244
Lemnius, Simon, 87–89, 152, 247
Lening, Johannes (pseudonym:
Hulderichus Neobolus), 207, 213–14
Lessing, Gotthold Ephraim, 88
Leuven. See Louvain
Libius, Johann, 370
Lichtenburg, 126, 239, 274
Liegnitz, 183
Lindemann, Caspar, 20
Lindemann, Margaret, 20
Lindenau, Paul, 72, 155
Lindenau, Sigismund von (bishop of
Merseburg), 307
Lindenau, Sigismund von (cathedral
canon of Merseburg), 307
Link, Wenceslaus, 31–32, 144–45, 242,
285, 289, 311–13
Lippe (county), 314
Lissen, 276
Lochau, 8–9, 156, 242
Lodinger, Martin, 65
Löser, Hans von, 20
Lotther, Matthes, 37, 72, 153
Lotther, Michael (printer), 100
Louis V (elector of the Palatinate), 313
Louis (IV) the Bavarian (emperor), 227
Louvain, 331, 364, 366–67
Lübeck, 315
Lucius, Jacob, 268
Luder, Heinz (Luther's cousin), 239
Ludicke, Johann, 200
Ludwig (count of Eberstein), 316
Ludwig (XV) the Elder (count of
Öttingen), 142
Lufft, Hans (printer), 87, 97, 98, 100, 253
Luke (evangelist), 346
Lund, 203
Lüneburg, 33–34, 167, 183, 315, 317
Luther, Hans (Luther's son), 236–37,
253, 371, 377, 379

Luther, James (Luther's brother), 310,
369, 379
Luther, James (Luther's nephew), 238
Luther, Katherine, née von Bora, 18–21,
52, 55, 89, 162, 164, 186–88, 209–10,
217, 232, 235–44, 254, 262–63, 300,
371, 373–74, 377–79, *Plates X, XVII*
Luther, Magdalene (Luther's daughter),
236–38
Luther, Margaret (Luther's daughter), 21,
242, 379
Luther, Margarete (Luther's sister). See
Kaufmann, Margarete
Luther, Martin (Luther's son), 2, 20, 236,
371, 377, 379
Luther, Paul (Luther's son), 20, 371, 377

Maccabeus Scotus, Johannes, 228
Mackenrot, Paul (Luther's brother-
in-law), 369
Magdeburg, 26, 32, 85, 90, 100, 176, 183,
253, 297–98, 301, 309
Magdeburg (archdiocese/arch-
foundation), 297–99
Magdeburg, archbishop of. See Albrecht
II (margrave of Brandenburg); Johann
Albrecht (margrave of Brandenburg-
Ansbach)
Magenbuch, Johann, 232
Magnus (duke of Mecklenburg, adminis-
trator of Schwerin diocese), 126, 315
Mainz, 73, 87, 225, 299–300, 303
Mainz (archdiocese), 297
Mainz, archbishop/elector of. See
Albrecht II (margrave of Brandenburg)
Major, George, 118, 133, 246, 263, 367
Malachi (prophet), 97
Mansfeld, 32, 122, 160, 164–65, 167–68,
310, 369, 371, 374–75, 377
Mansfeld (county), 309
Mansfeld, counts of, 350, 369, 371,
377–79. *See also* Albrecht VII (count of
Mansfeld-Hinterort); Anna (countess
of Mansfeld-Hinterort); Dorothy
(countess of Mansfeld); Gebhard VII
(count of Mansfeld-Hinterort); Hoyer

Wolfgang (count of Anhalt-Köthen), 25,
90, 222–23, 310–11, 374
Wolfgang (palsgrave of Palatinate-
Zweibrücken), 313
Wolfhart, Bonifacius, 49, 55, 188
Wolkenstein, 72
Wolrab, Nicholas (printer), 100
Wörlitz, 26
Worms, 6, 53, 95, 169, 217–18, 223–24,
226, 364
Worms Colloquy, 169, 216–18
Worms, diet of (1521), 226, 359; (1545),
364, 367
Wrocław. See Breslau
Württemberg, 42, 46, 54, 122, 127, 183,
208. See also Ulrich I (duke of
Württemberg)
Württemberg Concord, 54
Wurzen, 292–93
Wycliffe, John, 83

Zahna, 6

Zápolya. See John (I) Zápolya (vaivode of
Transylvania)
Zechariah (prophet), 95, 144
Zeitz, 158, 231–32, 257, 262, 264,
300–302, 304, 306
Zerbst, 36, 87, 90, 310
Zettler, Bernhard, 272
Zeuner, Caspar, 294
Ziegler, Heinrich, *Plate XX*
Zoch, Lorenz, 32
Zöllsdorf (manor), 235, 241, 244, 262
Zulsdorf, Franz, 282
Zurich, 40, 46, 53–54, 56–58, 96, 327–31,
347, 355
Zwick, Conrad, 54
Zwick, Johannes, 49, 51–53
Zwickau, 26, 148, 188, 251, 271, 276,
278, 282–83
Zwilling, Gabriel, 242, 273, 275, 277
Zwingli, Ulrich, 34, 39, 48–50, 52, 54,
56–58, 77, 84, 104, 134–35, 195, 324,
327–31, 352

Subject Index to
Volumes 1–3

References to the indexes of the three individual volumes, which list persons and places, are indicated by *Vol. Index.*

37, 39, 44, 75–76, 84–85, 87, 89–93,
98, 100–101, 120–21, 138, 140, 204,
208–9, 224, 255, 273, 275–78, 281–83,
289–90, 324, 335–37, 349, 367,
377–78, 380–82, 397, 417, 431–32,
436, 449, 453. III 7, 10, 15, 21, 33,
35, 77, 90, 98, 109, 135, 158, 177,
181, 197, 205, 207, 235, 238–40,
249, 253–54, 256–57, 270, 274, 277,
279, 283–84, 310, 326, 328, 335,
342–43, 345, 356–57, 379

blessing the, II 335, 337

illegitimate, I 111. II 65, 91

Luther's, II 202–4, 206, 377. III 19–20,
118, 123, 175, 186–87, 236–38, 242,
244–45, 284, 378

Christ, I 2, 40, 42, 45, 55, 59, 61–62, 67,
71–82, 88–90, 92, 96–97, 117–18,
129, 131, 133–36, 138–39, 141–45,
147–48, 151–52, 156–58, 160–61,
163–64, 169, 171–73, 177, 185–89,
191–92, 195–98, 203, 208, 212, 214,
217–20, 223–26, 228–37, 241, 244,
251–53, 255–59, 261, 264, 268, 279,
281, 285–88, 291–94, 296, 304–8,
313, 319, 325, 327–30, 333–36, 340,
342–46, 348, 351–57, 362–64, 367,
369, 372, 376, 380–82, 386, 402,
404, 406–12, 415, 422, 425, 428–30,
432, 440, 445, 448–49, 453, 456,
458, 460, 469. II 4–5, 8–10, 12, 14,
16–18, 20–23, 26–29, 32, 34, 37,
43–44, 50–52, 55–59, 62–66, 69,
73–79, 82–84, 86–88, 93, 97, 100–101,
103–4, 109, 112–13, 116–18, 123–25,
127–29, 131, 133–34, 137, 139,
148–49, 151–58, 160–61, 163–64,
167–69, 171, 177–79, 185, 191, 193,
199–200, 203, 205–10, 215, 217, 219,
224, 227–29, 231–34, 245–47, 249,
252–53, 256–57, 265, 270, 274, 278,
286, 290, 294–95, 297–300, 303,
305–15, 318–24, 327–33, 335–38,
344, 346–47, 349–51, 355, 359, 361,
365–68, 370, 372, 376–79, 381–85,
388, 390–92, 395–97, 399, 402, 404–7,
409–10, 415–18, 426, 429, 431,

433–34, 441–42, 451–57, 459.
III 12, 14–15, 20, 22, 26–28, 31–36,
39–40, 42–46, 48–51, 55–57, 66,
68–70, 72, 74–79, 81–82, 96–97,
101, 103, 110–13, 117, 122, 124–25,
128–34, 136, 138, 140–41, 144, 148,
151, 153–54, 156, 158–59, 161–63,
165–66, 169, 176–78, 180, 183,
185–87, 189–90, 193–95, 197, 201–2,
209, 220–22, 224–30, 236, 238, 240,
242, 245, 250, 252, 257, 269–70,
272, 274, 283, 304–5, 309, 311,
314–15, 317, 319, 324–27, 329, 331,
333–38, 340–41, 342–51, 353–54,
356–57, 359–61, 366, 371–72,
375–77, 379–81

as judge, I 1, 49, 71, 73–82, 92, 96–97,
225, 227, 287, 293, 351, 387, 411.
II 19, 93, 178–79, 344, 360, 454,
457. III 10, 89, 91–92, 189, 333. *See
also* judge

as mystery, III 79, 140, 252, 326, 348

as sacrament, I 223

as the crucified, I 77, 134, 157, 233.
III 2, 132, 337, 341

Christ child, I 77

Christ, second coming of, III 9

Christendom, I 178, 221, 281, 344–45,
377, 390, 416, 434, 436–37, 456,
462. II 10, 70, 111, 153–55, 213,
215, 236, 311, 321, 418. III 48, 122,
180, 194, 196, 333, 354, 357,
359–60. *See also* Christianity

Christianity, I 41, 100, 145, 176, 239,
277–78, 296, 317, 417, 436, 458.
II 14, 45, 135, 204, 220, 226, 236,
273, 294, 367–68, 392. III 84, 253,
260, 339, 346, 350, 360, 367. *See
also* Christendom

Christians, true, I 61, 195, 280, 345. II 61,
84, 149, 292, 302, 322. III 76, 353

Christmas, I 13, 67, 73, 77, 151. II 6,
15–16, 33–34, 46, 51, 53, 126, 129,
134, 173, 224, 254, 285, 315. III 20,
28, 43, 140, 176, 245, 256, 284

Christology, I 78–79, 82, 294, 320, 408.
II 17, 76, 309, 314, 318–21, 324,

470. II 9–10, 12–13, 15, 27, 84, 86,
102, 209, 321, 364, 385, 392, 417.
III 74, 78, 162, 179–80, 189–90,
220–21, 299, 358–59
bull on, I 179–80, 188, 190, 206, 267
controversy over, I 112, 118, 175–221,
225, 230, 235, 237, 240, 258, 262,
291, 323, 339, 348, 358, 370–71,
411, 469. II 13, 392. III 85,
144
decretal on, I 261, 267, 269, 272, 325
instructions for sale of, I 180–82, 188,
190, 195
theses against Luther's theses, I 205–6,
209
theses on. *See* Luther, writings of: *On
the Power of Indulgences*
Industry, I 3, 5–6, 10, 12, 101, 110, 341.
II 34. III 261, 369. *See also*
commerce; economics; trade
Inflation, III 310
Ingratitude, II 15, 20, 145, 164, 262–63,
288, 311, 383, 439–40. III 5–6, 15,
154, 182, 201, 204, 256, 270, 285,
290, 292, 322, 352–53, 356
Inquisition, I 162. II 102
Insurrection, I 403. II 30–32, 81, 85, 111,
151, 155–56, 159, 161, 165–66, 267,
336, 345, 354, 358, 413, 419–20.
III 34, 67, 381. *See also* disturbances; revolt; unrest
Intercessions, II 5, 107, 207, 209, 258,
291, 362, 376, 382. III 14, 122, 292,
322
Interdict, I 155, 248, 256, 342, 374, 395,
398, 414, 422, 427. II 165
Interest, II 39, 96, 142–46, 189. III 32–33,
243, 257, 259–60
Interrogation, Luther's
at the Diet of Worms, I 421–23, 434,
436–47, 452–53, 455–64
by archbishop of Trier, I 272–73, 341–42,
402, 406, 418, 434, 443, 453
by Cajetan in Augsburg, I 250–57, 264,
299
by commission of imperial estates,
I 464–67, 469

by court of scholars, I 249, 269, 272–73,
433, 437, 464
Islam, II 365–67. III 354–55

Jackdaws, II 373
James, Epistle of, II 21, 50–52, 434
Jews. *See Vol. Index*
John, First Epistle of, III 79, 81
John, Gospel of, II 51, 105, 233, 307, 433
Journeys, Luther's, I 57, 157, 163, 213–17,
250–51, 260, 448–51, 470–72. II 29,
67, 69, 78, 82, 159, 174–75, 178–79,
205, 210, 260, 327, 334, 338, 349,
357–58, 370–72, 407, 424, 426, 432,
439, 444. III 97, 136, 178, 182–83,
199, 242, 262–64, 269, 288, 303,
306. *See also* Rome: journey to
Judge, I 1, 49, 71, 73–79, 92, 96–97, 203,
222, 225, 227, 243, 246, 256–58,
264, 269, 272, 287, 293, 311–12,
316, 320, 322–23, 331, 338, 347,
351, 387, 411, 414–15, 418, 428,
443, 472. II 19, 91, 93–94, 103, 109,
174, 176, 178–79, 281–82, 332, 344,
360, 398, 402, 433, 440, 454, 457.
III 8, 10, 69, 74, 89, 91–93, 120,
151, 173, 206, 241, 270, 272, 292,
319
God/Christ. *See* Christ: as judge
Judging, I 9, 76–77, 79–81, 87, 96, 134,
136, 138, 174, 233, 236, 315, 387.
II 52, 69, 74, 87, 245, 361. III 79
judging one's self, I 97, 222–23, 225,
227
Jurisprudence, I 29, 39, 40, 44–45, 48.
III 118–19, 121. *See also* jurists
Jurists, I 28, 44–46, 84, 184, 187–88,
204–5, 240, 249, 251, 256, 258, 277,
289, 311–12, 329, 339, 346, 357,
373, 384, 398, 403, 414, 424, 430,
448, 453. II 26, 42, 45, 59, 93, 116,
123, 127–28, 198, 199, 242, 244,
263, 280–83, 338, 363, 381, 412,
444. III 4, 10, 13, 21–22, 68, 78,
91–93, 104, 118–21, 178, 188, 201, 239,
253–55, 260–61, 263, 270, 280, 282,
293, 373–74. *See also* jurisprudence

481

486

489

sacrifice of the, I 73, 75, 222, 381–83. II 28, 33, 63, 74, 76, 83, 85–86, 125–26, 166–67, 256, 313, 321, 327, 371, 383, 403, 417, 456. III 30, 75, 180, 223, 359, 366

Masters, I 1, 8, 20, 28–31, 33–37, 40–41, 43–44, 46–48, 50, 57–58, 85, 90–91, 120–21, 125–27, 172, 182, 201, 242, 245–46, 277–78, 309, 339, 464. II 32, 36, 77–79, 88, 157, 189, 200–201, 243, 274–76, 277, 306, 372, 374, 378, 401, 417, 442. III 14, 27, 77, 90–91, 151, 156, 210, 240, 254, 261, 289, 294, 372, 375

Mathematics, I 33. II 140

Medicine, I 29, 39, 119, 153, 279, 352. II 2, 140, 208, 374, 429–30. III 113, 121–22, 131, 185, 229–32

medication, II 2, 372. III 22, 185, 374, 376

Medieval, I 11, 15, 52, 54, 74–75, 79, 91, 94, 99, 101, 105, 117, 134, 137, 151, 154, 222, 227, 277, 344, 356, 358, 360, 369, 371, 426, 474. II 118, 134, 148, 257, 320. III 147, 156, 220, 222, 245, 346. See also Middle Ages

Meditations, I 84, 131, 145, 148, 151, 351, 359, 408. III 14, 143. See also passion, meditation on

Men, teachings of, I 436. II 1, 18, 20, 33, 52, 63, 69, 84, 86, 89, 131, 163, 228, 264, 371. III 23, 111, 126, 181, 220, 288, 309, 366, 380

Mendicancy, mendicants, I 26, 28, 51–52, 54–55, 100, 126, 159, 190, 286, 330, 373–74, 389, 391, 398. II 21, 39, 71, 99, 139. III 78. See also beggars, begging

Merchants, I 181, 401. II 142, 144–45, 174, 199, 289, 349, 382. III 11, 32, 66, 84

Mercy, I 58, 69, 71, 76, 81, 95, 133–34, 144, 152, 183, 189, 195, 214, 222–23, 226–29, 231, 248, 261, 280, 293–94, 302, 354, 359–61, 428. II 8, 10, 19, 24, 56, 89, 180–81, 186–88, 206–7, 220, 227, 234, 236, 287, 289, 353,

359, 365, 378, 383, 405, 453, 456–57. III 3, 26, 102, 109, 149, 151, 176, 178, 194, 254, 259, 274, 322–23, 343–45, 369

"sharp mercy," III 343–45

Merit, treasury of surplus, I 176, 183, 185, 196, 212, 224, 236, 250, 253, 255–56, 261, 302–3, 391

Merits, I 49, 67, 81, 94, 96, 136, 139, 152, 156–57, 165, 170, 177, 185, 188–89, 194, 196, 212, 224–25, 228, 232, 253, 255–56, 325, 366, 382, 387. II 53, 83, 222–23, 231–33, 255, 268, 321, 362, 403, 434, 454. III 48, 259

Messiah, II 113. III 140, 337–39, 341–43, 345, 347–50

Metaphysics, I 33

Middle Ages, I 27, 53, 83, 93, 111–12, 146, 176–77, 211, 227, 309, 382. II 75, 134, 260. III 189. See also medieval

Middle class, II 382. See also burghers; citizenry

Military service, II 118, 342–44. III 195

Mining, I 3–6, 10, 12. III 369

Ministers, II 11, 36, 74, 76, 272, 284, 287, 290, 330, 381, 436, 441–42, 447. III 31, 50, 76, 125, 138, 279, 372

supply of, II 139

Ministry, ecclesiastical/spiritual, I 156. II 11, 69–70, 73–74, 88, 327–28, 336, 341, 381, 445–47. III 21, 27, 37, 76, 124–25, 130, 154, 197, 220, 250, 257, 270, 274, 305, 358

office of. See office: ministerial

Miracle, I 35, 104, 134, 154, 158, 205, 293, 460. II 79–80, 172, 200, 306, 347, 391, 421, 432. III 111, 113, 140, 187, 197, 216, 230, 242, 346, 375

Miracle men, III 4

Moderation, I 66. II 175, 188, 217, 219, 319. III 40, 231, 236, 269

Monastery, I 1, 5, 7–8, 11, 17–19, 21, 25–27, 30–31, 36, 41–64, 66–70, 72,

46–47, 50–53, 55, 74, 84, 87, 94,
104, 108, 117–18, 120, 123, 133,
150–51, 168, 213, 221, 231, 245,
277, 342, 347, 363. III 78–79, 81,
84, 95, 98, 100–103, 105, 107–8,
110, 112, 139, 142, 162, 205, 270,
285, 345. *See also* Bible; Scripture
Nobility, nobles, I 54, 265, 297, 346,
368–69, 371, 374–75, 377, 401–2,
405, 414–15, 419, 448, 451, 456.
II 21, 71, 85, 98, 100, 139, 188,
190–91, 195, 205, 260–63, 272,
300, 343, 355, 373, 382, 391, 402,
426, 436, 438–40, 446, 450, 455.
III 1, 5–6, 8, 11, 32, 71, 87, 91, 111,
118, 122–23, 126, 134, 211, 238,
259–60, 269–72, 280, 285, 292–94,
302–3, 305, 308, 311, 316, 321,
353–54, 356–57, 369–70, 379
Nominalism, I 29, 34–35, 38, 41, 43, 51,
91, 121, 136, 277. III 163. *See also*
Occamism; Scholasticism
Novices, master of the, I 57, 59–61, 68
Novitiate, I 58–61
Nuns, I 328. II 85, 94–102, 104, 141,
150, 190, 195, 197–99, 201, 203–4,
206, 281, 418. III 6–7, 11, 70, 175,
239, 272. *See also* monasticism

Oath, I 29, 93, 126, 128, 373, 461. II 73, 88,
179–80, 371. III 36, 67, 69, 303, 305
Obedience, I 6–8, 19, 29–31, 47, 49,
61–62, 101, 105, 125, 139, 146,
148–49, 154, 173, 223, 258–59, 291,
295, 304, 306, 335, 355, 364,
367–68, 371, 398, 404, 409, 419,
430, 438, 465, 472. II 23–24, 44–45,
93, 98, 115, 117, 127, 161, 179–80,
183, 186, 197, 204, 222, 264, 268,
282, 335, 341, 347, 351, 354, 368,
370, 406, 408, 412–13. III 67, 70,
139, 149, 161, 197, 202, 206, 228,
245, 292, 311
Obscenity, III 89, 362
Observants, I 53, 98, 105, 127, 148, 373.
See also reform congregation
Occamism, I 36–37, 165

Occult, I 12. III 255
Offerings, II 26, 39, 71, 261, 289
Office, I 31, 45, 54, 57, 64, 66, 72–73,
110, 125–26, 147–48, 155, 158,
160–61, 179, 191, 224, 235, 265,
268, 291, 307–8, 311, 318–19, 326,
329, 331, 343–45, 348, 357, 386,
391, 397, 406–8, 425, 432, 462–63,
473–74. II 2, 11, 14, 22, 26, 28, 36,
38, 42, 57–59, 66, 69–70, 72–74,
83–85, 116–18, 129, 140, 146, 153,
156, 162, 179–81, 187, 189, 193,
248–49, 254, 263, 266–67, 282, 284,
297, 316, 321, 327–28, 336, 338–39,
341–42, 345, 350, 364–65, 373, 381,
400, 434, 443–47, 450. III 4, 7, 41,
68, 72, 75–76, 92, 115, 124–26, 150,
155, 157, 167–68, 180–81, 197, 220,
223, 249–51, 270, 274, 276–77, 279,
294, 297, 302–7, 311, 315–17, 358,
360, 371, 380–81
ministerial, I 72–73, 147, 155, 224,
235, 268, 291, 319, 329, 345, 357,
379, 391, 397, 407–8, 425, 432.
II 69–70, 72–74, 129, 146, 191, 207,
248, 282, 284, 316, 321, 327–28,
336, 341, 364, 381, 446–47. III 7,
72, 75–76, 124–26, 157, 167, 197,
223, 227, 249–51, 270, 276–77, 294,
302, 304, 306–7, 315, 358, 371,
380–81. *See also* ministry, ecclesias-
tical/spiritual
secular, I 45, 113, 160. II 42, 116–18,
156, 181, 187, 191, 193, 207, 282,
321, 338, 341–42, 350, 364–65,
381–82, 400, 434, 444, 450. III 4,
92, 270, 297, 311
Officials (ecclesiastical), I 240, 363–65,
368, 373, 453, 455–56, 458–62.
II 81, 266, 288, 440
Old Adam, I 139, 229, 233, 361, 367.
II 150, 156, 165
Old Luther, III 229–35, 241, 250, 264
Old Testament, I 93, 291, 343, 345, 357,
380, 458. II 46–47, 50–51, 55–56,
98, 104, 113, 122–23, 152, 177, 185,
221–22, 230, 245, 256, 266, 281,

284, 397, 422, 433. III 4, 61, 95, 98,
102, 108, 111, 138–40, 205, 214,
317, 337, 344, 347–48, 350. *See also*
Bible; Scripture

Opinion, public, I 323, 399, 419–20, 433

Opinions, II 270, 422. III 29, 31, 36–38,
45, 59–60, 167, 173, 178–79, 188,
200–201, 207, 215, 224, 226, 279–80,
287–88, 322, 324, 332, 358

Opponents, Luther's, I 17, 36, 42, 75, 91,
121, 168, 176, 179, 198, 203–4,
210–13, 219, 233–34, 245, 253, 259,
267–68, 271, 283, 285–86, 290–91,
306, 309, 315–16, 319, 321, 331–33,
336, 339–40, 342, 344, 350, 364–65,
375, 377–79, 384, 395, 400, 409,
411, 418, 422, 426, 430, 434, 436,
438, 445, 447–48, 452, 456–57,
459–61, 463–65, 470. II 5–8, 18, 20,
22–23, 31–32, 43, 57–58, 62, 81–83,
85–88, 98, 107, 111, 124, 126, 135,
137–38, 146, 156, 159–61, 164–65,
171, 173, 175, 178, 181, 199, 213,
215, 218–19, 224, 226, 230, 234,
247, 249, 267, 276, 293–94, 299,
304–15, 317–18, 320–21, 324, 328,
330–31, 337, 348, 357–58, 360–61,
364–65, 371, 373, 375, 387, 395–99,
402–4, 407, 416–20, 434, 445, 451,
455. III 3, 33, 44–46, 49–50, 55–56,
58, 65, 70, 73, 78–80, 82, 84, 101–2,
108–10, 130–31, 137, 143–44, 152,
168–69, 180–81, 183, 187, 194, 201,
204, 226, 287, 295, 314, 327, 329,
352–53, 355, 358, 366, 379

Order (monastic)
rule of the, I 55, 59–60, 63, 66, 68–69,
85, 98, 148, 158
study in the, I 56–57, 90–91, 127, 155,
159, 215

Ordinance
coinage, II 291
common chest, I 374. II 70–71, 139,
260
common purchase, I 374, 376

Ordination, I 72, 179, 365, 381, 383–84.
II 11, 25, 73–74, 284, 321, 371.

III 75–77, 119, 124–27, 175, 181,
204, 215, 245, 272, 303–5, 358
Luther's, I 69, 74

Original sin, I 132, 164–65, 189, 225.
II 120, 234, 299, 320, 327–28, 332.
III 37, 132, 134, 218–19, 226. *See
also* sins

Our Father. *See* Lord's Prayer

Overwork, Luther's, I 159–60, 350. II 61,
433. III 142, 230–31

Pamphlets, I 247, 324, 330, 336, 350,
395, 401, 413, 449. II 4, 11, 53, 58,
61–62, 102, 174, 181, 200–201, 268,
346. III 59, 85, 188, 190, 213, 219,
222, 233, 250, 337, 341, 361

Papacy, I 47, 51, 75, 122, 146, 177, 209,
226, 256, 303, 305, 307–9, 311, 317,
320, 326, 333–34, 343–47, 349–50,
369–73, 376, 382, 389, 391, 398–99,
407, 421, 425–26, 430, 432, 442,
458–59. II 15, 53, 141, 163, 165,
228, 268, 294, 321, 351–52, 355,
365, 391, 395, 401, 404, 419–20,
432, 456. III 7, 96, 107, 109, 127,
138, 166, 173, 180, 184–85, 187–89,
191, 227–28, 278, 280, 317, 323,
336, 339, 357, 359–62, 366–67

Papal ass, I 79. II 98. III 177, 362

Papists, I 27, 222, 245, 256, 382, 410,
425, 439, 442, 445. II 16, 20, 32, 64,
73, 163, 167–68, 193, 234, 291, 307,
309, 314, 327, 336, 347–48, 350,
354, 361–62, 372, 380, 388, 413,
416, 420–21, 439, 450, 455. III 28,
34, 45, 54, 74–75, 79, 82, 108, 139,
143–44, 152, 177, 181, 201, 204,
206, 215–16, 220–22, 233, 288, 323,
335–36, 339, 352, 354–55, 357, 372

Parents, I 2, 5–10, 15, 26, 48–49, 58, 73,
183, 250, 355, 367–68. II 23–24, 37,
92–93, 100, 139–40, 197, 199, 204,
208, 276–77, 282–83, 377–78,
380–82, 417. III 10, 77, 119, 123,
236–38, 253–54, 272, 281–82

Parishes, I 1–2, 17, 26, 30, 32, 111, 117,
153, 155, 159, 168. II 68, 70, 157,

Renaissance, I 101, 117, 179, 278

Reorganization, reformatory, II 38, 58–60, 64, 70, 137, 139, 142, 239, 283, 341, 355

Repentance, I 68–69, 92, 97, 133, 136, 144, 154, 156, 165, 168, 170, 178, 184–85, 187–89, 191–92, 194–95, 198, 207–9, 219, 222–24, 230, 235–36, 243–44, 299, 322, 327, 345, 358, 391, 413, 425, 448. II 10, 52, 175, 185, 201, 206, 246, 264–66, 268, 288, 352, 365–66, 385, 452, 456. III 51, 96, 148–49, 158, 161–63, 170, 175, 177, 228, 256–58, 336, 353, 356, 380. *See also* penance; penitence

impenitence, I 66. II 367, 404. III 194, 341

Research, Luther, I 83, 94, 130–31, 136, 202, 222, 226. II 58, 267. III 334, 340

Reserved cases, I 180, 303, 327

Resignation, I 139, 141, 144, 228, 421. II 382, 439, 455. III 159, 166, 233, 250, 262, 264–65, 356, 375

Resistance, I 99, 101, 105, 153, 178, 263, 277, 334, 349, 416, 419. II 82, 84, 110, 137, 143–44, 154, 175, 302, 341, 344, 362–64, 411–13, 415–16, 420, 450, 459. III 46, 53, 96, 177, 256, 307, 313–14, 353, 355, 358

right of, II 4, 100, 154, 352, 411–12. III 179, 199–203

Resurrection, I 354, 360–61. II 62, 131, 134, 183, 322, 392, 426. III 12, 110, 159, 238, 242, 275, 284, 349

Revelation, book of, II 47, 50, 52–53, 324, 367. III 77, 103, 177, 379. *See also* Apocalypse

Revelations, I 95–96. II 137, 146, 149, 151, 153, 155–56, 227, 233, 285, 300

Revocation. *See* recantation

Revolt, I 10, 212, 295–96, 358, 363, 443, 456, 463. II 4, 17, 31, 110, 121, 152, 154, 172–75, 177–81, 183–84, 186, 190–91, 193–94, 241, 343, 360, 363, 394, 420, 456. III 4, 67, 202. *See also* disturbances; insurrection; unrest

Revolution, I 38, 83, 244, 285, 461. II 32, 156, 174–75, 179, 183, 392

Luther's, I 38, 83, 227, 239, 244, 308, 322, 383–84, 407, 424, 461, 472

Reward, concept of, II 53, 222, 231, 434

Rhetoric, I 12, 14, 29, 33, 37, 39, 43, 278–80. II 138, 242. III 82, 135

"Riding in," III 242

Righteousness, I 39, 45, 59, 71, 86–87, 90, 95–96, 132–39, 144–45, 147–48, 151–52, 156–57, 160, 163–66, 172–73, 176, 187, 222–31, 233–35, 241, 251, 255, 270, 288, 291–94, 325, 352, 354, 367, 385, 408–9, 432, 449. II 8, 17, 21, 50–52, 56, 117, 164, 186, 196, 233, 248, 265, 334, 372, 384, 390, 392, 413, 451–54, 457. III 32, 103, 112–13, 129, 132, 137, 139–40, 148–49, 163, 165, 224–25, 318, 335–36, 372, 380

Christ's, I 156, 223, 229, 354. III 131–32, 151, 224–25

God's, I 86–87, 95, 134, 144, 156, 176, 187, 222, 225–29, 291. II 50, 233, 457

righteous and sinner at the same time, I 135, 151. II 8. III 161

Rom. 1:17, I 86, 225–27, 229, 236, 255, 352, 366. III 113

Romans, Epistle to the, I 83, 136, 164, 225, 279, 281, 284, 307. II 8, 33, 50–52, 105, 120, 153, 216, 231, 233. III 79, 81, 88, 107–10, 129, 131–32, 149, 180, 225, 329, 335, 340, 370, 378

Rome
journey to, I 68, 73, 93, 98–104
sack of. *See* Sacco di Roma

Rosary, I 64, 213. II 120, 187. III 232

Sabbatarians, III 337–41, 346

Sacco di Roma, II 350, 355

Sachsenspiegel, II 166, 285

Sacrament(s), I 71–75, 92, 102, 104, 145–46, 167, 184, 190, 212–13, 223–25, 231, 235–36, 239, 241, 253, 255, 294, 306, 308–9, 332, 344, 350, 353, 355, 358–59, 361–62, 365, 380–85, 391, 394, 429, 432, 437, 440, 442, 444,

Scholasticism, I 14, 27–29, 36, 38–41,
43–44, 54, 71, 83–84, 86, 91, 95,
119–20, 131, 135, 137–39, 141–42,
151, 161, 163, 165–68, 170–73,
175, 177, 188, 192, 199, 207, 209,
212–13, 217–18, 228, 231, 233, 240,
244, 265, 276, 278–82, 285, 288,
291–92, 294, 306, 313, 316–17, 321,
324–25, 327, 332, 334, 339–41, 349,
359–60, 375, 402, 408, 414, 417,
423–24, 430. II 9, 87, 102, 117, 140,
148, 216, 223, 228, 231, 233, 241,
453. III 132, 148, 161, 180. See also
Nominalism; Occamism; Scotism;
Thomism

Schoolmasters, I 11, 278, 466. II 70, 138,
141, 273, 290, 381, 440, 456. III 71,
80, 110, 158, 196, 245–46, 258, 260,
272–74, 276, 278, 284, 287, 311,
314, 352, 374. See also teachers

Schools, I 2, 6, 8, 10, 12–20, 28–29, 33,
36, 57, 90–91, 94, 128, 155, 159,
166, 170–71, 182, 277–78, 280, 311,
373. II 23, 34, 71–72, 133, 138–42,
174, 203, 206, 241, 254, 262–64,
268, 276, 321, 377, 380–82, 440.
III 6, 30, 33, 50, 82, 158, 196–97,
221, 237, 254, 256, 271, 278, 290,
313, 316–19, 360

Scotism, I 120

Scripture, I 2, 60, 76, 83–84, 86–90, 95,
127, 131, 133, 135, 137, 142–45,
149–51, 163, 165–67, 169, 171, 174,
184, 187, 194, 200, 202, 208, 210,
212, 217, 220, 226, 243–44, 253–57,
259, 263–65, 269–70, 276, 279, 281,
283, 287–88, 291–92, 294, 296, 299,
302–3, 307–9, 313, 315, 319–22,
324–27, 329, 331, 333, 335, 339–47,
352, 369, 371–73, 376–79, 383, 387,
397, 402, 410–11, 414–15, 425–26,
430, 434, 436–38, 447, 449, 455,
458–61, 464–66, 468–70, 474. II 5,
7, 9, 11, 20, 36–37, 45, 69, 76, 84,
95, 97–98, 131, 140, 142, 152, 154–55,
161, 168, 201, 205, 209, 216, 232,
236, 249, 274, 277–78, 294, 308–11,

321, 323, 339, 391, 397, 401, 418,
452, 457. III 33, 42–43, 56, 68–69,
90–91, 96, 98, 100, 104, 111–12,
124, 127, 141, 143, 210, 214, 216,
225, 246, 305, 340, 342, 344, 347,
351, 366, 375, 380. See also Bible
clarity of, I 89, 350, 436. II 227, 236
fourfold sense of, I 89, 287
principle of, I 244, 264, 279, 468–69,
472. III 366

Seal, Luther's, II 393, 403. III 96

Sect, sectarians, I 36, 146, 344, 373.
II 73, 128, 138, 150–51, 151–52,
156, 159, 163, 173, 191, 193, 263,
291, 302–5, 313, 315, 338–39, 371,
446–47, 452, 456. III 4, 38, 42, 47,
103, 164–65, 312, 317, 337, 352

Secularization, II 79, 386, 450

Security, I 98, 133, 153, 186, 190–91,
198, 212, 234, 293, 452, 472. II 78,
127, 164, 187, 234–35, 265, 343,
367, 414. III 134, 162, 165, 353

Seelsorge, Seelsorger, I 54, 156, 239, 297,
349, 355. II 72, 123, 270, 437.
III 13, 156, 254, 275

Self–realization, I 409

Sequestration of Luther's books, I 437–38,
446–49, 455, 468, 471. II 105

Serfdom, II 174, 177. See also peasants

Sermons, I 1, 16, 20, 23, 27, 29, 76, 85,
94, 96, 128, 137–39, 142, 147, 150–56,
161–63, 180, 182, 184–90, 204,
207–9, 229–31, 240–41, 267, 281,
290–91, 295, 297, 306, 317, 319,
330, 341, 343–44, 350–68, 362–63,
365, 374–75, 380, 382–83, 385–87,
407, 427, 429, 446, 449, 467, 473.
II 6, 15–17, 20–22, 30, 32–34,
39–40, 45, 51, 58–59, 61–67, 69,
75–76, 78, 83–84, 87, 89–93, 95, 97,
99, 101–2, 104, 111, 114–23,
125–30, 142–45, 149–50, 153–54,
156, 159–61, 164–66, 173, 177–79,
183–86, 188, 200, 202, 205, 210,
224–25, 252, 254, 256–57, 264,
274–75, 280, 284–89, 291–93, 302,
305–8, 310, 315, 324, 334, 337,

341–42, 346, 366–68, 371–72,
381–82, 384, 389, 406–8, 412, 426,
430, 433–35, 438, 443–44, 446, 450.
III 2, 5, 12–13, 15–16, 23, 26–27,
31–32, 35–36, 38, 51, 65, 71–72, 79,
84, 87, 90, 92, 119–20, 124–25,
141–42, 154, 156, 159, 167, 178,
183–84, 200, 208, 229, 232–33, 239,
245, 249–52, 256, 258, 262, 269–70,
273, 276, 288, 304, 307, 309, 331,
333, 349–50, 366, 370–72, 378–79
on the catechism. *See* catechism,
  sermons on
Sermons, Luther's, I 1, 20, 76, 94, 128,
  142, 150–56, 161–63, 184–88, 204,
  207–9, 229–31, 240–41, 281, 290–91,
  295, 297, 306, 317, 319, 341, 343–44,
  350–51, 353, 355–56, 358–59,
  361–68, 375, 380, 382–83, 385–87,
  407, 413, 449, 473. II 6, 16, 45,
  58–59, 61–67, 69, 78, 83, 93, 97, 99,
  101, 111, 114–22, 125–30, 142–43,
  145, 149, 156, 159–61, 164–65, 173,
  177–79, 183–86, 188, 200, 202, 205,
  210, 224–25, 254, 256, 264, 275, 280,
  284, 286–89, 291–93, 302, 305–8,
  315, 324, 334, 337, 341–42, 346,
  371–72, 382, 384, 406–8, 412, 426,
  430, 433–35, 438, 444, 446. III 2, 5,
  12–13, 15–16, 23, 26–27, 35–36, 38,
  51, 71, 84, 87, 92, 119–20, 124–25,
  141–42, 159, 167, 178, 183–84, 200,
  208, 229, 232–33, 239, 249–51, 253,
  256, 258, 262, 269–70, 288, 304,
  307, 331, 333, 349–50, 366, 370–72
drafts, III 13, 142
funeral, II 183, 426
in his home, II 430, 433. III 12, 239,
  251
Invocavit, I 150. II 59, 61–64, 76, 83, 165
on baptism, III 12, 35–36, 38
on 1 Peter, II 58, 177. III 256
on the Decalogue, I 138–39, 152–54.
  II 142, 285
on the Gospel of John, II 285
on the Gospel of Matthew, II 285.
  III 250, 333, 272

on the Pentateuch, II 285
weekday, II 256, 433. III 249
Servants, I 2, 19, 183, 310, 368, 451. II 1,
  29, 191, 201–2, 208, 256, 274–75,
  277, 354, 374, 471, 456. III 13, 19–20,
  22, 77, 91–92, 123, 130, 141, 186,
  193, 240, 244–45, 254, 256–57,
  269–70, 277, 285, 304, 329, 340,
  347–50, 375–76, 380
Service, preaching, II 257
Sexuality, I 67. II 101. III 236
Shrove Tuesday, III 237, 245, 312. *See
  also* Mardi Gras
Sick, sickness. I 12, 181, 295, 353. II 65,
  123, 208–9, 259, 288, 291, 324, 456.
  III 7, 16, 21–23, 123, 209–10, 229,
  231–32, 237, 239, 253–56, 275, 283,
  290, 295, 343, 371, 380. *See also*
  plague
communion of the, II 123, 208.
  III 254, 283, 290, 295
Katy, III 235
Luther. *See* health, Luther's
Melanchthon, II 243. III 210, 216
Sins, I 62, 64–69, 71–75, 77, 79–82, 88,
  90, 97, 104, 117, 130, 132–36, 144,
  149, 151–52, 154, 157, 160, 164–66,
  173, 175–77, 180, 182, 185–87,
  189–94, 197, 208, 214–15, 221–22,
  224–25, 228–32, 235–36, 270, 288,
  293, 299, 303, 319, 325, 330, 351–55,
  359–63, 366–67, 373, 376, 380, 385,
  391, 408–9, 420, 430, 449. II 2, 5,
  8–9, 14, 18–20, 22, 26, 29, 33, 51–52,
  56, 59, 62, 65, 83, 87, 92, 95, 115,
  117, 119–21, 129, 134, 142–43,
  165–67, 169, 171, 180, 199, 215,
  220–21, 224, 227, 231, 233–34, 237,
  249, 252, 256–57, 263–64, 268,
  276–77, 285, 288, 290, 299, 306–7,
  313, 320–21, 327–28, 332, 346,
  371–72, 378–79, 383, 390, 392, 397,
  401–2, 412, 417–18, 422, 426, 431,
  451, 453–57, 459. III 14, 20, 28, 31–32,
  37, 66, 75, 79, 93, 102, 110–12, 122,
  129, 131–32, 134–35, 138, 140, 149,
  158–59, 161–62, 164–68, 180–81,

79, 99, 104, 114, 133, 135, 141, 144–45,
163, 203, 206, 225, 243, 248, 270,
274, 277, 284–85, 370, 374, 379–80,
382–84, 386, 388, 391, 403–4, 408,
429–30, 433, 436, 446, 452, 455.
III 2, 47, 51, 82, 84, 96–98, 101–2,
107–8, 134, 142, 156, 196, 233,
240–41, 250, 257, 272, 277, 280,
283, 285, 289, 314, 318, 332, 338–39,
366, 373, 375, 377, 380–82
Work (literary), I 13–14, 35, 71, 90–92,
97, 139, 141–42, 168–70, 184,
208–11, 225, 243, 250, 263, 278,
284–85, 287, 289, 307, 309, 324,
326, 331–33, 335, 343–44, 346–47,
349, 353, 376–78, 405–6, 413, 426,
428–30, 432, 436, 444, 464. II 6–10,
12, 14, 16, 18, 23, 27, 31, 34, 47, 65,
75–76, 79, 83–85, 87, 89, 92, 94, 98,
100, 102, 108, 113, 118–19, 126,
129, 140–41, 143, 145, 152, 164,
169, 176–78, 180–81, 185, 188, 191,
193, 201, 207, 216, 219, 222–27,
235, 237, 247, 250, 267, 282, 285–87,
304–5, 309–11, 315, 317, 319–20,
322, 325, 337–38, 351, 354, 364,
379–80, 382, 384–85, 401, 415, 448,
455. III 3, 46, 49, 74, 77, 80–81, 83,
89–90, 93, 95, 98, 100, 102, 107–8,
110, 136, 141–44, 165–66, 168, 175,
188–89, 191, 193, 213, 215, 219,
222, 245, 251–52, 299, 311, 323,
327–29, 331, 341–42, 347–48, 355,
357, 359, 361–62, 364, 366
Works, I 56, 62–67, 70, 73, 76–80, 97,
132, 134–36, 138–39, 148, 151–53,
158, 160, 163–66, 170, 172–73, 177,
182, 184, 186, 188, 191, 195, 208,
214, 222–25, 231–34, 236–37, 244,
253, 268, 270, 288, 291, 293–94,
317–19, 327, 329, 336, 339, 340,
356, 358–59, 362, 366–67, 380–81,
383, 385–87, 391, 407–9, 449, 465.
II 4, 6, 8, 16–18, 20–21, 24, 50–53,
58, 62, 67, 72, 76, 78, 80, 83, 86–88,
97–98, 115–16, 120, 129, 131, 140,
145, 152, 164–65, 167–69, 171, 181,

196, 222–24, 227, 229, 232–35, 245,
252, 266, 286–87, 289, 307, 320–21,
324, 338, 351, 381, 383–84, 392,
400, 402, 417–18, 438, 446, 452–54.
III 36, 49, 69, 76, 80, 98, 100, 102–3,
108, 110, 129–30, 132, 135, 140–44,
148–49, 151–52, 158, 161, 175, 178,
181, 190, 192–95, 220, 224–26, 228,
245, 250–51, 310, 323, 327–28, 355,
357, 359, 361
alien works, I 138–39, 152, 224–25,
233, 236, 293, 449
good works, I 56, 62–63, 66–67, 70,
73, 76–79, 94, 97, 103, 135, 148,
151, 164, 170, 172, 177, 182, 188,
191, 195, 208, 214, 224, 268, 270,
294, 317, 319, 327, 329, 339–40,
356, 359, 362, 366–67, 380–81, 383,
385, 391. II 8, 52, 62, 67, 78, 86–87,
116, 131, 222–23, 289, 338, 381,
383, 417–18, 446. III 76, 80, 103,
110, 129, 148–49, 151–52, 181,
224–25, 310
one's own works, I 157, 166, 186, 222,
225, 253, 293, 449
proper works, I 138–39, 152, 225, 293
Works-righteousness, I 251, 354. II 21,
196, 384, 452, 454. III 189
World view, Copernican, III 118
Worldly matter, II 282
Worship, I 10, 15, 17, 32, 53, 60, 63–64,
75, 77, 85, 87–88, 118, 145, 162,
185, 239, 312, 325, 343, 351, 361,
367, 374, 380–81, 385, 387–88, 416.
II 4, 15, 17–18, 29–30, 33–34, 47,
64, 69, 71–72, 98, 104, 119, 122–23,
125–28, 134, 149, 158, 163, 167,
242, 251–59, 263, 270, 274, 284,
287, 290, 292, 316, 345, 365, 383,
385, 390, 398, 402, 421, 423, 427,
447, 449. III 16, 23, 26–27, 29, 37,
41, 59, 62, 68, 72, 77, 102, 108,
124–25, 134, 137, 175, 203, 208–9,
220, 223, 227–29, 231, 269, 283,
294, 298, 302, 307, 311, 325, 330,
335, 337–40, 345, 378, 380. See also
liturgy